ENCYCLOPEDIA OF WESTERN RAILROAD

HISTORY

Encyclopedia of Western Railroad History

Volume III

OREGON   WASHINGTON

by
Donald B. Robertson

© 1995 by Donald B. Robertson

All Rights Reserved

Robertson, Donald B.
　Encyclopedia of western railroad history.

　Includes indexes.
　Contents: v. 1. The desert states -- v. 2. The mountain states -- v. 3. Oregon, Washington.
　1. Railroads--West (U.S.)--History.　I. Title.
TF23.6.R63　1986　　　　　385'.0979　　　　　86-9611
ISBN 0-87004-4305-6 (v. 1)
ISBN 0-87833-026-7 (v. 2)
ISBN 0-8700-4366-8 (v. 3):(acid-free)

**Lithographed and bound in the United States of America by
The CAXTON PRINTERS, Ltd.
Caldwell, Idaho 83605
160194**

CONTENTS

Preface xi

Part I: Development of the West

Western North America 1832 – 1845 (map) 1
Formation of the western United States 1845 – 1854 (map) 2
The pre-Civil War era 1854 – 1861 (map) 3
The Civil War era 1861 – 1865 (map) 4
Pre-railroad western history 5-6
Military forts of Territory/State of Oregon and Washington 7
Establishment of counties and post offices in Oregon and Washington 8-11
Ranking of western territories and states by population 1850 – 1940 11
Post offices in the eleven western territories/states 1860 – 1900 12
Compendium of the seventh to fourteenth censuses 13-14
Operations in Oregon and Washington 1880 – 1890 15
Railroad mileage in the eleven western territories/states 1855 – 1919 16
Maps of the western territories/states 1865 – 1890 17-22
Western railroads in 1909 23-26
Authorized construction and abandonments in Oregon and Washington 1921 – 1963 27-28

Part II: The Railway Age

Mileage constructed in the United States 29
Introduction of the world-wide railroad era. 30
Chronology of the development of railroad equipment 31
Notes on track, gauges and equipment 32
The major locomotive builders 33-34
The Whyte wheel classification system 35-36
Chronology of major events in the world, United States and the West 1840 – 1940 37

CONTENTS

Part III: Oregon

    Introduction 39
    Index .... 40 – 43
    Railroad maps of Oregon .... 44 – 53
    Road map of Oregon, 1880 53
    Graph 55
    The railroads .... 56 – 163
    Railroad changes from *Official Guide* .... 164 – 166
    Chronology of major events 171

Part IV: Washington

    Introduction 173
    Index .... 174 – 178
    Railroad maps of Washington Territory/State .... 179 – 186
    Road map of Washington Territory, 1880 187
    Graph 188
    The railroads .... 189 – 304
    Railroad changes from *Official Guide* .... 305 – 309
    Detail maps of Spokane and Pasco areas 310
    Detail map of western portion of Skagit County 311
    Detail map of west-central Washington 312
    Chronology of major events 313

Photograph Gallery   315 – 322

Index to Railroads in Volumes One, Two and Three   323 – 338

Denver Public Library - Western History Department #19561 *Photo by Otto C. Perry*
Union Pacific rotary snowplow #062 was photographed at La Grande on July 29, 1938.

Denver Public Library - Western History Department #18292 *Photo by Otto C. Perry*
Union Pacific #3604, a 2-8-8-0, smokes the sky at Pendleton with westbound train 258 of 61 cars on July 29, 1938

Index of Illustrations

Amtrak passenger train at Marion	319
Benson Timber Co. long spars at Clatskanie	59
Big Lake Box Co. log loader	68
Big wheels used to skid logs	163
Bloedel-Donovan Lumber Co. #14 at Sequim	196
Burlington Northern Railroad operations in central Oregon	71
Cable-powered skid road	234
Central Railroad of Oregon locomotive #12	151
Chicago, Milwaukee, St. Paul & Pacific Railroad Co. 2-6-6-2 #9104	199
Chicago, Milwaukee, St. Paul & Pacific Railroad Co. electric engines	198
Chicago, Milwaukee, St. Paul & Pacific Railroad Co. locomotive #9311	199
Chicago, Milwaukee, St. Paul & Pacific Railroad Co. motor car #5902	199
City of Prineville locomotive #7	64
Clemons Logging Co. logging camp and Climax	197
Clemons Logging Co. locomotive #6, a 2-6-6-2T	196
Columbia River scene from about 1862	168
Columbia River steamers at Cascade locks in 1906	167
Coos Bay, Roseburg & Eastern Railroad Co. locomotive #4	71
Corvallis & Eastern Railroad Co. locomotive #2	73
Corvallis & Eastern Railroad Co. locomotive #4	74
Cowlitz, Chehalis & Cascade Railway Co. locomotive #25	206
Crown Willamette Paper Co. passenger car	75
Crown Zellerbach Corporation #12 and Climax	225
Eufaula Logging Co. incline	212
Far West Lumber Co. locomotives in about 1907	309
Frazer Hotel in South Tacoma	317
Gasoline powered logging equipment in Deschutes County	161
Gilchrist Timber Co. locomotive #204	166
Goodyear Logging Co. mess car ready for Christmas	277
Grants Pass celebration of completing the track into California	99
Great Northern Railway Co. locomotive #2123, a 2-10-2	218
Great Northern Railway Co. locomotives at Spokane yard	219
Great Northern Railway Co. passenger trains in Washington	218
Hamilton Logging Co. single-pole bridge under construction	220
Hartford Eastern Railway Co. gasoline passenger car	221
Idaho & Washington Northern Railroad locomotive #31	224
Independence Logging Co. series of long trestles	320
Klamath Falls Municipal Railway on opening day	105
Limestone loaded on a truck semitrailer at Wilkeson	237
Mason County Central Railroad Co. locomotive #9 with log train	268
Mason County Central Railroad Co. newspaper ad in 1889	268
Motorized logging in western Washington	318
Mount Hood Railroad Co. fourth locomotive #1	93
Mumby Lumber & Shingle Co. gasoline powered lumber carriers	259
Nehalem Timber & Logging Co. property at Scappoose	95
Nehalem Timber & Logging Co. Willamette "Shay"	95
Northern Pacific Railway Co. 4-6-6-4 with freight train	238
Northern Pacific Railway Co. locomotive #5119 with freight train	235
Northern Pacific Railway Co. 2-8-2s with freight train	238
Northern Pacific Railway Co. 4-6-6-4 at Connell and coaling tower	239
Oregon & California Rail Road Co. construction train at Grave Creek	9
Oregon & California Rail Road Co. covered bridge	99
Oregon & California Rail Road Co. locomotive engines "A" and #33	100
Oregon & California Rail Road Co. passenger trains	101
Oregon & California Rail Road Co. report for 1876	98
Oregon & Southeastern Railroad Co. locomotives #3 and #4 with trains	103
Oregon Eastern Railway Co. floating dredger	108
Oregon Electric Railway Co. caboose #026	110
Oregon Electric Railway Co. diesel engine #52	109
Oregon Electric Railway Co. sleeping car	110
Oregon Improvement Co. docks at Seattle in 1890	224
Oregon Portage Rail Road scenes from about 1862	113
Oregon Railway & Navigation Co. freight tarrif for 1880	120

INDEX OF ILLUSTRATIONS

Oregon Steam Navigation Co. engine house	125
Oregon Steam Navigation Co. train at The Dalles in about 1862	167
Oregon Steam Navigation Co. train on trestle	125
Oregonian Railway Co. locomotive #7	128
Oxen used in Clatsop County logging	169
Oxen used in western Washington logging	178
Pacific National Lumber Co. electric yard crane	246
Palouse County map from 1888 local newspaper	203
Peninsular Railway Co. locomotive #3	273
Point Defiance, Tacoma & Edison Railway Co. steam dummy	251
Polson Logging Co. locomotive #3 at Hoquiam	248
Polson Logging Co. locomotive storage track at Hoquiam	250
Polson Logging Co. power shovel	249
Polson Logging Co. train dumping logs	249
Puget Sound Electric Railway Co. depot in Tacoma	318
Raft of logs on the Columbia River	170
Railway Age "flag" of July 6, 1876	33
Rayonier, Incorporated, diesel powered train on bridge	257
Robert Dollar small diesel with large load	43
Rogue River Valley Railroad Co. locomotive #2	89
Rogue River Valley Railway Co. passenger motor	89
Salem, Falls City & Western Railway Co. gasoline powered passenger car	134
Salem, Falls City & Western Railway Co. yard with rolling stock	168
Satsop Rail Road Co. ad for its general store	272
Seattle & Walla Walla Railroad & Transportation Co. locomotive engine #1	264
Seattle & Walla Walla Railroad & Transportation Co. #1 with picnic train	264
Ships in Puget Sound waters on Monday, April 4, 1892	314
Skid road powered by cable	234
Southern Pacific Railroad Co. cab-ahead #4027	36
Southern Pacific Railroad Co. locomotive making a large smoke effect	77
Southern Pacific Railroad Co. high bridge on Tillamook branch	322
Southern Pacific Railroad Co. 4-4-2 and 4-6-6-2 cab-ahead	143
Southern Pacific Railroad Co. locomotive #4339, a 4-8-2	143
Southern Pacific Railroad Co. passenger train with three engines on Dollarhide	137
Southern Pacific Railroad Co. views of two passenger trains at Portland	142
Spokane International Railway Co. locomotive #104 with passenger train	282
Spokane, Portland & Seattle Railway Co. 4-6-6-4 #902 with freight train	285
Spokane, Portland & Seattle Railway Co. passenger trains at Wishram	285
Studebaker Corporation ads for farm equipment in 1913	170
Sumpter Valley Railway Co. locomotive #251 in winter	169
Sumpter Valley Railway Co. locomotives #17 and #19 with freight movement	147
Sumpter Valley Railway Co. view of Baker City yard with engines	147
Tacoma & Lake City Railroad & Navigation Co. ad for real estate in 1889	289
Tacoma Railway & Power Co. cable winding machinery	294
Union Pacific Railroad Co. 2-8-8-0 locomotive #3604	vii
Union Pacific Railroad Co. diesel #949 with directors' special	149
Union Pacific Railroad Co. eastbound freight at John Day dam	321
Union Pacific Railroad Co. 4-6-2 #2894 with passenger train	315
Union Pacific Railroad Co. 2-8-8-0 #3525 with water tanks at Wallowa	315
Union Pacific Railroad Co. snowplow #062	vii
Union Pacific Railroad Co. unit coal train at Telocaset in 1992	319
Victorian hotel in Centralia	316
Victorian seminary in Tacoma	316
Willamette Pacific Railroad Co. bridge #6 under construction	156
Willamette River scenes with passenger vessels	80
Willamette River scenes with passenger vessels	81
Willamette River steam vessels (five) in Portland	28
Willamette River steamer built in 1857	317
Willamette Valley & Coast Rail Road Co. locomotive engine #1	158
Willamette Valley & Coast Rail Road Co. locomotive #7 on turntable	157
Willamette Valley & Coast Rail Road Co. locomotive #7 with mixed train	158
Willamina & Grande Ronde Railway Co. locomotive #680	162
Wynooche Timber Co. cable-powered skid road	234
Yakima Valley Transportation Co. service car in 1969	304

o 000 o

PREFACE

This book catalogs virtually every steam railroad that owned or operated ten or more miles of track as a common carrier in Oregon and Washington. Many minor operations, including diesel and electric railroads plus logging and mining companies, will be found, but in much less detail.

The emphasis of this work is on the beginnings of railroads. It rarely contains later changes and betterments. It can serve as a "place of beginnings" for students of western railroad history, now and in the future.

This is not a locomotive picture book and will not reveal that in 1903 road number seven received new flues, increased boiler pressure and larger drivers. That information gets into the range of operations and economics and was not part of the original history of construction.

What you will find is a distillation of tens of thousands of printed pages from such sources as *Poor's Manual of the Railroads of the United States* and *Interstate Commerce Commission Valuation Reports*. Additional major sources of information and data are found at the beginning of each state section and each company page.

Every attempt has been made to verify names, spellings, dates and places from several sources. *Poor's Manual* was my final court of law for much early data. It was like today's newspaper, cut, indexed and bound into a book each year and hence not subject to someone's memory or recall. A few (very few) errors were found in *Valuation Reports*; some of them were printed 75 or 100 years after the event, hence not current news as in the case of *Poor's* reports. Numerous old newspapers have been read to determine construction details and opening dates not found to have been recorded in standard reference works.

Beginning in 1888, the Interstate Commerce Commission (ICC) published *Statistics of Railways in the United States*, and this series was checked each year for each company to record mileage alterations, change of name, new owners, leases, mergers and abandonments. The phrase "First listed in ICC for," is found for most of the company entries and refers to this publication.

Maps of each territory or state begin with the year in which a few miles of track had been built. They advance by five year periods except when unusual activity was evident, and skip ahead during a lull. The last year is 1915; from that date forward there was little construction or short line railroad activity except for consolidations into the present majors.

Extensive use was made of United States Geological Survey maps from the 1880's to about 1960.

The author especially wishes to acknowledge the importance to him of the extensive collections of railroad information available in the Hopkins Transportation Library at Leland Stanford Junior University of which he has made active use since 1970.

Below is an example of the information to be found throughout the book; a few brief notes that follow should help the reader.

SACRAMENTO & JACKSON RAILWAY COMPANY Robert Hastings, **President**

Incorp.:	2/1/1890	**Operated:**	(7/90) to 12/26/69		**HQ city:**	Kansas City, Mo.
Disposition:	abandoned March 12, 1970					
Miles track:	24.31	**Gauge:**	36"			
Main line:	Hastings, California, to Jackson, Arizona Territory					
Rail wt.:	26/36 lbs.	**Max. grade:**	2.36%	**Const. began:**	grading	February 5, 1890
Const. comp.:	June 30, 1890			**First train operated:**		May 27, 1890

Locomotives:

Road No.	Name	Type	Dvr. In.	Bldr.	Bldr. No.	Date	Weight	Effort	Remarks
1	Edith	4-6-0	32	Brooks	1233	2/89	82,500	18,070	acquired 1/1890 - scrapped
2*	Judy	2-8-0	44	BLW	44801	1/17	98,750	21,870	sold in February, 1970

Freight traffic: mine, gold

Roster of 6/30/1910:
  1   locomotive
  1   passenger car
 33   ore cars

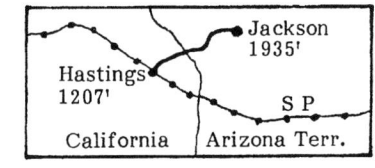

Bibliography: *Poor's 1911*, p. 123

In the example above, the "operated" date is an approximation, hence in parentheses; all inexact dates and numbers will be found in parentheses. Most small railroads were operated with used locomotives, as with "Edith" above. When an engine was purchased new, as with "Judy", a star (and cylinder data, if known) follows the road number.

PREFACE

Why the railroad was ever developed in the first place is partially explained by conditions that surrounded the founding of The San Francisco & San Jose Railroad Company in Civil War days.

> Roads between the two cities were not improved and there were no funds found available for the purpose. A stage coach service was started in 1850, but the trail was so poor that it gave up with the coming of the winter rains. When it did complete the journey, it took nine hours and the fare was $30 — a great deal of money then. Boating on San Francisco Bay could be overly exciting. Travelers with their own rigs often wandered in the fog and darkness and had to await for daylight to determine directions. By rail in 1864, the trip was a reasonably comfortable three and one half hours for the fifty miles and the fare was less than three dollars.

In the fairly flat and populated eastern states (and even to the Mississippi River area), the coming of the railroad meant yet another method of transportation. This was but a faster addition to their roads, canals, rivers and the ocean. In the deserts and mountains of the western territories none of these existed in a satisfactory manner. The rails did truly change a western wilderness into the populated areas of today. When there was no rail, there were very few people. The railroads were built and the population followed.

To make construction possible in the wild, high and unpopulated West, the Federal Government granted over 130 million acres for the railroad's building fund. About 90% of that land was west of the Mississippi. Nearly 12% of California and 15% of Montana Territory was owned by railroads. Southern Pacific Company is the largest private land holder in California. On the average this previously worthless granted land was sold for a bit over three dollars per acre, higher in the central states, very low in the desert. And in return, until 1946, the Government received rail services at 50% of the current rate for the movement of freight, mail and troops.

Before examining the locomotive roster lists, it should be noted that this data was taken almost exclusively from builder lists complied by The Railway & Locomotive Historical Society, Inc. The construction date may vary from other books; in most cases, driver diameter will be different. There was much rebuilding.

Builder lists today are in most cases nearly complete. There are, unfortunately, large gaps in Danforth-Cooke, Grant, Hinkley and Norris construction numbers, the originals having been lost with the passage of time.

In some cases town spellings do not agree with today's version. The information in this book was generally taken from reference sources of that era and what may appear to be spelling errors, hopefully, are not. Examples are Lovelocks, Nevada, and Las Cruzces (1854) and Las Cruces (1860), New Mexico Territory. McDermit, Nevada, is yet another.

Following this introduction will be found several sections which have no direct relationship to the history of a particular railroad company or even railroads in general. They are included as a matter of general interest and information, and will give a background and data on the development of the West and the beginning of the railroad era. This ancillary information includes development of railroad equipment, locomotive builders, census figures by town and territory, post office openings for selected early periods in the West.

Notes and comments about *Travelers' Official Guide* and *Official Guide of the Railways*.

The construction details, changes of name, etc., found in the back of each state section resulted from the use of 619 volumes of this publication from June, 1868, to December, 1919. Bound editions were found from January, 1874, to December, 1900, and 142 more between 1901 and 1919 for a total of 466. That left 153 which were on film in the New York (City) Public Library.

It should be understood that this excellent reference was not intended to be a permanent record, but to be used until next month when there would be a new copy. As a result, the bindings and paper were not the finest. When filmed, as many as ninety years had passed, and many showed the results of time and usage.

Between 1868 and 1870, virtually every timetable was dated; between 1871 and 1873 virtually none was. A great many of the covers (with the date) were missing, as were pages, indexes and page numbers. With this background in mind it will be understood that some of the "first published timetable" notations between 1868 and 1873 may not, in fact, be true. The compiler can not be sure that all editions were photographed and/or in proper date sequence.

It should be noted, further, that the term "first published timetable" refers to *Official Guide* only unless otherwise credited. Thus a railroad that was opened in 1862 would have a "first published timetable", by this definition, in the June, 1868, edition. In all cases, regardless of date, longer lines timetables will be truncated.

A list of towns with railroad stations first appeared in the December, 1871, edition; in December, 1872, construction news was added as a continuing feature.

ENCYCLOPEDIA OF WESTERN RAILROAD

HISTORY

INTRODUCTION 1.

Western North America from 1832 to 1845

The Formation of the Western United States from 1845 to 1854

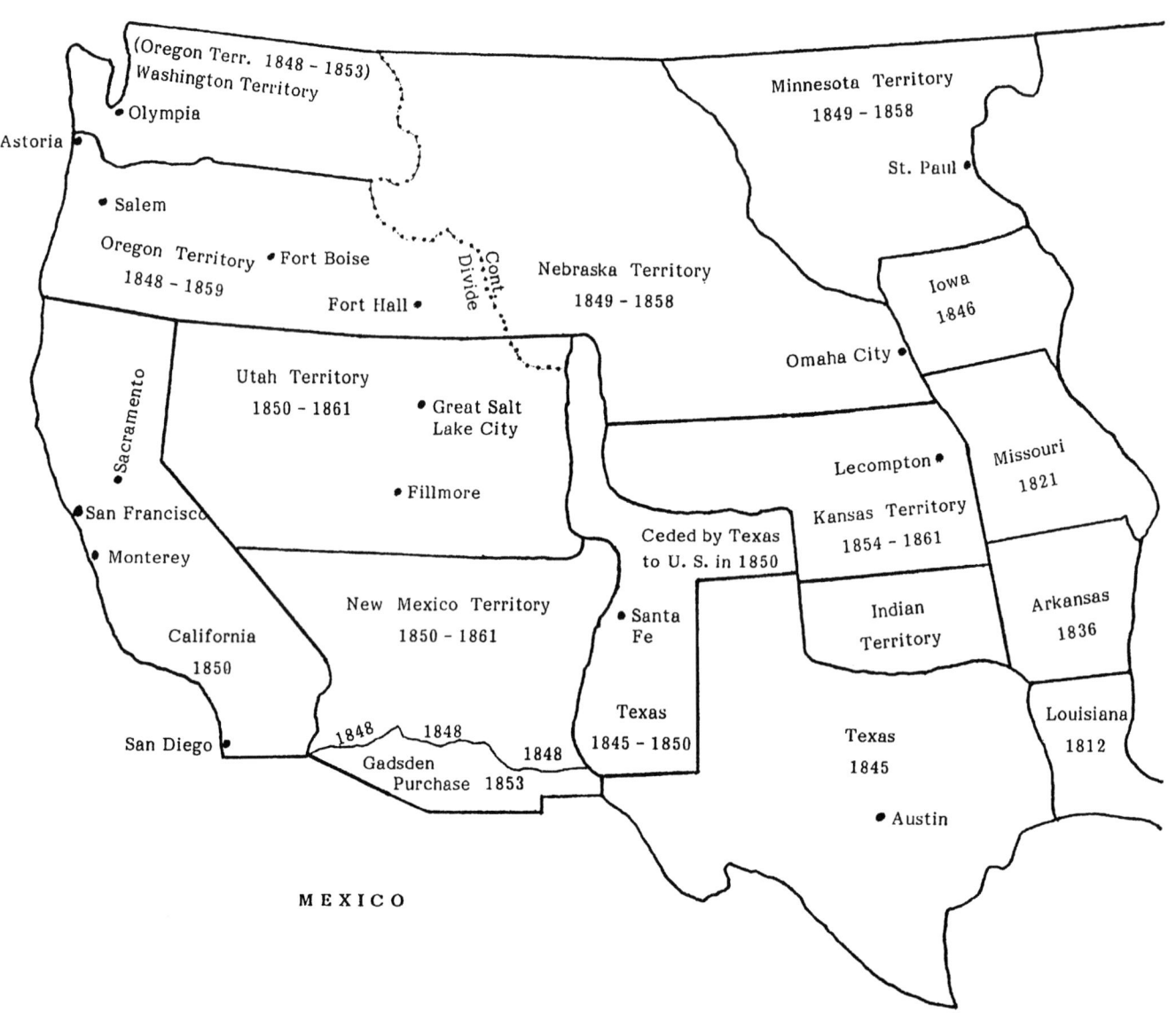

INTRODUCTION

The Pre-Civil War Era from 1854 to 1861

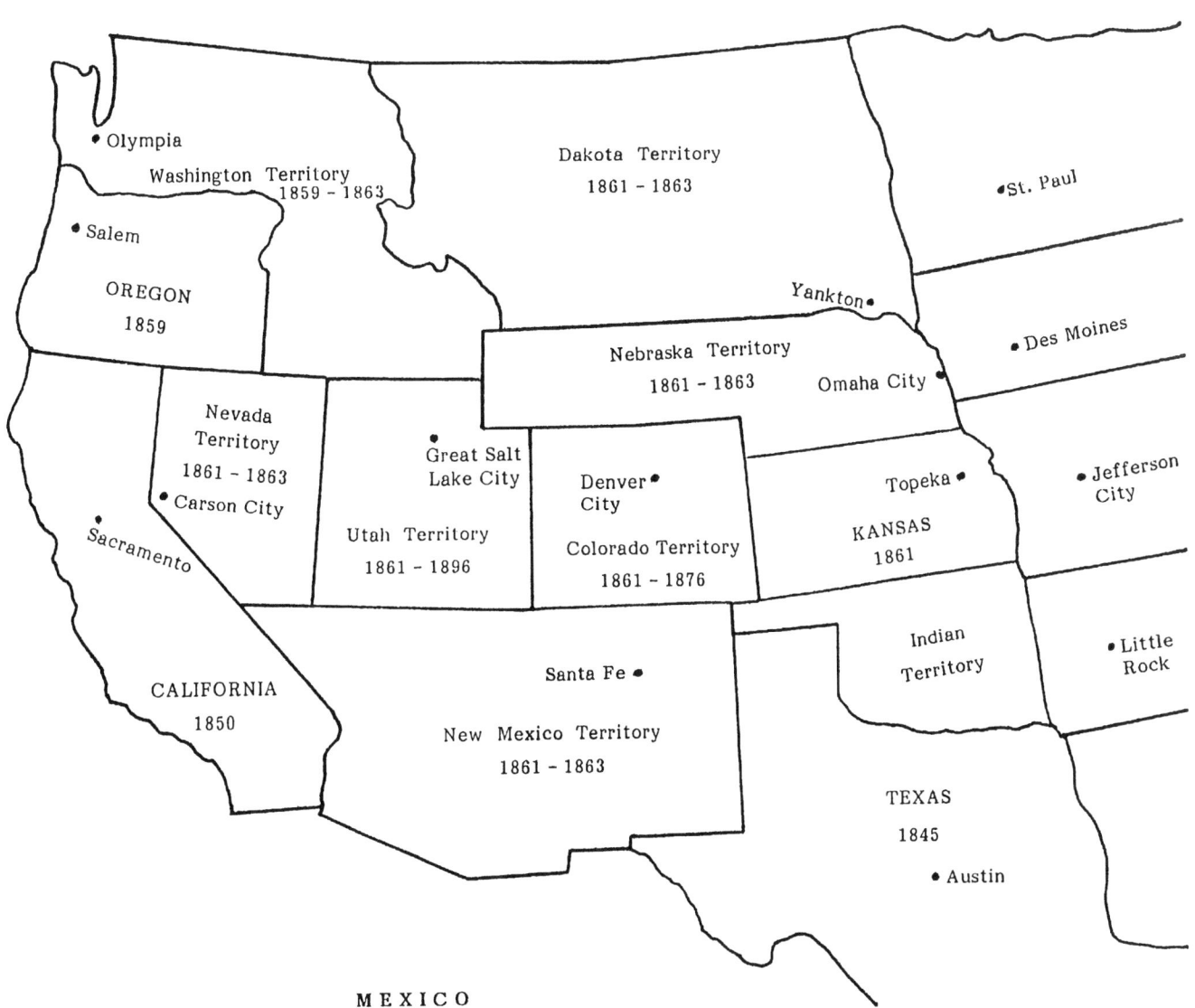

The Civil War Era from 1861 to 1865

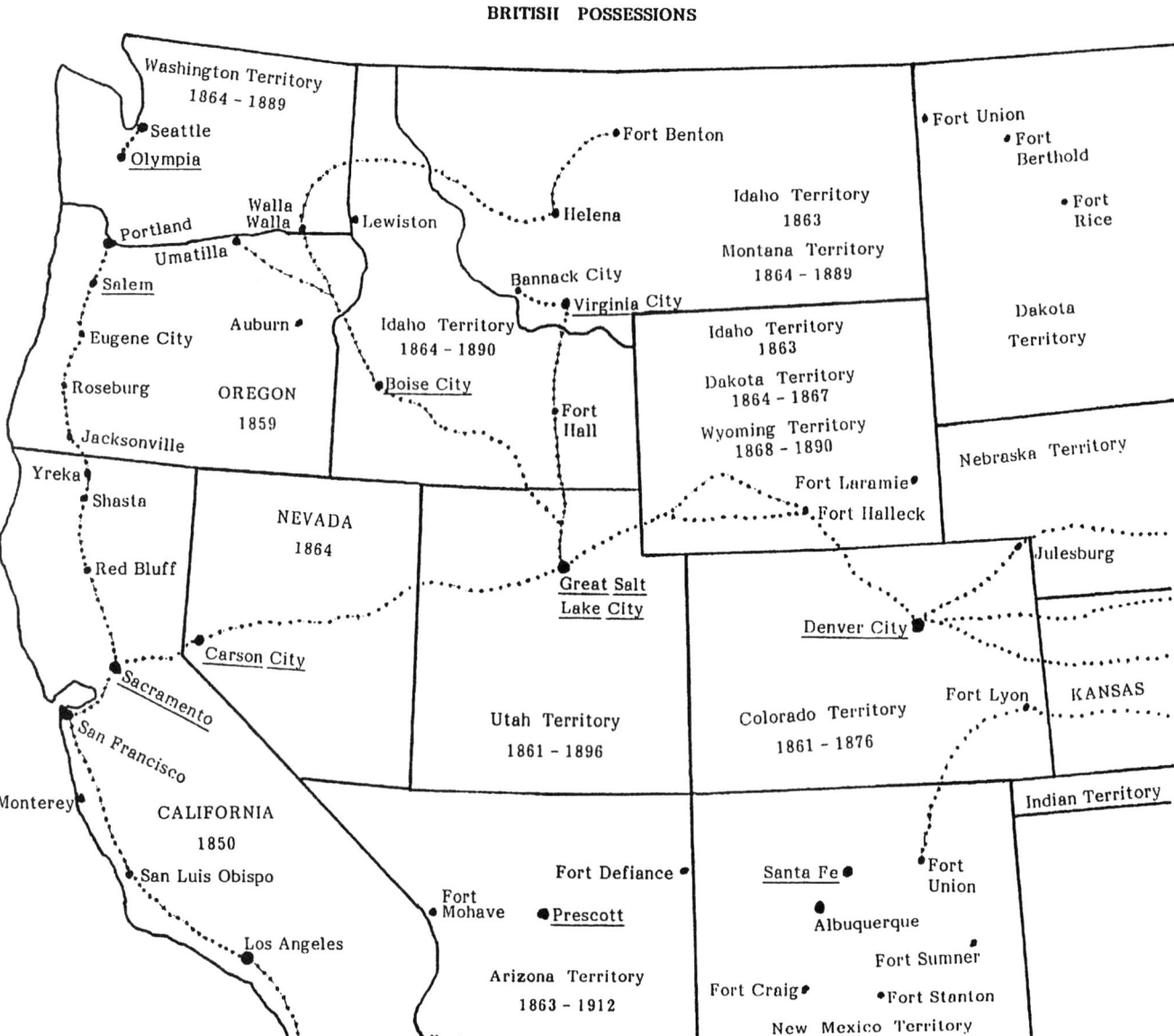

PRE-RAILROAD WESTERN HISTORY

Prehistoric people inhabited Oregon and Washington for well over ten thousand years before European discoveries brought a new era to their domain, but exploration of that diverse terrain lagged behind Spanish activity in California. Finally in 1542, Juan Cabrillo sent his sailing ship up California's coast to southern Oregon, or somewhere near there. Then Sir Francis Drake repeated Cabrillo's venture, entering a series of "most vile, thicke and stinking fogges" that darkened Oregon's seashore. Oregon and Washington thereafter were identified as Drake's New Albion - or New England. Another Spanish expedition penetrated some of Drake's Oregon fog in 1602-3, when Sebastian Viscaino and Martin Aguilar went out looking for Rogue River gold and spacious harbors along that obscure coast. They noticed a large river, but did not stop long enough to mine any gold. Further exploration ceased for another sixteen decades - a delay that left prehistoric inhabitants unmolested for another half dozen generations or so.

Peoples with exceptionally different cultures occupied Oregon and Washington in earliest times. Some had settled in relatively small areas where they developed dialects that persisted over many centuries. British Columbia, Washington, Idaho and western Montana shared tribes that had progressed from longer term coastal Salish settlements to larger new interior holdings where Pend Oreille (also referred to as Kalispell or Flathead), Spokane and Coeur d'Alene peoples had expanded over larger territories. Renowned for their totem poles and Potlatch feasts, coastal Salish and their interior associates spoke closely related languages that European travelers scarcely could recognize as speech of any kind. Other coastal Chinook and Athabascan villages lent variety to a western region where people did not need to travel extensively because they had a wealth of fish and vegetable resources that made for an easier life than other North American peoples enjoyed. They could just stay at home.

Interior plateau and desert peoples had a very different experience. They could have used railroads to considerable advantage. But from Spanish sources in New Mexico they acquired horses instead. Horse dealers soon wound up with an exceedingly large empire that extended clear into eastern Oregon, where Boise and Weiser bands of Northern Shoshoni advanced with their steeds. They formed part of a tribe with holdings reaching from New Mexico, western Texas, southern California and Colorado northward over plains and mountain areas past Wyoming and Montana into Alberta and Saskatchewan. Their lands included southern Idaho and much of Utah and Nevada. Mounted Shoshoni bands, whom Spaniards from New Mexico referred to as Comanche, distributed horses to many other tribes as well. (Shoshoni is a French and English term that designates people whom Spaniards called Comanche.) Another western group, known as Paiute, had a language and customs similar to their Shoshoni-Comanche neighbors; they were prominent in eastern Oregon and Nevada. Still different plateau peoples, such as Nez Perce, Cayuse and Umatilla, acquired Shoshoni horses and brought additional languages and living patterns to eastern Oregon and Washington. Many of these interior peoples traveled over wide areas hunting for buffalo, fishing for Snake and upper Columbia salmon and digging up vegetable products found in broadly scattered territories. Some mountain Shoshoni, however, found no advantage in embarking upon long seasonal migratory hunts, while other less adventurous upper Klamath people built permanent villages over rivers for easy canoe access that saved them from trips to distant lands.

Traditional prehistoric practices persisted in Oregon and Washington until a new eastern republic of former British colonies united in 1776 to initiate a new era in United States history with their Declaration of Independence from Great Britain. By that time, renewed coastal exploration had commenced from California bases. Juan Perez and Bruno Heceta had Spanish ships examining northwestern coastal shores more closely by 1774-6, and Heceta's sailors at last noticed Columbia River's Pacific outlet - almost simultaneously with Spanish discovery of San Francisco Bay through overland exploration. Then Captain James Cook's British navigators followed with a still more rewarding coastal survey in 1778. His vessel initiated a lucrative Pacific Northwest sea otter trade with China that soon attracted United States as well as British merchants. In 1786, Charles Barkley discovered Washington's Strait of Juan de Fuca, and in 1792, George Vancouver and Robert Gray undertook a lot more exploration. With a merchant ship from Boston, Gray sailed a few miles up a difficult lower Columbia River stretch, May 10, 1792, before embarking upon a significant Boston sea otter trade with China. Vancouver explored most of Puget Sound for British interests that soon became prominent.

Exploration of interior mountain and plateau lands of Oregon and Washington came from a new direction unconnected with Pacific coastal trade. In 1804-6, Meriwether Lewis and William Clark conducted a military and scientific expedition to examine upper Missouri and Columbia River lands as personal representatives of President Thomas Jefferson. Where possible, they took boats on their transcontinental journey westward. Their portage between navigable Missouri and Columbia tributaries turned out to require many more months than Jefferson had anticipated. After crossing a lot of difficult mountain country in Idaho, they finally reached Washington at the Snake River immediately below what would become Lewiston. Continuing on down to some Columbia gorge obstructions and past some Pacific coastal forests, they spent more time in Oregon than in any other state but North Dakota. Their scientific reports drew international attention to many Pacific Northwest wonders. Oregon, Washington and Idaho were not yet a United States' possession, but Lewis and Clark stimulated national interest in expansion into that region.

Aside from their extensive sea otter trade with China, fur hunters also approached Oregon and Washington from Rocky Mountain bases. Representing Montreal's North West Company of beaver trappers, David Thompson crossed from upper Saskatchewan posts to establish upper Columbia centers in British Columbia in 1807. Then he worked onward to later north Idaho in 1808 and built a post on Lake Pend Oreille in 1809. Spokane House (west of later Spokane Falls) followed as another major permanent trading center in Washington a year or two later. By that time, John Jacob Astor of New York was busy expanding his extensive beaver trade from his Great Lakes bases to Columbia River possibilities. He joined some North West Company beaver specialists in a project to found a major center that became Astoria, Oregon. He sent a ship out to open that Columbia sea port in 1810. Then Wilson Price Hunt's overland party followed a year later to set up a series of interior posts to provide fur resources for shipment from Astoria. His ambitious project led to competitive interior posts in Washington.

Complications intensified by serious War of 1812 hostilities and British naval operations defeated Astor's plan.

North West Company agents were induced to purchase his enterprise, and from that time on, Oregon and Washington had an extensive British and Canadian fur trade that survived efforts of Saint Louis operators to expand into their territory. Jim Bridger, Kit Carson and other celebrities from Saint Louis could not manage to operate effectively beyond Idaho's Snake country, but they succeeded in establishing routes that farmers and other emigrants could follow to reach Oregon and Washington after 1840. By that time, midwest farm lands suitable for settlement were largely occupied and new locations in western Oregon and Washington were becoming attractive.

Missionaries who came to serve Willamette Valley, Spokane, Cayuse and Nez Perce peoples after 1834 also facilitated farm settlements in Oregon and Washington. Hudson's Bay Company administrators had set up an agricultural company around Puget Sound in 1838 to supply their fur hunters as well as to trade in distant markets. By 1841, an emigrant brigade employed Red River ox carts to come out of Manitoba to join that farm settlement. A simultaneous - but smaller - party of midwestern agricultural emigrants bound for California from Missouri split up that summer. About half of that group opened an Oregon Trail route from Fort Hall to Willamette Valley. More followed in 1842, and a year later, Marcus Whitman brought out a much larger emigrant expedition with wagons that reached western Oregon. From then on United States farm settlements surpassed Canadian agricultural communities, and by 1846, Oregon and Washington became part of a United States possession. At that point, British Columbia was assigned to British control.

A large flood of emigration followed California gold discoveries in 1848, with a substantial share going to Willamette Valley where farmers prospered from supplying California markets. Improved transportation facilities were needed for Oregon as well as California, but Oregon had to depend upon ocean service. Emigrants could spend all summer driving their ox teams and wagons on their Oregon Trail trip, but more rapid communication clearly was in demand. Horses could move a lot faster for express service and for stages and freight lines, but they could go only short distances (12 to 20 miles) between stations. Then they needed relief and a chance to recuperate. Pack mules could go farther, but they did not provide a fast, long distance solution for most purposes either.

Railroads and telegraph lines had thrived in settled areas, and they offered what Oregon and Washington needed. How to utilize them in vast but empty areas of rugged mountains and arid plains posed problems that delayed them for years.

When mining commenced in southwestern Oregon in 1852, heavy freighting brought a greatly increased need for railroads. Mexican mule teams could supply placer miners without too much trouble, and they readily expanded from California into Oregon. Many large scale placer operations required heavy equipment like hydraulic giants - huge metal water hoses that washed out enormous pits from gold-bearing hillsides. But lode mines, blasted out of solid rock that ran deep into mountain interiors, required processing plants like stamp mills that could weigh 40 tons or more. Even when disassembled and hauled in large freight wagons, such devices required roads that ran great distances. A large party of freighters would have to spend weeks or months hauling mills from San Francisco or from remote rail terminals that had connections to Chicago. Places like Canyon City or John Day in eastern Oregon had to arrange for service from California, and still larger mill enterprises in nearby Idaho had to employ similar freight service from Umatilla and across eastern Oregon. In a particularly frustrating 1865 shipment of John Shoenbar's stamp mill from California to Silver City, Idaho, wagon drivers spent two weeks wandering somewhere around Goose Lake trying to find their way out of Nevada into - and across - eastern Oregon's deserts. Railroads proved essential for most important lode mines that managed to attain successful operating levels in remote or nearly inaccessible regions.

Oregon and Washington should have gained a transcontinental rail line far sooner than they did. Asa Whitney's widely publicized 1840 and 1844 proposals to build a railroad to a Pacific port would have done that. At a time before any Pacific destination was a United States' possession, he advocated an Oregon Trail route through South Pass and across Idaho's Snake plain to Willamette Valley. His plan focussed national attention upon an easier and naturally superior route, compared with one finally chosen in 1862 to reach California instead. By that time, gold mines had made California a much larger state than Oregon, which got by-passed for another two decades.

Merle Wells
An historian for
Idaho State Historical Society

INTRODUCTION 7.

The Military Forts of Territory/State of Oregon and Washington

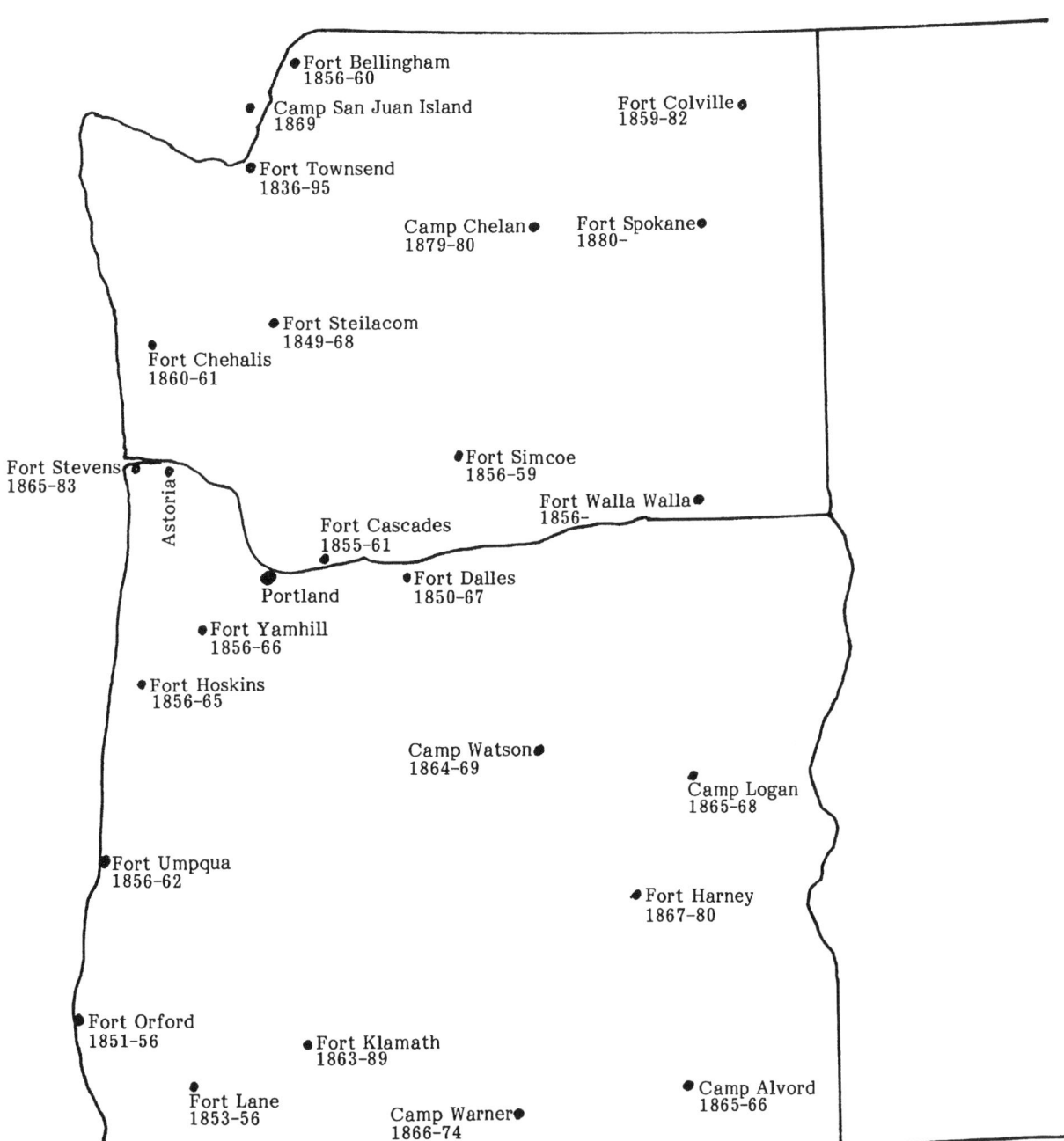

Establishment of Oregon Territory/State Counties and Post Offices

Counties

County	Date	County	Date
Clackamas	5 July 1843	Marion	5 July 1843
Washington	5 July 1843	Yamhill	5 July 1843
Clatsop	22 June 1844	Polk	22 December 1845
Benton	23 December 1847	Linn	28 December 1847
Umpqua	24 January 1851	Lane	28 January 1851
Douglas	7 January 1852	Jackson	12 January 1852
Tillamook	15 December 1853	Coos	22 December 1853
Wasco	11 January 1854	Columbia	16 January 1854
Multnomah	22 December 1854	Curry	18 December 1855
Josephine	22 January 1856	Baker	22 September 1862
Umatilla	27 September 1862	Grant	14 October 1864
Union	14 October 1864	Lake	24 October 1874
Klamath	17 October 1882	Crook	24 October 1882
Morrow	16 February 1885	Gilliam	25 February 1885
Wallowa	11 February 1887	Malheur	17 February 1887
Harney	25 February 1889	Sherman	25 February 1889
Lincoln	20 December 1893	Wheeler	17 February 1899
Hood River	23 June 1908	Jefferson	12 December 1914
Deschutes	13 December 1916		

Town	County	Date	Town	County	Date
Albany	Linn	8 January 1850	Amity	Yamhill	6 July 1852
Ashland	Jackson	27 October 1868	Astoria	Clatsop	29 March **1847**
Auburn	Baker	1 November 1862	Austin	Grant	28 August 1888
Avery's	Benton	8 January 1850	Baker City	Baker	27 March 1866
Bandon	Coos	12 September 1877	Bar	Baker	14 May 1886
Bend	Crook	18 January 1886	Brownlee	Baker	17 December 1910
Camp Harney	Grant	10 August 1874	Camp Lyon	Baker	2 August 1878
Camp Polk	Wasco	18 March 1875	Camp Watson	Grant	5 March 1875
Canby	Clackamas	16 August 1871	Canyon City	Wasco	23 April 1864
Clackamas	Clackamas	26 June 1876	Clarkville	Baker	27 September 1871
Clatskanie	Columbia	1 December 1871	Coquille	Coos	1 July 1870
Corvallis	Benton	18 February 1854	Cottage Grove	Lane	3 March 1855
Dairy	Lake	8 May 1876	Dallas	Polk	31 March 1854
Dalles	Jackson	5 November 1851	Dardanelles	Jackson	19 October 1852
Dayton	Yamhill	5 June 1851	Drain	Douglas	25 April 1872
El Dorado	Baker	11 September 1869	Empire City	Coos	27 March 1855
Eugene City	Lane	3 September 1853	Express Ranch	Baker	21 September 1865
Farwell Bend	Baker	19 March 1867	Forest Cove	Baker	4 June 1863
Fort Clatsop	Clatsop	8 March 1876	Fort Laramie	(to Wyo. Territory)	14 March 1850
Gardiner City	Umpqua	20 October 1853	Garibaldi	Tillamook	9 August 1870
Goble	Columbia	14 September 1894	Gold River	Jackson	18 April 1855
Goose Lake	Lake	24 September 1875	Grande Ronde	Polk	16 February 1861
Grant's Pass	Jackson	22 March 1865	Haines	Baker	26 November 1884
Hillsboro	Washington	5 August 1850	Hood River	Clackamas	30 September 1858
Humboldt Basin	Baker	29 June 1869	Huntington *	Baker	5 June 1882
Jacksonville	Jackson	18 February 1854	Jewell	Clatsop	23 December 1874
John Day City	Wasco	20 January 1865	Jordan Valley	Baker	13 February 1867
La Grande	Baker	28 May 1863	Lakeview	Lake	8 December 1876
Lebanon	Marion	5 June 1859	Leland	Jackson	28 March 1855
Linn City	Washington	8 January 1850	McMinnville	Yamhill	29 May 1855
Marshfield	Coos	22 June 1871	Marysville	Baker	28 March 1873
Milwaukie	Clackamas	1 February 1850	Mohawk	Lane	20 December 1862
Molalla	Clackamas	9 April 1850	Monmouth	Polk	25 February 1859
Mount Hood	Yamhill	14 October 1854	Myrtle Creek	Douglas	18 February 1854
Myrtle Point	Coos	29 December 1876	Nehalem	Tillamook	9 August 1870
New Albany	Linn	4 November 1850	New Era	Clackamas	5 January 1876
North Powder	Baker	15 May 1876	Norway	Coos	15 May 1876
Nyssa	Malheur	15 June 1889	Oakland	Umpqua	21 February 1852
Oceola	Multnomah	17 September 1860	Olney	Clatsop	12 March 1875
Ontario	Baker	19 March 1884	Oregon City	Clatsop	29 March **1847**
Oswego	Clackamas	3 May 1857	Oswego	Washington	31 March 1853
Owyhee	Baker	4 January 1886	Owyhee Ferry	Baker	19 March 1867
Pendleton	Umatilla	8 October 1869	Philomath	Benton	22 March 1889
Pilot Rock	Umatilla	2 December 1868	Pleasant Valley	Baker	28 September 1868
Pocahontas	Baker	4 August 1863	Port Clatsop	Clatsop	10 November 1852
Portland	Washington	8 November 1849	Port Orford	Jackson	2 March 1855

INTRODUCTION

Port Orford	Coos	27 March 1855	Prairie City	Grant	8 August 1870
Prineville	Wasco	7 September 1873	Rainier	Columbia	16 August 1854
Riverside	Malheur	21 November 1889	Robinette	Baker	3 May 1909
Roseburg	Douglas	27 January 1864	Rye Valley	Baker	27 September 1869
Salem	Marion	8 November 1849	Sandy	Multnomah	5 March 1862
Seaside House	Clatsop	23 July 1873	Silverton	Marion	31 July 1863
Skinner's	Benton	8 January 1850	Snake	Baker	5 April 1881
Sprague River	Lake	12 November 1873	St. Helens	Columbia	2 November 1853
Sumpter	Baker	29 September 1874	Sumter	Grant	24 June 1874
The Dalles	Wasco	22 March 1860	Tillamook	Tillamook	12 March 1866
Toledo	Benton	11 July 1868	Umatilla	Umatilla	28 May 1863
Union	Baker	8 May 1863	Union Mills	Clackamas	28 December 1875
Vale	Baker	20 February 1883	Vernonia	Columbia	11 March 1878
Westport	Clatsop	18 December 1863	White House	Baker	13 February 1867
Willamina	Yamhill	29 May 1855	Wingville	Baker	23 June 1871
Woodburn	Marion	28 December 1871	Yam Hill Falls	Yamhill	8 January 1850
Yaquina	Benton	22 April 1890			

* Huntington's first postmaster was James M. Huntington - not C. P. Huntington of the Central Pacific.

These post offices, originally in Oregon Territory, were split off into Washington Territory on 2 March 1853.

Cascades	Clark	5 November 1851	Columbia City	Clark	12 December 1850
Nisqually	Lewis	8 January 1850	Pacific City	Pacific	26 December 1850
Port Townsend	Thurston	28 September 1852	Seattle	Thurston	12 October 1852
Steilacoom	Lewis	6 July 1852	Vancouver	Clark	8 January 1850
Washougal	Clark	6 August 1852			

Courtesy of Southern Pacific Company
Oregon & California Rail Road work train on the Grave Creek trestle west of Grants Pass in 1883. The center is a Howe deck truss bridge; the trestle approaches are framed bents, as opposed to driven piles.

Establishment of Washington Territory/State Counties and Post Offices

Counties

County	Date	County	Date
Vancouver	20 August 1845	Lewis	21 December 1845
Clark (e)	3 September 1849	Pacific	4 February 1851
Thurston	12 January 1852	Jefferson	22 December 1852
King	22 December 1852	Pierce	22 December 1852
Island	6 January 1853	Chehalis	15 March 1854
Clallam	15 March 1854	Cowlitz	15 March 1854
Sawamish	15 March 1854	Skamania	15 March 1854
Wahkiakum	15 March 1854	Walla Walla	15 March 1854
Whatcom	15 March 1854	Kitsap	13 January 1858
Spokane	29 January 1858	Clickitat (Klickitat)	29 December 1859
Snohomish	14 January 1861	Stevens	20 January 1863
Mason	8 January 1864	Yakima	21 January 1865
Whitman	29 November 1871	San Juan	31 October 1873
Columbia	11 November 1875	Garfield	29 November 1881
Asotin	27 October 1883	Kittitas	24 November 1883
Lincoln	24 November 1883	Adams	28 November 1883
Douglas	28 November 1883	Franklin	28 November 1883
Skagit	28 November 1883	Okanogan	2 February 1888
Ferry	21 February 1899	Chelan	13 March 1899
Benton	8 March 1905	Grant	24 February 1909
Pend O'Reille	1 March 1911	Grays Harbor	15 March 1915

Town	County	Date	Town	County	Date
Aberdeen	Chehalis	10 April 1884	Ainsworth*	Franklin	22 December 1884
Anacortes	Skagit	2 October 1883	Asotin	Columbia	14 May 1880
Bellingham	Whatcom	17 October 1883	Black River	King	21 January 1867
Blaine	Whatcom	10 September 1885	Blakely	Kitsap	22 February 1867
Bothell	King	25 May 1888	Bruceport	Chehalis	29 April 1858
Brush Prairie	Clark	7 January 1876	Cascades	Clark	2 September 1853
Castle Rock	Lewis	1 June 1854	Cathlamet	Wahkiakum	27 February 1865
Cedarville	Chehalis	11 December 1860	Central Ferry	Columbia	19 July 1877
Centralia	Lewis	11 January 1884	Chehalis	Lewis	28 December 1876
Chehalis Point	Chehalis	19 November 1860	Chenowith	Skamania	4 May 1881
Chinook	Pacific	19 October 1852	Clallam Bay	Clallam	25 June 1890
Cle-Elum	Kittitas	13 January 1887	Colfax	Whitman	15 March 1872
Collins Landing	Skamania	2 April 1875	Columbia City	Clark	16 June 1854
Connell	Franklin	16 January 1887	Cosmopolis	Chehalis	17 March 1863
Coveland	Island	7 July 1857	Colville	Stevens	13 April 1883
Colville Valley	Walla Walla	21 June 1858	Cowlitz	Lewis	29 April 1854
Curlew	Spokane	28 May 1884	Davenport	Lincoln	28 August 1884
Dayton	Columbia	25 September 1872	Deming	Whatcom	5 November 1888
Edmonds	Snohomish	15 April 1889	Ellensburg	Yakima	7 April 1873
Elma	Chehalis	14 July 1862	Etna	Clark	3 February 1882
Eufaula	Cowlitz	19 October 1895	Everett	Snohomish	12 June 1891
Fairhaven	Whatcom	15 July 1889	Forks	Clallam	8 February 1884
Fort Colville	Walla Walla	21 June 1858	Fort Simcoe	Klickitat	9 August 1870
Fort Steilacoom	Pierce	20 December 1881	Fort Stevens	Thurston	18 November 1857
Fort Townsend	Jefferson	28 September 1852	Fort Willapa	Chehalis	29 April 1858
Franklin	Pierce	31 May 1862	Golden	Okanogan	27 November 1889
Goldendale	Klickitat	18 April 1872	Grand Mound	Thurston	21 January 1854
Gray's Harbor	Chehalis	2 January 1890	Hoquiam	Chehalis	13 December 1867
Humptulips	Chehalis	10 July 1890	Ilwaco	Pacific	18 July 1876
Kalama	Clark	24 January 1871	Kelso	Cowlitz	11 December 1886
Kennewick	Yakima	21 January 1885	Kent	King	29 October 1884
Kettle Falls	Stevens	30 June 1890	Klickitat	Klickitat	14 July 1870
La Crosse	Whitman	31 August 1896	Leavenworth	Okanogan	30 December 1892
Longview	Benton	3 May 1911	Lyle	Klickitat	28 March 1882
Maple Valley	King	14 December 1885	Marcus	Stevens	5 May 1884
Marshall	Spokane	26 March 1880	Medical Lake	Spokane	30 June 1884
Metaline Falls	Pend O'Reille	17 November 1910	Molson	Okanogan	14 July 1900
Montesano	Chehalis	19 November 1860	Monticello	Cowlitz	16 January 1855
Morton	Lewis	22 January 1891	Moses Lake	Douglas	10 March 1906
Mount Vernon	Whatcom	29 June 1877	Mukilteo	Snohomish	5 July 1861

Nahcotta	Pacific	18 January 1890	Neah Bay	Clallam	24 June 1874
New Kamilche	Mason	22 October 1890	Newport	Pend O'Reille	27 February 1905
New Tacoma	Pierce	6 July 1874	Nisqually	Pierce	13 December 1860
Oak Harbor	Island	28 February 1861	Oakland	Sawamish	24 April 1858
Oak Point	Thurston	18 February 1857	Old Tacoma	Pierce	16 May 1884
Olney	King	30 January 1889	Olympia	Lewis	26 May 1853
Orting	Pierce	13 March 1878	Ozette	Clallam	3 April 1891
Pacific City	Lewis	26 December 1850	Palouse	Whitman	20 May 1873
Pasco *	Franklin	23 September 1885	Pe Ell	Lewis	23 June 1891
Pinkney City	Spokane	17 December 1859	Pomeroy	Columbia	25 February 1878
Port Angeles	Clallam	6 June 1862	Port Discovery	Clallam	28 February 1861
Port Gamble	Kitsap	17 January 1872	Port Ludlow	Clark	2 December 1857
Port Madison	Kitsap	13 May 1858	Port Orchard	Kitsap	1 May 1861
Port Townsend	Jefferson	30 June 1865	Prosser	Yakima	20 March 1882
Pullman	Whitman	5 December 1881	Puyallup	Pierce	3 September 1874
Pysht	Clallam	15 January 1878	Quilcene	Jefferson	16 March 1889
Raymond	Pacific	23 February 1904	Renton	King	21 June 1876
Republic	Ferry	29 December 1897	Riparia	Columbia	17 November 1882
Ritzville	Whitman	28 June 1880	Rockford	Spokane	26 April 1880
Rockland	Skamania	20 November 1860	Rosalia	Stevens	5 September 1872
Ryderwood	Cowlitz	16 February 1924	Saint John	Whitman	31 October 1889
San Juan	San Juan	31 August 1874	Satsop	Chehalis	13 June 1870
Seabeck	Kitsap	17 January 1872	Seattle	King	11 August 1853
Sedro	Skagit	7 December 1885	Sedro-Woolley	Skagit	7 July 1899
Selah	Yakima	9 January 1871	Shelton	Mason	23 March 1886
Skagit	Whatcom	24 April 1872	Skagit Head	Island	21 April 1858
Snohomish	Island	28 February 1861	Snoqualmie	King	20 May 1871
Spokane	Spokane	24 July 1890	Spokane Bridge	Stevens	2 December 1867
Spokane Falls	Spokane	5 February 1877	Sprague	Spokane	6 December 1880
Starbuck	Columbia	8 February 1883	Steilacoom	Pierce	19 May 1853
Stella	Cowlitz	14 August 1884	Sultan City	Snohomish	24 July 1886
Tacoma	Pierce	25 March 1869	Tekoa	Whitman	27 July 1888
Tenino	Thurston	17 November 1873	Thornton	Whitman	14 April 1890
Tolt	King	4 December 1883	Toppenish	Yakima	3 March 1890
Touchet	Walla Walla	23 March 1864	Tumwater	Thurston	19 June 1866
Union Ridge	Clark	15 September 1865	Unionville	Whatcom	26 May 1862
Vancouver	Clark	10 December 1855	Vashon	King	12 April 1883
Waitsburg	Walla Walla	27 November 1871	Walla Walla	Walla Walla	8 September 1862
Wallula	Walla Walla	8 March 1877	Washougal	Clark	11 October 1853
Waterville	Douglas	1 November 1887	Wenatchee	Kittitas	5 May 1884
Wickersham	Whatcom	5 June 1891	Willapa	Pacific	24 April 1884
Woodinville	King	10 May 1882	Woolley	Skagit	5 May 1890
Yakima	Yakima	2 May 1870	Yelm	Thurston	31 August 1874

* Ainsworth was renamed Pasco

Ranking of Western Territories/States by Population - 1850 to 1940

	1850	1860	1870	1880	1890	1900	1910	1920	1930	1940
Arizona				46	44	47	47	46	46	43	43
California	29	26	24	24	22	21	12	8	6	5
Colorado		38	41	35	31	32	32	33	33	33
Idaho			44	46	46	46	45	43	42	42
Montana			43	45	45	43	40	39	39	39
Nevada		41	40	43	48	48	48	48	48	48
New Mexico	32	34	37	41	44	44	44	44	44	41
Oregon	34	36	38	37	38	36	35	34	34	34
Utah	35	37	39	39	41	42	41	40	40	40
Washington			42	42	34	34	30	30	30	30
Wyoming			47	47	47	47	47	47	47	47
Average:	32	35	40	40	40	40	38	37	37	37

ENCYCLOPEDIA OF WESTERN RAILROAD HISTORY

Post Offices in the Eleven Western Territories / States

The establishment (and abandonment) of post offices is yet another indication of development in the West and the arrival (and departure) of people.

All dates are as of June 30.

	Ariz.	Calif.	Colo.	Idaho	Mont.	Nevada	N.Mex.	Oregon	Utah	Wash.	Wyo.	totals
1860		356	21				21	96	52	52		598
1861		373	23			2	22	97	57	64		638
1862		404	39			7	23	93	58	67		691
1863	1	398	59	8		14	17	99	59	69		724
1864	1	408	53	17		19	15	99	74	67		753
1865	2	422	52	18	1	23	17	103	114	62		814
1866	7	446	59	25	10	32	23	107	104	64		877
1867	15	433	73	31	23	51	34	120	92	63		935
1868	15	444	75	31	36	43	43	129	97	66	1	980
1869	15	467	90	28	52	53	41	144	104	67	20	1,081
1870	21	506	94	25	68	59	40	157	120	77	27	1,194
1871	26	576	110	33	76	58	46	175	136	92	24	1,352
1872	31	592	132	42	96	70	47	220	155	109	30	1,524
1873	37	630	145	53	101	82	48	239	168	126	33	1,662
1874	34	683	167	66	94	86	55	244	166	138	34	1,767
1875	42	731	188	68	100	88	66	268	174	155	40	1,920
1876	39	763	212	74	94	92	72	291	171	148	44	2,000
1877	42	771	236	73	97	98	81	305	182	153	51	2,089
1878	54	814	265	92	116	97	96	329	190	171	55	2,279
1879	74	836	293	92	123	115	102	354	198	200	60	2,447
1880	85	889	351	101	148	125	114	371	214	233	75	2,706
1881	113	912	393	112	156	121	148	373	225	254	85	2,892
1882	115	947	438	130	185	132	172	397	218	282	81	3,097
1883	125	972	487	142	199	139	173	407	225	296	93	3,258
1884	137	989	505	170	207	143	172	448	239	331	98	3,439
1885	143	999	506	178	235	141	189	463	240	364	110	3,568
1886	137	1,058	490	200	251	139	211	496	240	385	122	3,729
1887	147	1,098	498	219	261	131	215	528	247	426	148	3,918
1888	156	1,204	557	213	296	136	227	564	230	453	173	4,209
1889	160	1,283	609	227	303	138	228	593	244	476	185	4,446
1890	170	1,355	676	260	348	148	256	653	253	602	226	4,947
1891	168	1,394	682	270	379	152	265	701	257	665	236	5,169
1892	183	1,439	708	300	418	161	277	749	272	766	253	5,526
1893	194	1,488	706	313	418	168	276	779	280	800	260	5,682
1894	185	1,520	673	317	406	166	292	778	290	809	250	5,686
1895	185	1,543	703	330	397	168	306	708	296	804	251	5,691
1896	181	1,560	699	355	404	173	297	797	301	801	262	5,830
1897	197	1,604	719	375	426	174	304	823	311	807	281	6,021
1898	201	1,642	743	411	458	181	310	860	331	813	301	6,251
1899	202	1,659	743	424	471	186	312	862	338	828	342	6,367
1900	221	1,657	751	448	497	188	322	890	339	850	317	6,480

Source: Report of the Postmaster-General.

INTRODUCTION

Compendium of the Seventh to Fourteenth Censuses

Oregon Territory

City	County	1850	1860	1870	1880	1890	1900	1910	1920
Albany	Linn			1,992	1,867	3,079	3,149	4,275	4,840
Ashland	Jackson		327		842	1,784	2,634	5,020	4,283
Astoria	Clatsop		252	639	2,803	6,184	8,381	9,599	14,027
Baker City	Baker				312	1,258	2,604	6,663	6,742	7,729
Bend	Crook						68	21	536	5,415
Brownsville	Linn				788	143	580	698	919	763
Burns	Harney						264	547	904	1,022
Coquille	Coos			94	210	176	494	728	1,398	1,642
Corvallis	Benton			1,231		1,128	1,527	1,819	4,552	5,752
Cottage Grove	Lane					967	1,527	974	1,834	1,919
Dallas	Polk			450	795	670	848	1,271	2,124	2,701
Dayton	Yamhill			426	587	368	304	293	453	448
Empire City	Coos			176	381	412	252	185	147	182
Eugene City	Lane			1,183	1,852	2,250	4,111	3,236	9,009	10,593
Forest Grove	Washington				922	547	668	1,096	1,772	1,915
Grants Pass	Josephine					551	1,432	2,290	3,897	3,151
Heppner	Morrow				133	895	675	1,146	880	1,324
Hillsboro	Washington				796	885	1,552	980	2,016	2,468
Hood River	Hood River			70	85	364	201	766	2,331	3,195
Jacksonville	Jackson			892		839	743	653	785	489
Joseph	Wallowa						249	237	725	770
Klamath Falls	Klamath						364	447	2,758	4,801
La Grande	Union				640	836	2,583	2,991	4,843	6,913
Lebanon	Linn				515		829	922	1,820	1,805
Linn City	Washington	125								
McMinnville	Yamhill			445	388	670	1,368	1,420	2,400	2,767
Marshfield	Coos				402	642	1,461	1,391	2,980	4,034
Medford	Jackson						967	1,791	8,840	5,756
Milton City	Washington	692								
Milwaukee	Clackamas			180	217	125	489	1,002	860	1,172
Myrtle Creek	Douglas			213	504	568	652	189	429	385
Newberg	Yamhill					481	514	945	2,260	2,566
North Bend	Coos								2,078	3,268
Oregon City	Clackamas	697		889	1,382	1,707	3,062	3,494	4,287	5,686
Pendleton	Umatilla				243	730	2,506	4,406	4,460	7,387
Portland	Multnomah	821		2,874	8,293	17,577	46,385	90,426	207,214	258,288
Prineville	Crook						460	656	1,042	1,144
Rainier	Columbia			85	116	372	238	522	1,359	1,287
Roseburg	Douglas			834		822	1,472	1,690	4,738	4,381
Salem	Marion			1,500	1,139	3,958	4,749	4,258	14,094	17,679
Silverton	Marion			617	801	229	511	656	1,588	2,251
The Dalles	Wasco			794	1,647	2,232	3,029	3,542	4,880	5,807
Umatilla	Umatilla				206	297	210	191	198	390
Union	Union				400	416	604	937	1,483	1,319
Woodburn	Marion					402	405	828	1,616	1,656
Totals:		13,294	52,465	90,923	174,768	317,704	413,536	672,765	783,389

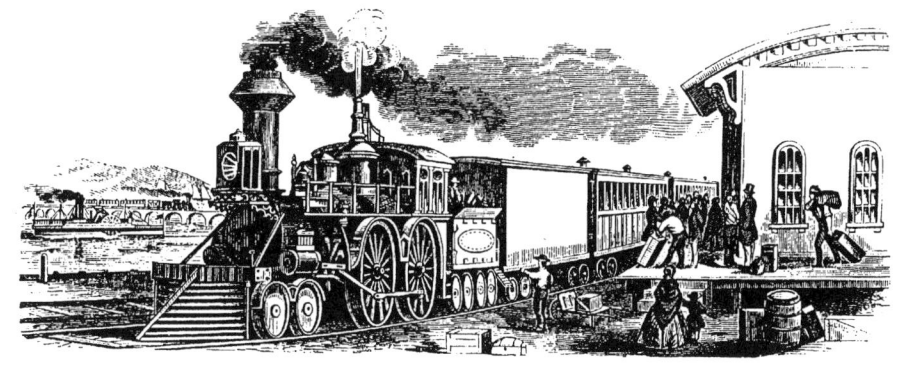

Compendium of the Eighth to Fourteenth Censuses
Washington Territory

City	County	1860	1870	1880	1890	1900	1910	1920
Aberdeen	Chehalis				1,638	3,747	13,660	15,337
Anacortes	Skagit				1,311	1,476	4,168	5,428
Asotin	Asotin				200	470	820	852
Auburn	King				740	489	957	3,163
Bellingham	Whatcom						24,298	25,588
Blaine	Whatcom				1,563	1,592	2,289	2,254
Buckley	Pierce					1,014	1,272	1,119
Centralia	Lewis				2,026	1,600	7,311	7,549
Chehalis	Lewis				1,309	1,775	4,507	4,558
Cheney	Spokane				647	781	1,207	1,252
Colfax	Whitman			444	1,649	2,121	2,783	3,027
Colville	Stevens	627	587	67	539	594	1,533	1,718
Cosmopolis	Chehalis				287	1,004	1,132	1,512
Davenport	Lincoln				386	1,000	1,229	1,112
Dayton	Columbia			996	1,880	2,216	2,389	2,695
Edmonds	Snohomish				384	474	1,114	936
Ellensburg	Kittitas				2,768	1,737	4,209	3,967
Elma	Chehalis				345	894	1,532	1,253
Everett	Snomomish					7,838	24,814	27,644
Fairhaven	Whatcom				4,076	4,228	renamed	Bellingham
Goldendale	Klickitat			545	702	738	1,203	1,274
Hamilton	Skagit				203	392	405	462
Hoquiam	Chehalis				1,302	2,608	8,171	10,058
Ilwaco	Pacific			85	517	584	664	787
Kalama	Cowlitz			129	325	554	816	1,228
Kelso	Cowlitz				354	694	2,039	2,228
Lynden	Whatcom				560	365	1,148	1,244
Marysville	Snohomish				262	728	1,239	1,244
Medical Lake	Spokane				617	516	1,730	2,545
Monroe	Snohomish					682	1,552	1,675
Montesano	Chehalis				1,632	1,194	2,488	2,158
Mount Vernon	Skagit				770	1,120	2,381	3,341
New Whatcom	Whatcom				2,140	6,834	renamed	Bellingham
North Yakima	Yakima				1,535	3,154	14,082	to Yakima
Oakesdale	Whitman				528	928	882	816
Olympia	Thurston		1,203	1,232	4,698	3,863	6,996	7,795
Orting	Pierce				623	728	799	972
Palouse	Whitman			148	1,119	929	1,549	1,179
Pasco	Franklin					254	2,083	3,362
Pomeroy	Garfield				661	953	1,605	1,804
Port Angeles	Clallam					2,321	2,286	5,351
Port Orchard	Kitsap	47	80	353	226	254	682	1,393
Port Townsend	Jefferson	264	593	917	4,558	3,443	4,181	2,847
Pullman	Whitman				868	1,308	2,602	2,440
Puyallup	Pierce			297	1,732	1,884	4,544	6,323
Renton	King				406	1,176	2,740	3,301
Republic	Ferry					2,050	999	781
Ritzville	Adams					761	1,859	1,900
Rosalia	Whitman				248	379	767	714
Roslyn	Kittitas				1,484	2,786	3,126	2,672
Seattle	King		1,107	3,553	42,837	80,671	237,194	315,312
Sedro-Woolley	Skagit					885	2,129	3,389
Shelton	Mason				648	833	1,163	984
Snohomish	Snohomish			149	1,993	2,101	3,244	2,985
South Bend	Pacific					711	3,023	1,948
Spokane Falls	Spokane			350	19,922	36,848	104,402	104,437
Sprague	Lincoln				1,689	695	1,110	822
Tacoma	Pierce	9	73	1,098	36,006	37,714	83,743	96,965
Tekoa	Whitman				301	717	1,694	1,520
Tenino	Thurston				339	341	1,038	850
Toledo	Lewis				276	285	375	324
Vancouver	Clark	660		1,722	3,545	3,126	9,300	12,637
Waitsburg	Walla Walla		107	248	817	1,011	1,237	1,174
Walla Walla	Walla Walla	722	1,514	3,588	4,709	10,049	19,364	15,503
Wenatchee	Chelan					451	4,050	6,324
Whatcom	Whatcom	77	258		4,059		to New	Whatcom
Yakima City	Yakima		23	267	196	287	263	18,539
Totals:			11,594	23,955	75,116	357,232	518,103	1,141,990	1,356,621

INTRODUCTION

Operations in Oregon and Washington - 1880 and 1890

	June 30, 1880 Oregon	June 30, 1880 Wash.	June 30, 1890 Oregon	June 30, 1890 Wash.
Astoria & South Coast Railroad Co.			15.78	
Bellingham Bay & British Columbia Rail Road Co.				3.00
Blanchard Railroad Co.				5.00
Cascades Railroad Co.		6.00		
Columbia & Grays Harbor Railroad Co.				4.00
Columbia & Puget Sound Railroad Co.				42.00
Fairhaven & Southern Railroad Co.				26.10
Ilwaco Railway & Navigation Co., The				16.00
Mosquito & Coal Creek Railroad Co.				2.63
Northern Pacific Railroad Co.		136.00	36.30	542.20
Central Washington Railroad Co.				87.50
Northern Pacific & Cascade Railroad Co.				18.60
Northern Pacific & Puget Sound Shore Railroad Co.				30.50
Spokane & Palouse Railway Co.				97.30
Tacoma, Orting & Southeastern Railroad Co., The				7.80
Olympia & Chehalis Valley Railroad Co., The				15.50
Oregon & California Rail Road Co.	197.57			
Oregon & Washington Territory Railroad Co.			44.68	117.40
Oregon Central Railroad Co.	46.70			
Oregon Pacific Rail Road Co.			141.80	
Oregon Railway & Navigation Co.	13.30			
Oregon Short Line & Utah Northern Railway Co.			15.41	
Oregonian Railway Co.			155.40	
Portland & Willamette Valley Railway Co.			28.30	
Puget Sound & Chehalis Railway Co.				6.00
Puget Sound & Grays Harbor Railroad Co.				20.00
Satsop Railroad Co.				24.00
Seattle & Walla Walla Railroad & Transp. Co.		20.00		
Seattle, Lake Shore & Eastern Railway Co.				155.80
Southern Pacific Co.				
Oregon & California Rail Road Co.			475.42	
Spokane Falls & Northern Railway Co., The				102.00
Thurston County Railroad Construction Co.		15.00		
Union Pacific Railway Co.				
Cascades Railroad Co.				6.00
Columbia & Palouse Railroad Co., The				142.07
Mill Creek Flume & Manufacturing Co.				12.59
Oregon Railway & Navigation Co.			504.36	136.51
Oregon Railway Extensions Co., The				47.84
Walla Walla & Columbia River Railroad Co.			5.34	30.18
Washington & Idaho Railroad Co.				62.59
Vancouver, Klickitat & Yakima Railroad Co.				10.00
Walla Walla & Columbia River Railroad Co.	11.00	35.00		
Western Oregon Railroad Co.	49.76			
Willamette Valley Railroad Co.	29.00			
Totals:	347.33	212.00	1,422.79	1,771.11

Source: Census of the United States - 1880 and 1890

Miles of Railroad Construction by Year and Company

	1863	1869	1870	1871	1872	1873	1875	1876	1877	1878	1879
Cascades	6.00										
Northern Pacific			114.00	114.23	165.00	136.50			31.00		54.00
Oregon & California		20.00	60.00	44.00	57.00	16.57					
Oregon Central					46.70						
Oregon Steam Navig.	13.30										
Seattle & Walla Walla								13.00	7.00		
Thurston County										15.00	
Walla Walla & C. R.							32.00				14.00
Western Oregon											49.76
Willamette Valley										29.00	

Railroad Development in the West

	1855	1856	1857	1858	1859	1860	1861	1862	1863	1864	1865	1866	1867
California	8	23	23	23	23	23	23	23	53	147	214	308	382
Colorado													b.(8)
Nevada													30
Oregon								4	19	19	19	19	19
Washington								a.(5)	a.(5)	a.(5)	a.(5)	a.(5)	a.(5)
Wyoming													82

	1868	1869	1870	1871	1872	1873	1874	1875	1876	1877	1878	1879	1880
Arizona											27	183	349
California	468	702	925	1,013	1,042	1,208	1,328	1,503	1,919	2,080	2,149	2,209	2,195
Colorado	b.(8)	b.(8)	157	328	483	603	682	807	957	1,045	1,165	1,208	1,570
Idaho							c.(2)	c.(2)	c.(2)	c.(2)	103	196	206
Montana												10	106
Nevada	402	402	593	593	611	629	650	650	627	627	629	720	739
New Mexico											8	118	758
Oregon	19	60	159	159	241	251	251	251	248	248	283	295	508
Utah	d.(5)	257	257	257	349	372	459	515	506	506	543	593	842
Washington	a.(5)	a.(5)	a.(5)	25	65	105	110	110	110	197	212	212	289
Wyoming	447	447	459	459	459	459	459	459	459	465	472	493	512

	1881	1882	1883	1884	1885	1886	1887	1888	1889	1890	1891	1892	1893
Arizona	497	713	866	906	906	989	1,060	1,095	1,095	1,095	1,098	1,162	1,162
California	2,309	2,636	2,881	2,911	3,045	3,264	3,656	4,126	4,205	4,328	4,485	4,624	4,629
Colorado	2,187	2,766	2,832	2,842	2,877	2,901	3,773	4,038	4,104	4,291	4,441	4,452	4,488
Idaho	276	494	777	811	795	808	848	868	929	946	960	1,073	1,090
Montana	271	633	1,035	1,047	1,047	1,062	1,687	1,804	1,972	2,196	2,291	2,668	2,722
Nevada	895	948	948	948	948	948	948	948	916	923	923	923	923
New Mexico	1,047	1,089	1,140	1,191	1,195	1,235	1,238	1,321	1,326	1,389	1,424	1,430	1,433
Oregon	573	756	950	1,165	1,181	1,222	1,291	1,412	1,413	1,456	1,504	1,522	1,512
Utah	877	1,062	1,124	1,134	1,139	1,139	1,134	1,153	1,177	1,265	1,336	1,357	1,364
Washington	472	472	598	675	776	934	1,037	1,319	1,686	2,005	2,309	2,765	2,810
Wyoming	576	625	625	616	617	745	877	902	942	1,003	1,049	1,150	1,158

	1894	1895	1896	1897	1898	1899	1900	1901	1902	1903	1904	1905	1906
Arizona	1,357	1,412	1,413	1,412	1,412	1,465	1,516	1,598	1,617	1,716	1,787	1,831	1,882
California	4,758	4,758	4,948	5,199	5,292	5,455	5,589	5,684	5,773	5,884	6,203	6,272	6,385
Colorado	4,539	4,503	4,509	4,576	4,609	4,617	4,650	4,741	4,802	4,852	4,990	5,093	5,239
Idaho	1,089	1,088	1,088	1,112	1,119	1,271	1,319	1,441	1,434	1,427	1,425	1,493	1,681
Montana	2,825	2,829	2,886	2,907	2,971	3,008	3,029	3,146	3,234	3,262	3,328	3,328	3,310
Nevada	923	916	916	908	920	920	920	960	961	957	1,187	1,282	1,546
New Mexico	1,510	1,505	1,502	1,502	1,613	1,778	1,779	2,031	2,349	2,450	2,441	2,597	2,789
Oregon	1,515	1,514	1,525	1,553	1,615	1,632	1,671	1,687	1,712	1,720	1,750	1,882	1,931
Utah	1,395	1,404	1,441	1,436	1,480	1,573	1,582	1,594	1,611	1,681	1,742	1,808	1,918
Washington	2,813	2,820	2,812	2,812	2,812	2,892	2,888	3,053	3,112	3,335	3,232	3,301	3,400
Wyoming	1,178	1,178	1,178	1,178	1,171	1,212	1,241	1,322	1,313	1,239	1,244	1,281	1,513

	1907	1908	1909	1910	1911	1912	1913	1914	1915	1916	1917	1918	1919
Arizona	1,935	1,935	2,052	2,168	2,190	2,156	2,283	2,273	2,291	2,416	2,424	2,479	2,498
California	6,702	7,039	7,188	7,373	7,512	8,104	8,183	8,368	8,451	8,439	8,359	8,268	8,393
Colorado	5,351	5,403	5,491	5,569	5,728	5,737	5,710	5,739	5,991	5,700	5,640	5,615	5,582
Idaho	1,835	2,022	2,061	2,398	2,551	2,556	2,664	2,749	2,878	2,829	2,861	2,884	2,947
Montana	3,468	4,013	4,120	4,249	4,361	4,358	4,497	4,847	4,954	4,859	4,954	5,037	5,032
Nevada	1,760	1,867	2,170	2,178	2,208	2,337	2,341	2,418	2,332	2,319	2,293	2,296	2,177
New Mexico	2,894	2,918	3,053	3,067	3,079	3,047	3,032	3,025	3,078	3,038	2,974	2,978	2,974
Oregon	1,971	2,089	2,153	2,378	2,602	2,686	2,774	2,912	3,083	3,226	3,232	3,298	3,315
Utah	1,959	1,963	1,981	1,994	2,056	2,029	2,083	2,098	2,039	2,143	2,145	2,161	2,175
Washington	3,717	4,180	4,364	4,768	4,892	5,179	5,290	5,247	6,161	5,685	5,650	5,612	5,546
Wyoming	1,554	1,624	1,608	1,662	1,704	1,677	1,680	1,821	1,891	1,918	1,924	1,931	1,930

The above are the official mileage figures from federal statistics; the author has added his unofficial figures as follows:

a. Cascades portage railroad on the Columbia River
b. The Union Pacific at Julesburg
c. Utah Northern to Franklin
d. Union Pacific to Wasatch

INTRODUCTION 17.

Western railroads in 1865

Western railroads in 1870

Western railroads in 1875

Western railroads in 1880

Western railroads in 1885

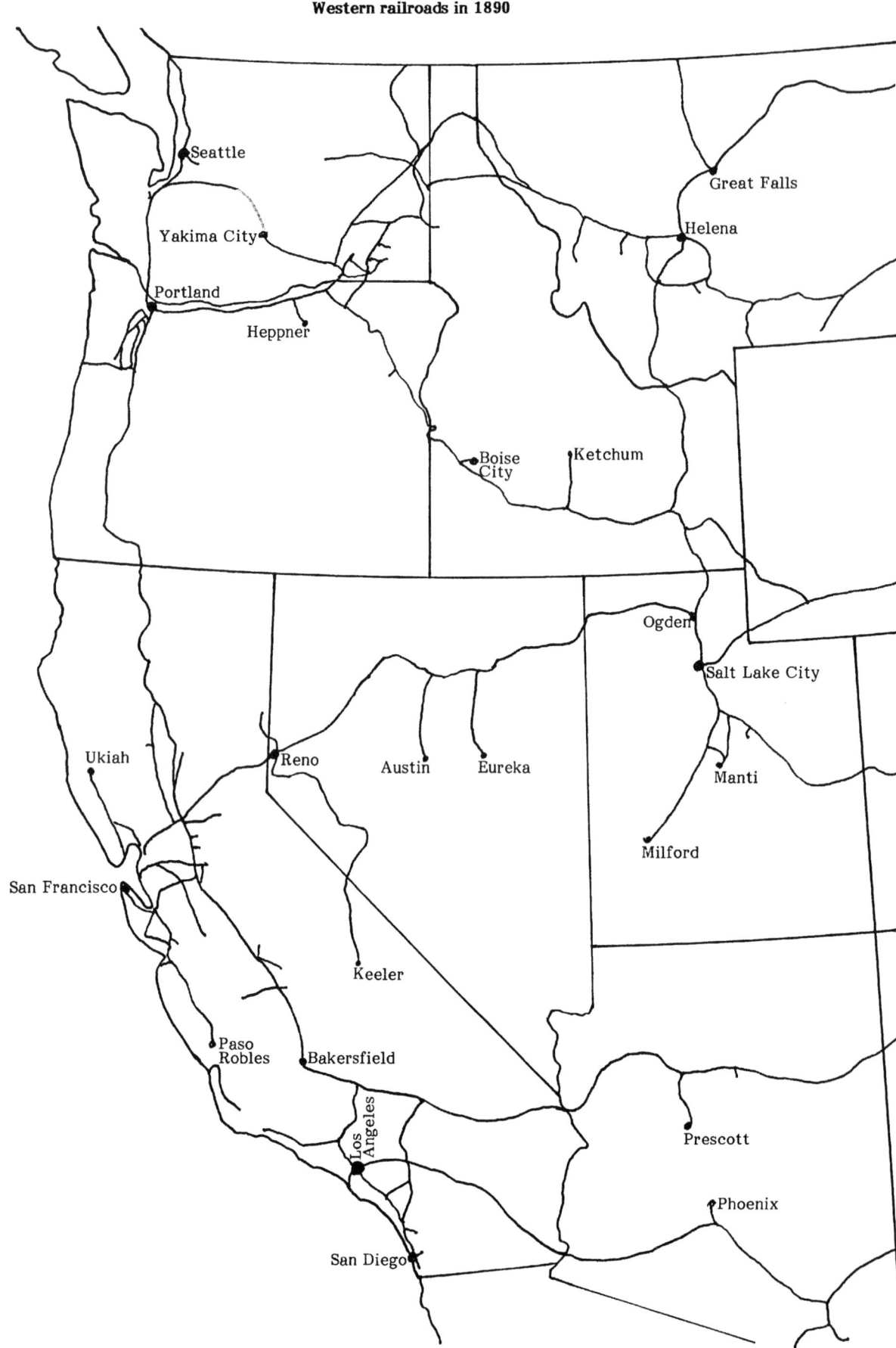
Western railroads in 1890

Railroads in the Eleven Western States

The following is the list of railroads recognized by and listed in Interstate Commerce Commission statistics, June 30, 1909.

	miles of track owned:	miles operated:	status:
Alamogordo Lumber Co's. Railroad	6½	not oper.	private
Amador Central Railroad Co.	12	12	indep.
Anderson & Bella Vista Railroad	16	16	lumber
Arcata & Mad River Railroad Co.	21	21	indep.
Argentine Central Railway Co.	16	16	indep.
Arizona & New Mexico Railway Co.	70	108	indep.
Lordsburg & Hachita Railroad Co.	39		subsid.
Arizona Southern Railroad Co.	20	20	indep.
Atchison, Topeka & Santa Fe Railway Co., The	6,693	7,458	indep.
Arizona & California Railway Co.	107	107	subsid.
Barnwell & Searchlight Railway Co.	23		subsid.
California Eastern Railway Co., The	45		subsid.
Eastern Railway Company of New Mexico, The	488	227	subsid.
Grand Canyon Railway, The	66	66	subsid.
Randsburg Railway Co.	29		subsid.
Santa Fe, Prescott & Phoenix Railway Co.	195	257	subsid.
Bradshaw Mountain Railroad Co.	36		subsid.
Prescott & Eastern Railroad Co.	26		subsid.
Western Arizona Railway Co.	22		subsid.
Bakersfield & Ventura Railroad Co.	25	25	indep.
Bay Point & Clayton Railroad Co.	10	10	indep.
Beaver, Penrose & Northern Railway Co.	6½	6½	indep.
Bellingham Bay & British Columbia Railroad	62	62	indep.
Blakely Railroad	28	28	private
Book Cliff Railroad Co.	12	12	indep.
Bucksport & Elk River Railroad Co.	8	8	indep.
Butte, Anaconda & Pacific Railway Co.	60	69	indep.
Butte County Railroad Co.		31	indep.
Chico & Northern Railroad Co.	31		subsid.
California Western Railway & Navigation Co.	21	21	indep.
Caspar, South Fork & Eastern Railroad	15	15	lumber
Central Arizona Railway Co.	24	24	indep.
Central Railroad of Oregon	14	14	indep.
Chicago & North Western Railway Co.	7,515	7,638	indep.
Wyoming & Northwestern Railway Co.	148	148	subsid.
Chicago, Burlington & Quincy Railroad Co.	8,733	9,021	indep.
Colorado & Southern Railway Co., The	1,042	1,250	subsid.
Colorado Railroad Co., The	42		subsid.
Colorado Springs & Cripple Creek District Railway Co., The	74	74	subsid.
Gilpin Railroad Co.	19	19	subsid.
Walsenburg & Western Railway Co.	1		subsid.
Chicago, Milwaukee & St. Paul Railway Co.			indep.
Chicago, Milwaukee & Puget Sound Railway Co.	1,262	not oper.	subsid.
Montana Railroad Co.	153	157	subsid.
Tacoma Eastern Railroad Co.	103	103	subsid.
Chino Valley Railway Co.	2	not oper.	private
Cimarron & Northwestern Railway Co., The	22	22	indep.
Coeur d'Alene Southern Railway Co.	18	18	lumber
Colorado & Southeastern Railway Co., The	7½	21	indep.
Colorado & Wyoming Railway Co., The	53	55	indep.
Colorado Eastern Railroad Co.	16	16	indep.
Colorado Midland Railway Co., The	261	338	indep.
Colusa & Lake Railroad Co.	22	22	indep.
Corvallis & Alsea River Railway Co.	24	24	indep.
Crescent City & Smith River Railroad	17	17	logging
Cripple Creek Central Railway Co.			
Florence & Cripple Creek Railroad Co., The	40	55	subsid.
Canon City & Cripple Creek Railroad Co., The	7¼		subsid.
Golden Circle Railroad Co., The	7		subsid.
Midland Terminal Railway Co., The	29	29	subsid.
Crystal River & San Juan Railroad Co.	7	11	indep.
Crystal River Railroad Co., The	32	21	indep.

Railroad			
Denver & Intermountain Railroad Co.	13	13	indep.
Denver & Rio Grande Railroad Co., The	2,529	2,598	indep.
Boca & Loyalton Railroad Co.	54	56	subsid.
Rio Grande Junction Railway Co., The - leased to D&RG + CM	62		
Rio Grande Southern Railroad Co., The	182	180	subsid.
Western Pacific Railway Co. (431 miles not opened)	712	281	subsid.
Denver, Boulder & Western Railroad Co.	46	47	indep.
Denver, Laramie & Northwestern Railway Co.	14	not oper.	indep.
Denver, Northwestern & Pacific Railway Co.	211	211	indep.
Diamond & Caldor Railway Co.	33	33	indep.
Eagle Salt Works Railroad Co.	12	13	private
El Paso & Southwestern Co.		348	indep.
Alamogordo & Sacramento Mountain Railway Co.	31		subsid.
Dawson Railway Co.	132		subsid.
El Paso & Northeastern Railway Co.	150		subsid.
El Paso & Rock Island Railway Co.	128		subsid.
El Paso & Southwestern Railroad Co.	343		subsid.
Morenci Southern Railway Co.	18	18	subsid.
Eureka & Freshwater Railway Co.	1	13	subsid.
Humboldt Logging Railway Co.	12		indep.
Eureka & Palisade Railway Co.	88	88	indep.
Eureka Hill Railroad Co.	7	7	indep.
Goble, Nehalem & Pacific Railway Co.	11	11	indep.
Golconda & Adelaide Railroad Co.	13	13	mine
Grande Ronde Lumber Co.'s Railroad	12	16	private
Great Northern Railway Co., The	6,369	6,878	indep.
Kootenay Railway & Navigation Co.			
Kootenai Valley Railway Co.	26	26	subsid.
Great Southern Railroad Co.	30	30	indep.
Great Western Railway Co.	67	67	indep.
Greenwood Railroad Co.	16	16	lumber
Gualala River Railroad	20	not oper.	lumber
Hetch Hetchy & Yosemite Valleys Railway Co.	25	25	lumber
Holton Interurban Railway Co.	10	10	indep.
Idaho & Washington Northern Railroad	51	51	indep.
Idaho Northern Railroad Co.	33	not oper.	indep.
Idaho Northern Railway Co.	58	59	indep.
Idaho Southern Railroad Co.	24	24	indep.
Iron Mountain Railway Co.	11	11	mine
Klamath Lake Railroad Co.	24	24	indep.
Lake Tahoe Railway & Transportation Co.	16	16	indep.
Laramie, Hahns Peak & Pacific Railway Co.	40	39	indep.
Las Vegas & Tonopah Railroad Co.	198	199	indep.
London, South Park & Leadville Railroad Co.	7	not oper.	private
Los Angeles & San Diego Beach Railway Co.	17	17	indep.
Ludlow & Southern Railway Co.	7½	7½	indep.
McCloud River Railroad Co.	76	76	indep.
Manitou & Pikes Peak Railway Co., The	9	9	indep.
Mill Valley & Mt. Tamalpais Scenic Railway Co.	11	11	indep.
Milner & North Side Railroad Co.	22	22	indep.
Missouri Pacific Railway Co., The	1,134	3,492	indep.
Pueblo & State Line Railroad Co., The	152		subsid.
Mono Lake Lumber Co's. Railroad (ex Mono Lake Ry. & Lbr.)	36	36	private
Mount Hood Railroad Co.	16	16	indep.
Nevada-California-Oregon Railway	184	184	indep.
Sierra Valleys Railway Co.	36	36	subsid.
Nevada Central Railroad Co., The	93	93	indep.
Nevada County Narrow Gauge Railroad Co.	26	26	indep.
Nevada Northern Railway Co.	165	165	indep.
Nevada Railroad Co.	10	not oper.	indep.
New Mexico Central Railroad Co.	116	116	indep.
New Mexico Midland Railway Co., The	11	11	indep.

INTRODUCTION 25.

Northern Pacific Railway Co.	6,219	6,087	indep.
Northwestern Improvement Co.			
North Yakima & Valley Railway Co.	14	14	subsid.
Port Townsend Southern Railroad Co.	41	41	subsid.
Washington Central Railway Co.	131		subsid.
Yellowstone Park Railway Co.	11	11	subsid.
Northwestern Pacific Railroad Co.	406	375	indep.
Northwestern Railroad Co.	41	not oper.	indep.
Ocean Shore Railway Co.	54	54	indep.
Oregon & Eureka Railroad Co.	5	37	indep.
(26.36 miles of Northwestern Pacific, known as Eureka & Klamath River Railroad, leased to and operated by Oregon & Eureka Railroad.)			
Oregon & Southeastern Railroad Co.	20	20	indep.
Pacific & Eastern Railway Co.	11	12	indep.
Pacific & Idaho Northern Railway Co.	78	78	indep.
Pacific Coast Co.			
Columbia & Puget Sound Railroad Co.	58	58	subsid.
Pacific Coast Railway Co. (11.3 miles electric)	96	96	subsid.
Pajaro Valley Consolidated Railroad Co.	42	42	indep.
Payette Valley Railroad Co.	13	13	indep.
Peninsular Railway Co.	18	30	logging
Simpson Railroad	12		subsid.
Pioche & Pacific Transportation Co.	17	17	indep.
Pittsburg Railroad Co.	5.66	not oper.	indep.
Placerville & Lake Tahoe Railway Co.	8	8	indep.
Portland & Southwestern Railroad Co.	12	12	logging
Puget Sound & Baker River Railway Co.	21	21	indep.
Rio Grande & Pagosa Springs Railroad Co.	30	30	indep.
Rio Grande & Southwestern Railroad Co.	33	not oper.	indep.
Rock Island Co., The			
Chicago, Rock Island & Pacific Railroad Co.			
Chicago, Rock Island & Pacific Railway Co., The	5,212	7,417	subsid.
Chicago, Rock Island & El Paso Railway Co.	112	112	subsid.
Rocky Mountain Railway Co.	14	not oper.	indep.
Rogue River Valley Railway Co.	6	6	indep.
Sacramento Valley & Eastern Railway	15	15	indep.
Saginaw & Manistee Lumber Co.'s Railroad	7	7	private
Saint Louis, Rocky Mountain & Pacific Railway Co.	106	106	indep.
Salem, Falls City & Western Railway Co.	13	50	indep.
Salt Lake & Los Angeles Railway Co.	15	15	indep.
Salt Lake & Mercur Railroad Co.	13	13	indep.
San Diego, Cuyamaca & Eastern Railway Co.	25	25	indep.
San Diego Southern Railway Co.	49	50	indep.
San Juan Pacific Railway Co.	7	not oper.	indep.
San Pedro, Los Angeles & Salt Lake Railroad Co.	983	1,105	indep.
Santa Fe, Raton & Des Moines Railroad Co.	16	not oper.	indep.
Santa Fe, Raton & Eastern Railroad Co., The	10	10	indep.
Saratoga & Encampment Railway Co.	45	45	indep.
Sheridan & Willamina Railroad Co.	5½	5½	indep.
Sierra Nevada Wood & Lumber Co's. Railroad	18	18	private
Sierra Railway Company of California	76	76	indep.
Silver City, Pinos Altos & Mogollon Railroad Co.	17	not oper.	indep.
Silver Peak Railroad Co.	17	17	indep.
Silverton, Gladstone & Northerly Railroad Co., The	7	7	indep.
Silverton Northern Railroad Co.	13	13	indep.
Silverton Railway Co.	21	21	indep.
Southern Pacific Company	12	5,633	indep.
Arizona & Colorado Railroad Co.	35	35	subsid.
Central Pacific Railway Co.	1,452		subsid.
California Northeastern Railway Co.	86		subsid.
Central California Railway Co.	5		subsid.
Coos Bay, Roseburg & Eastern Railroad & Navigation Co.	31	31	subsid.
Corvallis & Eastern Railroad Co.	141	141	subsid.
Gila Valley, Globe & Northern Railway Co.	125	125	subsid.
Independence & Monmouth Railway Co., The	2½	19	subsid.
Maricopa & Phoenix Railroad Co., The	46	46	subsid.
Nevada & California Railway Co.	422	422	subsid.
New Mexico & Arizona Railroad Co. (leased from AT&SF Ry.)	88		leased
Oregon & California Railroad Co.	665		subsid.

Southern Pacific Company - continued			
Pacific Railway & Navigation Co.	32		subsid.
Phoenix & Eastern Railroad Co.	94	95	subsid.
Arizona Eastern Railroad Co.	1		subsid.
Southern Pacific Railroad Co.	3,323		subsid.
Coast Line Railway Co.	12		subsid.
Inter-California Railway Co.	41		subsid.
Peninsular Railroad Co.	16		subsid.
Sacramento Southern Railroad Co.	8		subsid.
San Bernardino & Redlands Railroad Co.	7		subsid.
San Francisco & Napa Railway Co.	11		subsid.
South Pacific Coast Railway Co.	97		subsid.
Southern Utah Railroad Co.	3	not oper.	indep.
Spokane & British Columbia Railway Co.	36	36	indep.
Spokane & Inland Empire Railroad Co.	175	175	indep.
Spokane International Railway Co.	141	141	indep.
Spokane, Portland & Seattle Railway Co.	405	421	indep.
Astoria & Columbia River Railroad Co.	83	122	subsid.
Stone Canon Pacific Railroad Co.	22	22	indep.
Sugar Pine Railway Co.	15	15	indep.
Sumpter Valley Railway Co.	62	62	indep.
Sunset Railroad Co.	33	42	indep.
Sunset Western Railway Co.	15	15	indep.
Tacoma, Olympia & Chehallis Valley Railroad Co.	9	9	indep.
Tonopah & Goldfield Railroad Co.	100	109	indep.
Tonopah & Tidewater Company			
Bullfrog Goldfield Railroad Co.	82	83	subsid.
Tonopah & Tidewater Railroad Co.	173	181	subsid.
Twin Buttes Railroad Co., The	28	28	indep.
Uintah Railway Co., The	55	55	indep.
Union Pacific Railroad Co.	3,289	3,310	indep.
Ilwaco Railroad Co.	29	29	subsid.
Oregon & Washington Railroad Co.	6	6	subsid.
Oregon Railroad & Navigation Co., The	1,142	1,327	subsid.
Columbia River & Oregon Central Railroad Co.	45		subsid.
Columbia Southern Railway Co.	69		subsid.
Snake River Railroad Co., The	66		subsid.
Umatilla Central Railroad Co.	14		subsid.
Oregon Short Line Railroad Co.	1,178	1,509	subsid.
(Of "owned", 56.59 miles, Montana Union Ry., leased to and operated by Northern Pacific Railway Co.)			
Boise City Railway & Terminal Co.	8		subsid.
Malad Valley Railroad Co.	46		subsid.
Malheur Valley Railway Co.	14		subsid.
Minidoka & Southwestern Railroad Co.	74		subsid.
Saint Anthony Railroad Co.	53		subsid.
Salmon River Railroad Co.	86		subsid.
Wyoming Western Railroad Co.	23		subsid.
Yellowstone Park Railroad Co.	70		subsid.
Oregon, Washington & Idaho Railroad Co.	72	72	subsid.
United Verde & Pacific Railway Co.	26	26	indep.
Verdi Lumber Co's. Railroad	16	16	private
Virginia & Truckee Railway	67	67	indep.
Washington, Idaho & Montana Railway Co.	48	48	indep.
Wyoming & Missouri River Railroad Co.	18	18	indep.
Yellowstone Park Railroad Co.	27	27	indep.
Yosemite Short Line Railway Co.	6	not oper.	indep.
Yosemite Valley Railroad Co.	79	79	indep.
Yreka Railroad Co.	7½	7½	indep.
Zuni Mountain Railroad	42	42	private

Of the 240 names here listed, 126 were "railroads" and 114 "railways." Their ownership status was 128 "independent", 90 were "subsidiaries" and 22 were various others.

Source: Interstate Commerce Commission *Statistics of Railways in the United States*, June 30, 1909.

INTRODUCTION   27.

Record of Authorized Construction and Abandonments

Beginning in 1921, the Interstate Commerce Commission issued its "Annual Report" which listed authorized construction and abandonments. Many were for two or three miles; the following are the major ones. The mileage columns are for its authority; not all of them may have occurred.

year:	company name:	counties:	state:	build:	abandon:
1921	Spokane & British Columbia	Ferry	Wash.		36.300
1922	Oregon Trunk Ry.	Jefferson and Wasco	Oreg.		28.920
1923	Central Pacific	Klamath and Lane	Oreg.	118.000	
	Longview, Portland & Northern	Cowlitz and Lewis	Wash.	30.000	
1924	Wenatchee Southern Ry.	Benton, Chelan, Kittitas	Wash.	82.000	
	Oregon-Washington RR & Navig.	Harney	Oreg.	30.000	
	Valley & Siletz	Polk	Oreg.	1.500	
1925	Cowlitz, Chehalis & Cascade Ry.	Lewis	Wash.	14.000	
	Northern Pacific Ry.	Mason	Wash.	15.000	
	Port Townsend S. + PT & Puget Sound	Jefferson	Wash.		13.910
1926	Columbia & Cowlitz Ry.	Cowlitz	Wash.	6.000	
	Central Pacific	Klamath + Modoc, Calif.	Oreg.	36.000	
	Oregon, California & Eastern	Klamath and Lake	Oreg.	143.000	
	Oregon Trunk Ry.	Deschutes and Klamath	Oreg.	100.000	
1927	Oregon Trunk Ry.	Klamath	Oreg.	78.000	
	Great Northern Ry.	Chelan and King	Wash.	26.290	34.940
	Port Angeles Western	Clallam and Jefferson	Wash.	9.000	
1928	Great Northern Ry.	Deschutes and Klamath	Oreg.	47.000	
	Klickitat Log & Lumber Co.	Klickitat	Wash.		16.000
1929	Southern Pacific Co.	Polk	Oreg.		19.000
	Washington Western Ry.	Snohomish	Wash.		11.200
1930	Northern Pacific + O-WR&N	Grays Harbor and Jefferson	Wash.	64.500	
	Oregon-Washington RR & Navig.	Pacific	Wash.		28.100
	Port Angeles Western	Clallam and Jefferson	Wash.	24.000	
	Clackamas Eastern Railroad	Clackamas	Oreg.	4.000	
	Great Northern Ry.	Klamath + Lassen, Modoc and Siskiyou, Calif.	Oreg.	87.500	
	Oregon Electric Ry.	Linn	Oreg.	68.600	
1931	Great Northern Ry.	Deschutes	Oreg.	14.300	
	Great Northern Ry.	Klamath	Oreg.	.200	
	Oregon Electric Ry.	Lane	Oreg.	35.227	
	Great Northern Ry.	Okanogan	Wash.		23.490
1932	Sumpter Valley Ry.	Grant	Oreg.		14.200
1933	Carlton & Coast Railroad	Yamhill	Oreg.	9.500	
	Oregon Electric Ry.	Linn	Oreg.		5.200
	Hartford Eastern Ry.	Snohomish	Wash.		42.000
1934	Northern Pacific Ry.	Grant	Wash.	28.500	
	Oregon Electric Ry.	Washington	Oreg.	7.500	
	Edward Hines Western Pine Co.	Grant and Harney	Oreg.		48.000
1935	The Dalles & Southern	Wasco	Oreg.		41.790
	Great Northern Ry.	Ferry and Okanogan	Wash.		16.930
	Great Northern Ry.	Okanogan	Wash.		20.710
	CMStP&P-GN-LP&N-NP-OWR&N	Clark and Lewis	Wash.		19.350
	Pacific Coast Railroad	King	Wash.		11.900
1936	Carlton & Coast Railroad	Yamhill	Oreg.		3.841
	Des Chutes Railroad + Union Pacific	Sherman and Wasco	Oreg.		71.260
	Gold Coast Railroad Co.	Curry and Josephine	Oreg.	90.000	
	Oregon, Pacific & Eastern	Lane	Oreg.	3.000	
	Southern Pacific Co.	Lane	Oreg.		11.099
	Puget Sound & Cascade Ry.	Skagit	Wash.		3.800
1938	Willamette Valley Ry.	Clackamas	Oreg.		20.500
1940	Carlton & Coast Railroad	Yamhill	Oreg.		20.400
	Chicago, Milwaukee, St. Paul & Pac.	Snohomish	Wash.		15.100
	Great Northern Ry.	Ferry and Stevens	Wash.		21.240
1941	Great Northern Ry.	Spokane	Wash.	8.000	
	Oregon-Washington RR & Navig.	Grays Harbor	Wash.		15.260
	Oregon Electric Ry.	Multnomah and Washington	Oreg.		12.760

1943	Chicago, Milwaukee, St. Paul & Pac.	Benton	Wash.		25.105
	Chicago, Milwaukee, St. Paul & Pac.	Pierce	Wash.		14.000
	Chicago, Milwaukee, St. Paul & Pac.	Whatcom	Wash.		12.000
	Newaukum Valley Railroad	Lewis	Wash.		10.620
	Yakima Valley Transportation Co.	Yakima	Wash.		4.200
	Oregon, Pacific & Eastern	Lane	Oreg.		2.000
	Oregon Short Line	Sherman and Wasco	Oreg.		17.200
	Walla Walla Valley Ry.	Umatilla	Oreg.		4.910
1945	Great Northern Ry.	Des Chutes	Oreg.		15.410
	Great Northern Ry.	Spokane (+ Kootenai, Idaho)	Wash.		6.850
	Pacific Coast Railroad	King	Wash.		8.700
1946	Sumpter Valley Ry.	Baker and Grant	Oreg.		57.000
1947	Oregon, Pacific & Eastern	Lane	Oreg.		8.000
	Southern Pacific Co.	Marion	Oreg.		20.568
	Pacific Coast Railroad	King	Wash.		7.250
1948	Oregon, Pacific & Eastern	Lane	Oreg.	10.300	
1949	Yakima Valley Transportation Co.	Yakima	Wash.		1.850
1950	Oregon-Washington RR & Navig.	Umatilla	Oreg.	17.150	
	Oregon-Washington RR & Navig.	Morrow and Umatilla	Oreg.		23.800
	Spokane, Portland & Seattle	Washington	Oreg.		12.870
1951	Central Pacific + Southern Pac.	Douglas	Oreg.		19.540
	Southern Pacific Co.	Jackson	Oreg.	6.000	
	Willamina & Grande Ronde Ry.	Douglas	Oreg.	3.500	
1952	Great Northern Ry.	Spokane	Wash.		22.870
1953	Longview, Portland & Northern	Cowlitz and Lewis	Wash.		31.000
	Port Angeles & Western	Clallam	Wash.		63.300
1954	Oregon, Pacific & Eastern	Lane	Oreg.		4.160
	Waterville Railway Co.	Douglas	Wash.		4.467
1955	Cowlitz, Chehalis & Cascade Ry.	Lewis	Wash.		32.000
1957	California & Oregon Coast	Josephine	Oreg.		14.610
1958	Oregon Short Line	Baker	Oreg.		33.240
	Southern Pacific Co.	Benton and Lane	Oreg.		9.060
	Spokane, Portland & Seattle	Columbia	Oreg.		9.610
1959	Big Creek & Telocaset	Union	Oreg.		11.000
1960	Southern Pacific Co.	Lane	Oreg.		10.450
1962	Sumpter Valley Ry.	Baker	Oreg.		1.500
1963	Great Northern Ry.	Skagit	Wash.		9.240

Oregon State Library Collection WPA Series 4
Five Willamette River steamers at Ainsworth Dock, Portland, in 1876

The Railway Age

Railroad Mileage in the United States

Year	built	total	Year	built	total	Year	built	total
1830	23	23	1860	1,837	30,626	1890	5,427	166,703
1831	72	95	1861	660	31,286	1891	4,026	170,729
1832	134	229	1862	834	32,120	1892	4,441	175,170
1833	151	380	1863	1,050	33,170	1893	2,346	177,516
1834	253	633	1864	738	33,908	1894	1,899	179,415
1835	465	1,098	1865	1,177	35,085	1895	1,700	181,115
1836	175	1,273	1866	1,716	36,801	1896	1,654	182,769
1837	224	1,497	1867	2,249	39,050	1897	1,822	184,591
1838	416	1,913	1868	2,979	42,229	1898	2,219	186,810
1839	389	2,302	1869	4,615	46,844	1899	4,008	190,818
1840	516	2,818	1870	6,078	52,922	1900	3,444	194,262
1841	717	3,535	1871	7,379	60,301	1901	4,481	198,743
1842	491	4,026	1872	5,878	66,171	1902	4,195	202,938
1843	159	4,185	1873	4,097	70,268	1903	4,397	207,335
1844	192	4,377	1874	2,117	72,385	1904	5,059	212,394
1845	256	4,633	1875	1,711	74,096	1905	4,947	217,341
1846	297	4,930	1876	2,712	76,808	1906	5,294	222,635
1847	668	5,598	1877	2,274	79,082	1907	5,362	228,128
1848	398	5,996	1878	2,665	81,747	1908	3,918	232,046
1849	1,369	7,365	1879	4,809	86,556	1909	6,310	238,356
1850	1,656	9,021	1880	6,706	93,262	1910	4,751	243,107
1851	1,961	10,982	1881	9,846	103,108	1911	3,466	246,573
1852	1,926	12,908	1882	11,569	114,677	1912	243	246,816
1853	2,452	15,360	1883	6,745	121,422	1913	2,387	249,803
1854	1,360	16,720	1884	3,923	125,345	1914	2,302	252,105
1855	1,654	18,374	1885	2,975	128,320	1915	1,684	253,789
1856	3,643	22,016	1886	8,018	136,338	1916	257	254,046
1857	2,486	24,503	1887	12,876	149,214	1917	-420	253,626
1858	2,465	26,968	1888	6,900	156,114	1918	-97	253,529
1859	1,821	28,789	1889	5,162	161,276	1919	-377	253,152
						1920	-307	252,845

And in the Eleven Western States Only

Year	built	total	Year	built	total	Year	built	total
1855	8	8	1877	342	5,170	1899	809	25,823
1856	15	23	1878	421	5,591	1900	361	26,184
1857		23	1879	746	6,337	1901	1,073	27,257
1858		23	1880	1,737	8,074	1902	661	27,918
1859		23	1881	1,906	9,980	1903	605	28,523
1860		23	1882	2,214	12,194	1904	806	29,329
1861		23	1883	1,582	13,775	1905	839	30,168
1862	9	32	1884	471	14,246	1906	1,436	31,594
1863	45	77	1885	279	14,525	1907	1,552	33,146
1864	94	171	1886	722	15,247	1908	1,907	35,053
1865	67	238	1887	2,302	17,549	1909	1,188	36,241
1866	94	332	1888	1,432	18,986	1910	1,563	37,804
1867	194	526	1889	779	19,765	1911	1,079	38,883
1868	828	1,354	1890	1,132	20,897	1912	983	39,866
1869	527	1,881	1891	923	21,820	1913	671	40,537
1870	674	2,555	1892	1,306	23,126	1914	960	41,497
1871	279	2,834	1893	165	23,291	1915	1,652	43,149
1872	416	3,250	1894	611	23,902	1916	-577	42,572
1873	377	3,627	1895	25	23,927	1917	-116	42,456
1874	314	3,941	1896	291	24,214	1918	103	42,559
1875	356	4,297	1897	381	24,595	1919	10	42,569
1876	531	4,828	1898	419	25,014	1920	47	42,616

Introduction of the World-Wide Railroad Era

Country:	Opened:	Km. track in 1878:	State:	Miles:	Opened:	Miles in 1880:
Great Britain	9/27/1825	27,895	Illinois	24.00	1839	7,851
U.S.A.	4/17/1827	131,603	Pennsylvania	9.00	1827	6,191
Austria-Hungary	9/20/1828	18,161				
France	10/1/1828	24,164	New York	12.50	1831	5,991
			Ohio	22.50	1838	5,792
Belgium	5/5/1835	3,740	Iowa	39.00	1855	5,400
Germany	12/7/1835	31,628				
Russia	4/4/1838	22,750	Indiana	22.00	1842	4,373
Holland	4/13/1839	1,678				
Italy	10/3/1839	8,404	Missouri	6.00	1852	3,965
			Michigan	33.00	1836	3,938
Switzerland	6/15/1844	2,623	Kansas	40.00	1864	3,400
Denmark	9/18/1844	1,450	Texas	32.00	1854	3,244
Canada	3/19/1847	9,519	Wisconsin	21.50	1851	3,155
Spain	10/30/1848	6,695	Minnesota	10.00	1862	3,151
Mexico	10/8/1850	767	Georgia	9.00	1837	2,459
Peru	5/29/1851	1,852	California	22.50	1856	2,195
Chili	1/ /1852	1,689				
British India	4/18/1853	13,219	Nebraska	40.00	1864	1,953
Brazil	4/30/1854	2,753	Massachusetts	26.76	1835	1,915
Portugal	6/9/1854	1,079	Virginia	13.00	1831	1,893
Queensland	9/13/1854	688	Alabama	45.50	1834	1,843
Victoria	5/29/1855	1,693	Tennessee	30.00	1851	1,843
			New Jersey	14.00	1832	1,684
Sacramento Valley Rail Road (California)	8/17/1855		Colorado	87.00	1870	1,570
			Kentucky	29.00	1835	1,530
Egypt	1/26/1856	1,494	North Carolina	63.00	1833	1,486
Western Australia	4/16/1856	109	South Carolina	7.00	1830	1,427
			Dakota Territory	256.50	1873	1,225
Cape Colony	6/26/1860	1,069	Mississippi	14.00	1841	1,127
Roumania	10/4/1860	1,309	Maryland	15.00	1830	1,019
Turkey	10/4/1860	1,469	New Hampshire	6.22	1838	1,015
Mauritius	5/13/1862	106	Maine	11.00	1836	1,005
Paraguay	10/1/1863	72				
Tasmania	1/21/1864	276	Connecticut		1837	923
Argentine Republic	12/14/1864	2,317	Vermont	25.00	1848	914
South Australia	7/31/1865	730	Arkansas	5.00	1857	859
Ceylon	10/1/1865	180	Utah Territory	36.00	1869	842
Venezuela	2/9/1866	147	New Mexico Terr.	8.30	1878	758
Java	8/10/1867	344	Nevada	35.00	1868	739
Uruguay	1/1/1869	376	West Virginia	39.00	1842	691
Greece	2/18/1869	13	Louisiana	5.00	1831	652
			Florida	5.00	1836	518
New Zealand	2/19/1871	1,722	Wyoming Territory	106.00	1870	512
Japan	10/17/1873	109	Oregon	80.00	1870	508
			Arizona Territory	30.00	1879	349
			Indian Territory	35.50	1870	289
			Washington Terr.	6.00	1862	289
			Delaware	16.19	1832	275
			Rhode Island	50.00	1837	210
			Idaho Territory	61.00	1874	206
			Montana Territory	63.00	1880	106
			U.S.A. - total miles			98,296

How the United States opening mileages were established has not been determined by the chronicler.

Idaho Territory, 61 miles was the Utah Northern - and Brigham to Franklin was 61 miles - but by 1874 it had built south to Ogden and Franklin was then milepost 80, of which possibly three miles were in Idaho Territory.

Wyoming Territory, 106 miles, was the Denver Pacific, Cheyenne to Denver, about seven of those miles being in Wyoming; the Union Pacific had entered Wyoming Territory in 1867.

Utah Territory's 36 miles in 1869 was the Utah Central, but Union Pacific had opened over one hundred miles in 1868.

Source: *Poor's Manual 1889*, p. xi   *Encyclopaedia Britannica 1898*, vol. 28, p. 2502

Development of Railroad Equipment and Related History — A Brief Chronology.

1829	August 8 — First locomotive operation in America; the <u>Stourbridge Lion</u>, at Honesdale, Penna.
1830	Baltimore & Ohio Railroad Company was founded.
	The T-shaped rail was developed.
	First coal-burning locomotive engine was built — <u>Tom Thumb</u>.
	August 28 — First commercial railway placed in operation, Baltimore to Ellicotts Mills, with <u>Tom Thumb</u>.
1831	The United States mail first carried by railroad.
	First major use of the new T-rail when the Camden & Amboy Railroad was built.
	August 9 — Mohawk & Hudson Rail Road Co. passenger train, Albany to Schenectady, with <u>DeWitt Clinton</u>.
1836	Locomotive engine cab, rail sander and steam whistle developed.
1847	New York State required T-rail for all new construction; strap iron on wood rails remained on branches until 1860.
1848	A speed of sixty miles per hour was reached.
1851	September — Erie Railroad Co. used electric telegraph for train orders.
1852	November — First locomotive engine west of the Mississippi River.
1853	First union passenger station was opened — in Indianapolis.
1856	April 21 — Mississippi River was bridged by Rock Island Railroad Co, Rock Island, Illinois, to Davenport, Iowa.
1858	First Pullman designed sleeping car — it was operated from Chicago to Bloomington in 1859.
1863	First major purchase of steel rails, by Pennsylvania Railroad Co. Iron rails continued to be made until 1900.
	First dining car, but it had no galley.
1864	Railway Post Office service inaugurated August 28 on Chicago & North Western Railway. This service was abandoned June 30, 1977, when the last train operated from New York City to Washington, D. C.
1865	Most engines now built to burn coal rather than wood except for those for use in the far western areas of the U. S.
1866	Automatic block signal developed.
1867	The refrigerator car was patented.
1868	Janney knuckle coupler was invented.
	Horizontal oil tank car was introduced.
	First Pullman-quality dining car was built.
1869	First patent on Westinghouse air brake.
1870	The track water scoop.
1871	March — Gas lights replacing candles in Pullman cars.
	Pennsylvania Railroad Co. using Westinghouse air brakes.
	Electric semaphore placed in use.
1872	Barnum's Circus began using the railroads.
	A sleeping car with electric lights on New York Central Railroad.
1876	Six-wheel truck for heavy passenger equipment.
1881	Steam heated cars and the electric headlight developed.
1882	Extensive use of electric lights in passenger cars.
1883	November 18 — Railroads adopt standard time zones; cities and states soon follow.
1886	Standard gauge, 56½", [it came from England] became the gauge of all major new construction except in the western mountains where 36" was still in vogue.
1887	The rotary snow plough; Union Pacific Railway Co. purchased four.
	Greatest new mileage laid in one year, nearly 13,000 miles.
	The closed-vestibule passenger car placed in operation. First oil-burning locomotive tested.
1895	Southern Pacific Railroad Co. made its first fuel conversion from coal to oil.
	The electric locomotive perfected by Baltimore & Ohio.
1904	First all-steel passenger cars, on Pennsylvania Railroad.
1905	A Pennsylvania Railroad Co. train reached 127 miles per hour, in Ohio.
1906	All-steel coaches on the Southern Pacific Railroad Co.
1914	Radio used to dispatch trains.
1916	Maximum United States railroad mileage, 254,000; from that year on, more track was abandoned than constructed.
1919	There were 65,000 steam locomotives in the United States; then their numbers decreased.
1925	First diesel-electric engine constructed.
1931	Pullman Company offered air conditioned cars.
1933	Welded rail used by Delaware & Hudson Railroad Co.
1934	Nearly 50% of all steam locomotives in domestic use were of a 2-8-0 classification.
1939	November — The real birthdate of the diesel engine when General Motors Co. built a 5,400 horsepower locomotive.
1949	May — Lima Locomotive Works erected its last steam locomotive, a 2-8-4.
1953	Piggybacking of highway motor truck trailers became common. This was a case of "re-inventing the wheel." In 1895, the Oakland, San Leandro & Haywards [Calif.] electric railway carried loaded farm wagons to Oakland.
1954	Closed-circuit television train orders.
1955	Baldwin Locomotive Works built its last steam locomotive, a 2-8-2 for the Government of India.
1957	Airplanes carried more passengers than did the trains.
1960	The END OF STEAM came in March when virtually no steam locomotive was to be found in class I revenue service.
1971	May 1 — AMTRAK passenger service was established. This, in effect, re-established a nation wide passenger operation which had been gradually abandoned by the various private railroad companies.

Notes on Track, Gauges and Equipment

A typical narrow gauge (36") passenger car weighed 340 pounds per patron; a standard gauge (56½") weighed 722 pounds. The 36" gauge car had a 36" seat on one side and a 19" on the other with a 17" aisle; the seating reversed in the center to balance the load. A box car weighed 8,800 pounds, was 23½ feet long, had 20 inch wheels and carried 18,000 pounds. A platform (flat) car weighed 6,250 pounds and carried 20,000. At its zenith, there were 1,200 miles of 36" gauge track in operation in the West, mostly in the mountains of California, Colorado, Nevada, New Mexico and Utah. A total of 85 lines were built in California alone.

A narrow gauge curve of 220 feet radius was practical whereas a standard gauge curve would have to be a 955 foot sweep to develop the same amount of flange friction. Total construction and equipment costs were about 1/3d the price. The Colorado Central Rail Road Company estimated a long section of track at a standard gauge cost of $90,000 per mile in its rough area, then actually built this same section for only $20,000 per miles as a narrow gauge.

Great Western Railway in England was called a broad gauge -- and broad it was -- seven feet between the rails. Various broad gauges of 5½ and 6 feet were used in the United States and Canada. When the "Pacific Railway" was being organized, the president of the United States, A. Lincoln, was to establish the gauge, 56½ or 60 inches; 60 inch was in use in California at that time. Finally the matter was handed to Congress, which, on March 3, 1863, determined that Union Pacific and Central Pacific should be constructed at the 56½ inch gauge in use to this day.

In 1870 there were 23 different gauges from 36 to 72 inches in operation in the U. S. And later on, Maine loggers laid many miles of 24 inch gauge.

Some examples of central states and east of the Mississippi River broad gauges before 1870:

72 inch:
    Atlantic & Great Western Railway Co., 507 miles.
    Delaware, Lackawana & Western Railway Co., 251 miles.
    Erie Railway Co., 460 miles.

66 inch:
    Galveston, Houston & Henderson Railway Co., 51 miles.
    Houston & Texas Central Railway Co., 130 miles.
    Maine Central Railway Co., 138 miles.
    Pacific Railroad (in Missouri), 283 miles (standard gauged July 18, 1869).
    St. Louis & Iron Mountain Railroad Co., 196 miles (changed to 60" gauge in 1868, to standard gauge June 28, 1879).

60 inch:
    Kentucky Central Railway Co., 112 miles (narrowed to standard gauge on July 10, 1881).
    Virginia & Tennessee Railway Co., 204 miles.

58 inch:
    Pittsburgh, Fort Wayne & Chicago Railway Co., 468 miles.
    Central Ohio Railroad Co., 137 miles.

The term "standard gauge" was approved in 1886 and was intended to apply to new construction. It probably did serve this function, but much non-standard gauge track remained. The following tally is from the 1890 ICC statistics of railways (the first column is the gauge, the second is the frequency):

Gauge	Freq	Gauge	Freq	Gauge	Freq	Gauge	Freq
2'	4	3'-4"	4	4'-3"	1	4'-9¼"	4
2'-6"	1	3'-6"	15	4'-7½"	1	4'-10½"	1
2'-7"	2	3'-6½"	1	4'-8"	9	5'	2
2'-10"	1	3'-9"	1	4'-8¼"	2	5'-½"	1
3'	234	3'-10"	1	4'-8½"	1030	5'-3"	1
3'-1/4"	1	3'-11½"	1	4'-8 5/8"	1	5'-8"	1
3'-1"	1	4'	2	4'-8 3/4"	33	5'-9"	1
3'-2"	1	4'-1"	1	4'-9"	307	8'-4"	1

The major requirements for one mile of standard gauge track:

by rail weight (per yard)	40 lbs.	60 lbs.	80 lbs.
tons of rails	62	94	126
pounds of spikes	4,512	6,420	6,420
pounds of bolts	1,124	1,825	1,966
ties	3,017	2,640	2,348

plus angle bars, tie plates, anti-creepers, tools and the graded right-of-way.

Standards of Time

On November 18, 1883, standard time zones were established throughout the United States. Before then, each railroad had its own clock based, somewhat, on local sun time -- and that of a nearby division office. In 1874 when it was noon in Washington, D. C., it was as follows elsewhere:

New York City	12:12 p.m.	Denver	10:08 a.m.	Santa Fe	10:04 a.m.	Laramie	10:02 a.m.
Salt Lake City	9:40 a.m.	Sacramento	9:02 a.m.	San Francisco	8:58 a.m.	Portland	8:56 a.m.

The Locomotive Builders

The product was called a locomotive engine in the beginning and that name was retained by Poor's Manual until 1893. These were the major builders with some of their various changes of name, location, dates of activity and approximate production up until 1901 and after that date. Only Baldwin and Schenectady lasted for one hundred years or longer.

		built to 1901:	after 1901:	total:
American Locomotive Co., New York, N. Y. (A June, 1901, merger of the following):			51,900	51,900
Brooks Locomotive Works, Dunkirk, N. Y.	1869-9/1929	3,990	210	4,200
Danforth, Cooke & Co., Paterson, N. J.	1852-2/1926	2,720	80	2,800
Dickson Manufacturing Co., Scranton, Penna.	1858-5/1909	1,370	30	1,400
Manchester Locomotive Works, Manchester, N. H.	1856-6/1913	1,760	40	1,800
Pittsburgh Locomotive & Car Works, Allegheny City, Penna.	1867-9/1919	2,520	80	2,600
Rhode Island Works, Providence, R. I.	1866-12/1907	3,340	60	3,400
Richmond Locomotive Works, Richmond, Va.	1886-9/1927	870	130	1,000
Schenectady Locomotive Works, Schenectady, N. Y.	1848-6/1948	5,990	310	6,300
(The following was acquired in 1905):				
Rogers Locomotive and Machine Works, Paterson, N. J.	1835-8/1913	5,660	640	6,300
Baldwin Locomotive Works, Philadelphia, Penna.	1831-1954	19,950	50,550	70,500
Climax Manufacturing Co., Corry, Penna.	1888-1928	300	790	1,090
Davenport Locomotive Works, Davenport, Iowa	1902-1955		3,000	3,000
Smith - New Jersey - Union - then Grant Locomotive Works, Paterson, N. J.	1848-1893	1,800		1,800
Heisler Locomotive Works (Stearns Mfg. Co.), Erie, Penna.	1894-1945	50	800	850
Hinkley Locomotive Co., Boston, Mass.	1841-1890	1,830		1,830
Lima Locomotive Works, Lima, Ohio	1869-1949	650	6,950	7,600
McKay and Aldus, East Boston, Mass.	1864-1869	100		100
Wm. Mason Machine Works, Taunton, Mass.	1852-1890	770		770
National Locomotive Works (Dawson & Baily), Connellsville, Penna.	1873-1887	260		260
Long & Norris - Wm. Norris - then R. Norris, Philadelphia, Penna.	1834-1872	1,190		1,190
Porter, Bell & Co. (H. K. Porter Co.), Pittsburgh, Penna.	1866-1950	4,200	4,000	8,200
Portland Locomotive Works, Portland, Maine	1848-1894	625		625
Rome Locomotive & Machine Works, Rome, N. Y.	1880-1895	700		700
Taunton Locomotive Manufacturing Co., Taunton, Mass.	1847-1889	1,000		1,000
Union Iron Works, San Francisco, Calif.	1865-1881	30		30
The Vulcan Iron Works, Wilkes-Barre, Penna.	1874-1949	1,000	3,700	4,700
Willamette Iron & Steel Works, Portland, Oreg.	1922-1929		33	33
Central Pacific Railroad Co., Sacramento, Calif.	1873-1889	74		74
Southern Pacific Railroad Co., Sacramento, Calif.	1917-1930		113	113
Some seventy eastern railroads that built their own				
"Shay Locomotive Works", Lima, Ohio	1878-1945	670	2,100	2,770

The Lima Locomotive Works' geared "Shay" (patented June 14, 1881) was the real work-horse of the logger and miner.

Most builders had some changes of name, but Hinkley seems to have had the most. It started in 1841 as Hinkley and Drury. It became Boston Locomotive Works in 1848 - Hinkley, Williams & Co. in 1861 - Hinkley & Williams Locomotive Works in 1864 - Hinkley Locomotive Works in 1872 and Hinkley Locomotive Co. in 1880.

VOL. I. No. 4.   CHICAGO, THURSDAY, JULY 6, 1876. $4.20 PER YEAR.

Locomotive Engine Production by Major United States Builders

year	total	BLW	Norris	Rogers	Hink.	Taun.	Smith	Port.	Schen.	Danf.	Mason	Man.	Dick.	R.I.	Pitts.
1833	1	1					1848-								
1834	9	5	4				1851								
1835	20	14	6												
1836	52	40	12				N.J.								
1837	65	41	23	1			1852-								
1838	42	23	12	7			1865								
1839	43	25	7	11											
1840	22	8	7	7			Union								
1841	21	9	1	9	2		1866								
1842	32	14	2	6	10		Grant								
1843	31	12	1	9	9		1867-								
1844	48	22	5	12	9		1893								
1845	79	27	12	14	26										
1846	94	40	7	17	30										
1847	140	39	17	22	55	7									
1848	182	19	15	39	80	19	5	5							
1849	172	30	29	45	34	18	8	8							
1850	163	37	16	43	34	18	10	5							
1851	249	50	28	53	58	28	17	10	5						
1852	301	49	31	68	68	35	18	11	21						
1853	416	60	62	89	74	29	24	15	39	22	2				
1854	449	62	70	103	56	32	35	20	38	23	10				
1855	331	46	21	82	28	15	40	4	33	17	22	23			
1856	345	58	30	49	32	19	42	8	37	29	22	19			
1857	330	66	24	84	14	22	33	6	31	26	21	3			
1858	142	33	28	18	11	10	16	9	2	8	6	.			
1859	229	70	7	57	11	19	20	2	3	32	9	.			
1860	290	83	6	88	10	11	24	5	21	30	12	.			
1861	146	40	4	27	2	3	31	.	14	19	6	.			
1862	260	75	3	43	12	10	40	.	30	33	13	.	1		
1863	377	98	13	73	.	17	45	1	39	62	25	.	4		
1864	509	130	9	103	10	32	50	12	43	69	69	9	3		
1865	544	114	29	94	50	30	53	7	45	66	35	17	4		
1866	487	117	11	102	33	25	58	4	24	62	22	17	7	5	
1867	527	126	23	67	41	26	48	6	42	49	29	13	10	34	13
1868	588	123	7	84	49	27	57	14	57	32	24	38	8	49	19
1869	867	234	2	102	28	33	100	16	74	53	43	65	10	74	31
1870	1,028	279	14	140	6	36	101	12	74	76	46	68	18	80	46
1871	1,170	330	3	132	37	32	96	24	71	65	52	107	16	99	59
1872	1,500	421	30	174	66	43	111	24	98	72	42	121	35	124	68
1873	1,655	436	.	189	168	37	131	48	108	82	44	112	30	122	79
1874	546	162		19	49	15	60	36	9	33	22	44	14	72	7
1875	372	130		44	19	18	10	12	28	28	9	24	10	.	17
1876	498	228		16	8	8	12	13	32	29	16	34	22	9	13
1877	366	185		15	10	2	12	9	55	8	18	13	6	10	4
1878	561	286		44	20	14	46	5	25	12	9	6	16	36	12
1879	858	394		56	36	29	31	4	95	17	19	32	14	70	21
1880	1,389	520		116	50	44	57	16	114	65	23	62	39	113	65
1881	1,937	550		226	98	61	111	38	171	106	28	114	42	174	78
1882	2,226	568		267	103	50	90	44	188	195	27	122	51	233	74
1883	2,004	554		279	81	26	103	60	176	145	16	78	68	117	74
1884	1,062	430		78	19	12	20	16	93	89	3	33	63	42	46
1885	699	232		75	8	10	3	8	103	22	12	47	7	98	30
1886	1,333	550		100	5	4	21	6	187	37	13	28	31	128	53
1887	1,876	661		175	39	28	19	26	244	62	12	47	62	167	81
1888	2,138	733		210	62	22	56	14	240	57	.	67	57	240	89
1889	1,871	827		143	6	8	8	16	250	52	2	48	52	180	79
1890	2,332	954		205	.	.	6	12	358	69	1	43	69	180	106
	36,024	11,502	631	4,439	1811	986	1,835	613	3,350	1,236	754	1488	802	2,527	1,199

The figures above were taken from builder's records, some of which are fragmented; some totals are, therefore, approximate.

INTRODUCTION

The F. M. Whyte Wheel Classification System

0-2-2			
0-2-2-4		1908	Schenectady #44444
0-2-4		1871	Danforth, Cooke & Co.
0-4-0		1842	
0-4-2T		1878	Baldwin
0-4-4T	Forney	1866	
0-4-4-0		(1889)	C. W. Hunt & Co., Staten Island, N. Y.; until about 1900
0-6-2T		1879	
0-6-4T		1881	Hinkley #1362
0-6-6T		1875	Mason #547
0-6-6-0		1904	Baldwin #24827 for American Railroad of Porto Rico
0-6-6-0T		1892	Baldwin #12526 for Sinnemahoning Valley #3
0-8-0		1843	Hinkley #16; built until about 1950
0-8-2			Illinois Central Railroad Co. converted a 2-8-2
0-8-8-0		1907	Erie Railroad Co.; built until about 1920
0-10-0		1891	Baldwin #11586; built until about 1925
0-10-2	Union	1936	Baldwin #61907 for Union Railroad Co. #301
0-12-0		1863	Philadelphia & Reading shops
2-2-0	Planet	1831	Baldwin #1
2-2-2	Jenny Lind	1843	Hinkley #13
2-2-2T		1860	Norris #1000
2-2-4T		1865	California Pacific Rail Road Co. #15, named <u>Flea</u>
2-2-6		1861	Mason Machine Works
2-4-0	Porter	1844	Baldwin #214
2-4-2	Columbia	1873	Baldwin #3110; built until 1900
2-4-2T		1871	Grant Locomotive Works
2-4-4		1876	Baldwin #3964
2-4-4T		1872	Baldwin #3031
2-4-4-2C		1913	Schenectady #53970
2-6-0	Mogul	1850	Built until 1933
2-6-2	Prairie	1896	Built until 1930
2-6-4		(1910)	
2-6-4T		1892	Rogers #4797
2-6-6T		1878	Mason Machine Works for Denver, South Park & Pacific Railroad Co.
2-8-0	Consolidation	1866	Lehigh & Mahanoy Railroad Co. #63, named <u>Consolidation</u>
2-8-2	Mikado	1890	Baldwin #11284; built until about 1930
2-8-4	Berkshire	(1922)	New York Central Railroad Co.; built until about 1949
2-8-6T		1880	Mason Machine Works for Denver, South Park & Pacific Railroad Co.
2-10-0	Decapod	1867	Norris for Lehigh Valley Railroad Co.; built until about 1947
2-10-2	Santa Fe	1903	Built until 1927
2-10-4	Texas	1919	Baldwin #52237 for Atchison, Topeka & Santa Fe #3829; built until 1944
2-4-4-2		1909	Little River Railroad Co. (Tennessee)
2-6-6-0		1909	Virginian Railroad Co.
2-6-6-2		1906	Great Northern Railway Co.; built until 1949
2-6-6-4		1934	Pittsburgh & West Virginia Railroad Co.; built until 1950
2-6-6-6	Allegheny	1941	Chesapeake & Ohio Railway Co.; built until 1948
2-6-8-0		1909	Alabama Great Southern #300
2-8-8-0		1910	Union Pacific Railroad Co. #3700; built until 1925
2-8-8-2		1909	Southern Pacific Railroad Co. #4000; built until about 1950
2-8-8-4	Yellowstone	1928	Northern Pacific Railway Co. #5003; had 182 square foot grate area
2-8-8-8-2T		1913	Erie Railroad Co. owned three of them; had tractive force of 160,000 pounds
2-8-8-8-4T		1916	Baldwin #44448 for Virginian Railway Co. #700
2-10-10-2		1911	Atchison, Topeka & Santa Fe #3000 to 3009; had 38" cylinders
4-2-0	Jervis	1834	Baldwin #2 for Charleston & Hamburg Railroad Co.; built until 1868
4-2-2	Bicycle	1840	Baldwin #146; built until 1896
4-2-2-0		1849	Utica & Schenectady Railroad Co.; had 84" drivers
4-2-4		1859	Mason Machine Works for Cleveland, Painesville & Ashtabula #30
4-4-0	American	1837	Baldwin; built until 1928
4-4-2	Atlantic	1887	Schenectady #2405 for Atchison, Topeka & Santa Fe #738; built until 1935
4-4-4	Jubilee	1915	Philadelphia & Reading Railroad Co.; built until 1935
4-4-4-4		1934	Baltimore & Ohio Railroad Co.
4-4-6-2		1909	Baldwin #33708 for Atchison, Topeka & Santa Fe #1300
4-4-6-4		1942	Pennsylvania Railroad Co., class Q-2

35.

4-6-0	Ten Wheel	1847	Norris for Philadelphia & Reading Railroad Co.; built until 1935
4-6-0-0-6-4		1938	Union Pacific Railroad Co.; a 181-foot long steam turbine
4-6-2	Pacific	1889	Schenectady #2855 for Chicago, Milwaukee & St. Paul #796; built until 1948
4-6-4	Hudson	1927	New York Central Railroad Co.; built until 1948
4-6-4T		1866	Danforth, Cooke & Co.
4-6-4-4		1941	Pennsylvania Railroad Co. #6130
4-6-6T		1928	Schenectady for Boston & Albany Railroad Co. #400
4-6-6-2		1912	Southern Pacific Railroad Co. #4200; rebuilt from 2-6-6-2
4-6-6-4	Challenger	1936	Union Pacific Railroad Co.; built until 1944 and in use in 1990
4-8-0		1855	Baltimore & Ohio; built until 1933
4-8-0-4-8-0		1950	Norfolk & Western Railway Co.
4-8-0-4-8-4		1947	Chesapeake & Ohio steam turbine
4-8-2	Mountain	1911	Chesapeake & Ohio
4-8-4	Northern	1927	Northern Pacific #2600; built until 1946
4-8-8-2		1928	Baldwin for Southern Pacific #4100
4-8-8-4	Big Boy	1941	Schenectady for Union Pacific #4000-4024; tractive effort 135,375 pounds
4-10-0		1883	Central Pacific #237, named El Gobernador
4-10-2	Overland	1925	Brooks for Union Pacific #8000
4-12-2	Union Pacific	1926	Brooks for Union Pacific #9000; built until 1930
6-2-0	Crampton	1849	Norris for Camden & Amboy #28, 96" drivers; built until 1853
6-4-4-6		1939	Pennsylvania Railroad's largest passenger locomotive
6-8-6		1944	Pennsylvania Railroad #6200, a steam turbine

Two-truck, three-truck and four-truck geared locomotives from Lima, Climax, Heisler and Willamette.

Union Pacific Railroad Co. was the innovator with six new types to its credit, all of them heavy-weights. Pennsylvania Railroad Co. and Atchison, Topeka & Santa Fe Railway Co. had four each, and again, all heavy ones.

Courtesy of Southern Pacific Company
Cab-ahead #4027, photographed at Oakridge about 1927, was built by Baldwin in May of 1911 and weighed nearly 400,000 pounds. It was rebuilt simple in March, 1930, and scrapped near Portland in early 1949.

Chronology of Major Events in the World, United States and the West — 1840 to 1940

1840	William H. Harrison, Whig, the 9th President of the United States. U. S. population is 17,069,453.
1841	Upon the death of Harrison, John Tyler, Democrat, became the 10th President. First steam fire engine built.
1844	First electric telegraph line in the U. S., Washington, D. C., to Baltimore. James K. Polk, Democrat, 11th President.
1845	Republic of Texas admitted to statehood. The great clipper ship *Rainbow* was built.
1848	Treaty of Guadalupe-Hidalgo ended war with Mexico which started in 1846; U. S. acquires the southwest. Zachary Taylor, Whig, elected our 12th President. Gold discovered in California.
1850	Upon death of Taylor, vice president Millard Fillmore became 13th President. Population is now 23,191,876.
1851	May 19 — Erie Railroad Co. connects New York City with the Great Lakes, 483 miles.
1852	Franklin Pierce, Democrat, 14th President.
1853	Commodore Matthew C. Perry opens Japan to American trade. Baltimore & Ohio joins Ohio River to Altantic.
1855	First Atlantic Ocean telegraph cable laid. Isthmus of Panama crossed by a railroad.
1856	James Buchanan, Democrat, elected as the 15th President.
1859	First petroleum well drilled in the United States, at Titusville, Penna.
1860	Abraham Lincoln, Republican, 16th President. Population now 31,443,321.
1861	The Confederate States of America established. Central Pacific Rail Road Company is incorporated.
1862	First engagement of naval ironclads, *Merrimac* and *Monitor*. Union Pacific Railroad Company is incorporated.
1865	April 8 — Robert E. Lee surrenders to U. S. Grant in a home at Appomattox Court House, Virginia. April 15 — Abraham Lincoln assissinated; Andrew Johnson, 17th President.
1867	Alaska purchased for $7,200,000 from Russia. Nebraska becomes state number thirty-seven.
1868	General Ulysses Simpson Grant, Republican, 18th President.
1869	May 10 — Union Pacific and Central Pacific joined at Promontory, Utah Territory. The 103-mile Suez Canal placed in operation November 21 with a fleet of 45 steamers bound for Alexandria.
1870	United States population is now 38,558,371.
1872	General Grant is reelected President.
1873	A fireboat with an iron hull was built in Boston.
1874	July 4 — First steel arch bridge across the Mississippi River, at St. Louis, was dedicated; James B. Eads, builder.
1876	Rutherford B. Hayes, Republican, 19th President. A functional telephone is introduced.
1878	October 15 — Thomas A. Edison established the Edison Electric Light Company in New York City.
1880	James A. Garfield, Republican, 20th President. The census now shows 50,155,783.
1881	September 19 — Garfield assassinated; Chester A. Arthur took office as 21st President.
1882	Construction of the Panama Canal begun.
1884	Grover Cleveland, Democrat, our 22nd President.
1885	First electric street car line in the United States, in Baltimore. The New York *Tribune* got a linotype machine.
1886	October 28 — Statue of Liberty dedicated in New York City harbor.
1888	Benjamin Harrison, Republican, 23rd President.
1890	Sioux War, the last Indian battle, is fought. U. S. population now 62,947,714
1892	Grover Cleveland, Democrat, 24th President.
1893	June 27 — Four years of deep depression begin with New York stock market crash.
1896	William B. McKinley, Republican, is now President.
1897	Klondike, Alaska, gold rush begins; Skaguay (now Skagway) becomes important entry point.
1898	April 24 — Spain declares war on the United States; the battleship *Maine* had been sunk on February 15.
1899	February 14 — Congress approves the use of voting machines in national elections.
1900	McKinley reelected. Population 75,994,575.
1901	September 14 — McKinley is assassinated; Theodore Roosevelt is the 25th President.
1903	First aeroplane flight at Kitty Hawk, N. C. A Packard automobile driven from San Francisco to New York City.
1904	Theodore Roosevelt elected President. New York City subway opened October 27, City Hall to 145th Street.
1906	April 18 -- San Francisco earthquake and fire; over 500 lives lost.
1908	William Howard Taft, Republican, our 26th President.
1910	United States population is now 91,972,266.
1912	April 15 — The new steamship *Titanic* sank off of Newfoundland with loss of over 1,500 lives. Woodrow Wilson, Democrat, defeated Howard Taft (Republican) and Roosevelt (Progressive) to become 27th President.
1914	World War broke out; Austria declared war against Serbia. Panama Canal is opened.
1915	May 7 — The liner *Lusitania* sunk by a German submarine with the loss of 1,200 lives.
1916	Woodrow Wilson reelected. "Pancho" Villa raided the village of Columbus, New Mexico.
1917	Germany resumed unrestricted submarine attacks. Wilson requested declaration of war on April 2.
1918	The Central Powers collapse and World War ends.
1920	Warren G. Harding, Republican, 28th President. Population now 105,710,620.
1923	August 2 — President Harding died in San Francisco; Calvin Coolidge, Republican, became 29th President.
1924	Coolidge elected in his own right.
1927	May 21 — Col. Charles A. Lindberg made a solo airplane flight from New York to Paris.
1928	Herbert C. Hoover, Republican, became our 30th President.
1929	October 29 — New York stock market crash was followed by a world-wide depression lasting about ten years.
1930	London Naval Reduction Treaty signed. Population now 122,775,046.
1932	Franklin D. Roosevelt, Democrat, became 31st President.
1935	September 30 -- Hoover Dam on the Colorado River, largest in the world, completed and dedicated.
1936	Roosevelt is reelected.
1939	Second World War erupted in Europe; the United States entered in 1942.
1940	Roosevelt is reelected - and again in 1944!

OREGON

What is now Oregon was probably visited in 1579 by Sir Francis Drake and the coast was mapped in 1592 by Spain. On May 11, 1792, American merchant captain Robert Gray discovered the fabled "River of the West" and named it Columbia's River in honor of his three-masted vessel *Columbia Rediviva*. In 1805, the Lewis and Clark expedition explored the northwest to the mouth of the Columbia River. A native of New England built a house there in 1810; the following year, Astoria was established as a fur trading post. Two years later it was renamed Fort George.

The original "Oregon country" had an area of over 300,000 square miles. A treaty with Spain in 1819 established the present southern boundary of Oregon which was then the border with Spanish-ruled Mexico. A treaty of "joint occupation" was made in 1818 between the United States and Great Britian; the treaty of 1846 finished the matter of the border with Canada.

Real settlement of the area began in 1843 when some one thousand crossed from the Missouri River to Oregon City; many thousands more were to follow them over the Oregon Trail. A territorial government was established August 14, 1848, and it became state number 33 on February 14, 1859. Oregon City was the first seat of government in 1848 and into 1850 when the capital was moved to Salem; this lasted until 1855 when it shifted to Corvallis and then back to Salem, all in the same year. The first newspaper was printed at Oregon City on February 5, 1846; in 1850 Portland had its own publication.

The early schools were Willamette University in 1842, Pacific University in 1849 and Linfield College the same year. The federal census for 1850 shows a population of 13,294; the enrollments must have been quite small.

The major cities:	1890	1960		1890	1960
Portland	46,385	372,676	Ashland	1,784	9,119
East Portland	10,532		The Dalles	1,595	10,493
Astoria	6,184	11,239	Corvallis	1,527	20,669
Salem	4,749	49,142	Roseburg	1,472	11,467
Eugene	4,111	50,977	Marshfield City	1,461	7,084
Albany	3,079	12,926	Grants Pass	1,432	10,118
Oregon City	3,062	7,996	McMinnville	1,368	7,656
Baker City	2,604	9,986	Medford	967	24,425
La Grande	2,583	9,014	Forest Grove	668	5,628
Pendleton	2,506	14,434	Bend		11,936

The census figures for 1890 revealed that the population was 181,840 males and 131,927 females for an average of 3.3 persons per square mile. There were 1,186 Negroes, 9,540 Chinese, 25 Japanese and 1,258 civilized Indians.

The present area of the state is 96,030 square miles of which 1,470 are water surfaces. By 1960 the population density was 18.0 per square mile, quite a change from 0.1 in 1850. The highest point in Mount Hood, fifty miles east by south from Portland, and measures 11,245 feet above the ocean.

Fertile light soil, abundant rainfall and a temperate climate makes Oregon a true food factory. Many of its varied crops are canned or frozen. Major export crops include apples, pears, strawberries, filberts, walnuts, potatoes and wheat. Livestock raising and flower bulbs are also major industries. For the past hundred plus years the major source of employment has been logging and lumber products. Starting in the 1960s electronic equipment has become important and will become more so in the future with the decline of logging.

Major sources of railroad information:
Poor's Manual of the Railroads of the United States, 1868 - 1924
Travelers' Official Guide, 1868 - 1901
Official Guide of the Railways, 1902 - 1975
Interstate Commerce Commission *Statistics of Railways in the United States, 1888 - 1974*
Interstate Commerce Commission *Valuation Reports, 1918 - 1934*
United States Geological Survey maps
Railroad Gazette, 1871 - 1908
The Railway Age, 1876 - 1908
Railway Age Gazette, 1908 - 1940
Electric Railway Journal, 1893 - 1931
Chicago Railway Review, 1875 - 1926
American Railroad Journal, 1879 - 1963
Department of the Interior *Report of the Agencies of Transportation in the U. S., 1883*
Department of the Interior, Census Office *Report of Transportation Business in the U. S., 1895*
Oregon Railroad Commission reports, 1889 - 1953
Tillitson Special Collection at Leland Stanford Junior University

Index of Railroads in Oregon

	page:
Albany & Lebanon Railroad Company	56 s
Algoma Lumber Company	56
Anderson & Middleton Lumber Company of Oregon	56
Astoria & Columbia River Railroad Company	57
Astoria & Portland Railway Company	134
Astoria & South Coast Railroad Company	134
Astoria Southern Railway Company	58
Baker White Pine Lumber Company, The	145
Beaverton & Willsburg Railroad Company	58 s
Benson Logging & Lumbering Company	59
Benson Timber Company	59
Big Creek Logging Company	60
Blue Lake Logging Company	60
Blue Mountain Railroad, Inc.	192
Booth-Kelley Lumber Company, The	60
Bowman-Hicks Lumber Company	61
Brix Logging Company	61
Brooks-Scanlon Lumber Company	62
Brownlee-Olds Lumber Company	90
Burlington Northern Railroad Company see Montana	279
California & Oregon Coast Railroad Company, The	62
California Northeastern Railway Company	107
Carlton & Coast Railroad Company	63
Central of Oregon Ry. Company	121
Central Pacific Railway Company see California	
Central Railroad of Oregon	150
Central Railway Company of Oregon	150
Chambers Lumber Company, J. H.	56
A City of Prineville Railway	64
Clackamas Eastern Railroad Company	65 s
Clackamas Southern Railway Company	160
Clark & Wilson Lumber Company	65
Clatsop Railroad Company	66
Cobbs & Mitchell Lumber Company	66
Columbia & Nehalem River Railroad Company	85
Columbia River & Oregon Central Railroad Company	67
Columbia River Belt Line Railway	68
Columbia Southern Railway Company	69
Condon, Kinzua & Southern Railroad Company	69
Coos Bay Lumber Company	82
Coos Bay, Roseburg & Eastern Railroad & Navigation Company, The	70
Corvallis & Alsea River Railway Company	72
Corvallis & Eastern Railroad Company	72
Crossett-Western Company	74
Crown-Willamette Paper Company	74
Crown Zellerbach Corporation	74
Curtis Lumber Company	90
Dayton, Sheridan & Grande Ronde Railroad Company, The	158
Des Chutes Railroad Company	76
Dollar Company, Robert	76
Eastern & Western Lumber Company	77
A East Portland Traction Company	78
East Side Logging Company	77
Eugene & Eastern Railway Company	132
Flora Logging Company	79
Gales Creek & Wilson River Railroad Company	79
Georgia-Pacific Corporation	82
Glendale Lumber Company	76
Goble, Nehalem & Pacific Railway Company	65
Grande Ronde Lumber Company	145

"A" before the name means active in 1993.
"s" after the page number shows that the line was built (or owned) as a subsidiary.

	Great Northern Railway Company	see Montana	303
	Great Southern Railroad Company		148
A	Great Western Railway Company of Oregon, Inc.		83
	Hammond Lumber Company		90
	Hines Lumber Company, Edward		83
A	Idaho Northern & Pacific Railroad Company		83
	Independence & Monmouth Railway Company, The		84
	Ingham Lumber Company		76
	International Paper Company		85
	Isthmus & Coquille Railroad Company		70
	K-P Timber Company		85
	Kerry Timber Company		85
	Kinzua Pine Mills Company		69
	Klamath Falls Municipal Railway		104
	Klamath Lake Railroad Company	see California	
A	Klamath Northern Railway Company		86
	Koster Products Company		86
	La Dee Logging Company		86
	Lamm Lumber Company		87
	Lewis & Clark Railroad Company		66
	Lewis & Clark Railway Company		66
	Long-Bell Lumber Company		85
	Longview, Portland & Northern Railway Company		161
	Malheur Railroad Company		102
	Malheur Valley Railway Company		87
	Masten Logging Company, C. C.		88
	Medford & Crater Lake Railroad Company		127
	Medford Coast Rail Road Company		88
	Medford Corporation		90
	Medford Logging Railroad Company		90
	Mill City Mfg. Company		90
A	Mollala Western Railway Company		91
	Mount Emily Lumber Company		91
A	Mount Hood Railroad Company		92
	Mount Hood Railway Company		92
	Mount Hood Railway & Power Company		78
	Nevada-California-Oregon Railway	see Nevada	148
	North Bend Mill & Lumber Company		92
	Northern Pacific Railroad Company	see Montana	331
	Northern Pacific Railway Company	see Montana	331
	Northwestern Railroad Company		93
	Noyes-Holland Logging Company		94
	Olympia Terminal Railway Company		122
	Oregon & California Rail Road Company		96
	Oregon & Northwestern Railroad		102
	Oregon & Northwestern Railroad Company		102
	Oregon & Southeastern Railroad Company		102
	Oregon & Washington Territory Railroad Company		242
	Oregon-American Lumber Company		85
	Oregon, California & Eastern Railway Company		104
	Oregon Central & Eastern Railroad Company		104
	Oregon Central Railroad Company		106
	Oregon Central Rail Road Company		106
	Oregon City & Southern Railway Company		78
	Oregon Coast Range Lumber Company		130
	Oregon Eastern Railway Company		107
	Oregon Electric Railway Company		108
	Oregon Lumber Company		111
	Oregon, Pacific & Eastern Railway Company		111
	Oregon Pacific Railroad Company		157
	Oregon Portage Rail Road		112
	Oregon Railroad & Navigation Company, The		114
	Oregon Railway & Navigation Company		117
	Oregon Railway Company, Ltd., The (Oregon)		126
	Oregon Railway Extensions Company, The		243
	Oregon Short Line & Utah Northern Railway Company	see Utah	274

	Oregon Short Line Railroad Company	see Idaho	219
	Oregon Short Line Railway Company	see Idaho	223
	Oregon State Portage Railroad		119
	Oregon Steam Navigation Company		121
	Oregon Trunk Line, Inc.		121
	Oregon Trunk Railway		121 s
	Oregon-Washington Railroad & Navigation Company		122 s
	Oregon Water Power & Railway Company, The		78
	Oregon Western Railroad Company		126
	Oregonian Railroad Company		126
	Oregonian Railway Company, Ltd. (Scotland)		126
	Owen-Oregon Lumber Company		90
	Pacific & Eastern Railway Company		127
	Pacific Railway & Navigation Company		129
	Palmer Lumber Company, The George		61
	Pelican Bay Lumber Company		129
	Polk Operating Company		130
	Portland & Oregon City Railway Company		65
	Portland & Southwestern Railroad Company		130
	Portland & Willamette Valley Railway Company		131 s
	Portland & Yamhill Railroad Company		131 s
	Portland, Astoria & Pacific Railroad Company		151
	Portland City & Oregon Railway Company		78
	Portland Electric Power Company		78
	Portland, Eugene & Eastern Railway Company		132 s
	Portland Lumber Company		94
	Portland Railway, Light & Power Company		78
	Portland Southern Railroad Company		65
	Portland Traction Company		78
A	Port of Tillamook Bay Railroad		133
	Rogue River Valley Railroad Company		88
	Rogue River Valley Railway Company		88
	Salem, Falls City & Western Railway Company		133
	Seashore Railroad Company		134
	Shaw-Bertram Lumber Company		135
	Sheridan & Willamina Railroad Company		135
	Shevlin-Hixon Lumber Company		136
	Silver Falls Timber Company		136
	Silverton Lumber Company		136
	Simpson Lumber Company		145
	Smith Lumber & Mfg. Company, C. A.		82
	Smith-Powers Logging Company		82
	Smith River & Northern Railway Company		137
	Southern Oregon Traction Company		88
A	Southern Pacific Transportation Company		138
	Spaulding Logging Company, Chas. K.		144
	Spaulding-Miami Lumber Company		144
	Spokane, Portland & Seattle Railway Company	see Washington	282
	Standard Logging Company		144
	Stoddard Bros. Lumber Company		145
	Stoddard Lumber Company		145
	Stout Lumber Company		145
	Sumpter Valley Railway Company		146
	Sunset Logging Company		148
	The Dalles & Southern Railroad Company		148
	Umatilla Central Railroad Company		149
	Union Pacific Railroad Company	see Idaho	233
	Union Railroad of Oregon		150
	Union Railway Company, The		150
	United Railways Company (Oregon)		151 s
	Vale & Malheur Railway Company		87
	Valley & Siletz Railroad Company		159
A	WCTU Railway Company		152
	Walla Walla & Columbia River Railroad Company	see Washington	292
	Walla Walla Valley Railway Company	see Washington	293
	Walla Walla Valley Traction Company	see Washington	293

OREGON

43.

	Warren Spruce Company	152
	Washington & Columbia River Railway Company see Washington	295
	Weed Lumber Company	107
	Western Lumber Company	83
	Western Oregon Lumber Company	153
	Westfir Lumber Company	83
	Weyerhaeuser Company	153
	Wheeler, C. H.	154
A	Willamette & Pacific Railroad Company	154
	Willamette Pacific Railroad Company	155
	Willamette Valley & Coast Rail Road Company	156
	Willamette Valley Railroad Company	158
	Willamette Valley Railroad Company - 2d	159
	Willamette Valley Railway Company	160
A	Willamette Valley Railway Company - 2d	161
	Willamette Valley Southern Railway Company	160
	Willamina & Grande Ronde Railway Company	162
A	Willamina & Grand Ronde Railway Company	162
A	Wyoming & Colorado Railroad Company	163
	Yeon & Pelton Company	94

Photo by Ed Austin
Robert Dollar Company's imp with the big load was a 45 ton, 300 h.p., General Electric #17730, built December, 1942. The photograph was taken January 30, 1981 with the usual lack of sunshine.

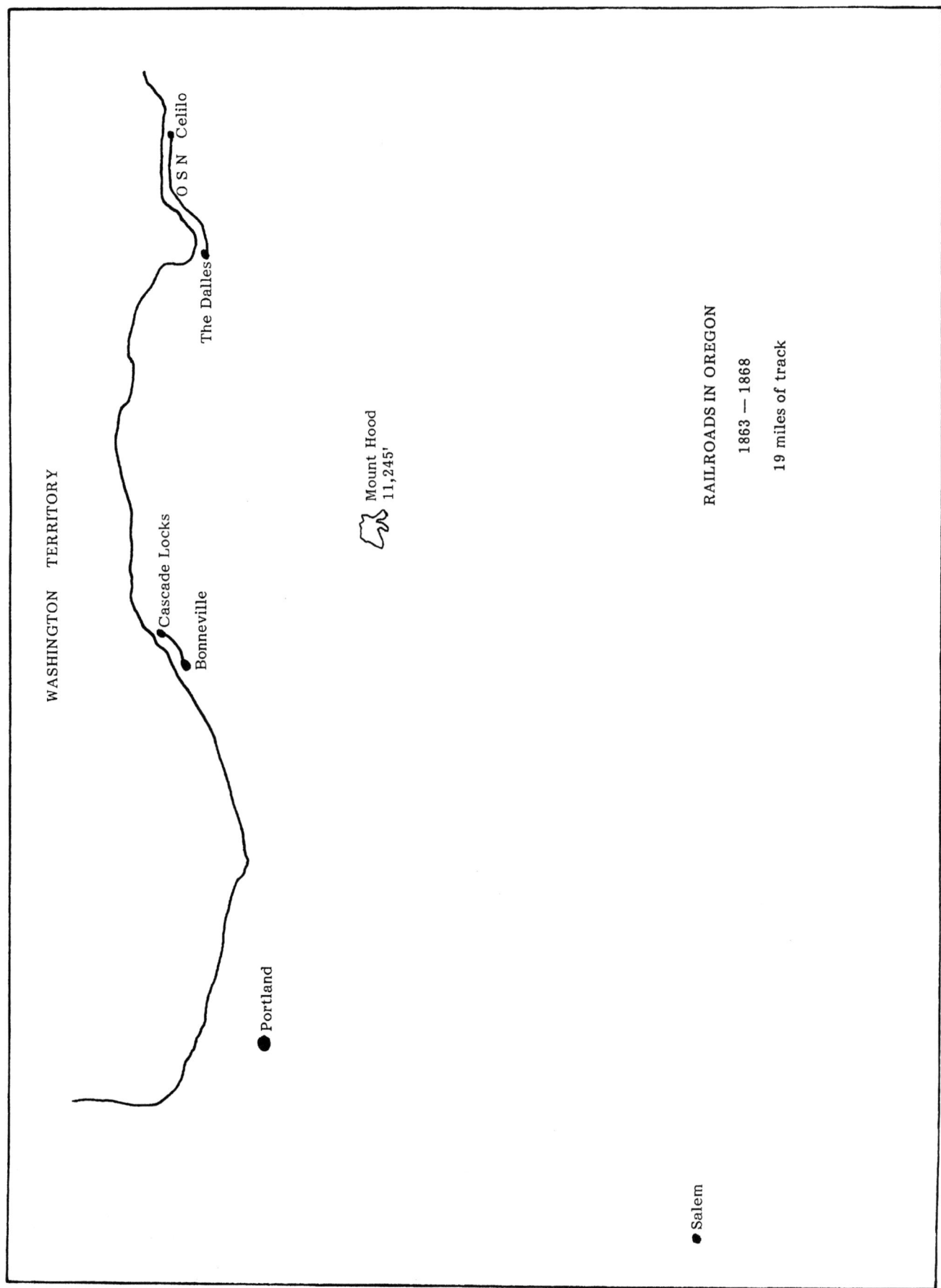

OREGON

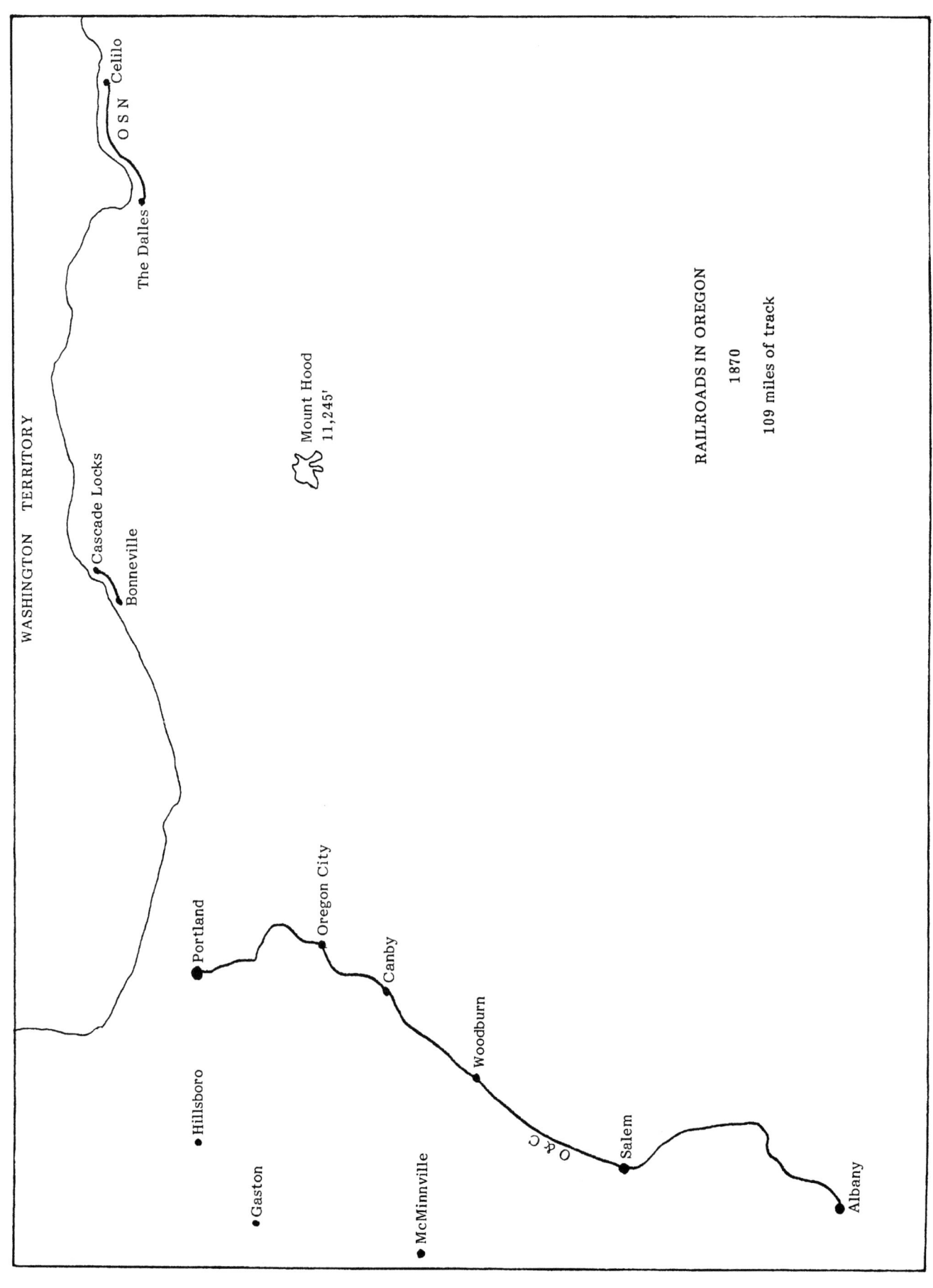

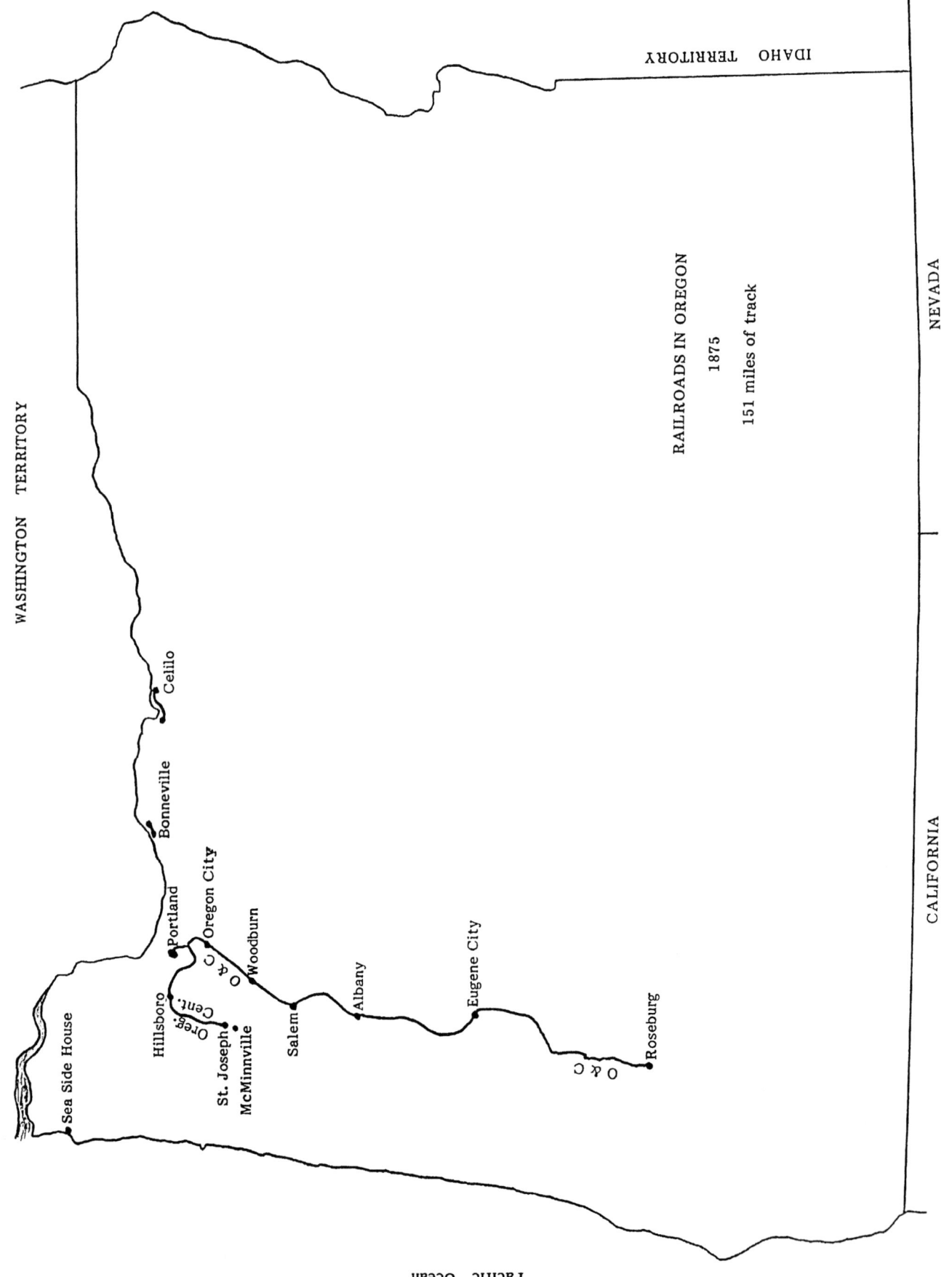

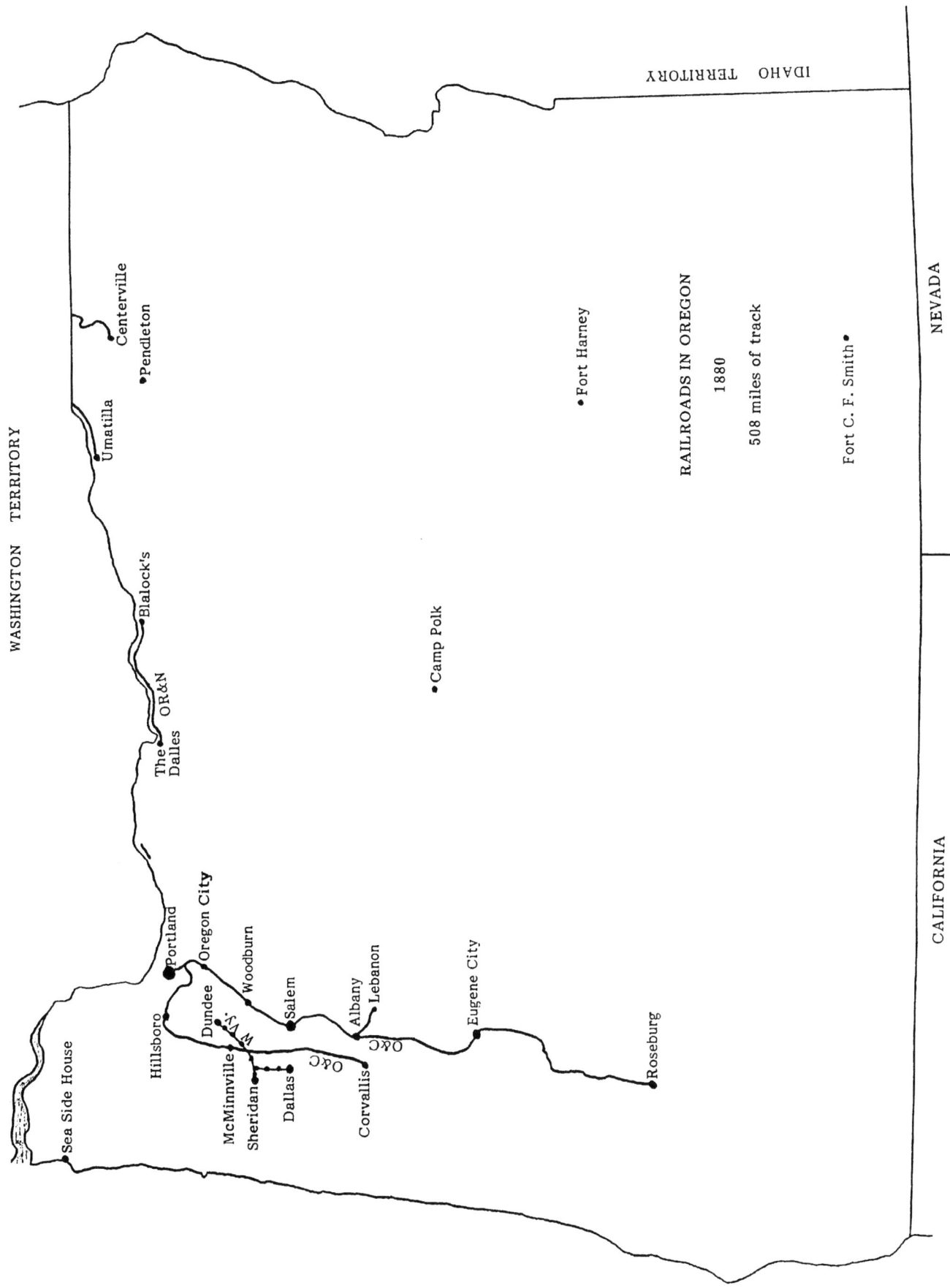

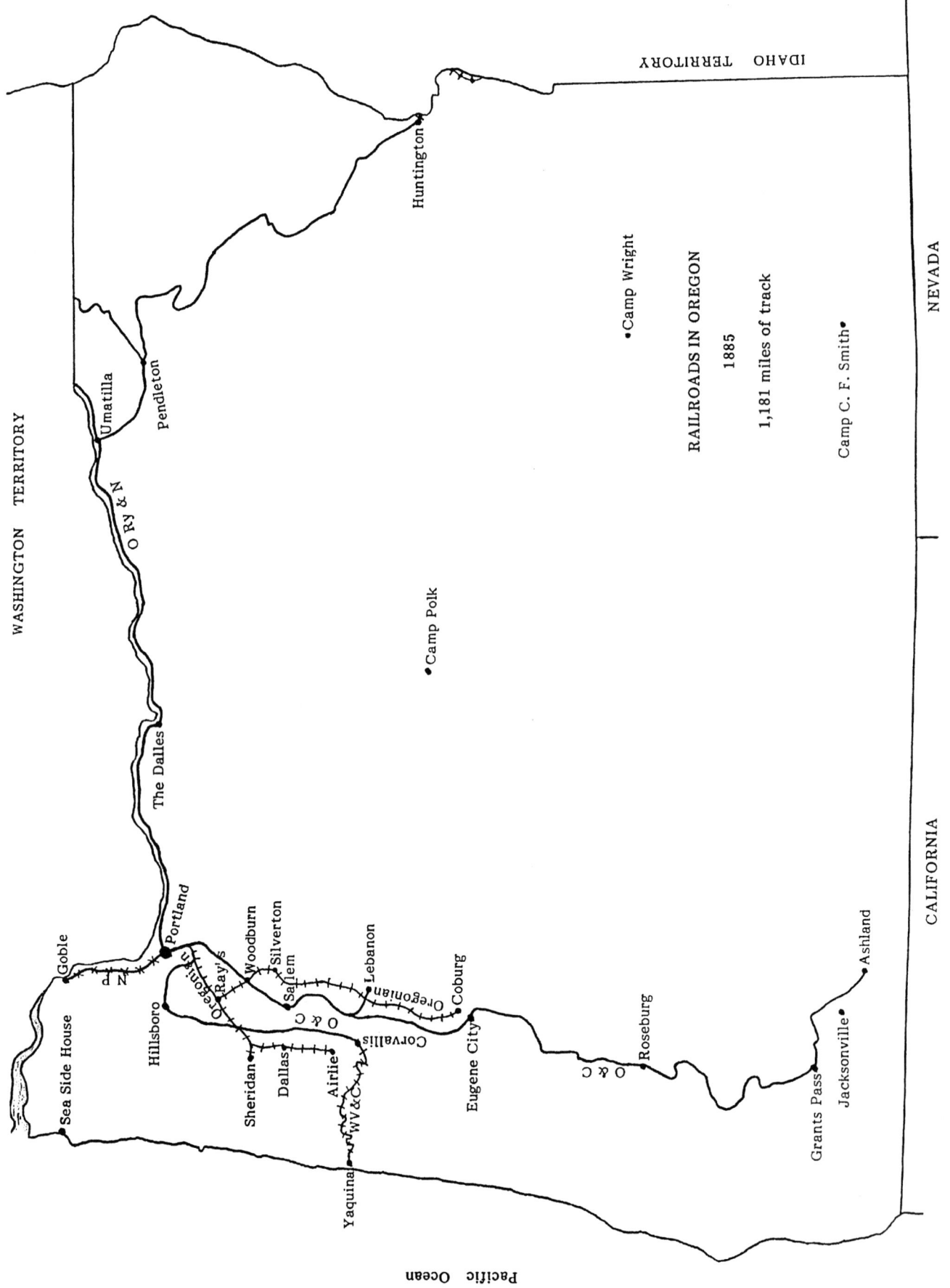

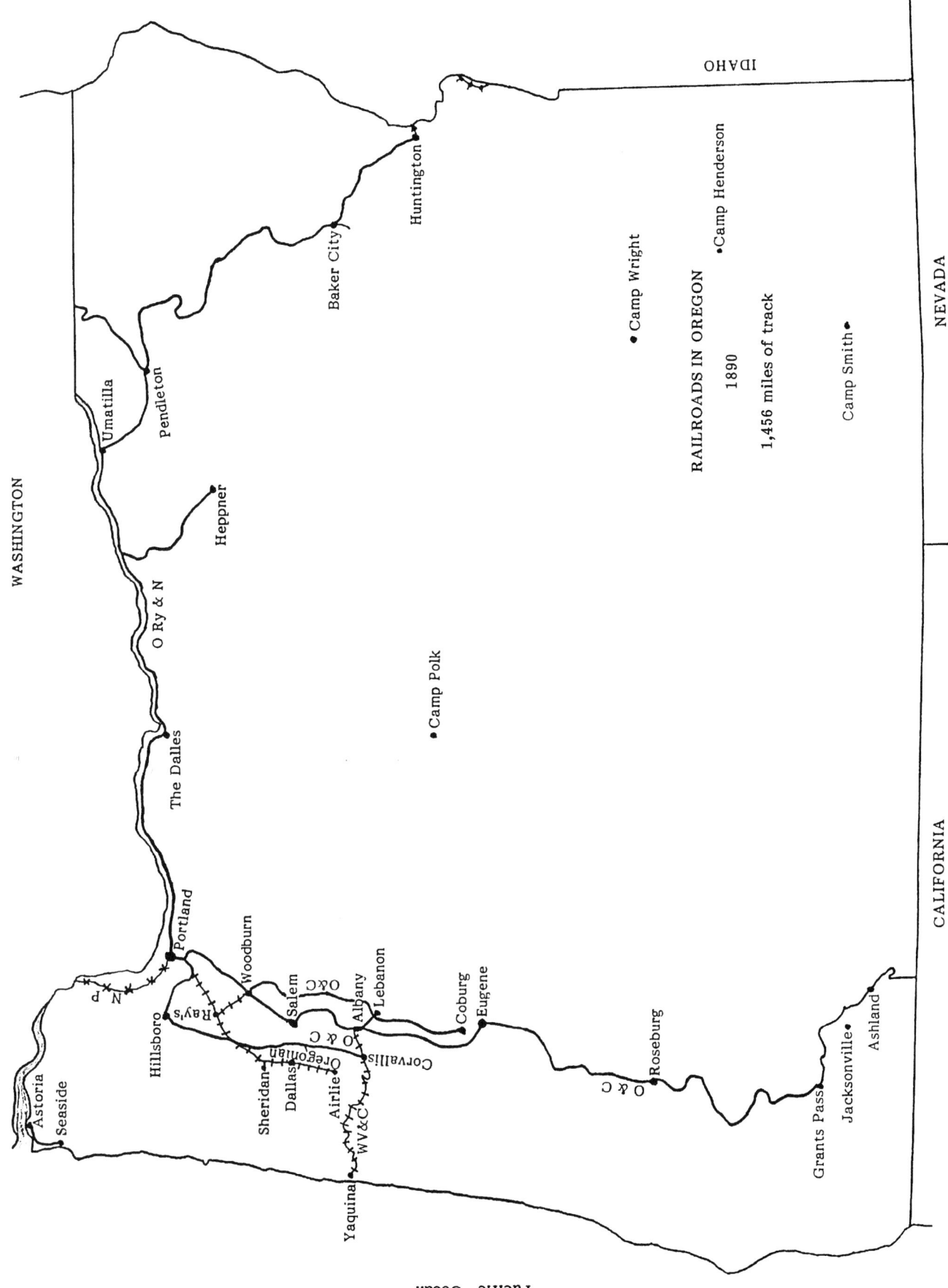

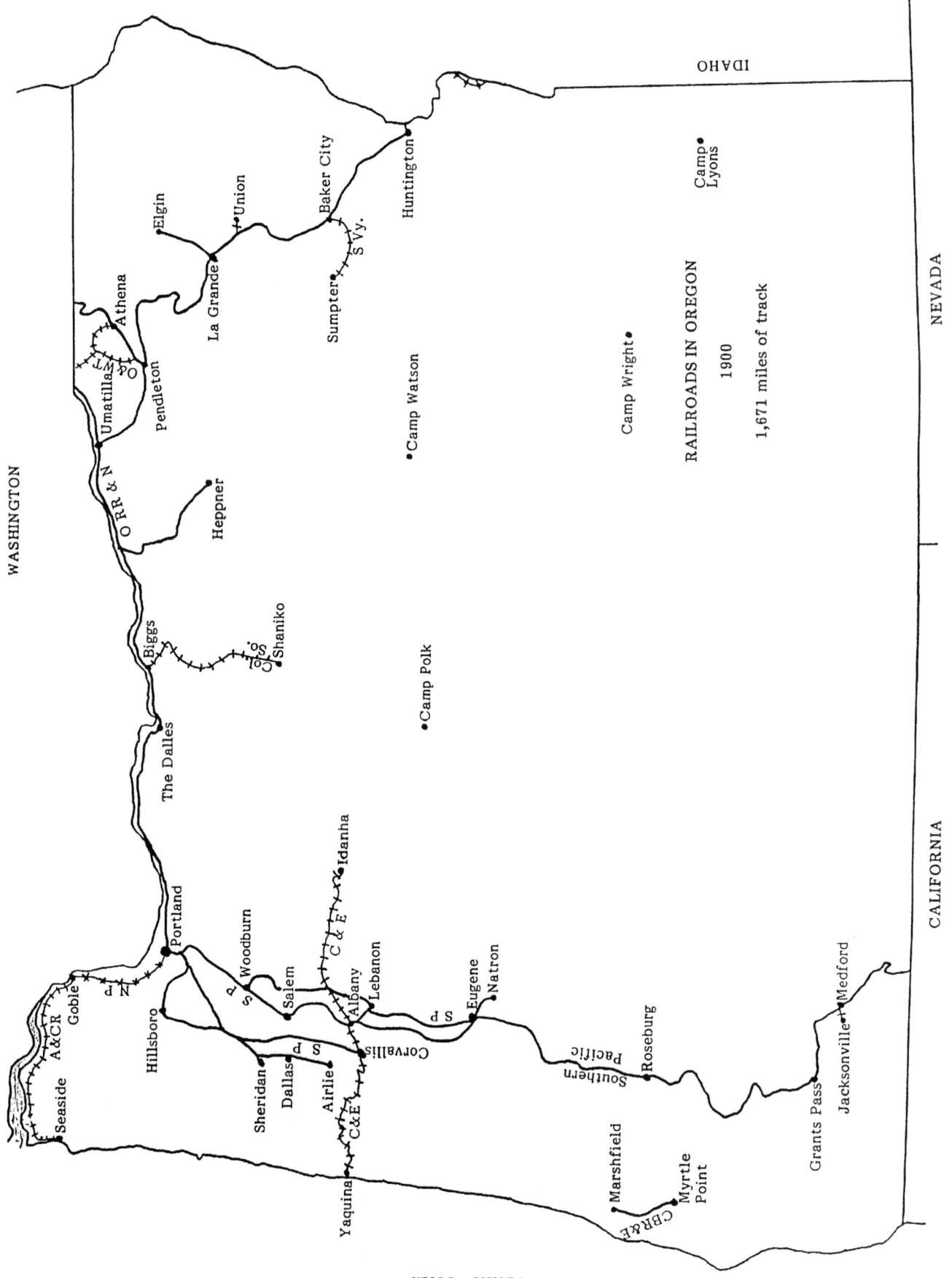

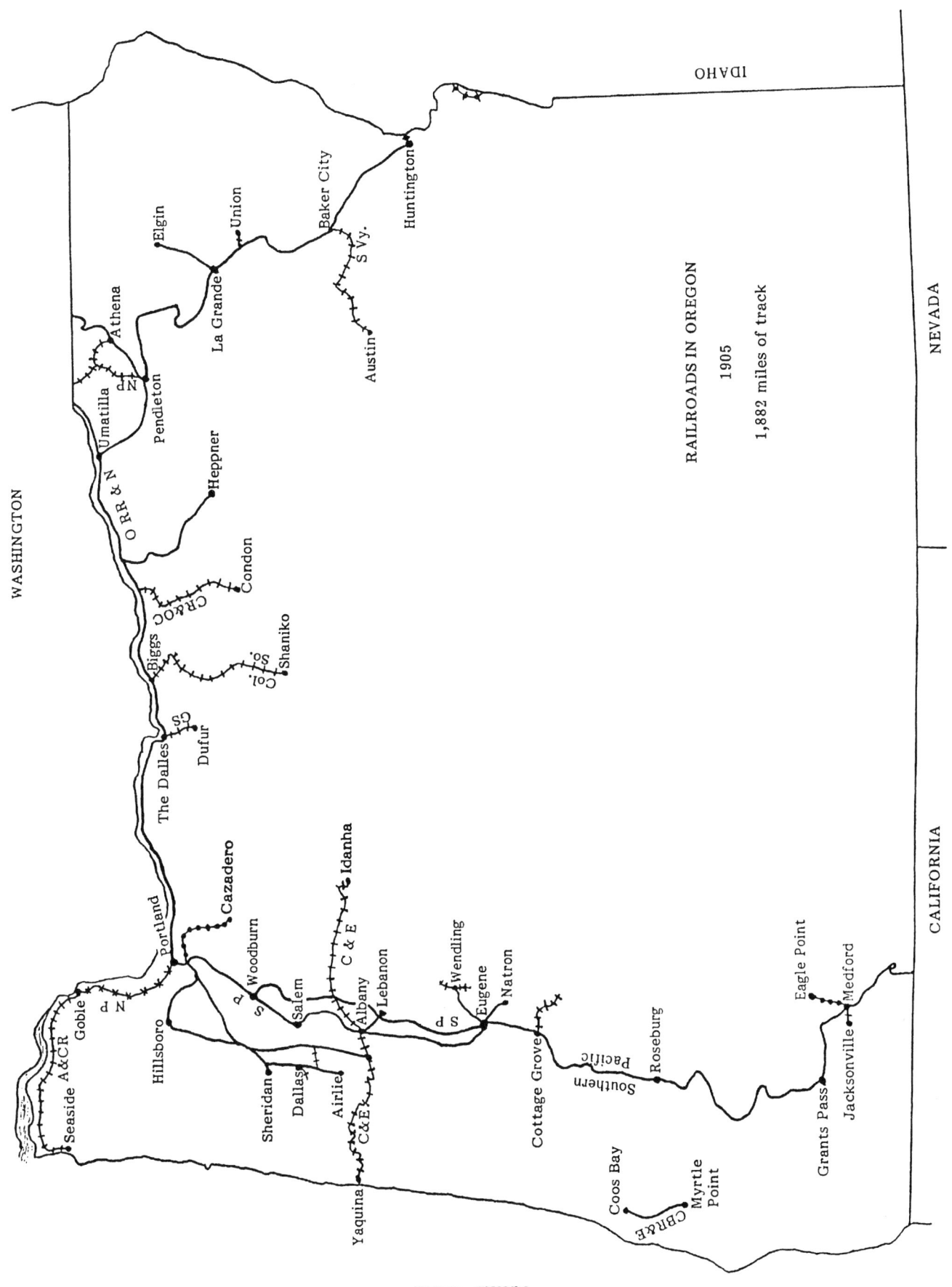

RAILROADS IN OREGON
1905
1,882 miles of track

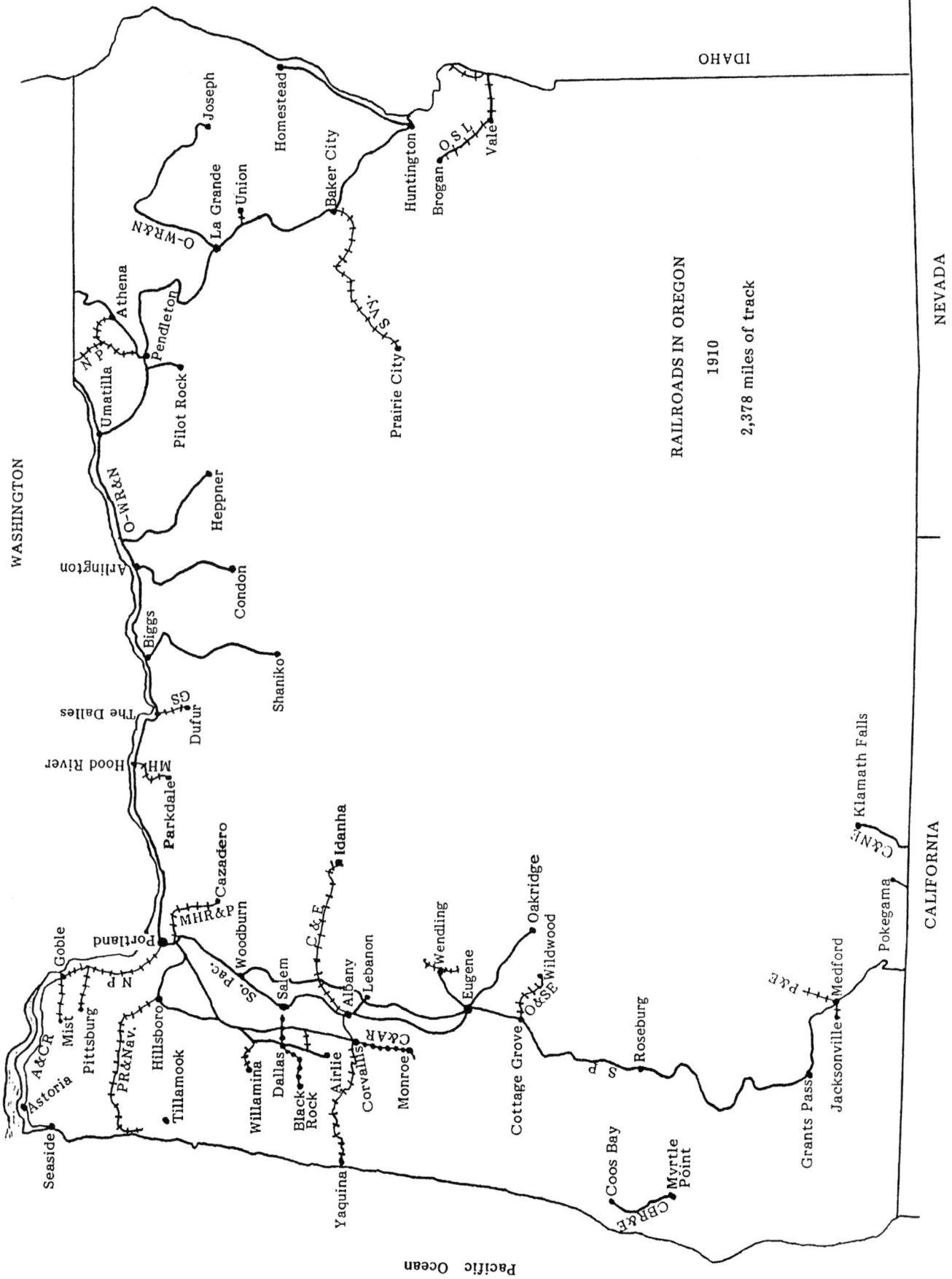

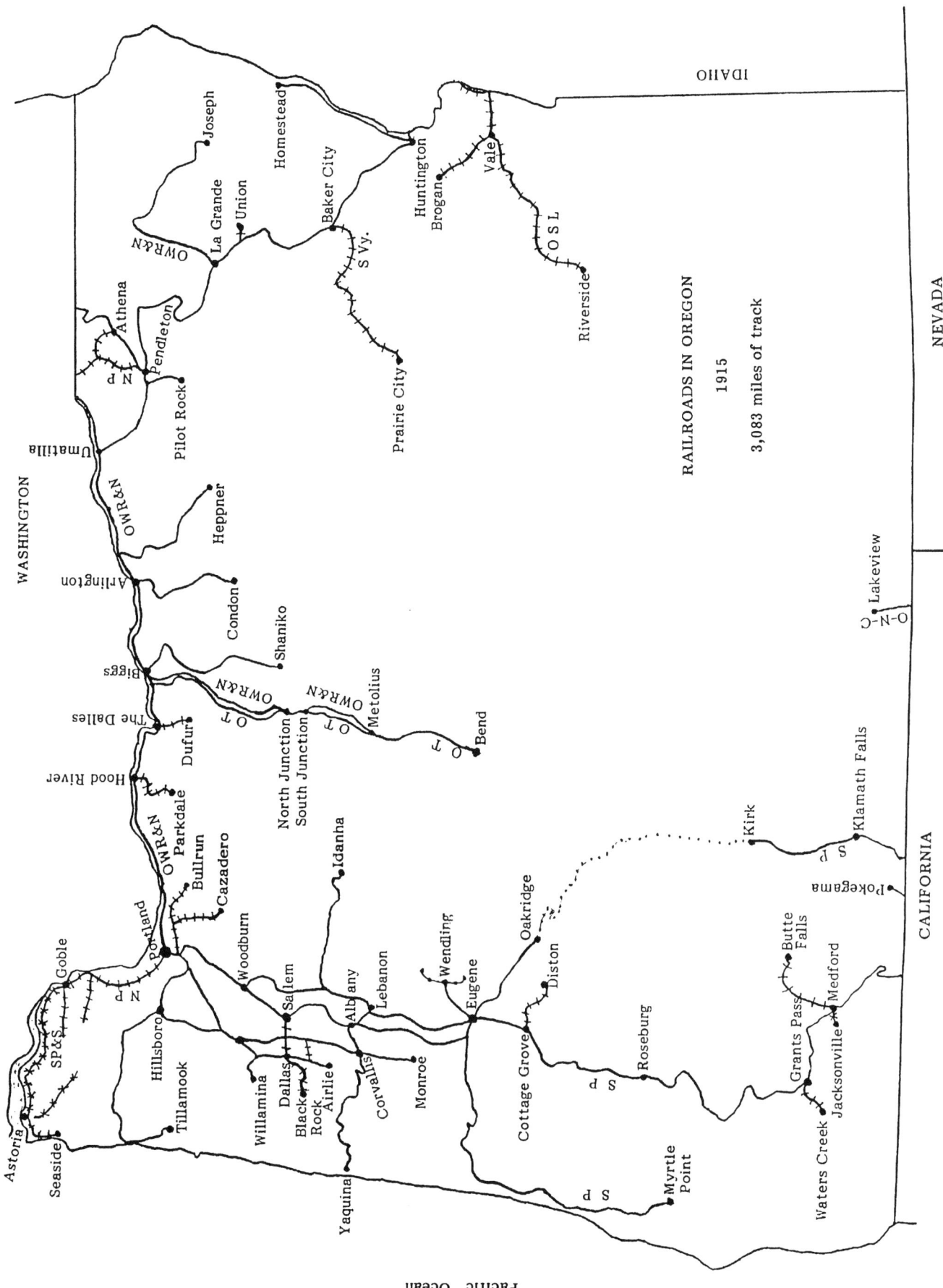

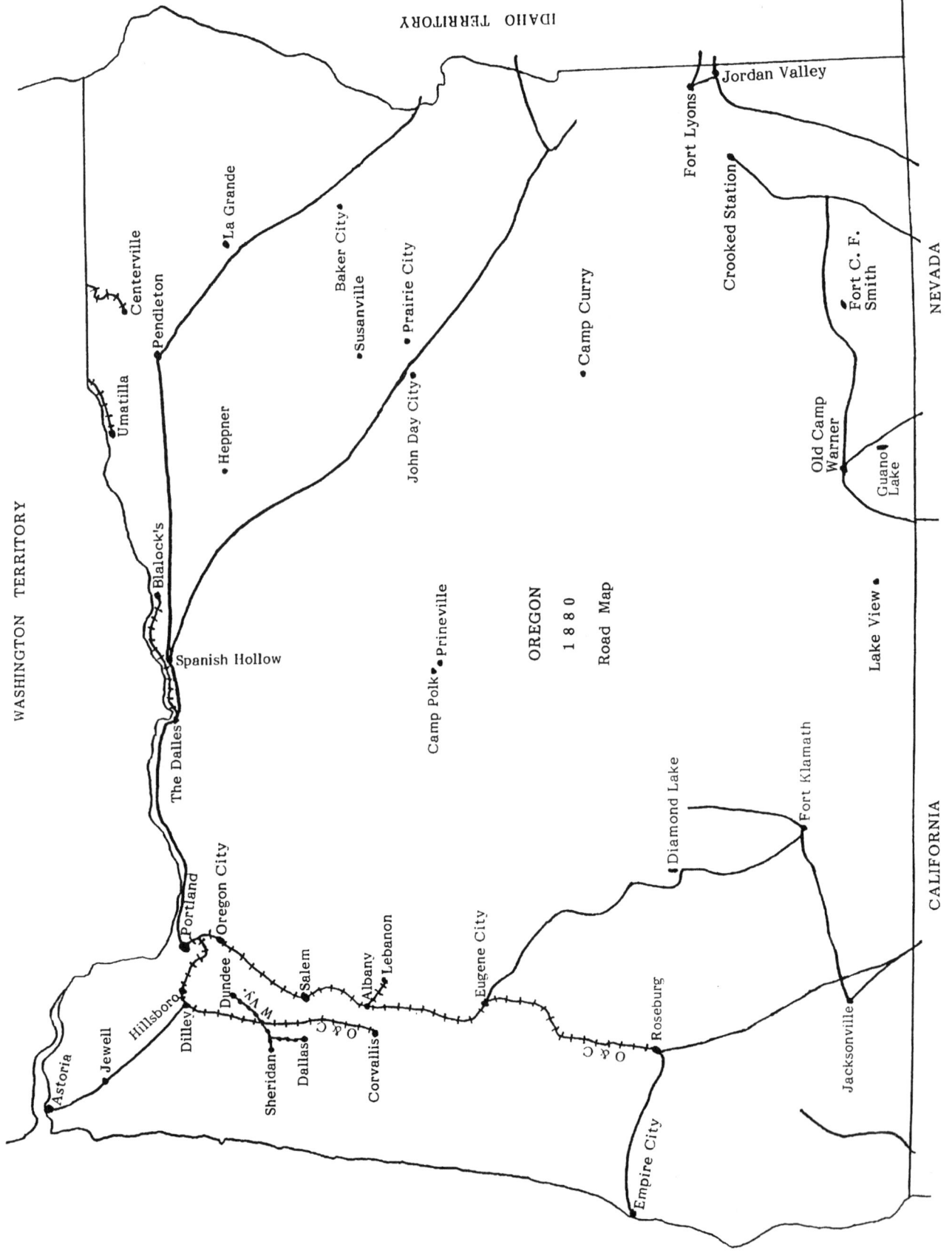

OREGON 55.

Miles of railroad track and population in Oregon

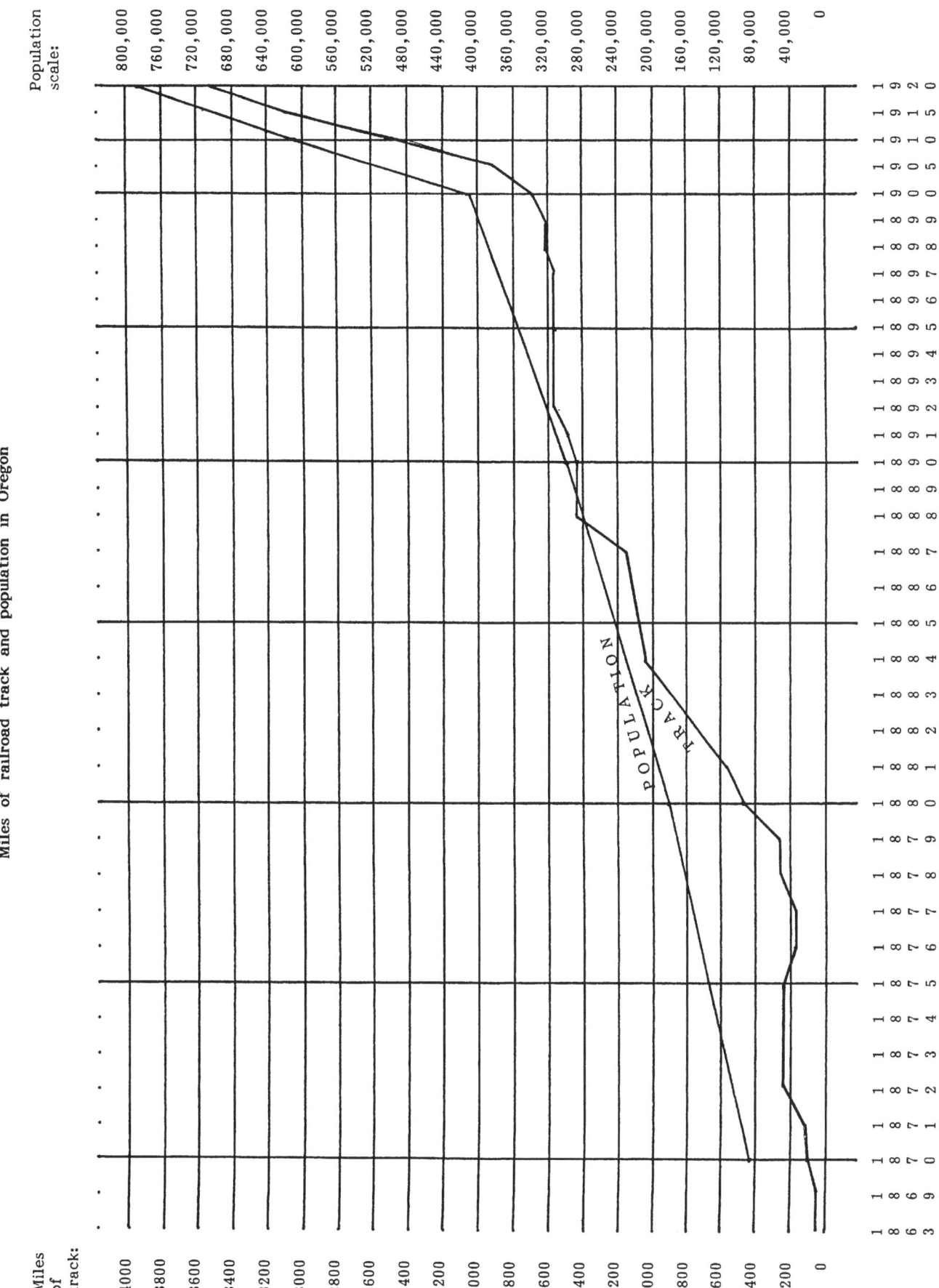

ALBANY & LEBANON RAILROAD COMPANY

R. Koehler, **President**

Incorp:	2/28/1880	**Operated:** 10/1/80 to 5/6/81
HQ city:		Portland
Disposition:	sold to Oregon & California Rail Road Company on May 6, 1881	
Miles track:	11.58	**Gauge:** 56½"
Main line:	Albany Jct. to Lebanon	
Rail wt.:	50 lbs. - iron	**Max. grade:** 0.500%
Const. began:	grading (June 7, 1880)	
	laying rails August 23, 1880	
Const. comp.:	(October 1, 1880)	**First train operated:** September 22, 1880
Freight traffic:	common carrier, agriculture	

This was a non-operating subsidiary and hence owned no equipment in its own name.

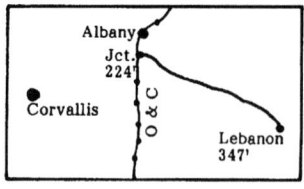

Bibliography: *Poor's 1881, p. 817*   Oregon PUC report 1890, p. 263   *Valuation 45, p. 422*
Albany - *State Rights Democrat* - May 28 to August 27, 1880

ALGOMA LUMBER COMPANY

President

Incorp:	1/29/1912	**Operated:** 1903 to 1943	**HQ City:**	Klamath Falls
Disposition:	abandoned			
Miles track:	30	**Gauge:** 56½"		
Main line:				
Rail wt.:	60 lbs.	**Max. grade:** 4.0%	**Const. began:** grading	

Locomotives:

Road No.	Cyln.	Type	Dvr. in.	Bldr.	Bldr. No.	Date	Weight	Effort	Remarks
1		2-4-4T	46	BLW	34845	6/10	110,000		ex South San Francisco Belt #4
2*	17x24	2-6-2	44	BLW	42012	5/15			
3		4-4-0	63	BLW	2935	9/72	61,600	10,350	acq. 4/1909 ex Oregon & Cal. #15
4		3T Shay	35	Lima	2754	4/14	157,000	31,500	4/1927 to Klamath Timber Co.

Freight traffic: logging

ANDERSON & MIDDLETON LUMBER COMPANY OF OREGON

President

Incorp:		**Operated:** 1923 to 1928	**HQ city:**	Cottage Grove
Disposition:	abandoned			
Predecessor:	J. H. Chambers Lumber Company		**from:** 1911 to 1923	
Miles track:	22	**Gauge:** 56½"		
Main line:	Cottage Grove into the forest			
Rail wt.:	56 lbs.	**Max. grade:** 8.0%	**Const. began:** grading	

Locomotives:

Road No.	Cyln.	Type	Dvr. in.	Bldr.	Bldr. No.	Date	Weight	Effort	Remarks
1		2-4-0	30	Porter	1236	12/90			
1-2d*		2-6-2T		BLW	58206	2/25	126,860	22,100	to Oregon, Pacific & Eastern #1
2*	17x24	2-6-2	44	Schen.	66351	5/25	126,000		
3		0-6-0T		Porter	4211	9/08			
4		4-4-0	54	Cooke	1728	9/86	71,200	10,250	sold in 1927
5?		2T Shay	32	Lima	1946	4/07	90,000	20,350	to Wheeler-Olmstead Lumber Co.

OREGON 57.

6?		2T Shay	32	Lima	2601	10/12	100,000	22,575	ex Phoenix Lumber Co. (Wash.)
7		2-6-0	48	BLW	2719	3/72	55,000		to Medford Corp. #7
8		2 truck	38	Heisler	1349	10/16	150,000		
9		3T Shay	32	Lima	1787	12/06	120,000	29,975	acq. 3/1914 ex Salt Lake & Mer.
		3T Shay	36	Lima	3276	3/25	140,000	30,350	12/1927 to Tidewater Timber Co,
		3 truck	36	Willam.	21	2/26	175,000	36,000	1935 to Western Lumber Co.

Freight traffic: logging

Roster of 12/31/1926:
- 2 rod engines
- 2 geared engines
- 60 sets logging trucks
- 1 tank car
- 22 miles of track; 30° maximum curve

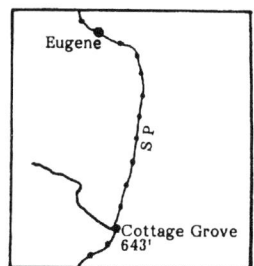

ASTORIA & COLUMBIA RIVER RAILROAD COMPANY

F. B. Clarke, President

Incorp: 4/4/1895 **Operated:** 5/16/98 to 3/1/11 **HQ City:** Astoria

Disposition: merged into Spokane, Portland & Seattle Railway Company on March 1, 1911

Predecessor: Seashore Railroad Company **Incorp.:** 5/17/1893 to 8/27/1897

Miles track: 100.42 **Gauge:** 56½"

Main line: Goble to Seaside

Rail wt.: 50/75 lb. steel **Max. grade:** 1.25% **Const. began:** grading (September 1, 1896)
laying rails (August 1, 1897)

Const. comp.: May 17, 1898 **First train operated:** May 16, 1898, to Astoria

Locomotives:

Road No.	Cyln.	Type	Dvr. in.	Bldr.	Bldr. No.	Date	Weight	Effort	Remarks
1		0-6-0	49	BLW	8617	6/87	125,730	13,575	ex N.P. #988 - to SP&S #6
4		4-4-0	54	Cooke	1731	9/86	135,500	13,540	acq. 1896 ex Corv. & E. - to SP&S #52
6		'	62	Rogers	3410	11/83	133,700	13,100	ex Oregon Pacific #3 - to SP&S #53
7		'	'	'	3411	'	'	'	ex Oregon Pacific #2 - to SP&S #54
8*	18x24	'	69	Schen.	4644	12/97	176,900	17,225	to SP&S #55
16*	20x26	4-6-0	63	Cooke	2375	1/98	138,600	24,675	to SP&S #153
17*	'	'	'	'	2376	'	'	'	to SP&S #154
18*	'	'	'	'	2377	'	'	'	to SP&S #155
19*	'	2-8-0	50	Pitts.	29459	8/04	146,000	31,825	to SP&S #370

Freight traffic: common carrier, lumber

Roster of 6/30/1907:
- 9 locomotives
- 26 passenger cars
- 195 freight cars

First published timetable:
May 17, 1898
8:40 a.m. Astoria 11:55
         Goble   9:00 a.m.
8:50 a.m. Astoria
10:03   Seaside 18 miles

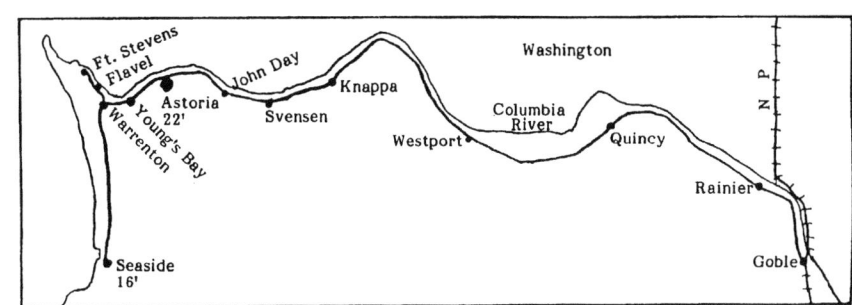

All locomotives were oil burners (in a wood burning era and state) and all rolling stock was equipped with air brakes and automatic couplers.

First listed in ICC for 6/30/97 as an operating independent with five miles owned, not in use. One year later it was 81 miles owned and 120 being operated; it had trackage rights over Northern Pacific to Portland. Very small adjustments in mileage through 1908, ending with 83 miles owned and 122 operated. By 6/30/09 it was an operating subsidiary of Spokane, Portland & Seattle Railway Company until merger in 1911.

Bibliography: *Poor's 1907*, p. 863   Oregon PUC report 1907   *Valuation 41*, p. 330

ASTORIA SOUTHERN RAILWAY COMPANY

Watson Eastman, **President**

Incorp:	5/3/1910	**Operated:** 1910 to 1943	**HQ city:**	Astoria
Disposition:	abandoned December 31, 1943			
Miles track:	18	**Gauge:** 56½"		
Main line:	Olney to Jewell			
Rail wt.:	60 lbs.	**Max. grade:**	**Const. began:** grading	1910
Const. comp.:	1928		**First train operated:**	1910

Locomotives:

Road No.	Cyln.	Type	Dvr. in.	Bldr.	Bldr. No.	Date	Weight	Effort	Remarks
1*	10x12	2T Shay	29½	Lima	2333	6/10	84,000	16,900	to Koster Products Co.
2	"	"	"	"	2490	6/12	"	"	1/1922 to Clark County Timber Co.
3	"	"	32	"	2840	4/16	107,000	22,575	to Big Creek Logging Co. at Wauna
18		2-8-2	44	BLW	43220	"	135,500	27,100	ex Columbia & Nehalem #118
53		2-8-0	50	"	53037	3/20	195,000	35,000	3/1944 to Cowlitz, Chehalis & Cas

Freight traffic: common carrier, logging

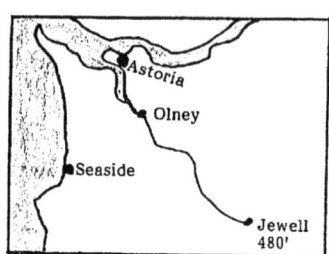

First listed in ICC for 6/30/11 as an operating independent with six miles owned and in use. Gradually extended to 15 miles by 12/31/16 and to 18 miles in 1928. In 1933 it owned 11 miles, but operated 24.

The property was owned by Western Cooperage Company until 1923 and then by Tidewater Timber Company after that.

Bibliography: *Morning Astorian* - May 12 to September 10, 1910

BEAVERTON & WILLSBURG RAILROAD COMPANY

D. W. Campbell, **President**

Incorp:	11/6/1906	**Operated:** 7/17/08 to 6/30/16	**HQ city:**	Portland
Disposition:	merged into Southern Pacific Company on June 30, 1916			
Miles track:	10.35	**Gauge:** 56½"		
Main line:	Beaverton to Cook and Lake Oswego to Willsburg Junction			
Rail wt.:	lbs.	**Max. grade:** 0.50%	**Const. began:** grading	(September 20, 1907)
			laying rails	1908
Const. comp.:	(July 31, 1908)		**First train operated:**	(July 17, 1908)

Freight traffic: common carrier

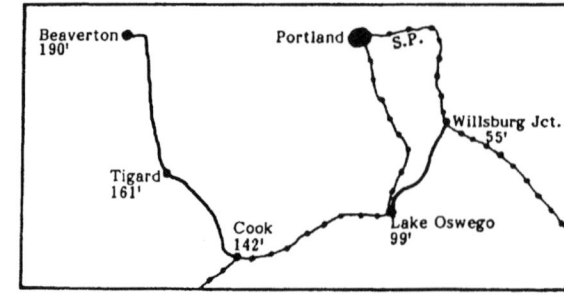

The property was leased March 31, 1910, to the Oregon & California Rail Road Company for operation and hence had no rolling stock in its own name.

First listed in ICC for 6/30/10 as a ten-mile non-operating subsidiary of Southern Pacific Company. By 6/30/11 it was shown as a subsidiary of Oregon & California and then unchanged through 6/30/16.

Bibliography: *McMinnville News Reporter* - September 20, 1907, p. 1

OREGON 59.

BENSON TIMBER COMPANY

S. Benson, **President**

Incorp:	6/10/1911	**Operated:** (6/19/11) to 1936		**HQ city:**	Portland
Disposition:	abandoned				
Predecessor:	Benson Logging & Lumbering Company		**Incorp.:** 12/23/1895 to (6/19/11)		
Miles track:	16	**Gauge:** 56½"			
Main line:	Clatskanie into the woods				
Rail wt.:	lbs.	**Max. grade:** 10.0%	**Const. began:** grading		

Locomotives:

Road No.	Cyln.	Type	Dvr. in.	Bldr.	Bldr. No.	Date	Weight	Effort	Remarks
8		2-6-2		BLW	29822	12/06			ex Benson at Oak Point, Wash.
11*	12x12	2T Shay	32	Lima	1953	10/07	120,000	26,850	to Portland locomotive dealer
776*	10x10	'	28	'	776	12/03	66,000	13,700	to H. H. Martin Lumber Co.
779*	14½x12	3T Shay	36	'	779	11/03	170,000	27,150	to Portland dealer
809*	10x12	2T Shay	29½	'	809	9/03	74,000	15,625	to Florence Logging Co.
879*	'	'	'	'	879	4/04	'	'	to Warren Spruce Company
2229*	'	'	'	'	2229	12/09	84,000	16,900	to Brighton Mills
2230*	'	'	'	'	2230	'	'	'	to Big Creek Logging Co. #4
2231*	'	'	'	'	2231	'	'	'	
2415*	'	'	29	'	2415	3/11	'	'	

Freight traffic: logging

Roster of 6/30/1908:
- 5 geared locomotives
- 1 rod engine
- 25 logging cars
- 9 miles of track

Special Collections Div. - Univ. of Washington Libraries   Clark Kinsey photo #75
Benson Timber Company long spar logs at Clatskanie bend under the weight of numerous loggers.

The editor of the Snohomish newspaper, *The Eye*, must have had in mind the scene above when he wrote October 31, 1891, that with the opening of the Great Northern Railway it will be possible to ship long ship's timbers to Philadelphia or Norfolk in three weeks vs. the present three months by boat. He added that Northern Pacific Railroad can handle nothing longer than that which will fit on two flat cars.

BIG CREEK LOGGING COMPANY

								President
Incorp:		**Operated:** 1912 to 1923					**HQ city:**	Knappa
Disposition:	abandoned							
Miles track:	28	**Gauge:** 56½"						
Main line:	Along Big Creek							
Rail wt.:		**Max. grade:**		**Const. began:** grading				

Locomotives:

Road No.	Cyln.	Type	Dvr. in.	Bldr.	Bldr. No.	Date	Weight	Effort	Remarks
1*		2 truck		Climax	1183	10/12	124,000		to Western Oregon Lbr. Co.
2		2T Shay	29½	Lima	2230	12/09	84,000	16,900	used at Olney
2-2d*	13¼x15	3T Shay	36	'	2689	7/13	160,000	35,100	used at Knappa
2-3d*	10x12	2T Shay	29½	'	2864	1/17	92,000	16,900	used at Knappa
3	'	'	32	'	2840	4/16	107,000	22,580	to Crossett Western #3
4*	11x12	'	'	'	2834	'	'	'	to Crossett Western #4
5*	'	'	'	'	2934	11/17	'	'	to Crossett Western #5
6*	'	'	'	'	2949	3/18	'	'	to Crossett Western #6
7*	'	'	'	'	3052	2/20	'	'	to Crossett Western #7
8*	'	'	'	'	3073	4/20	'	'	to Crossett Western #8

Freight traffic: logging   Road numbers three through eight were used a Wauna.

BLUE LAKE LOGGING COMPANY

					President
Incorp:	2/9/1924	**Operated:** 1922 to 1938		**HQ city:**	Cochran
Disposition:	abandoned				
Miles track:	18	**Gauge:** 56½"			
Main line:					
Rail wt.:	75 lbs.	**Max. grade:** 4.0%	**Const. began:** grading		

Locomotives:

		Type	Dvr. in.	Bldr.	Bldr. No.	Date	Weight	Effort	Remarks
		2T Shay	32	Lima	854	3/04	90,000	18,750	acq. 1923 ex Wheeler Logging - SCR 1938
		'	29½	'	1870	1/07	74,000	16,900	ex Spaulding Logging - to Wheeler Logging
		'	32	'	2829	1/16	107,000	22,580	ex C. H. Wheeler - SCR 10/1940
		3T Shay	36	'	2941	10/17	150,000	30,350	acq. 11/1928 ex Wheeler - sold 1/1932
		'	'	'	3084	6/20	160,000	35,100	acq. 8/1930 ex McCormick Lbr. - sold 3/34
3		2 truck	42	Heisler	1155	2/09			acq. 1926 ex Rainier Logging - sold 1928
		'	40	'	1432	4/20	130,000		ex La Dee Logging Company

Freight traffic: logging

BOOTH-KELLY LUMBER COMPANY, THE

					President
Incorp:	6/17/1898	**Operated:** (11/1/08) to 1945		**HQ city:**	Springfield
Disposition:	abandoned December 31, 1945				
Miles track:	26	**Gauge:** 56½"			
Main line:	Wendling into the forest				
Rail wt.:	60 lbs.	**Max. grade:** 3.7%	**Const. began:** grading	(June 16, 1908)	
Const. comp.:	1919		**First train operated:**	1908	

Locomotives:

Road No.	Cyln.	Type	Dvr. in.	Bldr.	Bldr. No.	Date	Weight	Effort	Remarks
1*	16x24	2-6-2	44	BLW	32943	8/08			
2*	17/24x26	2-6-6-2T	'	'	34215	1/10	200,000		converted wood to oil
3 ?				Climax	2516				
4*	17x24	2 truck	40	Heisler	1327	3/16	126,000		
5		3T Shay	36	Lima	2274	3/10	140,000	29,800	to Flora Logging Co. #5
6*	17/26x24	2-6-6-2T	44	BLW	53143	4/20			
7*	13¼x15	3T Shay	36	Lima	3144	11/20	199,200	35,100	to Day Lbr. Co. (Wash.)
7-2d*		3 truck	'	Willamette	8	5/23			

Freight traffic: common carrier, logging

OREGON   61.

Roster of 6/30/1910:
  1   rod engine
 60   flat cars
  5   logging trucks

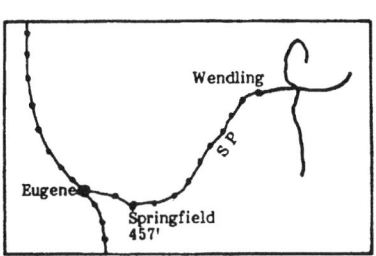

First listed in ICC for 6/30/10 as an independent with seven miles owned and operated. It was extended to 15 miles in 1914, to 20 miles in 1917 and to 26 by 12/31/19 where it remained unchanged for ten years. It was reduced to 12 miles in 1930, then gradually increased to 18 miles in 1937 and to 19 in 1941.

BOWMAN-HICKS LUMBER COMPANY   President

Incorp:		**Operated:** 1906 to 1936		**HQ city:**	La Grande
Disposition:	abandoned				
Predecessor:	George Palmer Lumber Company, The		**Incorp.:** 4/29/1904 to 10/24/1922		
Miles track:	65	**Gauge:** 56½"			
Main line:	Wallowa into the forest				
Rail wt.:	60 lbs.	**Max. grade:** 7.0%	**Const. began:** grading		

Locomotives:

Road No.	Cyln.	Type	Dvr. in.	Bldr.	Bldr. No.	Date	Weight	Effort	Remarks
1*	11x12	2T Shay	32	Lima	1894	3/07	90,000	20,350	
2*	12x15	3T Shay	36	'	2144	3/09	112,500	30,400	to Kosmos Logging Company
3*	15x17	'	40	'	2845	11/16	230,000	44,100	10/1937 to Kosmos Logging Co.
4		'	36	'	3008	8/18	146,000	30,350	10/1939 sold for scrap

The locomotives above were George Palmer Lumber Co.; the following were Bowman-Hicks Lumber.

Road No.	Cyln.	Type	Dvr. in.	Bldr.	Bldr. No.	Date	Weight	Effort	Remarks
1		2 truck	33	Heisler	1085	5/05	50,000		ex Nibley-Mimnaugh Lumber Co.
2*	10x10	2T Shay	28	Lima	814	8/03	66,000	13,700	
3		2 truck	36	Heisler	1151	8/09	80,000		ex Nibley-Mimnaugh Lumber Co.
4		'	'	'	1377	6/18	94,000		
7		'		'	1084	/03			ex Morrison-Knudson, Boise, Ida.

Freight traffic: logging

Roster of 6/30/1910:
(Palmer Lumber Co.)
  2   geared engines
  9   miles track at Elgin

Palmer Lumber Co. had a maximum of 38 miles of track northeast of La Grande.

BRIX LOGGING COMPANY   President

Incorp:	10/14/1925	**Operated:** 10/14/25 to 2/21/40		**HQ city:**	Holbrook
Disposition:	abandoned				
Miles track:	16	**Gauge:** 56½"			
Main line:					
Rail wt.:		**Max. grade:** 5.5%	**Const. began:** grading		

Locomotives:

Road No.	Cyln.	Type	Dvr. in.	Bldr.	Bldr. No.	Date	Weight	Effort	Remarks
3		3T Shay	36	Lima	2269	2/10	140,000	29,800	ex Stimson Mill Co. - scrapped 1/1940
5		'	'	'	2083	10/08	160,000	35,100	ex Northwestern Lbr. Co. - 1/1940 to dealer
11		2T Shay	32	'	2984	7/18	100,000	22,850	ex Kanppton Logging Co. - scrapped 1/1940

Freight traffic: logging

BROOKS-SCANLON LUMBER COMPANY

President

Incorp:	11/20/1915	Operated:	1915 to 1956	HQ city:	Bend
Disposition:	abandoned				
Miles track:	100	Gauge: 56½"			
Main line:	Bend to Sisters				
Rail wt.:	60/70 lbs.	Max. grade: 2.5%	Const. began: grading		

Locomotives:

Road No.	Cyln.	Type	Dvr. in.	Bldr.	Bldr. No.	Date	Weight	Effort	Remarks
1		2-6-0	58	Schen.	2872	8/89			1925 to City of Prineville Ry.
2*	18x24	2-8-2	44	BLW	56291	3/23	150,200		
3*	12x15	3T Shay	36	Lima	2965	2/18	146,000	30,350	scrapped in 1953
4*	18x24	2-8-2	44	BLW	52726	12/19	145,000		
4-2d		'	48	'	51907	4/25			ex Shevlin-Hixon Lumber Co.
5*	18x24	'	44	'	55399	5/22	144,000		1956 to Georgia-Pacific #5
6*	'	'	'	'	56290	3/23	'		
7*		2-8-2T	'	'	58362	4/25	145,000	28,600	1939 to Valley & Siletz #56
8		4-6-0	56	Rogers	5443	10/99	129,000	22,610	acq. 6/1924 ex Mobile & Ohio
9*		2-8-2T	44	BLW	58361	4/25	145,000	28,600	
50*	18x24	2-6-0	'	Lima	5923	2/20	121,000	27,000	
101*		B-B		ALCO	79538	/52			660 h.p. switcher
102*		'		'	79774	'			660 h.p. switcher

Freight traffic: logging

Roster of 12/31/1926:   It was incorporated in Minnesota.
- 4   rod engines
- 1   geared engine
- 152 sets logging trucks
- 9   flat cars
- 3   box cars
- 10 tank cars

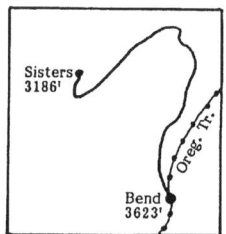

CALIFORNIA & OREGON COAST RAILROAD COMPANY, THE

Robert E. Twohy, President

Incorp:	12/3/1913	Operated:	9/7/14 to 10/31/54	HQ city:	Grants Pass
Disposition:	abandoned November 26, 1956				
Miles track:	14.507	Gauge: 56½"			
Main line:	Grants Pass to Waters Creek				
Rail wt.:	56/62 lbs.	Max. grade:	Const. began: grading	January 2, 1913	
			laying rails	(June 22, 1914)	
Const. comp.:	1915		First train operated:	September 7, 1914	

Locomotives:

1	4-4-0	56	Rogers	2079	10/72	133,500	10,524	acq. 3/13/1911 ex S.P. #1524 - SCR 1942
201	2-8-0	51	Cent. Pac.	48	11/87	113,350	27,080	acq. 4/21/1911 ex S.P. #2508 - SCR 1942
301	2-8-2	46	BLW	35780	12/10	167,000	33,000	acq. 1927 ex Hetch Hetchy #3-SCR (1950)
103	'	48	"	59126	4/26	180,000	37,500	acq. 1941 ex Pac. Port. Cem.-SCR 1957

Freight traffic: common carrier, lumber, copper

Roster of 12/31/1943:
- 2   locomotives
- 29 freight cars

Published timetable dated:
January 20, 1916 - daily

2:00 p.m.	Grants Pass		6:00
2:16	Simmons	5	5:39
2:40	Wilderville	10	5:20
2:44	Prairie Creek	11	5:11
3:00	Waters Creek	15	5:00 p.m.

Also a daily except Sunday trip in the morning.

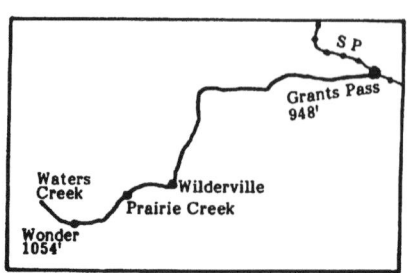

OREGON 63.

The track was acquired by the carrier June 26, 1915, from its owner, the City of Grants Pass. The remaining 4.61 miles to Waters Creek was built in 1915 by Twohy Bros. Company.

First listed in ICC for 6/30/14 as an operating independent with two miles owned and in use. It was extended to ten miles by 6/30/15 and to 15 miles owned and operated by 6/30/16. A class III carrier, it was placed in receivership on February 19, 1925, but continued to operate its 15 miles of track each year through 1942. In 1943 the track was reduced to 14 miles and again owned by Grants Pass, but operated by Pacific Portland Cement Company and still in receivership from 1925.

The property cost $342,427 to construct and $73,478 to equip. Passenger service ended in 1924. On February 5, 1957, the ICC authorized the abandonment of 14.610 miles of track.

Bibliography: *Poor's 1924*, p. 128   Grants Pass - *Rogue River Courier* - January 3 to December 19, 1913   *Valuation 46*, p. 722
Grants Pass - *The Oregon Observer* - June 10 to September 9, 1914

CARLTON & COAST RAILROAD COMPANY

C. E. Ladd, President

| Incorp: | 2/24/1910 | Operated: | 7/1/12 to (1939) | HQ city: | Carlton |

Disposition: abandoned May 10, 1940

Miles track: 13.841   **Gauge:** 56½"

Main line: Carlton into the forest

Rail wt.: 56 lbs.   **Max. grade:** 3.5%   **Const. began:** grading   July 16, 1910

Locomotives:

Road No.	Type	Dvr. in.	Bldr.	Bldr. No.	Date	Weight	Effort	Remarks
1	2-6-0	57	BLW	6256	6/82	75,000	14,480	acq. 2/1910 ex O.R.&N. #19
2	4-4-0	'	McK/Ald		8/68	33,500	10,524	acq. 8/25/1911 ex S.P. #1484
4	3T Shay	36	Lima	3009	10/18	146,000	30,350	1942 to Diamond Match (Calif.)
8	'	'	'	3144	11/20	199,200	35,100	4/1943 to Portland dealer
11	2-8-2	48	BLW	41299	4/14			sold in April, 1945
55	'		Porter	6860	2/24			sold in 1940
70	3T Shay	36	Lima	2642	2/13	140,000	30,350	sold to Portland dealer
1604	2-6-0	57	BLW	6700	4/83	68,700	14,480	acq. 2/21/1913 ex S.P. #1604

Freight traffic: common carrier, logging

Roster of 6/30/1912 - 6/30/1917:

locomotives	3	2
passenger car	1	1
freight cars	25	66

Published timetable dated:
March, 1929 - daily exc. Sunday
11:30 a.m. Carlton   9:00
            Pike
            Cedar Creek
            Chesterbrook
12:30 p.m. Tillamook Gate 14 8:00 a.m.

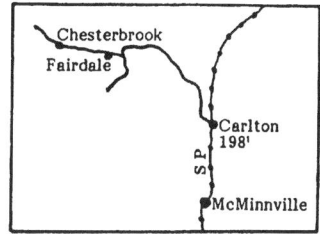

Construction work was performed by Carlton Consolidated Lumber Company (also incorporated February 24, 1910) under a contract dated April 16, 1910. The first six miles were through flat agricultural land; maximum curvature was 15 degrees. The carrier also used two locomotives owned by the lumber company. The road cost $300,467 to build and $54,562 to equip.

First listed in ICC for 6/30/11 as an operating independent with 15 miles owned and in use. This class III carrier remained in the 14 to 15 mile range through 1935. By 12/31/36 it had been extended to 23 miles, then reduced to 20 miles in 1938. It was not in operation at year end of 1939 and ICC authorized abandonment of 20.400 miles in 1940.

Bibliography: *Poor's 1918*, p. 1720   Oregon PUC report 1912, p. 67   *Valuation 114*, p. 161
McMinnville - *News-Reporter* - July 22 and 29, 1910

CITY OF PRINEVILLE RAILWAY

							Owner:	City of Prineville
Incorp:	not		**Operated:**	8/4/18 to			**HQ city:**	Prineville
Disposition:	in operation 1993							
Miles track:	18.34		**Gauge:**	56½"				
Main line:	Prineville Jct. to Prineville							
Rail wt.:	60 lbs.		**Max. grade:**			**Const. began:**	grading	April 20, 1917
							laying rails	May 28, 1918
Const. comp.:	August 4, 1918					**First train operated:**		(August 1, 1918)

Locomotives:

Road No.	Type	Dvr. in.	Bldr.	Bldr. no.	Date	Weight	Effort	Remarks
1*	motor				/18			24-place gasoline passenger car - scrapped in 1925
2	2-6-0	58	Schen.	2872	8/89			acq. 1925 ex Brooks-Scanlon Lbr. Co.
3	2-8-0							acq. 1938
4	'	51	Rome	429	10/88	217,610	25,600	acq. 1940 ex O.W.R.&N. #160
5	2-8-2T	41	BLW	53146	4/20	124,500	21,100	acq. 1941 ex Weyerhaeuser Timber #2
6	2-8-0	55	Rogers	5657	9/01	179,000	41,540	acq. 7/7/1945 ex Great Northern #1102
7	0-6-0	51	Manch.	44741	12/07	148,000	31,200	acq. 1946 ex Spokane, Port. & S. #2
985	B-B		EMD	19569	6/54			1750 h.p.
989	'		'	20029	11/54			'

Freight traffic: common carrier, lumber

Roster of 12/31/1920:
  1   locomotive
  2   passenger cars

Published timetable dated:
  March, 1929 - daily
  5:15 a.m.   7:45 p.m.   Prineville
  7:00   9:00   Prineville Jct.

The line cost $254,365 to construct, $6,615 for a locomotive and $15,310 for three passenger cars. It leased rails from Oregon-Washington Railroad & Navigation Co. valued at $36,291 and $35,349 worth from Oregon Trunk Railway.

First listed in ICC for 12/31/18 as an operating independent with 18 miles owned and in use as a class III common carrier. In 1959 it was upgraded to class II. Passenger service was discontinued in 1939.

Bibliography: Prineville - *Crook County Journal* - April 5, 1917 to July 25, 1918

Valuation 43, p. 399

California State Railroad Museum Library

City of Prineville Railway number seven in May of 1950

CLACKAMAS EASTERN RAILROAD COMPANY   President

Incorp:	7/17/1929	**Operated:** 4/26/30 to 5/26/30		**HQ city:**	Portland

Disposition: sold to Southern Pacific Company on May 26, 1930 - and abandoned November 1, 1939

Predecessors:	Portland Southern Railroad Company	**Incorp.:**	2/13/1923	to	12/1/1928
	Portland & Oregon City Railway Company		6/26/1913		2/13/1923

Miles track: 19   **Gauge:** 56½"

Main line: Clackamas to Molalla

Rail wt.: lbs.   **Max. grade:**   **Const. began:** grading   (May 17, 1915)

                                                        laying rails (September 6, 1915)

Const. comp.: June 1, 1930   **First train operated:** (November 29, 1915)

Freight traffic: common carrier, logging

Portland Southern Railroad Company was a foreclosure sale to the carrier. In 1930 the ICC authorized construction of the final 4.000 miles of track.

First listed in ICC for 12/31/30 as a 17-mile subsidiary of the Southern Pacific Company.

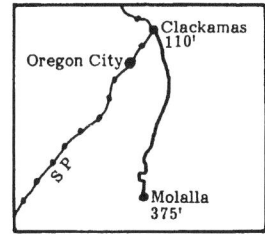

Bibliography: *Oregon City Courier* - September 23 to December 16, 1915

CLARK & WILSON LUMBER COMPANY   O. M. Clark,   President

Incorp:	11/3/1906	**Operated:** 1905 to 1943		**HQ city:**	Linnton

Disposition: abandoned

Predecessor:	Goble, Nehalem & Pacific Railway Company	**Incorp.:**	3/8/1902	to	6/30/1922

Miles track: 98   **Gauge:** 56½"

Main line: Goble into the forest

Rail wt.: 56 lbs.   **Max. grade:** 2.2%   **Const. began:** grading   May 8, 1900

Locomotives:

Road No.	Cyln.	Type	Dvr. in.	Bldr.	Bldr. No.	Date	Weight	Effort	Remarks
1		4-4-0	62	Hinkley	1476	1/82	71,300	12,826	acq. 1/1901 ex O.R.&N. #49
1-2d*	10x12	2T Shay	29½	Lima	1830	2/07	74,000	16,900	
2		4-4-0	57	BLW	6044	2/82			acq. 2/1903 ex O.R.&N. #35
2-2d*	10x12	2T Shay	29½	Lima	991	3/05	74,000	15,625	
4*	11x12	'	32	'	2983	9/18	107,000	22,570	

The locomotives above were Goble, Nehalem & Pacific; Clark & Wilson are below.

2		2T Shay	29½	Lima	991	3/05	74,000	15,625	
2-2d		3 truck	36	Willam.	6	5/23			ex Multnomah Lumber Co. #4
2-3d		3T Shay	'	Lima	3271	1/25	183,900	30,350	acq. 9/1937 ex Markham/Callow
3*	16x24	2-6-2		Davenp.	893	7/09			
3-2d		2T Shay	32	Lima	1818	2/07	90,000	20,300	acq. 1917 ex Nehalem Tbr. #3
4		'	'	'	2983	9/18	107,000	22,570	
4-2d		'	'	'	1943	8/07	100,000	'	acq. 1926 ex Nehalem Tbr. #4
5*	19x24	2-8-2		Porter	6728	9/22			
5-2d		3T Shay	36	Lima	2367	11/10	140,000	29,800	acq. 1926 ex Nehalem #5-2d
6		2T Shay	32	'	2601	10/12	100,000	22,575	acq. 1926 ex Nehalem Tbr. #6
6-2d*		2-8-2T	42	BLW	58825	11/25			to Portland & Southwest #18
6-3d*		'	'	'	58419	5/25			to Portland & Southwest #20
7		3 truck	36	Willam.	19	11/25			ex Nehalem Timber #7
15		2-6-2	44	BLW	28465	6/06			ex Portland & Southwest #1
16		2-8-2T	'	Brooks	64148	2/23	190,000	35,200	ex Portland & Southwest #16
17		2-8-2	48	BLW	57201	9/23	179,000	34,400	ex Portland & Southwest #17

Freight traffic: common carrier, logging

Rosters of	6/30/1906	– 12/31/1913:
locomotives	2	3
passenger car	1	
freight cars	13	26

The western terminal was Mooreville in 1907. The track from Goble had 1,480 feet of assent and 880 of decent.

All Clark & Wilson Shays were shown as headquartered in Scappoose. The company's state franchise was cancelled on January 7, 1952.

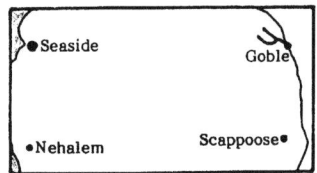

Goble, Nehalem & Pacific Railway Co. was first listed in ICC for 6/30/01 as an operating independent with 3.5 miles owned and in use. It was gradually extended to 7 miles in 1905, 8 miles in 1908 and to 11 by 6/30/09. In 1911 it was 6 miles and leased to Columbia Timber Co. By 1916 it was 10 miles in length and operated by the Clark & Wilson Lumber Co. It was down to 8 miles when purchased by Clark & Wilson in 1922.

Bibliography: *Poor's 1907*, p. 865 and *1914*, p. 1533

CLATSOP RAILROAD COMPANY   President

Incorp:	2/21/1934	**Operated:**	6/22/34 to 1938		**HQ city:**	Astoria
Disposition:	abandoned August 23, 1938					
Predecessors:	Lewis & Clark Railroad Company			**Incorp.:**	10/27/1922 to	6/21/1934
	Lewis & Clark Railway Company				3/5/1918	1/20/1923
Miles track:	24	**Gauge:**	36"	**Date standardized:**		
Main line:	Clatsop south along the Lewis & Clark River					
Rail wt.:	lbs.	**Max. grade:**		**Const. began:**	grading	(March 11, 1918)
					laying rails	(April 4, 1918)
Const. comp.:				**First train operated:**		(April 21, 1918)

Locomotives:

Road No.	Type	Dvr. in.	Bldr.	Bldr. No.	Date	Weight	Effort	Remarks
1	2 truck	40	Heisler	1432	4/20	130,000		
2	2-6-0							
3	2T Shay	36	Lima	3164	2/16	142,800	24,000	ex Eufaula Co.; to La Dee Logging Co.

Freight traffic: logging

On December 31, 1921, Lewis & Clark Railway Company owned 21 miles of track; a year later is was 18 miles.

Lewis & Clark Railroad Company was first listed in ICC for 12/31/31 as an 18-mile operating independent; it was extended to 23 miles in 1926.

In 1934 Clatsop Railroad Company was 16 miles, but then increased to 24 miles in 1935.

A bridge 105 feet tall was built in June of 1918.

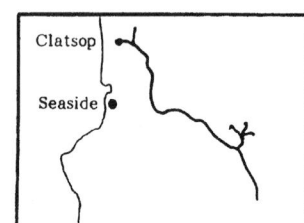

Bibliography: *Morning Astorian* - March 13 to August 28, 1918

COBBS & MITCHELL LUMBER COMPANY   President

Incorp:		**Operated:**	3/20/20 to 6/30/47		**HQ city:**	Valsetz
Disposition:	abandoned					
Miles track:	20	**Gauge:**	56½"			
Main line:						
Rail wt.:	56 lbs.	**Max. grade:**	7.0%	**Const. began:**	grading	

Road No.	Cyln.	Type	Dvr. in.	Bldr.	Bldr. No.	Date	Weight	Effort	Remarks
1		2T Shay	26	Lima	554	3/98	40,000	12,475	ex Falls City Lumber & Logging Co.
2*	10x12	'	29½	'	3168	10/21	78,000	13,320	
100		'	'	'	1989	9/07	74,000	16,900	acq. 4/1920 ex Siletz Lbr. & Log. #100
102		'	32	'	701	4/02	80,000	15,500	acq. 3/1920 ex Siletz Lbr. & Log.
103		2 truck	'	Willam.	30	4/27			ex Skamania Logging Co. #103
104		3 truck	36	'	1	11/22			ex Coos Bay Lbr.; to Valsetz Lbr. Co.

Freight traffic: logging

The various locomotives were shown as located at:
- 1   Falls City
- 1   Valsetz
- 2   Hoskins
- 100   Hoskins
- 102   Valsetz
- 103   Valsetz
- 104   Valsetz

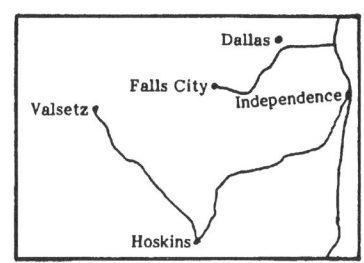

COLUMBIA RIVER & OREGON CENTRAL RAILROAD COMPANY

J. P. O'Brien, **President**

Incorp: 8/21/1903   **Operated:** 1905 to 12/23/10   **HQ city:** Portland

Disposition: merged into Oregon-Washington Railroad & Navigation Company on December 23, 1910

Miles track: 45.31   **Gauge:** 56½"

Main line: Arlington to Condon

Rail wt.: lbs.   **Max. grade:** 3.2%   **Const. began:** grading September 13, 1904

laying rails February 25, 1905

Const. comp.: (July 31, 1905)   **First train operated:** July 3, 1905

Locomotives:

364*	22x30	2-8-0	57	BLW	27241	1/06	189,700	43,300	to O.-W.R.&N. #364
365*	'	'	'	'	27242	'	'	'	to O.-W.R.&N. #365

Freight traffic: common carrier, lumber

First published timetable:
July 1, 1905 - daily exc. Sunday
2:40 p.m. Arlington 11:30
6:15 Condon 8:00 a.m.

First listed in ICC for 6/30/05 as an operating independent with 45 miles owned, not in use. It was leased on July 1, 1906, and then appeared as an operating subsidiary of the Oregon Railroad & Navigation Company until it was sold and merged in 1910.

Construction accounts were found in *Railway Age*:
September 23, 1904, p. 441
March 24, 1905, p. 514
June 9, 1905, p. 893

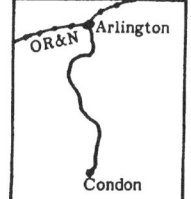

Bibliography: *Poor's 1910*, p. 1273   *Arlington Appeal* - March 2 to June 29, 1905   Oregon PUC report 1907, p. 105

COLUMBIA RIVER BELT LINE RAILWAY

							President
Incorp:	12/10/1909	**Operated:** 1907 to 1920				**HQ city:**	Blind Slough
Disposition:	abandoned						
Miles track:		**Gauge:** 56½"					
Main line:	Garibaldi along the Kilches River						
Rail wt.:	lbs.	**Max. grade:** 8.0%			**Const. began:** grading		

Locomotives:

Road No.	Cyln.	Name	Type	Dvr. in.	Bldr.	Bldr. No.	Date	Weight	Effort	Remarks
5*			2 truck		Climax	801	/07	84,000		
7		Snookum	2-4-4-2	48	BLW	33463	6/09	162,650	24,800	to Carlisle-Pennell Lbr. Co.
	17x22	Siwash	2-6-2T	44	'	36570	5/11	119,600	20,300	
801*		Molly	3 truck	36	Climax	1509	8/20	160,000	35,200	to Hammond-Tillamook Lbr.
2501*	21x26	Big Jack	2-8-0	50	BLW	53037	3/20	159,000	35,000	to Tideport Logging Co. #5

Freight traffic: logging

Roster of 6/30/1910:
- 2 rod engines
- 20 logging trucks
- 3 flat cars
- 3 miles of track

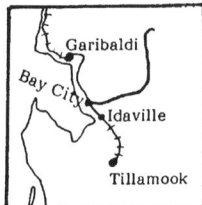

Headquarters in 1907 was at Svensen, eight miles east of Astoria. In 1910 it was Albert and at Idaville in 1920.

It appears that the owner, The Whitney Company, logged at two sites.

Special Collections Div. - Univ. of Washington Libraries   Clark Kinsey photo #183
Big Lake Box Company's McGiffert log loader with tractors at Sprague River

OREGON 69.

COLUMBIA SOUTHERN RAILWAY COMPANY
E. E. Lytle, **President**

Incorp:	3/5/1897			**Operated:**	10/6/97 to 12/23/10			**HQ city:**	Portland

Disposition: merged into Oregon-Washington Railroad & Navigation Company on December 23, 1910

Miles track: 69.46   **Gauge:** 56½"

Main line: Biggs to Shaniko

Rail wt.: 56 lbs.   **Max. grade:**   **Const. began:** grading   June 21, 1897
                                                                laying rails July 29, 1897

Const. comp.: May 13, 1900   **First train operated:** October 3, 1897

Locomotives:

1		4-4-0	62	Hinkley	1468	12/81	71,400	12,826	acq. 9/1897 ex O.R.&N. #21
2		4-6-0	54	Manch.	1110	12/83	178,860	16,223	acq. 12/1898 ex O.R.&N. #117
3*	20x28	2-8-0	51	BLW	20192	3/02	164,000	36,180	1903 to Butte County (Calif.) #1
10		2-6-0	55	Brooks	2409	11/93	108,300	22,762	ex Butte, A. & P.; to O.-W.R.&N.

Freight traffic: common carrier, agriculture

Roster of 6/30/1903:
   3   locomotives
   3   passenger cars
   1   baggage car
   2   box cars

First listed in ICC for 6/30/98 as an operating independent with nine miles owned and in use. It was extended to 27 miles by 6/30/99 and to 70 miles by 6/30/00; this continued through 1905. By 6/30/06 it was listed as a 69-mile operating subsidiary of Oregon Railroad & Navigation Co. It became a non-operating subsidiary by 6/30/07 and then unchanged until sale and merger in 1910.

First listing in *Official Guide*:
December, 1897
"Biggs to Shaniko, 10 miles"

Published timetable dated:
July 1, 1898 - daily exc. Sunday
5:00 a.m. Biggs   8:15
5:40   Wasco   7:30 a.m.

Published timetable dated:
May 6, 1900 - daily
1:34 p.m. Biggs   11:37
3:51   Grass Valley   9:33   38.5
5:32   Shaniko   8:00 a.m. 70.0

Opening dates by section:
Biggs to Wasco   10   October 6, 1897
to Moro   18   January 13, 1899
to Grass Valley   11.5   March 27, 1900
to Shaniko   30   May 13, 1900

The road cost $1,034,283 to build and $27,488 to equip. It was originally projected south to Prineville, 127 miles, for the lumber traffic.

Operations for year ending June 30, 1906:
  passenger revenue $49,476
  freight income   116,532
  other   12,287
  expenses   89,273
  net   41,183

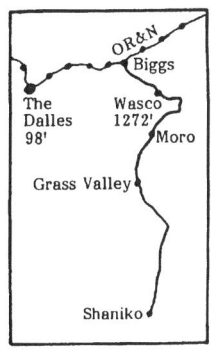

Bibliography: *Poor's 1904*, p. 641   Oregon PUC report 1907, p. 106   *Valuation 44*, p. 274
Spokane - *Spokesman-Review* - October 4, 1897   *The Railway Age* - June 25, August 6 and October 4, 1897

CONDON, KINZUA & SOUTHERN RAILROAD COMPANY
J. W. A. Luce, **Gen. Mgr.**

Incorp:	5/8/1928		**Operated:**	4/1/29 to 11/19/76	**HQ city:** Kinzua

Disposition: abandoned

Predecessor: Kinzua Pine Mills Company   from: 1927 to 5/1/1928

Miles track: 23.932   **Gauge:** 56½"

Main line: Condon to Kinzua

Rail wt.: 50/60 lbs.   **Max. grade:** 3.0%   **Const. began:** grading   April 1, 1927
                                                                       laying rails June 22, 1927

Const. comp.: December 31, 1928   **First train operated:**

Locomotives:

1		0-4-0T		Vulcan	3427	8/24	42,000		ex Kinzua Pine Mills - scrapped
1		2T Shay	32	Lima	3213	5/23	117,000	22,580	ex Portland Elect. Power #3
3		3T Shay	36	Lima	3276	3/25	140,000	30,350	acq. 8/1943 ex Tide. Tbr. Co. #3
5	Goose	motor bus		Mack		/22			retired in 1951
102*	18½x16	3 truck	40	Heisler	1595	12/29	198,000	43,600	sold in 1961
104*		B-B		G.E.	30845	3/51	140,000	660 h.p.	1976 to St. Regis Paper (Mont.)

Freight traffic: common carrier, lumber

Roster of 12/31/1930:
    1   locomotive
    1   passenger car
    2   freight cars

Published timetable dated:
    April 1, 1929 - motor car
    8:30 a.m.   Condon   7:32
    9:59   Kinzua   6:00 p.m.

The line cost $410,927 to construct and equip.

This class III common carrier was first listed in ICC for 12/31/29 as an operating independent with 24 miles owned and in use; then unchanged until abandonment in 1976.

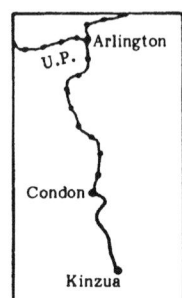

Bibliography: *Condon Globe-Times* - June 17 to September 23, 1927   *Valuation 43*, p. 556

COOS BAY, ROSEBURG & EASTERN RAILROAD & NAVIGATION COMPANY, THE

T. R. Sheridan, President

Incorp: 6/19/1890   **Operated:** (8/16/93) to 7/1/15   **HQ city:** Marshfield

Disposition: sold to Southern Pacific Company on July 1, 1915

Predecessor: Isthmus & Coquille Railroad Company   **Incorp.:** 1/1/1873 to 1890

Miles track: 28.01   **Gauge:** 56½"

Main line: Marshfield to Myrtle Point

Rail wt.: 56 lbs.   **Max. grade:** 2.05%   **Const. began:** grading (October 1, 1890)

                                                                                                                  laying rails (October 12, 1891)

Const. comp.: (August 12, 1893)   **First train operated:** (February 15, 1893)

Locomotives:

Road No.	Type	Dvr. in.	Bldr.	Bldr. No.	Date	Weight	Effort	remarks
1	4-4-0	63	Cuyahoga		/76	53,400	5,710	acquired 8/1893
2	"	69	"		/72	63,800		acquired 8/1893
3	"	63	BLW	4054	3/77	49,000	11,230	ex S.P. #1303-2d
4	4-6-0	55	Schen.	1636	12/82	67,200	16,230	acq. 7/1907 ex S.P. #2090
5	"	"	"	1587	9/82	82,000	"	acq. 5/1907 ex S.P. #2074

Freight traffic: common carrier, agriculture, coal and lumber

Roster of 6/30/1913:
    5   locomotives
    2   passenger cars
  175   freight cars

First published timetable:
    October 16, 1893 - Mon-Wed-Fri
    8:00 a.m. Marshfield
                Cedar Point
                Coquille   18
                Myrtle Point 31
Connection with stage to Roseburg.

First listed in ICC for 6/30/92 as an operating independent with ten miles owned, not in use. It was extended to 15 miles by 6/30/93, 26 miles in 1894, 28 in 1895 and to 31 by 6/30/96 and always "not in operation." For 6/30/99 it was shown as 27 miles and in operation.

Placed in receivership January 1, 1900. By 6/30/07 it was an operating subsidiary of Southern Pacific Co. Mileages varied from 28 to 32 through 1914. In 1915 it was 28 miles owned and 50 operated.

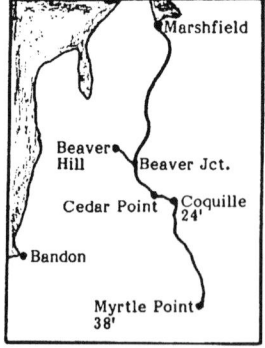

The Beaver Hill branch was completed August 22, 1894. The carrier never had an outside rail link; on July 24, 1916, Marshfield was connected to Eugene with construction of Southern Pacific's Willamette Pacific Railroad Company.

Bibliography: *Poor's 1914*, p. 1611   *Chicago Railway Review* - September 9, 1890   *Valuation 45*, p. 359
The Railway Age - October 4, 1890, p. 704 - October 23, 1891, p. 821 - November 6, 1891, p. 859

California State Railroad Museum Library
Coos Bay, Roseburg & Eastern locomotive #4 at the Marshfield coal bunker on Mill Slough in March of 1914

Photo by Ed Austin
The new (highpower electric line) and the old (Northern Pacific Railway car) are mixed with three types of Burlington Northern Railroad diesel engines at Moody, Oregon, looking south on Oregon Trunk Line route; date was April 9, 1977.

CORVALLIS & ALSEA RIVER RAILWAY COMPANY

Stephen Carver, **President**

Incorp:	7/19/1907	**Operated:** 6/5/09 to 7/20/11	**HQ city:**	Corvallis
Disposition:	sold to Portland, Eugene & Eastern Railway Company on July 20, 1911			
Miles track:	28.08	**Gauge:** 56½"		
Main line:	Corvallis to Monroe			
Rail wt.:	50 lbs. steel	**Max. grade:** 2.33%	**Const. began:**	grading August 6, 1907
				laying rails (December 4, 1907)
Const. comp.:	1909		**First train operated:**	

Locomotives:

Road No.	Cyln.	Type	Dvr. in.	Bldr.	Bldr. No.	Date	Weight	Effort	Remarks
1		2T Shay	29½	Lima	884	5/04	92,700	15,625	ex Wisconsin Logging & Timber Co.
2*	15x12	2 truck	36	Heisler	1151	8/09	72,000		

Freight traffic: common carrier, lumber

Roster of 6/30/1909:
    1   locomotive
    8   freight cars

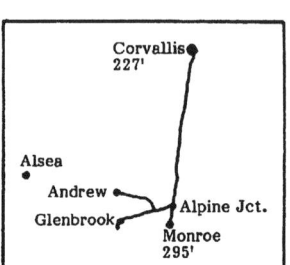

First listed in ICC for 6/30/08 as an operating independent with 11 miles owned, not in use. By 6/30/09 it was 24 miles owned and operated. It was extended to 30 miles by 6/30/10.

Construction notes from *The Railway Age:*

November 8, 1907	Twelve miles graded; rails are at Corvallis.
December 27, 1907	Corvallis to Bruce, ten miles, built in 1907.
April 24, 1908	Fourteen miles of track has been laid.

Bibliography: *Poor's 1909*, p. 717   Oregon PUC report 1909   *Valuation 45*, p. 369
The Corvallis Times - August 2 to December 6, 1907

CORVALLIS & EASTERN RAILROAD COMPANY

J. K. Weatherford, **President**

Incorp:	12/15/1897	**Operated:** 1/25/98 to 7/1/15	**HQ city:**	Albany
Disposition:	sold to the Southern Pacific Company on July 1, 1915			
Predecessors:	Oregon Central & Eastern Railroad Company		**Incorp.:** 4/12/1895	to 1/25/1898
	Willamette Valley & Coast Rail Road Company		7/6/1874	4/12/1895
Miles track:	140.74	**Gauge:** 56½"		
Main line:	Yaquina to Idanha			

Locomotives:

1	4-4-0	56	Rogers	3445	12/83	49,000	13,590	ex O.C.&E. #4 - to S.P. #1300-2d
2	'	55	Cooke	1342	11/81	45,000	13,000	ex O.C.&E. #1 - to S.P. #1301-2d
3	'	54	'	1730	9/86	64,000	13,540	ex O.C.&E. #14
4	'	'	'	1728	'	'	'	ex O.C.&E. #12 - to S.P. #1302-2d
5	'	'	'	1729	'	'	'	ex O.C.&E. #13 - to S.P. #1303
6	'	'	'	1725	6/86	'	'	ex O.C.&E. #11 - to S.P. #1304-2d
7	'	'	'	1724	'	'	'	ex O.C.&E. #10 - to S.P. #1305-2d
8	'	'	'	1722	'	'	'	ex O.C.&E. #8 - 1900 to Tacoma Eastern
9	'	'	'	1723	'	'	'	ex O.C.&E. #9 - 1902 to Oregon & S.E.

Freight traffic: common carrier, lumber

Rosters of 6/30/1903 - 6/30/1913:

locomotives	7	9
passenger cars	7	4
box cars	164	17
flat cars	79	96

A. B. Hammond, San Francisco lumberman, was the president in 1900.

First listed in ICC for 6/30/98 as an operating independent with 142 miles owned and in use; it remained unchanged through 6/30/07. The line was sold to E. H. Harriman on December 18, 1907. For 6/30/08 it was shown as a 141-mile operating subsidiary of Southern Pacific Railroad Co. A class II carrier, it was extended to 146 miles in 1912, then back to 141 miles in 1913. It then remained unchanged until its sale in 1915.

All locomotives and passenger cars had air brakes and automatic couplers; about half of the freight cars were so equipped.

OREGON
73.

Published timetable dated:
September 19, 1900 - daily exc. Sunday
6:10	a.m.	Yaquina	6:45	
8:52		Nashville	3:53	
12:15	p.m.	Albany	12:45	p.m.
7:00	a.m.	Albany	5:45	
10:05		Niagara	1:35	
11:20		Detroit	12:10	p.m.
		Idanha		

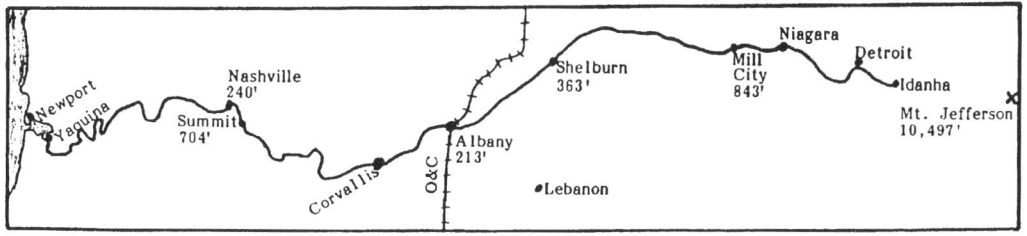

Bibliography: *Poor's 1904*, p. 642   Oregon PUC report 1907   *Valuation 44*, p. 352

Oregon State Library collection - Trover 10-2
Corvallis & Eastern Railroad Co. #2 is being refueled, possibly at Norton, west of Nashville.

California State Railroad Museum Library
Corvallis & Eastern Railroad Company locomotive #4 was photographed in 1910 at Albany.

CROSSETT-WESTERN COMPANY
                                                                                President

Incorp:			**Operated:**	1912 to 1941			**HQ city:**		Wauna
Disposition:	abandoned								
Miles track:	32		**Gauge:**	56½"					
Main line:	woods lines at Knappa, Olney and Wauna								
Rail wt.:	60/75 lbs.		**Max. grade:**	7.0%		**Const. began:**	grading		

Locomotives:

Road No.	Cyln.	Type	Dvr. in.	Bldr.	Bldr. No.	Date	Weight	Effort	Remarks
2		2T Shay	29½	Lima	2230	12/09	84,000	16,900	ex Big Creek Log. #2 used at Olney
2		3T Shay	36	'	2689	7/13	160,000	35,100	ex Big Creek Log. #2 used at Wauna
3		2T Shay	32	'	2840	4/16	107,000	22,580	ex Big Creek Log. #3
4		'	'	'	2834	'	'	'	ex Big Creek Log. #4
5		'	'	'	2934	11/17	'	'	ex Big Creek Log. #5
6		'	'	'	2949	3/18	'	'	ex Big Creek Log. #6
7		'	'	'	3052	2/20	'	'	ex Big Creek Log. #7 used at Knappa
7-2d		2-6-2T	44	BLW	57636	2/24	120,500	22,100	ex Columbia & Nehalem River #126
8		2T Shay	32	Lima	3073	4/20	107,000	22,580	ex Big Creek Log. #8
10*	10x24	2-8-0	50	BLW	35870	1/11			
10-2d*	18x24	2-8-2T	44	Montr.	67652	2/29	168,000	28,500	
11*	'	'	'	Schen.	68057	9/23	'	'	

Freight traffic: logging   For logging camp locations, see map on next page.

CROWN ZELLERBACH CORPORATION
                                                           President

Incorp:			**Operated:**	1928 to 3/37		**HQ city:**		Seaside
Disposition:	abandoned							
Predecessor:	Crown Willamette Paper Company					**from:** 1914		**to** 1928
Miles track:	30		**Gauge:**	56½"				
Main line:	Young's River Bay into the forest							
Rail wt.:	60 lbs.		**Max. grade:**			**Const. began:**	grading	

OREGON

Locomotives:

Road No.	Cyln.	Type	Dvr. in.	Bldr.	Bldr. No.	Date	Weight	Effort	Remarks
2	?	2 truck	33	Climax	417	/03	100,000	22,000	ex White River Lbr. Co. #2
3*		'	'	'	1493		90,000	19,800	used at Seaside
3-2d		2T Shay	36	Lima	3164	2/21	120,000	24,000	acq. 4/1934 - sold 3/1935
3		3 truck	35	Climax	1630	7/23	140,000	30,800	
5*		'	'	'	1631	'	'	'	used at Seaside
6		'	'	Willam.	13	1/24	'	30,350	
7		2 truck	30	Climax	650	/06	70,000	15,400	
8		2T Shay	29½	Lima	2747	1/14	84,000	16,900	acq. 10/1920 ex Hammond #6
11		'	36	'	3272	4/25	150,200	27,300	4/1934 from Floristan, Calif.
12*	17/26x24	2-6-6-2T	44	BLW	60771	4/29			
14*		3 truck	36	Willam.	14	4/24			
16		2-6-6-2T	44	BLW	60871	6/29			ex Curtis Lbr. #5-SCR 1959

Freight traffic: logging

Roster of 12/31/1925:
    4   locomotives
    8   flat cars
   65   sets logging trucks

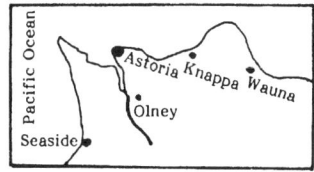

Special Collections Div. - Univ. of Washington Libraries   *Clark Kinsey photo #857*
Crown Willamette Paper Company's well-ventilated passenger car being pulled by a Shay

DES CHUTES RAILROAD COMPANY

		E. H. Harriman, **President**
Incorp: 2/2/1906	**Operated:** 6/1/11 to 12/30/87	**HQ city:** Portland
Disposition:	merged into Union Pacific Railroad Company on December 30, 1987	
Miles track: 95.260	**Gauge:** 56½"	
Main line:	Des Chutes Jct. to Metolius	
Rail wt.: 75 lbs.	**Max. grade:** 1.5%	**Const. began:** grading July 8, 1909
		laying rails November 1, 1909
Const. comp.: September 24, 1911 – at Metolius		**First train operated:**

Freight traffic: common carrier, agriculture

Published timetable dated:
May 7, 1916 – daily
```
1:35 p.m.   Sherman
3:05        Fargher          43
4:20        North Junction   72
4:45        South Junction   82
5:45        Madras          101
6:00        Metolius        107
7:45        Bend            148
```
The line cost $6,241,930 to construct and equip.

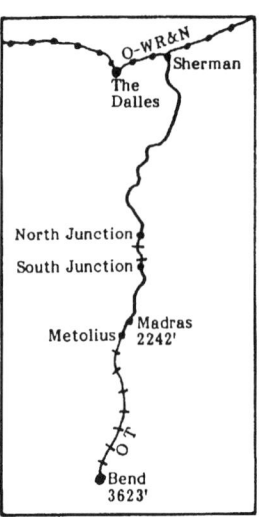

First listed in ICC for 6/30/10 as an operating independent with 21 miles owned, not in use. By 6/30/11 it was a non-operating subsidiary of Oregon-Washington Railroad & Navigation Co. with 91 miles owned; it had been leased to O-WR&N on May 31, 1911. It was extended to 95 miles by 6/30/12 and so remained for over 20 years. Reduced to 24 miles in 1936 and then unchanged through 1972.

The carrier had a joint trackage agreement with Oregon Trunk Railway to operate between North Junction and South Junction and from Metolius to Bend.

Present-day Union Pacific records state that it was "Operated under lease dated September 24, 1911 – Line from Sherman, Ore., to North Jct., Ore., 71.26 miles, and from South Jct., Ore., to Metolius, Ore., 24.04 miles. Total 95.30 miles."

Bibliography: *Poor 1912,* p. 1363   *Railway Age Gazette* - August 13 and November 5, 1909   *Valuation 44,* p. 250

ROBERT DOLLAR COMPANY

		President
Incorp:	**Operated:** 1931 to	**HQ city:** Glendale
Disposition:	track intact, but not in use in 1993	
Predecessors:	Ingham Lumber Company	**from:** 1932 to 4/1946
	Glendale Lumber Company	**Incorp.:** 1/30/1902 1932
Miles track: 12	**Gauge:** 56½"	
Main line:	Glendale east along Cow Creek	
Rail wt.: lbs.	**Max. grade:**	**Const. began:** grading 1909

Locomotives:

Road No.	Cyln.	Type	Dvr. in.	Bldr.	Bldr. No.	Date	Weight	Effort	Remarks
1*	11x10	2 truck	30	Heisler	1197	3/10	38,000		
2		2T Shay	29	Lima	2559	6/13	64,000	14,150	ex Beebe Lumber Co. #1
2-2d		2-6-2	46	BLW	55735	10/22			acq. 12/1930 as Glendale 2
3		2-6-2T	44	Schen.	67544	11/27	128,000		ex Lorrane Lumber Co.
2978		2T Shay	32	Lima	2978	5/18	100,000	22,580	acquired 6th hand
		B-B		G.E.	29345	3/48	90,000	380 h.p.	acq. (11/1979)

Freight traffic: logging

Roster of 6/30/1910:
```
1   geared engine
3   logging cars
3   flat cars
```

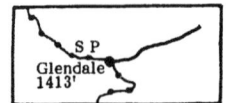

OREGON

EASTERN & WESTERN LUMBER COMPANY

					President
Incorp:	8/6/1902	Operated:	1906 to 1929	HQ city:	Portland
Disposition:	abandoned				
Miles track:	30	Gauge:	56½"		
Main line:	Astoria into the forest				
Rail wt.:	lbs.	Max. grade:	7.0%	Const. began:	grading

Locomotives:

Road No.	Cyln.	Type	Dvr. in.	Bldr.	Bldr. No.	Date	Weight	Effort	Remarks
4		2T Shay	32	Lima	2980	7/18	100,000	22,570	
5*	10x12	'	30½	'	1627	2/06	74,000	16,300	8/1921 to Donovan Dubois Lbr. Co.
5-2d		3 truck	36	Willam.	5	3/23			ex Eufaula Co. #5
6*	10x12	2T Shay	30½	Lima	1626	1/06	74,000	16,300	to Eufaula Co. #6 (Washington)

Freight traffic: logging

EAST SIDE LOGGING COMPANY

					President
Incorp:	1/20/1921	Operated:	1923 to 1933	HQ city:	Keasey
Disposition:	abandoned				
Miles track:	22	Gauge:	56½"		
Main line:					
Rail wt.:	60 lbs.	Max. grade:	8.0%	Const. began:	grading

Locomotives:

Road No.	Cyln.	Type	Dvr. in.	Bldr.	Bldr. No.	Date	Weight	Effort	Remarks
1 ?		2T Shay	32	Lima	1902	3/07	90,000	20,350	acq. 7/1929 ex North Fork Log.
4 ?		'	28	'	1732	7/06	56,000	15,150	to Sunset Logging Co. #4
5 ?		'	30½	'	1627	2/06	74,000	16,300	to Sunset Logging Co.
55*		3 truck	36	Willam.	29	4/28			to Sunset Logging Co. #55
102*		'	'	'	14	4/24			to Crown Willamette Paper Co.
107*		2 truck	32	'	25	9/26			to Sunset Logging Co. #25

Freight traffic: logging

Its state franchise was cancelled on January 18, 1937.

Photo by John E. Davis
Southern Pacific cab-forward entering the siding at Abernathy, Oregon, on the Cascade line in about 1946.

EAST PORTLAND TRACTION COMPANY Richard A. Samuels, **President**

Incorp:	10/15/1987	**Operated:**	4/1/91	to		**HQ city:**	Milwaukie
Disposition:	in operation 1993						

Predecessors:		**Incorp.:**		**to**	
	Portland Traction Company		7/25/1930	to	3/31/1991
	Portland Electric Power Company		(4/14/1924)		12/31/1944
	Portland Railway, Light & Power Company		1/1/1906		(4/14/1924)
	Mount Hood Railway & Power Company		10/29/1906		12/31/1915
	Oregon Water Power & Railway Company, The		7/1/1902		6/28/1906
	Portland City & Oregon Railway Company		1/31/1900		6/30/1902
	Oregon City & Southern Railway Company		1892		1900

Miles track:	72.53	**Gauge:**	56½"	
Main line:	Portland to Bull Run, Cazadero and Oregon City			
Rail wt.:	40/56 lbs.	**Max. grade:**	**Const. began:**	grading (September 12, 1892)
				laying rails (October 13, 1892)
Const. comp.:			**First train operated:**	January 28, 1893

Locomotives:

Road No.	Cyln.	Type	Dvr. in.	Bldr.	Bldr. No.	Date	Weight	Effort	Remarks
107		4-4-0							
112		"	57	BLW	6034	2/82	41,950		acq. 4/1903 ex O.R.&N. #34
114		0-6-0	50	Schen.	3424	2/91	90,000	18,500	ex Northern Pac. Term. #2
1*	11x12	2T Shay	32	Lima	3206	3/23	117,000	22,580	used at Estacada
2*	"	"	"	"	3207	"	"	"	
3*	"	"	"	"	3213	5/23	"	"	
4*	"	"	"	"	3214	"	"	"	
100*		B-B		EMD	16899	2/52	198,000	600 h.p.	
200*		"		"	17709	3/53	"	"	
5100		"		G.E.	30034	3/49	140,000	"	acq. 1989 ex S.P. #5100
5104		"		"	30167	6/49	"	"	acq. for parts ex S.P. #5104

Major business: common carrier, passengers, lumber

Roster of 6/30/1905:
    3   locomotives
  28   passenger cars
110   freight cars

First published "timetable":
May 1, 1907 - 7 round trips per day
Portland to Cazadero   37 miles
Portland to Oregon City   15
Operated by electricity and three steam engines.

The major track sections were:
  Montavilla to Troutdale   10.50 miles
  Golf Jct. to Cazadero   31.44
  Portland to Canemah Park   14.56
  Lineman Jct. to Ruby Jct.   2.06
  Ruby Jct. to Bull Run   13.97
  Portland to Lents Jct.   4.54

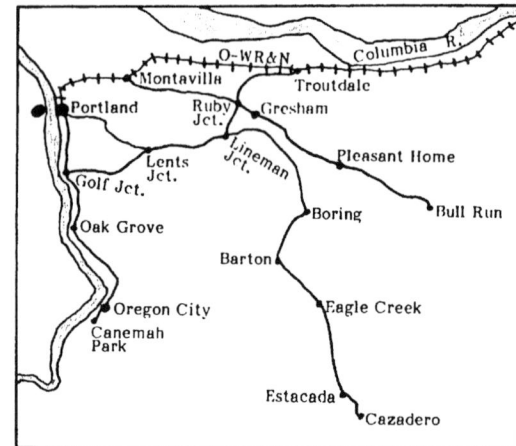

The traction data above and map are from June, 1916, *Official Guide of the Railways*.

The original company built from Portland to Oregon City, but became insolvent in 1900.

A note from *Electric Railway Journal*, April 12, 1913: (referring to Mount Hood Railway & Power Co.) Montavilla to Bull Run, 20 miles, was operated by steam until March 1, 1913. The company plans to electrify the 12 miles from Gresham to Bull Run.

Montavilla to Troutdale was abandoned in 1926; Boring to Cazadero passenger service ended November 26, 1932.

The present-day operation is from East Portland to Golf Jct. and Milwaukie, 5.287 miles, to provide switching services for Burlington Northern, Southern Pacific and Union Pacific; it now features 90 pound rails and a maximum grade of 6.025%.

Bibliography: *Poor's 1905*, p. 1094   *Oregon City Enterprise* - October 21, 1892 to March 3, 1893   Direct communication

FLORA LOGGING COMPANY

Incorp:	11/29/1922		**Operated:**	1923 to 1/26/39		**HQ city:**		Carlton
Disposition:	abandoned							
Miles track:	20		**Gauge:**	56½"				

Main line:

Rail wt.: lbs.   **Max. grade:** 6.0%   **Const. began:** grading

Locomotives:

Road No.	Cyln.	Type	Dvr. in.	Bldr.	Bldr. No.	Date	Weight	Effort	Remarks
1		2-6-0	57	BLW	6256	6/82			ex Carlton & Coast #1
2		2T Shay	28	Lima	646	4/01	56,000	11,120	acq. 7/1923 ex Mt. Tamalpais #3
3		2-8-2T	44	Brooks	65378	3/24	188,500	35,000	ex Sugar Pine Lbr. Co. #3
4		2-6-6-2S	'	BLW	56738	7/23			ex Curtis Lumber Co. #4
5		3T Shay	36	Lima	2274	3/10	140,000	29,800	ex Booth-Kelley Lumber Co. #5
6		2T Shay	32	'	2745	4/14	100,000	22,580	acq. 11/1923 ex Westport Lumber
7*		3 truck	36	Willam.	10	7/23			
8 ?		2T Shay	'	Lima	2050	10/08	120,000	23,850	ex Multnomah Lbr.; sold 4/1943
9		2-6-2T		Vulcan	3503	/25			sold in 1940
11*	18x24	2-8-2		Porter	6860	2/24			

Freight traffic: logging

GALES CREEK & WILSON RIVER RAILROAD COMPANY

John Pearson, **President**

Incorp:	4/2/1917	**Operated:** 1/1/20 to 12/31/43	**HQ city:**	Portland
Disposition:	sold to Spokane, Portland & Seattle Railway Company on January 1, 1944			
Miles track:	12.728	**Gauge:** 56½"		

Main line: Wilkesboro to Glenwood

Rail wt.: 56/60 lbs.   **Max. grade:** 1.5%   **Const. began:** grading (April 27, 1917)

laying rails (May 1, 1918)

Const. comp.: (December 31, 1919)   **First train operated:** (September 15, 1918)

Locomotives:

1	4-6-0	51	Schen.	3263	/90	125,000	24,546	acq. 1918 ex Colorado Midland #47
2	'	'	'	2421	/87	'	'	ex Colorado Midland #28-SCR 1928

Freight traffic: common carrier, lumber

Roster of 12/31/1920:
  2 locomotives
  4 freight cars

First listed in ICC for 12/31/18 as an operating road with 11 miles owned and in use. It was extended to 13 miles in 1919. This class III carrier (jointly owned by Northern Pacific and Great Northern) was then unchanged through 12/31/43, then the note "property acquired by SP&S Ry. Co. 1/1/44."

A listing in *Official Guide* dated November 25, 1928, (under SP&S heading) states "freight only."

The property cost $602,871 to construct and $33,913 to equip. There was one steel bridge 141 feet long.

In addition to the main line there were 2.237 miles of yard tracks and sidings for a total of 14.965 miles.

Bibliography: *Poor's 1924*, p. 273   *The Banks Herald* - April 12 to October 25, 1917 and March 21 to October 3, 1918   *Valuation 44*, p. 824

Oregon State Library Collection - #753

A Willamette River scene from 1851

Oregon State Library Collection - #809
Success in the foreground, *E. N. Cook* on the right and unidentified vessel in the Oregon City locks in 1869

Oregon State Library Collection - #750
Hudson's Bay Company's [1670-] 109-ton *Beaver* was the first steam vessel on the Pacific Coast in 1836; it appears to have been assembled at Astoria. The photograph dates from that period.

Oregon State Library Collection - #868 *WPA Series 4*
The passenger vessel *Governor Grover* in the locks at Oregon City in 1873

GEORGIA-PACIFIC CORPORATION

President

Incorp:		**Operated:** 7/56 to 6/8/72	**HQ city:**	Marshfield
Disposition:	abandoned			
Predecessors:	Coos Bay Lumber Company		**Incorp.:** 7/11/1914 to 7/1956	
	Smith-Powers Logging Company		**from:** 1908 1919	
	C. A. Smith Lumber & Mfg. Company		1919	
Miles track:	75	**Gauge:** 56½"		
Main line:	Marshfield to Powers			
Rail wt.:	lbs.	**Max. grade:**	**Const. began:** grading	

Locomotives:

Road No.	Cyln.	Type	Dvr. in.	Bldr.	Bldr. No.	Date	Weight	Effort	Remarks
1*	8x12	2T Shay	28	Lima	1944	7/07	56,000	15,150	to Coos Bay Lumber Co. #4
2	'	'	29½	'	1827	1/07	74,000	16,900	to Coos Bay Lbr. & Coal Co.
3	'	'	28	'	169	8/87	56,000	11,525	scrapped
4		2 truck	36	Heisler	1124	2/07	74,000		ex Peninsula Lumber Co. #3
5		'	31	Climax	445	10/03	70,000		ex C. A. Smith Lumber #1
6*	10x12	2T Shay	29½	Lima	2542	4/12	84,000	16,900	
7*	'	'	'	'	2650	3/13	'	'	
8*	17x15	2 truck	38	Heisler	1349	10/16	150,000		to Bradley Woodward Lumber Co.
9		2T Shay	29½	Lima	2998	10/18	85,000	16,900	ex Warren Spruce Co. #9
100*	18x24	2-8-2	44	BLW	38271	9/12			ex C. A. Smith Lumber Co.
102*	'	'	'	'	38965	12/12			ex C. A. Smith Lumber Co.
103*	'	'	'	'	39698	4/13			ex C. A. Smith Lumber Co.

The locomotives above were Smith-Powers Logging Co. - the following were Coos Bay Lumber Co.

Road No.	Cyln.	Type	Dvr. in.	Bldr.	Bldr. No.	Date	Weight	Effort	Remarks
1		2 truck	36	Heisler	1112	11/06	74,000		ex Great Northern Logging Co.
2		2T Shay	28	Lima	489	5/95	56,000	13,180	acq. 1922 ex Salt Lake & Merc.
9*	20x24	2-8-2T	44	Schen.	68720	12/35	205,000		
10*	12x15	3 truck	36	Willam.	1	11/22			to Cobbs & Mitchell #104
10-2d*	20x24	2-8-2T	44	Schen.	68548	12/30	197,000		
11*	'	'	'	'	68276	12/29	190,000		
12*	'	'	'	'	68487	4/30	196,000		
101*	18x24	2-8-2	'	BLW	55911	12/22			
120		2-6-2T	'	'	43213	4/16	118,000	22,100	ex Pac. White Cedar Co. #120
201		2T Shay	29	Lima	3223	7/23	83,000	17,660	ex Coos Cedar Co. - SCR 1954

Georgia-Pacific Corp.

Road No.	Cyln.	Type	Dvr. in.	Bldr.	Bldr. No.	Date	Weight	Effort	Remarks
5		2-8-2	44	BLW	55399	5/22	144,000		acq. 1956 ex Brooks-Scanlon #5

Freight traffic: logging

Roster of 6/30/1910:
- 4 geared engines
- 20 logging cars
- 21 miles of track

The main line mileposts were:
- Coquille 16.0
- Myrtle Point 25.8
- Powers 44.5

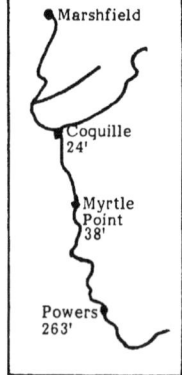

Smith-Powers Lumber Co. was first listed in ICC for 6/30/13 as an operating independent with two miles owned, not in use; it was being operated by 6/30/15. It was extended to 23 miles owned (plus 22 owned by subsidiary C. A. Smith Lbr. & Mfg. Co.) and 70 miles operated by 12/31/16. This combination was succeeded in 1919 by Coos Bay Lumber Co.

Coos Bay Lumber Co. was first shown in 1919 with 40 miles owned and 66 miles operated. It was increased to 55 miles owned, 80 operated, in 1923 as a joint operation with Southern Pacific Company. In 1924 it was reduced to 19 miles owned and operated. The carrier was acquired by Pacific States Lumber Co. in 1925.

An undated map in September, 1958, *Western Railroader* shows Georgia-Pacific track from Yaquina and Toledo north to Siletz, then northeast to a point due west of Monmouth. Use of that track is reported to have ceased on December 31, 1959.

OREGON 83.

GREAT WESTERN RAILWAY OF OREGON, INC.

David Lafferty, **President**

Incorp.:	9/6/1990	Operated:	1/18/86 to	HQ city: Lakeview
Disposition:	in operation 1993			
Miles track:	54.4	Gauge:	56½"	
Main line:	Alturas to Lakeview			
Rail weight:	75/132 lbs.	Max. grade:	1.16%	
Freight traffic:	common carrier, agriculture, lumber			

Locomotives:

Road No.	Type	Bldr.	Bldr. No.	Date	Weight	Effort	Remarks
1617	B-B	EMD		/53	250,000	1,500 h.p.	ex B.N. #1617
1621	"	"		/53	"	"	ex B.N. #1621
3416	"	"				1,750 h.p.	ex U.P. #3416

The property was acquired from Southern Pacific Company on January 22, 1986, by the County of Lake, Oregon.

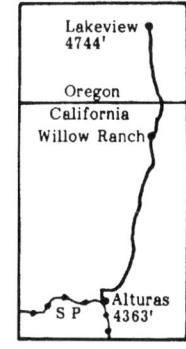

Bibliography: Direct communication

EDWARD HINES LUMBER COMPANY

President

Incorp:		Operated:	1946 to 1955	HQ city:	Westfir
Disposition:	abandoned				
Predecessors:	Westfir Lumber Company			from: 1936 to 1946	
	Western Lumber Company			1923 1936	
Miles track:	20	Gauge:	56½"		
Main line:					
Rail wt.:	62 lbs.	Max. grade:	2.0%	Const. began:	grading

Locomotives:

Road No.	Type	Dvr. in.	Bldr.	Bldr. No.	Date	Weight	Effort	Remarks
1	2T Shay	32	Lima	2652	5/13	100,000	22,550	ex Silver Falls Timber Co. #2
2	3 truck	36	Willam.	21	2/26	175,000	36,000	to Medford Corporation #7
4	2-8-0	"	BLW	6749	5/83			
10*	2-6-2T		"	60389	2/28			
2186 ?	4-6-0	55	R.I.	1965	2/88	88,500	18,550	acq. 8/1924 ex S.P. #2186

Freight traffic: logging

IDAHO NORTHERN & PACIFIC RAILROAD COMPANY

G. A. Gillette **President**

Incorp.:	9/22/1993	Operated:	11/14/93 to	HQ city: Emmett, Idaho
Disposition:	in operation 1993			
Miles track:	83.55 (in Oregon)	Gauge:	56½"	
Main line:	La Grande to Joseph			
Rail wt.:	133 lbs.	Max. grade:	2.60%	

Locomotives:

Freight traffic: lumber, agriculture
In Idaho, lines are operated from Nampa to Cascade and Weiser to Rubicon plus Emmett to Payette.
The ruling grade is 1.60% in Oregon.

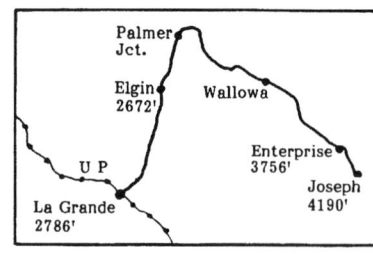

Bibliography: Direct Correspondence

Official Open and Prepay Station List

INDEPENDENCE & MONMOUTH RAILWAY COMPANY, THE

A. Nelson, **President**

Incorp:	3/23/1889	**Operated:** 8/24/90 to 8/31/18		**HQ city:**	Independence
Disposition:	operations discontinued on September 1, 1918				
Miles track:	2.50	**Gauge:** $56\frac{1}{2}"$			
Main line:	Independence to Monmouth				
Rail wt.:	40 lbs.	**Max. grade:**	**Const. began:**	grading	(May 1, 1890)
				laying rails	(June 24, 1890)
Const. comp.:	1890		**First train operated:**		August 24, 1890

Locomotives:

Road No.	Type	Dvr. in.	Bldr.	Bldr. No.	Date	Weight	Effort	Remarks
1*	0-4-2T	33	BLW	11045	7/90			Independence - gone by 1905
15 ?	2-4-2	41	'	9743	1/89	40,000	6,717	acq. 4/1905 ex S.P. #15
1011	0-4-0	51	'	6755	5/83	52,700	10,880	acq. 3/14/1905 ex S.P. #1011
1426	4-4-0	56	Rogers	1551	9/68	60,250	16,770	acq. 10/17/1904 ex S.P. #1426
1427	'	'	'	1539	'	'	'	ex S.P. #1427
1607	2-6-0	57	BLW	6826	6/83	68,700	14,480	acq. 11/22/1909 ex S.P. #1607

Major business: common carrier, passengers

Rosters of 6/30/1896 - 6/30/1912:
locomotives	1	3
passenger cars	1	4
freight car	1	

First published "timetable":
March, 1905
Independence
Monmouth   2.5 miles
Airlie   11.0

Independence
Airlie   9.0
There were three round trips daily on both routes.

First listed in ICC for 6/30/92 as an operating independent with 2.4 miles owned and in use. It was extended to 2.5 miles by 6/30/93 and so continued through 1903. By 6/30/04 it was 2.5 miles owned and 18.5 operated; the same in 1905. By 6/30/07 it was an operating subsidiary of Southern Pacific Company with 2.5 miles owned and 19 operated.

This class III common carrier increased its "operated" to 32 miles in 1912 and then back to 19 miles by 6/30/15. This was the last alteration until service was discontinued in 1918.

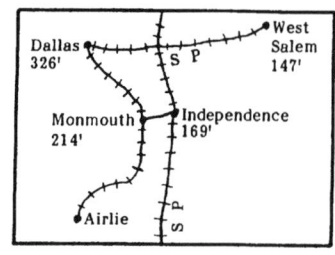

The extended operation in 1912 was Independence to West Salem, 13.09 miles, and Dallas to Airlie, 16.30 miles. The carrier had a trackage agreement with Southern Pacific Company to operate passenger service on these minor routes.

A truly modest operation, in 1896 it reported operating revenue of $1,792. The road was valued at $22,703, real estate of $1,000 and $800 worth of fuel for a total valuation of $24,503.

Bibliography: *Poor's 1897*, p. 261 and *1914*, p. 1536

The Independence West Side - January 31 to July 14, 1890

Oregon PUC 1892, p. 423

OREGON

INTERNATIONAL PAPER COMPANY

President

Incorp:		Operated: 1956 to 1957		HQ city:	Vernonia
Disposition:	abandoned				
Predecessors:	Long-Bell Lumber Company		from:	1953 to	1956
	Oregon-American Lumber Company		Incorp.:	12/31/1934	7/14/1953
Miles track:	35	Gauge: 56½"			
Main line:					
Rail wt.:	60 lbs.	Max. grade: 4.5%	Const. began:	grading	1922

Locomotives:

Road No.	Cyln.	Type	Dvr. in.	Bldr.	Bldr. No.	Date	Weight	Effort	Remarks
102		2T Shay	29½	Lima	2490	2/12	84,000	16,900	acq. 5/1928 ex Clark County Timber
103*	12x15	3T Shay	36	'	3181	6/22	166,600	30,350	scrapped in 1958
104*	18x24	2-6-2T	44	BLW	56851	8/23			
105*	'	2-8-2	'	'	58193	1/25			preserved
106*		3 truck	36	Willam.	26	1/27			scrapped in 1957
107		3T Shay	'	Lima	1812	3/07	160,000	35,100	acq. 6/1948 ex U.P. #61 - SCR 1956

Freight traffic: logging

K - P TIMBER COMPANY

A. S. Kerry, Owner

Incorp.:	9/4/1925	Operated: 9/11/25 to 1938		HQ city:	Kerry
Disposition:	abandoned on February 1, 1939				
Predecessors:	Kerry Timber Company		from:	1915 to	1925
	Columbia & Nehalem River Railroad Company		Incorp.:	2/15/1913	9/11/1925
Miles track:	53	Gauge: 56½"			
Main line:	Kerry into the forest				
Rail wt.:	60 lbs.	Max. grade: 8.0%	Const. began:	grading	(February 17, 1913)
			First train operated:		July 1, 1915

Locomotives:

Road No.	Cyln.	Type	Dvr. in.	Bldr.	Bldr. No.	Date	Weight	Effort	Remarks
1 ?		2 truck	30	Climax	648	/06	46,000		acquired 2d hand
2 ?		2T Shay	29½	Lima	1665	4/06	74,000	16,900	acquired 6th hand
3 ?		'	'	'	1851	3/07	'	'	acquired 6th hand
114		0-6-0	50	Schen.	3424	2/91	90,000	18,500	ex Portland Ry., L. & P. #114
115*	12½x14	2 truck	33	Climax	1337	4/15	100,000	22,000	
116*	'	'	'	'	1333	9/16	'	'	
117*	18x24	2-8-2	44	BLW	41710	9/14	135,500	27,100	to Weyerhaeuser #109
118*	'	'	'	'	43220	4/16			to Astoria Southern #18
119		2-6-2	'	'	36044	2/11			ex Day Lumber Co. #2
120*	17x24	2-6-2T	'	'	43213	4/16	118,000	22,100	to Port Orford Cedar Co.
121		2 truck	33	Climax	1341	5/15	110,000	24,200	ex Jefferson County Logging Co.
122*	14½x16	3 truck	35	'	1451	10/17	140,000		
123		2 truck	33	'	1289	2/15	100,000		ex Brix Bros. #5
124*	17x24	2-6-2T	44	BLW	49223	7/18	120,500	22,100	to Kern & Kibbe #1
125*	18x24	2-6-2	'	'	52790	1/20	160,000	31,800	8/1937 to Santa Maria RR #125
126*	17x24	2-6-2T	'	'	57636	2/24	120,500	22,100	to Crossett-Western #7-2d
127		2T Shay	32	Lima	3068	3/20	100,000	22,580	ex Green Mountain Logging #11

Freight traffic: logging

Roster of 12/31/1919:
- 7 rod engines
- 3 geared engines
- 5 flat cars
- 154 sets of logging trucks

ICC listings for Columbia & Nehalem River:

	owned:	operated:
6/30/14	8.00	
6/30/15	14.00	
6/30/16	24.00	16.00
12/31/16	27.00	27.00
12/31/20	30.00	30.00
12/31/22	33.32	28.50

Bibliography: *Pacific News* - #88, February, 1969

KLAMATH NORTHERN RAILWAY COMPANY

		Owner: Gilchrist Timber Co.
Incorp:	7/2/1940	Operated: 1/1/42 to
Disposition:	in operation 1993	HQ city: Gilchrist
Miles track:	10.612	Gauge: 56½"
Main line:	Gilchrist Jct. to Gilchrist	
Rail wt.:	62/80 lbs.	Max. grade:
Const. began:	grading 1925 ?	
Const. comp.:	(November 14, 1938)	First train operated:

Locomotives:

Road No.	Cyln.	Type	Dvr. in.	Bldr.	Bldr. No.	Date	Weight	Effort	Remarks
204*	20x24	2-6-2	48	BLW	33238	3/09			new as Gilchrist-Fordney (Miss.)-SCR 1955
205*		B-B		G.E.	32304	6/55	140,000	600 h.p.	replacement for #204
206*		B		BLW	40755	2/54	80,000	275 h.p.	
207*		B-B		G.E.	41290	12/82	250,000	1,000 h.p.	

Freight traffic: lumber

Roster of 12/31/1942:
  1 locomotive

According to ICC, Klamath Northern Railroad Company was incorporated in 1940 and purchased the track of Gilchrist Timber Co. (incorporated March 30, 1925); 11 miles owned and operated. In the volume for 1951 this class II carrier was listed as "Railway." The property was operated by the timber company through 1941.

Crown Pacific Railroad, Inc., was incorporated September 20, 1991, to operate the property. Peter W. Stott was the president with headquarters in Portland

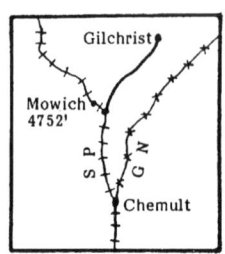

KOSTER PRODUCTS COMPANY

		President.
Incorp:		Operated: 1919 to 1939
		HQ city: Vernonia
Disposition:	abandoned	
Miles track:	11	Gauge: 56½"
Main line:	Astoria into the forest	
Rail wt.:	56/60 lbs.	Max. grade: 7.0%
Const. began:	grading	

Locomotives:

No.		Type		Bldr.	Bldr. No.	Date	Weight	Effort	Remarks
1		2T Shay	29½	Lima	2333	6/10	84,000	16,900	ex Astoria Southern; to U.S. Spruce
4		"	32	"	1821	1/07	90,000	20,350	ex Silverton Lbr.; to Interstate Logging Co.
5		3T Shay	"	"	1762	10/06	130,000	29,850	acq. 1922 ex California Barrell Co. #5
6		2T Shay	29½	"	2967	3/18	120,000	23,890	acq. 6/1920 ex California Barrell Co. #6
7		"	32	"	830	8/03	90,000	18,750	acq. 8/1929 ex Noyes-Holland #7

Freight traffic: logging

LA DEE LOGGING COMPANY

		President
Incorp:	3/18/1918	Operated: 1918 to 1934
		HQ city: Kerry
Disposition:	abandoned	
Miles track:	5	Gauge: 56½"
Main line:	woods lines - see locomotive listing	
Rail wt.:	60 lbs.	Max. grade:
Const. began:	grading	

Locomotives:

No.			Type		Bldr.	Bldr. No.	Date	Weight	Effort	Remarks
1	?	Kerry	3T Shay	36	Lima	2966	2/18	146,000	30,350	acq. 6/1923 ex Hudson Motor Car Co. #1
2	?	Birkenfeld	2T Shay	29½	"	3000	3/19	85,000	16,900	acq. 1/1920 ex Christenson Logging Co.
3	?	Astoria	"	36	"	3164	3/21	142,800	24,000	ex Lewis/Clark RR #3; to Crown Zeller.
4	?	Estacada	"	29½	"	3227	8/23	101,700	20,850	acq. 1931 ex Carstens Log. #4-sold 1933
5	?		2 truck		Climax	802	/07	70,000	20,350	ex Sorenson Logging Co. #3
6		Astoria	2T Shay	30½	Lima	1626	1/06	74,000	16,300	acq. 9/1930 ex Eastern/Western Lbr. #6
7	?	Kerry	2 Truck	40	Heisler	1432	4/20	130,000		ex Eastern & Western Lumber Co.

Freight traffic: logging

OREGON 87.

LAMM LUMBER COMPANY

President

Incorp:	10/7/1914	**Operated:**	1915 to 1944		**HQ city:**	Modoc Point
Disposition:	abandoned					
Miles track:	50	**Gauge:**	56½"			
Main line:	Chinchalo into the forest					
Rail wt.:	50/70 lbs.	**Max. grade:**	4.0%	**Const. began:**	grading	1914

Locomotives:

Road No.	Cyln.	Type	Dvr. in.	Bldr.	Bldr. No.	Date	Weight	Effort	Remarks
1		2T Shay	26½	Lima	798	4/03	64,000	14,950	acq. 1914 ex Clark Cr. Log; scr 1943
2		2 truck	40	Heisler	1254	5/12	120,000		wrecked in 1931
2-2d		2T Shay	29½	Lima	2722	10/13	84,000	16,900	ex Pelican Bay Lbr. #2 - scr 1951
3*	19x24	2-8-2	44	BLW	61306	4/30	158,700	31,900	1944 to California Western #44
4		2-6-2	48	Cooke	62515	/20	144,000	29,900	1944 to Ventura County Ry. Co. #3

Freight traffic: logging

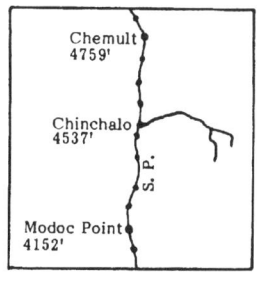

MALHEUR VALLEY RAILWAY COMPANY

W. H. Bancroft, **President**

Incorp:	1/26/1906	**Operated:**	(6/14/06) to 12/23/10		**HQ city:**	New York, N.Y.
Disposition:	merged into Oregon-Washington Railroad & Navigation Company on December 23, 1910					
Predecessor:	Vale & Malheur Valley Railway Company			**Incorp.:**	6/28/1905 to 9/10/1906	
Miles track:	37.33	**Gauge:**	56½"			
Main line:	Malheur Jct. to Brogan					
Rail wt.:	lbs.	**Max. grade:**	1.00%	**Const. began:**	grading (December 18, 1905)	
					laying rails May 8, 1906	
Const. comp.:				**First train operated:**	(June 11, 1906)	

Freight traffic: common carrier, agriculture

First published timetable:
(as Oregon Short Line RR)
June 16, 1907
9:20 a.m.   Ontario   2:30
10:00   Vale   1:50 p.m.

First listed in ICC for 6/30/06 as an operating independent with 14 miles owned and in use. The carrier was leased to Oregon Short Line Railroad Co. on January 15, 1907, and became a non-operating subsidiary.

Regarding the construction from Vale to Brogan (23.74 miles), the Willows River Land and Irrigation Co. purchased the right-of-way and paid a contractor to do the grading.

The maximum grade between Ontario and Vale is 0.525%.

Details about purchase of the predecessor are brief. Current Union Pacific Railroad Co. records show that "Sept. 10, 1906, "assets" sold to Malheur Valley Railway Company (voucher No. 796)." 10

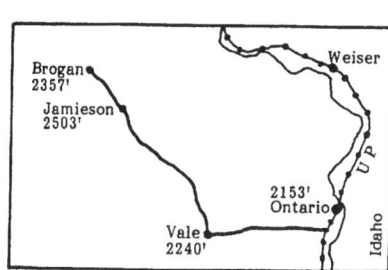

Bibliography: *Poor's 1910*, p. 1272   Vale - *Malheur Gazette* - October 26, 1905 to June 14, 1906   *Valuation 44*, p. 281
Oregon PUC report 1907, p. 120   Montana PUC report 1908, p. 178

MASTEN LOGGING COMPANY, C. C. President

Incorp:	4/3/1907	**Operated:**	1898 to 1910		**HQ city:**	Rainier
Disposition:	abandoned	(or sold to St. Helens Mill Company?)				
Miles track:	8	**Gauge:**	84"	**Date standardized:**		March, 1901
Main line:	Svensen into the woods					
Rail wt.:	lbs. (wood)	**Max. grade:**	4.0%	**Const. began:**	grading	1898

Locomotives:

Road No.	Cyln.	Type	Dvr. in.	Bldr.	Bldr. No.	Date	Weight	Effort	Remarks
1*		2 truck	26	Climax	183	12/98	28,000		to Silver Lake Railway & Lbr. Co.
1-2d*	'	'	'	'	248	3/01	58,000	13,200	to Sorenson Logging Co. #2
1-3d*	10x12	2T Shay	29½	Lima	1850	4/07	74,000	16,900	1/1909 to St. Helens Logging Co. #1
2*	'	'	'	'	2365	8/10	84,000	'	11/1910 to St. Helens Mill Co. #2

Freight traffic: logging

Roster of 6/30/1908:
- 2 geared engines
- 6 logging cars
- 5 miles of track at Cox Creek with headquarters at St. Helens

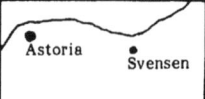

MEDFORD COAST RAIL ROAD COMPANY W. S. Barnum, **Owner**

Incorp:	11/6/1919	**Operated:**	1919 to 1925		**HQ city:**	Medford
Disposition:	abandoned in 1930					
Predecessors:	Southern Oregon Traction Company			**Incorp.:**	7/15/1913 to	1919
	Rogue River Valley Railway Company				8/3/1899 to	6/30/1915
	Rogue River Valley Railroad Company				7/1/1895	8/2/1899
	Rogue River Valley Railway Company				2/7/1891	6/30/1895
Miles track:	6.26	**Gauge:**	56½"			
Main line:	Medford to Jacksonville					
Rail wt.:	26 lbs. steel	**Max. grade:**		**Const. began:**	grading	(January 12, 1891)
					laying rails	(January 26, 1891)
Const. comp.:	(February 12, 1891)			**First train operated:**		February 15, 1891

Locomotives:

	Cyln.	Type	Dvr. in.	Bldr.	Bldr. No.	Date	Weight	Effort	Remarks
1*	8x14	2-4-0T	30	Porter	1236	12/90			re# 5
2									gasoline engine passenger car - re# 1
2-2d		2-4-0	48	Cooke	1718	5/86			acq. 2/1891 ex Willamette Vy. & Coast
3		4-4-0	56	'	1720	'	96,900	13,450	acq. 1911 ex Oregon & Eureka - scr 1925
4		2 truck	31	Climax	886	5/08	80,000		ex Fruit Growers Supply Co. (Calif.)
6		0-4-4T	42	BLW	6292	7/82	40,300		acq. 12/1907 ex Manhattan Ry. #148
7		2-6-0	36	Porter	292	2/78	36,000		ex Columbia & Puget Sound RR #6

Major business: common carrier, passengers

Roster of 6/30/1906:
- 2 locomotives
- 3 passenger cars
- 1 baggage car
- 1 box car
- 5 flat cars

First published timetable:
February, 1891
8:30 a.m. Jacksonville
Medford 10:00 a.m.
Plus two other round trips daily.

First listed in ICC for 6/30/91 as an operating independent with 5.5 miles owned and in use. Extended to six miles by 6/30/94. After its sale in 1915 (and called a "traction" company) it was no longer included in ICC statistics.

Income statement for first five months ending June 30, 1891:
  passenger income $1,449.75
  freight revenue   310.28
Cost of road, equipment 41,160.11
H. Honeyman was president.

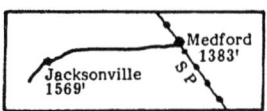

Poor's Manual 1907, still reports 26 pound rails; the 1914 edition states that 56 pound are now in use.

Southern Oregon Traction Company opened a street car service in Jacksonville on March 20, 1914, and on March 27, 1916, took over the common carrier railroad service to Medford. Its state operating franchise was cancelled on January 5, 1920. November 5, 1925, the Oregon PUC authorized sale of the carrier to the City of Medford for $12,000; presume that the city made the purchase.

Bibliography: *Poor's 1892,* p. 548   *Ashland Tidings* - January 2 to February 20, 1891   Oregon PUC report 1894, p. 279

Southern Oregon Historical Society #13437
The number two motor could offer passenger and mail service for less cost than a locomotive and passenger car.

Southern Oregon Historical Society #14790
Rogue River Valley number two, probably at Jacksonville. Track in foreground is innocent of ballast.

MEDFORD CORPORATION

					President
Incorp:	12/2/1932	**Operated:** (11/14/32) to (2/11/61)		**HQ city:**	Medford
Disposition:	abandoned - scrapping started March 21, 1961				
Predecessors:	Owen-Oregon Lumber Company		**from:**	1924	**to** 1935
	Medford Logging Railroad Company		**Incorp.:**	9/25/1924	1930
	Brownlee-Olds Lumber Company			8/20/1920	1924
	Pacific & Eastern Railway Company			5/27/1907	1/30/1919

Miles track: 65 **Gauge:** 56½"
Main line: Medford to near Mt. McLoughlin
Rail wt.: 56/60 lbs. **Max. grade:** 2.2% **Const. began:** grading

Locomotives:

Road No.	Owner	Type	Dvr. in.	Bldr.	Bldr. No.	Date	Weight	Effort	Remarks
1*	Brownlee	2-6-2	44	Porter	6696	2/22			scrapped
2	Owen	3 truck	36	Willam.	2	5/23	140,000		scrapped in August, 1959
3*	'	2-8-2	44	BLW	58045	10/24	152,000	30,000	sold 2/1965 Calif. Western #45
4*	'	3 truck	36	Willam.	18	2/25	175,000	30,350	8/1959 to display at Medford
5	'	3T Shay	33	Lima	3060	3/20	160,000	'	acq. 5/1928 - scrapped
6	'	2-8-2T	44	Brooks	65378	3/24	188,500	35,200	ex Consol. Tbr. #2 - scr 1952
7		2-6-0	48	BLW	2719	3/72	55,000		ex English Lumber Co. - scrapped
7-2d	Medford	3 truck	36	Willam.	21	2/26	175,000	36,000	1965 to display Dunsmuir, Calif.
8*	'	B-B		BLW	75481	/52		800 h.p.	

Freight traffic: logging

Roster of 12/31/1926:
  2 rod engines
  2 geared engines
  4 flat cars
 40 logging flats
 42 miles of track

Medford was a Delaware corporation

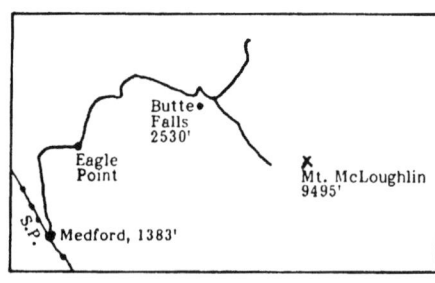

MILL CITY MFG. COMPANY

					President
Incorp:	3/16/1936	**Operated:** 1934 to 1947		**HQ city:**	Mill City
Disposition:	abandoned				
Predecessors:	Hammond Lumber Company		**from:**	1/1911	**to** 1934
	Curtis Lumber Company			1905	1/1912

Miles track: 35 **Gauge:** 56½"
Main line: Detroit along the Breitenbush River
Rail wt.: lbs. **Max. grade:** **Const. began:** grading 1905

Locomotives:

Road No.	Cyln.	Type	Dvr. in.	Bldr.	Bldr. No.	Date	Weight	Effort	Remarks
1*	12x12	2T Shay	36	Lima	994	3/05	110,000	22,275	
2*	11x12	'	32	'	1940	10/07	90,000	'	to Union Timber, Oakville, Wn.
2-2d*	17x14	2 truck	40	Heisler	1198	3/10	120,000		to Vancouver Plywood/Veneer #2
3*	10x12	2T Shay	29½	Lima	2738	1/14	84,000	16,900	abandoned in the woods in 1934
4*	17/26x24	2-6-6-2T	44	BLW	56738	7/23	211,130		to Flora Logging Co. #4
5*	'	'	'	'	60871	6/29	220,000	37,600	to Crown-Willamette #16
6*	'	'	'	'	60870	'	'	'	

Freight traffic: logging

Roster of 6/30/1910:
  2 geared engines
 25 flat cars
 10 miles of track

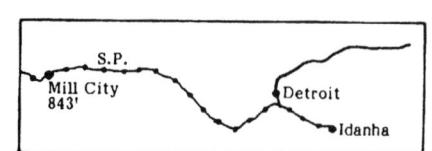

OREGON

MOLALLA WESTERN RAILWAY COMPANY

Richard A. Samuels, **President**

Incorp.:	2/11/1993	Operated: 2/22/93 to	HQ city: Milwaukie
Disposition:	in operation 1993		
Miles track:	10.46	Gauge: 56½"	
Main line:	Molalla to Canby		
Rail weight:	75 lbs.	Max. grade: 1.10%	
Freight traffic:	common carrier		

Locomotives:

187	B-B	EMD		/46		ex B.N. #187
801	'	'	13305	8/51	800 h.p.	ex B.N. #199

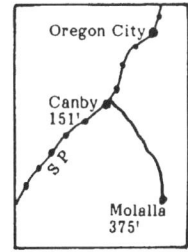

Bibliography: Direct communication

Official Open and Prepay Station List

MOUNT EMILY LUMBER COMPANY

Moser Bros. Logging Co. **Owner**

Incorp:	12/15/1924	Operated: 1924 to 1955	HQ city: La Grande
Disposition:	abandoned		
Miles track:	40	Gauge: 56½"	
Main line:			
Rail wt.:		Max. grade: 7.25%	Const. began: grading

Locomotives:

Road No.	Cyln.	Type	Dvr. in.	Bldr.	Bldr. No.	Date	Weight	Effort	Remarks
1		3T Shay	36	Lima	3233	9/23	160,000	35,100	ex Independence Logging Co. #1
1-2d*	18x24	2-8-2T	44	Brooks	66276	3/25	168,000	28,500	to Long-Bell #805 at Longview, Wn.
2*	'	'	'	'	66277	'	'	'	to Long-Bell #804 at Longview, Wn.
4		3 truck	36	Willam.	15	6/24	175,000	36,240	to Long-Bell #700
5		2T Shay	32	Lima	2614	1/13	100,000	22,550	ex Deep River Log. #5 - sold 9/1942

Freight traffic: logging

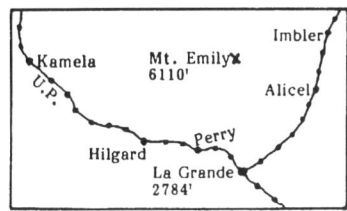

MOUNT HOOD RAILROAD COMPANY

| | | | | | | Jack Mills, | President |

Incorp.:	11/2/1987	Operated:	11/2/87 to		HQ city:	Hood River
Disposition:	in operation 1993					
Predecessors:	Mount Hood Railway Company			Incorp.:	4/30/1968 to	11/1/1987
	Mount Hood Railroad Company				2/23/1905	10/15/1968
Miles track:	21.162	Gauge:	56½"			
Main line:	Hood River to Parkdale					
Rail wt.:	45/75/100 lbs.	Max. grade:	3.4%	Const. began:	grading	(April 3, 1905)
					laying rails	(Dec. 15, 1905)
Const. comp.:	December 31, 1909			First train operated:		May 1, 1906

Locomotives:

Road No.	Cyln.	Type	Dvr. in.	Bldr.	Bldr. No.	Date	Weight	Effort	Remarks
1		2-8-0	49	BLW	1804	12/68	93,000	21,140	acq. 11/1904 ex U.P. #1251
1-2d*	8x12	2T Shay	26½	Lima	951	4/05	36,000	8,160	named Bud
1-3d		4-4-0	57	Manch.	1088	11/82	50,850	12,412	acq. 1915 ex O.W.R.&N. #58
1-4th*		2-8-2	44	BLW	55397	5/22	139,000		
2		2-8-0	49	'	1802	12/68	93,300	21,140	acq. 11/1904 ex U.P. #1252
3*	8x10	2T Shay	26½	Lima	1892	5/07	48,000	13,300	
11*		2-8-2		BLW	53486	7/20	135,000		to Oregon Lumber Co.
36			57	'	36333	4/11	208,450	47,945	acq. 1947 ex U.P. #2136
100*	15x12	2 truck	36	Heisler	1440	7/20	94,000		scrapped in 1954
50*		B-B		Schen.	78317	/50		660 h.p.	
88		'	40	EMD	19948	2/55	240,000	1,750 h.p.	ex S.P.
89		'	'	'	25301	5/59	'	'	ex Minnesota Vy.

Freight traffic: common carrier, lumber

Roster of 6/30/1910:
- 2 locomotives
- 3 passenger cars
- 13 freight cars

Published timetable dated:
October 17, 1915 - daily
8:00 a.m. Hood River 1:30 p.m.
10:15 Parkdale 11:45 a.m.

The original carrier was owned by Oregon Lumber Co. at Baker.

Hood River to Dee, 16.4 miles, was opened May 1, 1906. The southern section was built between March and December, 1909, and placed in operation on January 1, 1910.

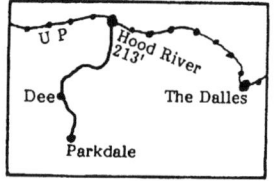

First listed in ICC for 6/30/06 as an operating independent with 16 miles owned and in use. This class II carrier was extended to 22 miles owned and operated by 6/30/11; it was reduced to 21 miles in 1931. The volume for 1968 states "sold assets to Union Pacific 10/15/68." From then on it was shown as a 21-mile class II operating subsidiary of Union Pacific Railroad Company. The road cost $463,287 to construct and $29,634 to equip.

Bibliography: *Poor's 1924*, p. 426   *Hood River Glacier* - March 9 to May 11, 1905   *Valuation 106*, p. 572

NORTH BEND MILL & LUMBER COMPANY

| | | | | | | | President |

Incorp:		Operated:	1900 to 1923	HQ city:	North Bend
Disposition:	abandoned				
Miles track:	7	Gauge:	56½"		
Main line:					
Rail wt.:	45 lbs.	Max. grade:		Const. began:	grading

Locomotives:

1		2T Shay	29½	Lima	765	4/03	74,000	15,625	ex Simpson Lbr. Co. #1; sold in 1916
2		'	'	'	2302	3/10	84,000	16,900	ex McDonald & Vaughan; sold in 1916
3		'	'	'	2303	'	'	'	ex Simpson Lbr.; 1916 to Buehner Lbr.
4		'	'	'	2518	5/12	'	'	ex Dollar Lbr.; to Stout Lbr. Co. #4
2978*	11x12	'	32	'	2978	5/18	100,000	22,580	to Stout Lumber Co. #2978

Freight traffic: logging

Roster of 6/30/1910:
- 1 geared engine
- 4 logging cars
- 1¼ miles of track

California State Railroad Museum Library *Gerald M. Best Collection*
Mount Hood's fourth number one is shown putting wood smoke into the Oregon sky.

NORTHWESTERN RAILROAD COMPANY
W. H. Bancroft, President

Incorp: 5/12/1906	**Operated:** 7/1/10 to 10/16/11		**HQ city:** New York, N.Y.

Disposition: sold to Oregon-Washington Railroad & Navigation Company by deeds dated 12/23/1910 and 10/16/1911

Miles track: 57.8   **Gauge:** 56½"

Main line: Blakes Jct. to Homestead

Rail wt.: lbs.   **Max. grade:**   **Const. began:** grading   see text below
                                              laying rails

Const. comp.: (June 1, 1910)   **First train operated:**

Freight traffic: common carrier, agriculture and mining

Published timetable dated:
January 2, 1916 - O-WR&N branch
```
11:25 a.m.  Blakes Jct.
12:12 noon  Home       12.4 miles
 1:25 p.m.  Robinette  32.9
 2:10       Brownlee   39.7
 3:10       Homestead  57.8
```

First listed in ICC for 6/30/09 as an operating independent with 42 miles owned, not in use. By 6/30/10 it was shown as a 58-mile subsidiary of Oregon Short Line Railroad Company, not in operation. It was sold to and merged into Oregon-Washington Railroad & Navigation Company on December 23, 1910, and October 16, 1911. The price was $2,640,000.

When was construction work begun? Numerous times, it seems, if one is to believe some of the notes from the public press that follow.

March 3, 1899, Spokane, Washington paper reported that 'mile of grade is completed from the new townsite of Nagle, 2.5 miles from Huntington near the Snake River bridge.'

March 9, 1899, a front page account in the Boise, Idaho, paper 'men being put on as fast as secured, will work a thousand, construction train to be put on shortly.'

July 3, 1899, again from Spokane 'seven hundred men are employed on the grades, 43 miles ready for ties and rails next month; to be 73 miles long.

May 14, 1906, from Walla Walla, Washington, we learn that 'eight carloads of machinery being delivered at Huntington this week. It mentions 12 surveyors will use a barge on the Snake to cross survey the old route.'

August 9, 1907, *Hillsboro Independent* states 'work going slowly, not enough men, but will begin to lay rails next week.'

December 26, 1907, from nearby Weiser, Idaho, a statement 'grading is nearly completed; expect to resume work soon.'

January 6, 1908, from nearby Baker City tells us that '18 cars of rails and ties for 40 miles are on hand; to build eight miles soon.'

January 30, 1908, same newspaper 'many tons of Russian rails are on the ground, many ties on the grade, but awaiting a better business outlook.'

February 13, 1908, from Weiser '43 miles northward from Huntington is graded and partly ironed; to reach Homestead this year.'

May 23, 1908, again from Weiser ' road under construction; last fall 30 miles of road were constructed from Huntington.

September 24, 1908, the Weiser paper reports 'construction work is progressing much more rapidly than earlier this year.

October 29, 1909, issue of *Railroad Age Gazette* tells us that 39.61 miles of rails have laid and 13.86 more graded. On June 6, 1910, the trade newspaper reports 'completed; to be turned over to operating department soon.'

And finally on June 15, 1910, *Salt Lake Mining Review* states that road is being operated into Homestead by Utah Construction Company, but expect to turn over to Oregon Short Line about July 1, 1910.

Bibliography: *Poor's 1910*, p. 1275   Oregon PUC report 1909   *Valuation 44*, p. 285

NOYES-HOLLAND LOGGING COMPANY

						President
Incorp:	12/14/1915	**Operated:**	(12/15) to 1926		**HQ city:**	Kerry
Disposition:	abandoned					
Predecessors:	Portland Lumber Company	(42" gauge)		**Incorp.:**	2/1/1902 to	1923
	Yeon & Pelton, Inc.				1901	1905

Miles track: 13   **Gauge:** 42" at Rainier and 56½" at Kerry

Main line:

Rail wt.: 56 lbs.   **Max. grade:** 6.0%   **Const. began:** grading

Locomotives:

Road No.	Owner	Type	Dvr. in.	Bldr.	Bldr. No.	Date	Weight	Effort	Remarks
1	Y&P	0-6-2		BLW	9847	2/89			
2	'	2 truck	31	Climax		(/02)	90,000		
3	'	0-6-2		BLW	9973	4/89			
4	'	2-6-0		'	10683	3/90			
5*	'	2 truck	31	Climax	457	12/03	90,000	19,800	to Morgan Lumber Company
5*	PL	2T Shay	32	Lima	1821	1/07	'	20,350	8/1929 to Silverton Lbr. Co. #4
7	N-H	'	'	'	830	8/03	'	18,750	8/1929 to Koster Products Company

Freight traffic: logging

Roster of 6/30/1910:
- 2   geared engines
- 3   rod engines
- 70   logging trucks
- 2   flat cars
- 11   miles of 42" track

Both predecessors operated at Rainier.

The three Baldwins were ex Willamette Bridge Railway Company.

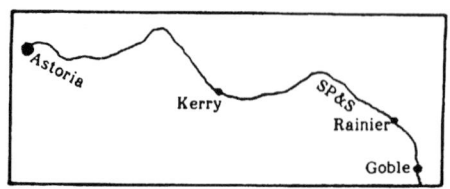

Special Collections Div. - Univ. of Washington Libraries Clark Kinsey photo #2301
Nehalem Timber & Logging Co. Willamette "Shay" c/n 19, shown at Scappoose, was purchased new.

Special Collections Div. - Univ. of Washington Libraries Clark Kinsey photo #2310
Nehalem Timber & Logging Co. headquarters at Scappoose with the cook house left of center

OREGON & CALIFORNIA RAIL ROAD COMPANY

Ben Holladay, **President**

Incorp: 3/17/1870   **Operated:** 9/5/70 to 1/3/27   **HQ city:** Portland

Disposition: sold to the Southern Pacific Company on January 3, 1927

Purchased:

	miles	Incorp.:	to
Portland & Yamhill Railroad Company	28.34	6/14/1892	7/22/1893
Oregonian Railroad Company	153.11	4/19/1890	7/31/1893
Albany & Lebanon Railroad Company	11.58	2/28/1880	5/6/1881
Western Oregon Railroad Company	49.70	1/27/1879	10/9/1880

Predecessors:

Oregon Central Railroad Company	46.80	11/21/1866	10/6/1880
Oregon Central Rail Road Company	20.08	4/22/1867	3/29/1870

Miles track: 680.228   **Gauge:** 56½"

Main line: Portland to California state line

Rail wt.: 35/56 lbs.   **Max. grade:** 3.75%   **Const. began:** grading (March 8, 1870)

laying rails (July 19, 1870)

Const. comp.: December 17, 1887 - main line   **First train operated:** September 5, 1870

Freight traffic: common carrier, agriculture

Rosters of   12/31/1870 - 12/31/1875 - 6/30/1890:

locomotive engines	6	14	49	- 44 w/air brakes
passenger cars	9	11	57	57 w/air brakes
freight cars	100	207	707	165 w/air brakes
fruit cars			24	24 w/air brakes

Second published timetable:
September 14, 1870 - daily

7:00 a.m.	East Portland		3:45	
7:30	Milwaukee	6	2:55	
8:20	Oregon City	15	2:30	
9:07	Canby	24	1:45	
10:30	Waconda	39	12:20	p.m.
11:03	End of track	45	11:45	a.m.

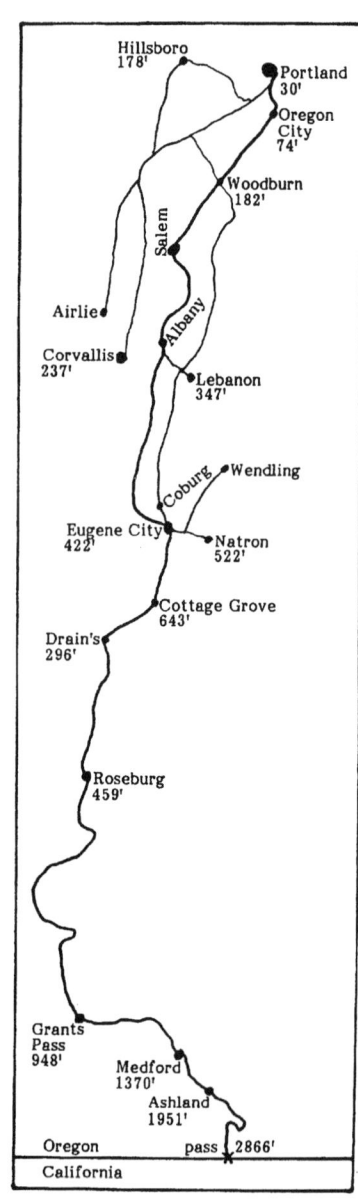

This admonition followed: "For the government and information of employees only" and "carefulness is enjoined upon all Employees. Always take the safe side in case of any uncertainty."

Published timetable dated:
September 21, 1873

8:15 a.m.	Portland		4:20	
9:17	Oregon City	16	3:13	
11:03	Salem	53	1:34	
12:18 p.m.	Albany	81	12:18	p.m.
2:45	Eugene City	124	9:53	
5:07	Drain's	161	7:24	
7:15	Roseburg	200	5:15	a.m.

Opening dates by track section:

to Salem	September 29, 1870
Albany	December 25, 1870
Eugene City	October 15, 1871
Roseburg	December 3, 1872
Grants Pass	December 2, 1883
Ashland	May 4, 1884
California line	December 17, 1887

Operations for the year ending December 31, 1875 - Henry Villard, President:

passenger earnings	$187,520.54
freight income	306,285.64
expenditures	340,803.42
net earnings	205,327.42
cost of construction	4,711,886.84
cost of rolling stock	454,890.65

Oregon & California Rail Road built 402.21 miles and the acquired companies contributed 309.61, less 29.13 miles abandoned between 1890 and 1910.

The line had 14 tunnels totalling 12,290 feet plus 543 trestles and bridges. In 1890 the carrier's locomotives burned 30,777 cords of hard wood costing $2.78 each. The line from Coburg to Natron, 12.90 miles, was opened September 2, 1891, and 15.95 miles from Mohawk Junction to Wendling on January 1, 1901. The carrier remained in *Official Guide* until October, 1889.

OREGON

The carrier was leased to Southern Pacific Company on July 1, 1887, and was listed in ICC for 6/30/89 as a 475-mile non-operating subsidiary. It was extended to 555 miles by 6/30/91, to 653 miles in 1894 and 670 in 1901. It was 680 miles in 1914, then "property conveyed by deed 1/3/1927."

Bibliography: *Poor's 1877-78,* p. 885   Oregon PUC report 1890, p. 263   *Valuation 45,* p. 292
Salem - *The Daily Oregon Statesman* - March 8 to July 28, 1870

Locomotive engines:

Road No.	Name	Cyln.	Type	Dvr. in	Bldr.	Bldr. No.	Date	Weight	Effort	Remarks	1891 renumbering
1	Oregon		4-4-0	62	BLW	2001	11/69	31,900		ex Ore. Cent.	to S.P. #1106
2	Portland	'	'	'	'	2002	'	'		ex Ore. Cent.	' 1107
3	Stephens	'	'	60	Hink.	199	9/48	36,600	9,560		' 1172
4*	Clackamas	16x24	'	57	BLW	2145	5/70	'	10,350		' 1173
5*	Salem	'	'	'	'	2146	'	41,950	'		' 1243
6*	Albany	'	'	'	'	2149	'	'	'		' 1244
7*	Harrisburg	'	'	'	'	2548	9/71	'	'		' 1245
8*	Eugene	'	'	'	'	2547	'	'	'		' 1246
9*	Junction	'	'	63	'	2696	2/72	'	'		' 1247
10*	Hallett	'	'	'	'	2697	'	'	'		' 1248
11*	Eugene	'	'	'	'	2892	8/72	'	'		' 1249
12*	Santiam	'	'	'	'	2934	9/72	'	'		' 1250
13	Couch		4-6-0	52	Sm&Pk		11/53	40,000		ex Ore. Cent.	' 1508
14	Dallas		4-4-0					30,700		ex Ore. Cent.	' 1108
15*	Umpqua	16x24	'	63	BLW	2935	9/72	41,950	10,350		' 1251
16*		'	'	'	'	2895	8/72	'	'		' 1252
17*		'	'	'	'	4519	1/79	'	'		' 1253
18*		'	'	'	'	4557	3/79	'	'		' 1254
19*		'	'	'	'	4574	'	'	'		' 1255
20			2-6-0	53	'	5029	3/80	65,000	15,573	ex Western Oregon	' 1512
21*		16x24	4-4-0	57	'	6018	1/82	41,950	10,700		' 1256
22*		17x24	'	61	'	6580	1/83	48,000	13,100		' 1355
23*		'	'	'	'	6582	'	'	'		' 1356
24*		'	'	'	'	6663	3/83	'	'		' 1357
25*		'	'	'	'	6669	'	'	'		' 1358
26*		'	'	'	'	6674	'	'	'		' 1359
27*		'	'	'	'	6675	'	'	'		' 1360
28*		'	'	'	'	6757	5/83	'	'		' 1361
29*		'	2-6-0	57	'	6216	5/82	68,700	14,480		' 1513
30*		'	'	'	'	6217	'	'	'		' 1514
31*		'	'	'	'	6697	4/83	'	'		' 1515
32*		'	'	'	'	6700	'	'	'		' 1516
33*		'	'	'	'	6824	6/83	'	'		' 1517
34*		'	'	'	'	6825	'	'	'		' 1518
35*		'	'	'	'	6826	'	'	'		' 1519
36*		'	'	'	'	6839	7/83	'	'		' 1520
37*		'	'	'	'	6702	4/83	70,000	16,820		' 1756
38*		'	'	'	'	6703	'	'	'		' 1757
39*		'	'	'	'	6715	'	'	'		' 1758
40*		'	'	'	'	6712	'	'	'		' 1759
41*		'	'	'	'	6716	'	'	'		' 1760
42*		'	'	'	'	6719	'	'	'		' 1761
43*		15x24	0-4-0	51	'	6755	5/83	52,700	10,800		' 1011
44*		19x30	2-8-0	'	C.P.	47	11/87	96,500	27,080		' 1907
45*		'	'	'	'	48	'	'	'		' 1908
46*		'	'	'	'	49	'	'	'		' 1909
47*		'	'	'	'	50	'	'	'		' 1910
48*		'	'	'	'	64	6/88	'	'		' 1911
49*		'	'	'	'	65	'	'	'		' 1912
1285*		20x26	0-6-0	57½	Lima	6753	4/24	155,000	31,020	same S.P. road numbers	
1286*		'	'	'	'	6754	'	'	'		'
1287*		'	'	'	'	6755	'	'	'		'
1288*		'	'	'	'	6756	'	'	'		'
1289*		'	'	'	'	6757	'	'	'		'
1290*		'	'	'	'	6758	'	'	'		'
1291*		'	'	'	'	6759	'	'	'		'
1292*		'	'	'	'	6760	'	'	'		'
1293*		'	'	'	'	6761	'	'	'		'
1294*		'	'	'	'	6762	'	'	'		'

OREGON AND CALIFORNIA RAILROAD.

Line of Road.—Portland, Oregon, to Roseburg, Oregon..............200 miles. Sidings and other tracks, 7.5 miles. Gauge, 4 feet 8½ inches. Rail, 50 and 56 lbs.

The Oregon Central Railroad Company of Salem was organized under the Act of Congress passed July 25, 1866. By this Act the company became the recipient of a 20-mile wide land grant, estimated to contain 3,500,000 acres, and of this, up to June 30, 1876, there had been certified to them 236,525.97 acres. The present company, successors of the Oregon Central of Salem, was chartered March 17, 1870. The road was completed between the present termini December 25, 1869. The Oregon Central Railroad, as now existing, runs from Portland, on the east side of the Willamette River, about 50 miles, and will ultimately be connected with the O. and C., at or near Eugene.

Rolling Stock.—Locomotive engines, 14. Passenger cars, 11; baggage, mail and express cars, 4; and freight cars, 227—viz.: box, 167; stock, 10; and platform, 50. Service cars, 2.

Operations for the year ending December 31, 1876.—Train movement—passenger, 181,820; and freight, 71,801, or a total of 253,621 miles. Service trains run, 35,925 miles. Passengers carried, 98,350; freight moved, 61,653 tons. Fiscal results:

Earnings.		*Expenditures.*	
From Passenger Traffic	$187,773 53	For Maintenance of Way, etc.	$110,485 37
" Freight Traffic	338,036 84	" Rolling Stock	18,522 42
" Mail and Express Service	29,385 01	" Transportation	178,454 69
" Minor Sources	21,596 04	" Miscellaneous Purposes	49,238 64
Total	$576,791 42	Total	$356,701 12

Balance—net earnings, $220,090.30, or less taxes ($25,245.31), $194,844.99; interest on funded debt (2 per cent.), $194,844.99.

Financial Statement.—Capital stock, none; funded debt, $10,950,000; and other liabilities, $28,464.09—total liabilities, $10,978,464.09. Cost of railroad and appurtenances, $5,938,470.75; cost of rolling stock, $480,725.27; and real estate, including buildings, $155,860.44—total property, $6,575,056.46; materials and fuel on hand, $51,782.38; bills receivable, $6,005.71; current accounts, $203,013.24; and cash, $10,355.03. Total property and assets, $6,846,212.82; excess of liabilities, $4,132,252.27.

The funded debt consists of 1st mortgage 7 per cent. bonds, issued April 15, 1870, and redeemable April 1, 1890, interest payable April and October, $10,950,000. This issue covers the whole length of the line completed and projected, being at the rate of $30,000 per mile on 365 miles.

Directors (elected April 10, 1877).—Henry Villard, New York, N. Y.; S. F. Chadwick, Salem, Oregon; C. H. Lewis and Hans Thielson, Portland, Oregon; James H. Foster, Albany, Oregon; Cyrus A. Dolph and Richard Koehler, Portland, Oregon.

HENRY VILLARD, *President*..................New York City, N. Y.
Richard Koehler, *Vice-President*..................Portland, Oregon.

Treasurer and Secretary......A. G. Cunningham.	*Road Masters* { 1st Div............T. De Clarke.
Gen. Superintendent..............J. Brandt, Jr.	{ 2d Div............J. D. McKinnon.
Chief Engineer..............Richard Koehler.	*Master Mechanic*..................A. Brandt.
Gen. Ticket and Freight Agent..................E. P. Rogers.	

PRINCIPAL OFFICE AND ADDRESS....................Portland, Oregon.

Oregon State Library Collection
Grants Pass - Trover 10-6
A gathering at Grants Pass to celebrate opening of the track to link Oregon with California on December 12, 1887.

Oregon State Library Collection
A covered bridge is shown being built over the North Umpqua River north of Roseburg; the photograph was probably taken in 1872 and in the summer judging from the low water.

California State Railroad Museum Library *Gerald M. Best Collection*
Oregon & California #33, Baldwin 6/1883, is all wooded and ready to depart Shedd

Oregon State Library Collection
Oregon & California "A" was built in San Francisco in 1862 for the Cascades Railroad Company on the north side of the Columbia River; it was then used on the subject line as a construction engine. It was photographed at Scio about 1895. It had 34 inch drivers and weighed 9,700 pounds. Date of scrapping is not known.

California State Railroad Museum Library
A short Oregon & California passenger train with number three, <u>Stephens</u>, in about 1875

Courtesy of Southern Pacific Company
Oregon & California Rail Road Company #8, <u>Eugene</u>, is shown at Myrtle Creek in about 1885.

OREGON & NORTHWESTERN RAILROAD COMPANY

				Owner:	Edw. Hines Lumber Co.
Incorp:	4/14/1934	**Operated:**	4/14/34 to 3/6/84	**HQ city:**	Hines

Disposition: connecting Union Pacific track was flooded; abandoned in April, 1990

Predecessors: Oregon & Northwestern Railroad   1930   4/13/1934

Malhuer Railroad Company   **Incorp.:** 11/5/1923 to 6/20/1930

Miles track: 51   **Gauge:** 56½"

Main line: Burns to Seneca

Rail wt.: lbs.   **Max. grade:**   **Const. began:** grading /1923

laying rails August 5, 1926

Const. comp.: 1929   **First train operated:**

Locomotives:

Road No.	Type	Dvr. in.	Bldr.	Bldr. No.	Date	Weight	Effort	Remarks
1	2-8-0	48	Schen.		/10	125,000		acq. in 1924
2	2-6-0							
4	3T Shay	36	Lima	3337	6/29	174,000	34,150	new as Edw. Hines Western Pine-scr 1960
5	2-8-0	51	Schen.	48057	/10	125,000	28,160	acq. in 1924
7	2T Shay	32	Lima	3345	11/29	120,000	25,830	acq. 7/1937 - 1961 to South Dakota
26*	2-8-2	56	BLW	61089	9/29	210,000		purchased new as Oregon & Northwestern
27	'	44	'		/10			
1400	'	55	Richm.	66919	6/26	282,000	55,900	acq. 1945 ex Longview, Portland & Nor.
2260	'	63	BLW	45765	6/17	214,050	53,625	acq. 2/1947 ex U.P. #2260
2261	'	'	'	45766	'	'	'	acq. 2/1947 ex U.P. #2261
1	C-C		'	75826	5/53	360,000	1,600 h.p.	acq. 2/1955
2	'		'	74916	9/50	330,000	'	acq. 10/1964 ex S.P. #5239
3	'		'	75470	5/52	'	'	acq. 6/1968 ex S.P. #5274
4	'		'	75449	3/52	324,000	'	acq. 8/1969 ex S.P. #5253

Freight traffic: common carrier, logging

Roster of 12/31/1930:
    2 locomotives
    200 freight cars

An Oregon Short Line Railroad Co. timetable dated June 2, 1916, shows operation from Ontario to Riverside, 93 miles. The line was extended to Crane, mp 127, in January, 1917. Burns became milepost 157 when the track was completed to that point on September 24, 1924.

This class II common carrier was first listed in ICC for 12/31/29 as an operating independent with 50 miles owned, not in use; by 1930 it was 47 miles owned and 50 in operation (to Hines). The figure became 50 miles each in 1934 and then unchanged through 1972.

Published "timetable" dated:
May, 1932 - freight only
Hines	
Burns	3 miles
Summit	25
Seneca	51

There was this addition:
"Passengers and express routed via Blue Mountain Stage Co. Motor Busses."

It appears that Edward Hines Lumber Co. owned all locomotives in its own name with the exception of road numbers 26 and 27 which were acquired by Oregon & Northwestern Railroad.

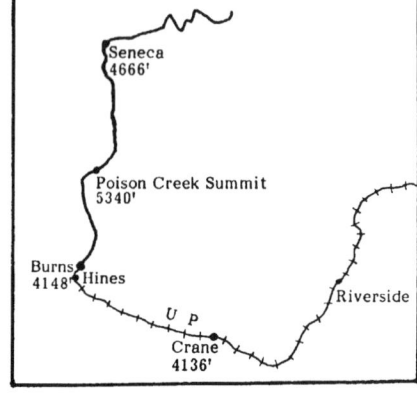

Bibliography: *Burns Times-Herald* - November 10, 1923 to August 7, 1926

OREGON & SOUTHEASTERN RAILROAD COMPANY

					George W. Crosby, **President**
Incorp:	4/19/1902	**Operated:**	(8/4/02) to 12/31/13	**HQ city:**	Cottage Grove

Disposition: sold to Oregon, Pacific & Eastern Railway Company on January 1, 1914

Miles track: 19.882   **Gauge:** 56½"

Main line: Cottage Grove to Disston

Rail wt.: 56 lbs.   **Max. grade:**   **Const. began:** grading May 6, 1902

laying rails (May 31, 1902)

Const. comp.: (May 19, 1906)   **First train operated:** (August 1, 1902)

OREGON

Road No.	Type	Dvr. in.	Bldr.	Bldr. No.	Date	Weight	Effort	Remarks
1	4-4-0	57	BLW	6019	1/82			
2	2-6-0	48	'	2094	3/70	55,000		
3	'		Danf.	885	10/72	75,000		acq. 1909
4	4-4-0	54	Cooke	1728	9/86	71,200	13,540	acq. 7/11/1902 ex Corvallis & Eastern #4
5	'	57	BLW	6044	2/82			originally O.R.&N. #35
6	2-6-0	'	'	6217	5/82	68,700	14,480	acq. 1902 ex S.P. #1602
9	4-4-0	54	Cooke	1723	6/86	64,000	13,540	acq. 1902 ex Corvallis & Eastern #9

Freight traffic: common carrier, agriculture, logging, mine

Roster of 6/30/1905:
   2 locomotives
   2 passenger cars
  33 freight cars

First listed in ICC for 6/30/03 as an operating independent with 15 miles owned and in use. It was extended to 18 miles by 6/30/04 and to 20 miles owned and operated by 6/30/06; a class III common carrier.

First published timetable:
September, 1903
7:30 a.m. Cottage Grove 11:30
9:05   Wildwood   10:00 a.m.

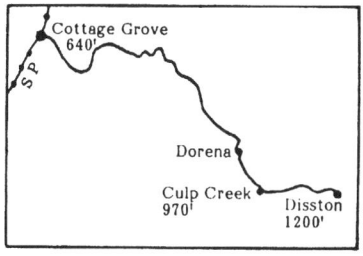

It appears that Wildwood was west of the Layng Creek bridge and once that stream was crossed, the station became Culp Creek, yet today, Culp Creek is west of the creek. Possibly Wildwood was simply renamed. The carrier was officially opened to Wildwood, 16.6 miles, on July 27, 1903.

There were five Howe-truss bridges and 23 pile-trestles. The line cost $309,505 to build and $38,724 to equip.

The actual date of sale was July 7, 1913, to be effective at the end of the year.

Bibliography: *Poor's 1906*, p. 652   *Cottage Grove Leader* - May 2 to July 4, 1902   *Valuation 106*, p. 605

California State Railroad Museum Library   *Gerald M. Best Collection*
Oregon & Southeastern #3 with logs and #4 with passenger coach, at Cottage Grove

OREGON, CALIFORNIA & EASTERN RAILWAY COMPANY

R. E. Strahorn, **President**

Incorp:	10/6/1915	**Operated:** 7/1/19 to 4/29/90	**HQ city:** Klamath Falls
Disposition:	operations discontinued on April 29, 1990		
Predecessor:	Klamath Falls Municipal Railway		to 6/30/1919
Miles track:	66.68	**Gauge:** 56½"	
Main line:	Klamath Falls to Bly		
Rail wt.:	75 lbs.	**Max. grade:** 1.25%	**Const. began:** grading July 6, 1917
			laying rails (Sept. 4, 1917)
Const. comp.:	April 30, 1929	**First train operated:**	July 14, 1918

Locomotives:

Road No.	Type	Dvr. in.	Bldr.	Bldr. No.	Date	Weight	Effort	Remarks
1	4-4-0	57	Manch.	1099	2/83	147,760	9,947	ex O.W.R&N. #65-arrived Aug. 18, 1917
2	2-6-0	50	BLW	9019	1/88	132,000	19,165	acq. 1920 ex Spokane International #12
3	2-8-0		Pitts.		/88	198,000		acq. 1924
201	C-C		EMD	34527	9/62		1,600 h.p.	ex Union Pacific #639
202	'		'	34239	7/62		'	' 633
203	'		'	34538	8/62		'	' 640
204	'		'	34228	9/61		'	' 628
205	'		'	34536	9/62		'	' 638
301	'		'	34238	5/62		'	' 629
302	'		'	34237	2/62		'	' 636

Freight traffic: common carrier, logging

Roster of 12/31/1927:
- 3 locomotives
- 1 passenger car
- 119 freight cars

Published "timetable" dated:
February, 1941
"Tariffs filed and traffic handled between Klamath Falls and Bly, Ore. (64.93 miles).
R. A. McCandless, president - Seattle."

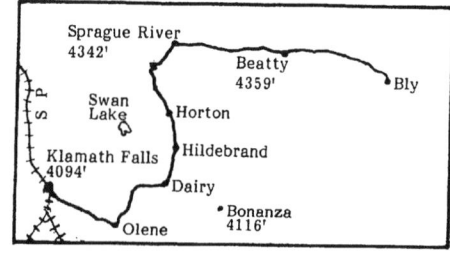

Klamath Falls Municipal Railway (owned by the City of Klamath Falls) was first listed in ICC for 12/31/17 as an operating independent with three miles owned, not in use; by 12/31/18 it was ten miles owned and operated. When acquired by the new owners the mileage was 19.068.

The subject carrier was first listed in 1919 as an operating independent with 20 miles owned and in use. It was gradually extended to 42 miles in 1923, but did not operate that year. For the year 1926 it was shown as a 42-mile operating subsidiary of Southern Pacific Company. In 1928 it had a joint ownership of Southern Pacific-Great Northern. In 1929 it was again independent with 65 miles owned and operated, then revised to 66 miles in 1965. The property was sold to Weyerhaeuser Company on January 1, 1975.

Construction details:
Dairy to Sprague River	20.932 miles	October, 1919, to October 12, 1923
Sprague River to Bly	26.550	April 2, 1927 to December 1, 1928

Poor's 1924 states that it is operating to Sprague River, 40 miles, and is building to Bonanza, 7 miles, and has surveys to Bend, 150 miles; also a two-mile branch to Swan Lake.

Bibliography: *Poor's 1924*, p. 1529   Klamath Falls - *The Evening Herald* - May 6 to September 7, 1917

OREGON CENTRAL & EASTERN RAILROAD COMPANY

A. B. Hammond, **President**

Incorp:	4/12/1895	**Operated:** 4/13/95 to 1/25/98	**HQ city:** Corvallis
Disposition:	sold to Corvallis & Eastern Railroad Company on January 25, 1898		
Predecessor:	Willamette Valley & Coast Rail Road Company	**Incorp.:**	7/6/1874 to 4/13/1895
Miles track:	140.74	**Gauge:** 56½"	
Main line:	Yaquina to Idanha		

OREGON

Road No.	Type	Dvr. in.	Bldr.	Bldr. No.	Date	Weight	Effort	Remarks
1	4-4-0	55	Cooke	1342	11/81	45,000	13,000	
2	"	62	Rogers	3411	11/83	49,000	13,100	1896 to Astoria & Columbia R. #7
3	"	"	"	3410	"	"	"	1896 to Astoria & Columbia R. #6
4	"	56	"	3445	12/83	"	13,590	
6	"	54	Cooke	1719	5/86	64,000	13,540	1898 to Yreka Railroad #2
7	"	"	"	1720	"	"	"	1898 to Eureka & Klamath R. #10
8	"	"	"	1722	6/86	"	"	
9	"	"	"	1723	"	"	"	
10	"	"	"	1724	"	"	"	
11	"	"	"	1725	"	"	"	
12	"	"	"	1728	9/86	"	"	
13	"	"	"	1729	"	"	"	
14	"	"	"	1730	"	"	"	
15	"	"	"	1731	"	"	"	1896 to Astoria & Columbia R. #4

Freight traffic: common carrier, lumber

Roster of 6/30/1896:
- 12   locomotive engines
- 7   passenger cars
- 322 freight cars

First published timetable:
July, 1895 (still dated 7/11/94)

7:00 a.m.	Yaquina		5:20	
	Summit	46 miles		
11:15	Corvallis	72		
11:50	Albany	84	12:35 p.m.	
1:30 p.m.	Albany	0	11:05	
	Mill City	35		
	Niagara	42		
5:50	Detroit	54	6:30 a.m.	

On December 22, 1894, Hammond and his Montana lumber associates purchased Oregon Pacific Railroad Co. and Willamette Valley & Coast Rail Road Co. at a sheriff's sale. The property was valued at $3,147,328.56 and it consisted of an operation with three tunnels totalling 1,975 feet plus 284 trestles and bridges of 42,285 feet; they paid $100,000.

First listed in ICC for 6/30/95 as an operating independent with 143 miles owned and in use. It was reorganized as Corvallis & Eastern Railroad Co. on December 15, 1897, to be effective the following January.

First published timetable showing operation to Idanha was dated November 17, 1895. The carrier also operated a line of steamboats on the Willamette between Portland and Corvallis.

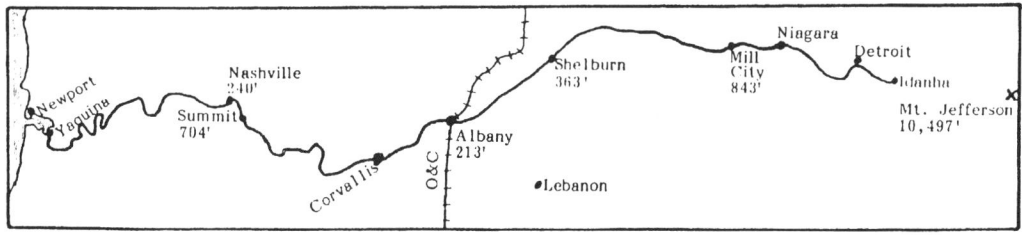

Bibliography: *Poor's 1896*, p. 345   Oregon PUC report 1895, p. 146   *Valuation 45*, p. 354

California State Railroad Museum Library
Klamath Falls Municipal Railway locomotive and passenger car at Klamath Falls on opening day, July 14, 1918; the operation was also known as the Strahorn Railroad in honor of its promoter.

OREGON CENTRAL RAILROAD COMPANY T. R. Cornelius, **President**

Incorp:	11/21/1866	**Operated:** 1/4/72 to 8/31/80	**HQ city:**	Portland
Disposition:	consolidated into Oregon & California Rail Road Company on September 1, 1880			
Miles track:	46.80	**Gauge:** 56½"		
Main line:	Portland to St. Joseph			
Rail wt.:	56 lbs. English iron	**Max. grade:** 3.750%	**Const. began:**	grading April 15, 1868
				laying rails (October 23, 1871)
Const. comp.:	November 3, 1872		**First train operated:**	(December 25, 1871)

Locomotive engines:

Road No.	Cyln.	Name	Type	Dvr. in.	Bldr.	Bldr. No.	Date	Weight	Effort	Remarks
1*	15x22	Oregon	4-4-0	62	BLW	2001	11/69	31,900		to Oregon & Calif. #1
2*	'	Portland	'	'	'	2002	'	'		to Oregon & Calif. #2
3		Couch	4-6-0	52	Smith/Perk.		11/53	40,000		ex Pennsylvania RR #76
4		Dallas	4-4-0	60				30,700		to Oregon & Calif. #14

Freight traffic: common carrier

Roster of 6/30/1880:
- 4 locomotive engines
- 2 passenger cars
- 40 freight cars

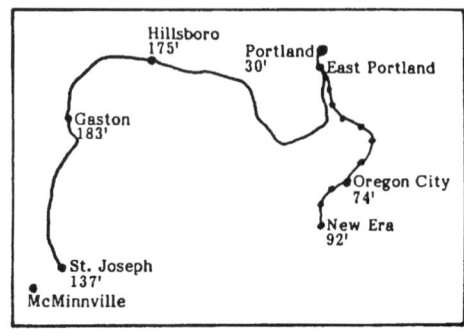

Published timetable dated:
June, 1879 - daily exc. Sunday

2:30 p.m.	Portland		10:30
	Hillsboro	20	
	Gaston	32	
6:30	St. Joseph	48	6:30 a.m.

The carrier cost $1,105,641 to construct and $96,566 to equip. It was being operated into Hillsboro by December 30, 1871.

The company's track was leased September 1, 1879, to Western Oregon Railroad Company.

Bibliography: *Poor's 1880*, p. 996   Oregon PUC report 1890, p. 263   *Valuation 45*, p. 420
Olympia - *Washington Standard* - November 4 and December 30, 1871
Oregon City Enterprise - October 27, 1871 to January 5, 1872

OREGON CENTRAL RAIL ROAD COMPANY Ben Holladay, **President**

Incorp:	4/22/1867	**Operated:** did not to 3/29/70	**HQ city:**	Salem
Disposition:	consolidated into Oregon & California Rail Road Company on March 29, 1870			
Miles track:	20.08	**Gauge:** 56½"		
Main line:	East Portland to New Era			
Rail wt.:	50/56 lbs. iron	**Max. grade:** 1.5%	**Const. began:**	grading April 16, 1868
				laying rails October 26, 1869
Const. comp.:	December 24, 1869		**First train operated:**	December 31, 1869

Locomotive engine:

3		Stephens	4-4-0	60	Hinkley	199	9/48	36,600	9,560	arr. 11/1869 ex Michigan Central

Freight traffic: common carrier

Bibliography: Olympia - *Washington Standard* - January 1, 1870   *Valuation 45*, p. 420

OREGON 107.

OREGON EASTERN RAILWAY COMPANY

E. E. Calvin, **President**

Incorp:	8/21/1905	**Operated:** 12/18/11 to 2/29/12		**HQ city:** San Francisco
Disposition:	sold to and merged in Central Pacific Railway Company on February 29, 1912			
Predecessors:	California Northeastern Railway Company		**Incorp.:** 7/6/1905 to 12/18/1911	
	Weed Lumber Company		7/29/1905	

Miles track: 112.99 **Gauge:** 56½"

Main line: Weed to Chiloquin

Rail wt.: lbs. **Max. grade:** 1.00% **Const. began:** grading February 24, 1903
laying rails September 1, 1906

Const. comp.: May 1, 1912 **First train operated:** September 1, 1906

Locomotives:

Road No.	Cyln.	Type	Dvr. in.	Bldr.	Bldr. No.	Date	Weight	Effort	Remarks
1		4-4-0	60	Portland	382	3/81	70,000		ex N.P. - 6/1909 to Amador Central #1
3*	17x24	2-6-2	44	BLW	30509	3/07	124,000	21,400	to Long Bell Lumber Company #3
3-2d		2-8-0	51	'	11478	12/90	106,700	24,100	1910 to Southern Pacific #2500-2d
4*	17x24	2-6-2	44	'	30519	3/07	124,000	21,400	to Long Bell Lumber Company #4
5		0-6-0T	40	'	17684	4/00	75,000	17,750	ex McCloud River Railroad Co. #5
12*	19x24	0-6-0	50	Cooke	30526	/05	122,000		

Freight traffic: common carrier, logging

Published timetable dated:

December, 1908 - daily
7:00 a.m. Weed
12:00 m Worden 67 miles
12:30 p.m. Worden (by stagecoach)
1:15 Blidel 71
1:30 Blidel (by lake boat)
3:30 Klamath Falls 86

Of the track owned by California Northeastern, 67.45 miles were in California and 45.54 in Oregon.

Weed Lumber Co. built a logging line from Weed to Grass Lake, 24.84 miles, between 1903 and 1905. California Northeastern Railway began construction September 1, 1906. The track was placed in operation from Grass Lake to Bray, 14.15 miles, September 6, 1907, to Dorris, 24.64 miles, on May 1, 1908, to Calor, 4.31 miles, August 25, 1908, and to Worden, 4.10, on November 25, 1908. Ady, 2.80 miles, was reached January 1, 1909, and extended into Klamath Falls, 11.31 miles, on May 20, 1909 for a total of 86.15 miles.

California Northeastern Railway Co. was first listed in ICC for 6/30/05 as an operating independent (owned by Weed Lumber Co.) with 22 miles owned and in use. It was extended to 25 miles by 6/30/06 and leased to Southern Pacific Company on September 1, 1906, as a non-operating subsidiary. It was increased to 64 miles by 6/30/08 and to 86 by 6/30/09, then unchanged through 6/30/11 and sold.

Oregon Eastern Railway Co. was first shown in ICC for 6/30/10 as a non-operating subsidiary of Southern Pacific Company with two miles owned, but was extended to 52 miles by 6/30/11 and then sold in 1912 to Central Pacific.

Oregon Eastern Railway Co. completed 26.89 miles from Klamath Falls to Chiloquin and owned two sections of road under construction on the date of sale to Central Pacific; they were Chiloquin to Kirk, 13 miles, and Natron to Oakridge, 34 miles. The section to Oakridge was completed by Central Pacific in May, 1912, and to Kirk in September. Closing the 110-mile gap between the two did not resume until October, 1923, and was placed in operation September 1, 1926.

Bibliography: *Poor's 1910*, p. 1354

Valuation 45, p. 413

California State Railroad Museum Library
Oregon Eastern Railway Co. "orange peel" floating dredger James Grady at work near Klamath Falls of May 5, 1910.

OREGON ELECTRIC RAILWAY COMPANY

Francis B. Clarke, **President**

Incorp:	5/15/1906	**Operated:** 1/21/08 to 8/ /81		**HQ city:**	Portland
Disposition:	consolidated into Burlington Northern, Incorporated, in August, 1981				
Miles track:	192.78	**Gauge:** 56½"			
Main line:	Portland to Eugene				
Rail wt.:	lbs.	**Max. grade:**	**Const. began:**	grading	July 11, 1906
				laying rails	(August 12, 1907)
Const. comp.:	(October 31, 1912) - main line		**First train operated:**		January 20, 1908

Locomotives:

Road No.	Type	Bldr.	Bldr. No.	Date	Weight	Effort	Remarks
1		G.E.		/07	80,000		
2		"		"	"		
3*		"	3219	/10	100,000		
4*		"	3295	"	"		
5*		"	3806	10/12	"		
6*		"	3807	"	"		
21*		"	3808	8/12	120,000		
22*		"	3809	"	"		
23*		"	3810	"	"		
24*		"	3811	"	"		
	0-4-4-0	Schen.	51067	/12			
	"	"	51068-74	"			

Major traffic: common carrier, passengers

Roster of 12/31/1939:
    10   electric motors
    25   freight cars

OREGON

First published timetable:
January 22, 1908 - *Weekly Oregon Statesman* - Salem

8:00 a.m.	Salem	5:00	
11:00	Portland	2:00	p.m.
2:00 p.m.	Salem	11:00	
5:00	Portland	8:00	a.m.

The initial excursion was Portland to Salem, 50.7 miles, on January 20, 1908. Salem to Albany, 26.7 miles, was opened July 4, 1912, and to Eugene, 121.1 miles from Portland, on October 15, 1912. The Forest Grove branch, 19.45 miles, was opened January 3, 1909. Albany to Lebanon, 13.65 miles, was joint trackage with Southern Pacific Company. Lebanon to Sweet Home, 15.46 miles, was placed in operation about January 24, 1931. Sweet Home to Dollar was 15.48 miles.

A 2,430-foot steel span was erected just south of Wilsonville to reach the west side of the Willamette River. The operation was 600 volts at first, but increased to 1,200 in 1912. Passenger service was terminated about June 30, 1933, and all electrical service on July 10, 1945.

The subject carrier was an operating subsidiary of Spokane, Portland & Seattle Railway Company. It was reclassified by ICC on January 1, 1933, from electric to steam. In 1933, the ICC authorized abandonment of 5.20 miles in Linn County and in 1941, 12.76 miles in Multnomah and Washington Counties.

The Portland station was at Front and Jefferson Streets.

While Oregon Electric was in fact a "short line" it offered unusual services for the traveling public. In 1916, a sleeping car could be boarded in Portland at 9:30 p.m. which then departed at 11:45 p.m. for arrival in Eugene at 6:50 a.m., but the passenger could remain in the car until 8. Northbound was 12:05 a.m. departure and 6:55 a.m. into Portland. Four trains offered buffet meals for parlor car passengers.

Bibliography: *Poor's 1914*, p. 1484
Salem - *Weekly Oregon Statesman* - June 15, 1906 to January 21, 1908
Oregon Historical Society *Quarterly*, vol. 44

California State Railroad Museum Library
Oregon Electric Railway Company number 52 at Portland in October, 1948

California State Railroad Museum Library
Oregon Electric sleeper <u>Santiam</u> is seen in this 1913 photograph at Portland; the car was retired in 1918.

California State Railroad Museum Library
Oregon Electric Railway Co. rear-end car #026 was photographed at Portland on May 21, 1938.

OREGON 111.

OREGON LUMBER COMPANY
President

Incorp:	10/25/1886		**Operated:**	1898 to 1943			**HQ city:**	Baker
Disposition:	abandoned							
Miles track:	30		**Gauge:**	36"				

Main line:

Rail wt.:	lbs.	**Max. grade:**	7.0%	**Const. began:**	grading	1898

Locomotives:

Road No.	Cyln.	Type	Dvr. in.	Bldr.	Bldr. No.	Date	Weight	Effort	Remarks
1		2T Shay	28	Lima	226	11/88	56,000	13,180	acq. 1898 ex Utah Central #226
1-2d*	8x10	'	26½	'	1983	7/07	'	12,600	re# 103 in 1921; scrapped 1/1929
7		3T Shay	36	'	3345	11/29	134,000	22,830	acq. 7/1937 ex N.M. Lbr. Co.
100*	15x12	2 truck		Heisler	1510	11/24	100,000		scrapped in 1950
105		'	29	Climax	1533	5/19	60,000		ex Sumpter Valley #8 - scr 1947

Freight traffic: logging

OREGON, PACIFIC & EASTERN RAILWAY COMPANY
J. H. Chambers, **President**

Incorp:	10/14/1912	**Operated:**	1/1/14 to 1990	**HQ city:**	Cottage Grove
Disposition:	rail transportation discontinued - abandoned November 22, 1993				
Predecessor:	Oregon & Southeastern Railroad Company		**Incorp.:**	4/19/1902 to 12/31/1913	
Miles track:	19.882	**Gauge:**	56½"		

Main line: Cottage Grove to Disston

Locomotives:

Road No.	Cyln.	Type	Dvr. in.	Bldr.	Bldr. No.	Date	Weight	Effort	Remarks
1		4-4-0	57	BLW	6019	1/82			
1-2d		2-6-2T		'	58206	2/25	126,860	22,100	acq. 1928 ex Anderson & Middleton #1
3		2-6-0		Danf.	885	10/72	75,000		
4		4-4-0	54	Cooke	1728	9/86			
5		'	57	BLW	6044	2/82			
5-2d		2-8-0	51	Brooks	63549	10/22	199,000	42,900	acq. 1972 ex Magma Arizona #5
6		2-6-0	57	BLW	6217	5/82			
7		'	53	'	5029	3/80	65,000	15,573	acq. 1916 ex Salem, Falls C.&W. #7
8		4-6-0	54	R.I.	2025	7/88	85,700	18,330	acq. 1924 ex S.P. #338 - SCR 1941
9		4-4-0		Cooke	1723	6/86	64,000	13,540	
9-2d		3T Shay	32	Lima	1787	12/06	120,000	26,975	acq. 1928 ex Anderson & Middleton #9
9-3d		2-6-2T	48	Richm.	45884	4/09	123,000		acq. 1941 ex Winston Lumber Co. #26
19		2-8-2		BLW	42000	4/15	178,400	35,700	acq. 1971 ex Yreka Western #19
10*				G.E.		5/52			out of service in 1977
11				'		/41			acq. 1953 ex Monongahela Connecting
12				'		/55			acq. 1973 ex Port of Tacoma #702
14				'		/49			ex S.P. #5109
14½				Plymouth		/30			ex Feather River Railway Co.
21		B-B		ALCO	70204	7/41		660 h.p.	acq. 1976 ex San Francisco Belt Ry.
100				Budd		/54			ex S.P. #100 - sold in 1978

Freight traffic: common carrier, lumber

Roster of 12/31/1917:
- 3 locomotives
- 3 passenger cars
- 45 freight cars

Published timetable dated:
May, 1916 - daily exc. Sunday

8:00 a.m.	Cottage Grove		1:00 p.m.
10:35	Rujada	m.p. 21	10:40 a.m.

In March, 1929, a mixed train operated to Rujada on Monday-Wednesday-Friday.

First listed in ICC for 6/30/14 as an operating independent with 24 miles owned and in use. This class III carrier was reduced to 20 miles in 1930. It was placed in receivership and a truseee was appointed on November 6, 1937. It was extended to 21 miles in 1951, to 24 miles in 1953, then reduced to 17 in 1970.

A railway post office service was operated from April 1, 1917, until March, 1929. In 1924, Anderson & Middleton Lumber Co. purchased the carrier from J. H. Chambers Lumber Co. In that same year, the five-mile Upton branch was removed and track built along Herman Creek; this last-named branch was abandoned in February, 1938.

Regular passenger service was terminated in July, 1930. A seven-mile branch was built from Walden in 1948. Culp Creek to Disston was abandoned in January, 1954; the Walden branch was scrapped in October, 1970. For the past several years, tourists were carried each summer.

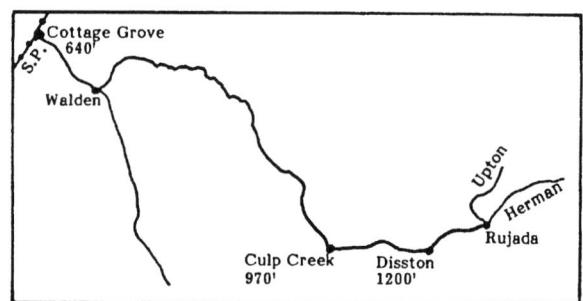

Bibliography: *Poor's 1918*, p. 1993   Direct communication   *Valuation 106*, p. 598

OREGON PORTAGE RAIL ROAD

Joseph S. Ruckel, **Owner**

Incorp:	not ?	**Operated:**	(11/58) to 4/20/63	**HQ city:**	Bonneville
Disposition:	ceased operation on a routine basis				
Miles track:	4.5	**Gauge:**	60"		
Main line:	Bonneville to Cascade (now Cascade Locks)				
Rail wt.:	lbs.	**Max. grade:**		**Const. began:**	grading (September 2, 1858)
					laying rails (October 1, 1858)
Const. comp.:	(May 16, 1861)			**First train operated:**	(November, 1858)

Locomotive engines:

1* Oregon Pony 0-4-0 34 Vulcan 3/62 9,700 810 stored at The Dalles (5/11/1863) - 10/18/66 to San Francisco
2
3

Freight traffic: common carrier, military and emigrants

Roster of 11/6/1862:
  1   locomotive engine
  1   passenger car
 20   freight cars

A portage wagon road was built at this site and opened about August 15, 1855. The original rails for the tramway were 6 x 6 fir stringers; the ties were covered with planks to provide a walkway for the three or four horses needed to move the small four-wheel cars.

During a one year period (May, 1860, to April, 1861) the carrier moved 5,314 tons of freight. The largest month was May (843 tons) and the low point was January (133 tons). A ton was 40 cubic feet in most cases.

The Pony [diminuitive of "iron horse"] arrived in Portland from San Francisco on March 31, 1862, and cost $4,000. It was set up and the trial run and excursion was on May 10, 1862; it was placed in operation ten days later.

It is known that Ruckel (also found as "Ruckle") had a partner, Harrison Olmstead, and probably four other partners/investors. The property was sold to Oregon Steam Navigation Company on November 6, 1862, for $155,000.

The carrier was largely built over the Columbia River on piles which had a habit each spring of washing out sections of the track.

After April 20, 1863, traffic was handled by the Cascades Railroad Company on the Washington Territory side of the river.

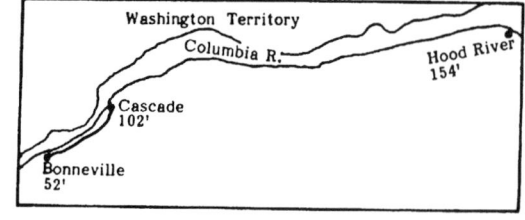

Bibliography: Oregon City - *Oregon Statesman* - May 20, 1861   *The Quarterly* of Oregon Historical Society, vol. xxv - #3

Oregon State Library Collection Views 10-11
The headquarters building and Eagle Creek bridge looking down stream toward Bonneville in about 1862

Oregon State Library Collection Oregon 302 - Hood River County
Oregon Portage Rail Road bridge across Eagle Creek with some type of loading device, probably in 1862

OREGON RAILROAD & NAVIGATION COMPANY, THE

E. McNeill, President

Incorp:	7/16/1896	**Operated:** 8/18/96 to 12/23/10

HQ city: Portland

Disposition: sold to Oregon-Washington Railroad & Navigation Company on December 23, 1910

Predecessors:

	Incorp.:	to
Columbia & Palouse Railroad Company, The	6/29/1892	9/6/1910
Walla Walla & Columbia River Railroad Company	12/28/1868	9/6/1910
Mill Creek Flume & Manufacturing Company	3/1/1880	10/26/1903
Oregon Railway Extensions Company, The	5/25/1888	8/17/1896
Washington & Idaho Railroad Company	7/7/1886	8/17/1896
Oregon Railway & Navigation Company	6/13/1879	8/17/1896

Miles track: 1,138.74   **Gauge:** 56½" (also 13.4 miles of 36" gauge - Walla Walla to Dixie, Dudley)

Main line: Portland to Huntington and Pendleton to Spokane

Rail wt.: 56/75 lbs.   **Max. grade:** 2.84%   **Const. began:** grading

laying rails

Const. comp.:

First train operated: August 18, 1896

Freight traffic: common carrier, agriculture and mining

Roster of 6/30/1897:

110	locomotives
38	passenger cars
1,940	box cars
294	flat cars
136	coal cars
259	stock cars
193	furniture cars
3	steamships (Portland-San Francisco)
2	steam tugs
16	river steamers (Riparia to Lewiston and Portland to Eugene)

First published timetable:

May 17, 1896

7:00 p.m.	Portland		
4:00 a.m.	Walla Walla		
1:20 p.m.	Spokane	448 miles
4:45 a.m.	Walla Walla		
6:40	Pendleton		
12:10 p.m.	Baker City		
2:00	Huntington	466 miles

First listed in ICC for 6/30/97 as an operating independent with 863 miles owned and 1,059 miles in use. By 6/30/98 it was an operating subsidiary of Union Pacific Railroad Company. The "owned" mileage changed little, but the "operated" figure increased to 1,264 in 1908 and to 1,327 in 1909. By 6/30/10 the mileages were 1,143 owned and 1,491 operated. It was reorganized as Oregon-Washington Railroad & Navigation Company in 1910.

The track was acquired as follows:

Foreclosures:	
Oregon Railway & Navigation Co.	642.76 miles
Oregon Railway Extensions Co., The	68.73
Washington & Idaho Railroad Co.	154.19
Direct purchases:	
Columbia & Palouse Railroad Co., The	144.80
Walla Walla & Columbia River Railroad Co.	35.52
Mill Creek Flume & Manufacturing Co.	13.51
Construction:	94.34
Less revisions and abandonments	-15.11
Total mileage:	1,138.74

Its major construction was Dayton to Turner, Wash., 11 miles, about June 30, 1903, and Elgin to Joseph, 63 miles, about December 1, 1908.

Locomotives:

Road No.	Type	Dvr. in.	Bldr.	Bldr. No.	Date	Weight	Effort	Remarks
10	4-4-0	55	Danf.	1046	1/77	50,000		7/1900 sold
11	2-6-0	37	BLW	5034	3/80	48,000		3/1900 to Tacoma Eastern
12	0-6-0T		Altoona	250	10/74			3/1900 sold
13	'		'	357	3/77			7/1902 to Central RR of Oregon
14	0-4-0	48	BLW	6239	6/82	55,600		
15	2-6-0	50	'	2094	3/70	60,500		8/1905 to Salem, Falls C. & W. #3
16	'	'	'	2719	3/72	'		2/1903 to English Logging Co.
17	'	'	Danf.	884	10/72	71,500		5/1906 to Rucker Bros.
18	'	'	'	885	'	'		5/1906 to Sumner Lumber Co.
19	'		57	BLW	6256	6/82	75,000	14,480	2/1910 to Carlton Logging Co.

OREGON

No.	Type	Dr.	Builder	C/N	Date	Weight	TE	Disposition
30	4-4-0	57	BLW	5509	2/81			2/1902 scrapped
31	'	'	'	5511	'			9/1905 to Ocean Shore Ry. (Calif.)
32	'	'	'	6019	1/82			2/1903 to Salem, Falls C. & W.
33	'	'	'	6033	2/82			2/1903 to Salem, Falls C. & W.
34	'	'	'	6034	'			4/1903 to Oregon Water Pwr. & Ry.
35	'	'	'	6044	'			2/1903 to Goble, Nehalem & Pacific
36	'	'	'	6046	'			3/1902 scrapped
37	'	'	'	6128	4/82	68,200		5/1903 to Columbia R. & Nehalem
38	'	'	'	6211	5/82	'		2/1903 sold to Pat McCoy
39	'	'	'	6212	'	'		5/1902 to English Logging Co.
40	'	62	Hinkley	1466	12/81	71,400	12,826	11/1905 to Ocean Shore Ry. Co.
41-43	'	'	'	1467-69	'	'	'	
44	'	'	'	1470	'	'	'	5/1902 to Seattle Mill Co.
45	'	'	'	1465	'	'	'	1/1906 to Labell Lumber Co.
46	'	'	'	1477	1/82	'	'	4/1906 burned at Umatilla
47	'	'	'	1473	'	'	'	5/1902 to Swigert & Campbell
48	'	'	'	1474	'	'	'	3/1902 to P.S.E. Co., Tacoma, Wash.
49	'	'	'	1475	'	'	'	1/1901 to Goble, Nehalem & Pacific
50	'	'	'	1476	'	'	'	
53	'	57	Manch.	1083	10/82		9,947	1/1902 scrapped
54	'	'	'	1084	'		'	1907 condemned
55	'	'	'	1085	'		'	3/1906 to M. E. Rodgers
56-58	'	'	'	1086-88	11/82			
59	'	60	'	1093	1/83	53,800	11,230	8/1906 to East Side Lumber Co.
60-62	'	'	'	1094-96	2/83	'	'	
63	'	'	'	1097	'	'	'	11/1901 scrapped
64	'	'	'	1098	'	'	'	
65	'	54	'	1099	'	48,600	12,412	
66	'	'	'	1100	4/83	'	'	
67	'	'	'	1101	'	'	'	3/1910 exploded
68-70	'	'	'	1102-04	'	'	'	
71-72	4-6-0	'	'	1105-06	'	71,000	16,223	
73	'	'	'	1107	5/83	'	'	
74-75	'	'	'	1108-09	7/83	'	'	
76	'	'	'	1110	10/83	'	'	12/1898 to Columbia Southern Ry. #2
77-78	'	'	'	1111-12	'			
79	4-4-0	63	BLW	6827	6/83	55,300	12,412	
80	'	'	'	6831	'	'	'	
81	'	'	'	6829	'	'	'	
82-86	2-8-0	51	Rome	429-33	1/89	116,950	25,600	
87	2-6-0	58	Schen.	2868	/89	91,500	17,973	8/1909 to Idaho Northern Railroad
88-95	'	'	'	2869-76	'	'	'	
130-135	4-6-0	63	Rome	507-12	10/89		17,534	
136-139	'	'	Cooke	2067-70	1/91	112,950	22,666	
140-147	'	'	'	2059-66	12/90	'	'	
148-151	'	57	'	2321-24	10/95		27,916	
152-156*	'	'	'	2379-83	12/97	125,600	29,465	
160	2-8-0	51	Rome	429	10/88		25,600	
161-164	'	'	'	430-33	'			#161 to Idaho Northern 8/1909
165	'	50	BLW	5793	8/81	92,000	22,750	ex U.P. #1260
166	'	'	'	5943	12/81	'	'	ex U.P. #1265
167	'	'	'	5962	'	'	'	ex U.P. #1267
168	'	'	Cooke	1368	10/82	'	'	ex U.P. #1268
169	'	'	'	1370	'	'	'	ex U.P. #1270
170	'	'	Taunton	882	2/83	104,180	'	ex U.P. #1283
190-193*	4-6-2	77	Schen.	30035-38	9/1904	222,000	29,920	
194-196*	4-6-2C	'	BLW	25687-89	5/05	143,000	28,265	
197*	'	'	'	25717	'	'	'	
198-199*	'	'	'	28613/18	7/06	'	'	
200-202*	2-8-0	55	Brooks	3075-77	11/98	148,920	33,474	
205-210*	4-6-0	63	'	45045-50	4/08	198,000	36,570	
211-213*	'	'	BLW	33712/23	8/09	161,000	33,390	
214-216*	'	'	'	33741-43	9/09	'	'	
300-302*	2-8-0VC	57	'	19103/64	6/01	167,340	34,649	
303-306*	'	'	'	19301-04	7/01	'	'	
307-309*	'	'	'	19341-43	8/01	'	'	
310-313*	'	'	'	21768/840	3/03	'	'	
314*	'	'	'	21920	4/03	'	'	
340-344	'	'	'	21011/197	9-11/02	181,200	40,900	ex U.P. #1512-13-17-20-21
350-355*	2-8-0	'	'	25271/94	3/05	187,000	43,300	
356-359	'	'	'	27205-08	1/06	189,970	'	
360-365	'	'	'	27237-42	'	'	'	

115.

366-373*	2-8-0	57	BLW	30245-252	2/07	189,790	43,300	
374-375	"	"	"	30280-81	"	"	"	
376-378*	"	"	"	31251-53	7/07	"	"	
379-381*	"	"	"	31298-300	"	"	"	
382-385*	"	"	"	31325-28	"	"	"	
386-388*	"	"	Brooks	44978-80	2/08	208,000	"	
400-405*	4-6-0VC	63	BLW	19173/234	7/01	145,300	26,744	
440*	2-8-2	57	"	34978	7/10	208,450	47,950	to O.-W.R.&N. #500
450*	2-8-8-2C	"	"	34016	11/09	394,000	94,880	re# 3800
451*	"	"	"	34017	"	"	"	re# 3801
452*	"	"	"	34018	"	"	"	re# 3802

Second numbers and replacements:

20	0-6-0	51	Cooke	2265	9/95	98,000	19,440
21*	"	"	BLW	25523	4/05	146,400	27,915
22*	"	"	"	25571	"	"	"
23*	"	"	"	25575	"	"	"
24*	"	"	"	25605	5/05	"	"
25*	"	"	"	18704	2/01	129,000	"
26*	"	"	"	18705	"	"	"
27*	"	"	"	21731	3/03	"	"
28*	"	"	"	30676	4/07	140,000	27,375
29*	"	"	"	30677	"	"	"
30*	"	"	"	30678	"	"	"
31*	"	"	"	33788	9/09	"	"
32*	"	"	"	33789	"	"	"

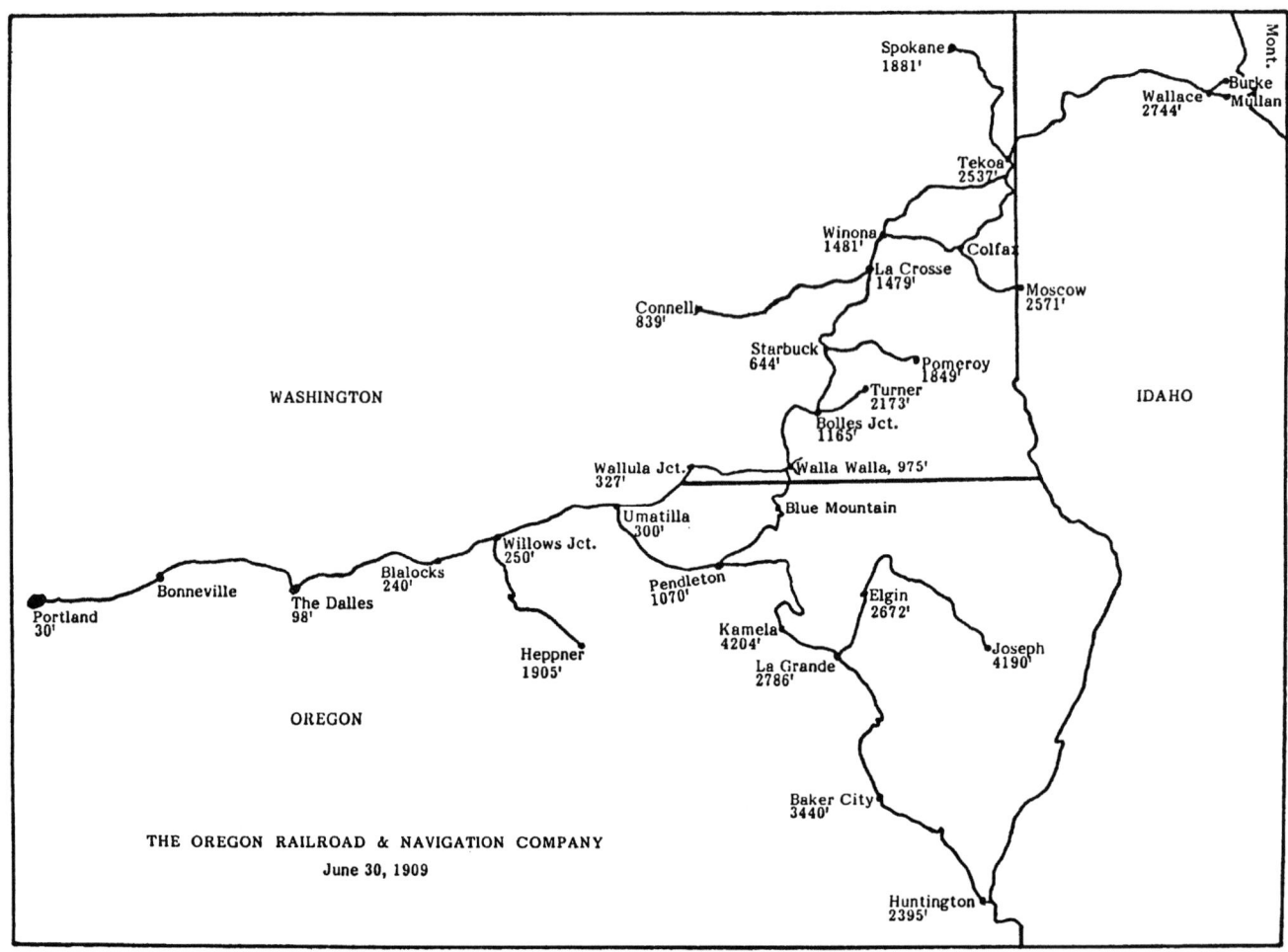

THE OREGON RAILROAD & NAVIGATION COMPANY
June 30, 1909

Bibliography: *Poor's 1897*, p. 248 Oregon PUC report 1896, p. 182 *Valuation 44*, p. 253

OREGON RAILWAY & NAVIGATION COMPANY   Henry Villard, **President**

Incorp: 6/13/1879   **Operated:** 7/1/79 to 8/18/96   **HQ city:** Portland
Disposition: sold to The Oregon Railroad & Navigation Company on August 18, 1896
Predecessor: Oregon Steam Navigation Company   **Incorp.:** 10/12/1862 to 3/31/1880
Miles track: 642.76   **Gauge:** 56½" (and 13.4 miles of 36")
Main line: Portland to Huntington and Pendleton to Winona
Rail wt.: 35/56/75 lbs.   **Max. grade:** 2.840%   **Const. began:** grading (February 9, 1880)
                                                                         laying rails (August 9, 1880)
Const. comp.: 1884   **First train operated:** November 21, 1880
Freight traffic: common carrier, agriculture and mining

Rosters of   6/30/1881 − 6/30/1887 − 12/31/1893:   Published "timetable" for Oregonian lines operated by OR&N
  locomotive engines   19   74   100   November 9, 1881
  passenger cars   21   31   33   East Side division:
  freight cars   423   1,485   2,818   Portland to Woodburn   41 miles
  miles of track   172.5   752.1   1,059.3   Silverton   51
                                                                                 Lebanon Jct.   88
First published timetable: Brownsville   101
  Undated in April, 1881, *Official Guide*   West Side division:
  "mail"   "mixed"   Portland to Whites   46
  6:00 a.m.   7:00 p.m.   The Dalles   Sheridan Jct.   54
  9:51   10:48   Blalock's   Sheridan   61
  then by steamboat to arrive   Dallas   67
  1:00 p.m.   4:00 p.m.   Umatilla   Airlie   83
  5:15   8:55   Walla Walla   July 12, 1882
  This was less than 12 hours via the "mail"   East Side now to Coburg   121
  and over 25 hours on the "mixed."   Status as of October 1, 1885:
                                                                 Portland to Huntington   404 miles
Published timetable dated: Wallula Jct. via W. W. to Riparia 87
  July 24, 1881 (all-rail schedule)   Palouse Jct. to Moscow   117
  8:20 p.m.   The Dalles   Bolles Jct. to Dayton   13
  11:23   Blalock's   46 miles   Walla Walla to Blue Mountain   20
  2:56 a.m.   Umatilla   99   Pendleton to Centerville   17
  5:10   Wallula Jct.   126   total: 658
  7:00   Walla Walla   157   Elijah Smith was the president.
  9:50   Dayton   196

Additional schedules showed the progress.   Timetables dated November 30, 1890, show all main
  April 30, 1882   line track (Portland to Huntington and Spokane Falls),
    Bonneville to Dayton   242   1,044.7 miles, being operated as a part of Oregon Short
  November 26, 1882   Line & Utah Northern Railway Company.
    Portland to Dayton   283
     and on to Riparia   301   The main line was opened from The Dalles to Cascades
  July 20, 1884   on March 17, 1882, and westward to Portland October
    Portland to La Grande   305   3 of the same year. Umatilla to Pendleton was completed
  November 23, 1884   on September 11, 1882, and to Huntington November
    Portland to Huntington   404   25, 1884.

Listed in first ICC (6/30/88) as an operating subsidiary of Union Pacific Railway Company with 608 miles owned and
752 miles in use. By 6/30/90 it was 641 miles owned and 1,029 operated; by 6/30/96 it was 640 miles owned and 1,059
operated. It was reorganized on July 16, 1896, and sold as noted above.

Assorted construction notes:
  Railroad Gazette:
    February 6, 1880   Celilo to Wallula has been surveyed; grading to begin soon.
    May 21, 1880   Walla Walla & Columbia River Railroad is being extended down river to Grande Ronde
                          Landing to bypass the Umatilla rapids; once track is built east to this point, it will be
                          made standard gauge.
  The Railway Age:
    August 26, 1880   Ships with English rails have arrived.
    September 2, 1880   Grading to Wallula is completed and tracklaying commenced at Celilo. Graders have
                          moved to Texas Ferry on the Snake River and then to work Grange City to Walla Walla.
  Idaho Tri-Weekly Statesman: [Boise City]
    April 28, 1881   Last Sunday the 36" track from Wallula Jct. to Umatilla was made standard gauge.
    May 27, 1881   The first broad gauge train arrived in Walla Walla last evening. Track laying to Dayton
                          will begin tomorrow.
    August 9, 1881   On August 4th track laying started at Bolles towards Grange City, 26 miles. Head of
                          track to reach Colfax in September.

Locomotive engines:

Road No.	Type	Dvr. in.	Bldr.	Bldr. No.	Date	Weight	Effort	Remarks
1	4-2-4T	55	Danf.	240	/62	35,000		Ainsworth; scrapped (10/1885)
2	'	'	'	241	'	'		Bradford' scrapped (10/1885)
3	4-4-0	'	'	472	/66	50,000		Ruckel; roundhouse fire 11/7/1886
4	'	'	'	473	'	'		Reed; retired about 1891
5	'	54	'	1046	1/77	'		Thompson
6	'	'	'	1047	'	'		Sprague; retired about 1891
7*	2-6-0	37	BLW	5031	3/80	48,000		retired about 1891
8*	'	'	'	5037	4/80	'		retired about 1891
9*	'	'	'	5032	3/80	'		retired about 1891
10*	'	'	'	5038	4/80	'		retired about 1891
10-2d	'	55	Brooks		/93		22,762	acquired about 1895
11*	'	37	BLW	5034	4/80	48,000		
12*	4-4-0	41	Rogers	2575	2/80			retired about 1891
13*	'	'	'	2576	'			retired about 1891
14*	'	57	BLW	5509	2/81			
15*	'	'	'	5511	'			
16-17	vacant							diverted to Northern Pacific
18*	4-4-0	62	Hinkley	1465	12/81	71,400	12,826	
19*	'	'	'	1466	'	'	'	
20*	'	'	'	1467	'	'	'	
20-2d	0-6-0	51	Cooke	2265	9/95	98,000	19,440	
21*	4-4-0	62	Hinkley	1468	12/81	71,400	12,826	
22*	'	'	'	1469	'	'	'	
23*	'	'	'	1470	'	'	'	
24-25	vacant							diverted
26-30*	4-4-0	62	Hinkley	1473-77	1/82	71,400	12,826	
31	vacant							diverted to Oregon & California
32*	4-4-0	57	BLW	6019	1/82			
33-36*	'	'	'	6033/46	2/82			
37	0-6-0T		Altoona	250	10/74			acquired May, 1881
38	'		'	357	3/77			acquired May, 1881
39	2-6-0	50	Danf.	884	10/72	71,500		acq. 1881 ex Virginia & Truckee #15
40	'	'	'	885	'	'		acq. 1881 ex Virginia & Truckee #16
41	'	'	BLW	2094	3/70	60,500		acq. 1881 ex Virginia & Truckee #6
42	'	'	'	2719	3/72	'		acq. 1881 ex Virginia & Truckee #10
43*	4-4-0	57	Manch.	1087	11/82		9,947	
44*	'	'	'	1088	'		'	
45*	'	'	BLW	6127	4/82	68,200		retired about 1891
46*	'	'	'	6128	'	'		
47*	'	'	'	6211	5/82	'		
48*	'	'	'	6212	'	'		
49-50	vacant							diverted to Oregon & California
45-2d*	4-6-0	63	Rome	507	10/89	92,350	17,534	
46-2d*	'	'	'	508	'	'	'	
47-2d*	'	'	'	509	'	'	'	
48-2d*	'	'	'	510	'	'	'	
49*	'	'	'	511	'	'	'	
50*	'	'	'	512	'	'	'	
51*	2-6-0	57	BLW	6256	6/82	75,000	14,480	
52*	0-4-0	48	'	6239	'	55,600		
53*	4-4-0	57	Manch.	1083	10/82		9,947	
54*	'	'	'	1084	'		'	
55*	'	'	'	1085	'		'	
56*	'	'	'	1086	'		'	
57*	'	'	'	1087	11/82		'	
58*	'	'	'	1088	'		'	
59*	'	60	'	1093	1/83	53,800	'	
60-64*	'	'	'	1094-98	2/83	'	'	
65*	'	54	'	1099	'	48,600	12,412	
66-70*	'	'	'	1000-04	4/83	'	'	
71-75*	4-6-0	'	'	1105-09	4/7/83	71,000	16,223	
76-78*	'	'	'	1110-12	10/83	'	'	
79-81*	4-4-0	63	BLW	6827/31	6/83	55,300	12,412	
82-86*	2-8-0	51	Rome	429-433	1/89	116,950	25,600	
87-95*	2-6-0	48	Schen.	2868-76	/89	91,500	17,973	
136-139*	4-6-0	62	Cooke	2067-70	1/91	112,950	21,300	
140-147*	'	'	'	2059-66	12/90	'	'	
148-151*	'	57	'	2321-24	10/95	119,400	27,916	

OREGON 119.

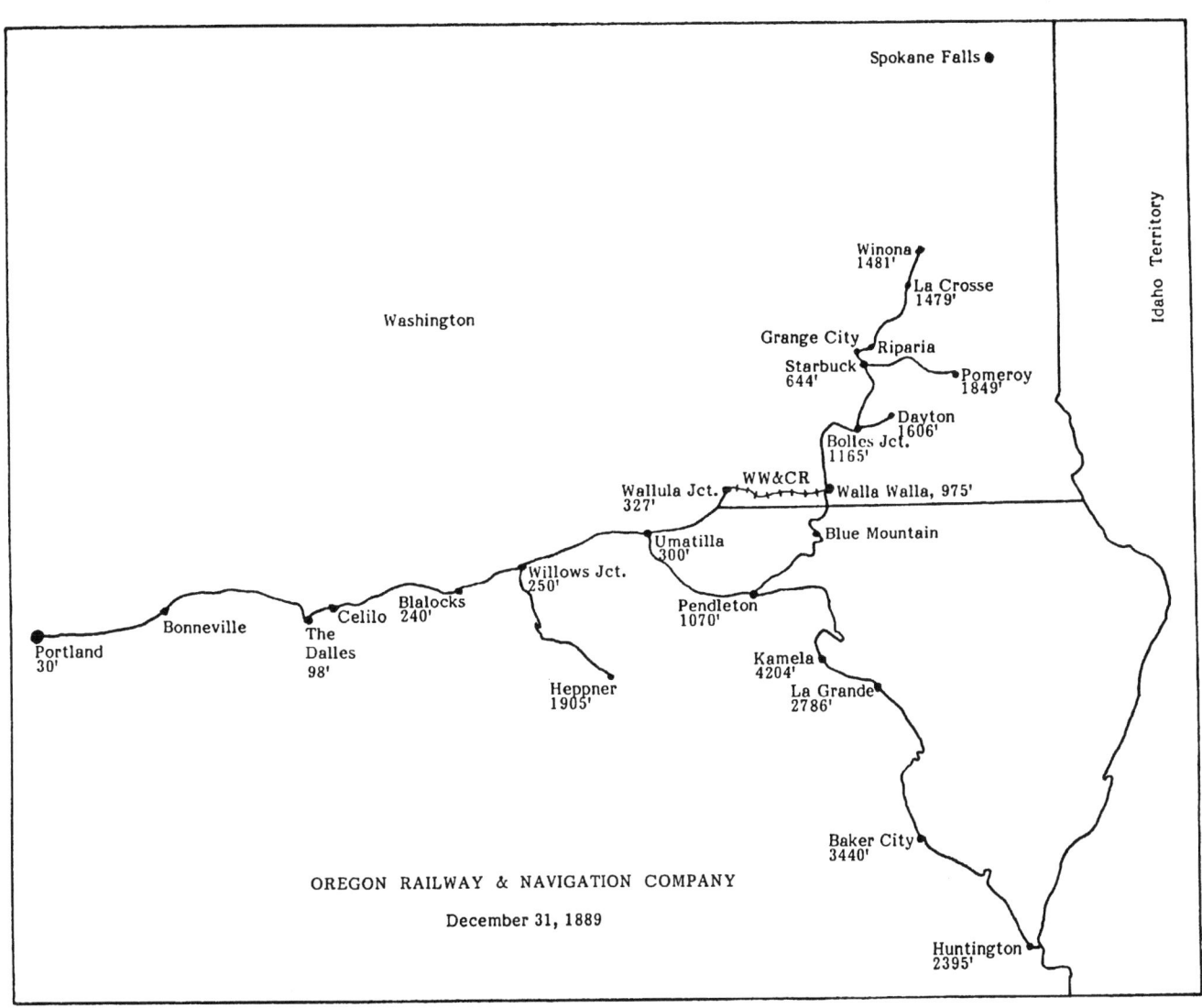

Bibliography: *Poor's 1880*, p. 998 Oregon PUC report 1891, p. 30 *Valuation 44*, p. 258
The Dalles - *The Weekly Mountaineer* - January 1 to November 25, 1880
Walla Walla Union - March 27, 1880

OREGON STATE PORTAGE RAILROAD

State of Oregon, **Owner**

Incorp: not **Operated:** 6/3/05 to 1915 **HQ city:** Salem
Disposition: abandoned
Miles track: 12 **Gauge:** 56½"
Main line: Big Eddy to above Celilo Falls
Rail wt.: **Max. grade:** **Const. began:** grading (February 1, 1905)
laying rails (March 13, 1905)
Const. comp.: (February 16, 1907) **First train operated:** June 3, 1905

Locomotives:

Road No.	Name	Type	Dvr. in.	Bldr.	Bldr. No.	Date	Weight	Remarks
1*	Lewis	2-6-0		Daven.	403	11/04		to Portland & Oregon City Railroad Co.
2		4-4-0		Manch.				ex O.R.&N. - to Portland & Oregon City
3				BLW			80,000	acq. 2/1911 from Railway Equipment Co.

Freight traffic: common carrier, portage
First listed in ICC for 6/30/05 as a ten-mile operating independent; it was extended to 12 miles by 6/30/11.

Bibliography: *Railway Age* - February 3, 1905 - March 24, 1905 - May 19, 1905 - June 9, 1905

OREGON
Railway & Navigation Co.

Freight and Passenger Tariff

To take effect February 1st, 1880.

This Tariff supersedes all others and all Special Rates. The Company reserves the right to vary therefrom at its pleasure.

Upper Columbia and Snake Rivers.

Up freight, not otherwise specified, per ton measurement.

Portland to Dalles................	$ 8 00	Portland to Blue Mountain Station.............	$26 50
do Columbus...................	13 00	do Ainsworth............................	27 50
do Umatilla....................	18 00	do Tucannon.............................	30 00
do Walla Walla and Whitman.....	25 00	do New York Bar, Penewawa & Almota.	32 50
do Milton Station...............	25 50	do Lewiston.............................	35 00

Special Rates.

FROM PORTLAND TO	Dalles	Columbus	Umatilla	Whitman and Walla Walla	Milton Station	Blue Mountain Station	Ainsworth	Tucannon	New York Bar, Penewawa and Almo	Lewiston
Separators, set up, 6-horse............	40 00	56 00	70 00	90 00	92 00	95 50	95 00	100 00	110 00	120
do do 8-horse............	45 00	60 00	80 00	102 00	104 00	108 00	107 00	112 00	125 00	135
do do 10-horse...........	50 00	72 00	90 00	114 00	116 00	121 00	120 00	125 00	137 50	150
do do 12-horse...........	55 00	80 00	100 00	126 00	128 50	133 50	131 00	135 00	147 50	160
Reapers and Harvesters, knocked dwn..	8 00	12 00	15 00	20 50	21 00	21 75	21 00	22 00	25 00	27 50
Headers, do	18 00	26 40	33 00	40 00	41 00	42 50	42 50	45 00	50 00	55
Mowers, do	7 00	9 60	12 00	15 00	15 50	16 00	16 00	17 50	18 75	20
Farm Wagons, 3¼ in axle under set up,	9 00	11 20	14 00	18 00	18 40	19 10	19 00	20 00	22 00	23
do do do knockd dn its b..	7 50	8 00	10 00	14 50	14 80	15 37	15 00	16 00	18 00	20
do 3¼ do over set up.....	12 00	14 00	17 50	24 00	24 50	25 50	25 00	24 00	26 50	27 50
do do knockd dn its b..	9 00	10 00	12 50	18 00	18 40	19 10	19 00	18 50	20 50	22 50
Header Wagons, knocked down lots 5...	6 00	6 40	8 00	12 00	12 25	12 75	13 00	14 00	16 00	18
Spring Wagons and Buggies, withot tp..	10 00	12 00	15 00	19 00	19 50	20 25	20 00	21 50	23 00	25
do do with top..	12 00	14 00	17 00	21 00	21 50	22 25	22 00	24 00	25 00	27
Hacks..................................	15 00	20 00	25 00	30 00	31 00	32 00	32 50	35 00	37 50	40
Sulkies................................	5 00	6 00	7 50	12 00	12 25	12 75	13 00	14 00	16 00	18
Drills, Seeders and Cultivators, set up..	7 00	10 00	12 50	17 00	17 50	18 10	17 50	18 50	20 50	22 50
Gang or Sulky Plows, set up...........	5 00	6 00	7 50	11 00	11 25	11 75	11 50	12 50	13 75	15
Walking Plows, knocked down.........	75	1 00	1 25	1 80	1 85	1 90	1 90	2 00	2 25	2 50
do set up................	1 50	2 00	2 50	3 50	3 60	3 70	3 50	3 60	4 00	4 50
Gang Harrows.........................	2 00	3 00	4 50	6 25	6 40	6 60	6 75	7 50	8 12	8 75
Sulky Rakes, knocked down...........	2 50	4 00	5 00	7 25	7 40	7 70	7 00	7 50	8 75	10

The Dalles - *The Weekly Mountaineer* - September 9, 1880, page two

OREGON STEAM NAVIGATION COMPANY   Capt. J. C. Ainsworth, **President**

Incorp:	10/21/1862	**Operated:**	12/1/62 to 3/31/80	**HQ city:**		Portland
Disposition:	sold to Oregon Railway & Navigation Company on March 31, 1880					
Predecessors:	Oregon Steam Navigation Company (Washington Territory)			**Incorp.:**	12/16/1860 to	12/5/1862
	Oregon Portage Rail Road				1861	11/6/1862
Miles track:	13.8	**Gauge:** 60"		**Date standardized:**		February 7, 1880
Main line:	The Dalles to Celilo and Bonneville to Cascade					
Rail wt.:	50 lbs.	**Max. grade:**		**Const. began:** grading		March 17, 1862
				laying rails		1862
Const. comp.:	(April 20, 1863)			**First train operated:**		1862

Locomotive engines:

Road No.	Name	Type	Dvr. in.	Bldr.	Bldr. No.	Date	Weight	Effort	Remarks
1*	Ainsworth	4-2-4T	55	Danforth	240	/62	35,000		to O.R.&N. #1
2*	Bradford	'	'	'	241	'	'		to O.R.&N. #2
3*	Ruckel	4-4-0	'	'	460	/66	50,000		to O.R.&N. #3
4*	Reed	'	'	'	461	'	'		to O.R.&N. #4
5*	Thompson	'	'	Cooke	1046	1/77	'		to O.R.&N. #5
6*	Sprague	'	'	'	1047	'	'		to O.R.&N. #6

Freight traffic: common carrier, portage

Its steamships operated to and from San Francisco to Astoria [established in 1811; a sawmill was built there in 1851 and a salmon packing plant in 1866] and to Portland and The Dalles. At that point they were stopped by a series of rapids in the Columbia River that extended to Celilo Falls. The subject portage road was to carry freight and passengers around these maritime obstructions. From Celilo to the east it was water travel again to eastern Washington Territory and northern Idaho Territory.

In May, 1861, the company sent its steamboat Colonel Wright loaded to capacity with freight and passengers for the new Idaho gold fields. Upon leaving Wallula, it entered the Snake River and thence into the Clearwater River at the future site of Lewiston and then 32 miles east of that point below the present town of Peck where the water became too hazardous. This initial trip of 290 miles was immediately followed by the inauguration of a regular schedule between Celilo and Lewiston.

Number 4, the Reed arrived about June 25, 1866. The telegraph line to Walla Walla was opened about June 4, 1870.

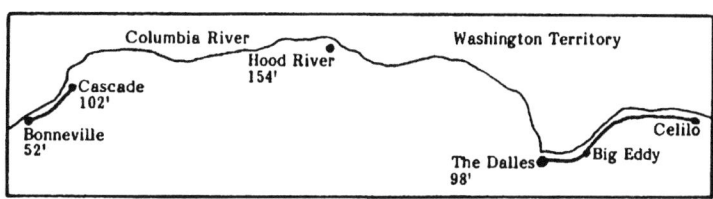

This mixed water and rail route must have been satisfactory, because by March, 1881, the carrier (Oregon Railway & Navigation Company had rails into Walla Walla (115 miles east of The Dalles), but didn't build west to Portland until November of 1882.

Bibliography: *Poor's 1879*, p. 952   Salem - *The Oregon Statesman* - March 30 to April 27, 1863   *Valuation 44*, p. 264

OREGON TRUNK RAILWAY   John F. Stevens, **President**

Incorp:	11/3/1909	**Operated:**	3/1/11 to 9/30/70	**HQ city:**		Portland
Disposition:	consolidated into Burlington Northern, Inc., on October 1, 1970					
Predecessors:	Central of Oregon Ry. Company			**Incorp.:**	6/18/1908 to	11/3/1909
	Oregon Trunk Line, Inc.				4/3/1906	11/3/1909
Miles track:	156.91	**Gauge:** 56½"				
Main line:	Wishram to Bend (and operating to Chemult, about 222 miles)					
Rail wt.:	90 lbs.	**Max. grade:** 1.0%		**Const. began:** grading		May 30, 1910
				laying rails		(October 13, 1910)
Const. comp.:	July 30, 1912			**First train operated:**		February 15, 1911

Locomotives:

156	4-6-0	63	BLW	23931	3/04	117,900	18,885	ex Spokane & Inland
157	'	69	Schen.	4703	2/98	155,600	25,623	ex Northern Pacific #201
158	'	'	'	4709	'	'	'	ex Northern Pacific #207

Freight traffic: common carrier, agriculture

Roster of 12/31/1917:
- 3 locomotives
- 10 tank cars

Published timetable dated:
May 1, 1916

Time	Station	Miles
10:30 p.m.	Fallbridge	
12:48 night	Oakbrook	39.9
2:56 a.m.	North Junction	75.4
5:00	Madras	110.0
5:25	Metolius	115.2
6:05	Opal City	127.0
6:55	Redmond	140.0
8:00	Bend	156.5

The Railroad Age Gazette, April 15, 1910, states "Construction bids to be opened April 18 for 111 miles; work is to start May 1."

The track was completed to Madras on February 15, 1911, and to Metolius on March first. The "gold spike" ceremony was held at Bend on October 5, 1911, but the track was not completed to that city until November first.

First listed in ICC for 6/30/11 as a class II operating subsidiary of Spokane, Portland & Seattle Railway Company (itself a subsidiary of Northern Pacific and Great Northern) with 130 miles owned and 127 in use; extended to 157 miles each by 6/30/12. In 1924, SP&S was listed as "independent" along with Oregon Trunk at which time 128 miles were owned and 152 operated. In 1955 it was 128 miles each and the same in 1970.

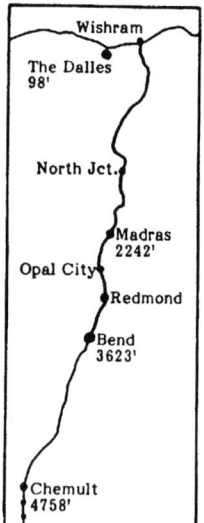

Bibliography: *Poor's 1914*, p. 1618

The Bend Bulletin - April 6, 1910 to March 8, 1911

OREGON - WASHINGTON RAILROAD & NAVIGATION COMPANY

Robert S. Lovett, **President**

Incorp:	11/23/1910	**Operated:** 12/24/10 to 12/31/35	**HQ city:**	Portland

Disposition: leased to Union Pacific Railroad Company on January 1, 1936

Predecessors:

Company	Incorp.	miles
Columbia River & Oregon Central Railroad Company	8/22/1903	45.31
Columbia Southern Railway Company	3/5/1897	69.46
Idaho Northern Railroad Company	1/10/1906	32.83
Ilwaco Railroad Company (36" gauge)	5/6/1907	28.65
Lake Creek & Coeur d'Alene Railroad Company	7/26/1906	14.18
Malheur Valley Railway Company	1/26/1906	37.33
Northwestern Railroad Company	5/12/1906	57.84
Olympia Terminal Railway Company	9/6/1911	7.43
Oregon & Washington Railroad Company	5/12/1906	25.30
Oregon Railroad & Navigation Company, The	7/16/1896	1,138.74
Oregon, Washington & Idaho Railroad Company	8/8/1903	72.03
Snake River Valley Railroad Company	3/3/1898	65.85
Umatilla Central Railroad Company	5/24/1906	14.21

All of the above were consolidated in on December 24, 1910, and are shown with the mileages contributed.

Miles track: 1,962.155   **Gauge:** 56½"

Main line: Portland to Huntington and Pendleton to Spokane

Rail wt.: 75/90 lbs.   **Max. grade:** 2.84%   **Const. began:** grading

laying rails

Const. comp.: 1924   **First train operated:** December 24, 1910

Freight traffic: common carrier, agriculture and mining

Rosters of

	12/31/1917	12/31/1923	+ 36" gauge
locomotives	302	312	4
passenger cars	275	243	14
freight cars	7,637	7,326	32

The company purchased 1,593.12 miles of track, constructed 369.31 and abandoned and revised 18.03 miles. The major construction was Ayer to Spokane and Vale to Burns, Oregon.

First listed in ICC for 6/30/11 as an operating subsidiary of Oregon Short Line Railroad Company with 1,760 miles owned and 1,856 in use. It was gradually increased to 2,011 miles owned and 2,224 operated by 12/31/20. Ten years later it was 2,006 miles owned and 2,337 operated. It was then leased to Union Pacific as a non-operating subsidiary. Mileage figures were again shown in ICC for 1955 at which time the carrier owned 1,850 miles; gradually reduced to 1,744 miles in 1972.

OREGON

123.

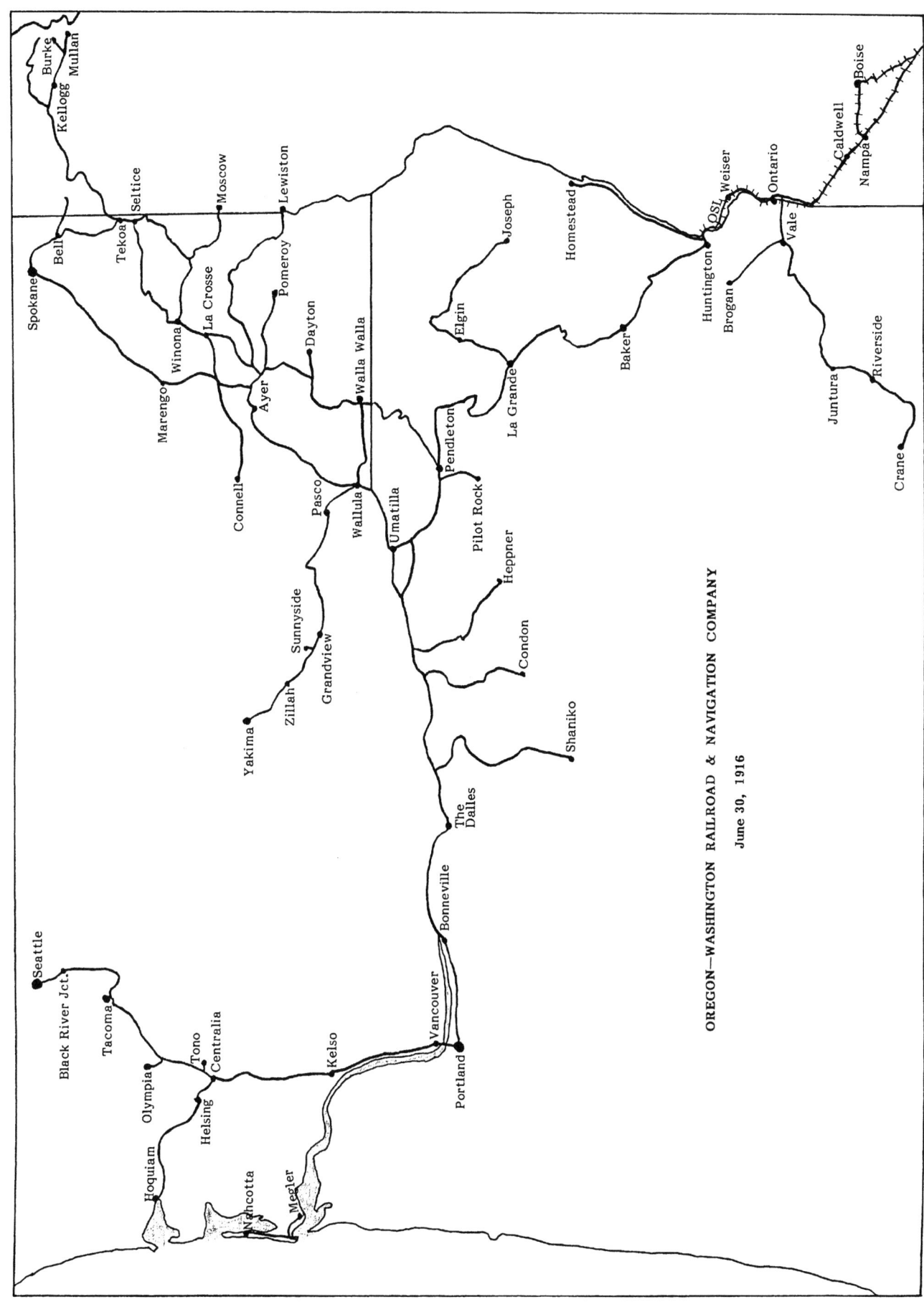

OREGON—WASHINGTON RAILROAD & NAVIGATION COMPANY
June 30, 1916

Locomotives:

Road No.	Type	Dvr. in.	Bldr.	Bldr. No.	Date	Weight	Effort	Remarks
10	2-6-0	55	Brooks	2409	11/93	102,200	22,762	1916 to Montana Western #10
20	0-6-0	51	Cooke	2265	9/95	98,000	19,440	
21-24	'	'	BLW	25523/605	4-5/05	146,400	28,915	
25-26	'	'	'	18704-05	3/01	129,000	27,915	
27	'	'	'	21731	3/03	'	'	
28-30	'	'	'	30676-78	4/07	140,000	'	
31-32	'	'	'	33788-89	9/09	'	'	
33-42*	'	'	'	36462/506	4/11	'	'	
44-49*	'	'	'	39637-42	4/13	145,000	'	
50-53*	'	'	Lima	1420-23	8/14	150,200	'	
54	4-4-0	57	Manch.	1086	10/82		9,947	1911 it was condemned
55	'	'	'	1085	11/82			
56-58	'	'	'	1086-88	2/83	53,800	12,412	
60	'	'	'	1094		'	'	
62	'	'	'	1096	'	'	'	
64	'	'	'	1098	'	'	'	
65	'	54	'	1099	'	48,600	9,947	8/1917 to Klamath Falls Ry.
66	'	'	'	1100	4/83	'	'	
68-70	'	'	'	1102-04	'	'	'	
71-73	'	'	BLW	6827/31	6/83	55,300	12,412	
80-87	'	62	R.I.	2444-51	9-10/90	68,600	16,782	
88-96*	4-4-2	81	BLW	36068-76	2/11	106,000	23,500	
97-102*	'	'	'	36113-18	'	'	'	
103-111	2-6-0	57	Schen.	2868-76	/89	91,000	17,973	
112-119	4-6-0	55	Manch.	1105-12	4-10/83	71,000	16,223	
130-135	'	63	Rome	507-12	10/89	92,350	17,534	
136-139	'	'	Cooke	2067-70	1/91	112,950	22,666	
140-147	'	'	'	2059-66	12/90			
160-164	2-8-0	51	Rome	429-33	10/89	116,950	25,600	
170-173	4-6-0	57	Cooke	2321-24	10/95	119,400	27,916	
174-178	'	'	'	2379-83	12/97	125,600	29,466	
179-184	4-6-0VC	63	BLW	19173/234	7/01	145,300	26,744	
190-193	4-6-2	77	Schen.	30035-38	9/04	222,000	29,920	
194-197	4-6-2C	'	BLW	25687/717	5/05	143,000	28,266	
198-200	4-6-2	'	'	28613/59	7/06	148,500	29,920	
201-207*	'	'	'	35948/57	1/11	'	'	
208-209*	'	'	'	36416-17	4/11	167,000	42,500	
210-215*	4-6-2S	'	Brooks	53349-54	4/13	'	'	
250-255	4-6-0	69	BLW	33712/43	8-9/09	159,000	33,390	
256-262*	'	'	'	36121/60	2/11	161,000	'	
300-305	'	63	Brooks	45045-50	4/08	198,000	36,570	
325-326	2-8-0	51	Schen.	43294-95	9/09	156,000	32,066	
327-329	'	55	Brooks	3075-77	11/98	148,920	33,747	
330-332	2-8-0VC	57	BLW	19103/64	6/01	167,340	34,649	
333-338	'	'	'	19301/43	7-8/01	'	'	
339-342	'	'	'	21768/840	3/03	'	'	
343	'	'	'	21920	4/03	'	'	
344	'	'	'	19303	7/01	'	'	
345-349	'	'	'	21011/197	10/02	181,200	40,900	
350-355	2-8-0	'	'	25271/94	3/05	187,000	43,300	
356-365	'	'	'	27205/42	1/06	'	'	
366-375	'	'	'	30245/81	2/07	189,970	'	
376-385	'	'	'	31251/328	7/07	'	'	
386-388	'	'	Brooks	44978-80	2/08	208,000	'	
500	2-8-2	'	BLW	34978	7/10	208,450	47,945	
501-520*	'	'	'	36324/51	3-4/11	'	50,470	
521-540*	'	'	'	36237/337		'	'	
541-555*	'	'	'	38293/361	9/12	'	'	
556-565*	'	63	'	39905-14	5/13	'	'	
700-702	2-8-8-2C	57	'	34016-18	11/09	394,000	94,880	
3620-3629	2-8-8-0C	'	Brooks	61910-19	8/20	490,000	106,900	
3803-3805*	'	'	'	63778-80	3/23	494,000	'	
5400-5404*	2-10-2	63	BLW	55903/96	1/23	291,000	70,450	
5405-5408*	'	'	'	56077-80	'	'	'	
9700-9707*	4-12-2S	67	Brooks	67596-603	7-8/28	368,500	96,650	

Bibliography: *Poor's 1914*, p. 1521   *Valuation 44*, p. 234

California State Railroad Museum Library   *Gerald M. Best Collection*
Oregon Steam Navigation Company engine house and turntable at Lower Cascade in 1867

Oregon State Library Collection   *Oregon 963*
Oregon Steam Navigation Company locomotive engine with four freight cars at The Dalles in 1863

OREGONIAN RAILROAD COMPANY

T. E. Stillman, **President**

Incorp: 4/19/1890	**Operated:** 5/20/90 to 7/31/93	**HQ city:** Portland

Disposition: sold to and merged in Oregon & California Rail Road Company on August 1, 1893

Predecessors:

	Incorp.:	to
Oregon Western Railroad Company	10/29/1889	5/20/1890
Oregonian Railway Company, Ltd. (Scotland)	5/4/1880	11/1/1889
The Oregon Railway Company, Ltd. (Oregon)	2/21/1880	12/11/1880
Willamette Valley Railroad Company, The	9/9/1878	4/2/1880
Dayton, Sheridan & Grande Ronde Railroad Company, The	11/17/1877	6/2/1879

Miles track: 153.11 **Gauge:** 36" **Date standardized:** 1893

Main line: Ray's Landing to Coburg and Dundee to Airlie

Rail wt.: 28/35 lbs. **Max. grade:** **Const. began:** grading April 19, 1880

laying rails (August 16, 1880)

Const. comp.: (August 31, 1882) **First train operated:** October 4, 1880

Locomotive engines:

Road No.	Type	Dvr. in.	Bldr.	Bldr. No.	Date	Weight	Effort	Remarks
1	2-4-0	31	National	259	5/78	21,200		Pioneer - ex Dayton, Sheridan & Grande Ronde #1
2	'	'	'	260	'	'		Progress - ex Dayton, Sheridan & Grande Ronde #2
4*	2-6-0	38	Pitts.	430	7/80	37,500		Brownsville - 12/28/03 to San Joaquin & S.N. #5
5*	'	35½	Porter	374	6/80	36,000		(7/1899) to Sierra Valley #3
6*	'	'	'	375	7/80	'		Dallas - 1/26/1895 to Sierra Valleys #1
7*	'	'	'	376	8/80	'		Scio - 1/26/1895 to Sierra Valleys #2
8*	4-4-0	44	BLW	5748	8/81	43,000		Scott - 12/28/1903 to San Joaquin & S.N. #4

(The above were narrow gauge - the following standard gauge)

10	4-4-0	56	Rogers	1551	9/68	38,400	16,770	ex Central Pacific #110 - to S.P. #1426
11	'	'	'	1539	8/68	'	'	ex Central Pacific #104 - to S.P. #1427
12	'	'	'	1543	'	'	'	ex Central Pacific #105 - to S.P. #1428
13	'	'	'	1550	9/68	'	'	ex Central Pacific #109 - to S.P. #1429

Freight traffic: common carrier, agriculture

Roster of 6/30/1888:
- 8 locomotive engines
- 6 passenger cars
- 3 mail and express
- 23 box cars
- 98 stock cars
- 116 platform cars
- 3 cabooses

The carrier was leased to Oregon Railway & Navigation Company on October 1, 1881, for operation by that company. It reverted to independent status on November 15, 1884.

Poor's 1889, page 894, states that "In January, 1887, connection was made with the Portland and Willamette Road, running from Dundee Jct. to Portland, 29.6 miles, and the roads are now operated as one."

First published timetable:
April, 1885
"Known since 1881 as Narrow Gauge Divn. of Oregon Railway & Navig. Now independent, in receivership. Thought to be running as follows."

West Side Division:
- 9:20 a.m. Portland
- 1:45 p.m. Whites
- 2:25 Sheridan Jct.
- 6:45 Airlie

(Whites to Airlie, 38 miles)
Also Sheridan Jct. to Sheridan

East Side Division:
??????????????

Published timetable dated:
October 5, 1885
"At last accounts the trains were running as follows:"

East Side Division:
- 12:50 p.m. Portland (via O. & C.)
  Woodburn
  Silverton
  West Stayton   6:30 a.m.
- 5:55 a.m. Thompson's for Coburg   miles 36
- 11:15 Coburg for Lebanon Jct.   32
- 3:50 p.m. Brownsville for W. Stayton 41
- 9:06 Lebanon Jct. for Brownsville 23

Station list and mile posts on Portland & Yamhill Railroad Company + Oregonian Railway Company:

Portland	0.0	Mt. Angel	49.7	South Santiam	83.8	Sheridan Jct.	50.2
Oswego	7.3	Silverton	53.9	Lebanon Jct.	90.8	Ballston	52.9
Tualatin	13.1	Howell Prairie	58.2	Brownsville	103.7	Sheridan	57.2
Newburg	26.4	Macleay	63.8	Coburg	123.0		
Dundee Jct.	28.8	Waldo Hills	66.1				
Fulquartz	31.2	Aumsville	69.1	Dayton	32.7	Perrydale	52.4
Ray's Landing	33.3	West Stayton	72.9	Lafayette	34.7	Dallas	63.0
St. Paul	35.4	North Santiam	75.0	Dayton Jct.	37.8	Monmouth	70.1
Woodburn	43.4	West Scio	78.3	Whites	44.8	Airlie	79.4

OREGON 127.

Details of the construction are scant. The following was taken from volume 45 of the *Valuation Reports* and expanded upon from newspaper articles.

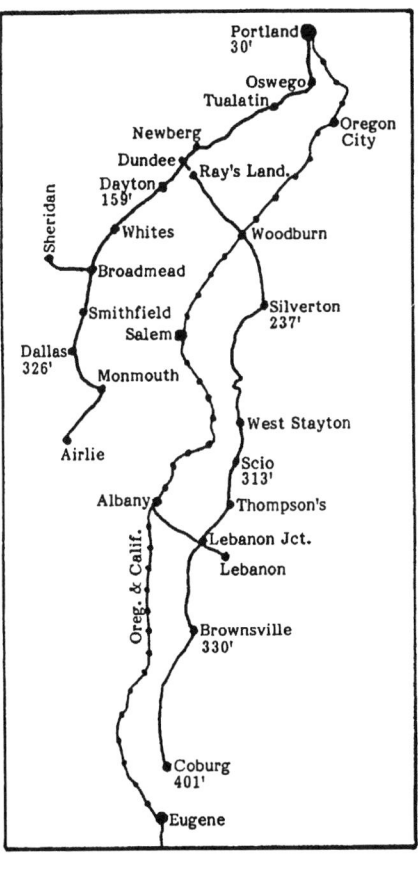

Dayton, Sheridan & Grande Ronde:
  Dayton to Smithfield, 22.95 miles.
  Broadmead (now Sheridan Jct.) to Sheridan, 7.24 miles.
  Total of 30.19 miles of narrow gauge track.

Willamette Valley Railroad:
  No construction; track mileage as above.

Oregon Railway Co. (Oregon):
  Dayton to Dallas, 26.95 miles, opened May 30, 1880.
  Sheridan Jct. to Sheridan, 7.24 miles.
  Total of 34.19 miles of narrow gauge track.

Oregonian Railway Co. (Scotland):
  Dundee to Airlie, 50.98 miles.
  Ray's Landing to Coburg, 89.24 miles.
  Branches aggregating 12.89 miles.
  This company completed 70 miles begaun by its predecessors and 48.92 miles of its own construction.

  The predecessor began construction April 19, 1880, at Silverton and built north and south, opening Ray's to Silverton, 20.6 miles, on October 4, 1880. It was extended to Scio on November 20, 1880, and to Brownsville December 28. The west side line was completed to Airlie in September, 1881, and on the east side to Coburg in July, 1882, and operating Dundee to Portland on November 26, 1887.
  The company owned 153.11 miles of narrow gauge track.

Oregon Western Railroad:
  No construction; track as above.

Oregonian Railroad:
  The east side section, 79.80 miles, was sold December 5, 1890, to Oregon & California; Ray's to Woodburn had been abandoned on a date not determined. The property was 57.50 miles of 36 inch track on July 31, 1893, when the company and the west side track was sold to the successor. The record is not clear, but it appears that the tracks were made standard gauge in 1890 and 1893 by Oregon & California Rail Road Company.

Listed in first ICC (6/30/88) as an operating independent with 147 miles owned and in use. It was increased to 152 miles owned and 182 operated (to Portland) by 6/30/89. It was reorganized at "Railroad" on May 21, 1890. By 6/30/91 it was a 57-mile non-operating subsidiary of the Southern Pacific Company. In 1891 the carrier consisted of a main line from Dundee to Airlie and to Sheridan, 58.198 miles; it had abandoned four branches totalling 15.326 miles.

Bibliography: *Poor's 1889*, p. 894   Oregon PUC report 1893, p. 60   *Valuation 45*, p. 423
              Salem - *Oregon Statesman* - June 4 to August 27, 1880

PACIFIC & EASTERN RAILWAY COMPANY   W. C. Morris, **President**

Incorp:	5/27/1907	**Operated:**	5/27/07 to 1/30/19	**HQ city:**	Portland
Disposition:	sold to Brownlee-Olds Lumber Company on August 20, 1920				
Predecessor:	Medford & Crater Lake Railroad Company		**Incorp.:**	12/29/1904 to 5/10/1907	
Miles track:	32.92	**Gauge:**	56½"		
Main line:	Medford to Butte Falls				
Rail wt.:	60/77½ lbs.	**Max. grade:**		**Const. began:** grading	April 4, 1905
				laying rails	August 15, 1905
Const. comp.:	April 1, 1911			**First train operated:**	November 5, 1905

Locomotives:

Road No.	Type	Dvr. in.	Bldr.	Bldr. No.	Date	Weight	Effort	Remarks
101	4-8-0	55	Rogers	5404	7/99	148,000	32,140	acq. 5/5/1910 ex Great Northern Ry. #736
102								
103	4-6-0	63	Rogers	5772	7/02	120,000	25,330	acq. 3/5/1910 ex G.N. #938-12/1912 to S.P.&S.

Freight traffic: common carrier, logging and fruit

Rosters of   6/30/1909 - 12/31/1917:

locomotives	3	3
passenger cars		4
freight cars	18	17

Published timetable dated:
November 10, 1907
8:00 a.m.   Medford   10:10
9:00   Eagle Point   9:00 a.m.
A. A. Davis, president

Published timetable dated:
July 4, 1915

9:00 a.m.	Medford		3:15
9:29	Table Rock	9	2:40
9:45	Eagle Point	12	2:25
10:30	Derby	23	1:30 p.m.
11:15	Butte Falls	33	12:45 noon

L. C. Gillman, president

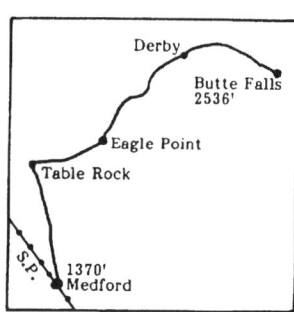

The track was completed to Eagle Point about August 1, 1906.

Medford & Crater Lake Railroad Co. was first listed in ICC for 6/30/06 as an 11-mile independent, not in operation. It was sold at a receiver's sale. Pacific & Eastern Railway Co. was first shown 6/30/07 as an independent with 11 miles owned and in operation. It was extended to 15 miles by 6/30/10. By 6/30/11 it was a 34-mile operating subsidiary, class III, of Spokane, Portland & Seattle Railway Co. It was then sold to Mr. M. D. Olds.

The cost of road and equipment was $2,081,727. It was originally projected some 70 miles more to Klamath Falls and a meeting with Great Northern Railway Company.

Bibliography: *Poor's 1910*, p. 1318   *Medford Mail* - March 17 to November 10, 1905
                 The Railway Age - April 7, 1905 - July 14, 1905 - August 3, 1906

Oregon State Library Collection
Oregonian Railway Company number 7, Scio, is shown in this undated photograph at Dallas, possibly on May 30, 1880, when the narrow gauge track was placed in operation to that point.

OREGON 129.

PACIFIC RAILWAY & NAVIGATION COMPANY

E. E. Lytle, President

Incorp: 10/13/1905 **Operated:** 1/1/12 to 7/1/15 **HQ city:** Hillsboro
Disposition: sold to Southern Pacific Company on July 1, 1915
Miles track: 91.20 **Gauge:** 56½"
Main line: Hillsboro to Tillamook
Rail wt.: 75 lbs. **Max. grade:** 3.37% **Const. began:** grading November 20, 1905
laying rails December 6, 1905
Const. comp.: June 30, 1911 **First train operated:** September 2, 1907

Locomotives:

Road No.	Type	Dvr. in.	Bldr.	Bldr. No.	Date	Weight	Effort	Remarks
1	4-4-0	63	BLW	5310	10/80	77,100	13,100	acq. 12/5/1905 ex Northern Pacific #839
2	'	'	'	2895	8/72	41,950	10,524	acq. 6/19/1907 ex Southern Pacific #1507
3	2-6-0	57	'	6824	6/83	68,700	14,480	acq. 6/14/1910 ex Southern Pacific #1605

Freight traffic: common carrier, lumber

Rosters of   6/30/1906 - 6/30/1914:
  locomotives   1   9
  passenger cars   2   3
  freight cars   10   23

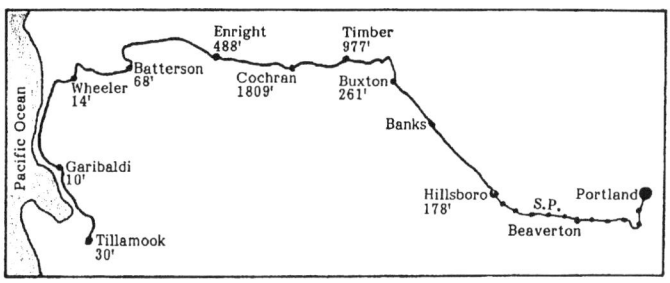

Published timetable dated:
  April 20, 1916 (as S.P. Lines)
  9:20 a.m.   Hillsboro
  10:08   Buxton   mp 16.24
  10:58   Timber   28.21
  11:33   Cochrane   35.03
  12:22   Enright   46.00
  2:34   Garibaldi   80.15
  3:20   Tillamook   90.18

A construction note from *Railway & Engineering Review* for November 20, 1909: Seventy miles have been graded; 35 miles of rails laid from Hillsboro to the west and 12 from Tillamook to the east. To be completed July 1, 1910.

First listed in ICC for 6/30/06 as an operating independent with ten miles owned, not in use. By 6/30/07 it was an operating subsidiary of Southern Pacific Company with 17 miles owned. It was 20 miles in 1908, 32 in 1909, 55 in 1910 and 78 miles by 6/30/11, still not in operation. By 6/30/12 it was 91 miles owned and 112 operated; in 1914 it was 91 miles each.

The first Portland to Tillamook train was operated on October 9, 1911; it had trackage rights with Soustherm Pacific Railroad Co. to operate to Portland, 21 miles east of Hillsboro. There were 13 tunnels and 11.6 miles of sidings.

The investment in land, construction and equipment was $5,768,268. The property was sold February 1, 1990, by the Southern Pacific Company to Port of Tillamook Bay Railroad.

Bibliography: *Poor's 1914*, p. 1553   *The Railway Age* - November 17 and December 8, 1905   *Valuation 45*, p. 362
  Hillsboro Independent - October 20 to December 8, 1905 and August 30, 1907
  Spokane - *Spokesman-Review* - October 10, 1911

PELICAN BAY LUMBER COMPANY

President

Incorp: 4/3/1911 **Operated:** 1911 to 1934 **HQ city:** Algoma
Disposition: abandoned
Miles track: 44 **Gauge:** 56½"
Main line: from Bly (on Oregon, California & Eastern) to the south
Rail wt.: 68 lbs. **Max. grade:** 4.0% **Const. began:** grading 1911

Locomotives:

1*	8x10	2T Shay	27½	Lima	2410	9/11	56,000	12,850	to Shaw-Bertram Lumber Co. #1
2*	10x12	'	29½	'	2722	11/13	84,000	16,900	to Lamm Lumber Co. #1
3*	19x26	2-6-2T	48	Cooke	62515	/20	146,000	29,900	
28		2T Shay	36	Lima	2268	2/10	120,000	23,850	ex Pacific Lumber Co. (Cal.) #28

Freight traffic: logging

POLK OPERATING COMPANY

				President
Incorp:	10/14/1926	Operated: 10/26 to 1943	HQ city:	Grande Ronde
Disposition:	abandoned			
Predecessor:	Oregon Coast Range Lumber Company		from: 1924	to 10/1926
Miles track:	21	Gauge: 56½"		

Main line:

| Rail wt.: | 56 lbs. | Max. grade: | 4.0% | Const. began: | grading | 1924 |

Locomotives:

Road No.	Type	Dvr. in.	Bldr.	Bldr. No.	Date	Weight	Effort	Remarks
1 ?	2T Shay	26½	Lima	1580	10/05	40,000	10,700	ex Spaulding-Miami Lbr. Co. #1 ?
5	3T Shay	36	"	2757	4/14	146,000	30,350	acq. 9/1924 ex Spaulding-Miami Lbr. #5
6	"	"	"	3096	7/30	179,000	35,100	acq. 2/1930
7	2T Shay	32	"	611	12/00	80,000	17,500	acq. 9/1924 ex Spaulding-Miami Lbr. #7
8	"	29½	"	2666	7/13	84,000	16,900	acq. 9/1924 ex Spaulding-Miami Lbr. #8

Freight traffic: logging

PORTLAND & SOUTHWESTERN RAILROAD COMPANY

				James B. Kerry,	President
Incorp:	12/19/1905	Operated: (8/28/06) to 1944		HQ city:	Linnton
Disposition:	abandoned December 31, 1945				
Miles track:	10.773	Gauge: 56½"			
Main line:	Boom to Scappoose and into the forest to Camp One				
Rail wt.:	45/60/85 lbs.	Max. grade: 2.35%	Const. began: grading	(March 19, 1906)	
Const. comp.:	(May 14, 1909)		First train operated:	(August 25, 1906)	

Locomotives:

1*	16x24	2-6-2	44	BLW	28465	6/06			to Clark & Wilson #15
2*	10x12	2T Shay	29½	Lima	1665	4/06	74,000	16,900	10/1908 to Seaside Lbr. & Mfg.
2-2d*	18/28x28	2-6-6-2	51	BLW	35785	12/10			
3*	11x12	2T Shay	32	Lima	1818	2/07	90,000	20,300	2/1913 to Nehalem Timber & Log.
4*	"	"	"	"	1943	8/07	100,000	22,575	2/1913 to Nehalem Timber & Log.
5*	12x15	3T Shay	36	"	2367	11/10	140,000	29,800	to Fir Tree Lumber Co. #5
16		2-8-2T	44	Brooks	64148	3/23	190,000	35,200	ex Sugar Pine Lbr. (Calif.)
17*		2-8-2	48	BLW	57201	9/23	179,000	34,400	
18		2-8-2T	42	"	58825	11/25			ex Clark & Wilson #6
20		"	"	"	58419	5/25			ex Bear Creek Logging Co. #4

Freight traffic: logging

Roster of 12/31/1919:
- 1 rod engine
- 3 geared engines
- 2 flat cars
- 75 logging trucks

First listed in ICC for 6/30/07 as an operating independent with 7.67 miles owned (from Chapman Landing to Alder Creek) and in use. It was gradually extended to 12 miles by 6/30/14 and to 17 owned and 11 operated in 1924. In 1926 it was 19 miles owned and 111 operated. In 1928 it was 11 miles each and then unchanged until abandonment.

The carrier was built by Chapman Timber Co. and owned by it until 1913 when it passed to Nehalem Timber & Logging Co. It was purchased in 1926 by Clark & Wilson Lumber Co.

The line cost $341,564 to build and $19,703 to equip.

Bibliography: *Poor's 1914*, p. 1879   Oregon PUC report 1907, p. 160   *Valuation 114*, p. 52

PORTLAND & YAMHILL RAILROAD COMPANY

L. R. Fields, President

Incorp:	6/14/1892	**Operated:** 8/5/92 to 7/31/93	**HQ city:**	Portland
Disposition:	sold to Oregon & California Rail Road Company on July 22, 1893, effective August 1			
Predecessor:	Portland & Willamette Valley Railway Company		**Incorp.:** 1/19/1885 to 8/5/1892	
Miles track:	28.34	**Gauge:** 36"	**Date standardized:**	1893
Main line:	Portland to Dundee			
Rail wt.:	40 lbs. steel	**Max. grade:** 2.74%	**Const. began:** grading (January 18, 1886)	
			laying rails August 2, 1886	
Const. comp.:	(December 31, 1886)		**First train operated:** October 9, 1886	

Locomotive engines:

Road No.	Type	Dvr. in.	Bldr.	Bldr. No.	Date	Weight	Effort	Remarks
1	2-4-0	31	Baily	259	5/78	21,200		ex Oregonian #1
2	'	'	'	260	'	'		ex Oregonian #2
1-2d	2-6-0	44	BLW	5121	5/80	39,000	6,557	acq. 1887 ex Utah & Northern #19
2-2d	'	48	Rome	21	4/83	65,000	12,250	acq. 1/1887 ex Cincinnati Northern #8
3	'	'	'	22	'	'	'	acq. 1/1887 ex Toledo, Cincin. & St. L. #49

Freight traffic: common carrier, agriculture

Rosters of   6/30/1891 - 6/30/1893:

locomotive engines	3	3
passenger cars	6	7
flat cars	73	94
box cars	3	3

First published timetable:

January 1, 1887

10:10 a.m.	Portland	
1:15 p.m.	Dundee Jct.	m.p. 28.8
2:30	Whites	42.8
3:13	Sheridan Jct.	50.2
4:50	Dallas	63.0
5:30	Monmouth	70.1
6:15	Airlie	79.4

Operations for year ending June 30, 1889:
  passenger earnings $28,584.80
  freight revenue   62,429.10

A report for the year ending June 30, 1893:

  The company carried 161,084 passengers from whom it collected $41,498.82 and had freight revenue of $63,127.60. The carrier replaced 10,952 ties at a cost of twenty-five cents each; fuel consumption was 2,041 cords which not cost $2.56 each.

  While the freight income remained largely unchanged from 1889, the passenger earnings improved markedly.

The original roadbed and bridges were constructed for a standard gauge line. The grading work began at Dundee.

The line was placed in commercial operation December 11, 1886, from Elk Rock (near Oswego) to Dundee. The major trestles: Clehalem Creek, 700 feet - Blair Creek, 1,000 feet - Rock Creek, 1,800 feet - Tualatin River, 180 feet.

In the year ending June 30, 1890, their small locomotive engines burned 3,090 cords of soft wood costing $2.20 each.

Listed in first ICC (6/30/88) as a 30-mile operating subsidiary of Oregonian Railway Co. By 6/30/89 it was shown as an independent with 46 miles owned and 31 operated and then reduced to 28 miles each by 6/30/90 and the same in 1891. The carrier was placed in receivership on February 2, 1892. By 6/30/92 it was a non-operating subsidiary of Southern Pacific Co. with 28 miles owned.

Portland & Yamhill was first shown for 6/30/93 as an operating subsidiary of Southern Pacific Co. with 28.5 miles owned and in use.

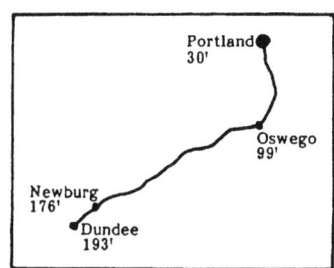

Bibliography: *Poor's 1889*, p. 899   Oregon PUC reports 1889 to 1894   *Valuation 45*, p. 293
McMinnville - *West Side Telephone* - July 2 to October 12, 1886
Oregon Historical Society *Quarterly* vol. 20 #2   *The Railway Age* - March 25 to December 23, 1886

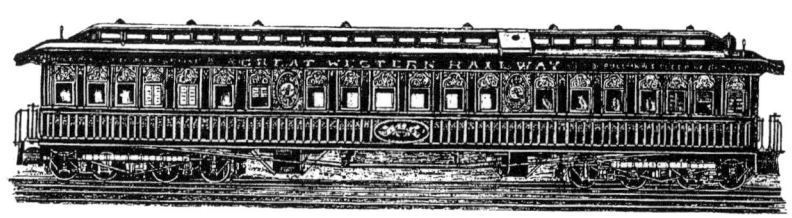

PORTLAND, EUGENE & EASTERN RAILWAY COMPANY

Alvadore Welch, **President**

Incorp:	11/25/1907	**Operated:** 12/27/07 to 7/1/15	**HQ city:**	Portland

Disposition: sold to the Southern Pacific Company on July 1, 1915

Predecessors:
Sheridan & Willamina Railroad Company	**Incorp.:**	5/4/1907 to	6/9/1913
Corvallis & Alsea River Railway Company		7/19/1907	7/20/1911
Eugene & Eastern Railway Company		5/11/1907	12/27/1907

Miles track:	107.76	**Gauge:**	56½"	
Main line:	Eugene to Corvallis			
Rail wt.:	75 lbs.	**Max. grade:** 2.33%	**Const. began:** grading	1907
			laying rails	July 18, 1907
Const. comp.:	(September 30, 1913)		**First train operated:**	September 26, 1907

Locomotives:

Road No.	Type	Dvr. in.	Bldr.	Bldr. No.	Date	Weight	Effort	Remarks
1	2T Shay	29½	Lima	884	5/04	92,700	15,625	ex Corvallis & A.R. #1 - sold 11/1915
2	2 truck	36	Heisler	1151	8/09	72,000		ex Corvallis & A.P. #2 - sold 11/1915
3	4-4-0	63	BLW	2697	2/72	61,600		scrapped in November, 1913
4								
100	0-4-4-0E	36½	BLW	38086	8/12		400 h.p.	ex Southern Pacific #200
101	'	'	'	38154	'		'	ex Southern Pacific #201
102	'	'	'	38298	9/12		'	ex Southern Pacific #202

Freight traffic: common carrier, agriculture and lumber

Roster of 6/30/1912:
- 2 locomotives
- 1 passenger car
- 38 freight cars

According to ICC *Valuation Reports,* the carrier constructed 34.41 miles and acquired 34.94 miles of electrical lines, but details and dates are unusually lacking and vague.

The company started construction of two steam lines in the summer of 1912. Monroe to Eugene, 22.45 miles, was opened September 4, 1913; Canby to Molalla, 10.45 miles, opened 16 days later.

The Eugene & Eastern Railway contributed 14.96 miles in and between Eugene and Springfield.

The carrier purchased electric lines as follows: on December 31, 1908, it took title to .87 miles in Albany - May 1, 1912, it got 11.67 miles in Salem from Portland Railway, Light & Power Co. and 7.44 from Walling to Tualatin River on January 31, 1913, from the last named company.

Corvallis & Alsea River provided 28.08 miles and Sheridan & Willamina Railroad Co. 5.35 miles making a total steam operation of 66.33 miles; electric lines totalled 34.94 miles. There were also constructed 6.49 miles of steam-operated branch line extensions which brought the declared total to 107.76 miles.

First listed in ICC for 6/30/15 as a class II operating subsidiary of Southern Pacific Company with 108 miles owned and 111 in use. It appears that ICC considered the carrier to be primarily an electric operation, hence the late date in being included.

Bibliography: *Poor's 1911,* p. 2405 Oregon PUC report 1909, p. 179 *Valuation 45,* p. 363
Corporate History of the Southern Pacific Company as of June 30, 1916
Salem - *Weekly Oregon Statesman* - September 27, 1907

OREGON 133.

PORT OF TILLAMOOK BAY RAILROAD

Port of Tillamook Bay, **Owner**

Incorp:	not	Operated: 3/27/86 to
Disposition:	in operation 1993	
Miles track:	94.4	Gauge: 56½"
Main line:	Hillsboro to Tillamook	
Rail wt.:	75/132 lbs.	Max. grade: 3.37%

HQ city: Tillamook

Locomotives:

Road No.	Type	Bldr.	Bldr. No.	Date	Weight	Effort	Remarks
3771	B-B	EMD				1,750 h.p.	acq. 9/93 ex S.P. #3771
4368	C-C	'	20203	4/55		1,800 h.p.	acq. 3/86 ex S.P. #4368
4381	'	'	19945	3/55		'	acq. 3/86 ex S.P. #4381
4405	'	'				'	acq. 9/93 ex S.P. #4405
4414	'	'	21314	4/56		'	acq. 3/86 ex S.P. #4414
4432	'	'				'	acq. 9/93 ex S.P. #4432

Freight traffic: common carrier, agriculture, lumber

Roster of 12/31/1993:
  6 locomotives

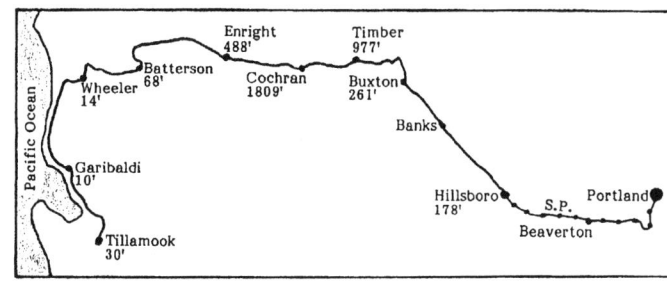

Bibliography: Direct communication

SALEM, FALLS CITY & WESTERN RAILWAY COMPANY

Louis Gerlinger, **President**

Incorp:	10/24/1901	Operated: 5/31/03 to 7/1/15
Disposition:	sold to Southern Pacific Company on July 1, 1915	
Miles track:	28.35	Gauge: 56½"
Main line:	Dallas to Black Rock and Dallas to Salem	
Rail wt.:	50/60 lbs.	Max. grade: 4.20%

HQ city: Salem

Const. began: grading (September 16, 1902)
laying rails December 12, 1902

Const. comp.: (March 14, 1913) at Salem   First train operated: May 31, 1903

Locomotives:

Road No.	Cyln.	Type	Dvr. in.	Bldr.	Bldr. No.	Date	Weight	Effort	remarks
1		4-4-0	57	BLW	6019	1/82	43,800		acq. 2/1903 ex O.R.&N. #32
1-2d		motor car		McKeen		/09			passenger, mail, Wells Fargo express car
2		4-4-0	57	BLW	6033	2/82	43,800		acq. 2/1903 ex O.R.&N. #33
2-2d		'	'	Taunton		/85	65,000		ancestry not known - scrapped 1/24/1917
3		2-6-0	48	BLW	2094	3/70			acq. 8/1905 ex O.R.&N. #15
4*	10x12	2T Shay	29½	Lima	1807	11/06	74,000	16,900	1917 to Spaulding Logging Co. #6
5*	12x12	'	36	'	1939	6/07	110,000	23,850	to Spaulding Logging Co. #5
6		2-6-0	57	BLW	6217	5/82	68,700	14,480	acq. 1916 ex O.P.&E. #6 - SCR 1/1917
7		'	53	'	5029	3/80	65,000	15,573	acq. 2/10/1909 ex S.P. #1600 - SO 5/16
8*	17x20	2-8-0	40	Lima	1008	4/06	89,000	22,110	to Southern Pacific #2501-2d

Freight traffic: common carrier, lumber

Rosters of 6/30/1906 - 6/30/1913:

locomotives	4	4
passenger	1	1
box cars	1	4
flat cars	25	97
motor car		1

First published timetable:
November 23, 1903 - daily exc. Sun.
7:45 a.m. Dallas   9:55
8:20   Falls City 9:20 a.m.

First listed in ICC for 6/30/03 as an operating independent with 9.5 miles owned and in use. It was increased to 13 miles each by 6/30/06 and 13 owned and 50 operated (joint trackage to Newberg) by 6/30/07; this continued through 1909. By 6/30/10 it was 27 miles owned and 64 operated; same in 1911. By 6/30/12 this class II common carrier was an operating subsidiary of Southern Pacific Company with 27 miles owned and 64 operated. By 6/30/15 it was 28 miles each.

Dallas to Falls City was completed on May 29, 1903; Falls City to Black Rock opened November 2, 1905. Dallas eastward to West Salem placed in operation October 1, 1909, and to Salem as shown above.

Published timetable dated:
April 20, 1916 - Southern Pacific
9:45 a.m.	Salem	
10:00	West Salem	1.8
10:33	Gerlinger	10.1
11:20	Dallas	15.1
11:35	Falls City	24.2
11:50	Black Rock	28.0

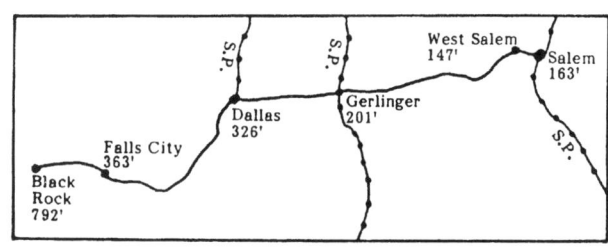

The road cost $792,569 to construct and equip. We can assume that the carrier built to Salem for water transportation on the Willamette River, but what was the attraction of joint trackage to Newberg for one train per day?

Bibliography: *Poor's 1907*, p. 870   Dallas - *Polk County Itemizer* - August 29, 1902 to June 5, 1903   *Valuation 45*, p. 370

Oregon State Library Collection   19 - 7 Trover Views
Salem, Falls City & Western Railway Co. gasoline passenger car about 1911

SEASHORE RAILROAD COMPANY   D. K. Warren, President

Incorp:	5/17/1893	**Operated:**	6/9/93 to 8/26/97		**HQ city:**	Astoria

Disposition: merged into Astoria & Columbia River Railroad Company on August 27, 1897

Predecessors:	Astoria & Portland Railway Company	**Incorp.:**	3/16/1892 to 5/17/1893
	Astoria & South Coast Railroad Company		8/18/1888 3/16/1892

Miles track: 15.78   **Gauge:** 56½"
Main line: Youngs Bay to Seaside
Rail wt.: 40/50 lbs.   **Max. grade:**   **Const. began:** grading   March 4, 1889
                                                            laying rails   May 11, 1889
Const. comp.: (June 30, 1890)   **First train operated:**   June 12, 1890

Locomotives:
2
26   Frank J. Taylor

OREGON   135.

Major business: passengers and lumber

Roster of 6/30/1896:
    2   locomotives (one leased)
    2   passenger cars
    2   box cars
   15   flat cars

First listed in ICC for 6/30/90 as an operating independent with 16 miles owned and in use. For 6/30/93 it was 15.78 miles each. By 6/30/95 it was 20 miles and controlled by Oregon Improvement Co. By 6/30/96 it was a 15.5 mile independent and then unchanged until its sale.

Notes from Oregon PUC reports:
   6/30/1890 - Not yet in operation.
   6/30/1891 - John Q. A. Bowlby, president; 15.78 miles in operation. Carried 12,919 passengers for $5,919.29 and had freight income of $1,881.86.
   6/30/1893 - It states that "Road and equipment purchased from Frank Patton and H. C. Thompson, the Astoria & South Coast Railroad Co. for $137,000." It included one locomotive, 10 passenger cars, 14 freight cars, a 74-foot draw bridge and 16 trestles with a total length of 7,957 feet.

A locally built three-compartment passenger car was called Dundee.

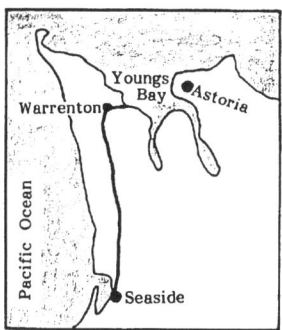

Bibliography: *Poor's 1892*, p. 11 and *1897*, p. 265   Oregon Historical Society - *Quarterly* - volumes 15 and 58
                Morning Astorian - January 30 to March 21, 1889 and April 1 to June 13, 1890

SHAW-BERTRAM LUMBER COMPANY   President

Incorp: 7/29/1920   **Operated:** 1920 to 1936   **HQ city:** Klamath Falls
Disposition: abandoned
Miles track: 30   **Gauge:** 56½"
Main line: Northwest from Oregon, California & Eastern junction south of Sprague River
Rail wt.: 40/50 lbs.   **Max. grade:** 5.0%   **Const. began:** grading   1920

Locomotives:

Road No.	Cyln.	Type	Dvr. in.	Bldr.	Bldr. No.	Date	Weight	Effort	Remarks
1		2T Shay	27½	Lima	2410	9/11	56,000	12,850	ex Pelican Bay Lumber Co. #1
2		2 truck	40	Heisler	1254	5/12	120,000		to Lamm Lumber Co. #2
3*	17¼x14	3 truck	38	'	1539	1/27	160,000	34,220	to Weyerhaeuser Timber Co. #3
3-2d	?	2T Shay	32	Lima	1946	4/07	90,000	20,350	acq. 8/1928 ex Braymill White Pine Co.
4*	13x15	3T Shay	36	'	3331	3/29	188,000	38,200	1/1936 to White River Lumber Co. #6
5		2T Shay	32	'	3249	1/24	124,000	22,580	acq. 10/1929 ex Snow Lbr.-sold 10/1937

Freight traffic: logging

SHERIDAN & WILLAMINA RAILROAD COMPANY   Jesse Edwards, **President**

Incorp: 5/4/1907   **Operated:** 11/11/07 to 6/9/13   **HQ city:** Portland
Disposition: sold to Portland, Eugene & Eastern Railway Company on June 9, 1913
Miles track: 5.35   **Gauge:** 56½"
Main line: Sheridan to Willamina
Rail wt.: 60 lbs.   **Max. grade:** 1.00%   **Const. began:** grading   (May 16, 1907)
                                                                                                   laying rails   1907
Const. comp.: 1907   **First train operated:**   1907

Locomotives:

| 6 | 4-4-0 | 63 | BLW | 2697 | 2/72 | 41,950 | 10,880 | acq. 12/30/1911 ex S.P. #1503 - to P.E.&E. #3 |

Freight traffic: common carrier, lumber

Roster of 6/30/1910:
- 2 locomotives
- 1 passenger car
- 9 freight cars

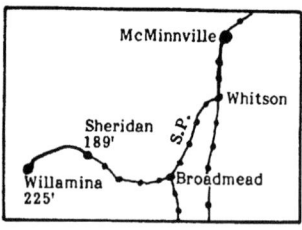

First listed in ICC for 6/30/07 as an operating independent with six miles owned, not in use. By the next year five miles were owned and operated. By 6/30/10 it was five miles owned and 13 (to Broadmead) operated. By 6/30/12 it was six miles each. The property was sold on March 1, 1913, to be effective June 9.

Portland, Eugene & Eastern operated the carrier from April 1, 1913.

The road cost a modest $45,325.19 to build and equip.

Bibliography: *Poor's 1911*, p. 1330   Valuation 45, p. 370

SHEVELIN-HIXON LUMBER COMPANY   President

Incorp:		**Operated:**	1916	to	1922	**HQ city:**	Bend

Disposition: abandoned

Miles track: 88   **Gauge:** 56½"

Main line:

Rail wt.: 60 lbs.   **Max. grade:** 2.6%   **Const. began:** grading   1915

Locomotives:

Road No.	Cyln.	Type	Dvr. in.	Bldr.	Bldr. No.	Date	Weight	Effort	Remarks
1*	11x12	2T Shay	32	Lima	2821	9/15	118,000	25,380	sold to Portland dealer
2*	18x24	2-8-2	44	BLW	43210	4/16			
3*	12x15	3T Shay	36	Lima	2941	10/17	150,000	30,350	to Eagle Lumber Co.
4*	20½x28	2-8-2	48	BLW	51907	6/19	175,500		
5*	18x24	"	44	"	55805	11/22	143,000		
6*	"	"	"	"	56111	1/23			
8*	"	"	"	"	57708	3/24	182,760		

Freight traffic: logging

SILVER FALLS TIMBER COMPANY   President

Incorp:	6/14/1912	**Operated:**	1913	to	1938	**HQ city:**	Silverton

Disposition: abandoned in 1938 when it had 35 miles of track

Predecessor: Silverton Lumber Company   **Incorp.:** 10/22/1906 to 2/1/1913

Miles track: 40   **Gauge:** 56½"

Main line: Silverton and Millwood into the forest

Rail wt.: 60 lbs.   **Max. grade:** 7.0%   **Const. began:** grading   (February 18, 1907)

Locomotives:

Road No.	Cyln.	Type	Dvr. in.	Bldr.	Bldr. No.	Date	Weight	Effort	Remarks
1									
2*	10x12	2T Shay	29½	lima	2208	8/09	84,000	16,900	to Hauser Construction Co.
		- The above were Silverton Lumber Co.; the following were Silver Falls Timber -							
1*	11x12	2T Shay	32	Lima	2566	11/12	100,000	22,500	to South Bend Mills & Timber Co.
2*	"	"	"	"	2652	5/13	"	"	to Western Lumber Co. #2
3*	"	"	"	"	2654	"	"	"	
4*	12x15	3T Shay	36	"	3016	9/18	140,000	30,350	
4-2d		2T Shay	32	"	1821	1/07	90,000	20,350	acq. 8/1929 ex Noyes-Holland
5		2 truck	33	Climax	1333	(/16)	100,000	22,000	ex Kerry Timber Co.
6		2-6-0	57	BLW	6216	5/82	68,700	14,480	acq. 2/1923 ex S.P. #1601
101*	20½x28	2-8-2	48	"	39394	3/13	176,000	35,500	1939 to McCloud River RR
102*	"	"	"	"	45753	6/17			
103*		2-6-2T	44	"	55482	6/22	134,500	22,100	to Peninsula Terminal Co. #103
104*	17x24	"	"	"	59137	4/26	"	"	to Peninsula Terminal Co. #104

Freight traffic: logging

OREGON   137.

Roster of 6/30/1910:
  1   rod engine
  1   geared engine
 18   flat cars

Mileages from Oregon PUC reports:

Silverton Lumber Co.			Silver Falls Timber Co.		
	owned	operated		owned	operated
6/30/07	5.0	5.0	6/30/13	22.5	.0
6/30/08	7.0	.0	6/30/14	26.0	26.0
6/30/09	9.0	9.0	6/30/15	30.0	.0
6/30/10	12.0	12.0	12/31/18	30.0	30.0
			12/31/26	40.0	40.0

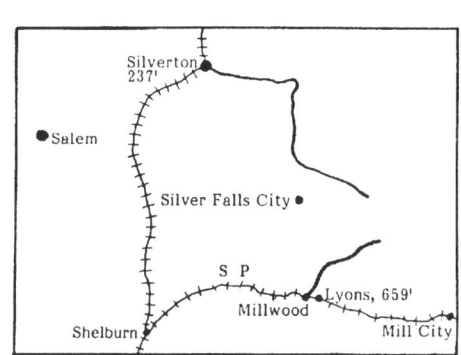

SMITH RIVER & NORTHERN RAILWAY COMPANY   California & Oregon Lumber Co., **Owner**

Incorp:		Operated: 1916 to 1925	HQ city: Brookings

Disposition: abandoned

Miles track: 30   **Gauge:** 56½"

Main line:

Rail wt.:   lbs.   **Max. grade:**   **Const. began:** grading   1916

Locomotives:

Road No.	Cyln.	Type	Dvr. in.	Bldr.	Bldr. no.	Date	Weight	Effort	Remarks
1		2T Shay	26½	Lima	2175	1/10	48,000	10,700	1916 acq. from dealer - sold in 1922
2		'	32	'	2413	1/11	100,000	22,575	ex Del Norte Railroad #6
3		'	26½	'	2284	4/10	48,000	10,700	acq. 11/1916 ex Nelson Logging Co.
4*	12x15	3T Shay	36	'	2889	11/16	146,000	34,100	sold to Portland dealer

Freight traffic: logging

Courtesy of Southern Pacific Company
Seven passenger cars being moved by three locomotives up the Dollarhide Trestle, now a fill, located at milepost 418 between the California line and Ashland at an elevation of 3259 feet. The road engine has a wood burner stack.

SOUTHERN PACIFIC TRANSPORTATION COMPANY D. J. Russell, **President**

Incorp:	2/20/1969	**Operated:**	11/26/69 to		**HQ city:**	San Francisco
Disposition:	in operation 1993					

Major predecessors:

	Incorp.:	to
Texas & New Orleans Railroad Company	12/24/1859	11/1/1961
Central Pacific Railway Company	7/29/1899	6/30/1959
Arizona Eastern Railroad Company	2/1/1910	9/23/1955
El Paso & Southwestern Railroad Company	7/8/1901	9/23/1955
El Paso & Rock Island Railway Company	12/11/1900	9/23/1955
Oregon & California Rail Road Company	3/17/1870	1/3/1927
Southern Pacific Railroad Company of New Mexico	4/14/1879	3/10/1902
Southern Pacific Railroad Company (of Arizona), The	9/20/1878	3/10/1902
Northern Railway Company	5/15/1888	4/14/1898
California Pacific Railroad Company	12/29/1869	4/14/1898
Southern Pacific Railroad Company	12/2/1865	10/12/1870
San Francisco & San Jose Rail Road Company	8/18/1860	10/12/1870

Miles track: 11,363 in 1969 **Gauges:** 56½" and 36"
Main lines: Ogden to Oakland and Portland to New Orleans
Rail wt.: 50 lbs. **Max. grade:** 2.200% **Const. began:** grading 1870
  laying rails 1870

Const. comp.:   **First train operated:** July 31, 1871 - Hollister

Freight traffic: common carrier, agriculture and lumber

Rosters of   6/30/1876 - 12/31/1877 - 12/31/1887 - 12/31/1888 - 6/30/1900 - 6/30/1906 - 12/31/1917:

	6/30/1876	12/31/1877	12/31/1887	12/31/1888	6/30/1900	6/30/1906	12/31/1917
locomotive engines	39	43	83	223	1,093	1,667	1,385
passenger cars	73	69	110	161	1,133	1,653	1,738
freight cars	670	949	1,632	5,091	29,465	44,284	33,797

Published timetable dated:
August 12, 1873
(as Southern Pacific Railroad of California)

8:40 a.m.		San Francisco	
9:19		Baden	mp 12
9:48		San Mateo	21
10:24		Menlo Park	33
10:48		Murphy's	41
11:10		San Jose	50
12:15 p.m.		Madrone	74
1:00		Gilroy	80
1:55		Pajaro	99
2:38		Salinas	118
4:20		Soledad	143
		and	
1:30 p.m.		Gilroy	80
1:40		Carnadero	83
2:30		Hollister	94
2:55		Trespinos	100

The Western Pacific Railroad Co. built from near Sacramento to Lathrop in 1869 at which point its line turned southwest to San Jose and Oakland. Central Pacific Railroad Co. built from Lathrop to Goshen between 1870 and 1872.

The carrier's first expansion was in the San Jose area as shown on the small map. Its first operation listed above, in 1870, was from Gilroy to Hollister. Predecessors had already constructed track from San Francisco to Gilroy.

Gilroy to Hollister	July 31, 1871	14
Carnadero to Pajaro	Nov. 27, 1871	16
Pajaro to Salinas	Nov. 1, 1872	19
Hollister to Trespinos (Tres Pinos)	August 12, 1873	6
Goshen to Tipton	July 25, 1872	21
Tipton to Delano	July 14, 1873	20
Delano to Sumner (Bakersfield)	October 26, 1874	32
Sumner to Caliente	April 26, 1875	22
Caliente to Keene's	May 26, 1876	14
Keene's to Mojave	August 9, 1876	32
Mojave to Tunnel (Lang)	September 6, 1876	58
Los Angeles to San Fernando	April 15, 1874	20
San Fernando to Tunnel	January 1, 1876	23
Los Angeles east to Spadra	April 15, 1874	28
Spadra to Colton	July 16, 1875	28
Colton to Indian Wells (Indio)	May 29, 1876	72
Indian Wells to Dos Palmas	March 3, 1877	31
Dos Palmas to Pilot Knob	April 29, 1877	79
Pilot Knob to Colorado River (at Yuma)	May 23, 1877	8
Sagus to Ellwood	December 21, 1887	92
Soledad to Templeton	November 16, 1886	78
Templeton to Santa Margarita	(March 15, 1889)	14
Santa Margarita to San Luis Obispo	(June 15, 1894)	16
San Luis Obispo to Guadalupe	(August 15, 1895)	25
Guadalupe to Surf	1896	26
Surf to Elwood	March 31, 1901	56

Construction to the east:

Mojave to Amboy	(Feb. 15, 1883)	156
Amboy to Needles	August 8, 1883	84
Goshen Jct. to Huron	July 1, 1877	40

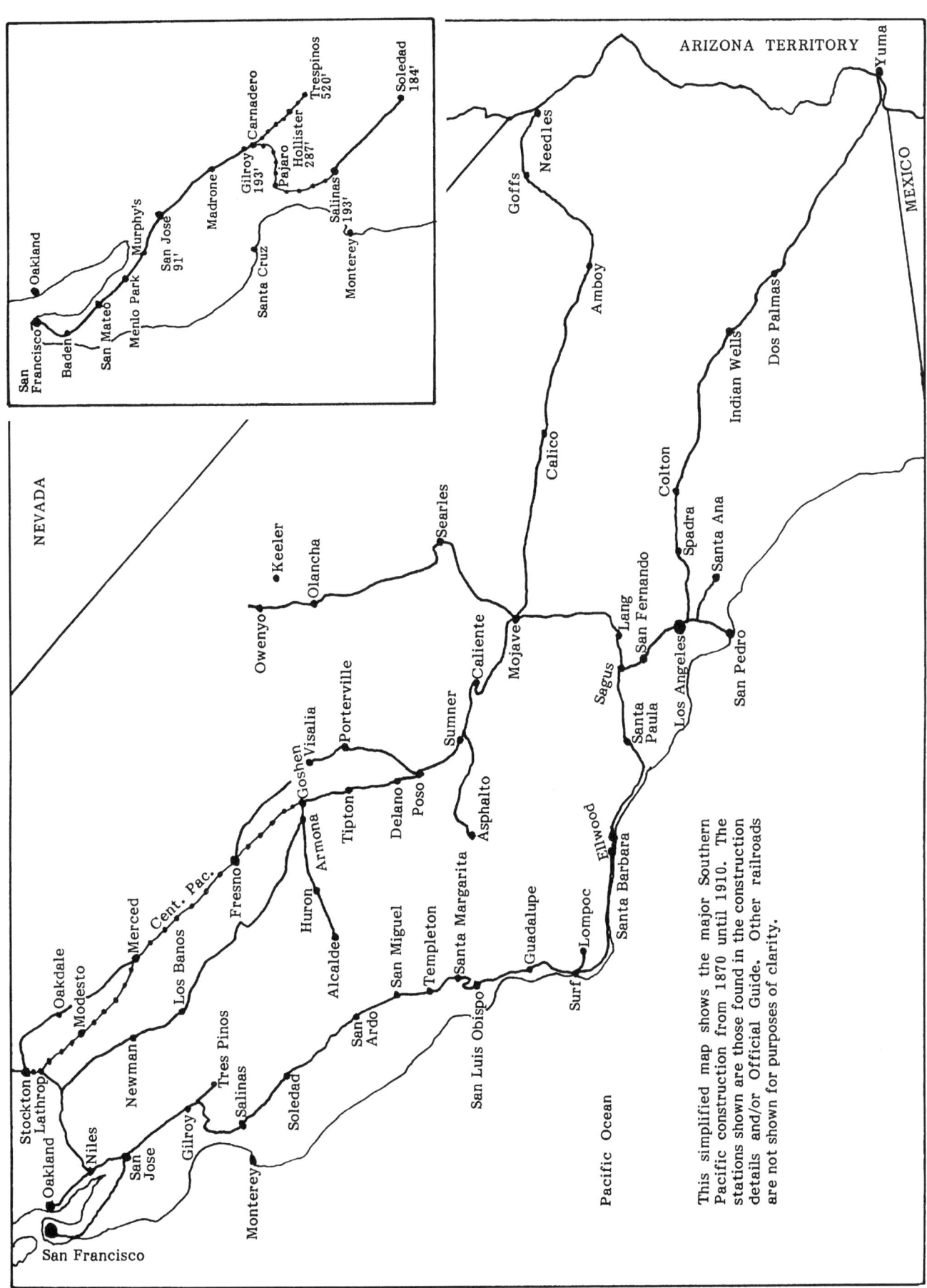

The Texas and Louisiana lines are outside of the scope of this volume, but a brief, and very simplified, listing of the major predecessors in the area is presented by way of background for this important part of the Sousthern Pacific system. The mileages represent no particular time frame, but approximate the carrier's original construction of main lines. There was also extensive mileage in Mexico.

Title:	Incorporated:	To:	Miles:
Texas & New Orleans Railroad Co.	12/24/1859	11/1/1961	4,322
Sabine & East Texas Railway Co.	8/3/1881	10/28/1882	103
Texas Trunk Railroad Co.	11/6/1879	11/25/1899	52
Houston East & West Texas Railway Co.	3/11/1875	3/1/1927	236
Houston & Shreveport Railroad Co.	9/9/1891	3/1/1927	40
Texas Midland Railroad Co.	12/16/1892	4/1/1928	125
Dayton & Goose Creek Railway Co.	7/24/1917	6/30/1934	25
Lake Charles & Northern Railway Co.	10/30/1906	3/1/1927	44
Louisiana Western Railroad Co.	3/30/1878	3/1/1927	198
Morgan's Louisiana & Texas Railroad Co.	4/1/1878	3/1/1927	432
Houston & Texas Central Railroad Co.	9/1/1856	9/30/1934	744
Waco & Northwestern Railroad Co.	8/6/1870	2/4/1873	55
Fort Worth & New Orleans Railway Co.	6/13/1885	8/22/1901	42
Austin & Northwestern Railroad Co.	4/20/1888	8/22/1901	106
Galveston, Harrisburg & San Antonio Railway Co.	7/27/1870	3/1/1927	2,037
Buffalo Bayou, Brazos & Colorado Railway Co.	2/11/1850	7/27/1870	86
San Antonio & Aransas Pass Railway Co.	8/28/1884	3/1/1927	728
Galveston, Houston & Northern Railway Co.	3/30/1899	9/28/1905	57
San Antonio & Gulf Railroad Co.	3/31/1897	8/9/1905	37
New York, Texas & Mexican Railway Co.	11/17/1880	8/8/1905	177
Gulf, Western Texas & Pacific Railway Co.	8/4/1870	8/8/1905	71

Southern Pacific Company was, for many years, a railroad operating company only. It was listed in first ICC (6/30/88) as operating 5,624 miles, the track being owned by, amongst others, these major western lines: Southern Pacific (Arizona), leased February 10, 1885 - Southern Pacific (California), leased March 1, 1885 - Southern Pacific (New Mexico), also leased March 1, 1885 - Central Pacific, leased April 1, 1885 - Oregon & California, leased July 1, 1887 - South Pacific Coast, leased July 1, 1887 - Northern Railway, leased June 1, 1889.

Its "operated" increased to 6,641 miles in 1894, then gradually declined to 5,248 miles by 6/30/01. By 6/30/08 it owned a short track, 12 miles, with the merger in of Bayshore Railway Co. By 6/30/10 the operated total was 6,139 miles.

Southern Pacific Railroad Company was first listed in ICC for 6/30/02 with 3,260 miles owned and nothing operated. It was formed by the consolidation on March 10, 1902, of Southern Pacific (Arizona), 393 miles, Southern Pacific (California), 2,703 miles and Southern Pacific (New Mexico) with 167 miles. This company was leased to Southern Pacific Company from December 31, 1901, through June 30, 1951. It remained in the 3100-3300 mile range until its merger into Southern Pacific Company on September 30, 1955.

	owned:	operated:		owned:	operated:
6/30/15	30	6,517	12/31/52	1,453	8,113
6/30/16	422	6,950	12/31/53	7,974	8,119
12/31/26	578	8,764	12/31/61	11,711	12,017
12/31/27	1,239	8,934	12/31/68	11,388	11,761
12/31/40	1,453	8,607	12/31/72	11,136	11,640

The mergers of 1955 must have been anticipated and that mileage taken into the 1953 "owned" column.

The major history of Southern Pacific is found in California and the locomotive rosters are found there; because of the continuing importance of this corporation to Oregon the development and structure is included here.

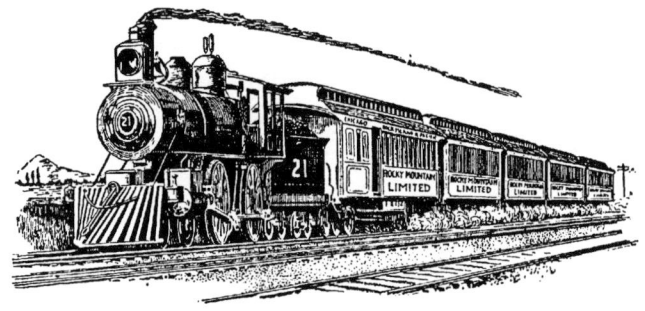

Bibliography: *Poor's 1877-78*, p. 673   California PUC report 1884, p. 127   *Valuation 45*, p. 162

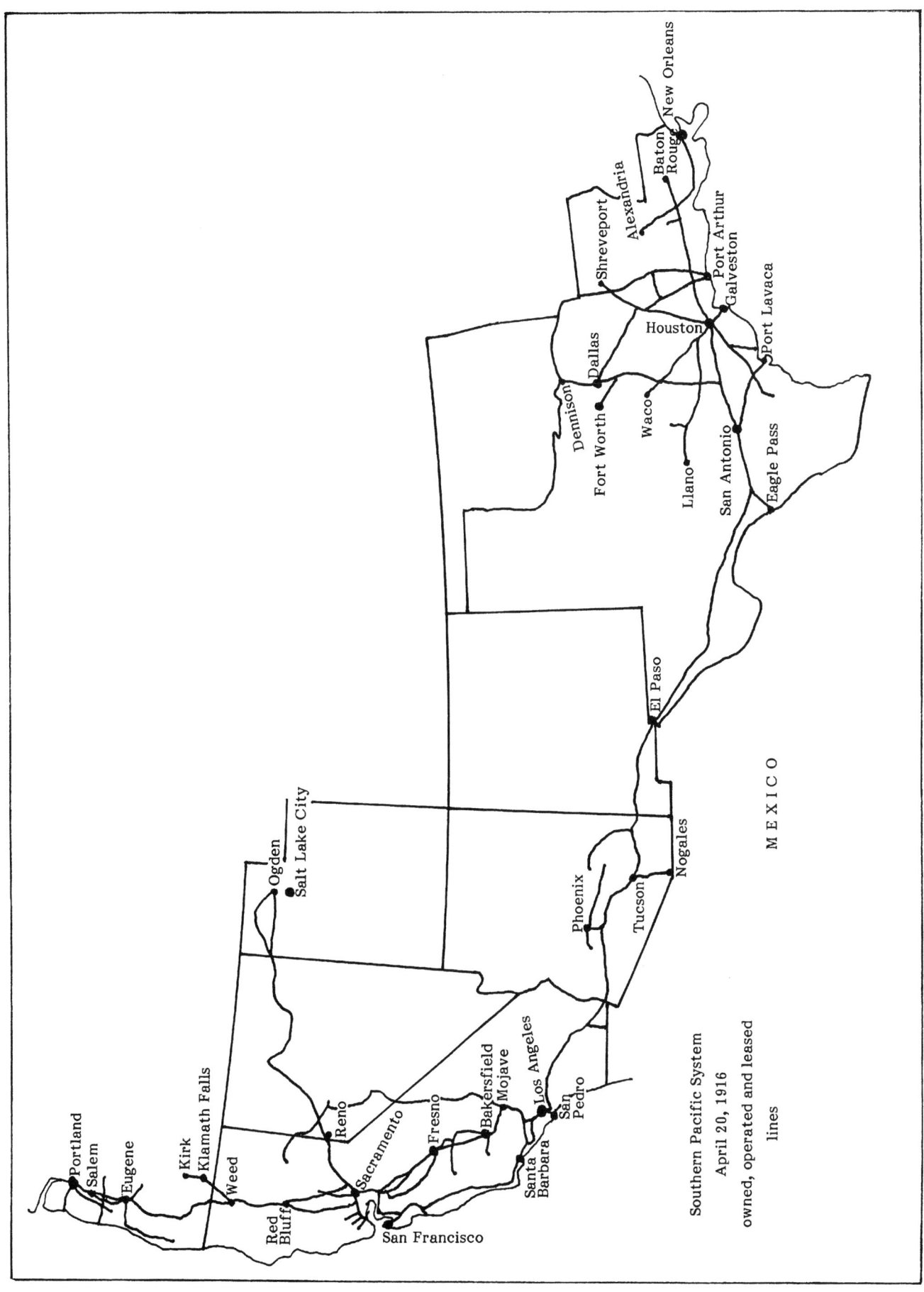

Denver Public Library - Western History Department *Photo by Otto C. Perry*
Southern Pacific #4363, a 4-8-2, with <u>Beaver</u> leaving Portland with 14 cars on July 29, 1940

Denver Public Library - Western History Department *Photo by Otto C. Perry*
<u>Klamath</u>, train 19, with #4313 at Portland July 29, 1940; clock tower is still used in 1993, likely the semaphore above is not.

OREGON

Denver Public Library - Western History Department *Photo by Otto C. Perry*
Southern Pacific high-driver (81") 4-4-2 photographed at Portland on June 6, 1926; built by Brooks in February of 1908

Denver Public Library - Western History Department *Photo by Otto C. Perry*
Southern Pacific train 13 engine 4-8-2 #4339 is taking on a load of water at Grants Pass; the date is June 7, 1926.

Denver Public Library - Western History Department *Photo by Otto C. Perry*
Cab-forward 4-6-6-2 photographed at Eugene on July 24, 1939; previous number was 4210.

SPAULDING LOGGING COMPANY, CHAS. K.

								President
Incorp:	5/15/1917		**Operated:**	5/05 to 1938			**HQ city:**	Newberg
Disposition:	abandoned							
Miles track:	20			**Gauge:**	56½"			
Main line:	along the Lukiamute River							
Rail wt.:	60 lbs.		**Max. grade:**	5.0%		**Const. began:**	grading	

Locomotives:

Road No.	Type	Dvr. in.	Bldr.	Bldr. No.	Date	Weight	Effort	Remarks
1 ?	2T Shay	26½	Lima	1580	10/05	40,000	10,700	ex Bell Logging Co. #1
	'	29½	'	1870	1/07	74,000	16,900	ex Ostrander Ry. & Timber Co.
5	'	36	'	1939	6/07	110,000	23,850	ex Salem, Falls City & Western #5
6	'	29½	'	1807	11/06	74,000	16,900	acq. 1917 ex Salem, Falls C. & W. #6
10*	2 truck	35	Climax	1093	5/11	114,000		

Freight traffic: logging

Roster of 6/30/1908:
    1   locomotive
    2   logging cars

SPAULDING—MIAMI LUMBER COMPANY

								President
Incorp:	11/18/1920		**Operated:**	1921 to 1924			**HQ city:**	Grande Ronde
Disposition:	abandoned							
Miles track:	21			**Gauge:**	56½"			
Main line:								
Rail wt.:	lbs.		**Max. grade:**			**Const. began:**	grading	

Locomotives:

1 ?	2T Shay	26½	Lima	1580	10/05	40,000	10,700	ex C. K. Spaulding - to Oregon Coast Range
5	3T Shay	36	'	2757	4/14	146,000	30,350	acq. 3d hand - 9/1924 to Oregon Coast Range
7	2T Shay	32	'	611	12/00	80,000	17,475	acq. 10/1920 ex Marys River Logging Co. #7
8	'	29½	'	2666	7/13	84,000	16,900	acq. 11/1920 ex Warren Spruce - to O. Coast R.
10	2 truck	35	Climax	1093	5/11	114,000		ex Chas. K. Spaulding Logging Co. #10

Freight traffic: logging

STANDARD LOGGING COMPANY

								President
Incorp:	1/15/1938		**Operated:**	1938 to 1944			**HQ city:**	Cochran
Disposition:	sold to Long-Bell Lumber Company on July 25, 1944							
Miles track:	22			**Gauge:**	56½"			
Main line:								
Rail wt.:	lbs.		**Max. grade:**			**Const. began:**	grading	

Locomotives:

1	2T Shay	29½	Lima	1870	1/07	74,000	16,900	acq. 3/1938 ex Wheeler Logging - SCR 8/1940
2	'	32	'	3206	3/23	117,000	22,580	acq. 4/1938 ex Portland Ry. & Power Co. #1
3	'	29½	'	1737	9/06	74,000	16,900	acq. 1/1939 ex Snow Lbr./Shingle - SCR 8/1940
4	3T Shay	40	'	1651	6/06	180,000	40,400	acq. 3/1938 ex Oregon Coast Logging Co. #4
5 ?	2T Shay	28	'	1742	7/06	90,000	20,300	acq. 1/1939 ex Oregon Tbr. & Lbr. #2 - SCR
11	3T Shay	36	'	3018	4/19	146,000	30,350	acq. 4/1938 ex Wheeler Lumber Co. #11
80	'	'	'	3286	3/25	196,000	35,100	acq. 6/1939 ex Fruit Growers #5 (Calif.)
108 ?	'	'	'	3254	4/24	209,800	40,400	acq. 1940 ex Cascade Tbr. #108 - sold 1946

Freight traffic: logging

OREGON 145.

STODDARD LUMBER COMPANY

President

Incorp:	1/30/1914	**Operated:** 1914 to 1943		**HQ city:** Baker
Disposition:	abandoned			

Predecessors:
The Baker White Pine Lumber Company	(36" gauge)	**Incorp.:**	8/1/1910	to 3/24/1929
Stoddard Bros. Lumber Company	(36" gauge at Perry)		1898	1914
Grande Ronde Lumber Company	(56½" gauge at Perry)		2/9/1889	1/1929

Miles track:	60	**Gauge:**	36" and 56½"
Main line:	Perry into the forest plus woods lines from Sumpter Valley Railway Co.		
Rail wt.:	40 lbs.	**Max. grade:** 8.0% **Const. began:** grading	

Locomotives:

Road No.	Cyln.	Type	Dvr. in.	Bldr.	Bldr. No.	Date	Weight	Effort	Remarks
		- Grande Ronde Lumber Co. -							
5		3 truck	38	Heisler	1501	3/24	160,000		to Big Creek & Telocaset #5
103*	10x12	2T Shay	29½	Lima	2241	11/09	84,000	16,900	to Stoddard Lumber Co. #103
104*	15x12	2 truck	36	Heisler	1496	1/24	100,000		to Stoddard Lumber Co. #104
105 ?		'	30	'	1091	6/06	44,000		to Meacham Lumber Co.
		- Stoddard Bros. Lumber Co. -							
1		2T Shay	26	Lima	244	6/89	26,000	7,250	acq. 1897 ex Sumpter Vy. #1
		- Baker White Pine Lumber Co. -							
1*		2 truck	28	Climax	1077	4/11	66,000		to Stoddard Lumber Co.
2*		'	'	'	1199	2/13	70,000		to Stoddard Lumber Co.
3		'	'	'		/15	'		
		- Stoddard Lumber Co. -							
3*		2 truck		Heisler	1360	5/17	72,000		56½" gauge - scrapped 1947
4*	14x12	'	33	'	1460	7/22	80,000		36" gauge - scrapped 1947

Freight traffic: logging

Roster of 6/30/1908:
(Grande Ronde Lumber Co.)
 2 geared engines
 6 flat cars
 12 miles track at Hilgard

Grande Ronde Lumber Co. was first listed in ICC for 6/30/07 as an eight-mile operating independent. It was 12 miles in 1909, 16 in 1923 and seven miles in 1928.

Various data from Oregon PUC reports:
Grande Ronde Lumber Co.
 1925 Fifteen miles of track, 52 lb. rail, two wood burners and 50 logging flats.
 1926 Twenty miles, 8% maximum grade, 30° curve, 3 geared engines and a 2100-foot incline with a 32° grade.
Baker White Pine Lumber Co.
 1919 Operating its tracks from Austin and Whitney.
 1925 32 miles of track with 30/56 lbs. rail, four wood burning engines.
 1926 Thirty miles, 3 geared engines, 135 logging flats, 6% grade, 36° curve.
Stoddard Lumber Co.
 1925 Ten miles of 36" gauge track.

STOUT LUMBER COMPANY

President

Incorp:		**Operated:** 1923 to 1926		**HQ city:** North Bend
Disposition:	abandoned			
Predecessor:	Simpson Lumber Company		**from:** 1900	to 1923

Miles track:	18	**Gauge:**	56½"
Main line:	Daniel's Creek into the forest		
Rail wt.:	50 lbs.	**Max. grade:** 4.0% **Const. began:** grading	

Locomotives:

Road No.	Cyln.	Type	Dvr. in.	Bldr.	Bldr. No.	Date	Weight	Effort	Remarks
1*	10x12	2T Shay	29½	Lima	765	4/03	74,000	15,625	to North Bend Mill & Lbr. #1
2*	'	'	'	'	2302	3/10	84,000	16,900	to McDonald & Vaughan Logging #2
3*	'	'	'	'	2303	'	'	'	to North Bend Mill & Lbr. #3
4	'	'	'	'	2518	5/12	'	'	ex North Bend Mill & Lbr. #4
10	'	'	'	'	2999	10/18	85,000	16,000	ex North Bend Mill & Lbr. #10
2978	'	'	32	'	2978	5/18	100,000	22,580	ex North Bend Mill & Lbr. #2978

Freight traffic: logging

SUMPTER VALLEY RAILWAY COMPANY

David Eccles, **President**

Incorp:	8/18/1890	**Operated:** 1891 to 4/11/47		**HQ city:**	Baker City
Disposition:	abandoned December 29, 1961				
Miles track:	79.41	**Gauge:** 36"			
Main line:	Baker City to Prairie City				
Rail wt.:	40/75 lbs.	**Max. grade:** 4.0%	**Const. began:**	grading (September 9, 1890)	
				laying rails (December 9, 1890)	
Const. comp.:	January 13, 1910		**First train operated:**	October 1, 1891	

Locomotives:

Road No.	Cyln.	Type	Dvr. in.	Bldr.	Bldr. No.	Date	Weight	Effort	Remarks
1		2T Shay	26	Lima	244	6/89	26,000	7,250	1897 to Stoddard Lumber Co.
1-2d		2-6-0	41	Brooks	530	4/81	45,800		acq. 1892 ex O.S.L.&U.N. #88
1-3d		'	44	BLW	19211	7/01	81,290	16,290	acq. 1910 ex Tonopah RR #2
2		'	41	Brooks		/81	45,800		ex Utah & Northern
2-2d		'	44	BLW	19210	7/01	81,290	16,290	acq. 1910 ex Tonopah RR #3
3		2-8-0	37	'	9519	9/88	82,080	15,460	acq. 1910 ex Tonopah RR #1
4		2-6-0	44	'	24689	9/04			acq. 1907 ex Tonopah RR #4
5		'	41	Brooks		/81	45,800		ex Utah & Northern - sold in 1912
6		4-4-0	44	BLW	4982	2/80			ex O.S.L.&U.N. #294
8		2 truck	29	Climax	1533	5/19	60,000		ex Hallack & Howard - SCR 1947
10		2-8-0	36	BLW	5164	6/80	56,000	12,450	ex Denver & R.G. #74-sold 1912
11		2-6-0	'	'	4429	9/78	39,000	6,557	ex Utah & Northern #7 - SCR 1942
12		'	41	Brooks		/81	45,800		ex Utah & Northern
13		'	'	BLW	5695	6/81	45,000		acq. 1890 ex Minn, Lyndale & M.
14		2-8-0	36	'	5930	11/81			ex Connotton Valley #13
14-2d		'	38	'	28806	9/06	81,500	16,300	acq. 1912 ex Eureka & Palisade #8
15		2-6-0	37	'	11075	6/90	78,580	14,320	acq. 1912 ex Eureka & Palis. #10
16*	17x22	2-8-2	42	'	42073	5/15	141,910	23,140	sold 10/25/1944 - sent to Peru
17*	'	'	'	'	42074	'	'	'	sold 10/25/1944 - sent to Peru
18*	'	'	'	'	42815	1/16	'	'	sold 10/25/1944 - sent to Peru
19*	19x20	'	44	Schen.	61981	5/20	128,000	19,000	1941 to White Pass & Yukon #81
20*	'	'	'	'	61980	'	'	'	1941 to White Pass & Yukon #80
50*	16x20	4-6-0	42	BLW	42865	2/16	113,900	18,650	sold 10/25/1944 - sent to Peru
101*	8x10	2T Shay	26½	Lima	1884	3/07	48,000	13,300	scrapped in 1940
101-2d*		A-A	30	Davenp.	2245	5/37	60,000	20,550	a diesel - 1961 to Edw. Hines Lbr.
102*	8x10	2T Shay	26½	Lima	1885	4/07	48,000	13,300	scrapped in 1940
250		2-6-6-2T	42	BLW	59261	6/26	236,300	42,000	4/1940 ex Uintah #250-sold 7/1947
251		'	'	'	60470	4/28	246,000	'	4/1940 ex Uintah #251-sold 7/1947
285		4-6-0	44	Grant	1230	4/79	37,500		acq. 8/1890 ex O.S.L.&U.N. #285

Freight traffic: common carrier, logging

Rosters of 6/30/1896 - 6/30/1909:

locomotives	4	15
passenger cars	1	19
freight cars	175	307

First published timetable:
September 1, 1892 - daily exc. Sunday
6:00 p.m.   Baker City   9:00
7:30   McEwen   7:30 a.m.

Published timetable dated:
January, 1916 - daily
8:30 a.m.   Baker
8:56   Salisbury   9.5 miles
9:39   McEwen   22.5
10:05   Sumpter   29.0
11:05   Whitney   43.4
11:40   Greenwood   51.0
12:40 noon Austin   59.2
2:10 p.m.   Prairie   80.1
(Tipton was now Greenwood)

First listed in ICC for 6/30/92 as an operating independent with 25 miles owned and in use. It was gradually extended to 37 miles by 6/30/97 and to 45 by 6/30/01. It reached 62 miles by 6/30/05 and remained unchanged through 1910. It was 81 miles each by 6/30/11. In 1931 this class II carrier owned 79 miles, but was reduced to 61 in 1933. It owned and operated 58 miles through 1946. It was sold to Oregon Lumber Co. in 1947 when the track had been reduced to two miles of mill switching at Baker. From 1949 to 1961, freight service was offered by highway motor trucks.

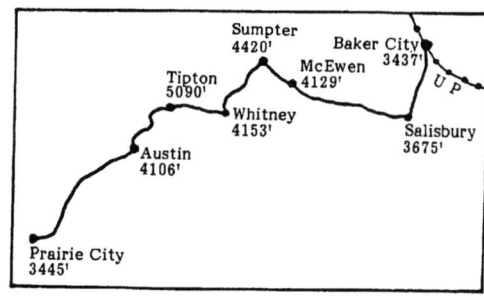

The railway was constructed over a twenty year period in the following sections:

Baker City to McEwen	22.60 miles	July 10, 1890	to	March 22, 1892
McEwen to Sumpter Jct.	6.42	November 4, 1896		May 1, 1897
Sumpter Jct. to Whitney	14.35	May 3, 1900		May 1, 1901
Whitney to Tipton	7.66	May 1, 1904		(August 20, 1904)
Tipton to Austin	8.19	July 1, 1904		(November 17, 1905)
Austin to Prairie City	21.08	July 8, 1909		January 13, 1910

All of the sections were released for operations in the same month that it was completed except for Austin to Prairie City which was formally opened on June 1, 1911.

The carrier cost $1,319,072 to construct and $207,070 to equip. Maximum curvature was 24°. Grading was frequently light, at some points it required just clearing and grubbing.

The locomotives were converted from wood to oil burners in 1940 upon arrival of the 2-6-6-2s; even with this "superpower", link-and-pin couplings continued to be used.

Bibliography: *Poor's 1897*, p. 266   Oregon PUC report 1895, p. 301   *Valuation 141*, p. 466
Baker City - *The Weekly Bedrock Democrat* - June 16 to December 8, 1890

Denver Public Library - Western History Department   *Photo by Otto C. Perry*
Sumpter Valley #17 leads a 13-car eastbound from Austin on July 28, 1938, with #19 smoking up the background pushing.

California State Railroad Museum Library
A general view of Sumpter Valley's Baker City yard and general store

SUNSET LOGGING COMPANY

									President	
Incorp:	6/12/1923			**Operated:**	1923 to 1949			**HQ city:**	Timber	
Disposition:	abandoned									
Miles track:	18			**Gauge:**	56½"					
Main line:										
Rail wt.:	60 lbs.			**Max. grade:**	6.0%			**Const. began:**	grading	1923

Locomotives:

Road No.	Type	Dvr. in.	Bldr.	Bldr. No.	Date	Weight	Effort	Remarks
3 ?	3T Shay	36	Lima	3164	2/21	142,800	24,000	acq. 3/1935 ex Crown Zellerbach #3
4	2T Shay	28	'	1732	7/06	56,000	15,150	ex East Side Logging Co. - SCR 1950
5 ?	'	30½	'	1627	2/06	74,000	16,300	ex East Side Logging Co. #5
25	2 truck	32	Willam.	25	9/26			ex East Side Logging Co. #107
55	3 truck	36	'	29	4/28			ex East Side Logging Co. #55

Freight traffic: logging

THE DALLES & SOUTHERN RAILROAD COMPANY

							Wasco Pine Lumber Co., **Owner**	
Incorp:	12/11/1933		**Operated:**	12/13/33 to 5/1/36		**HQ city:**	Portland	
Disposition:	abandoned							
Predecessor:	Great Southern Railroad Company					**Incorp.:**	3/3/1904 to 12/12/1933	
Miles track:	40.79		**Gauge:**	56½"				
Main line:	The Dalles to Friend							
Rail wt.:	60 lbs.		**Max. grade:**			**Const. began:**	grading	March 9, 1904
							laying rails	(May 10, 1905)
Const. comp.:	December 31, 1912					**First train operated:**		December 1, 1905

Locomotives:
Road
No.
1
2

Freight traffic: common carrier, lumber

Roster of 6/30/1913:
  2 locomotives
  2 passenger cars
  9 box cars
  3 stock cars
  9 flat cars

First published timetable:
June 15, 1908
  2:00 p.m. The Dalles 10:15
  4:00   Dufur   8:15 a.m.

Published timetable dated:
January, 1916 - daily
  8:00 a.m. The Dalles 3:45
             Dufur
  10:45   Friend   1:00 p.m.

Great Southern Railroad Co. was first listed in ICC for 6/30/06 as an operating independent with 30 miles owned and in use. This class III carrier was extended to 41 miles by 6/30/13, and then unchanged through 1932.

It was succeeded in 1933, ceased operations in 1936 and abandoned.

The line was completed to Dufur, 29.67 miles, on November 30, 1905. Construction was resumed in May, 1911, and completed in 1912 at a cost of $625,691 to build and $32,519 to equip.

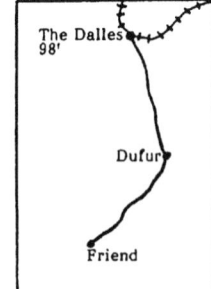

Bibliography: *Poor's 1914*, p. 1533   Oregon PUC report 1909, p. 115   *Valuation 130*, p. 682
The Railway Age - December 4, 1904 to December 1, 1905

OREGON

UMATILLA CENTRAL RAILROAD COMPANY E. H. Harriman, **President**

Incorp: 5/24/1906 **Operated:** 12/16/07 to 12/23/10 **HQ city:** Portland
Disposition: merged into Oregon-Washington Railroad & Navigation Company on December 23, 1910
Miles track: 14.21 **Gauge:** 56½"
Main line: Rieth to Pilot Rock
Rail wt.: lbs. **Max. grade:** **Const. began:** grading (May 13, 1907)
  laying rails (September 9, 1907)
Const. comp.: December 16, 1907 **First train operated:** December 16, 1907
Freight traffic: common carrier, agriculture

First published timetable:
  December 29, 1907
  8:45 a.m. Pendleton   3:15
  10:00   Pilot Rock 19 m 2:00 p.m.

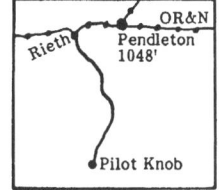

First listed in ICC for 6/30/08 as a non-operating subsidiary of Oregon Railroad & Navigation Co. with 14 miles owned; it had been leased to O.R. & N. on December 16, 1907. It then remained unchanged until merger in 1910.

Bibliography: *Poor's 1910*, p. 1273 Oregon PUC report 1909, p. 173 *Valuation 44*, p. 296
  Pendleton - *Daily East Oregonian* - June 11 to September 23, 1907

Photo by Ed Austin
Union Pacific directors' special train westbound at East Sandy, Oregon, on the afternoon of June 26, 1993

UNION RAILROAD OF OREGON   Edwin Wilcox, **President**

Incorp:	4/29/1927	**Operated:**	2/15/27 to 7/25/93		**HQ city:**	Union
Disposition:	ceased operations July 25, 1993					
Predecessors:	Central Railroad of Oregon			**Incorp.:**	3/22/1909 to	2/14/1927
	Central Railway Company of Oregon				6/2/1905	5/14/1909
	Union Railway Company, The				7/18/1890	6/26/1906
Miles track:	16.123	**Gauge:**	56½"			
Main line:	Union Jct. to Cove					
Rail wt.:	52/60 lbs.	**Max. grade:**		**Const. began:**	grading	March 27, 1906
					laying rails	(August 22, 1906)
Const. comp.:	(November 17, 1911)			**First train operated:**		

Locomotives:

Road No.	Type	Dvr. in.	Bldr.	Bldr. No.	Date	Weight	Effort	Remarks
1	0-6-0T		Altoona	357	3/77			acq. 7/1902 ex O.R.&N. #13
12	4-4-0	64	C&A		/90	82,000		acq. 3/1909 ex Chicago & Alton #142
1106	'	63	BLW	6827	6/83	170,500	12,412	ex O.R.&N. #79 - scrapped in 1940
101	A-A		Plymouth	3836	4/36		250 h.p.	its sole power in 1979

Freight traffic: common carrier, agriculture and lumber

Roster of 6/30/1913:
- 2 locomotives (one leased)
- 3 passenger cars (all leased)
- 2 box cars
- 2 stock cars

Published "timetable" dated:
August, 1908
  Union Jct.
  Union
  Richmond
  Cove   18 miles

Published timetable dated:
January, 1916
  12:05 p.m. Union Jct.
  12:15   Union   m.p. 2.5
  12:45 lv.   Union   2.5
  1:10   Richmond   8.0
  1:45   Cove   18.0
     also
  8:35 a.m.   Union
  8:50   Richmond   5.0
  9:00   Hot Lake   8.0

Union Jct. is 12 miles southeast of La Grande. The road cost $141,265 to construct.

ICC recorded the track in these sections: Union Jct. to Union, 2.291 miles - Valley Jct. to Cove, 10.540 miles - Richmond to Hot Lake, 3.292 miles.

The map below was drawn with these figures in mind, and very little else.

ICC data regarding operations:

6/30/1906	miles: 0.0
6/30/1907	12.46
6/30/1908	13.05
6/30/1909	13.67
6/30/1910	12.46
6/30/1912	16.36
12/30/1926	16.36
12/31/1927	2.10

On June 30, 1906, the local newspaper stated that the "Dinky" Road is now the property of the Central Company. On September first, it noted that laying steel on Central Railway, connecting the old "Dinky" line to Cove, had commenced this week. Must assume that these citations refer to The Union Railway Company of 1890.

ICC records show that 2.291 miles (Union Jct. to Union) were purchased in 1906 (track that had been operated by its former owned - unnamed - since 1890), then constructed in 1906 from Valley Jct. to Cove, 10.54 miles, and Richmond to Hot Lake. Judging by the operations figures above, the Hot Lake track was built at a later date. The December, 1911, *Official Guide* shows that this line had just being opened. The carrier's owners had interests in a medicinal springs spa at Hot Lake.

Interstate Commerce Commission *Valuation Reports,* vol. 106, p. 520, states: "The records of the company are in a chaotic condition. Some of the transactions are recorded in books kept in Boston, Mass. The last entry in these books is as of June 30, 1908. Another set of books kept in Union, Oreg., records transactions to Nov. 2, 1908. The two sets of books are not in harmony; each contains entries not in the other."

This confusion spread to the industry. *Poor's 1918* shows it with one mile of track; in 1919 it suddenly had 91 miles to Walla Walla, Wash. The June, 1916, *Official Guide* map of Oregon shows this Walla Walla track, which, of course, was not built. It also shows track to Sparta which is 26 miles east by north of Baker.

The Central Railway Company of Oregon was placed in receivership November 22, 1908, sold March 22, 1909, to Central Railroad of Oregon and the new name was placed in use on the 15th of May.

Bibliography: *Poor's 1914,* p. 1530   Oregon PUC report 1909, p. 104   *Valuation 106,* p. 511
Union - *Eastern Oregon Republican* - March 24 to November 10, 1906

California State Railroad Museum Library   *Gerald M. Best Collection*
Central Railroad of Oregon locomotive with fancy tender on a track with few ties and even less ballast

UNITED RAILWAYS COMPANY (OREGON)   John F. Stevens, President

Incorp: 1/17/1906	**Operated:** to 11/11/44		**HQ city:** Linnton	
Disposition:	merged into Spokane, Portland & Seattle Railway Company on November 11, 1944			
Purchased:	Portland, Astoria & Pacific Railroad Company	**Incorp.:** 7/29/1919 to 12/31/1923		
Miles track: 58.695	**Gauge:** 56½"			
Main line:	Linnton to Keasey (51.231 miles) plus tracks in Portland (7.464 miles)			
Rail wt.: 70/90 lbs.	**Max. grade:**	**Const. began:** grading (March 11, 1907)		
		laying rails (April 22, 1907)		
Const. comp.: March 31, 1923		**First train operated:**		

Locomotives:
United Railways Co.:

Road No.	Cyln.	Type	Dvr. in.	Bldr.	Bldr. No.	Date	Weight	Effort	Remarks
1		0-4-4-0		BLW	32061	10/07		400 h.p.	electric - to Yakima Transportation
Portland, Astoria & Pacific									
101*	20x28	2-8-2	48	Brooks	61857	8/20	174,000	36,680	to Weed Lumber Company
101*	'	'	'	'	61858	'	'	'	
102*	'	'	'	'	61859	'	'	'	

Freight traffic: common carrier, lumber and agriculture

Roster of 12/31/19223: - ICC
    (Portland, Astoria & Pacific)
    16   locomotives
    5   passenger cars
    8   freight cars

Published timetable dated:
    (United Rys. - electric)
    March 13, 1916
    8:35 a.m.   Linnton
    8:53   Burlington   4.4
    9:14   Helvetia   10.3
    9:50   Wilkesboro   19.1

Roster of 12/31/1925: - ICC
    (United Railways)
    12   locomotives
    10   passenger cars
    67   freight cars

Portland to Wilkesboro, 30.036 miles, was constructed between March, 1907, and April, 1911, by the United Railways Co.

March, 1911, *Official Guide* shows that Burlington to North Plains, 11.20 miles, has just been opened. In May, 1911, it was extended to Banks, 4.60 miles.

As of December 5, 1921, Portland, Astoria & Pacific Railroad Co. had graded 32 miles and laid about 9.5 miles of track. There were two tunnels, 4,111 and 1,137 feet, plus five Howe truss bridges. Must assume that it started at Wilkesboro to build north and west.

Portland, Astoria & Pacific was first listed in ICC for 12/31/21 as an operating independent (owned by Oregon-American Lumber Co.) with 4.5 miles owned, not in use; increased to 33 miles in 1922, still not in operation. By 12/31/23 it was 33 miles owned and 48 operated. The carrier was sold to United Railways Co. on December 8, 1921, but the corporation was not dissolved until December 31, 1923.

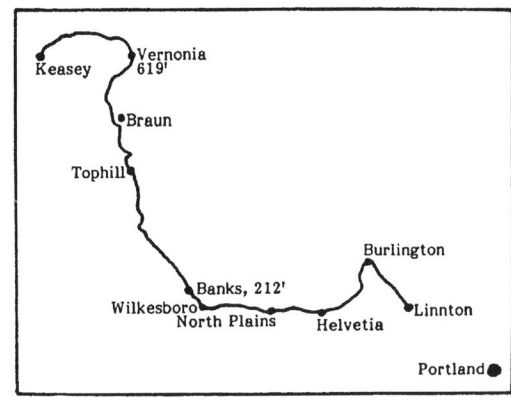

United Railways Co., being an electric line most of its life, was not listed in ICC until 1924 at which time it was shown as an operating subsidiary of Spokane, Portland & Seattle Railway Co. with 53 miles owned and 55 operated; it was 50 miles in 1943.

Bibliography: Oregon PUC report 1909   *Hillsboro Independent* - April 19 to June 28, 1907   *Valuation 46*, p. 648

WCTU RAILWAY COMPANY

Wm. L. Snelgrove, **President**

Incorp:	11/3/1954	**Operated:**	(11/16/54) to	**HQ city:** White City
Disposition:	in operation 1993			
Miles track:	13	**Gauge:**	56½"	
Main line:	White City switching and terminal			

Locomotives:

Road No.	Type	Dvr. in.	Bldr.	Bldr. No.	Date	Weight	Effort	Remarks
5117	B-B		G.E.	31162	9/51	140,000	660 h.p.	
5119	'		'	32284	5/55	'	'	

Freight traffic: forest products

The title White City Terminal & Utility Company was also found, possibly just to explain the initials.

The area was previously served by the Medford Corporation logging railroad. Camp White was established during World War II and after that sold as the site of an industrial complex. When its rail line to Medford was abandoned, Southern Pacific built a track from Tolo to White City.

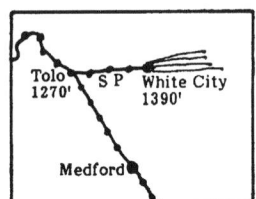

Bibliography: Direct communication   *The Pocket List of Railroad Officials*

WARREN SPRUCE COMPANY

President

Incorp:	1/11/1918	**Operated:**	1918 to 1920	
Disposition:	abandoned			
Miles track:	13	**Gauge:**	56½"	

Locomotives:

Road No.				Bldr.	Bldr. No.	Date	Weight	Effort	Remarks
1*	13x12	2 truck	33	Heisler	1373	5/18	72,000		to Skykomish Lbr. Co. - Index, Wash.
2 ?		2T Shay	29½	Lima	1712	7/06	74,000	16,900	ex Multnomah Lumber & Box #2
5*	10x12	'	'	'	2994	9/18	85,000	'	sold to Portland dealer
6*	'	'	'	'	2995	'	'	'	sold to Portland dealer
7*	'	'	'	'	2996	'	'	'	
8*	'	'	'	'	2997	10/18	'	'	to McCall Logging Co. #8
9*	'	'	'	'	2998	'	'	'	to Smith-Powers Logging Co.
10*	'	'	'	'	2999	'	'	'	to Black Diamond Lumber Co.
879	'	'	'	'	879	4/04	74,000	15,625	ex Benson Timber Co. #879

Freight traffic: logging

WESTERN OREGON RAILROAD COMPANY

R. Koehler, President

Incorp:	1/27/1879	**Operated:** 1/28/80 to 10/9/80	**HQ city:** Portland
Disposition:	consolidated into Oregon & California Rail Road Company on October 9, 1880		
Miles track:	49.70	**Gauge:** 56½"	
Main line:	St. Joseph to Corvallis		
Rail wt.:	50/56 lbs.	**Max. grade:** 1.193%	**Const. began:** grading (April 14, 1879)
			laying rails (August 18, 1879)
Const. comp.:	(April 30, 1880)		**First train operated:** September 1, 1879

Locomotive engines:

Road No.	Cyln.	Type	Dvr. in.	Bldr.	Bldr. No.	Date	Weight	Effort	Remarks
8*	17x24	2-6-0	53	BLW	5029	3/80	65,000	15,573	6/1881 to Oregon & California #20

Freight traffic: common carrier, agriculture and lumber

Roster of 6/30/1880:
    4 locomotive engines
    2 passenger cars
  43 freight cars

First published timetable:
  November 21, 1879
    6:30 a.m. Portland
  11:35 St. Joseph   m.p. 47
  12:00 m McMinnville   50
  12:30 p.m. Willamette Vy. RR crossing 54
  12:50 Unity   57
   3:00 Independence   76

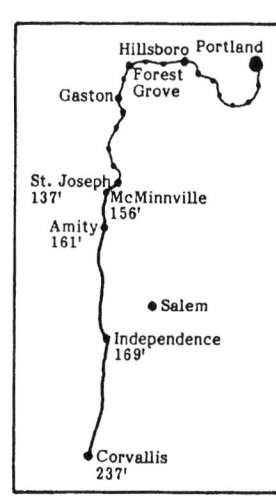

The portion from Portland to St. Joseph was owned by Oregon Central Railroad Company, but leased to the subject company on September 1, 1879, to operate the track.

Construction comments in April, 1880, *Official Guide*, states that the track is now opened to Corvallis, 21 miles. A published timetable dated June 22, 1880, shows Corvallis as 97 miles from Portland.

Bibliography: *Poor's 1881*, p. 820   *The Dallas Itemizer* - May 16 to October 10, 1879   *Valuation 45*, p. 422

WEYERHAEUSER COMPANY

President

Incorp:		**Operated:** 1928 to	**HQ city:** Klamath Falls
Disposition:	in operation in 1980		
Miles track:	120	**Gauge:** 56½"	
Main line:	Woods lines from Beatty, Klamath Falls, Springfield and Sutherlin		

Locomotives:

1	2-8-2	44	BLW	37496	1/12	140,000		ex Twin Falls Logging Co.
2	2-8-2T	41	'	53146	4/20			1941 to City of Prineville Ry. #5
3	3 truck	38	Heisler	1539	1/27	160,000		to Kosmos Timber Co. #10
4*	2-6-6-2	51	BLW	61781	/34	293,000	59,600	6/1952 to Sierra Railroad Co. #38
6	'	44	'	60412	3/28	210,000	42,500	ex Mud Bay Logging Co. #8
101*	B-B		'	74814	7/50		750 h.p.	diesel
102*	'		'	74815	'		'	diesel
103*	'		'	75254	5/51		800 h.p.	diesel
105*	'		'	75255	'		'	diesel

Freight traffic: logging

The track sections:
Beatty into the woods was opened in 1928.
Springfield, 31 miles, was built in 1949.
Sutherlin, about April, 1949, and 18 miles.
Klamath Falls past Aspen Lake reached about
40 miles before abandonment in 1956.

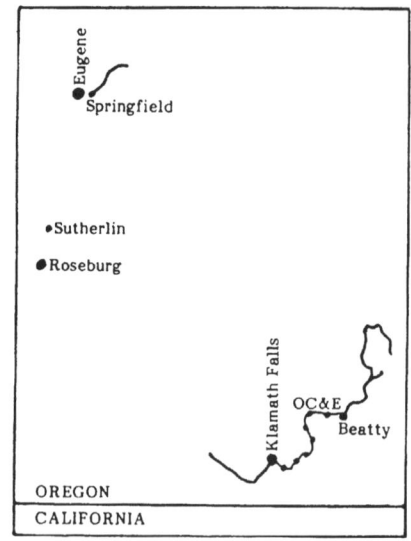

WHEELER, C. H.

								President
Incorp:			**Operated:**	1909 to 1935			**HQ city:**	Cochran
Disposition:	abandoned							
Miles track:	30		**Gauge:**	56½"				
Rail wt.:	60 lbs.		**Max. grade:**	5.0%				

Locomotives:

Road No.	Type	Dvr. in.	Bldr.	Bldr. No.	Date	Weight	Effort	Remarks
1 ?	2T Shay	29½	Lima	884	5/04	74,000	15,625	ex Portland, Eugene & Eastern #1
1-2d ?	"	"	"	1870	1/07	"	16,900	3/1938 to Standard Logging Co. #1
2 ?	2 truck	36	Heisler	1151	8/09	80,000		ex Portland, Eugene & Eastern #2
2-2d ?	2T Shay	29½	Lima	2864	1/17	92,000	16,900	ex Big Creek Logging Co. #2-2d
3 ?	"	32	"	854	3/04	90,000	18,750	acq. 8/1915 ex Francis Weist
3-2d ?	3T Shay	36	"	2941	10/17	150,000	30,350	ex Eagle Lumber Co.
4 ?	2 truck	31	Climax	886	5/08	80,000		acq. 1921 ex S. Oregon Traction Co. #4
10 ?	2T Shay	32	Lima	2829	1/16	107,000	22,580	ex Portland Lumber Co. #10
11	3T Shay	36	"	3018	4/19	146,000	30,350	4/1938 to Stoddard Logging Co. #11

Freight traffic: logging

WILLAMETTE & PACIFIC RAILROAD, INC.

						Mortimer B. Fuller, III,	**President**
Incorp:	2/9/93		**Operated:**	2/22/93 to		**HQ city:**	Albany
Disposition:	in operation 1993						
Miles track:	183.80		**Gauge:**	56½"			
Main line:	Newberg to Monroe and Albany to Toledo						
Rail wt.:	60/136 lbs.		**Max. grade:**	2.62%			

Locomotives:

Road No.	Type	Bldr.	Bldr. No.	Date	Weight	H-power	Remarks			Name
1801	B-B	EMD	25130	4/59	250,000	1,750	acq. 3/93 ex SP		#3855	Black Widow
1802	"	"	21362	4/56	"	"	"	1/93 "	5669	Lake Oswego
1803	"	"	22920	1/57	"	"	"	10/93 "	5738	Sherwood
2301	"	"	74602-1	10/74	261,000	2,300	"	5/93 ex AT&SFe	3600	Sheridan
2302	"	"	74602-2	"	"	"	"	" "	3601	Adair Village
2303	"	"	74602-3	"	"	"	"	" "	3602	Amity
2304	"	"	74602-4	"	"	"	"	" "	3603	Corvallis
2305	"	"	74602-5	"	"	"	"	" "	3604	Dallas
2306	"	"	74602-6	"	"	"	"	" "	3605	Dundee

OREGON 155.

2307	B-B	EMD	74602-7	10/74	261,000	2,300	acq. 5/93 ex AT&SFe #	3606	Independence
2308	'	'	74602-8	'	'	'	'	'	3607	Lafayette
2309	'	'	74602-9	'	'	'	'	'	3608	Philomath
2310	'	'	74602-10	'	'	'	'	'	3609	Monroe
2311	'	'	74602-11	'	'	'	'	'	3610	Newberg
2312	'	'	74602-12	'	'	'	'	'	3611	Albany
2313	'	'	74602-13	'	'	'	'	'	3612	Toledo
2314	'	'	74602-14	'	'	'	'	'	3613	McMinnville
2315	'	'	74602-15	'	'	'	'	'	3614	Willamina
2316	'	'	74602-16	'	'	'	'	'	3615	Beaverton
2317	'	'	74602-17	'	'	'	'	'	3616	Eugene

Freight traffic: forest products and agricultural

Roster of 12/31/1993:
20 locomotives
37 freight cars
4 cabooses

The carrier also has joint trackage rights with Southern Pacific from Albany to Eugene.

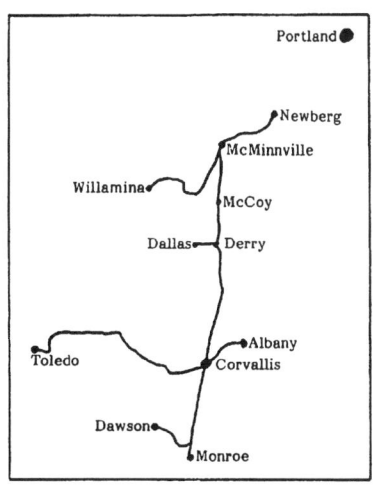

Bibliography: Direct communication

Official Open and Prepay Station List

WILLAMETTE PACIFIC RAILROAD COMPANY

Wendling-Johnson Lumber Co., **Owner**

Incorp:	6/14/1911	**Operated:** to 7/1/15	**HQ city:**	Florence

Disposition: sold to Southern Pacific Company on July 1, 1915

Miles track: 73.3   **Gauge:** 56½"

Main line: Eugene to Canary

Rail wt.: lbs.   **Max. grade:** 0.72%   **Const. began:** grading (November 27, 1911)
                                                                                                                 laying rails

Const. comp.: October 1, 1916, by Southern Pacific   **First train operated:** April 16, 1914

Freight traffic: common carrier, logging and agriculture

Published timetable dated:
May, 1916 - Southern Pacific
7:20 a.m. Eugene
10:00 Mapleton 58.0 miles
11:50 Gardiner 91.5
1:30 p.m. Reedsport 92.8
3:30 Marshfield 121.6

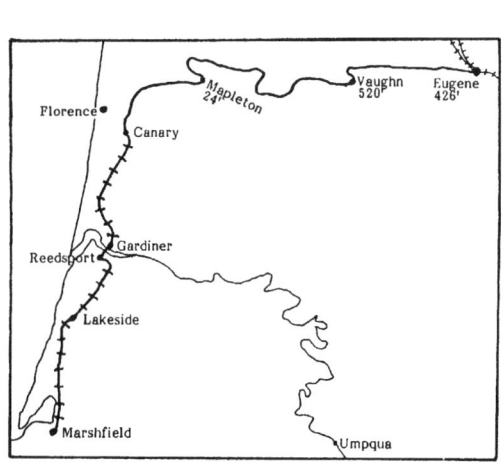

First listed in ICC for 6/30/13 as a Southern Pacific subsidiary with 13 miles owned, not in use; extended to 39 miles by 6/30/14 and to 72 miles by 6/30/15, still not in use.

A note in May, 1916, *Official Guide* states that from Eugene to Marshfield, 121.6 miles, have been completed with the exception of a bridge over the Umpqua River at Reedsport where a ferry is employed.

The first round trips were made on April 5, 1916, to Marshfield; the property was placed in operation by Southern Pacific on October 1, 1916.

The first train, April 16, 1914, was to Walton, 24.7 miles; opened to Nekoma on September 20 and to Mapleton November 19, 1914. These trains were operated by the construction department. This data was found in *Corporate History of Southern Pacific Company, Pacific System, of June 30, 1916*, page 20 of Southern Pacific Company.

Bibliography: Eugene - *Guard* - November 30, 1911   *Valuation 45*, p. 373   Spokane - *Spokesman-Review* - April 6, 1916:

California State Railroad Museum Library
Willamette Pacific span number six under construction on August 18, 1915; to Eugene is to the left

WILLAMETTE VALLEY & COAST RAIL ROAD COMPANY

Col. T. Egenton Hogg, **President**

Incorp:	7/6/1874	**Operated:** (4/1/85) to 12/22/94	**HQ city:**	Corvallis

Disposition: foreclosure sale to Oregon Central & Eastern Railroad Company effective April 13, 1895

Miles track: 141.80   **Gauge:** 56½"

Main line: Yaquina to Detroit

Rail wt.: 50/55 lbs. steel   **Max. grade:** 2.62%   **Const. began:** grading (December 17, 1883)

laying rails (March 11, 1884)

Const. comp.:   **First train operated:** April 11, 1884

Locomotive engines:

Road No.	Cyln.	Type	Dvr. in.	Bldr.	Bldr. No.	Date	Weight	Effort	Remarks
1		2-4-0		Grant	1261	4/79			Corvallis - to Bell. Bay & E. #2
1-2d*	17x24	4-4-0	55	Cooke	1342	11/81	45,000	13,000	
2-3*	'	'	62	Rogers	3411-10	11/83		13,000	
4*	'	'	56	'	3445	12/83	49,000	13,590	
5*	10x18	2-4-0	48	Cooke	1718	5/86			2/1891 to Rogue River Valley Ry.
6-7*	15x22	4-4-0	54	'	1719-20	'	64,000	13,540	
8-11*	'	'	'	'	1722-25	6/86	'	'	
12-15*	'	'	'	'	1728-31	9/86	'	'	

Freight traffic: common carrier, lumber

Rosters of   6/30/1887 - 6/30/1891:
locomotive engines	18	16
passenger, mail cars	12	12
flat cars	45	81
box cars	575	253
gondolas	100	

First published timetable:
December 15, 1885 - M-W-F
8:00 a.m. Yaquina
           Toledo   9 miles
           Nashville   41
           Blodgett's 52
3:33 p.m. Corvallis   72
Westbound trip was T-Th-Sat.

Published timetable dated:
April 16, 1893 - daily exc. Sun.
7:30 a.m.		Yaquina	
7:55		Toledo	m.p. 9.0
8:18		Elk City	18.0
9:22		Nashville	41.0
9:45		Summit	46.1
10:15		Blodgett	51.5
11:12		Corvallis	71.2
11:43		Albany	83.3
1:30 p.m.		Albany	
2:15		Shelburn	97.1
3:50		Mill City	118.9
4:30		Niagara	126.2
4:40		Halstead	127.9
5:40		Detroit	138.0

Ground was broken at Corvallis on May 17, 1877, with some grading and tunnel work done. The ceremony was repeated September 9, 1881. Rail laying began at Yaquina in the spring of 1884 and head of track reached Elk City, 20 miles, in September and into Corvallis on December 15, 1884.

The line was extended to Albany, and a connection with the main line of Oregon & California Rail Road Co., on February 1, 1887. Work resumed in about July, 1891. The first published timetable showing Halstead, 128 miles, was dated January, 1892. The next change was a schedule dated April 16, 1893, showing operations to Detroit, 138 miles. It appears that the final four miles, to Idanha, wasn't operated until about October, 1895, by the successor company.

Listed in first ICC (6/30/88) as an operating independent with 101 miles owned and in use. By 6/30/89 it was 136 miles; by 6/30/90 it was 142 miles owned and 128 operated. The "owned" remained constant, but the "operated" varied. In 1891 it was 138 miles, 128 in 1892 and 1893, then back to 138 by 6/30/94.

Oregon Pacific Rail Road Company, incorporated October 15, 1880, was the construction company and to operate the system until completed to Boise City, 600 miles east. As it never was, that company operated the line from first opening until October 28, 1890, when Col. T. E. Hogg was appointed receiver. He was replaced by E. W. Hadley on March 4, 1893, and, in turn, by Charles Clark on January 6, 1894.

The line had 1,975 feet of tunnels and 284 bridges and trestles totalling 42,285 feet (over eight miles). It is estimated that the carrier cost $4,250,000 to build and equip. Steamships were operated from San Francisco to Yaquina and also river steamers on the Willamette River from Corvallis and Albany to Portland.

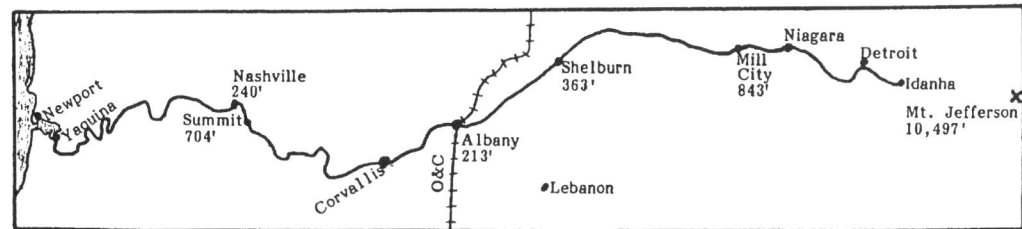

Bibliography: *Poor's 1889*, p. 894   Oregon PUC reports 1888 to 1895   *Valuation 45*, p. 355
The Corvallis Gazette - January 4 to April 18, 1884   *Railroad Gazette* - March 26, 1885

California State Railroad Museum Library   *Gerald M. Best Collection*
Willamette Valley & Coast number seven on the "armstrong" turntable at Yaquina in 1886

California State Railroad Museum Library   *Railway & Locomotive Historical Society Collection*
Willamette Valley & Coast Rail Road Company locomotive engine number one

Oregon State Library Collection   *Views 10-3 - Gift of George B. Abdill*
Willamette Valley & Coast number seven was photographed at Toledo in about 1887 with a four-car mixed train.

WILLAMETTE VALLEY RAILROAD COMPANY, THE

Joseph Gaston, **President**

Incorp:	9/9/1878 **Operated:** 6/2/79 to 4/1/80	**HQ city:** Portland
Disposition:	sold to The Oregon Railway Company, Ltd., on April 2, 1880	
Predecessor:	Dayton, Sheridan & Grande Ronde Railroad Company, The	**Incorp.:** 11/17/1877 to 6/2/1879
Miles track:	30.19 **Gauge:** 36"	
Main line:	Dayton to Sheridan and Smithfield	

OREGON 159.

Rail wt.: 28/35 lbs. - iron Max. grade: 2.24% Const. began: grading (June 6, 1878)
laying rails (July 22, 1878)

Const. comp.: was not First train operated: July 29, 1878

Locomotive engines:

Road No.	Name	Type	Dvr. in.	Bldr.	Bldr. No.	Date	Weight	Effort	Remarks
1*	Pioneer	2-4-0	31	National	259	5/78	21,200		arrived July 19, 1878
2*	Progress	'	'	'	260	'	'		both burned wood

Freight traffic: common carrier, agriculture

The carrier was placed in operation September 1, 1878; first service to Sheridan was October 24, 1878.

The line was graded from Smithfield to Dallas, four miles, and completed by the successor company on May 31, 1880.

The purpose of the road was to deliver farm products to the Yamhill River at Dayton for inexpensive water transportation to Portland.

A note from *The Railway Age* for August 7, 1878, states "This new narrow gauge road two weeks since received a 15-ton engine and rails to lay 12 miles of track."

ICC Valuation Reports describes the property as Dayton to Sheridan, 22.95 miles, and from Broadmead (now Sheridan Jct.) to Sheridan, 7.24 miles; it should have read Dayton to Smithfield, 22.95 miles.

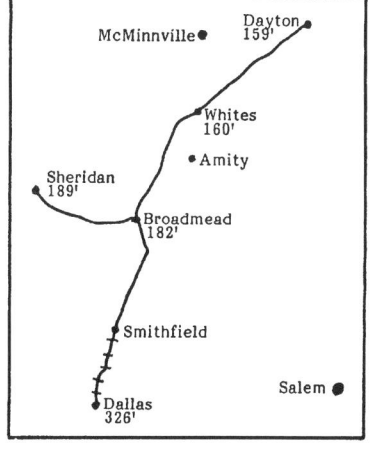

Bibliography: *Poor's 1880*, p. 999   McMinnville - *Yamhill County Reporter* - February 7 to August 15, 1878   *Valuation 45*, p. 426

WILLAMETTE VALLEY RAILROAD COMPANY

Ruth E. Root, **President**

Incorp:	10/11/1984	**Operated:**	1/1/85 to (10/17/92)	**HQ city:**	Hoskins

Disposition: permanently closed ?

Predecessor: Valley & Siletz Railroad Company   **Incorp.:** 1/20/1912 to 12/31/1984

Miles track: 40.06   **Gauge:** 56½"

Main line: Independence to Valsetz

Rail wt.: 56/90 lbs.   **Max. grade:** 3.2%   **Const. began:** grading (August 18, 1913)
laying rails (Nov. 17, 1913)

Const. comp.: December 31, 1917   **First train operated:** 1916

Locomotives:

Road No.		Type	Dvr. in.	Bldr.	Bldr. No.	Date	Weight	Effort	Remarks
10		2-6-0	37	BLW	5034	3/80	48,000		acq. 1913 ex Tacoma E. #1 - SCR 1919
17		2-8-2	48	'	57201	9/23	179,000	34,400	acq. 1947 ex Clark & Wilson-SCR 1957
50*	17x24	2-6-2	46	'	41379	5/14	120,800	23,070	scrapped in 1953
55*	19x24	2-8-2	'	Porter	6859	2/24	156,000	30,420	scrapped in 1955
56		'	44	BLW	58362	4/25	145,000	28,600	acq. 1939 ex Brooks-Scanlon - SCR 1955
57		'	48	'	34563	4/10	171,700	32,800	acq. 1942 ex Carlisle Lumber-SCR 1955
60		4-6-0	51	Pitts.		/88	100,600	17,500	acq. 1916 ex Spokane Intl. #9-SCR 1931
70		4-4-0	63	BLW	9465	9/88	72,500	11,600	acq. 8/22/18 ex S.P. #1500 - SCR 1922
5*		B-B		G.E.	32132	2/54	140,000	600 h.p.	diesel
7*		'		'	32133	'	'	'	(6/1985) to Santa Maria Valley
8		'		'	28340	12/46	88,000	380 h.p.	
11*		'		'		/55	140,000	600 h.p.	

Freight traffic: common carrier, lumber

Roster of 12/31/1924:
- 2 locomotives
- 3 passenger cars
- 20 freight cars

Initial construction work was begun in July, 1912. The 2.1 miles entering Valsetz was purchased May 20, 1920, from Siletz Lumber & Logging Co. A connecting line of 1.2 miles at Independence was built between September 12, 1923, and September 15, 1924.

First published timetable:
    January 1, 1918 - daily exc. Sunday
    10:55 a.m. Valsetz   10:30
    11:48   Hoskins   9:35 a.m.
                Hoskins   5:00
     1:20 p.m. Pedee   4:12
     2:05   Simpson   3:36
     2:40   Independence   3:00 p.m.
    Frank J. Cobbs was president

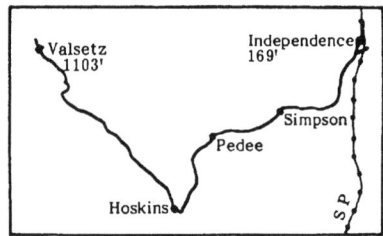

First listed in ICC for 6/30/14 as an operating independent with 13 miles owned, not in use. It was extended to 18 miles by 6/30/15, 25 miles by 6/30/16, 34 miles by 12/31/16, to 37 in 1918, 38 in 1919 and to 40 miles in 1920.

The carrier opened officially on January 1, 1918, as a common carrier. The total cost of construction was $1,335,278 and $121,612 to equip, $33,116 being paid for passenger cars, $18,591 for freight cars and $48,141 for the locomotives. In addition to the steam equipment, the road operated gasoline passenger cars numbered five, nine and ten; all were scrapped in 1945.

The mail contract was lost June 30, 1952, and, with that gone, passenger train service was discontinued. Rail service beyond Pedee, 16.3 miles, was terminated on March 12, 1979.

Bibliography: *Poor's 1924*, p. 721   *Valuation 43*, p. 353

WILLAMETTE VALLEY RAILWAY COMPANY

							President
Incorp:	10/6/1927	**Operated:**	(10/17/27)	to	(9/17/38)	**HQ city:**	Oregon City
Disposition:	abandoned ?						
Predecessors:	Willamette Valley Southern Railway Company			**Incorp.:**	1/24/1914	to	(10/16/1927)
	Clackamas Southern Railway Co.				12/11/1908		1914
Miles track:	45.1	**Gauge:**	56½"				
Main line:	Portland to Mount Angel						
Rail wt.:	lbs.	**Max. grade:**		**Const. began:**	grading	(March 23, 1914)	
					laying rails	(August 17, 1914)	
Const. comp.:	October 23, 1915			**First train operated:**		March 6, 1915	
Electric motors:							

Major business: passengers

Published timetable dated:
    February 27, 1916
    9:15 a.m. Portland
    9:33   Golf Jct.   m.p. 5.0
    9:55   Oregon City   13.2
    10:20   Beaver Creek   20.1
    10:26   Spangler   22.5
    10:40   Mulino   27.2
    10:52   Molalla   32.4
    11:10   Monitor   41.6
    11:20   Mount Angel   45.1
    There was also a 6:40 p.m. departure from
    Portland and two round trips from Oregon
    City to Mount Angel.
    Grant B. Dimick was the president.

A January, 1921, Southern Pacific system
map shows the end of track at Molalla.

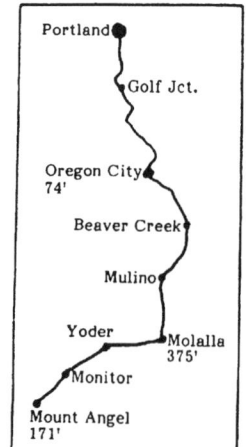

Bibliography: Oregon City - *Enterprise* - March 27, 1914   *Molalla Pioneer* - August 13 and 20, 1914
                Spokane - *Spokesman-Review* - March 7 to October 24, 1915

OREGON 161.

WILLAMETTE VALLEY RAILWAY COMPANY

					President	
Incorp:	1/26/1993	**Operated:**	2/22/93 to	**HQ city:**	Independence
Disposition:	in operation 1993				
Miles track:	83.	**Gauge:**	56½"		
Main line:	Woodburn to West Stayton and Albany Jct. to Mill City				
Rail wt.:	90/132 lbs.	**Max. grade:**	1.49%		
Freight traffic:	common carrier, agriculture and lumber				

Locomotives:
3859
4433

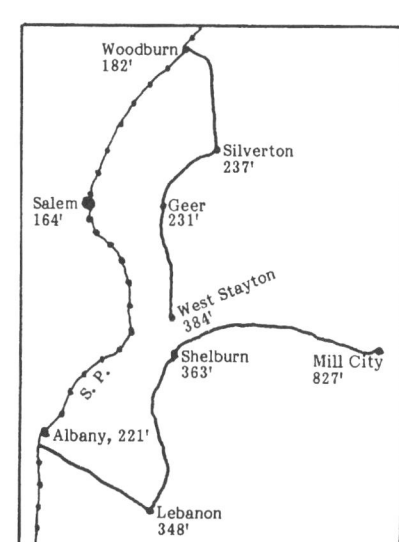

Bibliography: Direct communication   Official Open and Prepay Station List

Oregon State Library Collection   WPA 4 #732
Gasoline powered logging equipment that lays its own "tracks"; Deschutes County in about 1940

WILLAMINA & GRAND RONDE RAILWAY COMPANY

Ruth E. Root, President

Incorp:	1/27/1988		**Operated:**	3/5/88 to			**HQ city:**	Independence
Disposition:	in operation 1993							
Predecesssors:	Willamette Valley Railroad Company					**Incorp.:**	10/11/1984 to	3/5/1988
	Longview, Portland & Northern Railway Company						12/31/1954	3/29/1980
	Willamina & Grande Ronde Railway Company						6/20/1920	12/31/1954
Miles track:	5.2		**Gauge:**	56½"				
Main line:	Willamina to Fort Hill							
Rail wt:			**Max. grade:**			**Const. began:**	grading	1920

Locomotives:

Road No.	Type	Dvr. in.	Bldr.	Bldr. No.	Date	Weight	Effort	Remarks
680	2-8-0	50	BLW	44235	10/16			ex Louisiana & Pacific
681	2-6-2	47	"	54077	11/20			1953 to Mexicano del Pacifico
110	B-B		ALCO	74453	12/45	198,000	600 h.p.	used at Grande Ronde
111	"		"	76933	7/49	230,000	1,000 h.p.	used at Gardiner
112	"		"	79226	10/51	"	"	used at Gardiner

Freight traffic: common carrier, lumber

Roster of 12/31/1938: - ICC
  1 locomotive

Note the difference is spelling of title in 1920 and 1988.

The previous main line was nine miles from Willamina to beyond Grande Ronde; the branch at Reedsport, built in 1952, was three miles in length.

First listed in ICC for 6/30/20 as an operating independent with five miles owned, not in use. It was extended to eight miles in 1921 and "in operation" by 12/31/22. This class II carrier was owned by Miami Corporation in 1931. Mileage was listed as nine each in 1938.

In 1941 the property was owned by Long-Bell Lumber Company. It was extended to 12 miles each in 1952 and merged into Longview, Portland & Northern Railwlay Company on January 1, 1955; this last named was owned by International Paper Company. In 1951, the ICC authorized construction of 3.500 miles in Douglas County, Oregon.

The Longview, Portland & Northern Railway Company also operated in southwestern Washington from 1923 until 1981.

The precise line of succession is not known to the chronicler. The property was operated by Willamette Valley Railroad Company, but may or not have taken title to it. The two companies appear to be owned by the same principals.

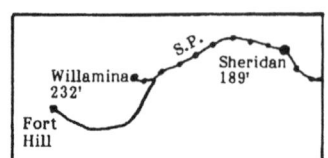

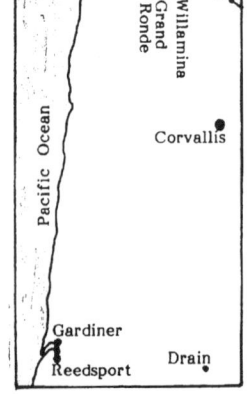

California State Railroad Museum Library
Willamina & Grande Ronde Railway Company number 680 at Grande Ronde in July, 1950

OREGON 163.

WYOMING & COLORADO RAILROAD COMPANY

David L. Durbano, **President**

Incorp:	1/18/1991	**Operated:** (2/1/90) to	**HQ city:**	Vale
Disposition:	in operation 1993			
Miles track:	154.8	**Gauge:** 56½"		
Main line:	Ontario Jct. to Burns			
Rail wt.:	131 lbs.	**Max. grade:**		
Freight traffic:	common carrier, agriculture			

Locomotives:

1608	B-B	EMD	/1952	1500 h.p.	acq. 1990 ex TP&W #103

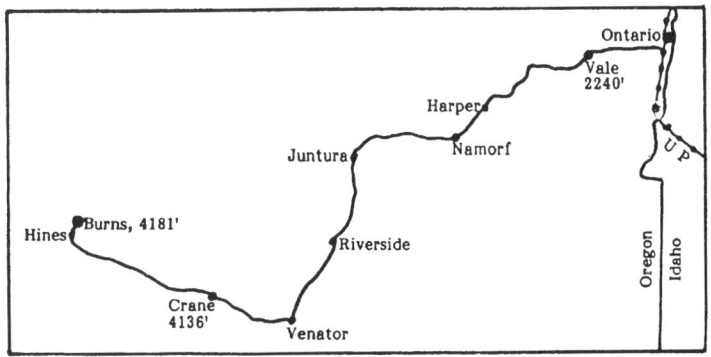

The line west of Crane was closed by flooding on March 8, 1984; several millions in federal funds were used to rebuild it.

The present operator used the full line for a couple of years, but as of July 1, 1992, no operations were performed beyond milepost 25 where a new quarry had opened. However, it was again reopened to Burns on November 10, 1893.

Locally, it is known as the Oregon Eastern Railway.

Southern Oregon Historical Society #2458
Big wheels (about 12 feet tall) were used to carry the front end of a load of logs over rough terrain such as creeks, rocks and other logs. They were drawn with by animals or tractors. Logs are being loaded onto a railroad car in this scene.

Extensions of old, opening of new roads, changes in name of roads, stations, @c. from *Official Guide*.

February, 1873
    Oregon & California — Opened from Oakland to Roseburg, 19 miles.

January, 1880
    Western Oregon — Completed and opened from Portland to Independence, 76 miles.

April, 1880
    Western Oregon — Independence to Corvallis opened, 21 miles.

December, 1880
    Oregon & California — The Western Oregon Railroad is now operated by this road and designated at West Side, Div., the main road being called the East Side Div.

September, 1881
    Oregonian Ry. — Operating Ray's Landing (Willamette River) south to Brownsville; Dayton to Monmouth; and Sheridan Jct. to Sheridan, a total of 115 miles.

June, 1882
    Oregon Ry. & Navig. — Bonneville to The Dalles, 46 miles, opened.

August, 1882
    Oregon Ry. & Navig. — Operating Oregon Railway from Brownsville to Coburg, 20 miles.

September, 1882
    Oregon & California — Roseburg to Myrtle Creek, 22 miles.

October, 1882
    Oregon Ry. & Navig. — Umatilla to Pendleton, 44 miles.

November, 1882
    Oregon & Calif. — Myrtle Creek to Riddle's, 6 miles.

January, 1883
    Oregon Ry. & Navig. — Bonneville to Portland, 41 miles.

June, 1883
    Oregon & California — Riddle's to Glendale, 37 miles.

August, 1883
    Oregon Ry. & Navig. — Pendleton southeast to Mikecha, 21.5 miles.

October, 1883
    Oregon Ry. & Navig. — Mikecha to Meacham, 28 miles.

January, 1884
    Oregon & California — Extended from Glendale southward to Grant's Pass, 34 miles.

May, 1884
    Oregon & California — Grant's Pass to Ashland, 45 miles.

August, 1884
    Oregon Ry. & Navig. — Meacham to La Grande, 25 miles.

December, 1884
    Oregon Ry. & Navig. — La Grande to Huntington, 99 miles.

May, 1885
    Oregonian Ry. — Operated since 1881 by Oregon Ry. & Navig. Co., but no longer is; in hands of a receiver.

May, 1886
    Oregon Ry. & Navig. — Spanish Hollow is now Biggs.

March, 1887
    Oregonian Ry. — Extended north from Ray's Landing to Portland and operating to Coburg, Sheridan and Airlie.

April, 1887
    Oregon Ry. & Navig. — Walla Walla to Blue Mountain and Pendleton, 47 miles.

January, 1888
    Southern Pacific — Opened from Siskiyou to Ashland, 17 miles.

January, 1889
    Oregon Ry. & Navig. — Willows Jct. to Heppner, 45 miles.

May, 1889
    Oregon Ry. & Navig. — Centerville, 18 miles north of Pendleton, is now Athena.

February, 1891
    Oregon Ry. & Navig. — La Grande to Elgin, 21 miles. (Actually it was The Oregon Railway Extensions Co.)

November, 1891
    Southern Pacific — Coburg to Natron, 13 miles.

OREGON

June, 1895
    Oregon Pacific Railroad -- It is now Oregon Central & Eastern Railroad Co.

January, 1896
    Oregon Central & Eastern -- Detroit to Idanha, 4 miles.

September, 1896
    Oregon Ry. & Navig. -- It is now Oregon Railroad & Navigation Co.

March, 1898
    Oregon Central & Eastern -- It is now Corvallis & Eastern Railroad Co.

June, 1898
    Astoria & Columbia River -- It is now in operation from Astoria eastward to Goble, 60 miles, and Astoria south to Seaside, 18 miles. Also a branch from Warrenton to New Astoria, 3 miles. Trains operate from Goble to Portland on Northern Pacific tracks.

October, 1899
    Astoria & Columbia River -- New Astoria, 10 miles west of Astoria, is now Fort Stevens.

February, 1901
    Southern Pacific -- Mohawk Jct. to Wendling, 16 miles.

December, 1901
    Sumpter Valley Ry. -- This road has been extended from Sumpter westward to Whitney, 14 miles.

October, 1904
    Sumpter Valley Ry. -- Road has been extended westward from Whitney to Tipton, 9 miles.

August, 1905
    Oregon Central Railroad -- Opened from Arlington south to Condon, 45 miles.

December, 1905
    Sumpter Valley Ry. -- Extended from Tipton to Austin, 8.2 miles.

July, 1907
    Malheur Valley Ry. -- Ontario west to Vale, 15 miles.

November, 1907
    Central Railway of Oregon -- Union Jct. to Valley Jct., 1.5 miles, and to Union, 2.4 miles; Valley Jct. to Cove, 10.5 miles.

February, 1908
    Oregon RR & Navig. -- Pilot Rock Jct. southward to Pilot Rock, 14 miles.

January, 1909
    Oregon RR & Navig. -- Elgin to Joseph, 63 miles.

July, 1909
    Southern Pacific -- Worden northeast to Klamath Falls, 14 miles.

October, 1909
    Corvallis & Eastern -- Extended from Detroit to Hoover, 2 miles.

November, 1909
    Salem, Falls City & Western -- Extended from Dallas eastward to Salem, 14 miles.

November, 1910
    Northwestern Railroad -- It has opened from Blake's Jct. northward to Homestead, 57.9 miles.

March, 1911
    Oregon Trunk Ry. -- Freight and passenger service opened March 1, 1911, over the line from Clark, Wash., to Madras.
    United Railways -- It has been extended from Burlington to North Plains, a distance of 11.2 miles.

April, 1911
    Malheur Valley Ry. -- Has been extended from Vale northwestward to Brogan, 23 miles.
    Sumpter Valley Ry. -- Now been extended from Austin westward to Prairie City, 21 miles.

May, 1911
    Oregon Trunk Ry. -- Metolius south to Opal City, 11.7 miles.
    United Railways -- North Plains to Banks, 4.6 miles.

July, 1911
    Oregon-Washington RR & Navig. -- Deschutes Jct. south to Madras, 101 miles.

August, 1911
    Southern Pacific -- Effective July 2, 1911, it operates Oregon Eastern Railway Co. from Klamath Falls to Chiloquin as a part of the Shasta Division.

December, 1911
    Central Railroad of Oregon -- Hot Lake branch, 8 miles, opened from Union to Hot Lake.
    Oregon Trunk Ry. -- Extended from Opal City to Bend, 29.5 miles.

June, 1912
  Southern Pacific — Extended and opened from Natron eastward to Oakridge, 33.6 miles.

July, 1912
  Portland, Eugene & Eastern — Corvallis south to Monroe, 16.4 miles, and branch, Monroe Jct. to Alpine, 2.7 miles.

August, 1912
  Oregon Electric Ry. — It has been extended from Salem south to Albany, 27 miles.

November, 1912
  Southern Pacific — Extended from Chiloquin northward to Kirk, 13.5 miles.

July, 1913
  Salem, Falls City & Western — Extended from West Salem to Salem, 1.4 miles.

October, 1913
  Portland, Eugene & Eastern — Has been extended from Monroe southward to Eugene, 24 miles, and a new line opened from Canby to Molalla, 11 miles

February, 1914
  Oregon, Pacific & Eastern — It has acquired Oregon & Southeastern Railroad Co. and assumed control and operation on January 1, 1914.

March, 1914
  Oregon Short Line — Extended from Vale to Juntura, 58 miles.

September, 1914
  Oregon Short Line — Extended from Juntura west to Riverside, 19 miles.

July, 1915
  Oregon Short Line — Opened passenger service between Ontario and Riverside, 93 miles.

January, 1916
  Rogue River Ry. — It is now operated by Oregon Southern Traction Co.

February, 1916
  Oregon-Washington RR & Navig. — A new line from Hinkle to Messner, 20 miles, is now used by certain through trains instead of via Umatilla.

May, 1916
  Willamette Pacific — From Eugene to Marshfield, 121.6 miles, has been completed with the exception of a bridge over the Umpqua River at Reedsport and Gardiner where a ferry is employed.

December, 1916
  Sumpter Valley Ry. — The station formerly known as Greenwood, 29 miles east of Prairie, is now Tipton.

February, 1917
  Oregon Short Line — Extended from Riverside to Crane, 34 miles.

November, 1929
  Oregon, California & Eastern Ry. — Sprague to Bly, 24.9 miles.

California State Railroad Museum Library
  Gilchrist Timber Co. number 204 at Gilchrist in August, 1938; it was predecessor of Klamath Northern Railway Co.

A local merchant had the railroad spirit as shown in this ad from *West Side Telephone* for September 10, 1886.

Steamers *Bailey Gatzert* and *Charles H. Spencer*, May, 1906, at lower entrance to Cascade Locks.

A four car train on Oregon Steam Navigation Co. at The Dalles in about 1862.

California State Railroad Museum Library   *Railway & Locomotive Historical Society Collection*
Salem, Falls City & Western yard with locomotive eight and passenger motor on the left

Oregon State Library Collection   Oregon 963
This is the full view of rugged scenery along the Columbia River; for center detail see page 125.

Oregon State Library Collection WPA 4 - Clatsop County - 297B
A scene from earliest days when logs were dragged out by several teams of oxen

California State Railroad Museum Library
Decades later, "iron horses" such as Sumpter Valley #251 pulling 21 cars were used; even the smoke looks frozen in the December 30, 1946, scene.

Studebaker started out building freight for the railroads, but changed to motor vehicles and competition for the carriers.
Grants Pass - *Rogue River Courier* - March 26 and April 18, 1913

Oregon State Library Collection

WPA 4 - #288

A seagoing log raft on the Columbia River heads for the Pacific Ocean

CHRONOLOGY

Some of the major events in the development of the Territory/State of Oregon.

1579	Sir Francis Drake sails north to what is now the southern part of Oregon.
1775	Bruno Heceta and party become the first known Europeans to land on northwestern soil.
1788	Captain Robert Gray arrives at Tillamook Bay with his sloop *Lady Washington*.
1793	Sir Alexander Mackenzie, the first white man to cross North America, arrives at the Pacific Ocean.
1803	President Thomas Jefferson purchases Louisiana Territory from France; it is termed Oregon Country.
1804	Captains Lewis and Clark begin expedition, guided by Toussaint Charbonneau, to the Pacific Ocean.
1811	John J. Astor's Pacific Fur Company established where Astoria now stands.
1812	South Pass through Rocky Mountains is discovered by Robert Stuart, Pacific Fur Co., and used by pioneers later.
1814	First livestock in the Pacific Northwest is brought from California by ship.
1818	Fort George (ex Astoria) returns to American ownership by Treaty of 1814; joint U. S. -British occupancy.
1827	First sawmill in the Pacific Northwest built by Dr. McLoughlin.
1828	Jedediah Smith, trapper and explorer-guide, reaches Pacific Northwest from California.
1828	First grist (flour) mills built by Hudson's Bay Company at Fort Vancouver and Fort Colville.
1829	Hudson's Bay Company post established at Willamette Falls, now Oregon City.
1832	Captain Benj. Bonneville and party of 110 men cross Rocky Mountains to reach Fort Walla Walla.
1833	First school at Fort Vancouver.
	First timber shipped from Oregon to China.
1834	Fort Hall, now in Idaho, established by Nathaniel Wyeth on his second expedition.
1836	The first steamboat on the Pacific Ocean is brought to Fort Vancouver.
	Alice Clarissa Whitman is the first white child to be born in Oregon Country.
1839	First printing press in the Northwest brought from Honolulu to Lapwai (now Idaho) to print Nez Perce primer.
	Father Blanchet establishes first Catholic mission in the town of St. Paul.
1841	First ship built by Americans, *Star of Oregon,* is launched.
1842	Willamette University, first west of the Mississippi River, is founded by Jason Lee.
1843	First large group over the Oregon Trail; about 900 settle in the Willamette Valley.
1845	George Abernethy is elected provisional governor.
1846	Treaty between U. S. and Great Britain establishes Oregon boundary.
	The first newspaper is printed at Oregon City.
1849	General Joseph Lane, first appointed territorial governor, arrives.
1851	City of Portland is incorporated.
1851	The first person of Chinese ancestry settles in Portland.
1853	The Typographical Society is the first labor union in Oregon.
1855	First telegraph company established in Oregon.
1856	Eastern Oregon closed to settlers by the army because of Indian wars.
1859	John Whiteaker becomes the first elected governor.
	Ladd and Tilton Bank, first in the state, is established.
1860	Daily stagecoach service from Portland to Sacramento.
1864	Salem becomes the seat of government by popular vote.
	California to Portland telegraph line opened.
1868	Corvallis College established, the first state-supported institution of higher education in Oregon.
1869	First public high school.
1872	Modoc Indian wars.
1876	University of Oregon opens in Eugene.
1878	Bannock Indian wars.
1882	State teachers colleges built at Monmouth and Ashland.
1883	Transcontinental railroad through the north is opened.
1902	Initiative and referendum laws adopted.
1905	Lewis and Clark Centennial Exposition is held in Portland.
1912	Women's suffrage voted into Oregon law.
1913	South jetty at the mouth of the Columbia River is completed.
1935	The state capitol, built in 1876, is destroyed by fire; new building completed in 1939.
1937	The major dam at Bonneville is now completed to provide hydroelectric power.
1941	Shipbuilding boom starts in Portland.
1954	McNary Dam on Columbia River dedicated by President Dwight D. Eisenhower.
1961	A freeway is completed between Salem and Portland.
1966	Oregon and Washington are linked at Astoria by opening of Astoria Bridge.
	Interstate highway links Washington, Oregon and California, known as I-5.
1968	John Day Dam, last remaining damsite on the Columbia, is dedicated by Vice President Hubert Humphrey.
1986	Metropolitan Area Express light rail service begins operation at Portland.
1992	Oregon Trail 150th anniversary is celebrated.

Source: *1993-94 Oregon Blue Book* provided by Oregon Historical Society.

WASHINGTON

The first white men to visit what is now Washington were Spanish and English seamen who had come north from California. In 1775 Bruno Heceta claimed this unknown region for Spain. English captain James Cook arrived in 1778, but not much was done in the way of exploration until 1792-94 when captain George Vancouver made extensive surveys of Puget Sound (named for one of his officers, Peter Puget) and Georgia Gulf.

American captain Robert Gray discovered the harbor which now bears his name; his discoveries plus those of Lewis and Clark in 1805 were the basis for United States claim to sovereignty. In 1811 the Canadian North West Company established a fur trading post near what would become Spokane Falls. In 1825 Hudson's Bay Company built Fort Vancouver. There followed a long period of joint-occupancy, but June 15, 1846, President Polk signed a treaty establishing the present boundary with British Canada.

In 1836 an Indian mission was opened by Marcus Whitman and Henry Spalding at what was to become Walla Walla; on November 29, 1847, Cayuse Indians massacred all 14 residents and burned the buildings. The Territory of Oregon was created in 1848, but on March 2, 1853, the area north of the Columbia River became Washington Territory; it included present-day north Idaho and western Montana to the continental divide. The first weekly newspaper, *Columbian*, was printed September 11, 1852, at Olympia. Whitman College opened its door in 1859 at Walla Walla. Gold seekers started to arrive in 1861 and many remained to become loggers and farmers. It became state number 42 on November 11, 1889.

The major cities:	1890	1960		1890	1960
Seattle	42,837	557,087	Snohomish	1,903	3,894
Tacoma	36,006	147,979	Dayton	1,880	2,913
Spokane Falls	19,922	181,608	Sprague	1,689	597
Walla Walla	4,709	24,536	Colfax	1,649	2,860
Olympia	4,698	18,273	Aberdeen	1,638	18,741
Port Townsend	4,558	5,074	Montesano	1,632	2,486
Fair Haven	4,076		Blaine	1,563	1,735
Whatcom	4,059	*34,688	North Yakima	1,535	43,284
Vancouver	3,545	32,464	Hoquiam	1,302	10,762
Ellensburg	2,768	8,625	Anacortes	1,131	8,414
Centralia	2,026	8,586	Pasco	480	14,522

* now Bellingham

The 1890 population was 349,390 v 75,116 in 1880, an increase of 365%; again, the people had followed the railroads.

The state is noted for Mount Rainier National Park and its mountain of 14,410 feet elevation, highest in the state. In the 1880s, Tacoma boosters called it Mount Tacoma. In 1960 the population density was 42 per square mile, the vast majority of them in a narrow band from Olympia to the Canadian boundary. For upwards of 150 years the state has depended heavily upon forest products for employment, but that dependence will be more moderate in the future. Other industries over the years have included ship building, Boeing aircraft, aluminum production from the abundant power of Grand Coulee Dam and others on the Columbia River and all manner of agricultural products and fisheries.

Major sources of railroad information:
    Poor's Manual of the Railroads of the United States, 1868 - 1924
    Travelers' Official Guide, 1868 - 1901
    Official Guide of the Railways, 1902 - 1975
    Interstate Commerce Commission *Statistics of Railways in the United States, 1888 - 1974*
    Interstate Commerce Commission *Valuation Reports, 1918 - 1934*
    United States Geological Survey maps
    Railroad Gazette, 1871 - 1908
    The Railway Age, 1876 - 1908
    Railway Age Gazette, 1908 - 1940
    Electric Railway Journal, 1893 - 1931
    Chicago Railway Review, 1875 - 1926
    American Railroad Journal, 1879 - 1963
    Department of the Interior, Census Office *Report of the Agencies of Transportation in the U. S., 1883*
    Department of the Interior, Census Office *Report of Transportation Business in the U. S., 1895*
    Washington Public Service Commission reports, 1906 - 1918
    Tillitson Special Collection at Leland Stanford Junior University

Index of Railroads in Washington

	Name	page:
	Admiralty Logging Company	189
	Armstrong, H. E.	208
	Baldridge Logging Company	189
	Bellingham & Northern Railway Company	189
	Bellingham Bay & British Columbia Rail Road Company	189
	Bellingham Bay & Eastern Railroad Company	190
	Bellingham Terminals & Railway Company	189
	Benson Logging & Lumbering Company	303
	Black Hills & Northwestern Railway Company	228
	Blakely Railroad Company	286
	Bloedel-Donovan Lumber Mills	191
A	Blue Mountain Railroad, Inc.	192
	Bolcom-Riley Logging Company	193
	Bolcom-Vanderhoof Logging Company	193
	Bradley Logging Company	208
	Bratnober-Waite Lumber Company	200
	Brock Logging Company, B. F.	213
	Brown's Bay Logging Company	189
	Buckley Logging Company	212
	Buffelen Lumber & Mfg. Company	193
	Burlington Northern Railroad Company see Montana	279
	Camas Prairie Railroad Company see Idaho	203
	Carlisle Lumber Company	193
	Carlisle-Pennell Lumber Company	193
	Carlsborg Mill & Timber Company	216
	Cascade Lumber Company	194
	Cascade Timber Company	195
	Cascades Railroad Company	195
	Cathlamet Timber Company	208
	Central Washington Railroad Company	297
	Chehalis & Cowlitz Railway Company	208
	Chehalis County Logging & Timber Company	260
	Chehalis Western Railroad Company	209
	Chelatchie Prairie Railroad Company	226
	Cherry Valley Logging Company	200
	Chicago, Milwaukee & Puget Sound Railway Co. see Montana	284
	Chicago, Milwaukee & St. Paul Railway Company see Montana	284
	Chicago, Milwaukee, St. Paul & Pacific Railroad Company see Montana	284
	Clallam County Railroad	250
	Clark County Timber Company	200
	Clear Lake Lumber Company	200
	Clemons Logging Company	201
	Coats-Fordney Logging Company	211
	Coats Logging Company, A. F.	211
	Coeur d'Alene & Spokane Railway Company, Ltd. see Idaho	205
A	Columbia & Cowlitz Railway Company	201
	Columbia & Palouse Railroad Company, The	202 s
	Columbia & Puget Sound Railroad Company	204
	Columbia & Red Mountain Railway Company	205 s
	Columbia Railway & Navigation Company, The	282
	Columbia River & Northern Railway Company	206
	Columbia Valley Railroad Company	222
	Connell Northern Railway Company	207 s
	Consolidated Lumber Company	207
	Copalis Lumber Company	193
	Cowlitz, Chehalis & Cascade Railway Company	208
	Crown Willamette Paper Company	208
	Crown Zellerbach Corporation	208
	Curtis, Milburn & Eastern Railroad Company	209
	Deep River Logging Company	210
	Deer Park Lumber Company	210
	Deer Park Railway Company	210
	Donovan-Corkery Logging Company	211

"A" before the name means active in 1993.
"s" after the page number shows that the line was built (or owned) as a subsidiary.

WASHINGTON

Eagle Gorge Logging Company	212
Eastern & Western Lumber Company	213
Eastern Railway & Lumber Company	213
Eastern Washington Railway Company, The	276 s
Eatonville Lumber Company	214
Elk Creek & Grays Harbor Railroad Company	211
English Lumber Company	214
Eufaula Logging Company	213
Everett & Monte Cristo Railway Company	231
Fairhaven & Southern Railroad Company	215
Farmers' Railway, Navigation & Steamboat Portage Company	282
Farmers' Transportation Company	282
Fiberboard Products, Inc.	216
Great Northern Lumber Company	217
Great Northern Railway Company see Montana	303
Green River & Northern Railroad Company	217 s
Hamma Hamma Logging Company	220
Hartford Eastern Railway Company	221
Idaho & Washington Northern Railroad see Idaho	209
Idaho Central Railway Company	278
Ilwaco Railroad Company	222
Ilwaco Railway & Navigation Company, The	222
Ilwaco Steam Navigation Company, The	222
Ilwaco Wharf Company, The	222
Independence Logging Company	260
Inland Empire Railroad Company	278
Inland Empire Railway Company	278
Inman-Poulsen Logging Company	222
Irving-Hartley Logging Company	216
Izett Lumber Company	216
Klickitat Log & Lumber Company	223
Klickitat Northern Railroad Company	223
Kosmos Timber Company	223
Lake Whatcom Logging Company	189
Lamb-Davis Lumber Company	217
Larson Company	191
A Lewis & Clark Railway Company	226
Lewis Mill & Timber Company	301
Little River Railway & Logging Company	232
Long-Bell Lumber Company	227
Longview, Portland & Northern Railway Company	226
Lyman Timber Company	274
McCormick Lumber Company, Charles R.	250
Manley-Moore Lumber Company	227
Marysville & Arlington Railway Company	228
Marysville & Northern Railway Company	286
Mason County Central Railroad Company	268
Mason County Logging Company	228
Melbourne & North River Railroad Company	201
Merrill & Ring Logging Company	229
Merrill & Ring Lumber Company	229
Mill Creek Flume & Manufacturing Company	229
Mill Creek Railroad Company	229
Miller Logging Company	230
Monroe Logging Company	230
Montana Rail Link, Inc. see Montana	324
Monte Cristo Railway Company	231
Mosquito & Coal Creek Railroad Company	213
Mud Bay Logging Company	232
Mutual Lumber Company	232
Natches Pass Railroad Company	258
National Lumber & Mfg. Company	260
Nelson Company, The Charles	232
Newaukum Railroad Company	193
Newaukum Valley Railroad Company	193
Nooksack Timber Company	258

North Coast Railroad Company, The		233
North Coast Railway		233
Northern Pacific & Cascade Railroad Company		233 s
Northern Pacific & Puget Sound Shore Railroad Company		235 s
Northern Pacific Railroad Company	236 and Montana	331
Northern Pacific Railway Company	see Montana	331
North Yakima & Valley Railway Company		240
O'Connell Lumber Company, M. T.		302
Olympia & Chehalis Valley Railroad Company, The		240
Olympia & Tenino Railroad Company		240
Olympia Railroad Union		240
Olympia Terminal Railway Company		122
Onalaska Lumber Company		193
Oregon & Washington Railroad Company		241 s
Oregon & Washington Territory Railroad Company		242
Oregon & Washington Territory Railroad Company, The		242
Oregon Railroad & Navigation Company, The		114
Oregon Railway & Navigation Company		117
Oregon Railway Extensions Company, The		243 s
Oregon, Washington & Idaho Railroad Company		243
Oregon-Washington Railroad & Navigation Company		122
Ostrander Railroad Company, The		244
Ozette Timber Company		256
Pacific & Eastern Railway Company		254
Pacific Coast Railroad Company		244
Pacific National Lumber Company		245
Pacific States Lumber Company		246
Page Lumber Company		193
Palouse River Railroad Company		192
Panther Lake Lumber Company		299
Parker-Bell Lumber Company		214
Pend Oreille Valley Railroad		247
Pend Oreille Valley Railroad, Inc.		247
Peninsular Railway Company		292
Phoenix Logging Company		247
Polson Brothers Logging Company		248
Polson Logging Company		248
Pope & Talbot Lumber Company		250
Port Angeles Western Railroad Company		250
Portland & Puget Sound Railroad Company		288
Portland & Seattle Railway Company		282
Portland, Vancouver & Yakima Railway Company		298
Port Ludlow, Port Angeles & Lake Crescent Railway		267
Port Townsend & Puget Sound Railway Company		252
Port Townsend Railroad		252
Port Townsend Southern Railroad Company		252
Puget Mill Company		250
Puget Sound & Baker River Railway Company		253
Puget Sound & Cascade Railway Company		254
Puget Sound & Grays Harbor Railroad Company		286
Puget Sound & Grays Harbor Railroad & Transportation Company		286
Puget Sound & Willapa Harbor Railway Company		254
Puget Sound Mills & Timber Company		232
Puget Sound Pulp & Timber Company		255
Puget Sound Shore Railroad Company, The		255
Rayonier, Incorporated		256
Republic & Kettle River Railway Company		275
Rucker Brothers Company		255
St. Paul & Tacoma Lumber Company		258
St. Paul, Minneapolis & Manitoba Railway Company, The	see Montana	303
St. Regis Pulp & Paper Company		258
Saginaw Timber Company		258
Sauk River Lumber Company		258
Satsop Rail Road Company		268
Schafer Brothers Logging Company		260
Seattle & International Railway Company		261
Seattle & Montana Railroad Company		261 s

WASHINGTON

Seattle & Montana Railway Company	261 s
Seattle & North Coast Railroad Company	262
Seattle & Northern Railway Company	263
Seattle & Walla Walla Railroad & Transportation Company	265
Seattle & West Coast Railway Company	265
Seattle Coal & Transportation Company, The	265
Seattle, Lake Shore & Eastern Railway Company	265
Seattle Lumber Company	268
Seattle, Port Angeles & Lake Crescent Railway	267
Seattle, Port Angeles & Western Railway Company	267 s
Seattle Southeastern Railway Company	246
Shelton Southwestern Railroad Company	268
Shelton Southwestern Railway Company, The	268
Simpson Logging Company	268
A Simpson Timber Company	268
Snake River Valley Railroad Company, The	273 s
Snohomish Logging Company	274
Snohomish, Skykomish & Spokane Railway & Transportation Company	231
Snohomish, Skykomish & Spokane Railway & Transportation Company, The	231
Snoqualmie Falls Lumber Company	274
Soundview Pulp Company	274
South Bend Mills & Timber Company	301
Spokane & British Columbia Railway Company	275
Spokane & Eastern Railway & Power Company	278
Spokane & Inland Empire Railroad Company	278
Spokane & Inland Railway Company	278
Spokane & Palouse Railway Company	276 s
Spokane & Seattle Railway Company	277 s
Spokane, Coeur d'Alene & Palouse Railway Company	278
Spokane Falls & Idaho Railroad Company see Idaho	223
Spokane Falls & Northern Railway Company, The	279
Spokane International Railroad Company	281
Spokane International Railway Company	281
Spokane Interurban System	278
Spokane, Portland & Seattle Railway Company	282
Springdale & Long Lake Railway Company	210
Standard Lumber Company	210
Standard Railway & Timber Company	287
Sterling Mill Company	299
Stimson Mill Company	286
Sultan Railway & Timber Company	287
Sunset Timber Company	301
Tacoma & Columbia River Railway Company	288
Tacoma & Lake City Railroad & Navigation Company	288
Tacoma Eastern Railroad Company	290
Tacoma, Lake Park & Columbia River Railway Company	288
Tacoma, Olympia & Chehalis Valley Railroad Company	213
Tacoma, Olympia & Grays Harbor Railroad Company	291
Tacoma, Orting & Southeastern Railroad Company, The	291s
Three Lakes Lumber Company	299
Thurston County Railroad Construction Company	240
Thurston County Railway Company	232
Toppenish, Simcoe & Western Railway Company	240
Twin Falls Logging Company	200
Union Lumber Company	291
Union Pacific Railroad Company see Idaho	233
Union River Logging Railroad Company	250
United Railroads of Washington, The	291s
Vance Lumber Company	228
Vancouver, Klickitat & Yakima Railroad Company	298
Walla Walla & Columbia River Railroad Company	292
Walla Walla Valley Railway Company	293
Walla Walla Valley Traction Company	293
Washington & Columbia River Railway Company, The	295
Washington & Great Northern Railway Company	295
Washington & Idaho Railroad Company see Idaho	242

A	Washington & Oregon Railway Company	298
	Washington Central Railroad Company, Inc.	296
	Washington Central Railway Company, The	297 s
	Washington Electric Railway Company	208
	Washington, Idaho & Montana Railway Company see Idaho	243
	Washington Pulp & Paper Company	216
	Washington Railway & Navigation Company	298
	Washington Southern Railway Company	269
	Washington Western Railway Company	299
	Waterville Railway Company	300
	Wenatchee Valley & Northern Railway Company	217
	Western Lumber Company	213
	Western Pine Lumber Company	223
	West Fork Logging Company	258
	Weyerhaeuser Company	300
	White River Lumber Company	301
	Willapa Harbor Lumber Mills	301
	Willapa Logging Railroad Company	301
	Wilson Bros. Company	260
	Winlock & Toledo Logging & Railroad Company	302
	Winlock Lumber Company	302
	Winlock-Toledo Lumber Company	302
	Wisconsin Logging & Timber Company	302
	Wood & Iverson	189
	Wright Logging Company, Stacey E.	255
	Wynoochee Timber Company	260
	Yakima & Pacific Coast Railroad Company	291
	Yakima Valley Transportation Company	303

Tacoma Public Library — *Washington industries #2447*
Oxen moving logs in western Washington at a site not recorded in about 1900

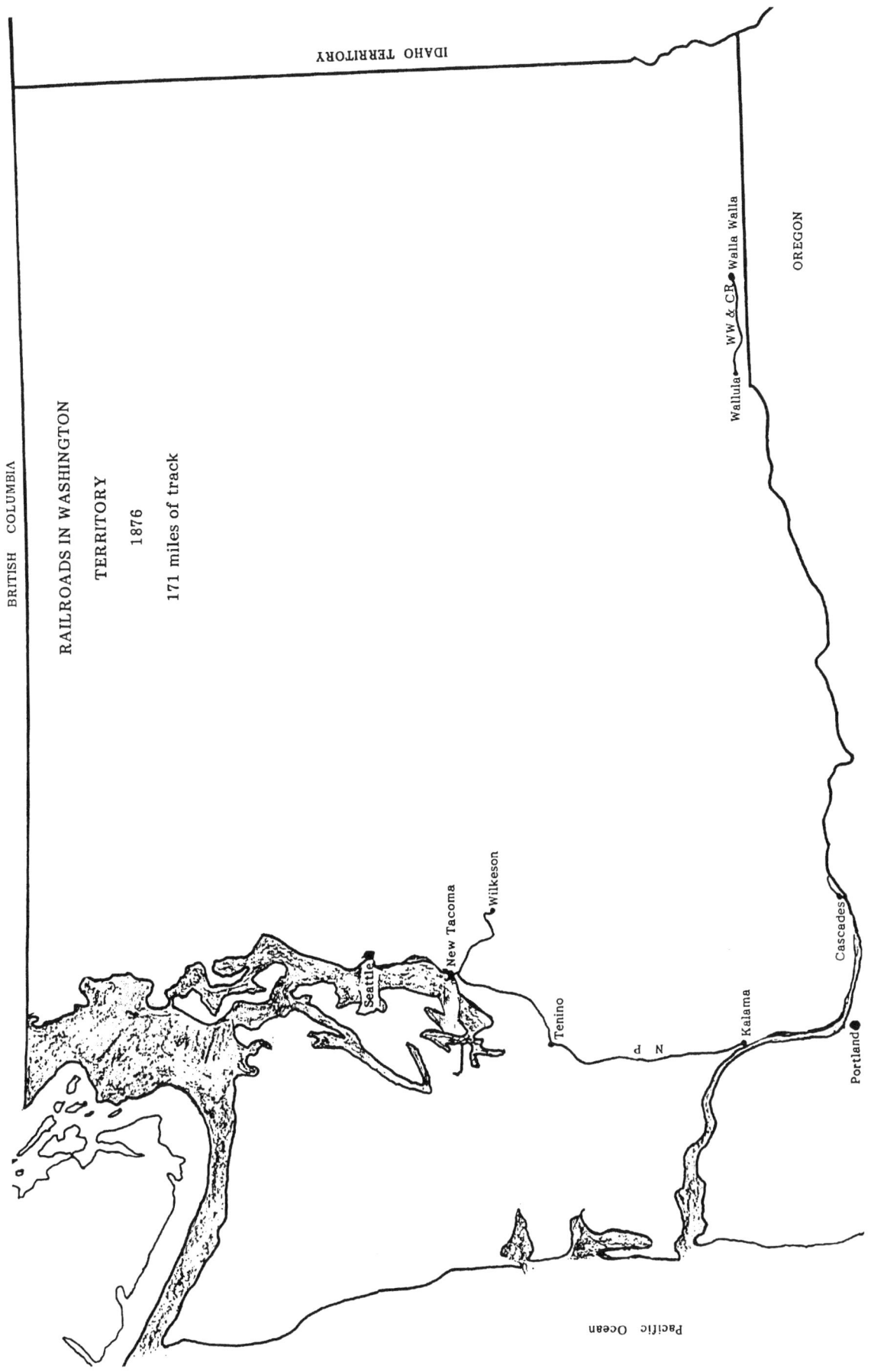

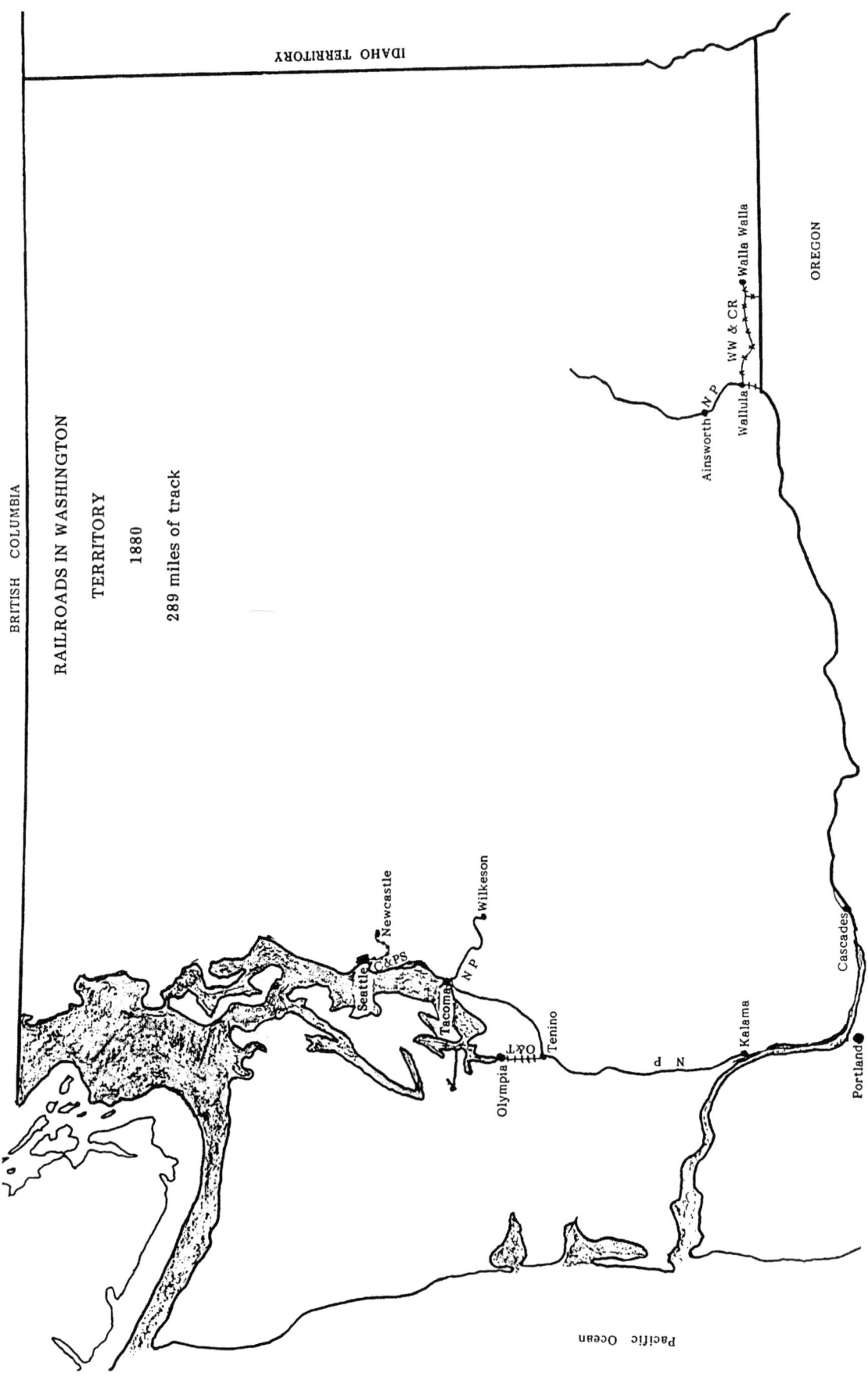

WASHINGTON

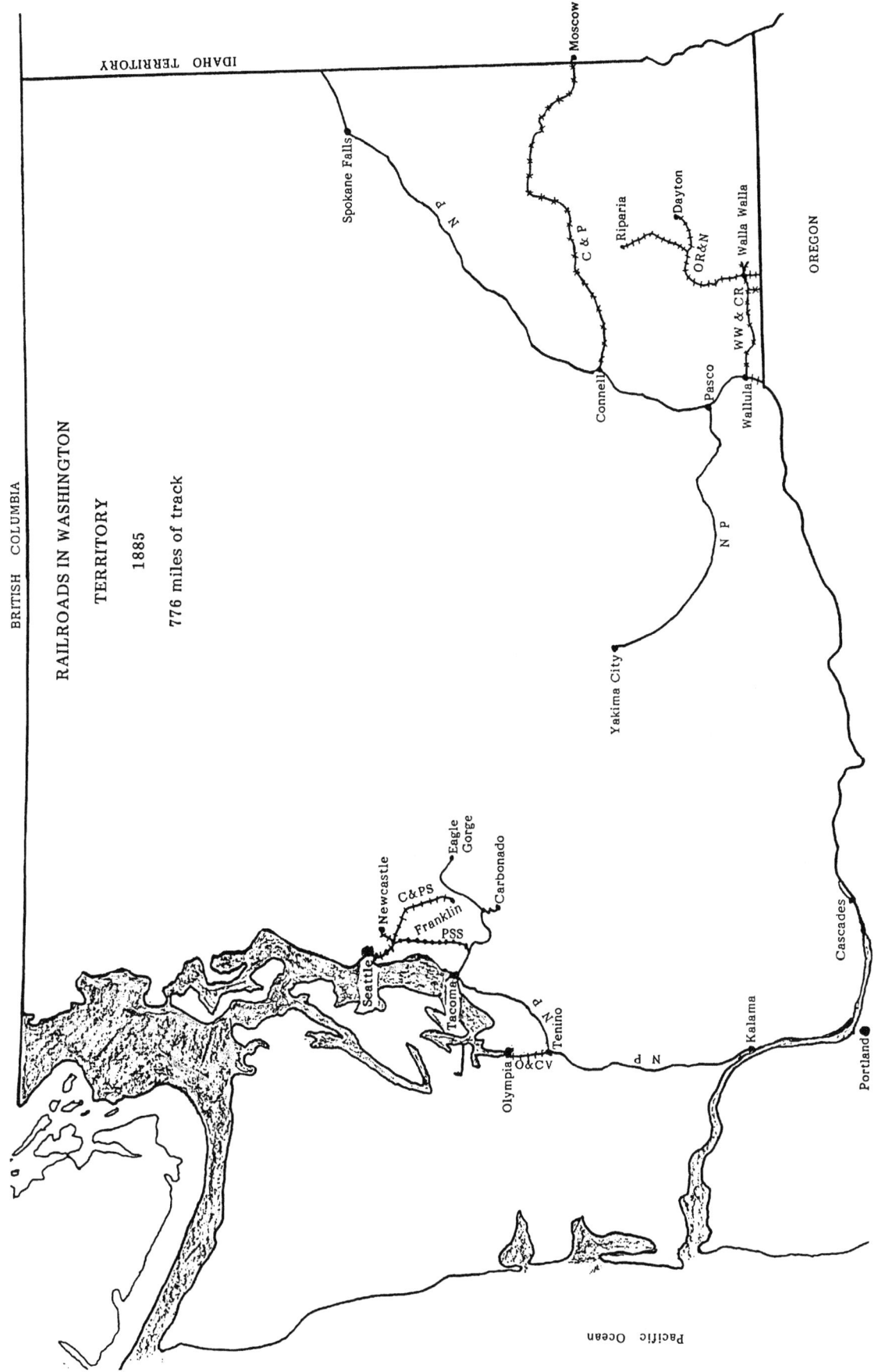

RAILROADS IN WASHINGTON TERRITORY

1885

776 miles of track

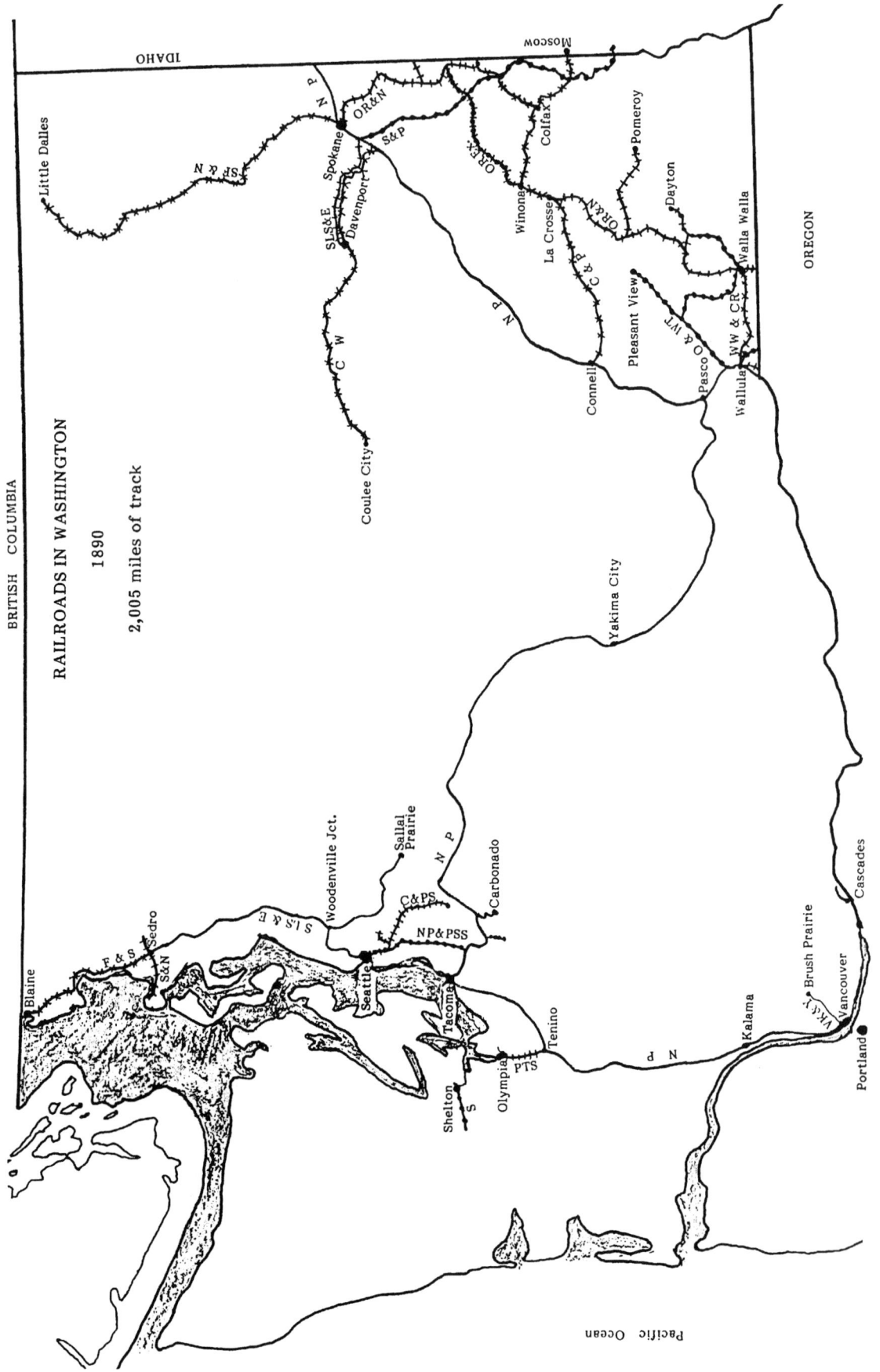

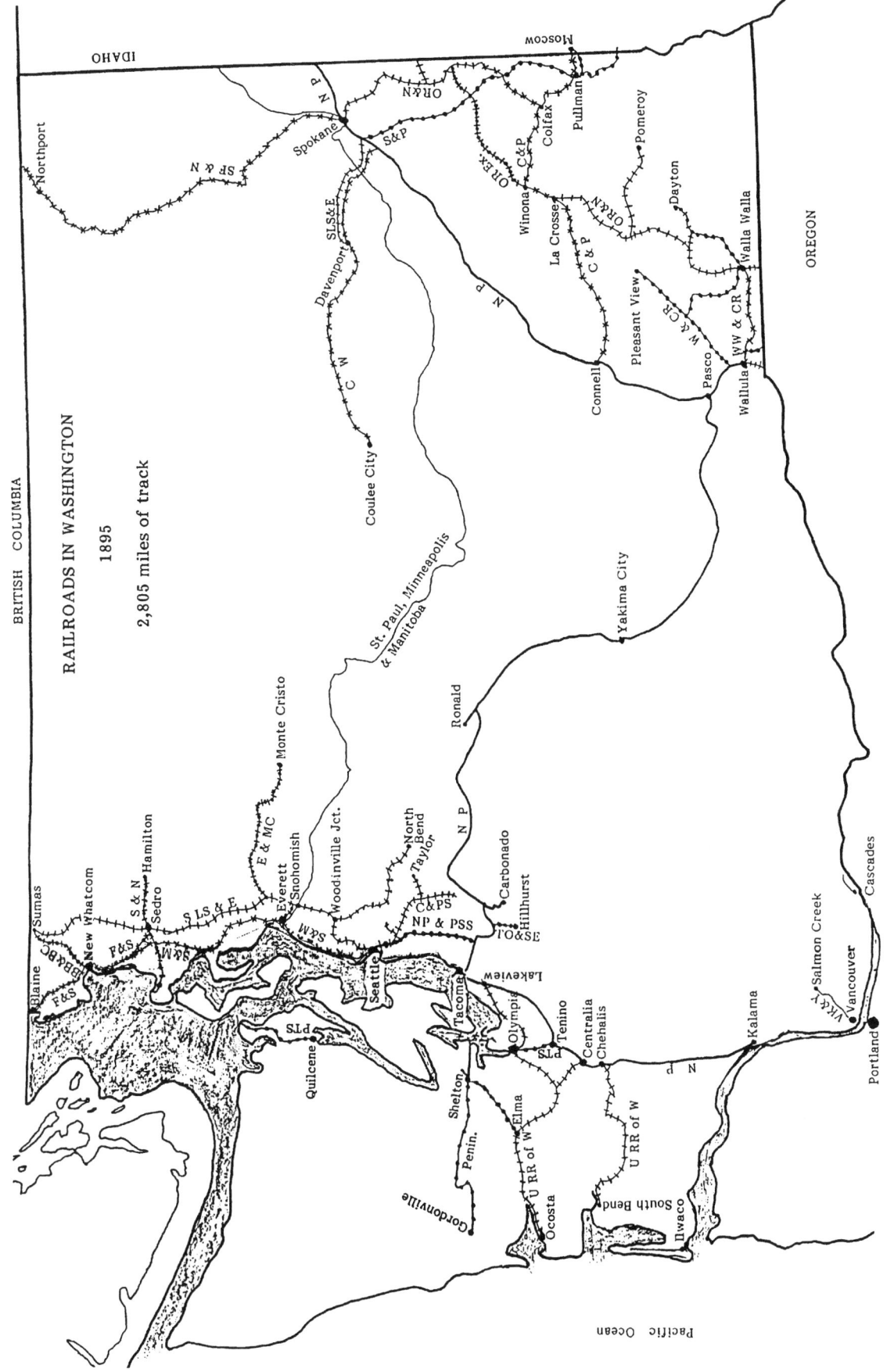

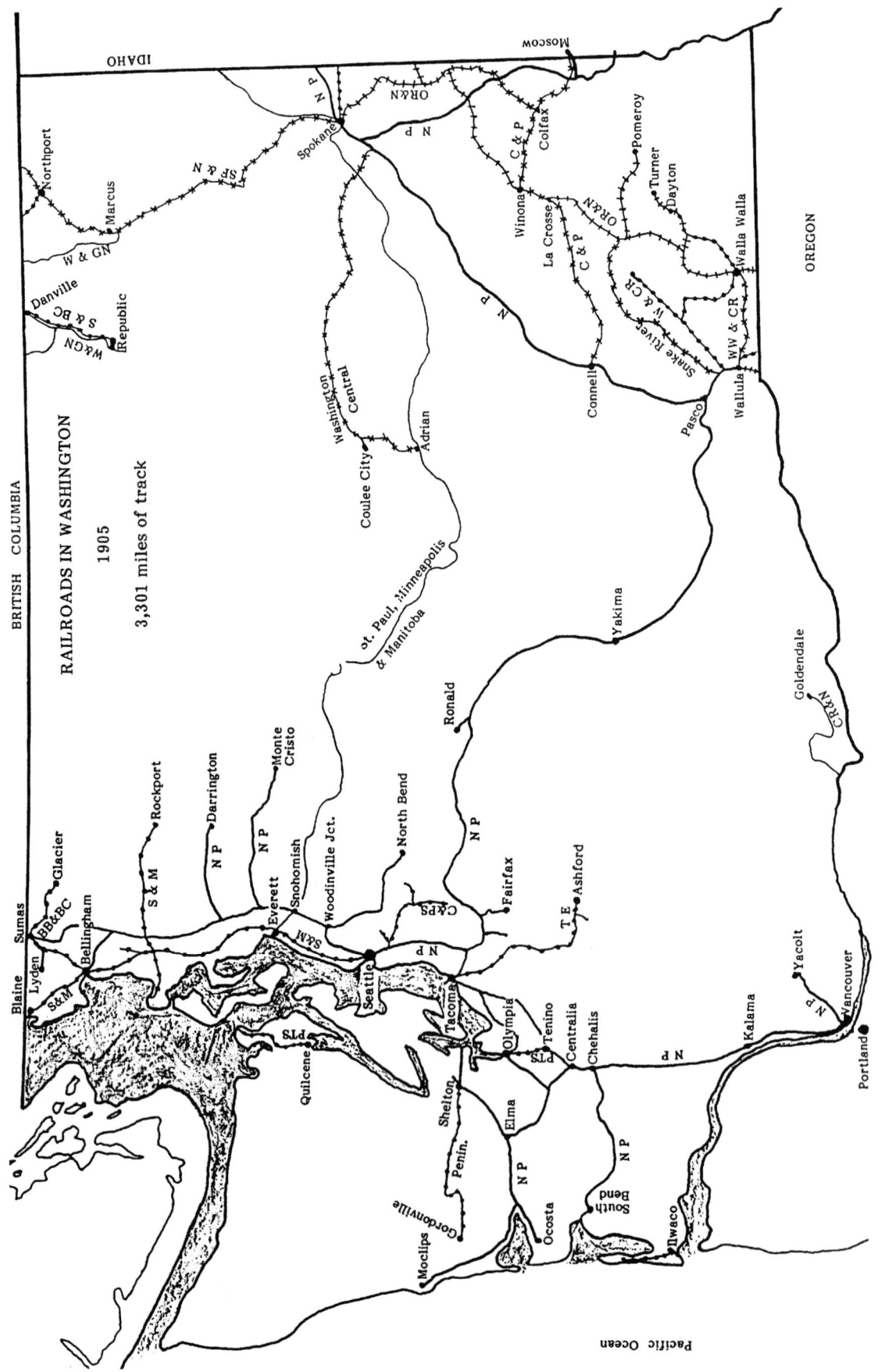

WASHINGTON

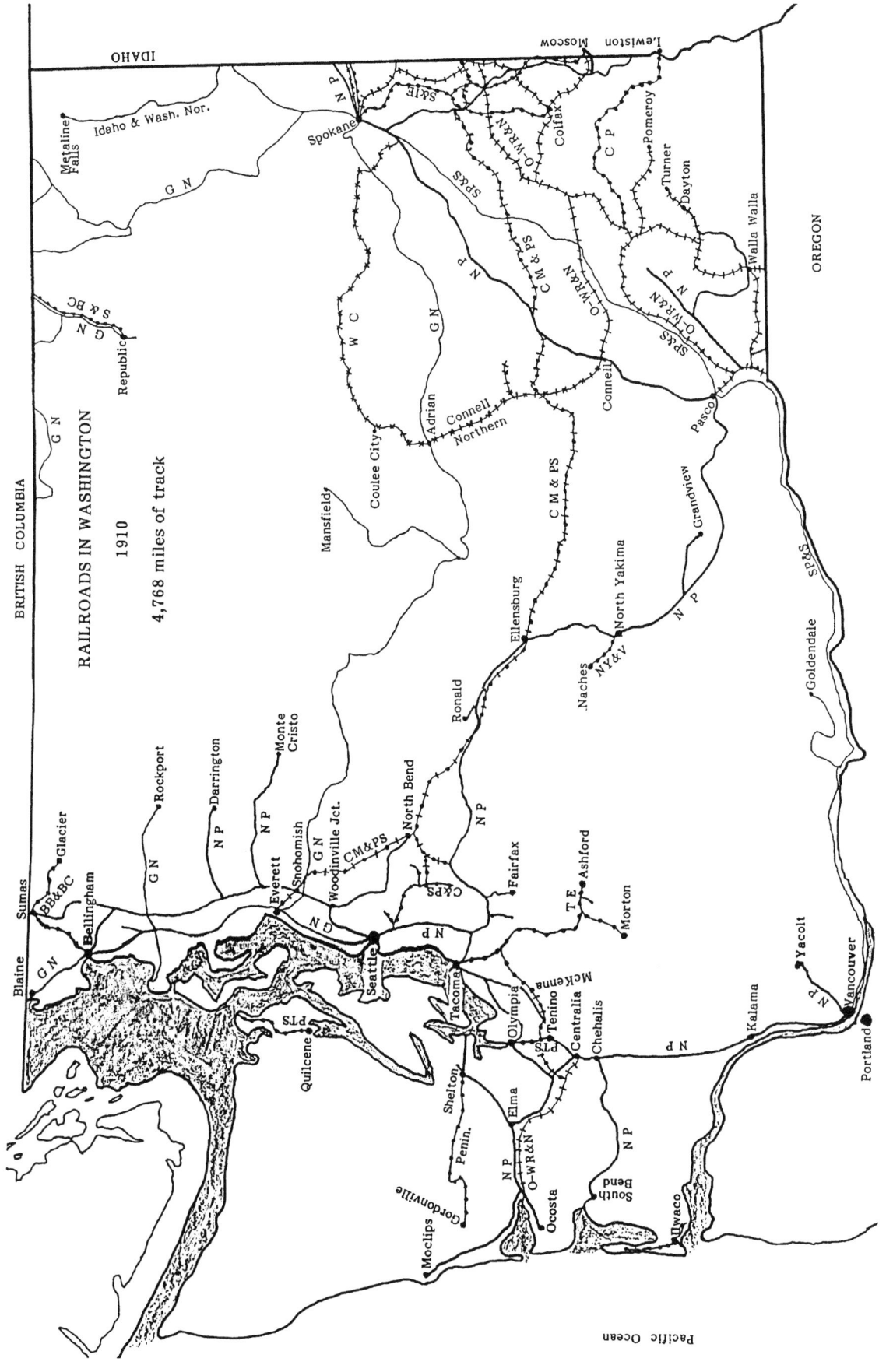

RAILROADS IN WASHINGTON
1910
4,768 miles of track

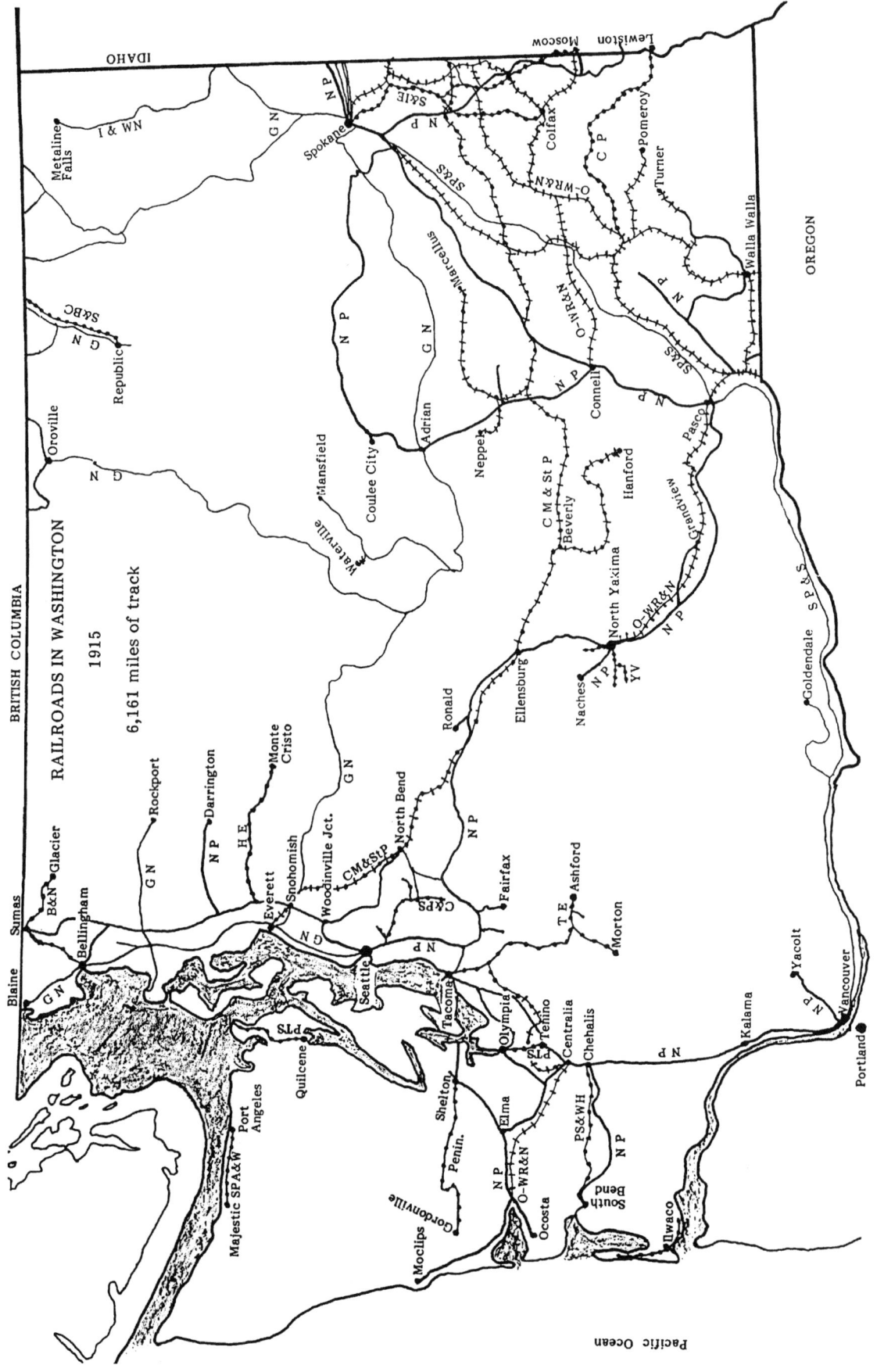

WASHINGTON

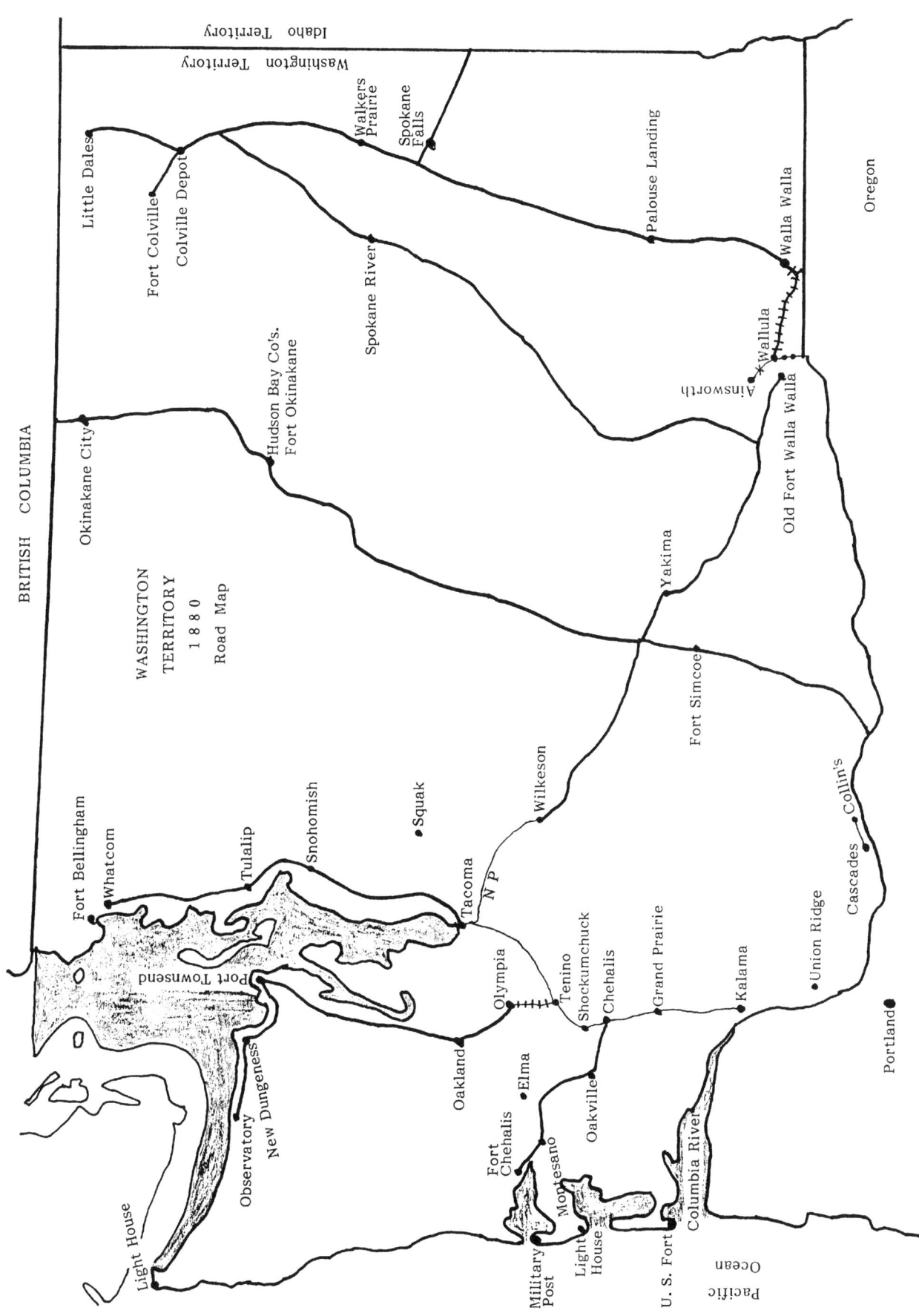

WASHINGTON TERRITORY 1880 Road Map

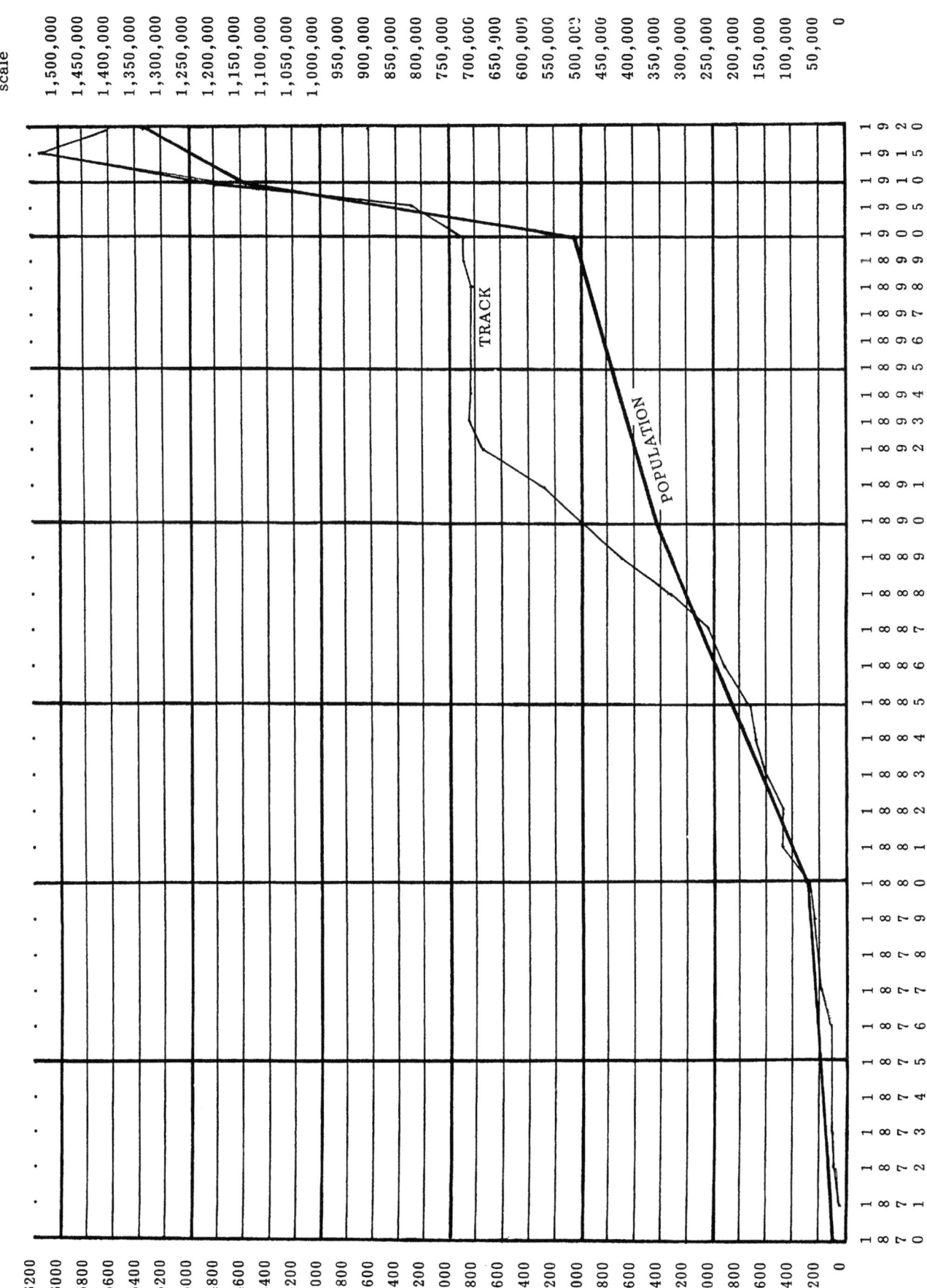

Miles of railroad track and population in Washington

WASHINGTON 189.

ADMIRALTY LOGGING COMPANY   President

Incorp:	5/23/1916	**Operated:**	1916 to 1922		**HQ city:**		Edmonds		
Disposition:	abandoned								
Predecessor:	Brown's Bay Logging Company	- 14 miles -	HQ at Seattle						
Miles track:	23	**Gauge:**	56½"						
Main line:	Meadowdale into the forest								
Rail wt.:		**Max. grade:**		**Const. began:**	grading		1916		

Locomotives:

Road No.	Cyln.	Type	Dvr. in.	Bldr.	Bldr. No.	Date	Weight	Effort	Remarks
1									
2*	11x12	2T Shay	32	Lima	2112	1/09	100,000	20,350	sold to R. C. Kinney Timber Co.
3*	'	'	'	'	2540	5/12	120,000	25,800	sold to McCush Logging Co.
4*	'	'	'	'	2578	10/12	'	'	sold to Discovery Bay Logging Co.
5*	'	'	'	'	2669	5/13	100,000	22,550	sold to Puget Mill Co.
6*	'	'	'	'	2970	3/18	'	'	(1924) to Puget Mill Co.
7 ?		3T Shay	36	'	3009	10/18	146,000	30,350	ex Anderson & Middleton

Freight traffic: logging

Roster of 6/30/1910:
    2   geared engines
    49   logging trucks
    2   flat cars
    7   miles of track at Meadowdale

BALDRIDGE LOGGING COMPANY   President

Incorp:	10/14/1927	**Operated:**	1927 to 1941		**HQ city:**		Stevenson	
Disposition:	abandoned							
Predecessor:	Wood & Iverson				**from:**	1903	**to**	1934
Miles track:	17	**Gauge:**	56½"					
Main line:	Snohomish and Hobart into the forest							
Rail wt.:		**Max. grade:**	6.0%	**Const. began:**	grading		1902	

Locomotives:

Road No.	Cyln.	Type	Dvr. in.	Bldr.	Bldr. No.	Date	Weight	Effort	Remarks
1*		2 truck	28	Climax	379	1/03	40,000	8,800	
2*		'	30	'	600	10/05	80,000	17,600	to Little River Logging & Ry. Co.
2-2d		2T Shay	26½	Lima	1637	12/06	46,000	13,500	acq. 7/1929
3*		3 truck	36	Climax	1151	4/12	150,000		to Baldridge Logging Co. #2
4*	15x16	'	'	'	1081	1/12	160,000	35,200	to Parker-Bell #4
4-2d*		'	'	'	1417	/16	'	'	
5		'	38	Heisler	1430	4/20	150,000		to Union Lumber Co.

Freight traffic: logging

Roster of 6/30/1910:
    1   geared engine
    15   logging trucks
    1   flat car
    5   miles of track at Snohomish

Wood & Iverson operated five miles of track at Snohomish from 1903 until 1912, then moved to Hobart, 17 miles, until its sale.

Baldridge Logging Co. used five miles at Stevenson from 1927 until June 30, 1932, and then at Hobart, six miles, from 1934.

BELLINGHAM & NORTHERN RAILWAY COMPANY   H. B. Earling, President

Incorp:	10/17/1912	**Operated:**	10/22/12 to 12/31/18	**HQ city:**		Bellingham
Disposition:	sold to Chicago, Milwaukee & St. Paul Railway Company on January 1, 1919					
Predecessors:	Bellingham Terminals & Railway Company			**Incorp.:**	5/3/1909 to	10/21/1912
	Bellingham Bay & British Columbia Rail Road Company				6/21/1893	10/21/1912
Miles track:	66.818	**Gauge:**	56½"			
Main line:	Bellingham to Glacier					

190. ENCYCLOPEDIA OF WESTERN RAILROAD HISTORY

Rail wt.:	50/56/60 lbs.		Max. grade:		Const. began:	grading	April 7, 1884
						laying rails	(May 6, 1884)
Const. comp.:	January 31, 1904 - main line				First train operated:		October 11, 1888

Locomotives:

Road No.	Cyln.	Type	Dvr. in.	Bldr.	Bldr. No.	Date	Weight	Effort	Remarks
1		0-6-0	36	Booth	9	/68	72,000		*Mills* - ex Black Diamond Coal/RR
2		"	44	BLW	2141	5/70	"		*Diamond* - ex Black Diamond Coal/RR
3*	17x24	4-4-0	62	"	11517	1/91			converted wood/coal/oil
4*	"	2-6-0	54	"	12231	9/91			to C.M.&St.P. #2952
5		2-8-0	50	"	5943	12/81	102,000	24,480	acq. 7/1900 ex U.P. #1265
6		2-8-0VC	"	"	13800	10/93	126,800	26,511	to C.M.&St.P. #7563
7		4-6-0		"					acq. 1902 ex Penna. RR #760
8		2-8-0	50	"	18718	3/01			ex Simpson Log.; to C.M.&St.P. #7564
9*	19x26	4-6-0	56	"	32348	12/07			to C.M.&St.P. #2265

Freight traffic: common carrier, logging

Rosters of 6/30/1897 - 12/31/1917:
- locomotives   4   9
- passenger cars 4   10
- freight cars 55   171

First published timetable:
November 22, 1891 - daily
- 9:00 a.m. New Whatcom 8:50
-            Everson   16
-            Sumas   23 7:15 a.m.

Published timetable dated:
April 2, 1916 - daily exc. Sun.
- 7:30 a.m. Bellingham   5:05
- 8:19   Everson   15.8
- 8:23   Hampton   17.1
- 8:39   Lynden   22.4
- 9:00   Hampton   17.1
- 9:45   Sumas   23.3
- 10:35   Columbia   30.3
- 11:10   Maple Falls 37.2
- 11:35   Glacier   44.4 2:30 p.m.

The site of "Welcome" and "Kulshan" appear to be the same, or very near by.

Operating figures for the year ending June 30, 1906:
- passenger income $56,778
- freight revenue   153,559
- expenses   157,891
- net   63,325
- cost of road   1,448,496
- equipment cost   256,833

The carrier was placed in commercial operation on July 3, 1890.

The road was opened to Sumas April 1, 1891, to Maple Falls in the summer of 1901 and to Glacier in January, 1904. The Lynden branch was placed in operation on January 16, 1904, and the 11.29-mile Kulshan line was completed in December, 1916. The July, 1917, *Official Guide* announced its completion.

First listed in ICC for 6/30/90 as an operating independent with three miles owned, not in use. By 6/30/91 it was 23 miles owned and operated. It was gradually increased to 42 miles by 6/30/01 and to 62 miles by 6/30/09. In 1910 it was 56 miles, the other six miles now being owned by Bellingham Terminals & Railway Co. which had been leased on October 1, 1909.

Listed 6/30/13 under the new name as a 64-mile operating subsidiary of Chicago, Milwaukee & St. Paul Railway Co. It was gradually extended to 80 miles by the end of December, 1917, and was a class II common carrier.

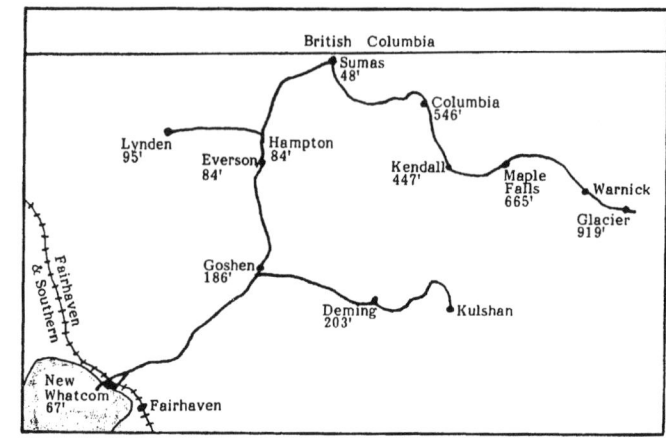

Bibliography: *Poor's 1898*, p. 265 and *1918*, p. 211   Snohomish - *The Eye* - May 10, 1884   *Valuation 44*, p. 766

BELLINGHAM BAY & EASTERN RAILROAD COMPANY   Hugh Eldridge, **President**

| Incorp: | 12/17/1891 | Operated: | 6/8/92 to 6/30/03 | HQ city: | New Whatcom |

Disposition: sold to and merged into Northern Pacific Railway Company on July 1, 1903

Miles track:	23.370	Gauge:	56½"
Main line:	New Whatcom to Wickersham		
Rail wt.:	40/56 lb. steel	Max. grade:		Const. began:	grading	(February 8, 1892)
					laying rails	May 14, 1892
Const. comp.:	February 15, 1902			First train operated:		June 8, 1892

WASHINGTON

Locomotives:

Road No.	Cyln.	Type	Dvr. in.	Bldr.	Bldr. No.	Date	Weight	Effort	Remarks
1		4-4-0	62	BLW	4925	1/80	58,300	10,900	acq. 5/1892 ex N.P. #315
2		2-4-0	40	Grant	1261	4/79		10,080	to N.P. #1072

Freight traffic: common carrier, coal and logs

Roster of 6/30/1901:
    2   locomotives
   34   freight cars
   20   logging flats

First? published "timetable":
May, 1902
"Irregular service for freight and passengers."
Fairhaven
Whatcom   m.p. 3
Larsen   7
Woodlawn   12
Park   19
Wickersham   23

First listed in ICC for 6/30/92 as an operating independent with 2.6 miles owned and in use. By 6/30/94 it owned 3.5 miles and operated 7.5. It was gradually increased to eight miles each by 6/30/00 and the same in 1901, but was extended to 26 miles each by 6/30/02. On 6/30/03 it was a 23-mile operating subsidiary of Northern Pacific Railway Company.

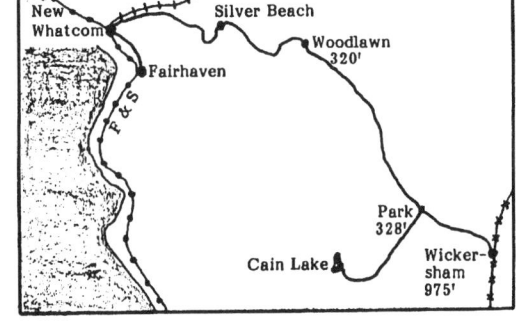

The official construction record is brief and incomplete. New Whatcom to Lake Whatcom, 2.4 miles, was placed in operation on June 8, 1892, and Woodlawn to Manning, 3.8 miles, on August 1, 1896.

The following construction notes from *The Railway Age* help to complete the chronology of events.

August 7, 1896	This road on July 27 began the construction of three miles of logging road on the northeast shore of Lake Whatcom, near Woodlawn.
January 1, 1897	This road has been extended from Woodlawn to Manning, three miles.
November 24, 1899	From Whatcom to Blue Canyon coal mines, four miles, is to be opened December 17th.
June 1, 1900	New Whatcom to Lake Whatcom, four miles has been completed.
October 18, 1901	Branch from Whatcom to Fairhaven, 1.75 miles, has been completed.
January 24, 1902	During 1901, the road was built from Silver Beach to Blue Canyon, 11.5 miles, and is being extended from Blue Canyon to Wickersham, five miles, plus a two-mile branch towards Cains Lake.
April 18, 1902	Fairhaven to Wickersham, 23.1 miles, was opened for operations on March 6th.

If we compare the January 24, 1902, entry with that of November 24, 1899, we must assume that the Blue Canyon coal mines, four miles from Whatcom, were not located at Blue Canyon, five miles from Wickersham.

Bibliography: *Poor's 1902*, p. 615   Bellingham Bay - *Weekly Express* - January 23 to March 26, 1892   *Valuation 25*, p. 492

BLOEDEL-DONOVAN LUMBER MILLS

President

Incorp:	1/30/1913	**Operated:** 1913 to 12/31/45	**HQ city:**	Bellingham
Disposition:	abandoned on December 31, 1945			
Predecessors:	Larson Company		from: 1912 to 1913	
	Lake Whatcom Logging Company		Incorp.: 8/19/1898 to 1913	
Miles track:	150	**Gauge:** 56½"		
Main line:	woods lines from Sekiu, Skykomish, Marysville and Park			
Rail wt.:	56/70 lbs.	**Max. grade:** 6.0%	**Const. began:** grading	1900

Locomotives:

1*	18x24	2-6-2	48	Schen.	45896	3/09			
1-2d* ?		3 truck	36	Climax	1648	1/24	160,000	35,200	used at Alger Camp; to Rayonier #1
1-3d ?		2 truck	33	Heisler	1373	5/18	72,000	18,750	at Skykomish; to Mason Cty. Log.
2		3T Shay	"	Lima	2908	5/17	150,000	33,100	at Sekiu; 4/1945 to Rayonier #2
3		"	36	"	2786	10/14	140,000	"	at Sekiu; 4/1945 to Rayonier #3
3-2d ?		3 truck	"	Climax	1479	10/17	160,000	35,200	ex Chinn Lumber Co. #3
4		2T Shay	32	Lima	820	9/03	90,000	18,750	acq. 1910; at Alger, then Sekiu
5*	12x15	3T Shay	36	"	2855	6/16	140,000	30,350	at Delvan, Sekiu; to Rayonier
6		2 truck	33	Heisler	1055	/01	50,000		used at Marysville
6-2d ?		"	30	Climax	692	7/06	90,000	19,800	ex Skykomish Lumber Co. #1
6-3d ?		"	36	Heisler	1288	10/13	88,000		at Skykomish, Sekiu; to Rayonier #6

7*	12x15	3T Shay	36	Lima	3012	4/19	140,000	30,350	at Sekiu; 4/1/45 to Rayonier #7
8*	17/26x24	2-6-6-2S	44	BLW	58064	11/24	212,000		to Rayonier #8
9*	'	'	'	'	58065	'	'		to Rayonier #9
10*	15¼x16	3 truck	36	Climax	1641	6/23	160,000	35,200	at Alger Camp; to Rayonier #10
11*	14¼x16	'	35	'	1632	8/23	140,000	30,800	at Skykomish; to Rayonier #11
14		2-6-6-2	51	BLW	60256	11/27	275,000	56,600	ex Larson Timber #14; to Rayonier
15*	13x15	3T Shay	36	Lima	3318	4/28	184,000	38,200	at Sekiu; 4/1/45 to Rayonier #15

Freight traffic: logging

Roster of 6/30/1910:
- 2 geared engines
- 2 rod engines
- 6 flat cars
- 38 sets logging trucks
- 28 miles of track from Park

Owned and operated mileages from ICC:

6/30/1914	11 + 11 leased from G.N. Ry.
12/31/1917	20
12/31/1919	35
12/31/1924	60
12/31/1925	90
12/31/1928	110
12/31/1930	150
12/31/1931	140
12/31/1932	90
12/31/1935	35
12/31/1940	30
12/31/1942	15 + 23 leased miles

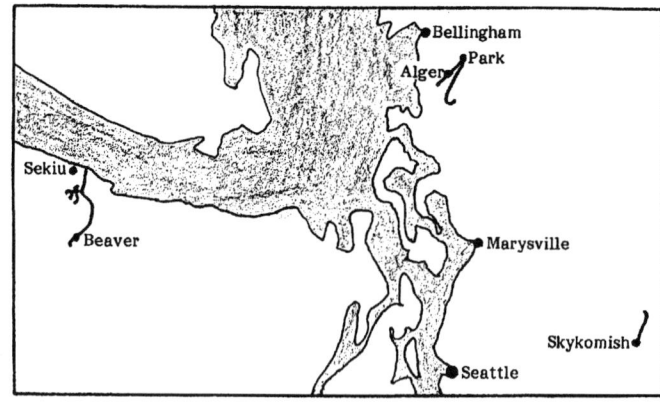

A construction note in March, 1907, *Western Lumberman* stated that six miles from Park (and a connection with Bellingham Bay & Eastern) to Alger had been completed.

BLUE MOUNTAIN RAILROAD, INC.   Charles R. Webb, **President**

Incorp:	10/27/1992	**Operated:**	11/20/92 to	**HQ city:** Walla Walla
Disposition:	in operation 1993			
Miles track:	204	**Gauge:**	56½"	
Main line:	Wallula to Dayton and Hooper to Moscow			
Rail wt.:		**Max. grade:**		

Locomotives:

Road No.	Type	Bldr.	Bldr. No.	Date	Weight	Effort	Remarks
784	B-B	EMD				2,500 h.p.	acq. 12/93 ex U.P. #784 - W.P. #3003
790	'	'				'	acq. 12/93 ex U.P. #790 - W.P. #3010
792	'	'				'	acq. 12/93 ex U.P. #792 - W.P. #3013
799	'	'				'	acq. 12/93 ex U.P. #799 - W.P. #3022

Freight traffic: common carrier, agriculture

The northern line is called Palouse River Railroad Company.

The Moscow line is being purchased; the Walla Walla section is leased from Union Pacific Railroad Company.

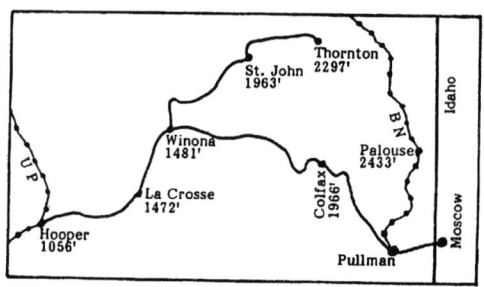
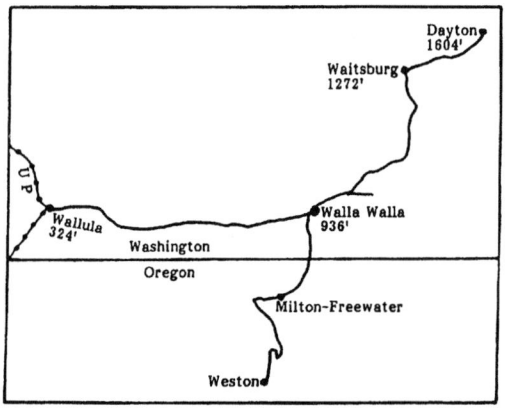

Bibliography: Direct communication   *Official Open and Prepay Station List*

WASHINGTON   193.

BOLCOM-VANDERHOOF LOGGING COMPANY   President

Incorp: 2/4/1909   **Operated:** 1909 to 1918   **HQ city:** Seattle
Disposition: abandoned
Predecessor: Bolcom-Riley Logging Company - Port Townsend with three miles of track   from: 1907 to 1908
Miles track: 10   **Gauge:** 56½"
Main line: Lochsloy and Acme into the woods
Rail wt.:   **Max. grade:**   **Const. began:** grading   1907
Locomotives:

Road No.	Cyln.	Type	Drv. in.	Bldr.	Bldr. No.	Date	Weight	Effort	Remarks
1*	10x12	2T Shay	29	Lima	2022	11/07	84,000	16,900	at Lochsloy; to Dungeness Logging Co.
2*	12x15	3T Shay	36	'	2236	10/09	140,000	29,800	at Lochsloy; to Skagit Mill Co.
3*	'	'	'	'	2269	2/10	'		used at Acme; to Stimson Mill Co.
4*	12x12	2T Shay	32	'	2345	7/10	120,000	23,850	used at Acme; sold into Br. Columbia

Freight traffic: logging

Roster of 6/30/1910:
    1   geared engine
    5   miles of track at Lochsloy

BUFFELEN LUMBER & MFG. COMPANY   President

Incorp:: 3/7/1913   **Operated:** 1922 to 1939   **HQ city:** Deming
Disposition: abandoned - corporation dissolved January 28, 1953
Predecessor: Page Lumber Company - at Buckley   from: 1901 to 1922
Miles track: 14   **Gauge:** 56½"
Main line: Eagle Gorge into the forest
Rail wt.: 45/56/60 lbs. **Max. grade:** 9.0%   **Const. began:** grading
Locomotives:

Road No.	Cyln.	Type	Drv. in.	Bldr.	Bldr. No.	Date	Weight	Effort	Remarks
1									
2*	15x12	2 truck	36	Heisler	1120	11/06	74,000		to Buffelen Lumber & Mfg. #2
2-2d		'	33	'	1092	8/06	56,000		to Libby, McNeil & Libby
4		3 truck	38	'	1430	4/20	150,000		to Wood & Iverson #5
5*	17x14	2 truck	40	'	1462	11/22	126,000		
6 ?		'		Climax	780	/07	70,000		to Moe Bros. Logging Co. #1
21 ?		3T Shay	36	Lima	1810	1/07	130,000	29,850	to Alpine Lumber Co. #21

Freight traffic: logging

Roster of 6/30/1910:
    1   geared engine
    2   rod engines
    6   miles of track at Eagle Gorge

CARLISLE LUMBER COMPANY   President

Incorp: 6/7/1922   **Operated:** 1924 to 1943   **HQ city:** Onalaska
Disposition: abandoned

Predecessors:	Carlisle-Pennell Lumber Company	10 miles	from:	1914	to	1924
	Newaukum Valley Railroad Company	11 miles	Incorp.:	10/5/1914		1943
	Newaukum Railroad Company			5/25/1914		10/4/1914
	Copalis Lumber Company	9 miles	from:	1914		1920
	Onalaska Lumber Company	6 miles		1916		1917

Miles track: 30   **Gauge:** 56½"
Main line: Napavine to Onalaska plus woods lines
Rail wt.: 56/60/66/72 lbs. **Max. grade:** 1.5%   **Const. began:** grading   June 1, 1914
                                                                     laying rails
Const. comp.:   **First train operated:**   July 20, 1916

Locomotives:

Carlisle Lumber Co.

Road No.	Type	Dvr. in.	Bldr.	Bldr. No.	Date	Weight	Effort	Remarks
3	3T Shay	29	Lima	461	5/94	140,000	30,675	renumbered 800
5	2T Shay	29½	'	3006	5/19	84,000	16,900	to Portland dealer
6	'	36	'	1825	3/07	110,000	23,850	
30	2-6-0		Vulcan	1894	/11			
900	2-8-2	48	BLW	38035	7/12	171,700		1943 to Red River Lumber Co. #104

Carlisle-Pennell Lumber Co.

| 2 | 3T Shay | 29 | Lima | 461 | 5/94 | 140,000 | 30,675 | |
| | 2T Shay | 36 | ' | 1825 | 3/07 | 110,000 | 23,850 | ex Copalis Lumber Co. |

Newaukum Valley Railroad Co. (W. A. Carlisle, president)

1	2-6-0	54	BLW	11942	6/91			acq. 7/16/15 ex Northern Pacific #525
1-2d	'		Vulcan	1894	/11			to Carlisle Lumber Co. #30
2	3T Shay	29	Lima	461	5/94	140,000	30,675	acq. 1915 ex Utah Copper Co.
7	2-4-4-2	48	BLW	33463	6/09	162,650	24,800	ex Whitney Co.; to Mud Bay Logging Co.
200	2-8-2	'	'	38035	7/12	171,700	35,100	ex Pacific & Idaho Northern Railway Co.
521	'	51	Brooks	54734	5/14	172,000	45,100	ex Chicago & Ill. Mid. #521-to S.P.
522	'	'	'	54735	'	'	'	ex Chicago & Ill. Mid. #522-to S.P.
901	'	48	BLW	34563	4/10	171,000	32,800	ex Marysville & N. #1-to Valley/Siletz
1000	'	'	Schen.	61535	1/20	195,000	35,700	acq. 1930; 1944 to Santa Maria (Calif.)

Onalaska Lumber Co.

2	3T Shay	29	Lima	461	5/94	140,000	30,675	
3 ?	2T Shay	32	'	854	3/04	90,000	18,750	ex Deep Creek Logging Co. #3
4 ?	'	29½	'	1802	11/06	84,000	16,900	ex Clark Creek Logging Co. #3
6 ?	'	'	'	2995	9/18	85,000	'	ex Warren Spruce Co. #6
427 ?	'	'	'	3006	5/19	84,000	'	ex Siems-Carey #427

Copalis Lumber Co.

| 2 ? | 2T Shay | 36 | Lima | 1825 | 3/07 | 110,000 | 23,850 | ex Lytle Logging & Mercantile Co. #2 |

Freight traffic: common carrier, logging

Roster of 12/31/1917:
    1   locomotive
    15   freight cars

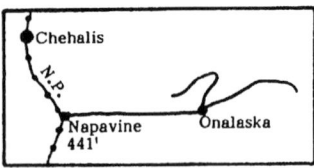

Construction was begun at Napavine. The "Const. began" and "First train operated" refer to Newaukum Valley Railroad Co. The cost of road and equipment to December 31, 1917, was $377,031.

Newaukum Valley Railroad Co. was first listed in ICC for 6/30/15 as an operating independent with 6.5 miles owned, not in use. By 6/30/16 it was 10.5 miles (the main line to Onalaska) owned and operated.

Bibliography: *Poor's 1918*, p. 2003   *Valuation 43*, p. 862

CASCADE LUMBER COMPANY   President

| **Incorp:** | 3/15/1902 | **Operated:** | 1908 to 1954 | **HQ city:** | Yakima |

Disposition: abandoned

Miles track: 42   **Gauge:** 56½"

Main line: Cle Elum to Casland and woods line from Easton

Rail wt.: 60 lbs.   **Max. grade:**   **Const. began:** grading

Locomotives:

1								
2 ?	2T Shay	29½	Lima	1790	1/07	74,000	16,900	acq. from Seattle dealer
214	3T Shay	36	'	2794	4/16	146,000	30,350	ex A. H. Guthrie & Co. #214
215	'	'	'	2906	4/17	150,000	'	ex A. H. Guthrie & Co. #215

Freight traffic: logging

Rosters of   6/30/1910 - 12/31/1919:
    geared engines   1   2
    rod engines   1
    flat cars   8
    miles of track   2 at Easton   30 at Cle Elum

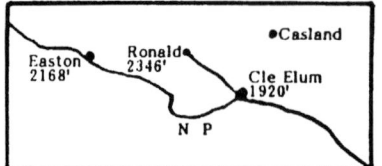

WASHINGTON   195.

CASCADE TIMBER COMPANY   President

| Incorp: | 1/23/1901 | Operated: | 1903 to 1942 | HQ city: | Reliance |

Disposition:	abandoned
Miles track:	30	Gauge:	56½"
Main line:	woods lines from Reliance and Selleck
Rail wt.:	56 lbs.	Max. grade:	8.0%	Const. began:	grading

Locomotives:

Road No.	Cyln.	Type	Dvr. in.	Bldr.	Bldr. No.	Date	Weight	Effort	Remarks
3		2 truck	40	Heisler	1201	5/10	120,000		acq. 2d hand; used at Reliance
3-2d		3 truck		Climax	1401	4/16	140,000	30,800	ex Reliance Lumber Co. #3
6		3T Shay	36	Lima	2544	7/12	180,000	40,400	acq. 1930; used at Reliance - scr 1942
107		2-6-2	44	BLW	55415	5/22		23,400	ex Pac. States Lbr. #107 - sold 7/1943
108*	14½x15	3T Shay	36	Lima	3254	4/24	209,800	40,400	used at Reliance; 1940 to Standard Log.
109*	13x15	'	'	'	3319	5/28	186,000	38,200	used at Selleck; 10/1941 to St. Paul/T.
5100		2-6-2	44	BLW	34918	7/10			acq. 7/1939 ex Pac. States Lbr. Co.

Freight traffic: logging

CASCADES RAILROAD COMPANY   Oregon Steam Navigation Co.,   **Owner**

| Incorp: | 12/16/1860 | Operated: | 5/1/60 to (1896) | HQ city: | Cascades |

Disposition:	abandoned about 1907
Miles track:	5.91	Gauge:	60" - reduced to 56½" in 1880 and to 36" about March 19, 1883
Main line:	Cascades to Upper Cascades
Rail wt.:		Max. grade:		Const. began:	grading	(April, 1859)
					laying rails	
Const. comp.:	October 13, 1862			First train operated:	April 20, 1863, by steam

Locomotive engines:

1		0-4-0	34	Vulcan	(2)	/61	9,700	810	
2		'	'	'	(7)				
1-2d		0-6-0		Porter	246	7/76	20,000		acq. 1881 ex Walla Walla & Col. R.
2-2d		'		'	283	1/78	28,000		acq. 1896 ex Walla Walla & Col. R.
7		2-4-0	42	'	289	2/78	20,000	5,600	acq. 1882 ex Mill Creek Flume #5

Freight traffic: portage, agricultural and mining

Roster of 6/30/1887:
    2   locomotive engines
    2   passenger cars
    4   combination cars
    29 box cars
    17 flat cars

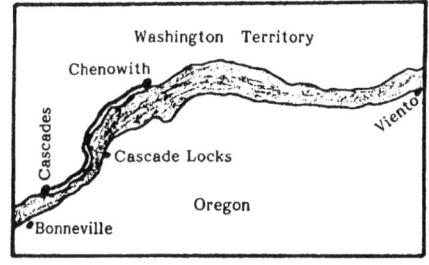

It appears that a two-mile mule-powered line was built on this site by Daniel and Putnam Bradford several years earlier.

First listed in ICC for 6/30/89 as a non-operating subsidiary of Oregon Railway & Navigation Co. with six miles owned. The property was purchased by Oregon Railroad & Navigation Co. on August 18, 1896, and probably not operated after that date. ICC for 6/30/97 states "not in operation" and this is repeated each year through 1907. Edition for 6/30/08 shows abandoned.

A Washington map of 1892 shows clearly the eastern terminal as Chenowith. A map of 1899 places Chenowith at the mouth of the Little White Salmon River, which would place it about two miles east of Viento, Oregon. Chenowith as shown on the map above is placed two miles east of Stevenson.

Bibliography: *Poor's 1888*, p.916   *Valuation 44*, p. 266

California State Railroad Museum Library   *Gerald M. Best Collection*
Bloedel-Donovan Lumber Co. #14 at Sequim in 1936

Special Collections Div. - Univ. of Washington Libraries   *Clark Kinsey photo #486*
Clemons Logging Company number six, a 2-6-6-2T, was built by Baldwin in January of 1924.

Special Collections Div. - Univ. of Washington Libraries *Clark Kinsey photo #494*
Clemons Logging Company Climax number 443 with an enclosed house and a barrel size spark arrester

Special Collections Div. - Univ. of Washington Libraries *Clark Kinsey photo #468*
Clemons Logging Company Shay with a load of logs and the whole camp on wheels

Denver Public Library - Western History Department #5123 Photo by Otto C. Perry
Chicago, Milwaukee, St. Paul & Pacific #10233, a General Electric 2-B+B, at Tacoma on October 2, 1931

Denver Public Library - Western History Department #5125 Photo by Otto C. Perry
Chicago, Milwaukee, St. Paul & Pacific #10252, a General Electric 1B+D+D+B1, in Tacoma October 2, 1931

WASHINGTON

Denver Public Library - Western History Department   #5247   *Photo by Otto C. Perry*
Chicago, Milwaukee, St. Paul & Pacific gasoline-electric passenger car #5902 at Tacoma on October 2, 1931.

Denver Public Library - Western History Department   #5221   *Photo by Otto C. Perry*
Chicago, Milwaukee, St. Paul & Pacific #9311 pulling train #16 with nine cars east of Spokane September 29, 1931.

Denver Public Library - Western History Department   #5108   *Photo by Otto C. Perry*
Chicago, Milwaukee, St. Paul & Pacific #9104, a 2-6-6-2, at Spokane on September 29, 1931

CHERRY VALLEY LOGGING COMPANY   Weyerhaeuser Co., **Owner**

Incorp: 7/6/1916 **Operated:** 1902 to 1930 **HQ city:** Everett
Disposition: abandoned - corporation dissolved January 19, 1948
Miles track: 45 **Gauge:** 56½"
Main line: woods lines from Tolt and Stillwater
Rail wt.: 56 lbs. **Max. grade:** 3.5% **Const. began:** grading 1902
Locomotives:

Road No.	Cyln.	Type	Dvr. in.	Bldr.	Bldr. No.	Date	Weight	Effort	Remarks
1		2T Shay	29½	Lima	486	2/95	64,000	14,075	ex Mosher & McDonald #2
1-2d		'	32	'	2030	11/07	100,000	22,600	ex Stillwater Lumber Co. #1
2*		2 truck	31	Climax	411	6/03	90,000	19,800	
2-2d*	13½x15	3T Shay	36	Lima	3090	8/20	189,000	35,100	to Weyerhaeuser Tbr. Co. #2 at Vail
3*	12x12	2T Shay	'	'	2671	5/13	110,000	23,900	to Weyerhaeuser Tbr. Co. #3 at Vail
101*	20½x28	2-8-2	48	BLW	39787	'	175,000	35,500	to Weyerhaeuser Tbr. Co. #101

Freight traffic: logging

Roster of 6/30/1910:
  1   geared engine
 30   logging trucks
  2   miles of track at Tolt

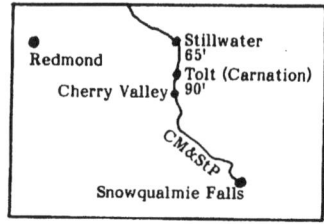

CLARK COUNTY TIMBER COMPANY   Weyerhaeuser Co., **Owner**

Incorp: 1/1/1904 **Operated:** 1917 to 1924 **HQ city:** Portland
Disposition: abandoned
Predecessor: Twin Falls Logging Company - 15 miles in 1906 **from:** 1903 to 1917
Miles track: 30 **Gauge:** 56½"
Main line: Yacolt into the forest
Rail wt.: 56 lbs. **Max. grade:** 4.5% **Const. began:** grading
Locomotives:

Road No.	Cyln.	Type	Dvr. in.	Bldr.	Bldr. No.	Date	Weight	Effort	Remarks
101*	20½x28	2-8-2	48	BLW	37539	2/12	173,000	35,300	to Weyerhaeuser #101
102		'	44	'	37496	1/12	139,000	27,000	ex Weyerhaeuser (Oregon) #1
103		'	'	'	37497	'	'	'	ex Weyerhaeuser (Oregon) #2
200*	12x15	3T Shay	36	Lima	2642	2/13	140,000	30,350	to Carlton & Coast #70
2-2d ?		2T Shay	29½	'	2490	2/12	84,000	16,900	acq. 1/1922 ex Astoria Southern #2

Roster of 6/30/1910:
  5   geared engines
 30   miles of track

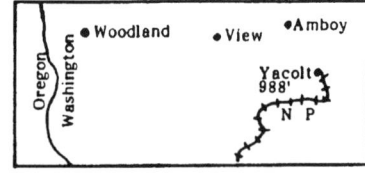

CLEAR LAKE LUMBER COMPANY   President

Incorp: 11/10/1902 **Operated:** 1903 to 1927 **HQ city:** Clear Lake
Disposition: abandoned
Predecessor: Bratnober-Waite Lumber Company **Incorp.:** 11/3/1899 to 12/31/1902
Miles track: 55 **Gauge:** 56½"
Main line: Clear Lake into the forest
Rail wt.: 56 lbs. **Max. grade:** 5.0% **Const. began:** grading 1900

Locomotives:

Road No.	Cyln.	Type	Dvr. in.	Bldr.	Bldr. No.	Date	Weight	Effort	Remarks
1		2T Shay	32	Lima	1940	10/07	83,600	22,575	acq. 4th hand; sold 6/1929
2*		2 truck	30	Climax	209	4/00	70,000	15,400	new as Bratnober-Waite #2
2-2d*?	13½x15	3T Shay	36	Lima	2837	6/16	160,000	35,100	to Puget Sound Pulp & Tbr. #2
3*		2 truck	30	Climax	371	12/02	70,000	15,400	new as Clear Lake Lumber #3
4*		'	'	'		3/07	80,000	17,600	
4-2d		2T Shay	32	Lima	2304	3/10	83,600	22,500	ex Miller Logging #4; sold
5*		2 truck		Climax		3/08			
5-2d*	12x12	2T Shay	36	Lima	2315	5/10	101,800	23,890	to Skagit Valley Lumber Co. #5
6*		2 truck		Climax	1063	12/10	114,000		new as Clear Lake Lumber #6
7 ?		'	30	'	636	2/06	56,000		ex Dickey & Angel Logging #3
8*	13½x15	3T Shay	36	Lima	3260	4/24	204,600	35,100	to Phoenix Logging Co. #8
9 ?		2 truck	30	Climax	900	7/08	80,000	17,600	ex Robe-Menzel Lumber Co. #2

Roster of 6/30/1910:
- 2 geared engines
- 24 logging trucks
- 1 flat car
- 8 miles of track

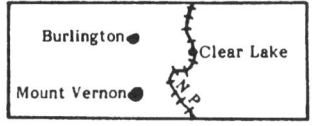

CLEMONS LOGGING COMPANY

Weyerhaeuser Co., Owner

Incorp:	2/19/1919	**Operated:** 2/1919 to 1936	**HQ city:**	Montesano
Disposition:	to Weyerhaeuser Timber Company			
Predecessor:	Melbourne & North River Railroad Company - 13 miles		**from:** 1903 **to** 2/1919	
Miles track:	75	**Gauge:** 56½"		
Main line:	Melbourne and Cosmopolis into the forest			
Rail wt.:	60 lbs.	**Max. grade:** 4.0%	**Const. began:** grading	1903

Locomotives:

	Cyln.	Type	Dvr. in.	Bldr.	Bldr. No.	Date	Weight	Effort	Remarks
1*		2 truck		Climax	443	9/03	100,000		to Murphy Timber Co. at Yacolt
2*	12x15	3T Shay	36	Lima	2008	11/07	140,000	29,800	used at Cosmopolis
3*		3 truck	'	Climax	1027	/10	160,000	35,200	to Discovery Bay Logging Co.
4*		'	'	'	1411	7/16	'	'	
	Clemons Logging Co.								
2*	18¼x16	3 truck	40	Heisler	1574	4/29	180,000		to Craig Mountain (Idaho) #6
4*		'	36	Climax	1555	12/19	160,000	35,200	to West Fork Logging Co.
5*		'	'	'	1602	/21	'	'	to West Fork Logging Co. #5
6*	17/26x24	2-6-6-2T	44	BLW	57601	1/24			
7*	18/28x24	2-6-6-2	'	'	58529	7/25	245,500	42,500	
8*	'	2-6-6-2T	'	'	60343	1/28			

Freight traffic: logging

Roster of 6/30/1910:
- 2 geared engines
- 21 logging trucks
- 5 miles of track

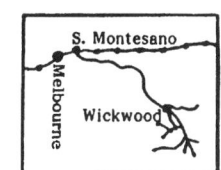

COLUMBIA & COWLITZ RAILWAY COMPANY

J. P. Weyerhaeuser, President

Incorp:	4/10/1925	**Operated:** 1/1/29 to	**HQ city:**	Longview
Disposition:	in operation 1993			
Miles track:	8.487	**Gauge:** 56½"		
Main line:	Columbia Jct. to Ostrander Jct.			
Rail wt.:	66/70/112 lbs.	**Max. grade:** 2.5%	**Const. began:** grading	(May 3, 1926)
			laying rails	June 23, 1926
Const. comp.:	December 31, 1928		**First train operated:**	January 1, 1929

Locomotives:

Road No.	Type	Dvr. in.	Bldr.	Bldr. No.	Date	Weight	Effort	Remarks
1	2-8-2	44	BLW	37496	1/12			ex Twin Falls Logging Co. #102
102	'	'	'	45248	2/17			ex East Oregon Lumber Co. #3
109	'	'	'	41710	9/14			ex Columbia & Nehalem River #117
120	2-6-6-2	50	'	61904	/36	373,000	59,600	scrapped
701*	B-B		EMD	18599	7/53		1,500 h.p.	
702	'		'	18604	8/53		'	ex Southern Pacific #2407

Freight traffic: common carrier, logging

Roster of 12/31/1930: - ICC
    1   locomotive
    0   cars

First published "timetable":
November, 1938
Columbia Jct.
Rocky Point
Ostrander Jct.

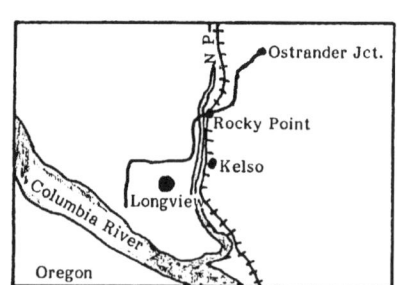

Connection was made at Rocky Point with Chicago, Milwaukee, St. Paul & Pacific, Great Northern Railway, Northern Pacific Railway and Union Pacific Railroad.

Of the total road, 2.97 miles of partially constructed line extending from the Cowlitz River, northeast of Ostrander Jct., were acquired by purchase on July 12, 1926, from the Weyerhaeuser Timber Co., by whom it was constructed between 1923 and 1925. The subject carrier completed construction of this segment and built 5.517 miles extending from Cowlitz River southwest to Columbia Jct. near Longview. This work included bridging the Cowlitz at Rocky Point, 240 feet long.

This class III carrier was first listed in ICC for 12/31/26 as an operating independent with 8.5 miles owned, not in use. By 12/31/29 it was 8.5 miles owned and operated. In 1947 it was nine miles owned and seven operated (with Weyerhaeuser Timber Co. operating the other two miles). In 1955 it was eight and six miles.

Bibliography: *Longview Daily News* - April 21 to June 23, 1926

Valuation 43, p. 584

COLUMBIA & PALOUSE RAILROAD COMPANY, THE

President

Incorp: 6/29/1882   **Operated:** 1/1/84 to 9/5/10   **HQ city:** Portland

Disposition: sold to The Oregon Railroad & Navigation Company on September 6, 1910

Miles track: 144.80   **Gauge:** 56½"

Main line: Connell to Moscow and Farmington

Rail wt.:   **Max. grade:**   **Const. began:** grading (January 1, 1883)
                                                                                laying rails (April 2, 1883)

Const. comp.: (October 31, 1886)   **First train operated:** 1883

Freight traffic: common carrier, agriculture

First published timetable:
November 24, 1884
Time	Station	m.p.
7:25 a.m.	Palouse Jct.	
10:30	Hooper	39.7
12:50 noon	Endicott	69.0
2:50 p.m.	Colfax	89.0

A published timetable dated October 1, 1885, shows operation to Moscow, 117 miles.

Farmington, 117 miles, is shown on a schedule dated October 27, 1886.

Listed in first ICC (6/30/88) as a non-operating subsidiary of Oregon Railway & Navigation Co. with 145 miles owned, then unchanged until its sale and merger in 1910.

Notes from *Railroad Gazette*:
March 2, 1883   Work will begin soon.
August 24, 1883   Forty-four miles of rails laid.

And from *The Railway Age*:
May 27, 1886   Work has been commenced at Colfax to build north.
September 2, 1886   It is reported completed to Farmington, about 27 miles.

Bibliography: *Poor's 1901*, p. 598   Oregon PUC report 1890, p. 208   *Valuation 44*, p. 270
Olympia - *Washington Standard* - March 23, 1883

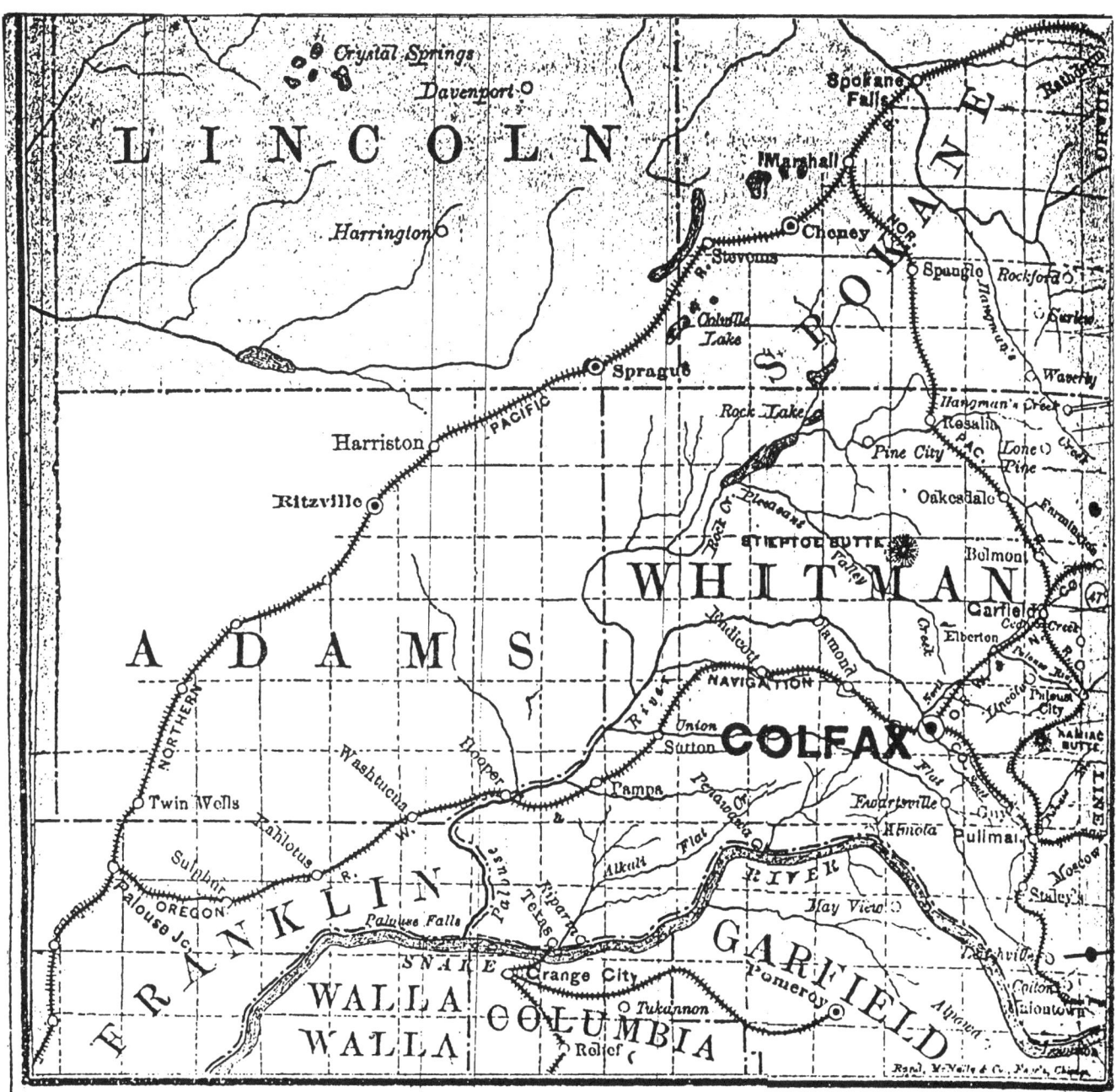

The Palouse Country, the grain belt of Eastern Washington, comprises all that country lying south of Cheney and east of the line of the Northern Pacific railroad, north of Snake river, in Washington territory, as shown by the above map. No section of the great northwest will equal this in its productiveness and fertility, and it is the recognized garden spot of Eastern Washington. With the exception of a patch of timber now and then scattered over its area, the Palouse Country is susceptible of being transformed into one vast grain field. Hardly one-sixth of its arable land is yet in cultivation; the remaining five-sixths awaits the industrious immigrant who wishes a home in the great west. The average grain yield is 30 to 40 bushels per acre of wheat, and of oats and barley 70 to 80 bushels. The Palouse Country is well watered by the Palouse river and its many tributaries, and numerous springs. Two lines of railroad cross the country, and another is in course of construction, commencing at Riparia on Snake river and extending northeast, crossing the O. R. & N. at Pampa and the N. P. at Oakesdale, its destinatition being the Cœur d'Alene mines. Construction has also commenced on an extension of the O. R. & N. road from Farmington to Spokane Falls, which will junction with the road to the mines about ten miles north of Farmington. In size Whitman county is about that of the state of Delaware, and is fully capable of sustaining a population equal to that state—150,000.

Colfax *Commoner* June, 1888

It appears that the predecessor of the chamber of commerce was the local newspaper editor.

COLUMBIA & PUGET SOUND RAILROAD COMPANY A. A. Denny, **President**

Incorp:	11/26/1880	**Operated:**	11/26/80 to 3/25/16	**HQ city:**	Seattle

Disposition: consolidated into Pacific Coast Railroad Company on March 26, 1916

Predecessors: Seattle & Walla Walla Railroad & Transportation Company **Incorp.:** 7/19/1873 to 11/25/1880
Seattle Coal & Transportation Company, The 2/26/1876 2/15/1878

Miles track:	60.26	**Gauge:** 36"		**Date standardized:**	November, 1897

Main line: Seattle to Newcastle and Franklin

Rail wt.: 35/85 lbs. **Max. grade:** 2.50% **Const. began:** grading (January 7, 1884)
laying rails (August 29, 1884)

Const. comp.: (May 15, 1893) **First train operated:** November 26, 1880

Locomotive engines:

Road No.	Cyln.	Type	Dvr. in.	Bldr.	Bldr. No.	Date	Weight	Effort	Remarks
1		0-6-4	33	Mason	552	8/85	50,000		ex Stockton & Ione - SCR 1895
2		4-4-0	36	Baily		5/77	26,000		
2-2d		0-4-0	30	BLW	5610	4/81			
3		2-6-2T	'	'	3603	5/74	20,000		
3-2d		2-6-0	42	Brooks		/81	57,400	12,975	1898 to White Pass & Yukon #1
4		0-6-0T	30	BLW	3713	4/75	20,000		
4-2d		2-6-0	42	Brooks		/81	57,400	12,975	sold in 1897
5		0-4-0T		Fulton		9/71			1883 to Mosquito & Coal Creek RR
5-2d		0-6-0	36	BLW	3771	8/75	(36,000)		sold in July, 1896
		0-4-0	30	'	4108	7/77			
6		2-6-0	36	Porter	292	2/78	36,000		1898 to Rogue River Valley (Oregon)
7		0-4-0T		'	114	2/72	15,000		sold in 1897
8*	15x20	2-8-0	37½	BLW	7597	5/85	63,000	15,100	1898 to White Pass & Yukon #5
9	'		36	Grant	1517	8/82	63,000	16,000	acq. 9/30/1887; 1898 to W.P.&Y. #3
10		4-4-0	42	BLW	4294	3/78	43,300	6,800	1897 to White Pass & Yukon #4

the above were narrow gauge; the following standard gauge:

Road No.	Cyln.	Type	Dvr. in.	Bldr.	Bldr. No.	Date	Weight	Effort	Remarks
1		4-4-0	62	Norris		/66	70,000		sold in 1900
4		4-6-0	54	BLW	11265	10/90	80,000		ex Port Townsend S. #4; sold in 1906
5		4-4-0	62	N.Y.	628	7/90	78,000	13,312	ex Port Townsend Southern #2
7*	19x24	2-8-0	50	BLW	15439	7/97	115,000		sold in 1916
8-2d*	'	'	'	'	15440	'	'		
9		4-4-0	62	N.Y.	629	7/90	78,000	13,312	ex Seattle & Northern #2 - SCR 1910
10*	17x24	0-6-0	50	BLW	15501	9/97	80,000	18,865	
11*	19x24	2-8-0	'	'	19298	7/01	121,650		
12*	'	'	'	'	22759	8/03	'		
14*	20x24	'	52	R.I.	41965	2/07	124,500		
15*	'	'	'	'	41966	'	'		
16*	'	'	'	Brooks	48294	7/10	138,000		
17*	19x26	0-6-0	51	'	48296	'	127,000	28,160	
18*	18x24	4-4-0	62	'	48295	'	110,000		

Freight traffic: common carrier, coal

Rosters of 6/30/1888 - 11/30/1891 - 6/30/1913:

locomotive engines	9	8	11
passenger cars	4	5	8
freight cars	211	44	152
coal cars		100	236

Published timetable dated:
March 5, 1890

7:15 a.m.	Seattle		
7:55	Black River Jct.	10	miles
8:10	Renton	13	
9:05	Cedar Mountain	19	
9:30	Maple Valley	23	
10:30	Black Diamond	31	
11:00	Franklin	34	
5:40 p.m.	Seattle		
	Newcastle	19	

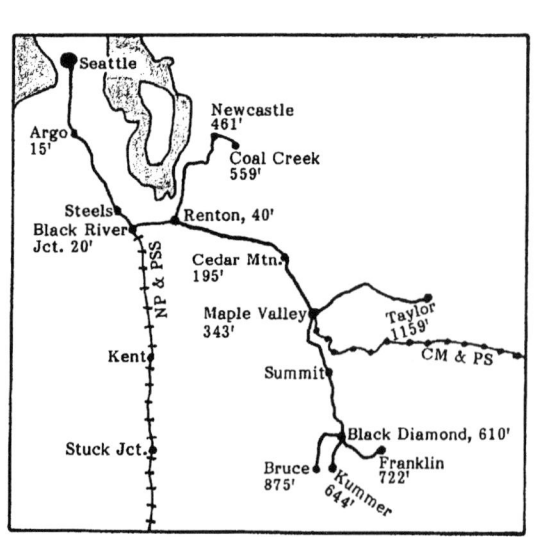

The main line was opened Renton to Franklin in December, 1884, and Newcastle to Coal Creek about December, 1891. It was opened Maple Valley to Taylor in about May, 1893. About April, 1897, Denny was renamed Bruce. The 1.65-mile Kummer track opened by June 30, 1903.

The six miles between Black River Junction and Argo was three-railed, completed July 1, 1884, so that Northern Pacific & Puget Sound Shore Railroad Co. could operate into central Seattle. At Argo, the Northern Pacific track inclined to the west to its own depot. Under terms of a February 3, 1903, contract, the carrier granted to Northern Pacific trackage rights from Argo into its part of Seattle. In return, Northern Pacific gave it trackage rights from Argo to the coal export docks regions of Seattle. In 1909 an agreement was made with Chicago, Milwaukee & Puget Sound Railway Co. granting trackage rights for 20.37 miles from Maple Valley into Seattle.

Cost of road and equipment to November 30, 1886, was $1,025,471; ten years later it had grown to $1,935,849. Maximum grade to Newcastle was 2.50%, to Black Diamond it was 1.38% and 2.04% to Bruce (Denny).

Listed in first ICC (6/30/88) as an operating independent with 44 miles owned and in use; increased to 55 miles each by 6/30/91. On December 1, 1897, it became a non-operating subsidiary of the Pacific Coast Company, but again shown as an independent in 1906 and 1907. By 6/30/08 it was a 58-mile operating subsidiary of Pacific Coast Co.

A note in the Laramie, Wyoming, *The Daily Boomerang* for September 13, 1889, states that Columbia & Puget Sound has purchased four Oregon Short Line & Utah Northern narrow-gauge engines.

Bibliography: *Poor's 1892*, p. 179   *Seattle Daily Post-Intelligencer* - September 18, 1884

COLUMBIA & RED MOUNTAIN RAILWAY COMPANY

D. C. Corbin, President

Incorp:	1/25/1895	**Operated:**	12/16/96 to 6/30/07	**HQ city:**	Spokane Falls

Disposition: sold to Great Northern Railway Company on July 1, 1907

Miles track: 7.51   **Gauge:** 56½"

Main line: Northport to British Columbia boundary

Rail wt.: 56 lbs.   **Max. grade:** 3.0%   **Const. began:** grading (August 1, 1896)
                                                                  laying rails September 22, 1896

Const. comp.: December 10, 1896   **First train operated:** December 16, 1896

Locomotive:

Road No.	Cyln.	Type	Dvr. in.	Bldr.	Bldr. No.	Date	Weight	Effort	Remarks
9*	19x24	2-8-0	47	BLW	15013	8/96	113,300	26,640	to Spokane Falls & Northern #9

Freight traffic: common carrier, mining

First published timetable:
December 30, 1896
1:35 p.m.   Northport
2:37   Frontier   m.p. 6.8
3:25   Rossland   17.0

First listed in ICC for 6/30/97 as an operating subsidiary of Spokane Falls & Northern Railway Co. with 7.5 miles owned and in use. By 6/30/99, Spokane Falls & Northern was an operating subsidiary of Great Northern Railway Co., and, so in turn, was Columbia & Red Mountain. No further changes in status until its sale and merger in 1907.

Roster of 6/30/1906:
    1   locomotive
    1   passenger car
   18   freight cars

The locomotive was jointly owned with the 9.53-mile Red Mountain Railway Co. in Canada. The line cost $560,493 to build and equip. The grading contract was signed on July 20, 1896. Maximum curve was 22°. Northport is 34 miles from the Idaho-Washington boundary.

According to a press report of September 9, 1901, eighty-eight cars of steel are to be used in relaying the tracks between Northport and Rossland. By November 6 the job was nearly completed and only a few cars of heavy new rails remained to be placed.

The corporation was dissolved on January 3, 1911.

Bibliography: *Poor's 1904*, p. 567   *The Railway Review* - September 26, 1896   *Valuation 133*, p. 191
                The Spokesman-Review - September 12 and November 11, 1901
                Spokane - *The Chronicle* - September 4 and 25, 1896

COLUMBIA RIVER & NORTHERN RAILWAY COMPANY

Rufus Mallany, President

Incorp: 1/24/1902 **Operated:** 5/1/03 to 3/31/08 **HQ city:** Portland
Disposition: sold to and merged into Spokane, Portland & Seattle Railway Company on March 31, 1908
Miles track: 42.25 **Gauge:** 56½"
Main line: Goldendale to Lyle
Rail wt.: 56 lbs. steel **Max. grade:** 2.20% **Const. began:** grading (June 2, 1902)
laying rails (November 3, 1902)
Const. comp.: April 25, 1903 **First train operated:**

Locomotives:

Road No.	Type	Dvr. in.	Bldr.	Bldr. No.	Date	Weight	Effort	Remarks
1	4-4-0	57	Hinkley	1469	12/81	68,000	12,826	ex O.R.&N. #44; to S.P.&S. #51
2	'	63	Schen.	2785	2/89	99,000	18,480	ex U.P. #623; to S.P.&S. #50

Freight traffic: common carrier, lumber

Roster of 6/30/1906:
- 2 locomotives
- 2 passenger cars
- 44 freight cars

First listed in ICC for 6/30/03 as an operating independent with 41 miles owned and in use. It was extended to 43 miles each by 6/30/04 and then unchanged until its sale and merger.

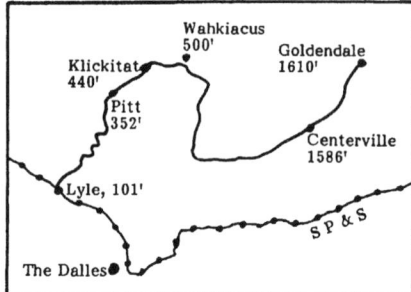

First? published timetable:
October, 1903
6:15 a.m. Goldendale 7:35
8:20 Lyle 5:30 p.m.

Construction notes from *Railroad Gazette*:
- April 25, 1902 Surveys are being made.
- May 30, 1902 Construction contract was let May 15, 1902.
- June 13, 1902 Grading contract to Goldendale awarded.
- October 3, 1902 Twenty-five miles have been graded, to lay rails soon. Some rails have now arrived and more due soon.

Bibliography: *Poor's 1905*, p. 620 Spokane - *Spokesman Review* - May 29 to July 7, 1902 *Valuation 41*, p. 30

California State Railroad Museum Library negative 11323B
Cowlitz, Chehalis & Cascade Railway Co. #25 at Chehalis in July, 1950

WASHINGTON

CONNELL NORTHERN RAILWAY COMPANY

Incorp: 6/1/1909 **Operated:** 11/1/10 to 6/25/14 **HQ city:** Connell **President**

Disposition: sold to Northern Pacific Railway Company on June 25, 1914

Miles track: 73.49 **Gauge:** 56½"

Main line: Connell to Adco

Rail wt.: **Max. grade:** **Const. began:** grading (October 18, 1909)
laying rails (February 14, 1910)

Const. comp.: (June 30, 1910) **First train operated:** November 1, 1910

Freight traffic: common carrier, agriculture

Published timetable dated:
April 9, 1916 - Northern Pacific
8:45 a.m.	Connell		
10:00	Bruce	m.p.	7
10:55	Bassett Jct.		31
11:45	Schrag		44
1:00 p.m.	Wheeler		39
2:50	Adrian		62

The official construction record is not detailed.
Connell to Adco	1909-1910	60.95 miles
Bassett Jct. to Schrag	1909-1910	12.54

A construction note from *Railway Age Gazette:*
October 29, 1909   Grading is now under way.

First listed in ICC for 6/30/10 as a non-operating subsidiary of Northern Pacific Railway Co. with 61 miles owned, not in use; it was shown as 74 miles by 6/30/14.

Bibliography: *The Pasco Express* - November 4, 1909 to February 10, 1910

Valuation 25, p. 505

CONSOLIDATED LUMBER COMPANY

Incorp: **Operated:** 1902 to 1916 **HQ city:** Elk **President**

Disposition: abandoned

Miles track: 18 **Gauge:** 36"

Main line: Elk into the forest

Rail wt.: **Max. grade:** **Const. began:** grading

Locomotives:

Road No.	Cyln.	Type	Dvr. in.	Bldr.	Bldr. No.	Date	Weight	Effort	Remarks
1		2T Shay	26	Lima	62	2/83	24,000	4,635	The oldest Shay in the West; 11/1919 to Oregon
2*	9x8	'	26½	'	1746	9/06	46,000	13,500	1916 to Edwards & Bradford at Elk
3*	8x12	'	28	'	2152	3/09	64,000	15,150	1916 to Edwards & Bradford
4*	8x10	'	27½	'	2569	6/12	56,000	12,850	1916 to Edwards & Bradford

Freight traffic: logging

Roster of 6/30/1910:
- 3 geared engines
- 41 logging trucks
- 6 flat cars
- 18 miles of track at Elk

COWLITZ, CHEHALIS & CASCADE RAILWAY COMPANY

W. E. Brown, President

Incorp:	6/24/1916	**Operated:** 1/1/18 to 1955	**HQ city:**	Chehalis
Disposition:	abandoned May 9, 1955			
Predecessors:	Washington Electric Railway Company		**Incorp.:** 9/9/1912 to 6/26/1916	
	Chehalis & Cowlitz Railway Company		1/17/1911 6/26/1916	
Miles track:	32.294	**Gauge:** 56½"		
Main line:	Chehalis to Cowlitz			
Rail wt.:	56/85 lbs.	**Max. grade:**	**Const. began:** grading (July 2, 1911)	
			laying rails September 20, 1911	
Const. comp.:	December 31, 1927	**First train operated:**	January 1, 1918	

Locomotives:

Road No.	Cyln.	Type	Dvr. in.	Bldr.	Bldr. No.	Date	Weight	Effort	Remarks
1		4-4-0	62	BLW	6920	8/83	88,100	13,100	acq. 5/1914 ex Northern Pacific #295
2		4-6-0	56	R.I.	2337	2/90	120,000	19,400	ex Seattle, Lake Shore & Eastern #15
5		'	'	Cooke	2223	6/92			ex Monte Cristo Railway #1
5-2d?		4-4-0	62	BLW	10692	3/90	88,000	13,100	acq. 2/14/1925 ex Northern Pac. #366
10		2-6-0	'	Schen.	39090	3/06	159,000	30,222	acq. 12/1927 ex C.M.St.P.&P. #2976
15*	20½x28	2-8-2	48	BLW	44106	9/16			to Puget Sound & Cascade Railway
20		4-8-0	55	Schen.	4524	2/97	184,200	33,075	acq. 9/1936 ex Northern Pacific #14
25		2-8-0	50	BLW	53037	3/20	195,000	35,000	acq. 3/1944 ex Astoria Southern #53

Freight traffic: common carrier, logging

Roster of 12/31/1924:
- 2 locomotives
- 2 passenger cars
- 71 freight cars

Published timetable dated:
May, 1929 - daily

6:45 a.m.	Chehalis		11:32
7:41	Onalaska Jct.	15	10:52
9:10	Cowlitz	32	9:25 a.m.

Also a 2:30 p.m. round trip

First listed in ICC for 6/30/16 as an operating independent with nine miles owned, not in use; by 12/31/16 it was 18 miles owned and not in operation. By 12/31/17 it owned and used 18 miles (to Lacamas, 18.32 miles). It was extended to 20 miles in 1927 and to 32 miles in 1928 with 34 miles operated. In 1932 this class II carrier owned and operated 32 miles. Toward the end of its life it was a joint venture of Northern Pacific, Great Northern, Oregon-Washington Railroad & Navigation and Chicago, Milwaukee, St. Paul & Pacific.

Construction data about the predecessors is fragmented, but it appears that Chehalis & Cowlitz built about four miles in 1911 and Washington Electric added about six miles to the end of the former's line. This 10.08 miles was sold to the carrier on June 26, 1916. The subject company then built 8.32 miles to Lacamas between 1916 and 1918.

Construction work was resumed in 1926 and 13.894 miles to Cowlitz River was completed December 31, 1927, and the completed line was placed in operation the following day.

The railroad cost $854,208 to build and $114,068 to equip. There were three Howe timber truss bridges. It used 3,200 untreated fir ties per mile and gravel for ballast.

Bibliography: *Poor's 1924, p. 217* *The Chehalis Bee-Nugget* - July 6 to October 5, 1911 *Valuation 46, p. 497*

CROWN ZELLERBACH CORPORATION

President

Incorp:		**Operated:** 1928 to 1958	**HQ city:**	Seattle
Disposition:	abandoned			
Predecessors:	Crown Willamette Paper Company	16 miles, 60 lb. rails, 4% grade	**from:** 1924 **to** 1928	
	Cathlamet Timber Company	14 miles, 40/56 lb. rails	1902 1923	
	Bradley Logging Company	8 miles of track	1908 1923	
	Armstrong, H. E.	2 miles of track	1901 1908	
Miles track:	60	**Gauge:** 56½"		
Main line:	Cathlamet into the forest			
Rail wt.:	40/90 lbs.	**Max. grade:** 6.0%	**Const. began:** grading	1901

Road No.	Cyln.	Type	Dvr. in.	Bldr.	Bldr. No.	Date	Weight	Effort	Remarks
1*	8x8	2T Shay	26	Lima	639	5/01	34,000	10,850	new as H. E. Armstrong #1
1-2d		'	28	'	671	10/01	56,000	9,875	acq. 1908 as Bradley #1
2*	10x12	'	29½	'	1631	2/06	74,000	16,900	new as H. E. Armstrong #2
3*	11x12	'	32	'	2176	5/10	100,000	20,350	new as Bradley Logging #3
6*		3 truck	36	Willam.	13	1/24			new as Crown Willamette
7		2T Shay	32	Lima	830	8/03	90,000	18,750	2d hand to Cathlamet Timber
11		3T Shay	36	'	3272	4/25	150,000	27,300	ex Crown Willamette (Ore.)
12*	17/26x24	2-6-6-2T	44	BLW	60771	4/29			
14		3 truck	36	Willam.	14	4/24			ex Crown Willamette (Ore.)
15		'	'	'	17	9/24	175,000	36,240	ex Long Bell #702
16		2-6-6-2T	44	BLW	60871	5/29			
17		2-8-2		Porter	7052	7/27			
101 ?		3 truck	36	Willam.	11	8/23			ex Smith Lbr/Shingle Co. #101

Freight traffic: logging

Roster of 6/30/1910:
  Bradley Logging Co.
  2 geared engines
  16 logging trucks
  9 miles of track at Cathlamet

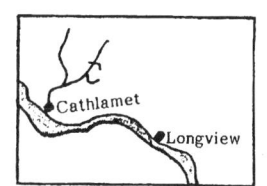

CURTIS, MILBURN & EASTERN RAILROAD COMPANY

									President

Incorp: 8/31/1973   **Operated:** 1/1/76 to (12/14/90)   **HQ city:** Chehalis

Disposition: operations discontinued - permanently ?

Predecessor: Chehalis Western Railroad Company   **Incorp.:** 2/28/1936 to 12/23/1975

Miles track: 165   **Gauge:** 56½"

Main line: Morton and Curtis to Puget Sound

Rail wt.:   **Max. grade:** 3.84%   **Const. began:** grading   1936

Locomotives:

492	B-B		F-M			
684	'		ALCO	60031	7/68	1,500 h.p.
817	'		EMD			2,000 h.p.
818	'		'			'

Freight traffic: logging

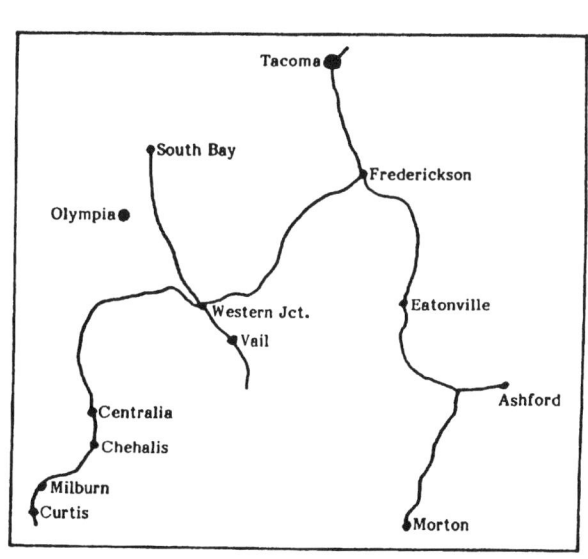

DEEP RIVER LOGGING COMPANY

Incorp:	7/19/1900	Operated: 1900 to 8/55	HQ city:	President Deep River
Disposition:	abandoned in August, 1955			
Miles track:	22	Gauge: 56½"		
Main line:	Deep River into the forest			
Rail wt.:	56/60 lbs.	Max. grade: 3.5%	Const. began:	grading May, 1900

Locomotives:

Road No.	Cyln.	Type	Dvr. in.	Bldr.	Bldr. No.	Date	Weight	Effort	Remarks
1		2T Shay	26	Lima	597	3/00	46,000	11,850	acq. 1904
2*	10x10	'	'	'	653	7/01	56,000	10,950	sold 6/1906 to Benson Logging Co. #5
3*	11x12	'	32	'	854	3/04	90,000	18,750	to Onalaska Lumber Co.
4*	10x12	'	29½	'	1630	1/06	74,000	16,900	sold to Seattle dealer
4-2d*	'	'	'	'	1869	4/07	'	'	sold to Portland dealer
5-2d*	11x12	'	32	'	2614	1/13	100,000	22,850	to Mount Emily Lumber Co. #5
7*	16x24	2-6-2	44	BLW	42199	7/15			
7-2d		2-4-4-2	48	'	33463	6/09	162,500	24,800	acq. 1935 ex Mud Bay Logging Co. #7
8*		2 truck	32	Climax	1600	9/21	100,000	24,200	scrapped
9		2T Shay	29½	Lima	1766	12/06	74,000	16,900	ex Benson Log. #9; 1910 to dealer
9-2d*		2-8-2ST	44	Brooks	65977	2/25	165,000	28,500	to Willamette Vy. Lbr., Dallas, Ore.
10		2T Shay	29½	Lima	1767	12/06	74,000	16,900	ex Benson Log. #10; 1910 to dealer
62		2-6-2		ALCO					scrapped
65		'	44	Brooks	65497	/24	118,000		ex B.W. Timber Co.
3000 ?		2T Shay	29½	Lima	3000	3/19	85,000	16,900	ex Benson Timber Co. #3000

Freight traffic: logging

Roster of 12/31/1919:
- 2 geared engines
- 1 rod engine
- 4 flat cars
- 22 miles of track

Deep River's luck has continued to be bad; the post office closed October 10, 1975. Zip code 98618 had joined the railroad in abandonment.

DEER PARK LUMBER COMPANY

Incorp:	3/9/1914	Operated: 1914 to 1956	HQ city:	President Deer Park		
Disposition:	abandoned					
Predecessors:	Deer Park Railway Company		Incorp.:	5/2/1928	to	1936
	Springdale & Long Lake Railway Company			4/21/1911		1920
	Standard Lumber Company		from:	1913		1914
Miles track:	52	Gauge: 56½"				
Main line:	Springdale into the forest					
Rail wt.:		Max. grade: 5.0%	Const. began:	grading		

Locomotives:

Road No.	Cyln.	Type	Dvr. in.	Bldr.	Bldr. No.	Date	Weight	Effort	Remarks
1		2T Shay	29½	Lima	2715	11/13	84,000	16,900	acq. 2/1922 ex Winton Lumber Co.
1-2d ?	'	'	'	'	2219	10/09	'	'	ex Moore Logging Co. #1
564	2-8-0	55	Brooks	2157	8/92	120,000	23,210		acq. 8/1928 ex Great Northern #564
1596*	3 truck	35	Climax	1596	7/22	140,000	30,800		

Freight traffic: logging

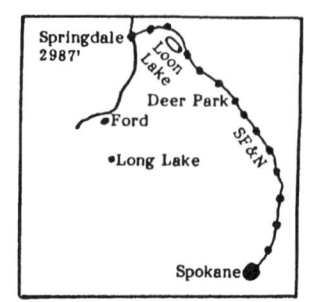

DONOVAN-CORKERY LOGGING COMPANY

					President
Incorp:	3/27/1923	**Operated:** 1923 to 1934		**HQ city:**	Aberdeen
Disposition:	abandoned				
Predecessors:	Coats-Fordney Logging Company			from: 1910	to 1923
	A. F. Coats Logging Company			1905	1910
Miles track:	50	**Gauge:** 56½"			
Main line:	along Wishkah River				
Rail wt.:	60 lbs.	**Max. grade:**	**Const. began:** grading		1905

Locomotives:

Road No.	Cyln.	Type	Dvr. in.	Bldr.	Bldr. No.	Date	Weight	Effort	Remarks
1*		2 truck	33	Climax	564	/05	100,000	22,000	
2*		"	"	"	768	3/07	"	"	
3*		3 truck	36	"	1169	7/12	150,000		
4*		2 truck		"		/12			
8*		3 truck	36	"	1670	7/25	160,000	35,200	

Freight traffic: logging

Roster of 6/30/1910:
- 2 geared engines
- 1 flat car
- 24 logging trucks
- 6 miles of track at Wishkah River

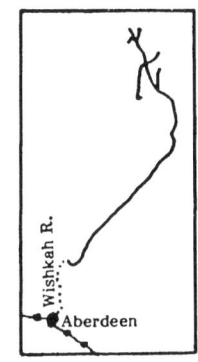

DOTY LUMBER & SHINGLE COMPANY

					President
Incorp:	2/17/1905	**Operated:** 1904 to 1928		**HQ city:**	Doty
Disposition:	abandoned				
Purchased:	Elk Creek & Grays Harbor Railway Company			from: 1913	to 1916
Predecessor:	Doty Lumber Company			1902	1904
Miles track:	12	**Gauge:** 56½"			
Main line:	Doty into the forest				
Rail wt.:	45/60 lbs.	**Max. grade:**	**Const. began:** grading		

Locomotives:

Road No.	Cyln.	Type	Dvr. in.	Bldr.	Bldr. No.	Date	Weight	Effort	Remarks
1 ?		0-4-2	35	BLW	10050	6/89			ex Mt. Tabor Street Ry. to Doty Lbr.
1-2d ?		2T Shay	29½	Lima	327	2/91		18,000	ex Utah Central to Doty Lbr/Shingle
2		"	28	"	766	3/03	56,000	13,700	6th hand to Doty Lumber & Shingle
3*	11x12	"	32	"	1509	3/05	90,000	18,750	
4*	10x12	"	29½	"	2357	7/10	84,000	16,900	
5* ?		2 truck	31	Climax	1007	3/10	76,000		
5-2d*	11x12	3T Shay	32	Lima	3070	3/20	100,000	25,830	

Freight traffic: logging

Roster of 6/30/1910:
- 2 geared engines
- 1 rod engine
- 2 flat cars
- 20 logging trucks
- 10 miles of track at Doty

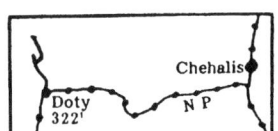

EAGLE GORGE LOGGING COMPANY President
Incorp: **Operated:** 1947 to 1955 **HQ city:** Eagle Gorge
Disposition: abandoned
Predecessor: Buckley Logging Company from: 1919 to 1947
Miles track: 8 **Gauge:** 56½"
Main line: Eagle Gorge into the forest
Rail wt.: **Max. grade:** **Const. began:** grading 1919
Locomotives:

Road No.	Type	Dvr. in.	Bldr.	Bldr. No.	Date	Weight	Effort	Remarks
1	2 truck	35	Climax	1515	6/18	120,000	26,400	ex Mutual Lbr. Co. #7; to Buckley #1
2*	3 truck	'	'	1549	11/19	140,000	30,800	
3	3T Shay	32	Lima	714	6/02	100,000	17,900	acquired 6th hand
4*	3 truck	39	Climax	1638	7/23	200,000	44,000	

Freight traffic: logging

Buckley Logging Co. owned 22 miles of track in 1930.

Special Collections Div. - Univ. of Washington Libraries *Clark Kinsey photo #1172*
Eufaula Logging Company's incline

EASTERN & WESTERN LUMBER COMPANY

						President
Incorp:	8/6/1902	**Operated:**	1902 to 1926	**HQ city:**		Portland
Disposition:	road abandoned by December 31, 1926					
Purchased:	Eufaula Logging Company			**from:**	1915	to 1926
Predecessors:	Western Lumber Company				1895	1902
	B. F. Brock Logging Company				1893	1902
	Mosquito & Coal Creek Railroad Company				1883	6/30/1904
Miles track:	15	**Gauge:**	36"	**Date standardized:**		(October, 1903)
Main line:	up Coal Creek and Mosquito Creek to Eufaula					
Rail wt.:	56 lbs.	**Max. grade:**	5.0%	**Const. began:**	grading	January 2, 1883
					laying rails	1883
Const. comp.:				**First train operated:**		(October 13, 1883)

Locomotives:

Road No.	Cyln.	Type	Dvr. in.	Bldr.	Bldr. No.	Date	Weight	Effort	Remarks
1		0-4-0		Fulton		9/71	14,000		acq. 5/1883 ex Seattle & W.W. - *Ant*
2		0-6-0ST		BLW			28,000		acq. 1890 - *Rattler*
3*		2 truck	29	Climax	272	/01	60,000	13,200	new as B. F. Brock Logging Co.
1-2d*	15x20	2-6-2T	38	BLW	24009	3/04	104,000		new as Eastern & Western Lumber Co.
2-2d*	17x24	2-6-2	44	'	27780	3/06			new as Eastern & Western Lumber Co.
3-2d*	12x12	2T Shay	36	Lima	3164	2/21	120,000	24,000	new as Eufaula; to Lewis & Clark RR
4*	11x12	'	32	'	2980	7/18	100,000	22,750	new as Eufaula; to E. & W. Lumber
5*	10x12	'	30½	'	1627	2/06	74,000	16,300	new as Eastern/Western; sold 8/1921
5-2d*		3 truck	36	Willam.	5	3/23	140,000		new as Eufaula; to E. & W. Lumber
6*	10x12	2T Shay	30½	Lima	1626	1/06	74,000	16,300	new as Eastern/Western; to Eufaula

(Baldwins second #1 and #2 built to 42" gauge - It had dual gauge? - or a different location?)

Freight traffic: logging

Roster of 6/30/1890:		Roster of 6/30/1910: (Eastern & Western)		Roster of 12/31/1925: (Eufaula Logging Co.)	
1	locomotive engine	3	geared engines	3	geared engines
4	freight cars	2	rod engines	2	rod engines
		40	logging trucks	74	logging trucks
		9	flat cars	9	flat cars
		11	miles of track at Eufaula		

Mosquito & Coal Creek Railroad Co. was first listed in ICC for 6/30/96 as an operating independent with 3.2 miles owned and in use. It was gradually increased to eight miles by 6/30/01 and to ten miles by 6/30/03. The property was owned by B. F. Brock and was renamed Eastern & Western Lumber Co. on July 1, 1904.

Eastern & Western Lumber Co., leased to the Eufaula Co., was an independent with 12 miles owned by 6/30/11 and 15 miles in 1923.

In 1926, the Eufaula Co. had 24 miles of track with a maximum grade of 7.5%, a 3,000 foot incline (with a maximum grade of 53%) and one of 2,500 feet with a 25% grade.

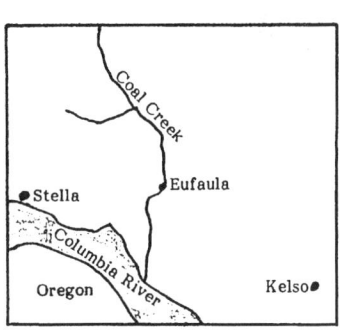

Bibliography: *Poor's 1890*, p. 1176

EASTERN RAILWAY & LUMBER COMPANY

						President
Incorp:	5/4/1903	**Operated:**	7/1/14 to 1940	**HQ city:**		Centralia
Disposition:	abandoned by December 31, 1941					
Predecessor:	Tacoma, Olympia & Chehalis Valley Railroad Company			**Incorp.:**	11/25/1889	to 6/30/1914
Miles track:	22	**Gauge:**	56½"			
Main line:	Centralia into the forest					
Rail wt.:		**Max. grade:**		**Const. began:**	grading	(June 1, 1890)
Const. comp.:				**First train operated:**		(1904)

Locomotives:

Road No.	Cyln.	Type	Dvr. in.	Bldr.	Bldr. No.	Date	Weight	Effort	Remarks
1		3T Shay	36	Lima	911	8/04	130,000	25,870	acq. 1915; 10/1942 to Agnew Lbr. Co.
2		2T Shay	28	'	766	3/03	56,000	13,700	ex Packwood Logging Co.
3*	13½x15	3T Shay	36	'	3142	12/20	160,000	35,100	10/1942 to S. A. Agnew Lbr. Co.
4		2 truck	40	Heisler	1106	11/06	104,000		ex Izett Bros.; to Angnew Lumber Co.
5		2T Shay	32	Lima	563	12/98	110,000	20,150	ex Salt Lake & Mercur #5
8		'	'	'	783	10/03	90,000	18,750	ex Northern Pacific #8; to Apex Timber
20 ?		4-4-0	62	Hinkley	1467	12/81	71,400	12,826	acq. 3/1902 ex O.R.&N. #20

Freight traffic: logging

Roster of 6/30/1910:
(Eastern Ry. & Lbr.)
- 1   geared engine
- 1   rod engine
- 12 sets logging trucks
- 15 flat cars
- 10 miles of track

Tacoma, Olympia & Chehalis Valley Railroad Co. started construction northwest from Centralia toward Elma, 32.57 miles, in 1890. The partially constructed line was deeded to Tacoma, Olympia & Grays Harbor Railroad Co. on September 10, 1890.

First listed in ICC for 6/30/99 as an operating independent with five miles owned, not in use. By 6/30/02 it was "rails removed, but road bed not abandoned." It reappeared by 6/30/04 with five miles owned and in operation. It was increased to eight miles in 1905, nine miles in 1907 and to ten miles each by 6/30/10. It was unchanged through 1913 and sold in 1914. It was 12 miles owned and operated in 1940 and then abandoned the next year.

EATONVILLE LUMBER COMPANY

Incorp: 10/12/1908	**Operated:** 1908 to 1940	**HQ city:** Eatonville	**President**
Disposition: abandoned - the corporation was dissolved June 13, 1941			
Miles track: 20	**Gauge:** 56½"		
Main line: Eatonville into the forest			
Rail wt.: 56 lbs.	**Max. grade:** 8.0%	**Const. began:** grading	

Locomotives:

Road No.	Cyln.	Type	Dvr. in.	Bldr.	Bldr. No.	Date	Weight	Effort	Remarks
1*	12x15	3T Shay	36	Lima	2281	3/10	150,000	30,350	
2*		'	'	'	3053	2/20	140,000	'	1/1944 to Tacoma Muni Belt Ry.
		2T Shay	32	'	714	6/02	100,000	17,900	acq. 2d hand
3 ?		'	29½	'	2031	9/08	84,000	16,900	acq. 4th hand
		3 truck	36	Climax	1672	9/25	160,000	35,200	ex Manley-Moore Lumber Co.
7		'	38	Heisler	1519	6/25	160,000		ex Manley-Moore Lumber Co. #7

Freight traffic: logging

Roster of 6/30/1910:
- 1   geared engine
- 8   flat cars
- 3   miles of track

The sawmill was opened on April 15, 1909.

ENGLISH LUMBER COMPANY

Incorp: (3/1901)	**Operated:** 1901 to 1946	**HQ city:** Mount Vernon	**President**
Disposition: abandoned			
Purchased: Parker-Bell Lumber Company		**Incorp.:** 6/28/1905 to 2/17/1922	
Miles track: 70	**Gauge:** 56½"		
Main line: Fir into the woods			
Rail wt.: 56/60 lbs.	**Max. grade:** 6.0%	**Const. began:** grading	1901

WASHINGTON 215.

Road No.	Cyln.	Type	Dvr. in.	Bldr.	Bldr. No.	Date	Weight	Effort	Remarks
1*	11x12	2T Shay	33	Lima	708	6/02	76,300	13,125	4/1920 to Goodro Logging Co.
2-2d		3T Shay	36	'	2837	6/16	160,000	35,100	used at McMurray
3*		2 truck	33	Climax	680	6/06	100,000	22,000	new as Parker-Bell; to Index Galena
3-2d		3T Shay	36	Lima	2643	7/13	160,000	35,100	ex Clear Lake #3; used at Fir
4		2T Shay	35	'	945	1/05	90,000	18,750	ex Skagit Vy. #4; used at Fir
4-2d?		3 truck	36	Climax	1081	1/12	150,000	35,200	ex P-Bell #4; to Silver Falls Log.
6*	12x12	2T Shay	'	Lima	2251	1/10	120,000	23,850	used at Hamilton; SCR 12/1942
7*	'	'	'	'	2630	12/12	103,665	22,550	used at Fir; SCR 2/1944
8		'	'	'	1878	3/07	110,000	23,850	used at Fir; sold to Seattle dealer
9		3T Shay	32	'	2533	4/12	120,000	25,830	acq. (1918); SCR 2/1944
10*	20½x28	2-8-2	48	BLW	53255	5/20	175,000		to Twin Falls Logging Co.
12*		3 truck	36	Climax	1581	'	180,000		new as Parker-Bell #5
13*	14x15	3T Shay	'	Lima	3198	1/23	201,500	40,400	used at Fir; 4/1945 to Puget SP&Tbr.
14		'	'	'	2704	2/14	140,000	30,350	acq. 1945; 6/1945 to P. Sound P&Tbr.
15		'	'	'	2709	10/13	160,000	35,100	1945 to Puget Sound Pulp & Tbr. Co.
16	?	2-6-0	48	BLW	2719	3/72	60,500		acq. 2/1903 ex O.R.&N. #16
39	?	4-4-0	57	'	6212	5/82	68,200		acq. 5/1902 ex O.R.&N. #39

Freight traffic: logging

Roster of 6/30/1910:
(English Lumber Co.)
  3 geared engines
 60 sets logging trucks
 10 flat cars
 24 miles of track at Conway

Roster of 6/30/1910:
(Parker-Bell Lumber Co.
  1 geared engine
  6 flat cars
  2 miles of track at Pilchuck

It was virtually unknown for a logger to have an engine #13.
Common carriers, almost always, but loggers almost never.

In 1919, Parker-Bell had 15 miles of track.

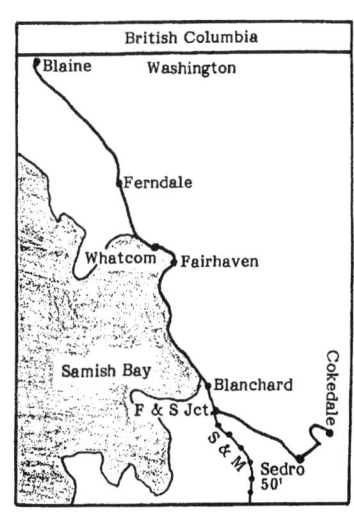

FAIRHAVEN & SOUTHERN RAILROAD COMPANY

Nelson Bennett, **President**

| **Incorp:** | 11/27/1888 | **Operated:** | 2/1/90 to 3/30/98 | **HQ city:** | Bellingham |

Disposition: sold to Seattle & Montana Railroad Company on March 30, 1898

Miles track: 56.80   **Gauge:** 56½"

Main line: Sedro to Blaine

Rail wt.: 56 lbs. steel   **Max. grade:** 1.0%   **Const. began:** grading (April 1, 1889)
                                                                                                                                                                             laying rails (July 15, 1889)

Const. comp.: (October 31, 1890) - main line   **First train operated:** February 1, 1890

Locomotive engines:

| 1* | 18x24 | 4-6-0 | 56 | Schen. | 2860 | 5/89 | 77,000 | 16,820 | to Seattle & Montana #298 |
| 2* | ' | ' | ' | ' | 2861 | ' | ' | ' | to Seattle & Montana #299 |

Freight traffic: common carrier, lumber and coal

Roster of 5/31/1890:
  2 locomotive engines
  4 box cars
 42 platform cars

First published timetable:
January 1, 1890
  7:00 a.m. Fairhaven   8:50
               Samish Lake 10
  7:50   Sedro   26   8:00 a.m.

The main line was 40.80 miles and the Cokedale branch 16.00. The carrier was connected on January 10, 1891, to the New Westminster Southern Railroad and by it to Vancouver.

The operation had a separate listing in *Official Guide* until November, 1891. In a timetable dated December 7, 1891, it was included with Seattle & Montana Railway Co. as one track from Seattle to Blaine.

First listed in ICC for 6/30/90 as an operating independent with 26 miles owned and in use. By 6/30/91 it was a 51-mile operating subsidiary of Great Northern Railway Co. By 6/30/93 it had been reduced to 41 miles and then unchanged until its sale.

Construction notes from *The Railway Age:*
March 22, 1889	Construction contracts have been let.
April 5, 1889	Thirty miles are under construction.
May 31, 1889	Steel rails have arrived at Tacoma.
August 16, 1889	One-half mile has been laid at Fairhaven.
June 28, 1890	Completed Fairhaven to Sedro, 27 miles are in operation.
August 30, 1890	Tracklaying from Fairhaven to Blaine began August 16th.
October 25, 1890	Track completed from Fairhaven to Blaine, 24 miles.
November 15, 1890	The coal branch - three miles above Sedro - is to be entended five miles; grading is completed and one mile has been railed.
December 6, 1890	Four-mile coal branch from Sedro south has been completed and to open at once.

And from *Railroad Gazette:*
February 7, 1890	Four trains daily now running from Fairhaven to Sedro on Skagit River, 25 miles.

Bibliography: *Poor's 1891*, p. 706   *Tacoma Morning Globe* - February 2, 1890   *Valuation 133*, p. 189
Snohomish - *The Eye* - July 13, 1889 to May 24, 1890

FIBERBOARD PRODUCTS, INC.

President

Incorp: **Operated:** 1927 to 1946   **HQ city:** Port Angeles

Disposition: abandoned

Predecessors:
Irving-Hartley Logging Company	6 miles, 60/90 lb. rails, 6.0% grade from: 1924	to	1927
Washington Pulp & Paper Company	25 miles at Neah Bay	1933	1942
Carlsborg Mill & Timber Company	30 miles, 56/65 lb. rails, 6.0% grade	1916	1942
Izett Lumber Company	6 miles at Brinnon	1904	1916

Miles track: 55   **Gauge:** 56½"

Main line: woods lines from Neah Bay, Port Angeles, Carlsborg and Brinnon

Rail wt.: 56/90 lbs.   **Max. grade:** 6.0%   **Const. began:** grading   1904

Locomotives:

Road No.	Cyln.	Type	Dvr. in.	Bldr.	Bldr. no.	Date	Weight	Effort	Remarks
1*		2 truck	30	Climax	652	5/06	70,000		new as Izett; to Morgan Lumber Co.
2*	12x12	2T Shay	36	Lima	1878	3/07	110,000	23,850	new as Izett; to English Lumber Co. #8
2-2d*		2 truck		Climax	916	4/09	96,000		new as Izett
3*		'	35	'	864	8/09	116,000		new as Izett
4		'	40	Heisler	1106	11/06	104,000		3d hand to Izett; to Eastern Ry. & Lbr.
8		2T Shay	29½	Lima	2747	1/14	87,000	16,900	acq. 9/1933 ex Crown Willamette (Oreg.)
9		'	32	'	2176	5/10	100,000	20,350	acq. 5/1933 ex Crown Willamette (Oreg.)

Roster of 6/30/1910:
Izett Lumber Co.
1	geared engine
8	logging trucks
1	flat car
4½	miles of track at Brinnon

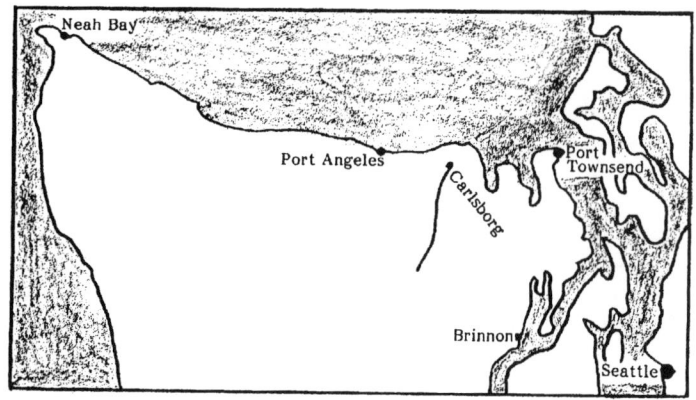

GREAT NORTHERN LUMBER COMPANY

Incorp:	12/26/1916	**Operated:** 1916 to 1926	**HQ city:**	Clinton, Iowa	**President**
Disposition:	abandoned – corporation dissolved January 27, 1940				
Predecessors:	Wenatchee Valley & Northern Railway Company		Incorp.:	10/15/1907 to	1/1/1920
	Lamb-Davis Lumber Company		from:	1906	1916
Miles track:	27	**Gauge:** 56½"			
Main line:	Leavenworth to Wenatchee Lake area				
Rail wt.:	65 lbs.	**Max. grade:**	**Const. began:** grading	(June 17, 1907)	

Locomotives:

Road No.	Cyln.	Type	Dvr. in.	Bldr.	Bldr. No.	Date	Weight	Effort	Remarks
101*	15x12	2 truck	36	Heisler	1112	11/06	74,000		new as Lamb-Davis Lumber Co.
102*	18x24	2-6-2	44	BLW	33285	3/09			new as Wenatchee Valley & North.
103*	17x14	2 truck	40	Heisler	1267	1/13	120,000		new as Wenatchee Valley & North.
1*	'	'	33	Climax	1357	/15	90,000	19,800	new as Great Northern Lumber Co.
2*	'	'	35	'	1443	/17	120,000	26,400	new as Great Northern Lumber Co.
1-2d*	11x12	2T Shay	32	Lima	3100	8/20	128,000	25,830	4/1921 to Mogul Logging Company
3004 ?		'	29½	'	3004	4/19	85,000	16,900	4/1922 to Hedlund Lbr. & Box Co.

Freight traffic: logging

Roster of 6/30/1913:
(Wenatchee Vy. & N.)
3 locomotives
31 freight cars
17 miles of track
L. Lamb, president

A construction note from *Western Lumberman* for July, 1907, states that Lamb-Davis Lumber Co. has started to build 25 miles of track from Leavenworth.

Wenatchee Valley & Northern was first listed in ICC for 6/30/08 as an operating independent with three miles owned, not in use. It was increased to 13 miles in 1909 and to 16 miles by 6/30/10, still not in use. By 6/30/11 it was 17 miles owned and operated. By 6/30/16 it was 27 miles owned, but not in operation. By 12/31/16 it had been sold to Great Northern Lumber Co.

Bibliography: *Poor's 1914*, p. 1629

GREEN RIVER & NORTHERN RAILROAD COMPANY

Incorp:	9/22/1890	**Operated:** 1890 to 4/21/98	**HQ city:**	Thomas F. Oakes, **President** St. Paul, Minn.
Disposition:	sold to Northern Pacific Railway Company on April 21, 1898			
Miles track:	11.90	**Gauge:** 56½"		
Main line:	Palmer to end of track			
Rail wt.:		**Max. grade:**	**Const. began:** grading	(May 14, 1888)
			laying rails	(Sept. 18, 1888)
Const. comp.:	(November 30, 1890)		**First train operated:**	

Freight traffic: common carrier, coal

The construction record is brief:

	dates:	miles:
Palmer Jct. to Kangley Jct.	5/1888 to 10/1888	2.90
Kangley Jct. to Kangley mine	8/1889 to 11/1889	1.50
Kangley Jct. to milepost 10.5	5/1890 to 11/1890	7.50

First listed in ICC for 6/30/91 as a non-operating subsidiary of Northern Pacific Railroad Co. with four miles owned; it was extended to 12 miles by 6/30/93. Then unchanged until its sale in 1896.

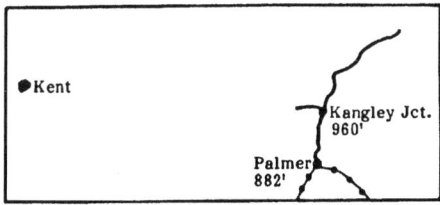

Construction notes from *Railroad Gazette*:

August 8, 1890	Track laying has commenced from Durham north to Raging River coal mines. Progress is slow because of the heavy stands of timber.
August 29, 1890	It is expected to have ten miles of track laid on the Durham extension early next week.
November 28, 1890	Seven miles of track has been laid from the junction of N. P. at Palmer toward Raging River; 500 men are at work.

Bibliography: *Poor's 1896*, p. 689

Valuation 25, p. 497

Denver Public Library - Western History Department #11994 *Photo by Otto C. Perry*
Great Northern train number five provides open window air conditioning along Puget Sound July 23, 1939

Denver Public Library - Western History Department #12023 *Photo by Otto C. Perry*
Great Northern train #2 of nine cars near Spokane with 4-8-2 #2510 on July 31, 1938

Denver Public Library - Western History Department #12017 *Photo by Otto C. Perry*
Great Northern #2123, a 2-10-2, with a 78-car eastbound freight near Odessa on September 30, 1931

Denver Public Library - Western History Department #11776 Photo by Otto C. Perry
Great Northern 0-6-0 #53 was photographed at Spokane on September 29, 1931.

Denver Public Library - Western History Department #11798 Photo by Otto C. Perry
Great Northern #838, a 0-8-0, at Spokane September 29, 1931

Denver Public Library - Western History Department #11883 Photo by Otto C. Perry
Great Northern super power 2-8-8-2 #2036 at Spokane on July 30, 1938

HAMMA HAMMA LOGGING COMPANY

Incorp:		**Operated:** 1922 to 1933			**HQ city:**	Bremerton	**President**
Disposition:	abandoned						
Miles track:	16	**Gauge:** 56½"					
Main line:	Eldon into the forest						
Rail wt.:	56 lbs.	**Max. grade:** 5.0%		**Const. began:**	grading		

Locomotives:

Road No.	Cyln.	Type	Dvr. in.	Bldr.	Bldr. No.	Date	Weight	Effort	Remarks
1		2T Shay	32	Lima	2581	8/12	100,000	22,575	acq. 4th hand; sold in 1940
2		3T Shay	36	'	2858	5/16	146,000	30,350	acq. 3d hand; sold 10/1938
4 ?		2T Shay	32	'	2578	10/12	100,000	22,575	acq. 4th hand; sold 3/1925
5		3T Shay	36	'	716	8/02	130,000	20,475	acq. 3d hand in 1923
7*	12x15	'	'	'	3194	10/22	170,000	30,350	sold in December, 1936

Freight traffic: logging

There was a 3,700-foot incline with a 37% maximum grade.
Eldon is 18 miles west of Bremerton.

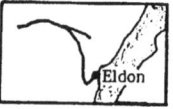

Special Collections Div. - Univ. of Washington Libraries   *Clark Kinsey photo #1449*
Hamilton Logging Co. (1907-1923) 132-foot high single-pole bridge under construction

HARTFORD EASTERN RAILWAY COMPANY

Puget Sound Pulp & Timber Co., **Owner**

Incorp:	5/14/1915	**Operated:** 6/1/15 to 5/33	**HQ city**	Everett

Disposition: abandonment authorized April 22, 1933, and scrapping began in 1935

Miles track: 41.809   **Gauge:** 56½"

Main line: Hartford to Monte Cristo

Rail wt.: 60 lbs.   **Max. grade:** 5.0%

Locomotive:

Road No.	Type	Dvr. in.	Bldr.	Bldr. No.	Date	Weight	Remarks
6	2-6-2	44	BLW	34840	6/10		1933 to Puget Sound & Cascade Ry. #6

Freight traffic: common carrier, logging and mining

Roster of 12/31/1918:
- 1 locomotive (leased)
- 4 passenger cars
- 9 freight cars

The maximum curve was 16°. There were six tunnels, but two of them were converted to open-cut because of slides.

First listed in ICC for 6/30/15 as a 42-mile operating independent. The track was leased from Northern Pacific Railway Co. until it was purchased in 1925. It was then unchanged through 1932, but did not operate in 1933 or 1934.

Bibliography: *Poor's 1918*, p. 2075

Valuation 106, p. 777

Special Collections Div. - Univ. of Washington Libraries
Hartford Eastern Railway Company gasoline passenger car with extra visibility trailer at Monte Cristo

ILWACO RAILROAD COMPANY

L. A. Loomis, **President**

Incorp:	5/6/1907	**Operated:** 6/13/07 to 12/22/10	**HQ city:**	Ilwaco

Disposition: sold to Oregon-Washington Railroad & Navigation Company on December 23, 1910

Predecessors:
Ilwaco Railway & Navigation Company, The	**Incorp.:** 8/16/1888	to	6/12/1907
Ilwaco Steam Navigation Company, The	2/23/1875		10/2/1888
Ilwaco Wharf Company, The	7/27/1874		11/22/1886

Miles track: 28.65 **Gauge:** 36"

Main line: Ilwaco to Nahcotta

Rail wt.: 35/60 lbs. **Max. grade:** **Const. began:** grading April 10, 1888

laying rails (June 5, 1888)

Const. comp.: May 22, 1908 **First train operated:** May 29, 1889

Locomotives:

Road No.	Cyln.	Type	Dvr. in.	Bldr.	Bldr. No.	Date	Weight	Effort	Remarks
1		2-6-0	42	BLW	4564	3/79	39,000	6,557	ex Utah & Northern #15; scrapped 1911
2*	12x18	'	40	Porter	1155	4/90		7,430	scrapped in 1908
3		2-4-0	42	'	289	2/78	20,000	5,600	ex Cascades Railroad #7; sold in 1900
3-2d		4-4-0	43	BLW	4224	12/77	45,500	7,837	ex S. Pac. Coast #26; scrapped 1937
4		2-6-0	42	'	5121	5/80	39,000	6,557	ex Portland & Willam. Vy. #1; scr 1941
5		4-4-0	43	'	4956	2/80	50,400	8,560	ex S. Pac. Coast #9; scrapped 1937
6		4-6-0	48	'	11925	5/91	74,000	12,430	acq. 2/1907 ex S. Pac. C. #23; scr 1931

Major business: common carrier, passengers

Roster of 4/30/1893:
- 2 locomotive engines
- 10 passenger cars
- 8 freight cars
- 1 sidewheel steamboat
- 1 steam tugboat

First published "timetable":
September, 1899
"Operating irregular schedule for freight and passengers from Ilwaco to Nahcotta, 16 miles."

Initially the carrier was engaged in steamboating only until the railroad to Nahcotta was added as shown above. The property was operated by the company from September 24, 1875, until June 12, 1907, and after that date by Oregon Railroad & Navigation Company.

Columbia Valley Railroad Company, incorporated February 16, 1899, was constructing a narrow gauge line from Ilwaco Jct. to Knappton; its uncompleted work was sold to the carrier on June 3, 1907. When finished, the branch was 13.39 miles long.

Track laying was begun with second hand rails from Utah & Northern Railway Co. which had been made standard gauge in 1887. The engine house was built at Nahcotta. Construction of the Megler line was started in March of 1907, completed May 22, 1908, and placed in operation on June 1.

Airbrakes and automatic couplers were adopted in 1903. In 1915, electric headlights replaced the oil and carbide lamps. The Megler line had a 910-foot tunnel; the dock area was 120 x 900 feet. Total cost of construction, equipment and boats to June 30, 1907, was $270,804. When the new branch opened, the Astoria ferry departed from that point.

First listed in ICC for 6/30/90 as an operating independent with 16 miles owned and in use. By 6/30/08 it was an operating subsidiary of Oregon Railroad & Navigation Co. with 29 miles owned and operated; then unchanged until its sale in 1910.

The line was abandoned September 9, 1930, and scrapping completed the following August.

Bibliography: *Poor's 1894*, p. 265   *The South Bend Journal* - September 20 to November 8, 1907   *Valuation 44*, p. 277

INMAN-POULSEN LOGGING COMPANY

President

Incorp:	**Operated:** 1906 to 1923	**HQ city:**	Portland

Disposition: abandoned

Miles track: 12 **Gauge:** 42"

Main line: woods lines from Kelso and Eufaula

Rail wt.: 60 lbs. **Max. grade:** **Const. began:** grading

WASHINGTON

Road No.	Cyln.	Type	Dvr. in.	Bldr.	Bldr. No.	Date	Weight	Effort	Remarks
1		2T Shay	26½	Lima	1637	12/06	46,000	13,500	acq. 2d hand; used at Mt. Solo
2*	10x10	"	28	"	1889	2/07	66,000	14,800	used at Eufaula
4*	"	"	29	"	2489	1/12	72,000	14,325	used at Eufaula; to Keasey, Oregon
5*	11x12	"	32	"	2957	1/18	108,000	22,580	used at Eufaula; 1924 to Oregon

Freight traffic: logging

Roster of 6/30/1910:
- 2   geared engines
- 1   rod engine
- 14   sets of logging trucks
- 1   flat car
- 7   miles of track at Kelso

KLICKITAT LOG & LUMBER COMPANY

St. Regis Paper Co., **Owner**

Incorp:		**Operated:** 7/5/22 to (1964)	**HQ city:**	Klickitat
Disposition:	abandoned			
Predecessors:	Klickitat Northern Railroad Company		**Incorp.:** 5/1/1914 to 1922	
	Western Pine Lumber Company	16 miles in 1919	**from:** 1909	7/5/1922
Miles track:	27	**Gauge:** 56½"		
Main line:	Klickitat into the forest			
Rail wt.:	56 lbs.	**Max. grade:** 4.5%	**Const. began:** grading	1909

Locomotives:

Road No.	Cyln.	Type	Dvr. in.	Bldr.	Bldr. No.	Date	Weight	Effort	Remarks
1*	6x10	2T Shay	22	Lima	2335	6/10	28,200	6,050	new as Western Pine Lumber Co.
2*	10x12	"	29½	"	2964	2/18	84,000	16,900	new as Western Pine Lbr.; SCR 8/1943
3	"	"	36	"	959	11/04	116,000	23,900	sold to dealer
4*	11x12	"	32	"	2976	5/18	120,000	25,830	new as Western Pine Lbr.; SCR 8/1943
5*	13½x15	3T Shay	36	"	3109	5/20	189,000	35,100	new as Western Pine Lbr.; SO 3/1930
5-2d	"	"	32	"	3336	5/29	140,000	25,830	ex J. Neils, Montana; SO 1964
6		3 truck	36	Willam.	34	12/29	150,000	39,300	ex J. Neils, Montana; to Rayonier
7		3T Shay	"	Lima	3346	11/29	180,000	38,200	acq. 5/1942 ex J. Neils, Montana

Freight traffic: logging

Klickitat Northern Railroad Co. was first listed in ICC for 6/30/16 as an operating independent with 16 miles owned and in use. In 1918 it was "purchased by Western Pine Lumber Co." and no longer included in ICC data.

In 1922, J. Neils Co. (Montana) purchased Western Pine Lumber Co. and its Klickitat Northern Railroad Co.; the combination became Klickitat Log & Lumber Co. This new firm was, in turn, sold to St. Regis Paper Co. in 1957.

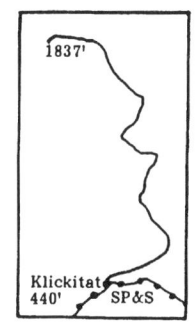

KOSMOS TIMBER COMPANY

U. S. Plywood Co., **Owner**

Incorp:	12/24/1941	**Operated:** 1939 to	**HQ city:**	Kosmos
Disposition:	abandoned after 1961			
Miles track:	90	**Gauge:** 56½"		
Main line:	Morton into the forest			

Locomotives:

Road No.	Cyln.	Type	Dvr. in.	Bldr.	Bldr. No.	Date	Weight	Effort	Remarks
1		2 truck	30	Heisler	1284	6/13	104,000		
1-2d ?		2-6-6-2T	51	BLW	61781	/34	245,000	42,500	ex Weyerhaeuser Timber Co. #4
2		3T Shay	36	Lima	2144	3/09	112,500	30,400	ex Bowman-Hicks Lumber #2
3		"	40	"	2845	11/16	202,600	44,100	acq. 10/1937 ex Bowman-H. #3
4		3 truck	38	Heisler	1316	11/15	150,000		ex Kent Lumber Co. #444
5*	18¼x16	"	40	"	1601	9/39	180,000		
6*		"	"	"	1602	"	"		
7		"	"	"	1593	11/29	"		ex Phelps-Dodge #7

8		3 truck	40	Heisler	1562	6/28	198,000	43,600	ex Weyerhaeuser Timber #101
9		3T Shay	36	Lima	3056	2/20	160,000	35,100	ex Mason County Logging #10
10		'	'	'	3347	4/30	188,800	38,200	acq. 4/1942 ex Mason Cty. #1
11		2-6-6-2T	44	BLW	59701	12/26			ex Weyerhaeuser Timber Co.
12		'		'	62065	/37	247,000	42,500	ex Weyerhaeuser Tbr. #112

Freight traffic: logging

The map on this page is but 20 miles of the track.

The subject company was sold to U. S. Plywood Co. in 1952.

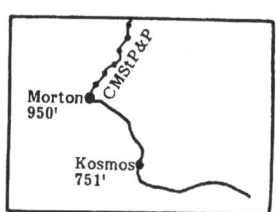

Baldwin Photo   *Collection of H. L. Broadbelt*
Idaho & Washington Northern Railroad #31 was built in 1909 with 73 inch drivers; it became Milwaukee #3135.

Tacoma Public Library TPL #1314   *F. Jay Haynes Collection*
Large steam powered/sailing ship docked in Seattle at Oregon Improvement Co. warehouse about 1890; city in background

WASHINGTON

Denver Public Library - Western History Department   #7281 *Photo by Otto C. Perry*
Crown Zellerbach Climax, built for Izett Lumber Co. in 1909, is shown near Longview on July 26, 1936

Denver Public Library - Western History Department   #7282 *Photo by Otto C. Perry*
Crown Zellerbach #12 was a 2-6-6-2T built in 1929 is shown near Longview on July 26, 1936.

LEWIS & CLARK RAILWAY COMPANY

Edward M. Berntsen, **President**

Incorp:	4/14/1987	**Operated:** 5/1/87 to		**HQ city:**	Battle Ground
Disposition:	in operation 1993				
Predecessors:	Chelatchie Prairie Railroad Company		**Incorp.:**	7/17/1980 to	8/29/1985
	Longview, Portland & Northern Railway Company			9/30/1922	7/22/1981
Miles track:	29.50	**Gauge:** 56½"			
Main line:	Rye to Chelatchie				
Rail wt.:	85 lbs.	**Max. grade:** 2.0%	**Const. began:**	grading	April 13, 1923
				laying rails	(July 16 1923)
Const. comp.:	1924		**First train operated:**		July 28, 1923

Locomotives:

Road No.	Cyln.	Type	Dvr. in.	Bldr.	Bldr. No.	Date	Weight	Effort	Remarks
20*		gas motor		Skagit		1/26			46-passenger; to Trona Railway #22
70*		0-6-0		BLW	57584	12/23			
75		'	50	Schen.	67100	9/26	146,000		acq. 1941 ex Los Angeles Jct. #200
650		2-6-2	47	BLW	54090	11/20			acq. 1940 ex Long-Bell #93-scr '55
670		4-6-0	51	Schen.	2418	/87	125,000	24,546	ex Colorado Midland #14
671		2-8-0	'	BLW	32208	11/07	194,050	45,170	acquired 4/1935
680		'	50	'	44235	10/16			ex Mount Hope Mineral Co. #3
681		2-6-2	'	'	54077	11/20			ex Calcasiau Long Leaf Lumber Co.
803		2-8-2ST	44	Brooks	66275	3/25	168,000	28,500	ex Long-Bell Lumber Co. #803
900		2-8-0	57	'	27752	4/03	186,000	36,825	ex Buffalo, Rochester & Pittsburgh
1400*	25x30	2-8-2	55	Richm.	66919	6/26	282,000	55,900	1945 to Oregon & Northwestern
1401*	'	'	'	'	66920	'	'	'	

Lewis & Clark Railway:

80		B-B		EMD	19494	1/54		800 h.p.
81		'		'	19495	'		'

Freight traffic: common carrier, logging

Roster of 12/31/1925: -ICC
- 5 locomotives
- 3 passenger cars
- 315 freight cars

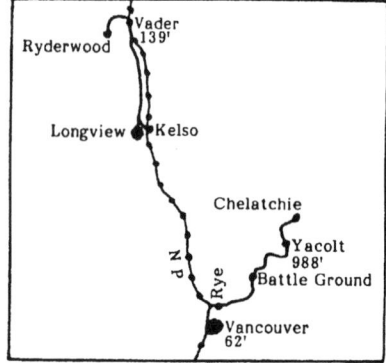

First listed in ICC for 12/31/1923 as an operating independent (owned by Long-Bell Lumber Co.) with four miles owned and in use. In 1924 it was 29 miles owned and ten in use. By 12/31/25 it was 30 miles owned and operated. In 1931 this class II carrier was reduced to seven miles owned, but 29 miles operated. It was abandoned on July 7, 1953.

The name was returned to ICC in 1961 with 42 miles owned and operated, 12 of those miles being in western Oregon and the balance between Vancouver and Chelatchie.

The track from Vancouver to Yacolt was acquired from the Northern Pacific Railway Co., so the subject had only to construct the north end of the line.

Poor's 1924 states that as of April 1, 1924, it operated seven miles from Vader to Ryderwood and three and a half miles from Longview Jct. to Longview. Also that construction was under way from Longview Jct. to Vader Jct. and to be completed for operation by January 1, 1925. This 22.85-mile main line was sold November 1, 1931, to Northern Pacific Railway, Great Northern Railway, Chicago, Milwaukee, St. Paul & Pacific Railroad and Oregon-Washington Railroad & Navigation.

A construction note from *Railway Age Gazette* dated July 26, 1924, states that a contract has been let for bridges between Kelso and Vader, 20 miles.

Bibliography: *Poor's 1924*, p. 2062   *Longview Daily News* - April 11 to July 30, 1923   Direct communication

WASHINGTON

LONG-BELL LUMBER COMPANY

Incorp:		Operated: 1924 to 1953	HQ city:	President Longview
Disposition:	abandoned			
Miles track:	56	Gauge: 56½"		
Main line:	woods lines around Longview			
Rail wt.:	60 lbs.	Max. grade: 7.0%	Const. began:	grading

Locomotives:

Road No.	Cyln.	Type	Dvr. in.	Bldr.	Bldr. No.	Date	Weight	Effort	Remarks
3		2-6-2	44	BLW	30509	4/07			ex Weed Lumber Co. #3
4		"	"	"	30519	"			ex Weed Lumber Co. #4
4-2d		3T Shay	40	Lima	1651	5/06	180,000	40,400	acq. 9/1945; used at Longview
5*	13½x15	"	36	"	3061	1/20	160,000	35,100	from Louisiana operations
6*	"	"	"	"	3071	"	"	"	from Louisiana operations
7		2-6-2	44	BLW	52851	"			ex Weed Lumber Co. #7
8		"	"	"	53347	6/20			ex Weed Lumber Co. #8
93		"	47	"	54090	11/20			from Louisiana operations
94		2T Shay	32	Lima	2943	10/17	130,000	26,850	used at Longview; to L-B in Calif.
95		2-6-2	46	BLW	31151	6/07			from Louisiana operations
96		"	"	"	31152	"			to Boise Western #2
100		2-8-2	48	Brooks	61857	/20	176,000	36,680	to Yreka Western #100 (Calif.)
101		"	44	"	65253	/23	165,000		ex Weed Lumber Co. #101
700*		3 truck	36	Willam.	15	6/24	175,000	36,240	to Mount Emily Lbr. #4 (Oreg.)
701*		"	"	"	16	8/24	"	"	to Rayonier, Inc. #4
702*		"	"	"	17	9/24	"	"	to Crown Willamette Paper Co.
800*	18x24	2-8-2ST	44	Brooks	66165	2/25	168,000	28,500	
801*	"	"	"	"	66166	"	"	"	
802*	"	"	"	"	66274	3/25	"	"	
803*	"	"	"	"	66275	"	"	"	to Longview, Portland & No. #803
804	"	"	"	"	66277	"	"	"	ex Mount Emily Lbr. #2
805	"	"	"	"	66276	"	"	"	ex Mount Emily Lbr. #1-2d
1000*		0-8-8-0		BLW	57597	1/24			
1001*		"		"	57598	"			
1008		3T Shay	36	Lima	3254	11/24	209,000	40,400	acq. 1946; used at Ryderwood

Freight traffic: logging

Roster of 12/31/1926:
- 7 rod engines
- 3 geared engines
- 6 tank cars
- 235 logging flats

The company operated 35 miles of track in 1926 and 65 miles in 1933; maximum curve was 20°.

In view of the fact that Long-Bell had operations at various locations in Louisiana, California, Oregon and Washington, this roster is, at best, in doubt - especially the rod engines.

MANLEY-MOORE LUMBER COMPANY

Incorp:		Operated: 1910 to 1934	HQ city:	President Fairfax
Disposition:	abandoned			
Miles track:	17	Gauge: 56½"		
Main line:	Melmont into the forest			
Rail wt.:	56 lbs.	Max. grade: 5.0%	Const. began:	grading 1910

Locomotives:

Road No.	Cyln.	Type	Dvr. in.	Bldr.	Bldr. No.	Date	Weight	Effort	Remarks
1 ?		2 truck	33	Climax	902	5/09	100,000	22,000	ex Oso Logging Co.
2 ?		"		"	1011	3/10	76,000		to Mutual Lumber Co.
3*	16x12	"	40	Heisler	1194	2/10	100,000		
4* ?	11x16	0-4-0		Porter	4820	1/11			
4-2d* ?		2 truck		Climax		3/12			
5 ?		3 truck	36	"	1377	3/16	160,000	35,200	ex Webb Logging & Timber Co.
6* ?		"	"	"	1672	9/25	"	"	to Eatonville Lumber Co.
7*	17x15	"	38	Heisler	1519	6/25	"		to Eatonville Lumber Co. #7

Freight traffic: logging

Roster of 6/30/1910:
- 1 rod engine
- 2 sets logging trucks
- 1½ miles of track at South Prairie

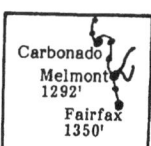

MARYSVILLE & ARLINGTON RAILWAY COMPANY

Ebey Logging Co., **Owner**

Incorp:	5/13/1907	**Operated:** 1909 to 1927	**HQ city:**	Seattle
Disposition:	abandoned			
Miles track:	16	**Gauge:** 56½"		
Main line:	Marysville into the forest			
Rail wt.:	56 lbs.	**Max. grade:** 6.0%	**Const. began:**	grading

Locomotives:

Road No.	Cyln.	Type	Dvr. in.	Bldr.	Bldr. No.	Date	Weight	Effort	Remarks
		2T Shay	33	Lima	631	3/01	80,000	18,575	ex Port Susan Logging; 1927 sold
		'	29½	'	1775	10/06	74,000	16,900	ex Wisconsin Lumber & Timber Co.
2*	12x12	'	36	'	2266	1/10	120,000	23,850	1927 to Seattle dealer
3		'	29½	'	1734	7/06	74,000	16,900	ex Port Susan Logging #3

Freight traffic: logging

Roster of 6/30/1910: There was a 4,800-foot incline with a 22% maximum grade.
   3   geared engines
  50   sets logging trucks
   5   flat cars
  16   miles of track at Arlington

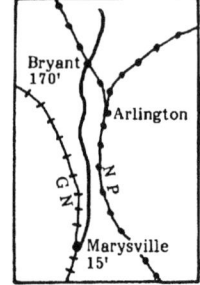

MASON COUNTY LOGGING COMPANY

President

Incorp:	7/25/1892	**Operated:** 1891 to 1941	**HQ city:**	Olympia
Disposition:	abandoned - corporation dissolved October 23, 1941			
Purchased:	Vance Lumber Company 9 miles in 1919	**from:**	(1906) to 1923	
	Black Hills & Northwestern Railway Company	**Incorp.:**	4/18/1903 to 6/30/1916	
Miles track:	85	**Gauge:** 56½"		
Main line:	Bordeaux Jct. into the forest			
Rail wt.:	56/67 lbs.	**Max. grade:** 8.0%	**Const. began:**	grading

Locomotives:

Road No.	Cyln.	Type	Dvr. in.	Bldr.	Bldr. No.	Date	Weight	Effort	Remarks
Black Hills & Northwestern Railway Co.:									
4*	14½x15	3T Shay	40	Lima	1651	6/06	180,000	40,400	7/1936 to Oregon Coast Logging Co.
6*	20½x28	2-8-2	48	BLW	34722	5/10			
7*	15x22	2-6-2ST	44	'	34666	'	86,000	17,000	sold in April, 1928
Vance Lumber Co.:									
3*	15x14	2 truck	38	Heisler	1248	2/12	100,000		used at Elma; to Malone Mercant.
4*	18x24	2-8-2	44	BLW	55804	11/22	144,330	27,800	1942 to Santa Maria Vy. (Calif.)
Mason County Logging Co.:									
1*	13x14	2 truck	30	Climax	210	4/00	80,000	17,600	used at Bordeaux; wrecked 5/2/1904
1-2d ?		'	33	Heisler	1373	5/18	72,000		ex Bloedel-Donovan #1
1-3d*	12x15	3T Shay	36	Lima	3347	4/30	188,800	38,200	4/1942 to Kosmos Timber Co.
2*	14½x12	'	'	'	688	5/02	130,000	19,400	to Bordeaux Lumber Co. #2
2-2d ?		2 truck	40	Heisler	1159	4/09	124,000		used at Bordeaux
3		'	38	'	1248	2/12	100,000		ex Malone Mercantile #3
9*	20½x28	2-8-2	48	BLW	41299	4/14	175,000		1945 to Carlton & Coast (Oregon)
10*	13½x15	3T Shay	36	Lima	3056	2/20	160,000	35,100	to Kosmos Timber Co. #9
11		2-4-2ST		Davenp.	536	1/07			
15		2-8-2	48	BLW	43563	6/16	179,000	35,000	ex Humbird Lbr.; sold 12/1941

Freight traffic: logging

WASHINGTON   229.

Rosters of 6/30/1910:

Mason County:		Vance Lumber:		Black Hills Ry.:	
3	rod engines	1	geared engine	3	geared engines
10	sets logging trucks	3	flat cars	1	rod engine
5	miles near Shelton	3½	miles at Elma	20	miles at Bordeaux

Roster of 12/31/1919:

Mason County:
- 5 rod engines
- 2 geared engines
- 30 logging flats
- 40 miles track at Bordeaux

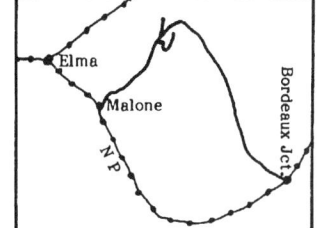

In 1892 it operated from a connection with Washington Southern Railway Co.

MERRILL & RING LOGGING COMPANY   President

Incorp:	6/4/1908	**Operated:**	1916 to 1944	**HQ city:**	Seattle
Disposition:	abandoned				
Predecessor:	Merrill & Ring Lumber Company			**Incorp.:**	8/26/1902 to 1916
Miles track:	30	**Gauge:**	56½"		
Main line:	Mukilteo and Pysht into the forest				
Rail wt.:	56/60 lbs.	**Max. grade:**		**Const. began:**	grading

Locomotives:

Road No.	Cyln.	Type	Dvr. in.	Bldr.	Bldr. No.	Date	Weight	Effort	Remarks
1		2T Shay	36	Lima	1817	2/07	110,000	23,850	acq. 2d hand; scrapped April, 1947
2	'	'	29½	'	2031	9/08	84,000	16,900	acq. 2d hand; used at Mukilteo
3*	11x12	'	32	'	2133	1/09	100,000	22,575	used at Mukilteo and Pysht
4*	'	'	'	'	2167	5/09	'	20,350	used as above; sold August, 1926
5*	12x15	3T Shay	36	'	3108	8/20	140,000	30,350	sold 12/1936 to Columbia Construction Co.
6*	'	'	'	'	3285	12/25	'	'	sold into British Columbia
7*	14½x15	'	'	'	3261	9/25	212,000	40,400	purch. 7/9/1927; sold in August, 1946

Freight traffic: logging

Roster of 6/30/1910:
- 4 geared engines
- 40 sets logging trucks
- 3 flat cars
- 12 miles of track at Everett

Mukilteo is five miles southwest of Everett.
Pysht is 32 miles west of Port Angeles.

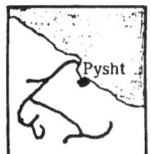

MILL CREEK RAILROAD COMPANY   President

Incorp:	10/19/1903	**Operated:**	12/10/03 to 9/8/05	**HQ city:**	Walla Walla
Disposition:	sold to and merged into Washington & Columbia River Railway Company on September 8, 1905				
Predecessor:	Mill Creek Flume & Manufacturing Company		**Incorp.:**	3/1/1880 to 12/10/1903	
Miles track:	13.51	**Gauge:**	36"	**Date standardized:**	January 16 to July 1, 1905
Main line:	Walla Walla to Dixie				
Rail wt.:	30 lbs. steel	**Max. grade:**	1.93%	**Const. began:**	grading (May 30, 1881)
					laying rails (July 18, 1881)
Const. comp.:	1882			**First train operated:**	(September 6, 1881)

Locomotive engines:

5	2-4-0	42	Porter	289	2/78	20,000	5,600	acq. 5/1881 ex Walla Walla & Columbia River
6	2-6-0	36	'	292	'	41,000		acq. 5/1881 ex Walla Walla & Columbia River

Freight traffic: common carrier, lumber

Roster of 6/30/1881:
- 1 locomotive engine
- 10 flat cars

The *Idaho Tri-Weekly Statesman* (Boise City) for May 28, 1881, states "One narrow gauge locomotive, 10 cars, and several miles of light iron have been sold to Mill Creek Flume & Mfg. Co. who will construct from Walla Walla up Mill Creek to the lumber flume at once." The 12.5-mile V-shaped flume was built of sawed lumber, the sides being 32 inches wide and the spread was 42 inches. It was able to handle 8x10s that were 65 feet long. One sawmill at the head of the flume was water powered and the other steam. The steepest pitch to the flume was 1.75 feet per hundred and the total fall was over 1,200 feet.

The original main line to Dixie was 10.79 miles and 1.65 miles to what was then called Dudley. Of the mileage in 1905, 7.01 of 10.79 miles between Walla Walla and Dixie was abandoned; the balance of 5.43 miles was converted to standard gauge. The abandonment may have been duplicate track from Walla Walla to Spring Creek. *Poor's 1907* shows that Washington & Columbia River Railway Co. was operating 6.13 miles from Mill Creek Jct. to Tracy. This could have been new track east of Walla Walla up Mill Creek rather than the Tracy to Dixie route.

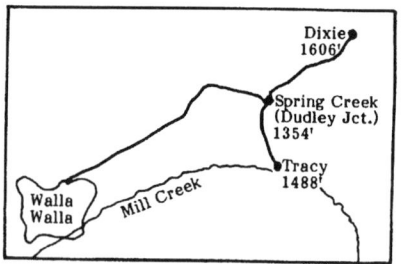

Mill Creek Flume & Manufacturing Co. was first listed in ICC for 6/30/90 as a non-operating subsidiary of Oregon Railway & Navigation Co. with 13 miles owned; control had been purchased by OR&N on August 18, 1886. On October 26, 1903, 1.07 miles were sold to The Oregon Railroad & Navigation Co. The major portion of the line was sold to Mill Creek Railroad Co. on December 10, 1903. It is unusual for portions of a minor route to be sold to subsidiaries of Union Pacific and Northern Pacific or any other major carrier.

Mill Creek Railroad Co. was first shown in ICC for 6/30/04 as a 12-mile non-operating subsidiary of Oregon Railroad & Navigation Co.; it appears that it should have stated Northern Pacific. The volume for 6/30/05 shows it as an operating independent with 12 miles owned, not in use.

Bibliography: *Poor's 1897*, p. 250   *Walla Walla Union* - June 4 to September 30, 1881   *Valuation 25*, p. 503

MILLER LOGGING COMPANY   President

Incorp:	6/2/1923	**Operated:** 1923 to 1940	**HQ city:**	Sedro Woolley
Disposition:	abandoned - corporation dissolved December 20, 1941			
Miles track:	25	**Gauge:** 56½"		
Main line:	Sultan into the forest			

Locomotives:

Road No.	Cyln.	Type	Dvr. in.	Bldr.	Bldr. No.	Date	Weight	Effort	Remarks
1		2 truck	36	Heisler	1131	10/07	74,000		ex Aloha Lumber Co.
2		3 truck	35	Climax	1349	10/15	140,000	30,800	ex Index-Galena #2
3 ?		2 truck	33	'	680	6/06	100,000	22,000	ex Index-Galena #1
4*	11x12	2T Shay	32	Lima	2304	3/10	'	22,500	to Clear Lake Lumber Co. #4
4-2d ?		2 truck	33	Heisler	1111	11/06	60,000		ex Lyle Logging & Mercantile Co.
4-3d ?		'	38	'	1334	5/16	104,000		ex Snohomish Logging Co. #5
5*	17¼x15	3 truck	'	'	1487	7/23	160,000		sold into British Columbia
6 ?		2 truck		Climax	904	10/08	80,000		ex Seattle-Issaquen Electric Co.
7 ?		3 truck		'	1471	/17			ex Christie Timber Co.

Freight traffic: logging

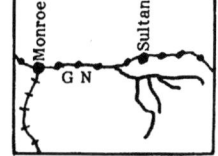

MONROE LOGGING COMPANY   President

Incorp:	6/17/1921	**Operated:** 1922 to 1947	**HQ city:**	Machias
Disposition:	abandoned			
Miles track:	25	**Gauge:** 56½"		
Main line:	near Machias to Lake Stevens area			
Rail wt.:	56/60 lbs.	**Max. grade:** 3.0%		

WASHINGTON   231.

Road No.	Cyln.	Type	Dvr. in.	Bldr.	Bldr. No.	Date	Weight	Effort	Remarks
1*	20x24	2-8-2		Porter	6797	7/23			to Puget Sound & Baker River Ry.
2*		3 truck	36	Willam.	2	1/23	140,000		to Owen-Oregon Lumber Co. #2
3		3T Shay	'	Lima	2653	7/13	'	30,350	scrapped in 1939
4		2T Shay	'	'	2597	10/12	120,000	23,900	9/1939 to Saulk River Lumber Co.
5		3T Shay	'	'	3074	5/20	160,000	35,100	acq. 2/1940; scrapped 8/1946

Freight traffic: logging

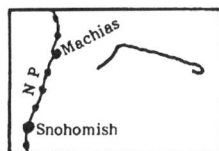

MONTE CRISTO RAILWAY COMPANY

E. T. Gates, President

Incorp:	8/27/1900	**Operated:** 8/19/00 to 7/31/03	**HQ city:** Everett

Disposition: sold to Northern Pacific Railway Company on August 1, 1903

Predecessors:	Everett & Monte Cristo Railway Company	**Incorp.:** 3/14/1892 to 8/18/1900
	Snohomish, Skykomish & Spokane Railway & Transportation Company	4/23/1891 12/15/1892
	Snohomish, Skykomish & Spokane Railway & Transportation Company, The	4/19/1889 4/22/1891

Miles track: 62.09   **Gauge:** 56½"

Main line: Everett to Monte Cristo

Rail wt.: 56/60 lbs. steel   **Max. grade:** 5.0%   **Const. began:** grading   July 19, 1891
                                                                                       laying rails   (Sept. 17, 1891)

Const. comp.: September 22, 1893   **First train operated:** April 1, 1892

Locomotives:

1*	21x26	4-6-0	56	Cooke	2223	6/92	137,000	29,100	to N.P. #366-2d
2*	'	'	'	'	2224	'	'	'	to N.P. #367-2d
3*	'	'	'	'	2225	'	'	'	to N.P. #368-2d

Freight traffic: common carrier, mine and lumber

Roster of 6/30/1895:
- 4 locomotives
- 3 passenger cars
- 100 freight cars

First published timetable:
October 22, 1893
- 8:00 a.m. Everett
- Snohomish 8
- Granite Falls 23
- Silverton 50
- 12:30 p.m. Monte Cristo 68

The construction record is brief and not detailed; all dates given as 1892 to 1893.

Snohomish, Skykomish & Spokane	Snohomish to Lowell	8.00
Everett & Monte Cristo	Lowell to Everett	3.41
Everett & Monte Cristo	Hartford to Monte Cristo	42.12
Seattle, Lake Shore & Eastern	Snohomish to Hartford, joint	8.20

The line was opened from Everett to Snohomish on April 1, 1892, and Hartford to Monte Cristo September 1, 1893

There were seven tunnels between Granite Falls and Robe; ties were set in concrete to anchor them from flooding by Stillaguamish River. In 1895, it converted to automatic couplers on all equipment.

First listed in ICC for 6/30/92 as an operating independent with 6.5 miles owned; a year later it was 40 miles owned and in use. It was increased to 55 miles owned and 63 operated by 6/30/94. In 1899 it was 62 miles owned and 70 operated, but by 6/30/01 it was 46 and 65 miles. By 6/30/03 it had become an operating subsidiary of Northern Pacific Railway Co. with the same mileage.

The Everett & Monte Cristo Railway Co. was placed in receivership on January 31, 1900, and sold as a foreclosure. The Everett to Snohomish track was sold to Seattle & International Railway Co. and the major line, Hartford to Monte Cristo, to Monte Cristo Railway Co.

Construction notes from *The Railway Age:*

Regarding Snohomish, Skykomish & Spokane:
- July 24, 1891 — To commence grading Monday next.
- September 25, 1891 — Nearly finished grading for ten miles.
- October 23, 1891 — Rail laying has begun at Snohomish to build to Puget Sound.
- October 30, 1891 — Nearly ten miles graded, 2% maximum grade; to carry coal and timber.

Bibliography: *Poor's 1897*, p. 261   Snohomish - *The Eye* - July 18 to November 25, 1891   *Valuation 25*, p. 493

MUD BAY LOGGING COMPANY

President

Incorp:	3/29/1910		**Operated:**	1906	to	1941		**HQ city:**	Olympia

Disposition: abandoned - corporation dissolved January 5, 1943

Purchased: Thurston County Railway Company   13 miles of track   **Incorp.:** 12/18/1911 to 1918

Miles track: 35 (in 1930)   **Gauge:** 56½"

Main line: Eld Inlet into the forest

Rail wt.: 56 lbs.   **Max. grade:**   **Const. began:** grading

Locomotives:

Road No.	Cyln.	Type	Dvr. in.	Bldr.	Bldr. No.	Date	Weight	Effort	Remarks
1		2-6-0T							
2		2 truck	36	Heisler	1102	9/06	74,000		ex Western Washington Logging #2
3		2-6-2T	44	BLW	33048	11/08	88,150	13,400	ex Western Washington Logging #3
4*	18x24	2-8-2		'	38836	11/12			
4-2d		3 truck	40	Heisler	1573	4/29	180,000		ex Weyerhaeuser Timber (Vail) #4
5*	13½x15	3T Shay	36	Lima	3084	6/20	160,000	35,100	sold January 7, 1925
6*	15½x14	2 truck	38	Heisler	1505	4/24	110,000	20,800	
7*	17x13	3 truck	'	'	1528	2/26	160,000	38,480	to Pacific National Lumber Co.
8*		2-6-6-2T	44	BLW	60412	3/28	210,000	42,500	displayed at Snoqualmie
		2-4-4-2	48	'	33463	6/09	162,650	24,800	ex Newaukum Vy. #7; to Deep River

Freight traffic: logging   Thurston County Railway was placed in operation about 1908.

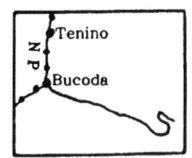

MUTUAL LUMBER COMPANY

President

Incorp:	2/24/1902		**Operated:**	1913	to	1943		**HQ city:**	Tenino

Disposition: abandoned - corporation dissolved December 26, 1946

Miles track: 24   **Gauge:** 56½"

Main line: Bucoda into the forest

Rail wt.:   **Max. grade:** 6.0%   **Const. began:** grading

Locomotives:

2	2 truck	31	Climax	1011	3/10	76,000		acq. 3d hand; scrapped
3	'	30	'	1003	2/10	80,000	17,600	acq. 2d hand; sold
4	'	33	'	411	6/03	90,000	19,800	acq. 4th hand; scrapped
5*	3 truck	36	'	1616	2/22	160,000	35,200	scrapped
6*	'	'	'	1643	8/23	'	'	scrapped
7*	2 truck	35	'	1515	6/18	120,000	26,400	to Buckley Logging Co. #1
8	3 truck	36	'	1670	7/25	160,000	35,200	ex Donovan-Corkery Logging Co. #8

Freight traffic: logging

NELSON COMPANY, THE CHARLES

President

Incorp:	10/1/1925		**Operated:**	1926	to	1929		**HQ city:**	Port Angeles

Disposition: abandoned - corporation dissolved May 13, 1937

Predecessors: Puget Sound Mills & Timber Company   25 miles of 36" gauge   **from:** 1907 to 1926

Little River Railway & Logging Company   6 miles standard gauge   1910   1916

Miles track: 7   **Gauge:** 56½"

Main line: Port Angeles into the forest

Rail wt.: 60 lbs.   **Max. grade:**   **Const. began:** grading

WASHINGTON

Locomotives:

Road No.	Cyln.	Type	Dvr. in.	Bldr.	Bldr. No.	Date	Weight	Effort	Remarks
1 ?		2 truck	36	Climax	160	12/97	50,000	11,000	ex Seattle Log; to PSM&T Co.
1-2d* ?	12x15	3T Shay	'	Lima	2661	3/13	140,000	30,350	new as PSM&T Co.; sold 9/1928
2 ?		2 truck	'	Climax	242	2/01	70,000	13,200	ex Seattle Log; to PSM&T Co.
2 ?		'	30	'	600	10/05	80,000	17,600	ex Wood/Iverson #2; to LRRy&L
		2T Shay	32	Lima	522	10/96	'	16,360	2d hand to PSM&T Co.; sold 2/31
		'	'	'	538	11/97	100,000	20,150	2d hand to PSM&T Co.; sold
		'	'	'	803	7/03	90,000	18,750	2d hand to PSM&T Co.
		'	29½	'	2603	12/12	84,000	16,900	2d hand to PSM&T Co.; to dealer
		'	36	'	2711	8/13	120,000	23,890	9/1918 to PSM&T Co.; sold 4/1929

Freight traffic: logging

Roster of 6/30/1910:
  (Puget Sound Mills & Timber Co.)
  2   geared engines
  4   rod engines
  125   sets logging trucks
  2   flat cars
  25   miles 36" track at Port Crescent

NORTH COAST RAILROAD COMPANY, THE

Robert E. Strahorn, **President**

Incorp: 4/14/1906   **Operated:** to 12/23/10   **HQ city:** Portland

Disposition: sold to Oregon-Washington Railroad & Navigation Company on December 24, 1910

Predecessor: North Coast Railway   **Incorp.:** 9/28/1905 to 10/11/1906

Miles track: 98.07   **Gauge:** 56½"

Main line: Attalia to North Yakima

Rail wt.:   **Max. grade:** 0.5%   **Const. began:** grading   January 2, 1906

laying rails   October 4, 1909

Const. comp.: March 24, 1911 (by O-WR&N)   **First train operated:**

Freight traffic: common carrier, agriculture

The company also partially completed another line, from Ayer Jct., via Marengo and Cheney, to Spokane; this route was completed by O-WR&N in the summer of 1914.

The name selected for this company is curious; Yakima is 175 miles from the Pacific Ocean.

A construction note from *Railway Age Gazette*:
  October 8, 1909
  Rails are now at Attalia and Kennewick; to lay soon.

Bibliography: *Walla Walla Statesman* - January 3, 1906 and October 7, 1909   *The Yakima Herald* - June 20, 1906 and October 6, 1909
Valuation 44, p. 283

NORTHERN PACIFIC & CASCADE RAILROAD COMPANY

President

Incorp: 8/23/1884   **Operated:** 5/6/89 to 4/21/98   **HQ city:** Tacoma

Disposition: sold to Northern Pacific Railway Company on April 21, 1898

Miles track: 19.11   **Gauge:** 56½"

Main line: Cascade Jct. to Carbonado and Spiketon and Crocker to Wingate

Rail wt.: 56 lbs.   **Max. grade:**   **Const. began:** grading   (June 11, 1888)

laying rails   1888

Const. comp.: (October 17, 1890)   **First train operated:** May 6, 1889

Freight traffic: common carrier, coal

First published timetable:
September, 1888
7:15 a.m.   South Prairie
            Cascade   1
            Wilkeson   6
8:35   Carbonado 9

The official construction record:
Constructed by Northern Pacific Railroad Co.:
    Cascade Jct. to Wilkeson   1877   5.23 miles
    Wilkeson to Carbonado   1880   3.60
    Cascade Jct. to Burnett   1881   1.87
Constructed by Northern Pacific & Cascade Railroad Co.:
    Extension beyond Wilkeson   1889   0.93 miles
    Crocker to Wingate   5/88 to 5/6/89   5.30
    Burnett to Spiketon   comp. 10/6/90   2.18

A construction note from *The Railway Age:*
December 28, 1888
    During 1888, 5.5 miles was laid from Crocker to Carbonado.

And from *Railroad Gazette:*
October 31, 1890
    The Burnett branch of the road has been extended 2.4 miles from Burnett to Pittsburgh mine.

The carrier was leased to Northern Pacific Railroad Co. October, 1, 1887.

Poor's 1887 shows South Prairie to Wilkeson and Carbonado plus South Prairie to Coal Fields, 10.4 miles.

Listed in first ICC (6/30/88) as a non-operating subsidiary of Northern Pacific Railroad Co. with ten miles owned and then it was extended to 19 miles by 6/30/89.

Bibliography: *Poor's 1896*, p. 689   Walla Walla - *Union* - June 2, 1888   *Valuation 25*, p. 498

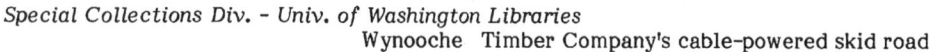

Special Collections Div. - Univ. of Washington Libraries   *Clark Kinsey photo #5190*
Wynooche Timber Company's cable-powered skid road

WASHINGTON

NORTHERN PACIFIC & PUGET SOUND SHORE RAILROAD COMPANY

				President
Incorp:	8/23/1884	Operated: 7/1/85 to 4/21/98	HQ city:	Seattle
Disposition:	sold to Northern Pacific Railway Company on April 21, 1898			
Predecessor:	Puget Sound Shore Railroad Company, The	Incorp.: 8/19/1882 to 10/31/1889		
Miles track:	43.05	Gauge: 56½"		
Main line:	Meeker to Seattle plus Kennydale and Kirkland branches			
Rail wt.:	56 lbs.	Max. grade:	Const. began: grading (August 5, 1890)	
			laying rails	
Const. comp.:	(July 18, 1891)	First train operated:		
Freight traffic:	common carrier			

First published timetable:
September, 1888
  9:50 a.m. Tacoma
             Puyallup   9 miles
             Meeker   11
 12:31 p.m. Seattle   41
There were two round trips daily.

The construction record is not detailed.
  Constructed by Northern Pacific Railroad Co.:
    Meeker to Stuck Jct.   deeded July 1, 1885   miles: 7.00
  Constructed by The Puget Sound Shore Railroad Co.:
    Stuck Jct. to Black River Jct.   1/1883 to 10/1/1883   13.85
    Black River Jct. to Seattle   1883 to 7/6/1884   10.10
  Constructed by Northern Pacific & Puget Sound Shore Railroad Co.:
    Black River Jct. to Kennydale   8/1890 to 7/4/1891   6.50
    Woodinville to Kirkland   8/1890 to 7/1891   5.60

Listed in first ICC (6/30/88) as a non-operating subsidiary of Northern Pacific Railroad Co. with seven miles owned; the carrier had been leased to Northern Pacific on October 1, 1887. It was extended to 30 miles by 6/30/90, to 46 miles by 6/30/93 and then reduced to 44 miles by 6/30/96.

Even though it was a "non-operating" subsidiary, some operating functions were performed in its name, but this ceased on August 31, 1896.

Construction notes from *Railroad Gazette*:
  July 4, 1890   Construction contract to build 20 miles around Lake Washington has been awarded.
  August 1, 1890   Locating survey, Black River Jct. to Kirkland, is being made and grading will commence shortly.
  August 8, 1890   One hundred men are at work grading.
  December 19, 1890 The Seattle belt line from Black River Jct. connecting with Seattle, Lake Shore & Eastern Railway at Gilman, 22 miles, is about completed.

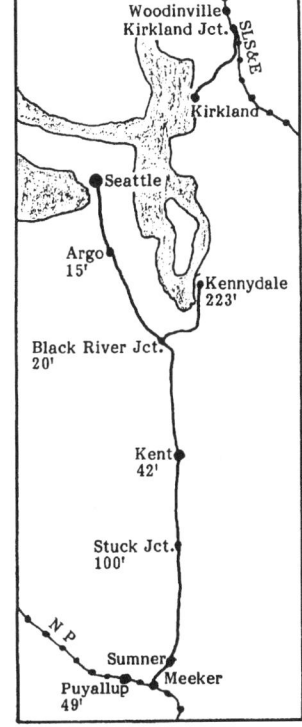

Bibliography: *Poor's 1889*, p. 1033

Valuation 25, p. 499

Denver Public Library - Western History Department   #14157 Photo by Otto C. Perry
Northern Pacific Railway #5119, a 4-6-6-4, with westbound freight near Providence on July 29, 1938

NORTHERN PACIFIC RAILROAD COMPANY

Incorporated on July 2, 1864

The full account of this early transcontinental is found in the Montana section; these pages are included here to chronicle a twenty year period and detail its construction on what amounted to three different fronts.

1870 — The company broke ground at Carlton, Minnesota, on February 15 and at Kalama, Washington Territory, in May. Tracklaying began at Carlton on August 15 and grading at Kalama December 16. This last named date may be in error. *Railroad Gazette* for May 27, 1871, states that rail laying had begun May 19, 1871; it is quite possible that it referred to "resumed" rather than "began." According to federal government figures, 114.00 miles was laid during the year ending June 30, 1870. To understand better the economic climate, the 1870 census figures were: Portland, 8,293 - Olympia, 1,203 - New Tacoma, 73 - Seattle, 1,107.

1871 — Laying of rails began October 5 and twenty miles placed in Washington Territory during the calendar year 1871. Engine number one was purchased July 18, 1870, for construction use at Carlton, but was soon shipped "around the Horn" and landed at Kalama in September. Company total for year ending June 30, 1871, was 114.23 miles of track.

1872 — The excursion on the western track was July 4 when a train was run to Evaline, 25.00 miles; placed in commercial operation about July 16. Total construction for the company was 165.00 miles.

1873 — The head of track reached Tenino, 65.00 miles, on August 15. The first train into New Tacoma, 40.10 miles further north, arrived at 3 p.m. December 16, although the track was not officially completed until March 15 of the next year. Total mileage for the company was 136.50.

1874 — A note in *Official Guide* for February states that Tenino to New Tacoma, 39 miles, has been opened for operation. The August edition said that Grand Prairie has become Winlock and that Steilacoom is now Lake View. Construction work for the year was zero; the Panic of 1872 had reached the railroad construction industry.

1875 — No news, comment or construction.

1876 — First published timetable dated February 21 listed the western operation: departure 11:20 a.m. from Kalama; 2:04 p.m. at Newaukum, 48 miles; 3:00 into Tenino, 66 miles, and to arrive in New Tacoma, 105 miles, at 5:00. The branch to Wilkeson, 31.00 miles, was ready on December 31, but not placed in operation for another ten months. Construction for the year was zero.

1877 — The mine branch to Wilkeson was opened on November first and a published timetable of even date (recorded in Kalama time) gave a 6:00 p.m. departure from New Tacoma to Puyallup, 9 miles, Orting, 19 miles, and 8:00 arrival at Wilkeson, 32 miles. Company total rail laying was 31.00 miles.

1878 — October *Official Guide* states that New Tacoma is now just plain Tacoma. No construction for the year.

1879 — Wallula to Ainsworth track work commenced on October second; also track from Ainsworth to Ritzville under construction. Company-wide total for the year, for work on the eastern section, was 54.00 miles.

1880 — Track completed Wallula to Ainsworth, 11.50 miles, and 45 miles beyond. Commenced work from Ritzville to Algoma, Idaho Territory. The census figures were: Portland, 17,577 - Olympia, 1,232 - Tacoma, 1,098 - Seattle, 3,533. Total new construction for the year was 77.00 miles.

1881 — Track was extended in June from Wilkeson to Carbonado, two miles, making the western total 139 miles. Ainsworth to Ritzville, 84.28 miles, completed. Opened to Spokane Falls on June 25. Ritzville to Algoma (six miles south of Sandpoint), 123.93 miles, was finished in November. Work was commenced at Algoma to cross the territory line and build toward the east.

1882 — After having been a "short line" for about eight years, the next published timetable, dated February 5, called for a 5:00 a.m. departure from Wallula Jct.; 3:15 p.m. arrival at Spokane Falls, 161 miles, and an 8:00 p.m. arrival at Pend Oreille, Idaho Territory, 228 miles; it was also called 354 miles from The Dalles, the closest point to Portland. Track was completed from Algoma to Montana Territory line, 43.90 miles. Commenced construction of Snake River bridge at Ainsworth.

1883 — Track headings being built from east and west met at Gold Creek, Montana Territory, 224.38 miles from territory line, on August 22. On the far west end, Carlton to Portland, 36.25 miles, was completed. Work started at Kennewick in July to build to Kiona, 25.20 miles; also in July, building northeast from Cascade Jct. Meeker to Stuck Jct., 7.00 miles, was completed to start a line to Seattle. A subsidiary, The Puget Sound Shore Railroad Co., completed 13.85 miles on October first from Stuck Jct. to Black River Jct. The first timetable, showing operations to Portland (via OR&N), 574 miles, was dated March 24, 1883.

1884 — Kiona to Yakima City, 59.85 miles was completed and being extended toward Ellensburg. A .94-mile Snake River bridge at Ainsworth completed. Pasco to Columbia River incline track of 2.08 miles was built. The Columbia River was never bridged at Kalama. With the Goble to Portland track completed on October nine, Portland became milepost "0" and Kalama became "40". The ferryboat *Tacoma*, 320 feet long, was placed in service; it carried 27 railroad cars and lasted for nearly 25 years. A rail connection from Kalama to Vancouver, started in 1902 was finished March 1, 1903. The river was bridged at Vancouver in 1908 and ferry service at Kalama terminated. On July 6, 1884, The Puget Sound Shore Railroad Co. opened 10.10 miles into Seattle.

1885 — Work commenced in July, 1883, from Cascade Jct. to Eagle Gorge, 24.10 miles, was finished.

1886 -- Track completed from Yakima City to Ellensburg, 39.60 miles. Started and completed in 1886 was a 40.28-mile extension to Eaton. Work was commenced on track northwest from Eaton, southeast from Eagle Gorge and on the Stampede Tunnel itself.

1887 -- Completed on July first were headings from Easton to Stampede switchback, 11.25 miles, and Eagle Gorge to switchback, 29.60 miles. The 7.10-miles of switchbacks over the Cascade Mountains were also completed the same day and were placed in operation ten days later. A published timetable dated November 20 shows a 9:30 a.m. departure from Ellensburg and a 5:20 p.m. arrival 133 miles later at Tacoma. At about this time, Northern Pacific ceased operating from the east to Portland via Oregon Railway & Navigation Co. tracks - begun in 1882 - and employed its own facilities to reach that city.

1888 -- Pasco to Kennewick bridge line over the Columbia River, 3.30 miles, was finished April 13, thereby creating an all-rail route from the Great Lakes area. The 2.92-mile Stampede Tunnel, opened for traffic May 27, was completed July first, thus making an all weather operation possible. A note in *Railroad Gazette* for June 1 states that while the Stampede Tunnel is open, the switchbacks will continue to be used for tourist [or all passenger trains?] trains.

1890 -- The census figures for this economic block: Portland, 46,385 - Olympia, 4,698 - Tacoma, 36,006 - Seattle, 42,837.

A few years after completion of the main lines to Portland and Seattle, the company began branch line construction, in the company name and also by subsidiaries. On July 1, 1909, a joint trackage agreement was signed with Union Pacific Railroad Co. whereby Oregon Railroad & Navigation Co. could operate its trains between Vancouver and Tacoma using Northern Pacific rails.

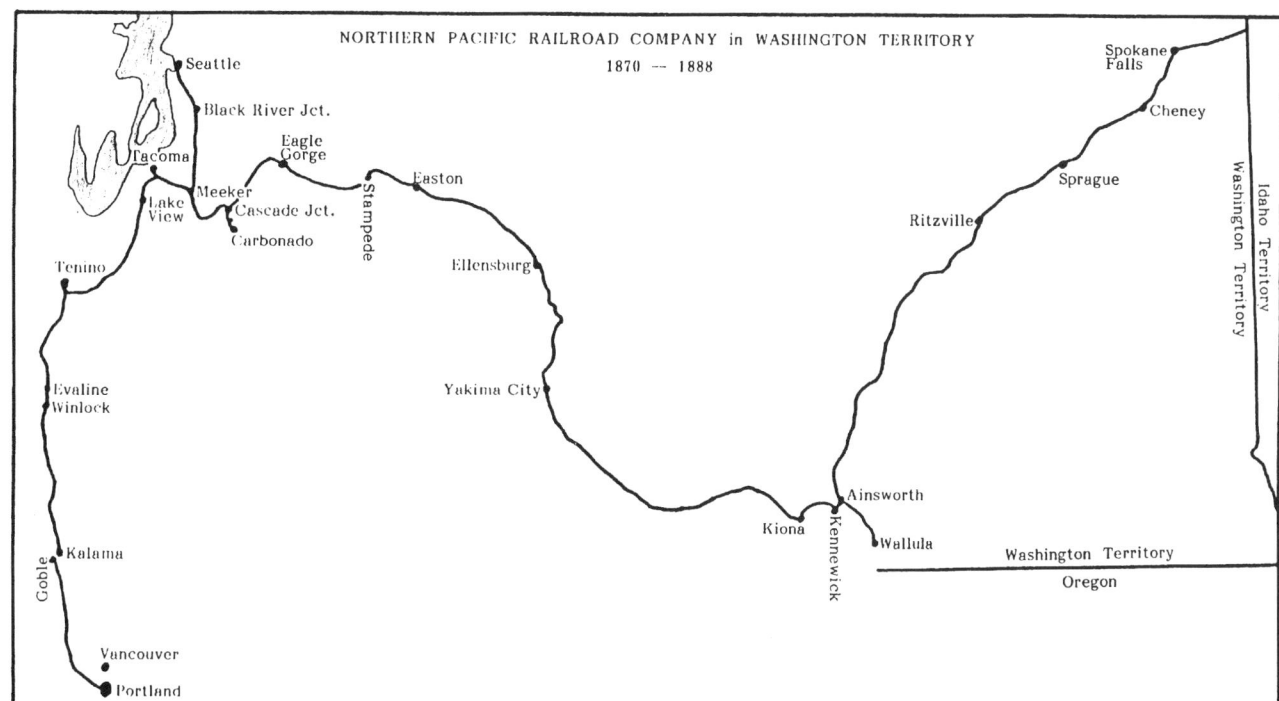

Tacoma Public Library B8490 *Boland Collection*
A semitrailer loaded with limestone at Wilkeson about 1923; probably a 1920 Republic truck.

Denver Public Library - Western History Department #14072 *Photo by Otto C. Perry*
Northern Pacific #1656 with helper #1613, both 2-8-2s, with nine-car westbound freight at Marshall on July 31, 1938

Denver Public Library - Western History Department #14155 *Photo by Otto C. Perry*
Northern Pacific #5113, a 4-6-6-4, with a 69-car westbound freight at Marshall on July 31, 1938; contrast with above.

Denver Public Library - Western History Department   *#14049 Photo by Otto C. Perry*
Northern Pacific #5115, a 4-6-6-4, at Connell on July 29, 1938, with strange panel on the tender

Denver Public Library - Western History Department   *#14028 Photo by Otto C. Perry*
Northern Pacific 2-8-8-2 #4018 at coal tower in Ellensburg on September 30, 1931

NORTH YAKIMA & VALLEY RAILWAY COMPANY

George Donald, **President**

Incorp:	7/24/1905	**Operated:** (7/15/06) to 6/24/14	**HQ city:**	North Yakima
Disposition:	sold to Northern Pacific Railway Company on June 24, 1914			
Purchased:	Toppenish, Simcoe & Western Railway Company		**Incorp.:** 5/5/1909 to 7/2/1912	
Miles track:	50.05	**Gauge:** 56½"		
Main line:	Naches to Moxee City and Granger to Parker			
Rail wt.:	66 lbs. steel	**Max. grade:**	**Const. began:** grading (April 9, 1906)	
			laying rails (May 14, 1906)	
Const. comp.:	August 11, 1912		**First train operated:** June 24, 1906	

Locomotives:

Road No.	Type	Dvr. in.	Bldr.	Bldr. No.	Date	Weight	Effort	Remarks
1	4-4-0	60	Portland	494	9/83	84,050	13,100	acq. 5/1906 ex N.P. #265
2	"	62	BLW	6955	10/83	88,100	"	acq. 4/1910 ex N.P. #735
3	"	"	"	10692	3/90	88,000	"	acq. 9/1910 ex N.P. #740
4	2-6-0	57	"	10315	9/89	104,000	17,400	acq. 8/1912 ex N.P. #468

Freight traffic: common carrier, agriculture

Rosters of   6/30/1906 - 6/30/1913:
  locomotives   1   3
  passenger cars   2   3
  freight cars   1   8

First published timetable:
  July 1, 1907 - daily ex. Sun.
  7:00 a.m.   North Yakima   5:50
                    Naches   5:00 p.m.

Poor's 1913 gives the terminals as:
  North Yakima to Naches City   13.00
  North Yakima to Moxee   8.79
  North Yakima to Selah   4.00
  Granger to Mellis   15.06

The official construction record:
North Yakima to Naches	7/1905 - 7/1906	13.07
North Yakima to Moxee	7/1909 - 10/1910	8.85
Granger to Flint	1909 - 11/1910	10.70
Flint to Yakima River	1910 - 1911	5.36
Yakima River to Parker	1911	1.00
Cowiche Jct. to Spitzenberg	1912	2.50

Partially constructed by Toppenish, Simcoe & Western:
  Wesley Jct. to Farron   8.57

First listed in ICC for 6/30/06 as an operating independent with nine miles owned, not in use. By 6/30/07 it was 14 miles owned and operated. By 6/30/08 it was a 14-mile operating subsidiary of Northern Pacific Railway Co. By 6/30/11 it was 33 miles owned and operated; in 1912 it was 37 owned and 41 operated. By 6/30/13 it became a 50-mile non-operating subsidiary. It was reduced to 47 miles by 6/30/14.

The carrier cost $1,153,942 to build and equip.

Construction notes from *The Railway Age*:
  October 20, 1905   A construction contract has been awarded.
  June 15, 1906   Twenty miles have been graded and ten miles of track laid.

Regarding Toppenish, Simcoe & Western Railway Co., a note in *Railroad Age Gazette* for January 28, 1910, states that a construction contract has been let for 17 miles of grading from Toppenish.

Bibliography: *Poor's 1907*, p. 1913   *The Yakima Herald* - April 11 to June 27, 1906   *Valuation 25*, p. 505

OLYMPIA & CHEHALIS VALLEY RAILROAD COMPANY, THE

John W. Sprague, **President**

Incorp:	8/6/1881	**Operated:** 8/1/81 to 9/11/90	**HQ city:**	San Francisco
Disposition:	sold to Port Townsend Southern Railroad Company on September 11, 1890			
Predecessors:	Olympia & Tenino Railroad Company		(not incorporated in Washington)	
	Thurston County Railroad Construction Company		**Incorp.:** 6/4/1877 to 7/31/1881	
	Olympia Railroad Union		1/5/1874 7/28/1877	
Miles track:	15.50	**Gauge:** 36"	**Date standardized:** September 9, 1890 (by PTS RR Co.)	
Main line:	Tenino to Olympia			
Rail wt.:	30/35 lbs.	**Max. grade:**	**Const. began:** grading (April 8, 1878)	
			laying rails July 2, 1878	
Const. comp.:	August 1, 1878		**First train operated:** August 1, 1878	

Locomotive engines:

Road No.	Cyln.	Type	Dvr. in.	Bldr.	Bldr. No.	Date	Weight	Effort	Remarks
1*	11x16	4-4-0	42	BLW	4294	3/78	43,300	6,800	E. N. Ouimette; 1890 to Col. & Puget Sound
2		0-4-0T		Porter	124	8/72	15,000		acq. 12/1881 ex WW&CR; SCR 6/1889
3*	12x16	2-6-0	37	BLW	7298	5/84	38,000		Olympia (all were woodburners)

Freight traffic: common carrier, coal and lumber

Roster of 6/30/1889:
    2   locomotive engines
    2   passenger cars
    6   freight cars

First published timetable:
(as Olympia & Tenino RR)
November, 1879
7:15 a.m. Olympia
8:45   Tenino
There were two round trips daily.
T. M. Reed was president at Olympia.

The name "Olympia & Tenino Railroad Co." was recognized by *Official Guide* and *Poor's Manual*, but not by Interstate Commerce Commission *Valuation Reports*. It may have had no legal status, but just a convenient trade style for the construction company, its actual owner.

Locomotive engine number one was built as Olympia & Tenino Railroad Co.

Listed in first ICC (6/30/88) as an operating independent with 15 miles owned and in use. Then unchanged until its sale in 1890.

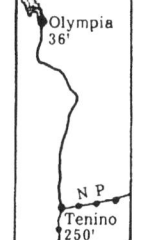

The Olympia & Chehalis Valley Railroad Co. was owned by Olympia Railroad & Mining Co. Its railroad property was sold for $192,000 to Port Townsend Southern Railroad Co.

Construction notes from *Railroad Gazette*:
    April 26, 1878   Grading is nearly finished.
    August 23, 1878   The operation is nearly completed and was placed in operation recently; it is to haul coal from Tenino to tidewater.

Bibliography: *Poor's 1880*, p. 1000   *The Olympia Transcript* - April 6 to August 3, 1878   *Valuation 116*, p. 362

OREGON & WASHINGTON RAILROAD COMPANY

Incorp: 5/12/1906   **Operated:** 2/1/08 to 12/22/10   **HQ city:** Portland   President

Disposition: sold to Oregon-Washington Railroad & Navigation Company on December 23, 1910

Miles track: 25.30   **Gauge:** 56½"

Main line: Wabash Jct. to Tono

Rail wt.:   **Max. grade:**   **Const. began:** grading   August 14, 1907
                                                                                    laying rails (November 9, 1907)

Const. comp.: January 30, 1908   **First train operated:** February 1, 1908

Locomotives:

1-6*	22x30	2-8-0	57	Brooks	44986-991	1/08	208,100	43,300	to O.-W.R.&N. #730-735
207-208		4-6-2	77	BLW		/10	422,480	38,635	

Freight traffic: common carrier, coal mine

It is always difficult to determine exact data on subsidiary lines - and this is no exception. As well as can be determined, this was the situation:

	miles owned:
Wabash Jct. to Tono	6.06
Centralia to Helsing Jct.	11.19
Black River Jct. to Seattle	9.20

The track operated appears to have been:
Centralia to Aberdeen	52.22
(joint trackage with Chicago, Milwaukee & Puget Sound from Helsing Jct. to Aberdeen)	
Vancouver to Tacoma	133.65
(joint trackage with Northern Pacific)	
Wabash Jct. to Tono	6.06
total operated:	191.93

First listed in ICC for 6/30/08 as an operating subsidiary of Union Pacific Railroad Co. with six miles owned and in use; same in 1909. By 6/30/10 it owned 21 miles and operated 192.

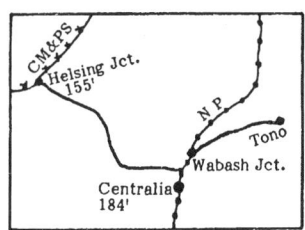

Construction notes from *The Railway Age*:
    September 6, 1907   Grading contracts have been let and work is under way.
    March 13, 1908   Two and one half miles of track has been laid.
And one from *Railway Age Gazette*:
    September 18, 1908   Work began September 5 on the eight-mile Seattle to Black River Jct. track.

Bibliography: *Poor's 1910*, p. 1288   *The Centralia Chronicle* - August 15, 1907 to February 1, 1908   *Valuation 44*, p. 288

OREGON & WASHINGTON TERRITORY RAILROAD COMPANY

Geo. W. Hunt, President

Incorp:	5/26/1887	**Operated:** (1/1/89) to 10/5/92		**HQ city:** Walla Walla
Disposition:	foreclosure sale to The Washington & Columbia River Railway Company on October 5, 1892			
Predecessor:	Oregon & Washington Territory Railroad Company, The	**Incorp.:**	3/4/1886 to 5/25/1887	
Miles track:	162.62	**Gauge:** 56½"		
Main line:	Pendleton to Dayton and Pleasant View			
Rail wt.:	56 lbs. steel	**Max. grade:** 2.197%	**Const. began:** grading (May 9, 1887)	
			laying rails (November 9, 1887)	
Const. comp.:	(December 15, 1889)		**First train operated:** (August 8, 1888)	

Locomotive engines:

Road No.	Cyln.	Type	Dvr. in.	Bldr.	Bldr. No.	Date	Weight	Effort	Remarks
1*	18x24	2-6-0	55	Grant	1784	12/88	98,500		to Northern Pacific #383
2*	'	'	'	'	1785	'	'		to Northern Pacific #384
3*	'	4-4-0	63	'	1780	4/88	94,400		
4*	'	'	'	'	1783	12/88	'		
7*	21x26	2-8-0	52	BLW	9614	11/88	136,000	28,650	to Northern Pacific #498
8*	'	'	'	'	9625	'	'	'	to Northern Pacific #499
9*	19x26	4-6-0	64	Grant	1766	3/88	110,300	18,700	
10*	'	'	'	'	1767	'	'	'	
11*	'	'	'	'	1768	'	'	'	

Freight traffic: common carrier, agriculture

First published "timetable":
December 20, 1888
Walla Walla Division:
  Hunt's Jct.
    to Eureka Jct.   22 miles
    to Pleasant View   42
  Eureka Jct. to Walla Walla   31
Pendleton Division:
  Hunt's Jct. to Junction   20
  Junction to Centerville   34
  Junction to Fulton   34

Published timetable dated:
November 28, 1889
  3:15 p.m.   Pendleton
  9:00   Walla Walla
  11:00   Dayton

The road cost $7,725,113 to construct and equip. There were 49.53 miles of track in Oregon.

Construction notes from *The Railway Age*:
- May 13, 1887 — Several hundred men building Wallula to Pendleton.
- March 2, 1888 — Twenty-two miles of rails have been laid.
- September 21, 1888 — Hunt's Jct. to Centerville, 35 miles, and to Fulton, 14 miles, are in operation; to bring in fall wheat crops.

Notes from *Railroad Gazette*:
- May 4, 1888 — Completed Wallula to Centerville, about 25 miles.
- August 10, 1888 — Completed to Eureka Flat.
- November 2, 1888 — Track has been completed to Walla Walla, 53 miles.

And from *Chicago Railway Review*:
- January 12, 1889 — A total of 121 miles was built in the year 1888.

The official construction record:

Hunt's Jct. to Fulton	1887 to 1888	34.10	
Smelts to Athena (Centerville)	1887	1888	14.39
Hunt's Jct. to Walla Walla	1888	12/1888	53.54
Eureka Jct. to Pleasant View	1888	1888	19.73
Walla Walla to Dayton	1889	1889	33.86
Fulton to Pendleton	1889	1889	7.00

First listed in ICC for 6/30/89 as an operating independent with 121 miles owned and in use; it was extended to 162 miles each by 6/30/90. It was placed in receivership on December 21, 1891, and sold at foreclosure April 20, 1892, to C. B. Wright who conveyed the property to The Washington & Columbia River Railway Co. on October 5, 1892.

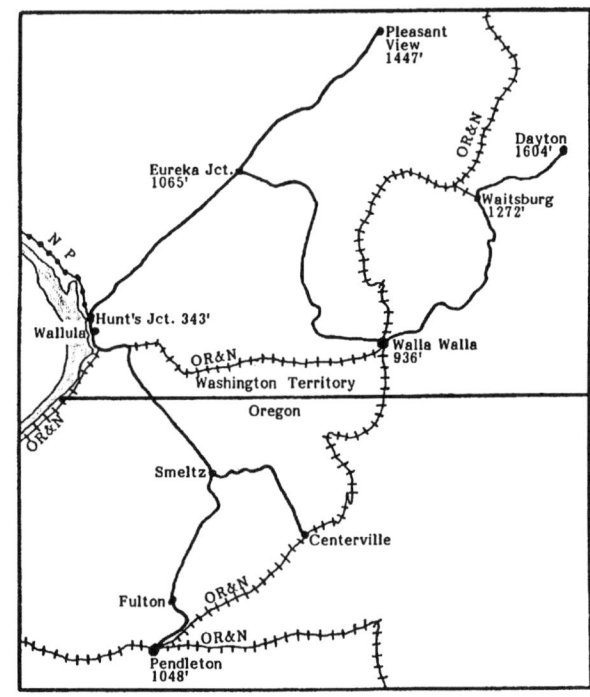

Bibliography: *Poor's 1892*, p. 831   Oregon PUC report 1893, p. 177   *Valuation 25*, p. 504
Walla Walla Weekly Union - July 9, 1887 to November 3, 1888

OREGON RAILWAY EXTENSIONS COMPANY, THE

Elijah Smith, **President**

Incorp:	5/25/1888	**Operated:** /89 to 8/17/96	**HQ city:**	Portland
Disposition:	foreclosure sale to Oregon Railroad & Navigation Company on August 17, 1896			
Miles track:	68.73	**Gauge:** 56½"		
Main line:	Winona to Seltice and La Grande to Elgin			
Rail wt.:		**Max. grade:**	**Const. began:** grading	(July 30, 1888)
			laying rails	(Sept. 24, 1888)
Const. comp.:	1890		**First train operated:**	(August 12, 1889)

Locomotive engines:

Road No.	Type	Dvr. in.	Bldr.	Bldr. No.	Date	Weight	Effort	Remarks
47	4-6-0	63	Rome	509	10/89	92,350	17,534	ex O.Ry.&N. #47-O.R.&N. #132
83	2-8-0	51	'	430	1/89	116,950	25,600	ex O.Ry.&N. #83-O.R.&N. #161
87	2-6-0	58	Schen.	2868	/89	91,500	17,973	ex O.Ry.&N. #87-O.R.&N. #87
88	'	'	'	2869	'	'	'	ex O.Ry.&N. #88-O.R.&N. #88

Freight traffic: common carrier, agriculture

Rosters of   6/30/1891 - 6/30/1894:
 locomotive engines   4
 passenger car   1   1
 freight cars   162   170

First listed in ICC for 6/30/90 as a non-operating subsidiary of Oregon Railway & Navigation Co. with 46 miles owned; it was extended to 69 miles the next year. No furthern changes until its sale in 1896.
There were 47.84 miles in Washington and 20.89 in Oregon.

First published "timetable":
 August 18, 1889
 "Operating from Seltice to
 Winona Jct., 47.7 miles."

First published timetable:
 January 1, 1891 - mixed
 4:00 p.m.   La Grande   10:15
 6:15   Elgin   8:00 a.m.

Poor's 1889 reports that by the end of 1888, track had been laid from Seltice Jct. to Oakesdale, 9.2 miles, and from Winona Jct. north for 1.5 miles to the Palouse River.

A construction note from *Railroad Gazette:*
 August 1, 1890   Grading is nearly completed to Elgin;
                   track laying to begin shortly.

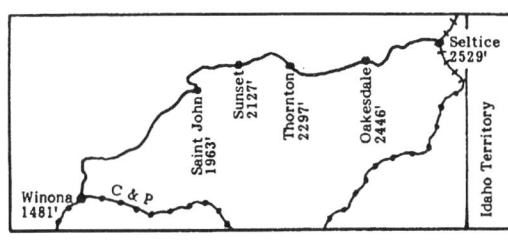

Bibliography: *Poor's 1892*, p. 1012 and *1895*, p. 902   Oregon PUC report 1890, p. 208   *Valuation 44*, p. 267

OREGON, WASHINGTON & IDAHO RAILROAD COMPANY

J. P. O'Brien, **President**

Incorp:	8/8/1903	**Operated:** 7/7/08 to 12/23/10	**HQ city:**	Portland
Disposition:	sold to Oregon-Washington Railroad & Navigation Company on December 23, 1910			
Miles track:	72.03	**Gauge:** 56½"		
Main line:	Riparia to Lewiston			
Rail wt.:	62 lbs.	**Max. grade:** 0.20%	**Const. began:** grading	(July 31, 1905)
			laying rails	(December 4, 1905)
Const. comp.:	July 7, 1908		**First train operated:**	(October 28, 1907)

Freight traffic: common carrier, lumber

First published timetable:
 August 5, 1908
 6:05 a.m.   Riparia   9:30
 9:00   Lewiston   6:40 p.m.

First listed in ICC for 6/30/06 as an operating independent with 15 miles owned, not in use. By 6/30/07 it owned 37 miles and it was extended to 72 miles by 6/30/08, still not in use. By 6/30/09 it was an operating subsidiary of Oregon Railroad & Navigation Co. with 72 miles owned and operated. It was sold as noted above and transferred to Camas Prairie Railroad Co.

The property cost $3,301,726 to buy the land and construct; this sum included $202,232 paid to The Snake River Railroad Co. for partial construction of the route. The subject was operated by the Camas Prairie Railroad Co. from December 3, 1909, until date of sale in 1910.

Construction notes from *The Railway Age:*
August 18, 1905   Grading has been commenced.
December 5, 1905 Rail laying has been commenced.

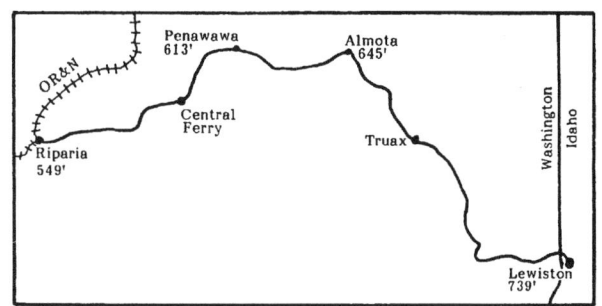

Bibliography: *Poor's 1909*, p. 657   *Walla Walla Evening Statesman* - December 4, 1905   *Valuation 44*, p. 287

OSTRANDER RAILROAD COMPANY, THE   President

Incorp:	2/21/1893	**Operated:**	1893 to 1940			**HQ city:**		Kelso
Disposition:	abandoned							
Miles track:	31	**Gauge:**	56½"					
Main line:	Ostrander into the forest							
Rail wt.:	40/56 lbs.	**Max. grade:**	3.7%			**Const. began:**	grading	

Locomotive engines:

Road No.	Cyln.	Type	Dvr. in.	Bldr.	Bldr. No.	Date	Weight	Effort	Remarks
1		2T Shay	26	Lima	349	4/90	40,000	9,125	acq. 2d hand; sold
2*	12x16	0-6-2ST	40	'	1020	11/05	72,500	18,000	
2-2d		2T Shay	32	'	2233	11/09	100,000	20,350	acq. 3d hand; sold
4*	13½x18	2-6-2T	37	BLW	32843	7/08	72,000		
4-2d		2T Shay	29	Lima	2605	6/13	64,000	14,150	ex Silver Lake Ry. & Timber
5*		3 truck	38	Heisler	1501	3/24	160,000		to Grande Ronde Lbr. Co. #5
5-2d		2T Shay	32	Lima	3152	2/21	112,700	22,580	acq. 2d hand; scrapped 8/1946
6*	10x12	'	'	'	1678	5/06	74,000	15,575	
7*	18/28x24	2-6-6-2T	44	BLW	59701	12/26	245,000	42,500	
		2T Shay	29½	Lima	1870	1/07	74,000	16,900	acq. 2d hand; sold
348		2 truck		Climax	642	2/06	40,000		acq. 2d hand; scrapped

Freight traffic: logging

Roster of 6/30/1910:
  2   geared engines
  1   rod engine
 64   sets logging trucks
  2   flat cars
  8½   miles track at Ostrander

PACIFIC COAST RAILROAD COMPANY   E. C. Ward, President

Incorp:	11/27/1897	**Operated:**	3/23/16 to 3/1/70	**HQ city:**	Seattle
Disposition:	sold to Burlington-Northern, Incorporated, on March 2, 1970				
Predecessor:	Columbia & Puget Sound Railroad Company			**Incorp.:**	11/26/1880 to 3/25/1916
Miles track:	55.23	**Gauge:**	56½"		
Main line:	Seattle to Franklin, Coal Creek and Taylor				

WASHINGTON   245.

Locomotives:

Road No.	Type	Dvr. in.	Bldr.	Bldr. No.	Date	Weight	Effort	Remarks
5	4-4-0	62	N.Y.	628	7/90	78,000	13,100	sold 1923
8	2-8-0	50	BLW	15440	7/97	115,000		SCR 1938
10	0-6-0	'	'	15501	9/97	80,000	18,865	sold 1941
11	2-8-0	'	'	19298	7/01	121,650		SCR 1938
12	'	'	'	22759	8/03	'		SCR 1950
14	'	52	R.I.	41965	2/07	124,500		SCR 1951
15	'	'	'	41966	'	'		SCR 1953
16	'	'	Brooks	48294	7/10	128,000		SCR 1953
17	0-6-0	51	'	48296	'	127,000	28,160	SCR 1951
18	4-4-0	62	'	48295	'	110,000		SCR 1939

Freight traffic: common carrier, coal

Roster of 6/30/1916:
- 10 locomotives
- 6 passenger cars
- 261 freight cars
- 236 coal cars

First published timetable:
May 7, 1916

8:25 a.m.	Seattle	
8:55	Renton	12
9:15	Cedar Mtn.	19
9:25	Maple Valley	23
10:04	Franklin	34

4:55 p.m.	Seattle	
5:47	Maple Valley	23
7:00	Hobart	26
7:20	Taylor	32

6:00 p.m.	Seattle	
6:30	Renton	12
6:50	Newcastle	19
7:00	Coal Creek	21

Abandonments:
1933	Renton to Coal Creek
1936	Black Diamond to Franklin
1945	Maple Valley to Taylor
1947	Maple Valley to Henry's
	This left Seattle to Maple Valley and Henry's to Black Diamond.

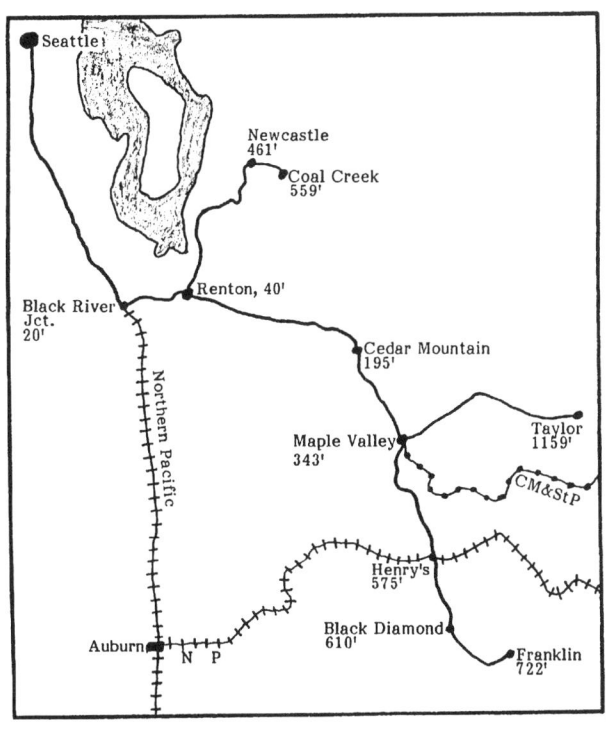

First listed in ICC for 6/30/16 as an operating subsidiary of Pacific Coast Co. with 56 miles owned and in use. It was reduced to 54 miles in 1919 and to 49 in 1929. The name was revised to "Pacific Coast R. R. Co." on November 26, 1930. This class II carrier was reduced to 43 miles in 1934, to 40 miles in 1936 and to 30 in 1945.

In 1951 it was an operating subsidiary of Great Northern Railway Co.

A listing in July, 1969, *Official Guide* shows: "Freight only amongst Seattle, Black River, Henry's, Maple Valley, Renton. Main line, 22.29 miles; branch lines, 9.74 miles."

Bibliography: *Poor's 1918*, p. 518

PACIFIC NATIONAL LUMBER COMPANY   President

Incorp:		**Operated:**	1905 to 1949	**HQ city:**	Tacoma
Disposition:	abandoned				
Miles track:	12	**Gauge:**	56½"		
Main line:	National into the forest				
Rail wt.:	56 lbs.	**Max. grade:**	7.0%	**Const. began:**	grading

Road No.	Cyln.	Type	Dvr. in.	Bldr.	Bldr. No.	Date	Weight	Effort	Remarks
1*	12½x12	2 truck	33	Heisler	1123	12/06	56,000		
2		2-6-2T		Cooke	64999	2/24			ex Hobi Timber Co. #2
4 ?		2 truck	36	Heisler	1147	12/08	84,000		
7 ?		3 truck	38	'	1528	2/26	160,000	38,480	ex Mud Bay Logging Co. #7

Freight traffic: logging

Roster of 6/30/1910:
- 1 geared locomotive
- 6 sets logging trucks
- 2½ miles of track

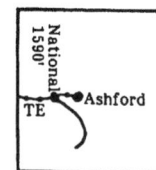

Tacoma Public Library
B7770 Boland Collection
Electric crane in stack yard of Pacific National Lumber Co. at National in about 1923

PACIFIC STATES LUMBER COMPANY

President

Incorp: 10/23/1908	**Operated:** 1905 to 1939		**HQ city:** Tacoma	
Disposition: abandoned				
Predecessor: Seattle Southeastern Railway Company	8.2 miles track	**Incorp.:** 9/13/1906 to 1913		
Miles track: 46	**Gauge:** 56½"			
Main line: Kangley into the forest				
Rail wt.: 56 lbs.	**Max. grade:** 6.5%	**Const. began:** grading		

Locomotives:

Road No.	Cyln.	Type	Dvr. in.	Bldr.	Bldr. No.	Date	Weight	Effort	Remarks
5*	16x24	2-6-2T	44	BLW	30659	4/07	114,000		new as Seattle Southeastern Ry.
6*	14½x15	3T Shay	36	Lima	2544	7/12	191,600	40,400	used at Selleck; sold in 1930
7 ?		2 truck	31	Climax	437	8/03	100,000		ex Chinn Bros.; scrapped
8 ?		'	'	'		(1916)	180,000		acq. 1920; scrapped
9*	18x24	2-8-2	44	BLW	55480	6/22			
107*	'	2-6-2	'	'	55415	5/22		23,400	1939 to Cascade Timber Co. #107
5100		'	'	'	34918	7/10			acq. 12/1927 ex C.M.StP.&P.

Freight traffic: logging

WASHINGTON   247.

PEND OREILLE VALLEY RAILROAD   Harold A. Bond, **Chmn.**

Incorp: not   **Operated:** 10/1/84 to   **HQ city:** Metaline Falls
Disposition: in operation 1993
Predecessor: Pend Oreille Valley Railroad, Inc.   **Incorp.:** 9/20/1979 to 9/30/1884
Miles track: 61.50   **Gauge:** 56½"
Main line: Newport to Metaline Falls
Rail wt.: 75/90 lbs.   **Max. grade:** 3.0%   **First train operated:** October 1, 1979

Locomotives:

Road No.	Type	Bldr.	Bldr. No.	Date	Weight	Effort	Remarks
101	B-B	EMD	20307	6/55	259,000	1,750 h.p.	ex B.N. # 1846
102	'	'	22718	2/57	246,200	'	ex B.N. # 1735

Freight traffic: common carrier, forest products

The initial corporation was dissolved December 17, 1984.

The ruling grade is zero, the maximum grade at the north end of the line.

The operation is a function of the County of Pend Oreille.

Present-day operations are conducted from Usk.

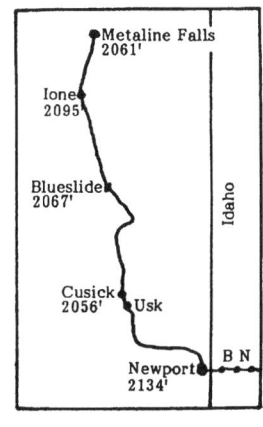

Bibliography: Direct communication

PHOENIX LOGGING COMPANY   President

Incorp: 10/6/1899   **Operated:** 1900 to 1939   **HQ city:** Seattle
Disposition: abandoned - corporation dissolved December 16, 1947
Miles track: 40   **Gauge:** 56½"
Main line: Potlatch into the forest and later at Hoodsport
Rail wt.: 40/56 lbs.   **Max. grade:** 4.2%   **Const. began:** grading

Locomotives:

Road No.	Cyln.	Type	Dvr. in.	Bldr.	Bldr. No.	Date	Weight	Effort	Remarks
1*	11x12	2T Shay	33	Lima	666	8/01	80,000	13,125	sold to Maytown Lumber Co.
2*		2 truck	'	Climax	284	/02	90,000	19,800	sold to Acme Logging Co.
2-2d		2T Shay	29½	Lima	2438	4/12	84,000	16,900	acq. 3d hand; sold to dealer in 1929
4		'	32	'	611	12/00	80,000	17,485	acq. 2d hand; sold into Oregon
4-2d*	13½x15	3T Shay	36	'	3200	2/23	193,000	35,100	used at Hoodsport; sold 11/1939
5*	12x12	2T Shay	'	'	1729	7/06	110,000	23,900	to Rucker Bros. #5
6*	'	'	'	'	1921	6/07	'	'	sold to Seattle dealer 12/1921
7*	'	'	'	'	2716	6/16	120,000	'	scrapped 6/1938
7-2d*	13½x15	3T Shay	'	'	3248	1/24	195,300	35,100	to Simpson Logging Co. #7
8	'	'	'	'	3260	4/24	204,600	'	acq. 2d hand; used at Hoodsport
9	'	'	'	'	3251	2/24	212,000	40,400	used at Hoodsport; sold 3/1940

Freight traffic: logging

Roster of 6/30/1910:
- 5   geared engines
- 85   sets logging trucks
- 2   flat cars
- 11   miles of track at Potlatch

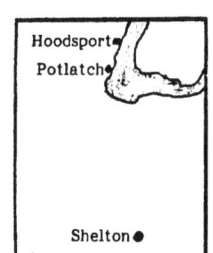

POLSON LOGGING COMPANY

								President
Incorp:	5/1/1903		**Operated:**	(5/11/03) to 8/30/48			**HQ city:**	Hoquiam

Disposition: sold to Rayonier, Incorporated, on August 30, 1948

Predecessor: Polson Brothers Logging Company   from: 1895 to (5/11/1903)

Miles track: 85   **Gauge:** 56½"

Main line: Hoquiam and Sekiu into the forest

Locomotives:

Road No.	Cyln.	Type	Dvr. in.	Bldr.	Bldr. No.	Date	Weight	Effort	Remarks
1		0-4-0T		Porter	84	7/70	24,000		acq. 1895 ex N.P. #1; 1932 to N.P.
1-2d		2-8-2	44	BLW	38967	12/12	140,000	27,000	to Rayonier #2 at Hoquiam
3		2T Shay	27½	Lima	2305	5/10	44,000	10,700	to Rayonier #3
11*		2 truck	33	Climax	303	3/02	90,000	19,800	to Grays Harbor Commercial Co.
12*		'	'	'	"2336"	/07	100,000	22,000	
18		4-6-0	56	BLW	18734	3/01			ex Arizona & New Mexico #18
33*	11x12	2T Shay	32	Lima	1614	11/05	90,000	20,500	to Rayonier #33 at Hoquiam
45*	15x24	2-6-2	44	BLW	27311	1/06	88,000	16,700	to Rayonier #45 at Hoquiam
51		2-8-0	50	'	10447	11/89			ex Northern Pacific #51
55*	12x12	2T Shay	32	Lima	1959	8/07	110,000	26,850	wrecked in runaway and scrapped
70*	18x24	2-8-2	44	BLW	55355	4/22	140,000	27,000	to Rayonier #70
90*	20x28	'	48	'	59071	3/26	197,000	35,700	to Rayonier #90
91*	13x15	3T Shay	36	Lima	3322	11/28	181,000	38,200	to Rayonier #91 at Hoquiam
99*	20x24	2-8-0	50	BLW	25416	3/05	136,000	29,200	to Rayonier #99
101*	18x24	2-8-2	44	'	38966	12/12	141,000	27,000	to Rayonier #101
191*	13x15	3T Shay	36	Lima	3343	10/29	187,000	38,200	to Rayonier #191
3100		2-6-6-2	55	BLW	34389	3/10	304,000	58,000	ex N.P. #3100; to Rayonier

Freight traffic: logging

Roster of 6/30/1910:
- 3 geared engines
- 4 rod engines
- 100 sets logging trucks
- 20 flat cars
- 20 miles of track at Hoquiam

The Hoquiam track was 55 miles.
The Sekiu line was 30 miles.

The corporation was dissolved on November 18, 1954.

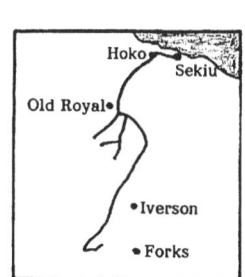
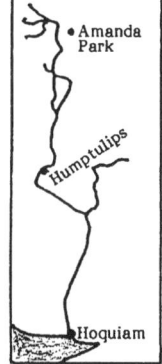

California State Railroad Museum Library   *Gerald M. Best Collection*
Polson Logging Co. number three at Hoquiam in 1903

Special Collections Div. - Univ. of Washington Libraries *Clark Kinsey photo #2772*
Polson Logging Company power shovel near Hoquiam with a half-track dump truck, useful in the rain forest

Special Collections Div. - Univ. of Washington Libraries *Negative #12,116*
Polson Bros. Logging Company number ten with a log train being dumped

Special Collections Div. - Univ. of Washington Libraries Clark Kinsey photo #2866
Polson Logging Company locomotive track at Hoquiam with its largest engine leading the way

POPE & TALBOT LUMBER COMPANY

								President
Incorp:	6/6/1936		**Operated:**	1936 to 1968			**HQ city:**	Port Gamble

Disposition: abandoned

Predecessors:	Charles R. McCormick Lumber Company	Port Gamble, 30 miles	**Incorp.:**	3/20/1925 to 1936
	Puget Mill Company	Port Gamble, 5 miles	**from:**	1883 1925
	Union River Logging Railroad Company	Union, 7 miles		1883 1901

Miles track: 50   **Gauge:** 56½"
Main line: Port Gamble north into the forest
Rail wt.: 60 lbs.   **Max. grade:** 6.0%

Locomotives:

Road No.	Cyln.	Type	Dvr. in.	Bldr.	Bldr. No.	Date	Weight	Effort	Remarks
1*	12x18	2-4-0		Porter	803	1/87			new as Puget Mill Co.
2*	9¼x14	0-4-2		'	946	6/88			new as Puget Mill Co.
1-2d		2T Shay	32	Lima	2669	5/13	100,000	22,550	from Puget Mill to McCormick #1
2-2d		'	'	'	2970	3/18	'	'	(1924) to Puget Mill; SCR 8/1942
4*	18x24	2-8-2	44	BLW	59284	6/26	144,330	27,800	new to McCormick; to P&T #100
101*	'	'	42	'	61159	12/29	169,000	29,100	new to McCormick

Freight traffic: logging   McCormick also had 15 miles at Castle Rock, 1930-1936, and 40 at Union, 1925-1936

PORT ANGELES WESTERN RAILROAD COMPANY

R. L. Stearns, **President**

Incorp:	2/11/1925	**Operated:**	8/25/25 to 1950	**HQ city:**	Port Angeles

Disposition: abandoned November 20, 1953
Predecessor: Clallam County Railroad   **from:** (1917) to 2/26/1925
Miles track: 36.092   **Gauge:** 56½"
Main line: Disque to Tyee
Rail wt.: 80 lbs.   **Max. grade:**   **Const. began:** grading   (June 29, 1918)
                                                              laying rails (October 26, 1918)
Const. comp.: 1938   **First train operated:**   1925 ?

Locomotives:

Road No.	Type	Dvr. in.	Bldr.	Bldr. No.	Date	Weight	Effort	Remarks
14	2-6-6-2T	51	BLW	60256	11/27	275,000	56,600	ex Larson Timber Co. #14
524 ?	2-8-2		Brooks	58451	/18	227,200	45,100	acq. 1942 ex Chi. & Ill. Mid. #524

Freight traffic: common carrier, logging

Roster of 12/31/1930:
   3   locomotives
 173   logging cars

Station list in September, 1928, *Official Guide:*
Tyee Lake	
Aero	m.p. 8.4
Sol Duc	18.0
Manganese	19.9
Ovington	24.0
Crescent	29.5
Disque	35.0

In September, 1940, it was Disque to Koller, 42.6 miles.

The official grand opening was set for Saturday, November 30, 1918, but the end of the World War negated it.

First listed in ICC for 12/31/25 as an operating independent with 36 miles owned and in use. By 1927, it was 35 miles owned and 53 operated (18 miles east to Port Angeles). In 1938 it was extended to 43 miles owned and 61 operated. This class II carrier then remained unchanged through 1950, but did not operate in 1951. A trustee was appointed March 24, 1952, and abandonment followed the next year.

The predecessor was owned by U. S. Spruce Corp., an agency of the federal government. Spruce was then used for aeroplane production. It built the original main line to Tyee in 1918 and 1919. The ICC authorized construction from Tyee to Forks on June 30, 1927, but the 43-mile maximum mileage would have placed the head of track about three miles north of Forks.

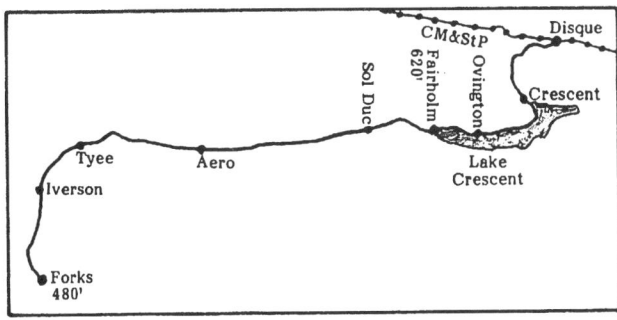

The cost of grading from Disque to Tyee was placed at $1,137,845 and excavation averaged about 33,000 cubic yards per mile. There was a tunnel of 504 feet and one of 154 feet. There were two Howe truss bridges having 150-foot spans over the Sol Duc River and several trestles. The total value of construction was $2,138,694 plus $322,060 for rolling stock.

Bibliography: *Poor's 1940,* p. 1606   *Port Townsend Weekly Leader* - January 3 to December 20, 1918   *Valuation 43,* p. 57

Tacoma Public Library
Point Defiance, Tacoma & Edison Railway Co. steam dummy and trailer near Point Defiance Park, Tacoma, circa 1890

PORT TOWNSEND RAILROAD

R. S. Fox and partners, **Owners**

Incorp:	not	**Operated:** 1/1/45 to 6/6/75	**HQ city:**	Seattle

Disposition: sold to Chicago, Milwaukee, St. Paul & Pacific Railroad Company on June 6, 1975

Predecessors:
Port Townsend Southern Railroad Company	**Incorp.:** 5/28/1929	to 12/31/1944
Port Townsend & Puget Sound Railway Company	6/1/1914	5/27/1929
Port Townsend Southern Railroad Company	9/11/1890	5/31/1914

Miles track: 27.304 **Gauge:** 56½"

Main line: Port Townsend to Quilcene

Locomotives:
Road
No.
1
2

Freight traffic: common carrier, lumber

Roster of 12/31/1917:
- 2 locomotives
- 1 passenger car
- 8 freight cars

Published timetable dated:
June 21, 1915
8:45 a.m.	Port Townsend	
9:40	Cooper's	14
10:05	Leland	20
10:35	Quilcene	26

Port Townsend & Puget Sound Railway Co. was first listed in ICC for 6/30/14 as a 29-mile operating company only; the track was leased from Port Townsend Southern Railroad Co. In 1925 the mileage was reduced to 12.5 when the track from Discovery Jct. to Quilcene was abandoned and removed. It was a class II common carrier.

Port Townsend Southern Railroad Co. was listed in ICC as a 12-mile operating independent from 1929 until 1944.

Port Townsen Railroad was first listed in ICC for 12/31/45 as a class III operating independent of 12 miles.

Connection was made at Discovery Jct. with Seattle, Port Angeles & Western Railway Co., a subsidiary of (and later purhcased by) Chicago, Milwaukee, St. Paul & Pacific Railroad Company.

The May, 1975, *Official Guide* shows Margaret N. Fox as the president.

Bibliography: *Poor's 1924*, p. 515

Valuation 116, p. 362

PORT TOWNSEND SOUTHERN RAILROAD COMPANY

W. H. Starbuck, **President**

Incorp:	9/28/1887	**Operated:** 8/30/90 to 5/31/14	**HQ city:**	Seattle

Disposition: leased to Port Townsend & Puget Sound Railway Company on May 31, 1914

Predecessor: Olympia & Chehalis Valley Railroad Company, The   **Incorp.:** 8/1/1881 to 9/11/1890

Miles track: 45.304 **Gauge:** 56½"

Main line: Tenino to Olympia and Port Townsend to Quilcene

Rail wt.: 56 lbs.   **Max. grade:**   **Const. began:** grading October 2, 1888

laying rails (June 9, 1890)

Const. comp.: (August 14, 1891)   **First train operated:** September 12, 1890

Locomotive engines:

Road No.	Cyln.	Type	Dvr. in.	Bldr.	Bldr. No.	Date	Weight	Effort	Remarks
1		4-4-0	62	Rome	629	7/90	78,000	13,100	ex Seattle & Northern #2
2*	17x24	'	'	'	628	'	'	'	1897 to Col. & Puget Sound #5
3*	'	4-6-0	54	BLW	11280	10/90	80,000		1902 to Northern Pacific #369
4*	'	'	'	'	11265	'	'		to Columbia & Puget Sound #4
6*	10x16	2-4-2T	40	Porter	1784	10/97	41,000		1902 to Northern Pacific

Freight traffic: common carrier, logging

Roster of 11/30/1891:
- 4 locomotive engines
- 2 passenger cars
- 26 freight cars

First? published timetable:
January, 1891
7:30 a.m.	Port Townsend
	Hooker's Lake 8:55 a.m.
	13 miles

WASHINGTON

First listed in ICC for 6/30/92 as an operating independent with 43 miles in use; it was owned by Oregon Improvement Co. December 1, 1897, it was purchased by The Pacific Coast Co. and became a non-operating subsidiary. It was increased to 46 miles by 6/30/99. Control passed to Northern Pacific Railway Co. on November 30, 1902, and from then until 6/30/13 it was a 41-mile operating subsidiary of Northern Pacific. By 6/30/14 it was 26 miles owned and 15 operated.

From an early date there was a three-mile branch from Olympia to Butlers Cove; it was abandoned in 1894. The original main line from Tenino to Olympia was sold to Northern Pacific Railway Co. on June 25, 1914. In May, 1917, Joshua Green acquired control of Port Townsend Southern from Northern Pacific. By then, it was Port Townsend to Quilcene, 27.304 miles.

The precise location of Hooker's Lake, the terminal of first operation, has not been determined; it appears to be the same as Discovery Jct. or very near that point.

Construction notes from *The Railway Age:*
    April 5, 1890   Grading is now under way.
    May 31, 1890   Tracklaying is to begin soon.
    July 19, 1890   Completed from Port Townsend to Quilcene.

Quilcene is 56 miles due north of Olympia.

Bibliography: *Poor's 1892*, p. 928   *Valuation 116*, p. 362

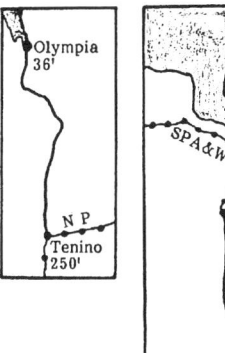
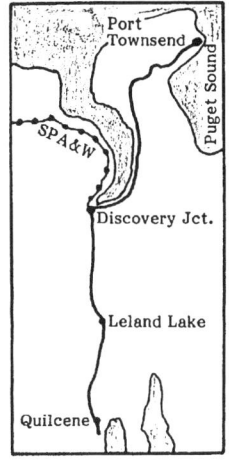

PUGET SOUND & BAKER RIVER RAILWAY COMPANY   Scott Paper Co., **Owner**

Incorp: 12/31/1907   **Operated:** 1907 to (1965)   **HQ city:** Hamilton

Disposition: abandoned - corporation dissolved January 17, 1966

Miles track: 27   **Gauge:** 56½"

Main line: Riverside to Dempsey

Rail wt.: 60/80 lbs.   **Max. grade:** 2.2%   **Const. began:** grading (December 17, 1906)
                                                                                                         laying rails   1907

Const. comp.: 1926   **First train operated:** (December 2, 1907)

Locomotives:

Road No.	Cyln.	Type	Dvr. in.	Bldr.	Bldr. No.	Date	Weight	Effort	Remarks
1*	16x24	4-6-0	44	BLW	31472	8/07	106,000		
2*	'	'	46	'	39058	1/13			displayed at Sedro Woolley

Freight traffic: common carrier, logging

Roster of 6/30/1910:
    1   locomotive
    5   logging cars
  20   miles of track

List of stations:
    Riverside
    G.N. Crossing   5.5 miles
    Sedro   8.5
    Minkler   14.5
    Lyman   16.5
    Hamilton   20.5
    Dempsey   25.0

The operation was owned by English & Dempsey until 1930, Lyman Timber Co. to 1937, Soundview Pulp Co. to 1951 and then Scott Paper Co.

First listed in ICC for 6/30/08 as an operating independent with 21 miles owned and in use. It was revised to 23 miles in 1914, to 21 miles in 1915, 23 miles in 1918 and 21 in 1919. In 1923 it was 25 miles owned and operated; in 1926 it was 27 miles, then down to 24 in 1932. Only three miles were operated in 1936, eight in 1937, closed down in 1938. It was reopened in 1939 with five miles. In 1942 it was declared "not a common carrier" and out of ICC reports.

Bibliography: *Mount Vernon Argus* - October 4, 1907

PUGET SOUND & CASCADE RAILWAY COMPANY

B. R. Lewis, **President**

Incorp:	7/1/1912	**Operated:** 9/16 to 1940	**HQ city:**	Mount Vernon
Disposition:	abandoned in 1942			
Miles track:	32	**Gauge:** 56½"		
Main line:	Mount Vernon to Clear Lake, Talc and up the Skagit River			
Rail wt.:	50/60 lbs.	**Max. grade:**	**Const. began:** grading	1916

Locomotives:

Road No.	Type	Dvr. in.	Bldr.	Bldr. No.	Date	Weight	Effort	Remarks
3 ?	2 truck	30	Climax	636	2/06	56,000		ex Dickey & Angel Logging Co. #3
6	2-6-2	44	BLW	34840	6/10			acq. 1933 ex Puget Sound Pulp & Paper Co. #6
200	2-8-2	48	'	44106	9/16			ex Cowlitz, Chehalis & Cascade #15 - preserved

Freight traffic: common carrier, logging

Roster of 12/31/1921:
2 locomotives
1 passenger car
68 freight cars

First listed in ICC for 6/30/16 as an operating independent with 15 miles owned and in use. It was increased to 18 miles by 12/31/18, back to 15 in 1919. By 12/31/21 it was 18 miles, extended to 27 in 1924, then unchanged through 1931. In 1932 this class III carrier was increased to 32 miles and reduced to 29 miles in 1936. It did not operate in 1938; returned again in 1939 and 1940, but not in 1941.

The railway's owners were: Skagit Logging Co., 1912 - 1913; Clear Lake Lumber Co., 1913 - 1929; Puget Sound Pulp & Timber Co., 1929 - 1940. The official distance from Mount Vernon to Talc, in 1917, was 15.929 miles.

For a map of the carrier, see previous page in conjunction with Puget Sound & Baker River Railway Company.

Bibliography: *Poor's 1920*, p. 1117   *Valuation 106*, p. 818

PUGET SOUND & WILLAPA HARBOR RAILWAY COMPANY

C. A. Goodnow, **President**

Incorp:	4/13/1913	**Operated:** 5/1/13 to 12/31/18	**HQ city:**	Raymond
Disposition:	sold to Chicago, Milwaukee & St. Paul Railway Company on December 31, 1918			
Predecessor:	Pacific & Eastern Railway Company	**Incorp.:** 10/22/1906 to 5/1/1913		
Miles track:	65.90	**Gauge:** 56½"		
Main line:	Maytown to Raymond			
Rail wt.:		**Max. grade:** 11.0%	**Const. began:** grading	(May 13, 1907)
Const. comp.:	1915		**First train operated:**	February 12, 1910

Locomotives:

Road No.				Bldr.	Bldr. No.	Date	Weight	Effort	Remarks
101*	15x12	2 truck	36	Heisler	1172	11/09	42,999		to Lebam Mill & Timber Co.
102*	17x24	2-6-2	44	BLW	34918	7/10			to C.M.&St.P. #5100
103*	17x14	2 truck	40	Heisler	1342	7/16	65,000		to Sunset Timber Co. #1
(The above were all purchased new by Pacific & Eastern Railway Co.)									
2123		4-6-0	63	R.I.	1763	3/87	111,100	18,753	
2130		'	'	Grant		/88	'	'	
2165		'	'	R.I.	2039	9/88	'	'	

Freight traffic: common carrier, lumber

Rosters of 6/30/1910 - 12/31/1917:
locomotives   2   4
passenger cars   3
freight cars   8   157
track at Willapa   7

Published timetable dated:
November 8, 1915 - daily
10:15 a.m. Maytown
10:30   Essex   m.p. 7.3
10:45   Centralia   13.9
10:55   Chehalis   17.5
11:45   Dryad   36.3
12:15 p.m. Bedford   49.1
12:27   P&E Jct.   54.4
12:32   Firdale   56.2
12:53   Willapa   63.1
 1:00   Raymond   65.9

The predecessor company built from Willapa to the east up Elk Creek between 1907 and 1910 to a point that would become P&E Jct. and operated this section from 1910 until September 11, 1915. On that date the property was taken over by Puget Sound & Willapa Harbor Railway.

A note in *Western Lumberman*, June, 1907, states "Building up Mill Creek for seven miles; three miles now graded from Raymond." In the September issue it stated that six miles were nearly completed and would open soon. The March, 1910, issue gave the February 12 opening date.

WASHINGTON 255.

First listed in ICC for 6/30/15 as an operating independent with 38 miles owned and in use; it was extended to 66 miles each by 6/30/16. By 12/31/16 it was an operating subsidiary of Chicago, Milwaukee & St. Paul Railway Co.

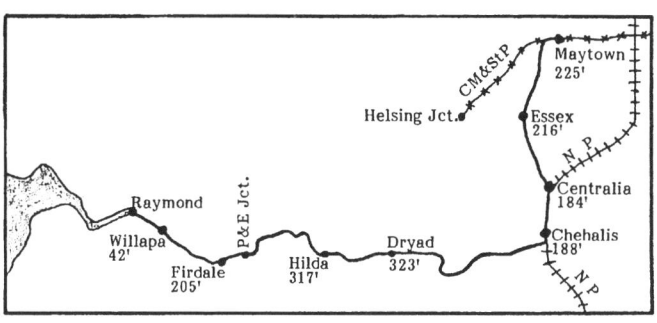

Bibliography: *Poor's 1918*, p. 213   *The South Bend Journal* - May 17, 1907   *Valuation 44*, p. 801

PUGET SOUND PULP & TIMBER COMPANY   President
Incorp: 7/2/1963   **Operated:** 1929 to 1952   **HQ city:**   Bellingham
Disposition: abandoned - corporation dissolved March 4, 1964
Predecessors: Rucker Brothers Company   from: (1905) to 1929
                   Stacey E. Wright Logging Company   1906   1909
Miles track: 40   **Gauge:** 56½"
Main line: Mount Vernon into the forest
Rail wt.:   56/60 lbs.   **Max. grade:**   **Const. began:** grading   1906

Locomotives:

Road No.	Cyln.	Type	Dvr. in.	Bldr.	Bldr. No.	Date	Weight	Effort	Remarks
1		2T Shay	32	Lima	1940	10/07	90,000	22,575	acq. 6/1929; used at Clear Lake
2		3T Shay	36	'	2837	6/16	160,000	35,100	ex Clear Lake Lbr. #2; at Mt. Vernon
3		'	'	'	2643	7/13	'	'	acq. 4th hand; used at Fir
4		2T Shay	32	'	2304	3/10	100,000	22,500	acq. 6/1929; used at Mount Vernon
5		'	36	'	2315	5/10	120,000	23,850	acq. 3d hand; used at Mount Vernon
6		2-6-2	44	BLW	34840	6/10			ex Rucker Bros. #3
8		3T Shay	36	Lima	3171	8/22	183,400	35,100	acq. 9/1938; used at Cedar Lake
13		'	'	'	3198	1/23	201,500	40,400	acq. 4/1945; used at Mount Vernon
14		'	'	'	2704	2/14	140,000	30,350	acq. 6/1945; used at Mount Vernon
15		'	'	'	2708	10/13	160,000	35,100	acq. 1945; used at Mount Vernon
100		2-8-2	44	BLW	38271	9/12			ex Smith-Powers Logging (Oregon)
Rucker Brothers Co.									
1 ?		2T Shay	36	Lima	2710	8/13	120,000	23,890	ex Hamilton Creek Railroad #1
3*	17x24	2-6-2	44	BLW	34840	6/10			to Puget Sound Pulp & Timber Co. #6
5		2T Shay	36	Lima	1729	7/06	110,000	23,900	ex Phoenix Logging #5; used at Oso
7*	12x15	3T Shay	'	'	2858	5/16	146,000	30,350	used at Hazel; to Discovery Bay Logging
17 ?		2-6-0		Danf.	884	10/72	75,000		acq. 5/1906 ex O.R.&N. #17
Stacey E. Wright Logging Co.									
1*	6x10	2T Shay	32	Lima	1743	8/06	20,000	4,500	to Joe Creek Shingle Co. #1
2*	11x12	'	'	'	1948	9/07	90,000	22,580	to Anderson & Middleton Lumber Co. #7

Freight traffic: logging

PUGET SOUND SHORE RAILROAD COMPANY, THE   Elijah Smith, **President**
Incorp: 8/19/1882   **Operated:** 7/6/84 to 10/31/89   **HQ city:**   Seattle
Disposition: sold to Northern Pacific & Puget Sound Shore Railroad Company on October 31, 1889
Miles track: 23.95   **Gauge:** 56½"
Main line: Stuck Junction to Seattle
Rail wt.:   56 lbs. steel   **Max. grade:**   **Const. began:** grading   (January 22, 1883)
                                                                                                laying rails   (January 28, 1884)
Const. comp.: July 18, 1889   **First train operated:**   June 17, 1884

Locomotives:

Road No.	Cyln.	Type	Dvr. in.	Bldr.	Bldr. No.	Date	Weight	Effort	Remarks
1*	17x24	4-4-0	62	Pitts.	862	4/88	84,265		became Northern Pacific #367
2									

Freight traffic: common carrier

Roster of 6/30/1888:
    2   locomotives
   12   freight cars

First published timetable:
July 1, 1887 - daily
   4:00 p.m.   Tacoma
   4:40   Puyallup   9
   5:30   Kent   24
   6:20   Seattle   41

A construction contract was signed September 2, 1882, to build a three-rail track from Argo to Black River Jct. with the existing narrow gauge Columbia & Puget Sound Railroad Co.; the work was completed on July 1, 1884.

Editorial section of March, 1887, *Official Guide* states "Puget Sound Shore RR (div. of Columbia & Puget Sound RR) opened Stuck Jct. to Seattle, 24 miles." Mr. Smith was president of Columbia & Puget Sound.

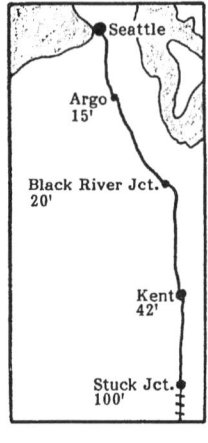

Listed in first ICC (6/30/88) as an operating independent with 23 miles owned and in use and it was extended to 25 miles each by 6/30/89. Volume for 6/30/90 states "Part of and owned by Northern Pacific & Puget Sound RR Co."

The official construction record is not very detailed.
   Stuck Jct. to Black River Jct.   January, 1883,   to   October 1, 1883   13.85 miles
   Black River Jct. to Seattle   1883   1884   10.10

An operations note from *The Railway Age:*
   July 3, 1884   The first passenger train passed over the Tacoma-Seattle branch on June 17, 1884, but the line is not yet in operation, however.

The last published timetable, dated October 6, 1889, shows the running time from Tacoma to Seattle as one hour and forty-five minutes.

Bibliography: *Poor's 1890*, p. 1176   *Seattle Post-Intelligencer* - July 18, 1889   *Valuation 25*, p. 499
                                       Snohomish City - *The Eye* - February 7, 1883 to June 21, 1884

RAYONIER, INCORPORATED   President

Incorp:	11/9/1937	**Operated:** (4/15/45) to		**HQ city:**	Hoquiam
Disposition:	abandoned - corporation dissolved June 14, 1968				
Purchased:	Ozette Timber Company		**Incorp.:**	5/23/1939 to	10/8/1954
Predecessor:	Polson Logging Company			5/1/1903	6/30/1948
Miles track:	100	**Gauge:** 56½"			
Main line:	woods lines from Sekiu and Hoquiam				
Notes:	Ozette Timber Company had 22 miles from Lake Pleasant to Lake Ozette. The Sekiu line was abandoned about August 31, 1971.				

Locomotives:

1	3 truck	36	Climax	1648	1/24	160,000	35,200	ex Bloedel-Donovan #1
1-2d ?	2T Shay	32	Lima	3100	8/20	128,000	25,830	ex Ozette Timber Co. #1 ?
2	3T Shay	33	'	2908	5/17	150,000	33,000	ex Bloedel-Donovan #2
2-2d	3 truck	36	Willam.	34	11/29	150,000	39,300	ex Neils Lumber Co. #6
3	3T Shay	'	Lima	2786	9/14	174,000	35,000	ex Bloedel-Donovan #3
3-2d	3 truck	'	Willam.	20	1/26	140,000	36,200	ex Ewauna Box Co. #4
4	2T Shay	32	Lima	820	5/03	90,000	18,750	ex Bloedel-Donovan #4
4-2d ?	3 truck	36	Willam.	16	8/24	140,000	36,200	ex Long-Bell #701
4-3d ?	2 truck	38	Heisler	1334	5/16	104,000		ex Ozette Timber Co. #4 ?
5	3T Shay	36	Lima	2855	6/16	140,000	30,300	ex Bloedel-Donovan #5
6	2 truck	'	Heisler	1288	10/13	88,000	18,800	ex Bloedel-Donovan #6
7	3T Shay	'	Lima	3012	4/19	140,000	30,300	ex Bloedel-Donovan #7
8	2-6-6-2T	44	BLW	58064	11/24	212,000	37,500	ex Bloedel-Donovan #8
9	'	'	'	58065	'	'	'	ex Bloedel-Donovan #9
10	3 truck	36	Climax	1641	6/23	160,000	35,200	ex Bloedel-Donovan #10
10-2d*	3T Shay	'	Lima	3348	4/30	188,000	38,200	ex Ozette Timber #10; 1945 to Rayonier
11	3 truck	35	Climax	1632	8/23	140,000	30,800	ex Bloedel-Donovan #11
14	2-6-6-2T	51	BLW	60256	11/27	275,000	56,600	ex Bloedel-Donovan #14
15	3T Shay	36	Lima	3318	4/28	184,000	38,200	ex Bloedel-Donovan #15

The above were used at Sekiu plus about 375 logging cars, 3 cranes and 25 tank cars, cabooses, etc.

WASHINGTON

Road No.	Type	Dvr. in.	Bldr.	Bldr. No.	Date	Weight	Effort	Remarks
2	2-8-2	44	BLW	38967	12/12	140,000	27,000	ex Polson Logging #1-2d; sold 1963
3	2T Shay	27½	Lima	2305	5/10	44,000	10,700	ex Polson Logging #3
14	2-6-6-2T	51	BLW	60256	11/27	275,000	56,600	from Clallam County operations
33	3T Shay	32	Lima	1614	11/05	122,400	25,830	ex Polson Logging #33
38	2-6-6-2	51	BLW	61781	/34	293,000	59,600	acq. 9/1955 ex Sierra Railroad #38
45	2-6-2	44	'	27311	1/06	88,000	16,700	ex Polson Logging #45
70	2-8-2	'	'	55355	4/22	140,000	27,000	ex Polson Logging #70
90	'	48	'	59071	3/26	197,000	35,700	ex Polson Logging #90
91	3T Shay	36	Lima	3322	11/28	181,000	38,200	ex Polson #91; sold (2/1958) Feather
99	2-8-0	50	BLW	25416	3/05	136,000	29,200	ex Polson Logging #99
101	2-8-2	44	'	38966	12/12	141,000	27,000	ex Polson Logging #101
110	2-6-6-2T	'	'	60561	7/28	222,000	37,500	ex Weyerhaeuser #110
111	'	'	'	62064	/36	247,000	42,500	ex Weyerhaeuser #110-2d
120	'	50	'	61904	'	373,000	59,600	ex Weyerhaeuser #120
191*	3T Shay	36	Lima	3343	10/29	188,000	38,200	ex Polson Logging #191
3100	2-6-6-2	55	BLW	34389	3/10	304,000	58,000	ex Polson Logging #3100

The above were used at Hoquiam plus approximately 600 logging flats, 3 cranes and 25 work cars.

Road No.	Type		Bldr.	Bldr. No.	Date			Remarks
90	C-C		BLW	75357	/51	1,600 h.p.		1986 to Trona Railway #54
201*	B-B		'	76136	9/56	1,200 h.p.		to U.S. Steel in Utah
202*	'		'	76137	'	'		to U.S. Steel in Utah
203	'		'	75912	10/53	'		ex McCloud R. #30; to U.S.S. in Calif.

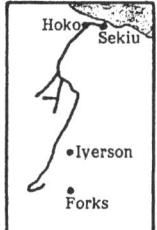
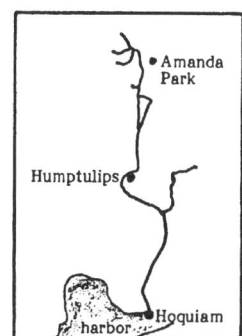

Tacoma Public Library
Rayonier, Incorporated, log train on steel bridge in about 1963
Richards Collection

ST. REGIS PULP & PAPER COMPANY

					President
Incorp:		**Operated:** 1943 to		**HQ city:**	Tacoma
Disposition:	abandoned				
Predecessors:	West Fork Logging Company	HQ at Mineral; 25 miles track	from:	1908 to 1955	
	St. Paul & Tacoma Lumber Company	HQ at Tacoma; 120 miles	Incorp.:	6/4/1888	1949
	Nooksack Timber Company	HQ at Deming; 12 miles track	from:	1922	1929
	Natches Pass Railroad Company	HQ at Buckley; 7 miles track	Incorp.:	7/16/1896	1910
Miles track:	23	**Gauge:** 56½"			
Main line:	woods lines from Ohop, Kapowsin, Kulshan and Nooksack				
Rail wt.:	60/85 lbs.	**Max. grade:** 6.0%	**Const. began:** grading		1896

Locomotives:

Road No.	Cyln.	Type	Dvr. in.	Bldr.	Bldr. No.	Date	Weight	Effort	Remarks
		St. Regis Pulp & Paper Co.							
83		3 truck	38	Heisler	1480	5/23	160,000		ex Potlatch Forests #83
91		"	40	"	1557	3/28	180,000	38,480	scrapped about 1958
92		"	"	"	1555	12/27	"	"	ex Potlatch Forests #91
		West Fork Logging Co.							
1*		2 truck		Climax	872	/08	104,000		to Stillwater Lumber Co.
2*		"	35	"	1335	10/15	120,000	26,400	to Lytle-Inch Logging Co.
3 ?		3 truck	36	"	1555	12/19	160,000	35,200	ex Clemons Logging Co. #3
4 ?		2 truck	30	"	778	/07	80,000	17,600	ex Bennett Logging Co. #1
5		3 truck	36	"	1602	/21	160,000	35,200	ex Clemons Logging Co. #5
91*	18¼x16	"	40	Heisler	1557	3/28	180,000	34,480	to St. Regis Pulp & Paper #91
		St. Paul & Tacoma Lumber Co.							
1*	12x12	3T Shay	32	Lima	565	1/99	100,000	24,175	used at Ohop; to Kuhn Logging #2
1-2d		2T Shay	29½	"	1917	5/07	74,000	16,900	used at Ohop; acq. 3d hand
2*	12x15	3T Shay	36	"	2166	5/09	140,000	29,800	used at Ohop
3*	"	"	"	"	2792	4/17	"	30,350	used at Ohop
3-2d ?		"	32	"	560	11/98	100,000	20,150	used at Ohop; sold in 1919
5*	14½x15	"	36	"	3126	11/20	180,000	40,400	used at Kapowsin
6		"	"	"	2642	2/13	140,000	30,350	used at Ohop
7*		0-8-8-0		BLW	56322	3/23			
702d ?		3 truck	35	Climax	1591	1/21	140,000	30,800	ex McCoy #2
8		3T Shay	36	Lima	3171	8/22	160,000	35,100	used at Kooksack; acq. 3/1941
9		"	"	"	2857	5/17	"	"	used at Ohop; scrapped in 1945
10*		2-6-6-2T	44	BLW	57600	1/24	208,000		
11*	13x15	3T Shay	36	Lima	3330	2/29	187,400	38,200	used at Kulshan; sold 10/1949
12		"	"	"	3319	5/28	186,000	"	used at Ohop; acq. 10/1941
		2 truck	33	Heisler	1335	5/16	64,000		ex Cabin Creek Lumber Co.
		Nooksack Timber Co.							
1 ?		3T Shay	36	Lima	2857	5/17	160,000	35,100	ex McCoy #1; to St. P.&T. #9

Freight traffic: logging

Rosters of 6/30/1910:

Natches Pass Railroad		St. Paul & Tacoma Lumber	
1	geared engine	1	geared engine
1	rod engine	14½	miles at Orting
11	miles at Buckley		

In each case, flat cars were leased from Northern Pacific.

After August, 1952, diesel power was used exclusively.

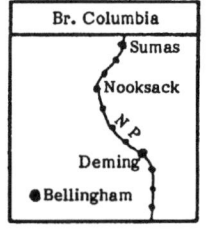
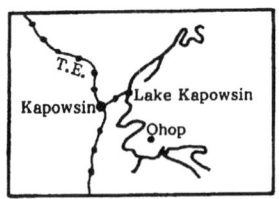

SAGINAW TIMBER COMPANY

					President
Incorp:	3/18/1908	**Operated:** 1909 to 1946		**HQ city:**	Elma
Disposition:	abandoned - corporation dissolved November 30, 1946				
Miles track:	40	**Gauge:** 56½"			
Main line:	woods line near Saginaw				
Rail wt.:		**Max. grade:** 5.0%	**Const. began:** grading		

WASHINGTON

Locomotives:

Road No.	Cyln.	Type	Dvr. in.	Bldr.	Bldr. No.	Date	Weight	Effort	Remarks
2*	18x24	2-8-2	44	BLW	38967	12/12			
3*		3 truck	35	Climax	1379	/16	140,000	30,800	
4*		2-6-6-2T	44	BLW	58272	3/25			to White River Lumber Co. #7
5		2 truck	35	Climax	1163	6/12	120,000	26,400	ex Lester Logging Co. #4
5-2d*		2-6-6-2T		BLW	60602	8/28			

Freight traffic: logging

The operation included a 2,000-foot incline with a maximum grade of 60%.

SAUK RIVER LUMBER COMPANY President

Incorp.:	4/1/1922	**Operated:**	1924 to 1952		**HQ city:**	Darrington
Disposition:	abandoned - corporation dissolved July 31, 1959					
Miles track:	35	**Gauge:**	56½"			
Main line:	Darrington into the forest					
Rail wt.:	66 lbs.	**Max. grade:**	7.0%	**Const. began:**	grading	

Locomotives:

No.	Cyln.	Type	Dvr. in.	Bldr.	Bldr. No.	Date	Weight	Effort	Remarks
2		2T Shay	36	Lima	2266	1/10	120,000	23,850	acq. 4/1928; scrapped 11/1939
2-2d		3T Shay	'	'	3053	2/20	140,000	30,350	acq. 2/1948
4 ?		2T Shay	'	'	2597	10/12	120,000	23,900	acq. 9/1939
12		'	29½	'	2278	2/10	84,000	16,900	acq. 4th hand; scrapped 11/1939
21 ?		3T Shay	36	'	1810	1/07	130,000	29,825	acq. 2d hand; sold
22*	14½x15	'	'	'	3282	6/25	180,000	40,400	sold into British Columbia
23*		3 truck	'	Willam.	22	3/26	140,000		

Freight traffic: logging

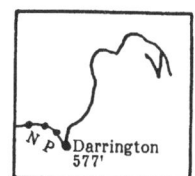

Special Collections Div. - Univ. of Washington Libraries Clark Kinsey photo #2121
Gasoline powered lumber carriers owned by Mumby Lumber & Shingle Company at Malone

SCHAFER BROS. LOGGING COMPANY

					President
Incorp:	3/26/1914	**Operated:** 1914 to 1955		**HQ city:**	Satsop

Disposition: abandoned - corporation dissolved March 22, 1956

Purchased:	Independence Logging Company	HQ: Aberdeen, 22 miles	from: 1920 to 1927
Predecessors:	National Lumber & Mfg. Company	HQ: Elma, 25 miles	1913 1927
	Wynoochee Timber Company	HQ: Hoquiam	1916 1924
	Chehalis County Logging & Timber Company	HQ: Cosmopolis, 13 miles	12/5/1902 1923
	Wilson Bros. Company	HQ: Aberdeen, 10 miles	(1907) 1920

Miles track:	150	**Gauge:**	56½"
Main line:	Brady into the forest		
Rail wt.:	56/60 lbs.	**Max. grade:** 6.0%	**Const. began:** grading

Locomotives:

Road No.	Cyln.	Type	Dvr. in.	Bldr.	Bldr. No.	Date	Weight	Effort	Remarks
		Schafer Bros.							
1*	17x24	2 truck	40	Heisler	1304	10/14	124,000		used at Brady
2		2T Shay	29½	Lima	865	8/04	74,000	15,625	acq. 3/1929; used at Satsop
3		2 truck	31	Climax	1585	5/20	90,000		acq. 2d hand; used at Satsop
4		2T Shay	29½	Lima	1918	6/07	74,000	16,900	acq. 3/1929; used at Dryad
5		'	36	'	1857	3/07	110,000	23,850	ex Grays Harbor Comm.; used at Brady
6*	19x24	2-8-2		Porter	6494	5/20			
7*	18x24	2-6-2T	44	BLW	58010	9/24	154,000		
8		'	'	'	55913	12/22			ex Wynoochee Timber Co. #4
9		'	'	'	57212	9/23			ex Wynoochee Timber Co. #3
10		'	'	'	55344	4/22			ex National Lbr. & Mfg. #3
11		2T Shay	36	Lima	2272	3/10	120,000	23,890	acq. 5th hand; used at Brady
12		'	32	'	2821	9/15	118,000	25,830	used at Brady; sold in 1938
20*		B-B		Schen.	78412	10/50		1,000 h.p.	1955 to Simpson Timber Co.
21		3T Shay	36	Lima	3225	6/23	169,900	30,350	acq. 2d hand; used at Brady
31		2 truck	40	Heisler	1267	1/13	120,000		ex Great Northern Lbr.; used at Brady
		2T Shay	26	Lima	338	2/91	26,000	5,150	acq. 3d hand; used at Brady
		'	'	'	2210	9/09	36,000	8,200	ex National Sash & Door Co.
997		0-6-0	49	BLW	7023	11/83	63,000	13,800	ex Northern Pacific #997
		Independence Logging Co.							
1		3T Shay	32	Lima	565	1/99	100,000	24,175	acq. 6/1920; sold in 1923
1-2d*		'	36	'	3233	9/23	190,000	35,100	to Mt. Emily Lbr. Co., Oregon
2*	12x15	'	'	'	3271	1/25	183,900	30,350	to Markham & Callow #2
3 ?		'	'	'	2160	4/09	140,000	29,800	ex Wilson Bros.
		National Lumber & Mfg. Co.							
2 ?		2T Shay	36	Lima	2272	3/10	120,000	23,890	4/1922 to Chehalis County Logging Co.
3*	17x24	2-6-2T	44	BLW	55344	4/22			to Schafer Bros. #10
4*	12x15	3T Shay	36	Lima	3225	6/23	169,900	30,350	to Schafer Bros. #21
		Wynoochee Timber Co.							
2		2-6-2	48	BLW	37125	10/11			ex Carlton Log. #6; to Schafer #26
2-2d ?		2 truck	40	Heisler	1201	5/10	120,00		ex Cascade Timber Co. #3
3*	18x24	2-6-2T	44	BLW	57212	9/23			to Schafer Bros. #9
4*	17x24	'	'	'	55913	12/22			to Schafer Bros. #9
		Chehalis County Logging & Timber Co.							
1*	12x12	2T Shay	36	Lima	1857	3/07	110,000	23,850	
		'	'	'	2272	3/10	120,000	23,890	acq. 4/1922; to Schafer Bros. #11
11 ?		2 truck	33	Climax	303	3/02	90,000	19,800	ex Polson Bros. Logging Co. #11
		Wilson Bros. Co.							
3 ?		3T Shay	36	Lima	2160	4/09	140,000	29,800	2/1920 to Independence Logging Co.

Freight traffic: logging

Rosters of 6/30/1910:

Chehalis County Logging & Timber Co.
- 1 geared engine
- 1 rod engine
- 7 miles of track at Montesano

Wilson Bros. Co.
- 1 rod engine
- 3 sets logging trucks
- 3 flat cars
- 4 miles of track at Independence Creek

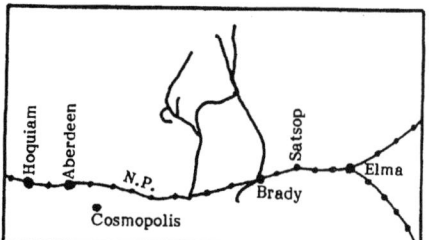

WASHINGTON   261.

SEATTLE & INTERNATIONAL RAILWAY COMPANY

Jno. H. Bryant, President

Incorp:	6/30/1896	**Operated:** 7/28/96 to 3/20/01	**HQ city:**	Seattle
Disposition:	sold to Northern Pacific Railway Company on March 21, 1901			
Predecessors:	Seattle, Lake Shore & Eastern Railway Company		**Incorp.:** 4/28/1885 to	7/1/1896
	Seattle & West Coast Railway Company		4/13/1887	3/24/1888
Miles track:	177.63	**Gauge:** 56½"		
Main line:	Seattle to Sumas			

Locomotives:

Road No.	Cyln.	Type	Dvr. in.	Bldr.	Bldr. No.	Date	Weight	Effort	Remarks
1		4-4-0	62	R.I.	1779	6/87	94,600	14,100	to Northern Pacific #1145
2		'	'	'	1780	'	'	'	to Northern Pacific #1146
3		'	'	'	1820	2/88	'	'	to Northern Pacific #1147
4		'	'	'	1937	'	'	'	to Northern Pacific #1148
7		2-8-0	'	'	1882	6/87			named White - to N.P. #48
8		'	50	Richm.	2496	/95			to Northern Pacific #47
9		'	56	R.I.	1883	6/87			to Northern Pacific #49
10		'	51	Rome	501	8/89			to Northern Pacific #84
11*	20x24	'	'	Schen.	5548	4/00	135,000	24,800	to Northern Pacific #45
12*	'	'	'	'	5559	3/00	'	'	to Northern Pacific #46
15		4-6-0	56	R.I.	2337	2/90	120,000	19,400	to Northern Pacific #365
16		'	'	'	2432	8/90	'	'	to Northern Pacific #388
17		'	'	'	2433	'	'	'	to Northern Pacific #389
101		4-4-0	62	'	2085	8/88	92,000	14,100	to Northern Pacific #1149
102		'	'	'	2086	'	'	'	to Northern Pacific #1150

Freight traffic: common carrier, lumber

Roster of 6/30/1898:

12	locomotives
15	passenger cars
46	box cars
205	flat cars
99	coal cars
147	logging cars

Published timetable dated:
(as Seattle, Lake Shore & Eastern)
April 30, 1893

8:35	a.m.	Seattle	
9:45		Woodinville Jct. m.p.	23.7
10:27		Snohomish	38.1
10:48		Hartford Jct.	46.3
11:23		Arlington	60.0
12:30	p.m.	Sedro	85.2
12:55		Woolley	85.9
1:30		Wickersham	97.5
2:10		Deming	110.7
3:00		Sumas	125.3
10:07	a.m.	Redmond	30.2
11:15		Fall City	52.5
11:27		Snoqualmie	56.2
11:35		North Bend	59.2
		Sallal Prairie	62.4

First listed in ICC for 6/30/97 as an operating independent with 168 miles owned and in use. By 6/30/00 it was 164 miles owned and 176 operated.

Control passed to Northern Pacific Railway Co. on April 1, 1898. The 11.43 miles of track from Snohomish to Everett was leased February 1, 1900, from Everett & Monte Cristo Railway Co.

Operating statesmen as of June 30, 1898:

passenger earnings	$127,194.09
freight income	266,058.01
other	23,821.37
operating expenses	286,776.32
net	130,297.15
taxes paid	62,789.24
interest on bonds	41,281.95
Coast of road and equipment	6,850,000.00

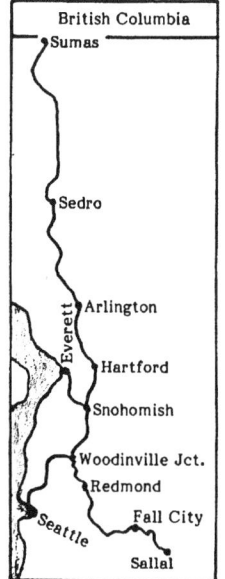

Bibliography: *Poor's 1899*, p. 653   *Valuation 25*, p. 502

SEATTLE & MONTANA RAILROAD COMPANY

Samuel Hill, President

Incorp:	3/29/1898	**Operated:** 3/31/98 to 6/30/07	**HQ city:**	Seattle
Disposition:	sold to Great Northern Railway Company on July 1, 1907			
Predecessors:	Seattle & Northern Railway Company		**Incorp.:** 8/9/1888 to	2/1/1902
	Seattle & Montana Railway Company		3/7/1890	3/30/1898
	Fairhaven & Southern Railroad Company		11/27/1888	3/30/1898

Miles track: 191.89 **Gauge:** 56½"
Main line: Seattle to Blaine
Rail wt.: **Max. grade:** **Const. began:** grading August 1, 1890
   laying rails May 26, 1891
Const. comp.: November 27, 1891 - main line **First train operated:** December 5, 1891
Locomotives:

Road No.	Type	Dvr. in.	Bldr.	Bldr. No.	Date	Weight	Effort	Remarks
139	4-4-0	63	Rome	629	7/90	49,000	13,100	ex Seattle & N. #2; to G.N. #139
199	'	'	R.I.	1296	12/82	59,000	14,690	acq. 6/30/1891 ex St.P.M.&M. #199
232	0-6-0	49	Hinkley	1765	8/88	83,000	16,850	acq. 4/3/1893; to G.N. #30
298	4-6-0	55	Schen.	2860	4/89	77,000	16,820	ex Fairhaven & Southern #1
299	'	'	'	2861	'	'	'	ex Fairhaven & S. #2; to G.N. #299
329	2-6-0	'	Rogers	4012	9/88	87,290	18,740	acq. 6/30/1891 ex St.P.M.&M. #329

Freight traffic: common carrier, lumber
First published timetable:
   (As Seattle & Montana Railway Co. and
   Fairhaven & Southern Railroad Co.)
   December 7, 1891
   9:30 a.m.   Seattle
   11:30   Everett   m.p.   33.0
   12:27 p.m. Mt. Vernon   67.9
   12:55   F&S Jct.   78.5
   1:13   Samish Lake   85.2
   1:38   Fairhaven   95.2
   1:45   New Whatcom   97.7
   3:25   Blaine   119.2
   5:00   S. Westminster   143.5

Constructed by Seattle & Montana Railway Co.:
   Seattle to near Burlington   1891   78.20
Constructed by Seattle & Montana Railroad Co.:
   Fairhaven to Belleville (re-building?)   1902 to 1906   18.82
   Branches and line changes   9.45

The cost of road and equipment was placed at $20,258,454.

Construction notes from *The Railway Age:*
   September 13, 1890   About 2,000 men are at work grading.
   February 7, 1891   To start laying rails at both ends on 2/10/1891
   June 6, 1891   Rail laying began May 26, 1891.
   July 18, 1891   Head of track 40 miles from Seattle.
   August 8, 1891   Track now six miles north of Marysville.
   August 15, 1891   Track now to Mount Vernon, 67.9 miles.
   October 23, 1891   The last spike was driven on October 12.
   December 4, 1891   Placed in operation November 27, Seattle to
                        F & S Junction, 78.5 miles.

No equipment roster or rail weight was found in *Poor's Manual.*

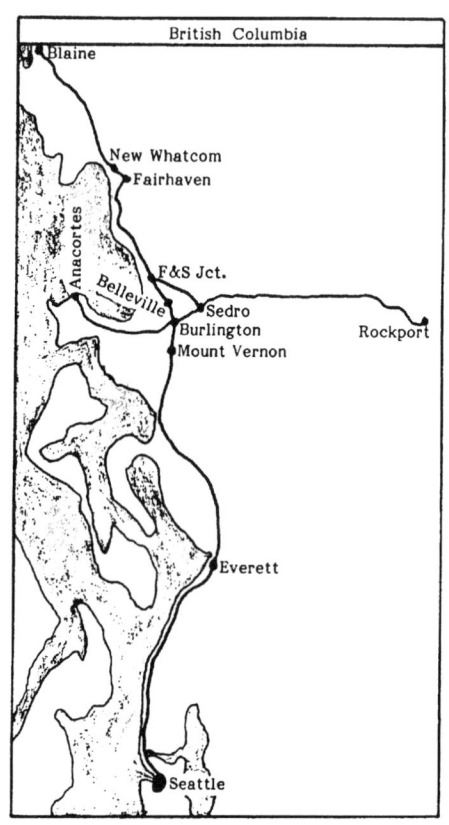

Seattle & Montana Railway Co. was first listed in ICC for 6/30/93 as an operating subsidiary of Great Northern Railway Co. with 78 miles owned and in use. By 6/30/98, as "Railroad", it had been increased to 137 miles owned and operated. By 6/30/99 it was a 135-mile non-operating subsidiary. It was reduced to 127 miles by 6/30/00 and to 119 by 1901. With the Seattle & Northern Railway Co. merger, the 1902 figure was 181 miles and 192 by 6/30/04.

Bibliography: *Poor's 1900,* p. 569   *Snohomish Eye* - August 14 to December 5, 1891   *Valuation 133,* p. 189

SEATTLE & NORTH COAST RAILROAD COMPANY   President
Incorp: 9/20/1979   **Operated:** 3/24/80 to 6/2/84   **HQ city:** Seattle
Disposition: bankrupt and abandoned - corporation was dissolved December 17, 1984
Miles track: 50.80   **Gauge:** 56½"
Main line: Port Angeles to Port Townsend

WASHINGTON 263.

Locomotives:

Road No.	Type	Bldr.	Bldr. No.	Date	Effort	Remarks
51	B-B	BLW	73042	11/46	660 h.p.	
102	'					
103	'					
502	C-C	EMD			1,750 h.p.	ex Chicago, Milw., St. P. & Pac.

Freight traffic: common carrier, lumber

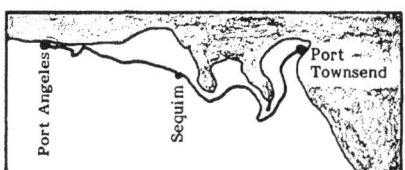

SEATTLE & NORTHERN RAILWAY COMPANY

Wm. H. Starbuck, President

Incorp:	8/9/1888	**Operated:**	11/25/90 to 2/1/02	**HQ city:**	Anacortes

Disposition: sold to Seattle & Montana Railroad Company on February 1, 1902

Miles track: 55.34 **Gauge:** 56½"

Main line: Anacortes to Rockport

Rail wt.: 56 lbs. **Max. grade:** 1.0% **Const. began:** grading (January 2, 1890)
laying rails March 17, 1890

Const. comp.: (December 31, 1900) **First train operated:** August 5, 1890

Locomotive engines:

Road No.	Cyln.	Type	Dvr. in.	Bldr.	Bldr. No.	Date	Weight	Effort	Remarks
1		4-4-0		Norris		/66	70,000		
1-2d*	17x24	'	63	Rome	627	7/90	49,000	13,100	
2*	'	'	'	'	629	'	'	'	to Seattle & Montana #139

Freight traffic: common carrier, lumber and coal

Roster of 11/30/1891:
    2   locomotive engines
    2   passenger cars
  37   freight cars

First published timetable:
    January 4, 1891
    6:30 a.m. Anacortes
                   Woolley   24 miles
                   terminus   30
    There were two more round trips daily.

The official construction details:
    Anacortes to Hamilton   1890 to February 1, 1891   34.14 miles
    Hamilton to Sauk   1900   18.84
    Sauk to Rockport   1901   2.36

Construction notes from *The Railway Age:*
    February 15, 1890   Twenty-three miles have been graded.
    April 5, 1890   Rail laying is under way. Maximum grade is 1%, using 50-pound rails.
    July 12, 1890   Now completed from Anacortes to Sedro.
    January 4, 1901   It has now been completed to Rockport, 55 miles.

And from *Railroad Gazette:*
    August 15, 1890   The road was placed in operation August 15, 1890, from Anacortes to seven miles beyond
                              Sedro; rail laying east of there will begin in 30 days.

First listed in ICC for 6/30/91 as an operating independent with 34 miles owned and in use. It was increased to 36 miles by 6/30/92, then back to 34 in 1895. By 6/30/98 it was shown as a non-operating subsidiary of The Pacific Coast Co. with 42 miles owned. It was extended to 46 miles by 6/30/99, then reduced to 37 miles by 6/30/00. By 6/30/01 it was again an independent, now with 57 miles owned and 61 operated.

Bibliography: *Poor's 1892*, p. 577   Anacortes - *Daily Progress* - March 5 to March 28, 1890   *Valuation 133*, p. 189

California State Railroad Museum Library   *Railway & Locomotive Historical Society Collection*
Seattle & Walla Walla Railroad & Transportation Co. #1, the Denny, was built by Mason in 1875

California State Railroad Museum Library   *Railway & Locomotive Historical Society Collection*
The Denny with a string of platform cars converted to passenger excursion duty; as the photograph is undated, it may have been on the Seattle & Walla Walla or the successor Columbia & Puget Sound Railroad Company.

SEATTLE & WALLA WALLA RAILROAD & TRANSPORTATION COMPANY

A. A. Denny, President

Incorp:	7/19/1873	**Operated:** 2/8/77 to 11/25/80	**HQ city:**	Seattle
Disposition:	renamed Columbia & Puget Sound Railroad Company on November 25, 1880			
Acquired:	Seattle Coal & Transportation Company, The		**Incorp.:** 2/26/1876 to 2/15/1878	
Miles track:	22.50	**Gauge:** 36"		
Main line:	Seattle to Newcastle			
Rail wt.:	35 lbs.	**Max. grade:** 2.50%	**Const. began:** grading	May 1, 1874
			laying rails	(Nov. 13, 1876)
Const. comp.:	(December 29, 1877)		**First train operated:**	February 8, 1877

Locomotive engines:

Road No.	Name	Type	Dvr. in.	Bldr.	Bldr. No.	Date	Weight	Effort	Remarks
1	A. A. Denny	0-6-4T	33	Mason	552	9/75	50,000		acq. 10/1876 ex Stockton & Ione
2*	Al-Ki	4-4-0	36	Baily		5/77	26,000		new as Seattle & Walla W. #2
2-2d*		0-4-0	30	BLW	5610	4/81			new as Seattle Coal & T. #2
3*	G. C. Bode	2-6-2T	'	'	3603	5/74	20,000		reblt. from Seattle Coal 0-6-0T
4*	Georgina	0-6-0	'	'	3713	4/75	'		new as Seattle Coal & T. #3
5*	Ant	0-4-0T		Fulton		9/71	14,000		new as S.C.&T. #1; sold 5/1883
6*	Seattle	'	30	BLW	4108	7/77			new as S.C.&T. #4

Freight traffic: mine, coal

Roster of 6/30/1880:
- 5 locomotive engines
- 2 passenger cars
- 60 freight cars

First published timetable:
March 12, 1880

7:30 a.m.	Seattle	1:00 p.m.	
8:30	Newcastle	11:30 a.m.	

The first train to operate by steam from Seattle (by Ant rather than horse) was February 29, 1872, likely from Lake Union south to Pike Street. Owner of the track is not clear, but probably Seattle Coal Co. which built a track in June, 1870.

The Mason engine arrived in Seattle on October 19, 1876. The first train to Renton was run as shown above and the line was placed in commercial operation October 15, 1877.

ICC data shows that the carrier built 3.5 miles from Seattle to Argo between 1873 and 1876; this was probably a wood-rail tram line and was being rebuilt with iron rails in 1875. As an engine was purchased in 1871, 1874 and 1875 we must assume that some commercial operation was going on pre-1877 when it was officially opened.

Construction notes from *Railroad Gazette:*

May 23, 1874	Grading contract for five miles has been awarded.
September 26, 1874	Fifteen miles of line ready for the ties.
March 23, 1877	Now completed to Renton, 15 miles, and opened for business.
July 20, 1877	Grading contract to Newcastle, 6.5 miles, has been let.
September 21, 1877	Track laying has resumed; a steady grade of 100 feet per mile.
January 18, 1878	Completed to Newcastle, 21.5 miles.

Bibliography: *Poor's 1880*, p. 1000   Olympia - *Transcript* - March 9, 1872   *Valuation 25*, p. 507

SEATTLE, LAKE SHORE & EASTERN RAILWAY COMPANY

J. R. McDonald, President

Incorp:	4/28/1885	**Operated:** 5/19/88 to 6/30/96	**HQ city:**	Seattle
Disposition:	name changed to Seattle & International Railway Company on July 1, 1896			
Purchased:	Seattle & West Coast Railway Company		**Incorp.:** 4/13/1887 to 3/24/1888	
Miles track:	216.27	**Gauge:** 56½"		
Main line:	Seattle to Sumas and Spokane Falls to Davenport			
Rail wt.:	60 lbs.	**Max. grade:**	**Const. began:** grading	(March 9, 1887)
			laying rails	(Sept. 5, 1887)
Const. comp.:	March 15, 1892		**First train operated:**	(October 25, 1887)

Locomotive engines:

Road No.	Name	Cyln.	Type	Dvr. in.	Bldr.	Bldr. No.	Date	Weight	Effort	Remarks
1*	Yesler	17x24	4-4-0	62	R.I.	1779	6/87	94,600	14,100	to Seattle & Int. #1
2*	Gilman	'	'	'	'	1789	'	'	'	to Seattle & Int. #2
3*		'	'	'	'	1820	2/88	'	'	to Seattle & Int. #3
4*		'	'	'	'	1937	'	'	'	to Seattle & Int. #4
6*	McDonald	16x20	2-4-4T	50	'	1990	6/88			
7			2-8-0	56	'	1882	6/87			acq. 1888 ex Minn. & P. #21
8*		20x24	'	50	Richm.	2496	/95			to Seattle & Int. #8
9	Smith		'	56	R.I.	1883	6/87			acq. 1888 ex Minn. & P. #22
10*		11x16	0-4-4T	42	'	2036	7/88			
11*	Cannon	17x24	4-4-0	62	'	2085	8/88	92,000	14,100	to Seattle & Int. #101
12*	Mohr	'	'	'	'	2086	'	'	'	to Seattle & Int. #102
13*		14x20	0-4-4T	50	'	2210	6/89	76,000	9,140	to Northern Pacific #1071
15*		19x24	4-6-0	56	'	2337	2/90	120,000	19,400	to Seattle & Int. #15
16*		'	'	'	'	2432	8/90	'	'	to Seattle & Int. #16
17*		'	'	'	'	2433	'	'	'	to Seattle & Int. #17

Freight traffic: common carrier, lumber and coal

Rosters of 12/31/1888 - 6/30/1895:

locomotive engines	12	12
passenger cars	10	13
box cars	46	52
coal cars	32	106
platform cars	128	216

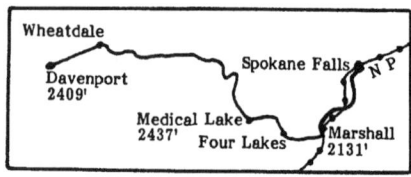

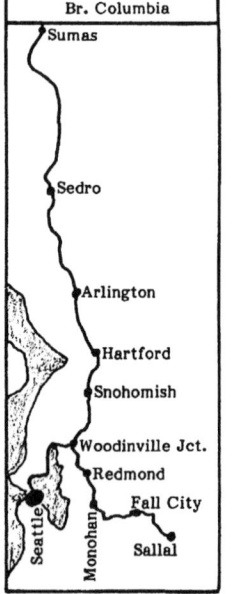

First published timetable:

April 15, 1888 - mixed train

7:00 a.m.	Seattle	
7:36	Union Bay	m.p. 9
8:30	Winsor	21
8:42	Snohomish Jct.	24
9:38	Redmond	30
10:12	Monohan	38
10:30	Gilman	42

Also a 2:20 p.m. departure

Construction notes from *Railroad Gazette*:

Jan. 28, 1887	Surveying is being done.
March 1, 1887	Grading contract let.
April 1, 1887	Ground was broken March 21.
Nov. 4, 1887	First train, Seattle to Squak, 25 miles, operated last week.
July 27, 1888	Opened Seattle to Snohomish, 23 miles, on July 16; about 45 miles of Spokane Falls track is completed.

Published timetable dated:

January 4, 1891

9:15 a.m.		Seattle	
10:20		Woodinville Jct.	23.6
12:15	p.m.	Arlington	59.9
1:25		Sedro	85.2

and

10:37	a.m.	Redmond	30.2
12:20	p.m.	Sallal Prairie	62.4

The official origin of the track as taken from ICC *Valuation* reports:

Partially constructed by Seattle & West Coast Railway Co. and completed by the carrier,

Woodinville to Snohomish	1887-1888	14.40

Constructed by the subject carrier:

Seattle to Sallal Prairie	1887-1888	63.32
Snohomish to Sumas	1888-1891	88.50
Spokane Falls to Davenport	1888-1889	50.05

Dates that various sections were placed in commercial operation:

Seattle to Woodinville Junction	May 19, 1888	23.18
Woodinville Junction to Fall City	May 19, 1888	28.85
Woodinville Junction to Snohomish	July 3, 1888	15.83
Fall City to Sallal Prairie	December, 1889	10.00
Snohomish to Hartford	June 1, 1890	7.90
Hartford to Sedro	November 25, 1890	38.90
Sedro to Sumas	May 1, 1891	40.10
Spokane Falls to Wheatdale	October 15, 1888	44.34
Wheatdale to Davenport	July 1, 1889	5.80

A construction note from *The Railway Age* dated October 14, 1887, states that 23 miles of rails have been laid and that road is intended to carry coal.

The track from Sedro to Sumas seems to have been finished about April, 1891, but not operated until March 15, 1892. A published timetable dated April 3, 1892, shows operation to Sumas. There is also discrepancy regarding building and opening dates to Sallal Prairie. Other than the extreme south and north ends, the dates coincide quite well.

WASHINGTON 267.

Three used passenger cars arrived in Seattle on September 12, 1887, from Philadelphia, Wilmington & Baltimore Railroad.

A note from *The Pullman Herald* for Nov. 24, 1888, states that the first train operated from Spokane on November 17 for ten miles.

The editorial comments from *Official Guide* helps complete the picture on a month to month basis.

May, 1888	Opened from Seattle to Gilman, 42 miles
January, 1889	Gilman to Raging River, 9.5 miles, placed in operation.
March, 1890	Snohomish north to Blackmans, 6 miles, is now in use.
June, 1890	Opened South Bend to Sallal Prairie, 3.2 miles.
August, 1890	Now operating Spokane Falls to Davenport, 50 miles, and Blackmans to Arlington, 16 miles.
December, 1890	Has been extended from Arlington to Sedro Junction, 26 miles.
June, 1891	Opened from Sedro to Sumas, 40 miles.
October, 1891	Sedro Junction is now Woolley.
May, 1892	The carrier is now being operated as a portion of Northern Pacific.

Listed in first ICC (6/30/88) as an operating independent with 55 miles owned and in use. It was extended to 67 miles each by 6/30/89 and to 156 miles by 6/30/90. By 6/30/91 it was an operating subsidiary of Northern Pacific Railroad Co. with 227 miles owned and operated. The "owned" remained at 227 miles through 6/30/96, but the "operated" dropped to 177 miles by 6/30/94 and remained there until it was reorganized in 1896.

The company was placed in receivership June 26, 1893, and sold as a foreclosure on May 16, 1896. The 50-mile Spokane Falls portion was conveyed to Spokane & Seattle Railway Co. by deed dated July 28, 1896. The balance (and major part) went to Seattle & International Railway Co., also by deed dated July 28.

Bibliography: *Poor's 1895*, p. 291   Snohomish City - *The Eye* - March 5 to 26, 1887   *Valuation 25*, p. 492
Seattle - *The Daily Press* - September 21 and October 24, 1887

SEATTLE, PORT ANGELES & WESTERN RAILWAY COMPANY

						President	
Incorp:	1/20/1915	**Operated:**	(4/10/16) to 12/31/18		**HQ city:**	Port Angeles	

Disposition: sold to Chicago, Milwaukee & St. Paul Railway Company on December 31, 1918

Predecessors:	Seattle, Port Angeles & Lake Crescent Railway	**Renamed:** 12/31/1911 to 1/25/1915
	Port Ludlow, Port Angeles & Lake Crescent Railway	**Incorp.:** 11/27/1911 12/19/1911

Miles track: 71.551   **Gauge:** 56½"

Main line: Discovery Junction to Majestic

Rail wt.:   **Max. grade:**   **Const. began:** grading   August 18, 1914
                                                         laying rails (November 2, 1914)

Const. comp.: (March 29, 1918)   **First train operated:** (November 23, 1914)

Freight traffic: common carrier, lumber

Notes from *Railway Age Gazette*:
August 21, 1914   Seattle, Port Angeles & Lake Crescent has 27 miles under construction from Port Angeles west.
June 4, 1915   Seattle, Port Angeles & Western has been opened from Port Angeles to the west for 26 miles.

Official construction details are brief.

Port Angeles to Majestic	23.60	miles	1914 to	January, 1915
Discovery Junction to Port Angeles	38.20		1915	May, 1916
Majestic to three miles beyond Twin Rivers	6.77		1916	1918

In the October 24, 1913, issue of Port Angeles *Tribune-Times* is a photograph showing a long shot of a completed grade with ties in place over at least a portion of the 25-mile section total; at least five miles of this sum was to the west of Port Angeles. No mention is made of the railroad involved, but likely Chicago, Milwaukee & St. Paul Railway Co.

The carrier owned only four pieces of work equipment; all common carrier rolling stock was provided by the parent company. The westernmost end of the line appears to have been called Earles at milepost 74.70 - as shown in June, 1916, *Official Guide*.

First listed in ICC for 6/30/16 as an operating subsidiary of Chicago, Milwaukee & St. Paul Railway Co. with 62 miles owned and in use. This class II then remained unchanged until its sale and merger in 1918.

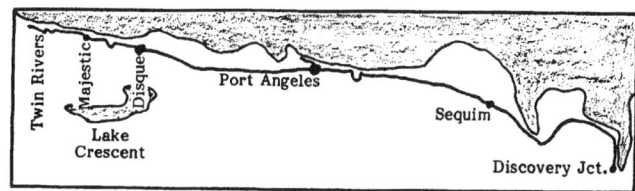

Bibliography: *Poor's 1918*, p. 195   *Port Townsend Weekly Leader* - July 30 to November 26, 1914   *Valuation 44*, p. 751
Port Angeles Olympic Leader - September 18 to December 4, 1914
Port Angeles - *Tribune-Times* - August 7 to December 18, 1914

SHELTON, MASON COUNTY, W. T. FRIDAY, MAY 24, 1889.

Mason County Central Railroad Co.s'
NEW SAWMILL.

—— MANUFACTURERS OF ——

FIR and CEDAR Lumber of All Grades,
SHINGLES, PICKETS ETC.

FLOORING and RUSTICS a Specialty

Dimension lumber and building materials cut on short notice at Reasonable Rates.   Office at Sawmill,

M. LEWIS, Manager.   - -   Front St., Shelton, W. T.

Special Collections Div. - Univ. of Washington Libraries
Mason County Central Railroad Company number nine with a load of logs bound for Shelton about 1890

SHELTON SOUTHWESTERN RAILWAY COMPANY, THE

John Snyder, **President**

Incorp:	4/27/1898	**Operated:**	5/1/98 to (1902)		**HQ city:**	Shelton
Disposition:	abandoned by June 30, 1905					
Predecessors:	Shelton Southwestern Railroad Company			**Renamed:**	7/27/1891 to	4/30/1898
	Mason County Central Railroad Company			**Incorp.:**	7/25/1889	7/27/1891
Miles track:	20	**Gauge:**	56½"			
Main line:	Shelton to Summit					
Rail wt.:	40 lbs.	**Max. grade:**	2.0%	**Const. began:**	grading	(August 5, 1889)
					laying rails	(Sept. 2, 1889)
Const. comp.:	1900			**First train operated:**		1890

Locomotives:

Road No.	Cyln.	Type	Dvr. in.	Bldr.	Bldr. No.	Date	Weight	Effort	Remarks
2		2-6-0	52	Cooke	1193	/81	112,000		ex Cincin, N.O. & T.P. #554
4 ?		2-4-2T	42	BLW	7669	8/85	62,000		Skookum; acquired 3/1898
6*	15x24	2-6-0	50	'	13675	8/93			probably diverted
9		4-4-0		'					Bertha

Freight traffic: common carrier, logging

Roster of 6/30/1895:
    2   locomotives
   30   logging cars

Construction notes from *The Railway Age*:
    February 1, 1890   About 100 men are building a six-mile extension; Allen C. Mason is the owner.
    October 30, 1891   Now eight miles out from Shelton into the timber; to add ten miles to Northern Pacific at Kamalchie.
    November 27, 1891   Will build to Summit next spring.

Poor's 1897, p. 266, gives the succession date as September 1, 1892.

Mason County Central Railroad Co. was first listed in ICC for 6/30/91 as an operating independent with 6.5 miles owned and in use; the track was laid with 30-pound rail. It was reorganized as Shelton Southwestern Railroad Co. on July 27, 1891.

Shelton Southwestern Railroad Co. was first shown for 6/30/92 as an operating independent with six miles owned and in use; it was extended to 12 miles each by 6/30/93. The carrier was placed in receivership on April 1, 1894. Mileage was increased to 20 by 6/30/00 and then unchanged through 6/30/02. By 6/30/03 it was ten miles owned, not in use. By 6/30/04 it had been reduced to three miles and inactive.

Cost of road and equipment to April 1, 1891, (with 6.5 miles of track) was placed at $57,140.32. There were net earnings of $4,949.30 in that fiscal year.

Bibliography: *Poor's 1891*, p. 764   Shelton - *The Mason County Journal* - May 17, 1889 to February 7, 1890

SIMPSON TIMBER COMPANY

Thomas F. Gleed, **President**

Renamed:	4/10/1956	**Operated:**	4/10/56 to		**HQ city:**	Shelton
Disposition:	in operation 1993					
Predecessors:	Simpson Logging Company			**Incorp.:**	6/27/1895 to	4/10/1956
	Peninsular Railway Company				6/12/1895	2/21/1936
	Washington Southern Railway Company				3/1/1891	6/12/1895
	Seattle Lumber Company				5/17/1884	2/28/1891
	Satsop Rail Road Company				11/30/1883	2/18/1891
Miles track:	49	**Gauge:**	56½"			
Main line:	Shelton to Gordonville					
Rail wt.:	40/60 lbs.	**Max. grade:**	3.0%	**Const. began:**	grading	(Sept. 15, 1884)
					laying rails	(April 13, 1885)
Const. comp.:	1893			**First train operated:**		1885

Locomotives:

Road No.	Cyln.	Type	Dvr. in.	Bldr.	Bldr. No.	Date	Weight	Effort	First owner and remarks
1*	9½x14	0-4-2T	33	Porter	681	6/85			Satsop; C. F. White preserved
1-2d*		0-4-4-0		Simpson	1	/97			flat car with engine and boiler
1-3d		2 truck		Climax	239	12/00	70,000	15,400	
2*	14x20	2-6-0		Porter	802	1/87			Satsop; Agnes
2-2d*	12x14	2 truck		Climax	189	6/99	70,000	15,400	Simpson
2-3d*	12x12	2T Shay	36	Lima	2587	8/12	120,000	23,850	Simpson
2-4th*	16x22	2-8-2T	41	BLW	53146	4/20	124,500	21,100	Simpson; to Fredson Bros.
3*	15x24	4-6-0	54	'	10657	2/90			Satsop; William Shorter
3-2d*	11x14	2 truck		Climax	200	/99	70,000	15,400	Simpson; Irene
3-3d*	20½x28	2-8-2	48	BLW	60838	5/29	186,000	35,400	Peninsular; William Shorter
4*		0-4-4-0		Penins.	2	/99			a flat car with engine and boiler
4-2d*		2 truck	33	Climax	1279	2/14	90,000	19,800	Peninsular; sold in 1918
4-3d*	16x16	3 truck	36	'	1589	11/21	160,000	35,200	Simpson; 1937 to Weyerhaeuser
5		2 truck	'	Heisler	1003	8/96	60,000		Tollie
5-2d		4-6-0		BLW					to Mason County Logging Co.
5-3d*	19x24	2-8-2	44	'	42639	11/15	149,000	30,100	Peninsular; scrapped in 1950
6*		0-4-4-0		Penins.	1	/98			a flat car with engine and boiler
6-2d*	16x24	2-6-2	46	BLW	27312	1/06	100,000	18,100	Simpson; to Kern & Kibbe
7*	'	4-6-0	'	'	30606	4/07	98,200		Simpson; Sol Simpson
7-2d*	15¼x16	3 truck	36	Climax	1371	11/15	160,000	35,200	Simpson; to Wallace Lumber Co.
7-3d		3T Shay	'	Lima	3248	1/24	195,300	38,200	Ed Elliott
8*	20½x28	2-8-2	48	BLW	35036	8/10	173,000	33,350	Peninsular; E. Frank Brown
9*	18x24	'	44	'	35079	'	132,400	24,100	Peninsular; Benjamin Snider
10*	11x12	2T Shay	32	Lima	2622	2/13	100,000	22,580	Simpson; to Fredson Bros.
10-2d*	12½x15	3 truck	36	Willam.	33	10/28	149,100	39,300	Simpson; 1949 to Ozette Timber Co.
11*	20½x28	2-8-2	48	BLW	44224	10/16	179,100	32,350	Peninsular; Frank Wandell
12*	19x24	2-8-2T	42	'	56634	6/23	180,000	32,500	Simpson; Wm. E. Parker
13*	18/28x24	2-6-6-2T	44	'	59173	5/26	234,100	42,500	Simpson; Sophus Jacobson
20		B-B		ALCO	78412	10/50		1000 h.p.	acq. 1956; City of Montesano
60		'		Whitcm.	60660	11/46	130,000	550 h.p.	acq. 1958; Lee Wills
900*		'		EMD	20609	5/55	230,000	900 h.p.	Simpson; City of Elma
1070		0-6-0	51	Manch.	41879	/07	149,000	31,000	acq. 4/1958 ex N. Pacific #1070
1200*		B-B		EMD	20634	4/56	247,300	1200 h.p.	Simpson; City of Shelton
1201*		'		'	20635	5/56	248,300	'	Simpson; City of McCleary
1202		'		'	25046	3/59	245,700	'	acq. 1948; City of Montesano

A locomotive list is at best art and guess; few of us today have any personal knowledge of what happened and when. In the case of the present subject, the era of steam lasted from 1885 to 1985 and involved overlaps between Peninsular and Simpson. In the case of large common carriers, #1 was purchased, it wore out and may have been replaced with #1-2d. Loggers frequently kept the number found on the acquired engine. As a result of all of these variables, the early road numbers assigned above are in most cases guesswork and little else.

Freight traffic: common carrier, logging

Rosters of 6/30/1889 - 6/30/1913:

locomotives	3	6
freight cars	90	203

First published timetable:

February, 1892

7:00 a.m.	Shelton		5:50	
	Summit	6		
	Nahwatzel	16		
	Windsor	23		
8:50	Satsop	30	4:00 p.m.	

J. R. McDonald was the president.

November, 1893
as above plus
  11:30 a.m. Gordonville, 60 miles

Published timetable dated:

November, 1895

7:00 a.m.	Shelton	
8:50	Satsop	30
9:25	Pierce	37
10:00	Shiller	42
10:45	Anderson	50
11:40	Gordonville	60

A. H. Anderson was the president.

It appears that Shelton was located on Big Skookum Bay and that Satsop owned five miles of track on December 31, 1886.

Satsop Rail Road Co. was listed in first ICC (6/30/88) as an operating independent with 19 miles owned and in use; the carrier was owned by Anderson, Healy and McDonald. It was extended to 24 miles by 6/30/89.

Washington Southern Railway Co. was first included 6/30/91 with 20 miles owned and operated. It was reduced to 17 miles by 6/30/93 and then increased to 30 miles by 6/30/94; the same in 1895.

Peninsular Railway Co.

	owned:	operated:	owned:
6/30/1896	36	36	by
6/30/1897	25	25	Simpson
6/30/1899	15	15	Railroad,
6/30/1903	30	30	a
6/30/1904	26	26	subsidiary
6/30/1906	26	34	8
6/30/1909	18	30	12
6/30/1913	21	31	10
12/31/1926	16	42	26
12/31/1929	16	52	38

And then unchanged until merger in 1936.

Simpson Railroad Co. was first listed in ICC for 12/31/36 as an independent with 49 miles owned and operated. It was revised to 48 miles in 1937 and then unchanged until declared "not a common carrier" in 1948 and removed from these data.

The map to the right is not spectacular, but it is a copy - the original is in the National Archives - of the survey chart for work done between June 14 and September 13, 1886; the surveyor was F. H. Whitworth. It was drawn to be submitted to the Department of the Interior to obtain right-of-way through public lands for a distance of 13 18/00 miles under act of March 3, 1875. The application was signed by Isaac Dobson, president of Satsop Rail Road Co. and approved by the federal agency on January 25, 1887. The company also petitioned for 19 88/00 acres for station, engine house and yard tracks at the lake.

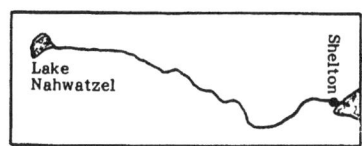

The maps below are a text book example of the difficulty of presenting a true and meaningful map of a logging railroad. We have here three versions of what are presumed to be true maps of the same thing, but they look very different. The first map below, 1890, shows "Satsop" in three different locations; the one at the bottom is the site of the present town of that name. There are three branches of the Satsop River, so we may assume that the other "Satsops" refer to river crossings.

The second map was from Northern Pacific Railway Co. land department dated 1897. May we assume that the names mentioned with various sections of track refer to joint operating agreements? The third was designated as Peninsular Railway Co. by Geo. F. Cram and dated 1899. Logging roads are poorly documented, but this operation was truly a special puzzle.

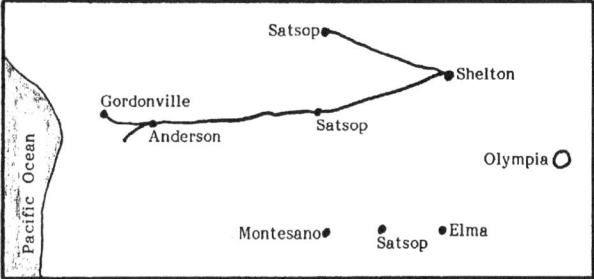

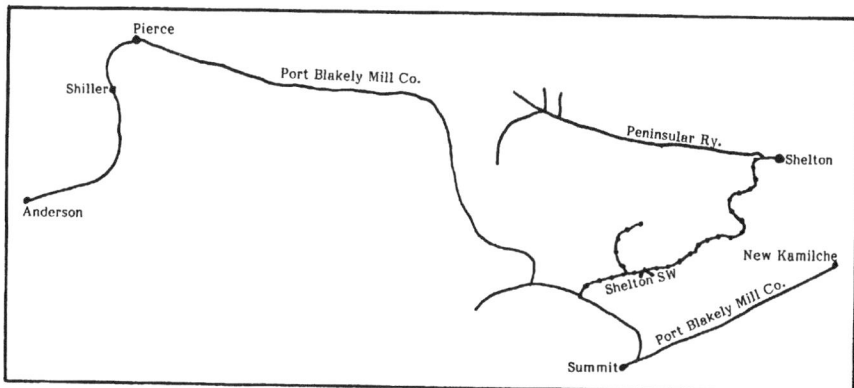

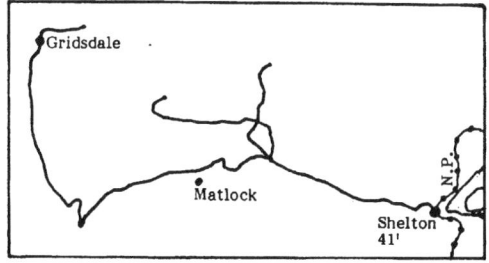

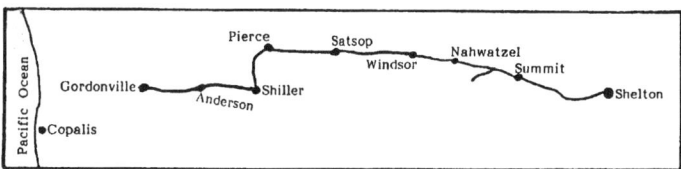

In 1938, the carrier operated over a 400-foot high steel trestle; it was a record height at the time.

The map above on the left is the present configuaration of the track; it is 31 miles long.

Bibliography: *Poor's 1890*, p. 1176   Olympia - *Washington Standard* - July 17, 1885   *Logging to the Salt Chuck*

SATSOP

RAILROAD COMPANY'S STORE

GENERAL MERCHANDISE,

WHOLESALE AND RETAIL.

OUR : IMMENSE : STOCK

Complete in Every Department, is Being

Sold Cheaper Than Ever!

From a Complete Logging Camp. Outfit to a Needle. Anythlg Can be Found in Our Store.

Groceries, Hard and Tinware, Glassware, Crockery, Logging Camp Supplies. Our stock of Flannels, Prints, Hosiery, Boots, Shoes and Gents' Clothing and Furnishing Goods is Complete. Patent Medicines, Candies, Notions, Etc.

CALL AND BE CONVINCED

SATSOP RAILROAD COMPANY,
SHELTON, WASHINGTON TERRITORY.

The Mason County Journal - Friday, May 24, 1889

For a needle or a logging camp ....

WASHINGTON   273.

SNAKE RIVER VALLEY RAILROAD COMPANY, THE   Henry Failing, **President**

Incorp: 3/3/1898   **Operated:** 12/1/99 to 12/23/10   **HQ city:** Portland

Disposition: sold to Oregon-Washington Railroad & Navigation Company on December 23, 1910

Miles track: 65.85   **Gauge:** 56½"

Main line: Wallula to Grange City

Rail wt.:   **Max. grade:**   **Const. began:** grading   (March 13, 1899)
                                                                        laying rails   (August 7, 1899)

Const. comp.: (December 31, 1899)   **First train operated:**   1899

Locomotives:

Road No.	Cyln.	Type	Dvr. in.	Bldr.	Bldr. No.	Date	Weight	Effort	Remarks
200-202		2-8-0	55	Brooks	3075-77	11/98	148,900	33,747	to O.-W.R.&M. #327-29
356-359*	22x30	'	57	BLW	27205-08	1/06	189,970	43,305	to O.-W.R.&N. #356-59
360-363*	'	'	'	'	27237-40	'	189,700	'	to O.-W.R.&N. #360-63

Freight traffic: common carrier, agriculture

First published timetable:
December 1, 1899
11:20 p.m.   Wallula
1:10 a.m.   Grange City

Construction notes from *The Railway Age:*

March 17, 1899	Grading is in progress; W. W. Cotton is president.
June 9, 1899	To begin track laying in early July.
August 18, 1899	Eighteen miles of track has been laid.
November 3, 1899	On October 25, 1899, only ten more miles of rails to be laid to completion.

First listed in ICC for 6/30/00 as a non-operating subsidiary of Oregon Railroad & Navigation Co. with 66 miles owned. The carrier was leased to the owner on July 1, 1907.

Bibliography: *Poor's 1910*, p. 1273   *The Walla Walla Statesman* - November 18, 1899   *Valuation 44, p. 292*
                The Spokesman-Review - March 1 to September 9, 1899   *The Walla Walla Watchman* - November 18, 1899

Wyoming State Museum
Peninsular Railway Co. #3, the William Shorter, was photographed in April, 1922, at Shelton.

SNOHOMISH LOGGING COMPANY   President

Incorp:	4/25/1900			**Operated:**	1901	to	1919	**HQ city:**	Snohomish
Disposition:	abandoned – corporation dissolved July 1, 1929								
Miles track:	15			**Gauge:**	56½"				
Main line:	Snohomish into the forest								

Locomotives:

Road No.	Cyln.	Type	Dvr. in.	Bldr.	Bldr. No.	Date	Weight	Effort	Remarks
1 ?		2T Shay	28	Lima	242	6/89	56,000	13,180	acq. 3d hand; scrapped 4/1926
3*	10x12	'	29½	'	1655	2/06	74,000	16,900	sold in 1923
4*	'	'	'	'	1918	6/07	'	'	sold in October, 1923
5*	'	'	'	'	2301	4/10	84,000	'	sold into British Columbia
5-2d*	15½x14	2 truck	38	Heisler	1334	5/16	104,000		to Miller Logging Co. #4
6*	15x12	'	36	'	1354	9/17	94,000		to McMillian Lumber Co. #47

Freight traffic: logging

Roster of 6/30/1910:
- 4 geared engines
- 37 logging trucks
- 11 miles of track

SNOQUALMIE FALLS LUMBER COMPANY   President

Incorp:				**Operated:**	1916	to	1942	**HQ city:**	Snoqualmie
Disposition:	abandoned								
Miles track:	100			**Gauge:**	56½"				
Main line:	Snoqualmie into the forest								
Rail wt.:				**Max. grade:**	5.0%		**Const. began:**	grading	1916

Locomotives:

Road No.	Cyln.	Type	Dvr. in.	Bldr.	Bldr. No.	Date	Weight	Effort	Remarks
1*	18x24	2-8-2	44	BLW	44058	8/16			scrapped
2*	'	'	'	'	44276	10/16			scrapped
3*	12x14	2 truck	33	Climax	1331	8/16	90,000	19,800	scrapped
4*	11x12	2T Shay	32	Lima	2969	3/18	124,000	25,830	scrapped in August, 1941
5*	19x24	2-8-2	44	BLW	52235	8/19	149,000		scrapped
5-2d*	'	'	'	'	55325	4/22			
6*	18x24	2-6-2T	'	'	56323	3/23			to Weyerhaeuser Timber Co. #6

Freight traffic: logging

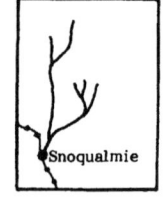

SOUNDVIEW PULP COMPANY   President

Incorp:				**Operated:**	1937	to	1951	**HQ city:**	Hamilton
Disposition:	abandoned								
Predecessor:	Lyman Timber Company		(25 miles in 1930)				**from:**	1903	**to** 1945
Miles track:	6			**Gauge:**	56½"				
Main line:	Hamilton into the woods								
Rail wt.:	56 lbs.			**Max. grade:**	6.0%		**Const. began:**	grading	1903

Locomotives:

1		2T Shay	36	Lima	2107	8/08	100,000	20,350	acq. 3d hand; sold August, 1942
2*	12x12	'	32	'	780	7/03	130,000	17,900	sold to dealer about Feb., 1921
3*	'	'	36	'	1881	5/07	100,000	23,850	to Soundview #2; scrapped 1936
4		'	'	'	2618	11/12	120,000	23,900	acq. 2d hand; to Soundview #4
5*	13½x15	3T Shay	'	'	3143	11/20	160,000	35,100	1945 to Soundview #5
6		'	'	'	3038	10/19	180,000	40,400	acq. 5/1930; to Soundview #4
7		2T Shay	'	'	2574	7/12	120,000	23,900	acq. 2d hand; to Soundview #3

Freight traffic: logging

Roster of 6/30/1910:
- 1 geared engine
- 1 rod engine
- 24 logging trucks
- 6 miles of track

SPOKANE & BRITISH COLUMBIA RAILWAY COMPANY

W. T. Beck, President

Incorp:	4/1/1905	**Operated:** 4/1/05 to 9/27/19		**HQ city:**	Republic
Disposition:	abandoned in 1921				
Predecessor:	Republic & Kettle River Railway Company		**Incorp.:**	8/28/1900 to 3/31/1905	
Miles track:	36.401	**Gauge:** 56½"			
Main line:	Danville to Republic				
Rail wt.:	56 lbs.	**Max. grade:**	**Const. began:**	grading (September 16, 1901)	
				laying rails (January 13, 1902)	
Const. comp.:	May 1, 1903		**First train operated:**	February 8, 1902	

Locomotives:

Road
No.
1
2
3

Freight traffic: common carrier, mine and lumber

Roster of 12/31/1917:
- 3 locomotives
- 2 passenger cars
- 16 freight cars

Published timetable dated:
November 1, 1915 - Tues. - Fri.
8:00 a.m.	Danville	
8:35	Curlew	m.p. 10
9:17	Karamin	20
19:00	Summit	28
10:30	Republic	35

Connected with Great Northern

It is interesting to note that the Washington & Great Northern Railway Co. built from Danville to Republic in 1902. The subject built an adjacent line, but made a physical connection only at Republic.

The carrier operated over an affiliate, Kettle Valley Railway Co. from Danville to Grand Forks, B. C., four miles, and to Lynch Creek, an additional 18 miles.

Construction notes from *Railroad Gazette:*
August 30, 1901	Construction contracts have been let.
February 21, 1902	Track has been laid to Curlew.
January 3, 1903	Danville to Republic opened for traffic.

Republic & Kettle River Railway Co. was first listed in ICC for 6/30/02 as an operating independent with 36 miles owned, not in use. By 6/30/03 it was 36 miles each. The company was reorganized and renamed in 1905, still a 36-mile independent. The "operated" increased to 58 miles by 6/30/08, then back to 36 in 1909. There were no further changes in this class III carrier through 12/31/1919. It was not operated in 1920 and abandoned the next year.

The cost of construction was $718,747 with rolling stock an additional $43,190. Early records were destroyed in August, 1908, when the depot at Grand Forks burned. For the period of March 1, 1909, until June 30, 1915, its revenues were $122,956 and expenses of $292,461. When taxes and interest were added, the deficit was $745,396.

Bibliography: *Poor's 1920*, p. 1307   Spokane - *Twice-A-Week Spokesman=Review* - January 27 to July 14, 1902   *Valuation 108*, p 210

SPOKANE & PALOUSE RAILWAY COMPANY A. M. Canton, President

Renamed:	3/1/1886	**Operated:** 11/1/86 to 2/21/99		**HQ city:** Spokane Falls
Disposition:	sold to Northern Pacific Railway Company on February 21, 1899			
Predecessor:	Eastern Washington Railway Company, The		**Incorp.:** 12/3/1885 to 3/1/1886	
Miles track:	149.80	**Gauge:** 56½"		
Main line:	Marshall to Genesee and Juliaetta			
Rail wt.:	56 lbs.	**Max. grade:**	**Const. began:** grading	April 9, 1886
			laying rails	(May 31, 1886)
Const. comp.:	(September 30, 1891)		**First train operated:**	October 1, 1886
Freight traffic:	common carrier, agriculture			

First published timetable:
   October 17, 1886 - mixed train
     2:20 p.m.   Spokane Falls
     3:20   Marshall   8.7 miles
     6:55   Belmont   51.7
   May 13, 1888
     operating to:
          Palouse   67.9
          Pullman   84.3
          Genesee   112.7
   December 7, 1890
     operating to:
          Moscow   94.5
   November 1, 1891
     operating to:
          Juliaetta   121.0

Dates that various sections were placed in operation:

Marshall to Belmont	42.96	miles	October 15, 1886
Belmont to Johnson	45.77		July 1, 1888
Johnson to Genesee	15.70		July 1, 1888
Junction to Farmington	6.09		December 10, 1890
Pullman to Juliaetta	40.55		September 15, 1891
Juliaetta to Lewiston	21.11		October 1, 1898

(The last named section was completed by Northern Pacific.)

Construction notes from *The Railway Age:*
April 13, 1888	The track is now laid to Genesee, Idaho Territory.
December 28, 1888	During 1888, 15.6 miles of track was laid.

And from *Railroad Gazette:*
August 29, 1890	Track from Pullman to Lewiston, 72 miles, has been completed for about 20 miles; also a branch from Belmont easterly to Farmington, about five miles, is being built.
November 14, 1890	The head of track is now between Moscow and Kendrick.
December 12, 1890	The Farmington line is completed and ready for traffic.

From local newspapers it was found that head of track reached Palouse City on October 31, 1887, and to Pullman about November 27.

Listed in first ICC (6/30/88) as a non-operating subsidiary of Northern Pacific Railroad Co. with 44 miles owned; it had been leased to N. P. on May 1, 1886, possibly the date that the first rail was laid. It was 104 miles by 6/30/89, 111 by 6/30/91, 149 by 6/30/92 and 153 by 6/30/93. It was then unchanged until merger into Northern Pacific Railway Co. on September 1, 1896, and its sale in 1899. The corporation was dissolved August 23, 1909.

Bibliography: *Poor's 1889*, p. 854   Spokane Falls - *The Morning Review* - April 10 to June 1, 1886   *Valuation 25*, p. 500
                   Walla Walla Weekly Union - November 12 and December 3, 1887

SPOKANE & SEATTLE RAILWAY COMPANY

John H. Bryant, **President**

Incorp:	6/30/1896	**Operated:**	7/28/96 to 10/3/00	**HQ city:**	Seattle

Disposition: sold to Northern Pacific Railway Company, part on March 17, 1899, and the balance October 3, 1900

Miles track: 50.05 **Gauge:** 56½"

Main line: Spokane to Davenport

Freight traffic: common carrier, agriculture

The track was constructed in 1888-1889 by Seattle, Lake Shore & Eastern Railway Co. The company was placed in receivership on June 26, 1893, and this eastern portion of its track was sold at foreclosure on May 16, 1896, to the subject carrier. The property was conveyed by deed dated July 28, 1896. The track had originally been intended to connect Spokane Falls with Seattle and thence into Canada.

The cost of construction was placed at $2,121,045, but the subject carrier must have purchased this stub-end track for a small fraction of that amount. Medical Lake to Davenport, 29.00 miles, was sold to Northern Pacific on March 17, 1899; Spokane to Medical Lake, 21.05 miles, was purchased October 3, 1900.

A Northern Pacific Railroad Co. schedule dated February 8, 1891, shows that this track is being operated as the "Spokane branch" with a round trip on Tuesday, Thursday and Saturday.

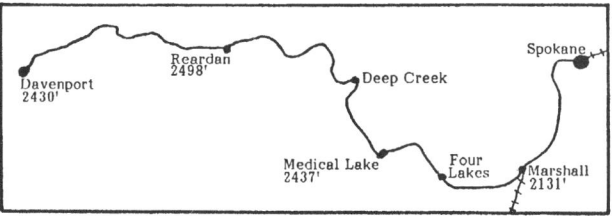

First listed in ICC for 6/30/97 as a non-operating subsidiary of Great Northern Railway Co. with 50 miles owned, but only 1.5 miles being operated (in Spokane) by Great Northern. By 6/30/98 it was 33 miles owned, 1.4 miles being used by Great Northern.

By 6/30/99 the subject was a non-operating subsidiary of Northern Pacific Railway Co. with 4.09 miles owned and 1.4 miles still being operated by Great Northern, around the Spokane depot, on a leased basis. It was shown to have been abandoned by 6/30/02 and the corporation dissolved on August 23, 1909.

Bibliography: *Poor's 1897, p. 266* Valuation 25, p. 492

Special Collections Div. - Univ. of Washington Libraries Clark Kinsey photo #1395
Goodyear Logging Company mess car at Clallam Bay decked out with Christmas bells

SPOKANE, COEUR D' ALENE & PALOUSE RAILWAY COMPANY

Jay P. Graves, President

Renamed: 12/11/1926 **Operated:** 11/26/26 to 4/30/34 **HQ city:** Spokane

Disposition: sold to Great Northern Railway Company on May 1, 1943

Predecessors:

		incorporated:	succession:
2.	Idaho Central Railway Company	9/15/1909	name changed to 1 on December 11, 1926
3.	Inland Empire Railroad Company	1/3/1920	sold to 1 on November 26, 1926
4.	Spokane & Eastern Railway & Power Company	1/3/1920	sold to 1 on November 26, 1926
5.	Spokane & Inland Railway Company		sold to 7 on December 31, 1906
6.	Spokane Interurban System	12/17/1904	name changed to 5 on January 10, 1905
7.	Spokane & Inland Empire Railroad Company		sold to 3 and 4 on November 1, 1919
8.	Inland Empire Railway Company	1/15/1906	name changed to 7 on November 7, 1906
9.	Coeur d'Alene & Spokane Railway Company, Ltd.	10/20/1902	sold to 7 on December 31, 1906

Miles track: 170.31 **Gauge:** 56½"

Main line: Spokane to Coeur d'Alene and Spokane to Moscow

Rail wt.: 70 lbs. **Max. grade:** **Const. began:** grading (June 24, 1905)

laying rails October 31, 1905

Const. comp.: September 15, 1908 **First train operated:** October 30, 1906

Locomotives:

Road No.	Type	Dvr. in.	Bldr.	Bldr. No.	Date	Weight	Effort	Remarks
2	4-6-0	63	BLW	23931	3/04	117,900	18,885	to Oregon Trunk #2
4	4-4-0	62	'	6972	10/83			ex Northern Pacific #739
500*	0-4-4-0E		'	27927	4/06	90,000	360 h.p.	new as S&IR #B-2; sold 1940
501*	'		'	31244	7/07	93,000	'	new as S&IE #501; sold 1940
502*	'	37	'	37513	2/12	101,400	600 h.p.	new as S&IE #502; sold 1940
503*	'		'	27735	3/06	103,900	500 h.p.	new as S&IR #A-1; sold 1940
603*	'		'	27823	'	100,000	600 h.p.	new as S&IR #B-1; SCR 1940
604*	'		'	27926	4/06	'	'	new as S&IR #A-2; SCR 1940
605*	'		'	27885	'	'	'	new as S&IR #C-1; SCR 1940
606*	'		'	27828	'	'	'	new as S&IR #C-2; SCR 1940
701*	'		'	31371	7/07	146,000	1,160 h.p.	new as S&IE #701; SCR 1940
702*	'		'	31372	'	'	'	new as S&IE #702; SCR 1940
703*	'		'	31435	'	'	'	new as S&IE #703; SCR 1940
704*	'		'	34397	3/10	'	'	new as S&EI #704; SCR 1940
706*	'		'	34398	'	'	'	new as S&IE #706

Major business: common carrier, agriculture and passengers

Roster of 6/30/1908:
- 6 locomotives
- 9 electric motors
- 24 passenger cars
- 461 freight cars

First published timetable:
November 8, 1906
- 7:30 a.m. Spokane
- 9:15 Waverly m.p. 34.0
- 6:30 a.m. Spokane
- 7:45 Coeur d'Alene 32.5

Published timetable dated:
June 1, 1907
- 7:00 a.m. Spokane
- Palouse 75.9
- 8:55 Rosalia 45.8

Published timetable dated:
October 7, 1907
- 8:05 a.m. Spokane
- 11:05 Colfax 76.7

Published timetable dated:
November, 1908
- 7:30 a.m. Spokane
- 11:00 Moscow 90.78

The track sections were as follows:

Coeur d'Alene to Spokane	32.41
Liberty Lake branch	2.21
Spokane to Moscow	90.78
Spring Valley to Colfax	36.71
Coeur d'Alene to Hayden Lake branch	8.20

The first operation listed above was for electrical traction to Waverly. Steam power was used for freight possibly in mid-July; official operation to Waverly began November 7, 1906.

Spokane & Inland Railway Co. was first listed in ICC for 6/30/06 as an independent with 33 miles owned, not in use. By 6/30/07, Spokane & Inland Empire Railroad Co. was shown with 123 miles owned and operated. It was 159 miles by 6/30/08, 175 miles in 1909 and 184 by 6/30/10. This class I carrier was declared to be an electric road by 6/30/12; as such, it was removed from these data. On January 1, 1942, it was reclassified from electric to steam and as such returned to these records as a class II operating subsidiary of Great Northern Railway Co. with 165 miles owned.

The subject carrier remained in *Official Guide*, "freight only", through January, 1970, but disappeared then with its merger into Burlington Northern Railroad Co.

A financial statement for Spokane & Inland Empire Railroad Co. dated June 30, 1908, shows that the cost of road and equipment was placed at $10,857,307.

Published timetable dated:
March 5, 1916

7:50	a.m.	Spokane	
8:35		Valleyford	16.8
9:09		Waverly	34.1
9:20		Spring Valley	40.1
9:52		Oakesdale	53.2
10:14		Garfield	65.0
10:35		Palouse	75.9
11:10		Moscow	90.4
9:37		Rosalia	45.8
9:56		Thornton	53.3
10:40		Colfax	76.7
6:35	a.m.	Coeur d'Alene	
6:53		Post Falls	8.5
7:14		Greenacres	19.1
7:50		Spokane	32.5
9:30	a.m.	Liberty Lake	
9:40		Greenacres	4.6
10:15		Spokane	16.8
9:15	a.m.	Hayden Lake	
9:35		Coeur d'Alene	8.2

There were three round trips daily from Spokane to Moscow and Colfax plus six round trips daily to Coeur d'Alene.

Construction notes from *The Railway Age*:
August 18, 1905	Grading is now in progress.
November 17, 1905	The grade is completed to Waverly.
December 15, 1905	Completed from Spokane to Freeman, 18 miles.
June 22, 1906	Will be opened to Waverly, 34 miles, in about two weeks.
November 23, 1906	It is now in operation to Waverly.

And from *Railroad Gazette*:
February 23, 1906	The line is graded to Waverly and 12 miles of track has been laid.
March 8, 1907	Has been opened from Waverly to Rosalia, 12 miles.
May 17, 1907	Extended from Spring Valley to Oakesdale, 13 miles.

Various operational notes from *Official Guide*:
July, 1907	Extended and opened Oakesdale south to Palouse, 22.7 miles.
September, 1907	Now from Rosalia south to Colfax, 30.9 miles.
October, 1908	It has been opened from Palouse to Moscow, 14.5 miles.

The Spokane to Coeur d'Alene track was acquired in 1906 from Coeur d'Alene & Spokane Railway Co., Ltd. Spokane & Inland Railway Co. built the seven miles to Moran and, judging from the 6/30/06 ICC report, to Waverly. At that point, Spokane & Inland Empire Railroad Co. made the great construction effort in 1907.

It is reported that Inland Empire Railroad Co. was organized to continue operations to Colfax and Moscow. And Spokane & Eastern Railway & Power Co. for the same purpose involving the Coeur d'Alene track. The Spokane & Inland Empire Railroad Co. was defunct and the operations were split up for seven years.

Bibliography: *Poor's 1909*, p. 1300 and *1922*, p. 514
The Spokesman=Review - June 23 to November 1, 1905 and October 16 to November 8, 1906

SPOKANE FALLS & NORTHERN RAILWAY COMPANY, THE Daniel C. Corbin, **President**

Incorp:	4/14/1888		Operated:	10/18/89 to 6/30/07		HQ city:	Spokane Falls
Disposition:	sold to Great Northern Railway Company on July 1, 1907						
Miles track:	140.60		Gauge:	56½"			
Main line:	Spokane Falls to British Columbia boundary						
Rail wt.:	56 lbs.		Max. grade:			Const. began:	grading (July 30, 1888)
							laying rails May 30, 1889
Const. comp.:	June 26, 1893					First train operated:	August 21, 1889

Locomotive engines:

Road No.	Cyln.	Type	Dvr. in.	Bldr.	Bldr. No.	Date	Weight	Effort	Remarks
1*	18x24	2-6-0	55	BLW	9968	4/89	77,000	16,820	to G.N. #478
2*	'	'	'	'	9972	5/89	'	'	to G.N. #479
3*	'	'	'	'	10036	6/89	'	'	to G.N. #480
4*	'	'	'	'	10037	'	'	'	to G.N. #477
5*	17x24	4-4-0	63	'	10833	4/90	52,000	13,100	to G.N. #142
6*	'	'	'	'	10830	'	'	'	to G.N. #141
7*	18x24	'	'	'	13803	10/93	56,100	14,690	to G.N. #231
8*	19x24	4-6-0	55	'	13807	'	85,000	20,090	to G.N. #948
9		2-8-0	47	'	15013	8/96	113,300	26,640	ex Col. & Red Mtn.; to G.N. #1094
10*	19x24	4-6-0	55	'	15059	9/96	85,000	20,090	to G.N. #949
11*	'	'	'	'	15248	3/97	93,850	22,760	to G.N. #970
12*	'	'	'	'	15249	'	'	'	to G.N. #971

Freight traffic: common carrier, lumber and mining

Rosters of	6/30/1891	– 6/30/1906:
locomotive engines	6	10
passenger cars	8	10
platform cars	125	115
other freight cars	55	88
rotary snow plow		1

First published timetable:
November 5, 1889
  8:40 a.m. Spokane Falls
  11:58 Summit m.p. 35
  4:55 p.m. Colville 88
additional schedules show advances
March 29, 1890
  Marcus 102
August 15, 1890
  Little Dalles 127
January 1, 1893
  Northport 131

Operations for year ending June 30, 1896:
  passenger earnings $130,807
  freight revenue 214,072
  other (mail, express) 13,921
  expenses 141,053
  net 217,747

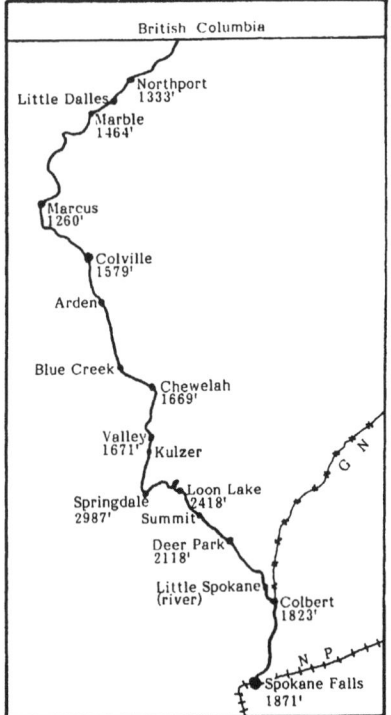

The construction record gives these opening dates:

Spokane Falls to Colville	October 18, 1889	88.10 miles
Colville to Little Dalles	1890	35.90
Little Dalles to Northport	December 31, 1892	6.40
Northport to Boundary	June 26, 1893	10.20
abandoned:		
Hillyard (Spokane) to Colbert	(1900)	10.06

The initial operation on August 21, 1889, was to Springdale.

The carrier was built unusually quickly - 48 miles to Springdale in less than three months and over a hundred miles in less than a year. And it also made a profit from an early date.

A timetable dated January 8, 1894, shows a mixed train being operated from Marcus to Kootenai, British Columbia, 96 miles. Operations in Canada were conducted by Nelson & Fort Sheppard Railway Co.

First listed in ICC for 6/30/90 as an operating independent with 102 miles owned and in use. It was extended to 127 miles each by 6/30/91 and to 141 by 6/30/94. The carrier was leased to Northern Pacific Railway Co. on July 1, 1898. It was listed 6/30/99 as an operating subsidiary of Great Northern Railway Co. with 141 miles owned. By 6/30/00 it was 132 miles owned and 141 operated. It was then reduced to 130 miles owned and 139 operated by 6/30/04.

Bibliography: *Poor's 1892*, p. 590   *Valuation 133*, p. 191 and 311

SPOKANE INTERNATIONAL RAILROAD COMPANY

Incorp:	4/1/1941	Operated: 10/1/41 to 12/31/87	HQ city:	Spokane
Disposition:	merged into Union Pacific Railroad Company on December 31, 1987			
Predecessor:	Spokane International Railway Company		Incorp.: 1/18/1905 to 9/30/1941	
Miles track:	139.889	Gauge: 56½"		
Main line:	Spokane to Eastport			
Rail wt.:	72/80 lb. steel	Max. grade: 1.0%	Const. began:	grading (July 3, 1905)
				laying rails (Dec. 4, 1905)
Const. comp.:	November 1, 1906		First train operated:	(November 1, 1906)

Locomotives:

Road No.	Cyln.	Type	Dvr. in.	Bldr.	Bldr. No.	Date	Weight	Effort	Remarks
1*	20x24	4-6-0	67	Rogers	42948	5/07	168,000	24,400	re# 101; retired in 1949
2*	19x24	'	'	'	42949	'	156,000	22,000	re# 102; retired about 1932
3*	'	'	'	'	43016	'	'	'	re# 103; wrecked 10/1/1949
4*	'	'	'	'	43017	'	'	'	re# 104; wrecked 7/28/1949
9		'	51	Pitts.		/88	100,000	17,500	acq. 1905; sold 1916
10		'	'	'		'	'	'	acq. 1905; sold 1913
11		2-6-0	50	BLW	9017	1/88	102,000	19,165	acq. 1905; sold 1923
12		'	'	'	9019	'	'	'	acq. 1905; sold 1920
21*	20x28	2-8-0	57	Rogers	40740	8/06	175,000	33,400	retired in 1949
22*	21x28	'	'	'	40741	'	191,000	36,800	re# 122; retired in 1949
23*	20x28	'	'	'	40742	'	175,000	33,400	scrapped in 1946
24*	21x28	'	'	'	41607	11/06	191,000	36,800	re# 124; retired in 1949
25*	20x28	'	'	'	41608	'	175,000	33,400	retired in 1949
26*	21x28	'	'	'	41609	'	191,000	36,800	re# 126; retired in 1949
51*	20x28	0-6-0	'	Cooke	48055	7/10	162,000	33,400	retired in 1949
52		'	51	Schen.	70417	11/42	158,000	40,000	acq. 6/1947; retired in 1949
907		2-8-0	57	Dickson	39806	/06	236,000	50,600	acq. 4/1943; scrapped 1947
908		'	'	Schen.	40546	/06	'	'	acq. 4/1943; scrapped 1947
916		'	'	'	40561	'	'	'	acq. 6/1943; scrapped 1947
936		'	'	'	40559	'	'	'	acq. 6/1943; scrapped 1947
1917		2-8-2	'	BLW	36395	4/11	270,400	47,945	acq. 3/1947; scrapped 1949
1936		'	'	'	38423	10/12	'	'	acq. 3/1947; scrapped 1949
2000		'	'	'	36362	4/11	'	'	acq. 6/1947; scrapped 1949
71-78*		B-B		Schen.	79594-601	/52		1,600 h.p.	diesels
200-202*		'		'	77166-168	9/49		1,000 h.p.	diesels
203-205*		'		'	77169-171	10/49		'	diesels
206-208*		'		'	77839-841	12/49		'	diesels
209-211*		'		'	79586-588	7/53		'	diesels

Freight traffic: common carrier, lumber and mining

Rosters of 6/30/1908 - 12/31/1917:

locomotives	14	14
passenger cars	6	9
freight cars	117	242

First published "timetable":
November, 1906
    C de'A Jct.
    Eastport   m.p. 120.0
for freight only

Published timetable dated:
July 1, 1907
3:30 p.m. Spokane
5:54 Sand Point 74.7
7:02 Bonners Ferry 109.6
8:20 Eastport 140.8
Also a 6:30 a.m. departure that made 19 stops and took 45 minutes longer to Eastport than the express.

Daniel C. Corbin was its first president and the construction contractor who built the track. The road cost $4,546,228 to build and equip. It had a modest 0.492% ruling grade.

For the year ending June 30, 1907 there was an operating loss of $301,126.

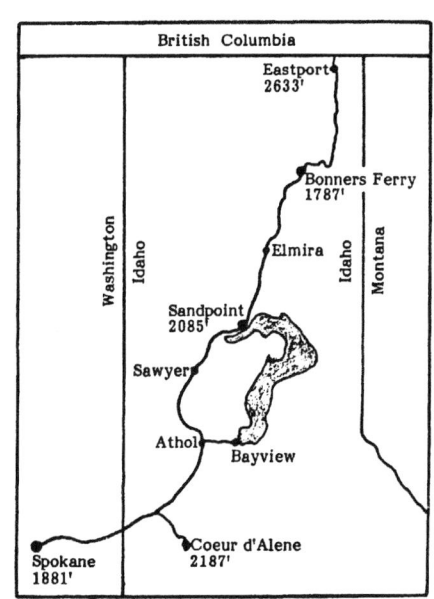

Construction notes from *The Railway Age*:
- October 6, 1905   About 1,200 men are at work on the grade.
- November 3, 1905   The maximum grade is 26 feet per mile; to use 72-pound rails.
- December 8, 1905   Rail laying has been commenced.

And from *Railroad Gazette*:
- July 28, 1905   Fifty miles of grade is ready for the rails.
- October 5, 1906   To be placed in operation for freight on October 25, 1906.
- June 14, 1907   Passenger service has been opened.

First listed in ICC for 6/30/06 as an operating independent with 30 miles owned; by 6/30/07 it was 141 miles owned and operated. On July 1, 1910, it leased the Coeur d'Alene & Pend Oreille Railway Co. and the "operated" figure became 163 miles. By 12/31/17 both carriers were a subsidiary of Canadian Pacific Railway Co.

This class I carrier became independent again in 1941 with 148 miles owned and 152 operated. By 12/31/58 it was an operating subsidiary of Union Pacific Railroad Co. In 1972, it was 148 miles owned and 150 operated.

Bibliography: *Poor's 1909*, p. 725   *The Spokesman=Review* - June 27 to December 7, 1905   *Valuation 110*, p. 173

Denver Public Library - Western History Department   #16141   Photo by Otto C. Perry
Spokane International #104 pulling Spokane Express on July 31, 1938, at Millwood - note the truss-rod coaches.

SPOKANE, PORTLAND & SEATTLE RAILWAY COMPANY

Francis B. Clarke, **President**

Renamed:	2/1/1908 **Operated:** 2/1/08 to 3/2/70	**HQ city:** Portland
Disposition:	consolidated into Burlington Northern Railroad Company on March 2, 1970	

Predecessors:

	Incorp./Renamed	From	To
United Railways Company (Oregon)	Incorp.:	1/17/1906	11/11/1944
Portland & Seattle Railway Company		8/23/1905	1/31/1908
Columbia River & Northern Railway Company		1/24/1902	3/30/1908
Astoria & Columbia River Railroad Company		4/3/1895	2/24/1911
Columbia Railway & Navigation Company, The	Renamed:	9/27/1890	7/14/1911
Farmers' Transportation Company		2/10/1890	9/27/1890
Farmers' Railway, Navigation & Steamboat Portage Company	Incorp.:	12/9/1885	2/10/1890

Miles track: 493.956   **Gauge:** 56½"
Main line: Spokane to Portland
Rail wt.: 56/85 lbs.   **Max. grade:** 0.80%   **Const. began:** grading   September 11, 1905
                                                                                                                laying rails   (Sept. 16, 1907)
Const. comp.: June 5, 1909 - main line   **First train operated:**   October 10, 1907

WASHINGTON

Freight traffic: common carrier, agriculture

Rosters of   6/30/1910 – 6/30/1916:

locomotives	46	70
passenger cars	30	115
freight cars	2	519
service cars	220	195

First published timetable:
December 15, 1907
7:00 a.m.   Pasco
2:30 p.m.   Cliffs   m.p. 111.9

Published timetable dated:
February 22, 1908
7:30 a.m.   Pasco
12:32 p.m.   Lyle   114.5
3:55   Vancouver   221.0

November 22, 1908
Pasco
Portland   230.8

May 3, 1909
Spokane
Pasco
Portland   377.5

The following operations dates are from *Official Guide*:

Pasco to Cliffs	111.8 miles	December 15, 1907
Cliffs to Lyle	33.6	January 15, 1908
Lyle to Vancouver	75.7	March 11, 1908
Vancouver to Portland	9.8	November 17, 1908
Pasco to Spokane	146.8	May 3, 1909

The Columbia Railway & Navigation Co. was first listed in ICC for 6/30/97 as a three-mile operating independent; this was unchanged through 1900. By 6/30/01 it was 12 miles owned and operated. From 1902 through 1906 it was "not operated." Edition for 1907 states "Reported to have been absorbed by Portland & Seattle Railway Company."

The Columbia Railway & Navigation Co. did some construction that resulted in its line in the vicinity of Wishram and Cliffs, but the "12 miles operated" is in doubt. According to *Valuation Reports*, this is what happened. "In the construction of its line eastward from Vancouver, the carrier acquired the uncompleted road of The Columbia Railway & Navigation Co., consisting of about nine miles of lightly constructed road on a located line of about 230 miles (note: the distance from Pasco to Portland). Such road was never operated by that company. Only parts of the nine miles of road were incorporated in the line of the carrier, and as these were entirely reconstructed, the mileage was considered as right of way acquired and is not included in the mileage of road purchased."

Portland & Seattle Railway Co. was first listed 6/30/07 in ICC as an operating independent with 68 miles owned, not in operation.

The subject carrier was listed 6/30/08 as an independent with 221 miles owned and in use. It was extended to 405 miles by 6/30/09 and 415 by 6/30/10. By 6/30/11 this class I line was an operating subsidiary of Northern Pacific Railway Co. (and also half owned by Great Northern Railway Co.) with 497 miles owned, 551 operated. In 1924, it was "independent" again with 495 miles owned and 555 operated.

By 12/31/1935 the mileages for Oregon Trunk Railway and United Railways Co. (both in Oregon) were added, the "owned" was then 850 miles and 947 miles operated. By 1950 it was 839 miles owned and 931 operated. In 1969 it was 813 miles owned, 922 in use. It was leased to Burlington-Northern Incorporated on March 2, 1970.

There were 22 tunnels through solid rock with an aggregate length of 16,663 feet, the longest being 2,476 feet. Ten were lined with concrete, five with timbers and seven left standing alone. Maximum curvature was 3° on the main line. The Columbia River bridge at Vancouver, 6,468 feet, and Willamette River bridge into Portland, 1,767 feet, were jointly owned by the carrier and Northern Pacific Railway Co.

The track sections:
    The main line, Spokane to Portland, was 377.5 miles.
    Oregon Trunk Railway, Fallbridge (Wishram), Washington, to Bend, Oregon, was 156.5 miles.
    The branch, Portland to beyond Seaside, added 119.1 miles,
    United Railways Co., Linnton to Wilkesboro, was 19.1 miles.

Oregon Electric Railway Co., with 141.8 miles from Portland to Eugene and Forest Grove, came under its control.

Locomotives:

Road No.	Type	Dvr. in.	Bldr.	Bldr. No.	Date	Weight	Effort	Remarks
1-5*	0-6-0	51	Manch.	2171-75	12/07	148,000	31,200	new as Portland & Seattle Ry.
6	'	49	BLW	8617	6/87	123,730	13,578	ex Astoria & Col. R. #1
7-8*	'	51	Schen.	54404-04	1/14	153,800	31,200	
50	4-4-0	63	'	2785	2/89	99,000	18,480	ex Columbia River & N. #2
51	'	62	Hinkley	1469	12/81	68,600	12,826	ex Columbia River & N. #1
52	'	54	Cooke	1731	9/86	64,000	13,540	ex Astoria & Co. R. #4
53-54	'	62	Rogers	3410-11	11/83	133,700	'	ex Astoria & Col. R. #6-7
55	'	69	Schen.	4644	12/97	176,900	17,227	ex Astoria & Col. R. #8
100-109	4-6-0	73	Schen.	35055/100	8/10	210,000	34,723	ex G.N. #1043-1052
150-151	'	'	BLW	36480-81	4/11	173,800	25,725	ex Astoria & Col. R. #150-151
152	'	69	Schen.	4710	2/98	155,600	25,623	ex N.P. #208 - SCR 5/1938
153-155	'	63	Cooke	2375-77	1/98	136,600	24,675	ex Astoria & Col. R. #16-18
156	'	'	BLW	23931	3/04	117,900	18,885	ex Spokane & Inland Empire #2
157	'	69	Schen.	4703	2/98	155,600	25,623	ex N.P. #251
158	'	'	'	4709	'	'	'	ex N.P. #257-SCR 5/1938
159	'	63	Rogers	5772	7/02	152,000	22,860	acq. 1921 ex Pacific & Eastern
160-161	'	73	BLW	34899-900	7/10	177,000	28,440	ex G.N. #1074-1075
162	'	'	'	34901	'	'	31,600	ex G.N. #1076
200	2-6-0	54	'	9546	10/88			ex N.P. #552-SCR 12/1928
201	'	55	Brooks	2371	8/93	119,000	18,760	ex G.N. #420

300	2-8-0	51	BLW	11949	6/91	159,900	33,800	ex N.P. #650
301	"	50	"	10445	11/89	"	"	ex N.P. #486
302	"	"	"	11948	9/91	"	"	ex N.P. #497
303-304	"	"	"	9506-07	9/88	150,000	"	ex N.P. #471-472
305	"	"	"	9515	"	159,900	"	ex N.P. #475-SCR 5/1937
315	"	"	"	9524	"	166,600	"	ex N.P. #480-SCR 5/1937
325	"	63	Schen.	5886	/01	198,000	36,700	ex N.P. #1255
326	"	"	"	5891	"	"	"	ex N.P. #1260
327-328	"	"	"	5882/92	"	"	"	ex N.P. #1251-1261
329	"	"	Richm.	25826	7/02	"	"	ex N.P. #1272
335-337	"	"	Schen.	27350/58	/03	197,000	39,200	ex N.P. #1283-1288-1291
338-339	"	"	"	27351/53	"	"	"	ex N.P. #1284-1286
350	"	55	Brooks	2107	7/92	136,000	23,210	ex G.N. #530
351	"	"	"	2116	"	"	"	ex G.N. #539
352	"	"	"	2154	8/92	"	"	ex G.N. #561
355-357	"	"	BLW	32392/478	12/07	195,000	41,540	ex G.N. #1256-1260-1261
358-360	"	"	"	32413/426	"	"	"	ex G.N. #1258-1259-1257
361-364	"	"	"	32391/485	"	"	"	ex G.N. #1262-1255-1264-1263
365	"	"	Rogers	38887	8/05	"	"	ex G.N. #1208
366	"	"	BLW	32191	11/07	"	"	ex G.N. #1228-SCR 1952
367-368	"	"	"	32243/362	"	"	"	ex G.N. #1240-1253-SCR 1955
370	"	51	Pitts.	29459	8/04	146,000	31,824	ex Astoria & Col. R. #19
450-453	2-6-2	69	BLW	30134/335	2/07	209,000	33,090	ex G.N. #1555-1565-1575-1577
454-456	"	"	"	30396/502	3/07	"	"	ex G.N. #1581-1583-1587
457	"	"	"	30568	4/07	"	"	ex G.N. #1593-SCR 5/1938
458	"	"	"	30999	6/07	"	"	ex G.N. #1638
459	"	"	"	30672	4/07	"	"	ex G.N. #1603-SCR 5/1937
460	"	"	"	30527	3/07	"	"	ex G.N. #1589-SCR 5/1937
461-464	"	"	"	30580/657	4/07	"	"	ex G.N. #1595-1597-1600-1601
465	"	"	"	30202	2/07	"	"	ex G.N. #1566-SCR 1948
466	"	"	"	28851	8/06	"	"	ex G.N. #1549-SCR 9/1948
500-502	2-8-2	63	"	39095/098	1/13	280,000	60,930	ex G.N. #3026-3028-3029
503	"	"	"	46163	8/17	"	"	ex G.N. #3099-SCR 8/1949
504-507	"	"	"	39092/157	1/13	"	"	ex G.N. #3039-3043-3023-3024
508	"	"	"	39297	2/13	"	"	ex G.N. #3064-SCR 8/1949
509-510	"	"	"	49158/226	7/18	"	"	ex G.N. #3121-3122
511	"	"	"	48468	4/18	"	"	ex G.N. #3108-SCR 11/1949
512	"	"	"	49731	9/18	"	"	ex G.N. #3134-SCR 11/1949
525	"	"	Schen.	46878	/10	265,000	50,600	ex N.P. #1698
530	"	"	Brooks	57957	/17	328,000	63,460	ex N.P. #1765
531-534	"	"	Brooks	52853/896	/13	320,000	"	ex N.P. #1704-1727-1744-1747
550-551	"	"	BLW	53793/835	10/20	319,700	64,310	ex G.N. #3211-3214
600-609*	4-4-2	73	"	33228/276	2-3/09	228,900	29,400	
620-626	4-6-2	"	G.N. Ry.		1927/29	283,400	38,580	
700-702*	4-8-4	"	BLW	62171-73	3/38	484,000	69,800	last BLW steam purchases
900-905*	4-6-6-4	69	Schen.	68990-95	5/37	621,000	104,270	
910-911*	"	"	"	71333-34	/44	"	"	last ALCO steam purchases
20*	B-B		BLW	62307	6/39		1,000 h.p.	first BLW diesel purchase
30-31*	"		"	62331-32	"		600 h.p.	
32*	"		"	64426	/42		1,000 h.p.	
33-34*	"		"	71539-40	11/45		"	last BLW diesel purchases
83	"		ALCO	80500	6/53	249,900	1,600 h.p.	acq. 4/1/1959 ex G.N. #231
84	"		"	80501	"	"	"	acq. 4/1/1959 ex G.N. #232

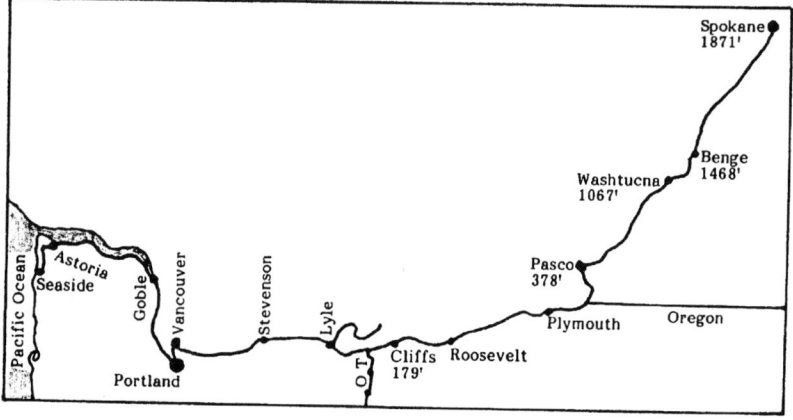

Bibliography: *Poor's 1910*, p. 1383 *Vancouver Columbian* - October 8 and 17, 1907 *Valuation 41*, p. 1
Walla Walla - *The Evening Statesman* - September 12, 1905 and September 27, 1907 *Pasco Express* - October 17, 1907

Denver Public Library - Western History Department   #16188   Photo by Otto C. Perry
Spokane, Portland & Seattle Railway Co. 4-8-4 #702 with 14-car train #1 at Wishram on July 28, 1940

Denver Public Library - Western History Department   #16169   Photo by Otto C. Perry
S., P. & S. #603, a 4-4-2 with 73-inch drivers, with passenger car on July 28, 1940, at Wishram

Denver Public Library - Western History Department   #16191   Photo by Otto C. Perry
S., P. & S. #902, a 4-6-6-4, is shown pulling 113 cars up river at Wishram on July 28, 1940 - and making little smoke.

STIMSON MILL COMPANY

								President
Incorp:		**Operated:**	1917	to	1926		**HQ city:**	Port Blakely
Disposition:	abandoned							
Predecessors:	Blakely Railroad Company					**Renamed:**	12/19/1896 to	1917
	Puget Sound & Grays Harbor Railroad & Transportation Company					**Incorp.:**	3/22/1886	12/18/1896
	Puget Sound & Grays Harbor Railroad Company						4/1/1886	(1893)
Miles track:	43	**Gauge:**	56½"					
Main line:	Kamilche to Montesano							
Rail wt.:	30/50 lbs.	**Max. grade:**		**Const. began:**	grading		(January 3, 1887)	

Locomotives:

Road No.	Cyln.	Type	Dvr. in.	Bldr.	Bldr. No.	Date	Weight	Effort	Remarks
4*	16x24	4-6-0	54	BLW	10149	7/89	76,000		new as Puget Sound & Grays H
5*	'	'	'	'	10151	'	'		new as Puget Sound & Grays H
5*		3 truck	36	Climax	1365	/16	160,000	35,200	new as Port Blakely Mill Co.
*	8x12	2T Shay	26½	Lima	838	2/04	56,000	14,950	new as Stimson Mill Co.
1-2d*	11x12	'	32	'	962	12/04	90,000	20,350	new as Port Blakely Mill Co.
7		2-4-2T		BLW					

Freight traffic: logging

Rosters of   6/30/1896 - 6/30/1910:
   locomotives   4   4
   passenger car 1
   logging cars   72   100
   freight cars   4   10

First? Published timetable:
Tacoma *Daily Ledger*
April 4, 1890
  7:00 a.m.   Kamilche   12:15 p.m.
  8:15   Elma   10:45
  9:00   Montesano   10:00 a.m.

Published timetable dated:
August 1, 1894
  9:00 a.m.   Kamilche
  9:28   Mountain   10 miles
  9:48   Summit   17
  10:00   Beck's Prairie   21
  10:24   Maple Grove   29
  10:48   Wright's   37
  11:00   Elma (with NP)   41
John A. Campbell, president

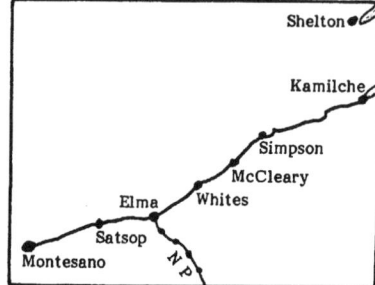

Puget Sound & Grays Harbor Railroad & Transportation Co. built from Montesano to Simpson, 20.80 miles, between about May 13, 1889, and September 13, 1890; this track was sold to The United Railroads of Washington on a date not yet determined.

Puget Sound & Grays Harbor Railroad Co. was listed in first ICC (6/30/88) as an operating independent with 12 miles owned and in use. It was extended to 20 miles by 6/30/89 and to 28 miles by 6/30/92. In the volume for 6/30/94 the "& Transportation Co." was added and the track was 24 miles.

Blakely Railroad Co. (owned by Port Blakely Mill Co.) was listed 6/30/97 as a 33-mile independent. It was increased to 38 miles by 6/30/99 and to 43 miles by 6/30/02. By 6/30/07 it was 30 miles, not in operation. By 6/30/08 it was 27 miles owned and in use, then gradually reduced to 15 miles by 12/31/16. The 1917 edition states "assigned to Stimson Mill Co. as logging equipment."

Bibliography: *Poor's 1897*, p. 845

STIMSON MILL COMPANY

								President
Incorp:	1/14/1890	**Operated:**	1891	to	1926		**HQ city:**	Seattle
Disposition:	abandoned - corporation dissolved November 23, 1962							
Subsidiary	Marysville & Northern Railway Company					**Incorp.:**	5/15/1905 to	1926
Miles track:	26.50	**Gauge:**	56½"					
Main line:	Marysville into the forest							
Rail wt.:		**Max. grade:**	6.0%	**Const. began:**	grading			1890

Locomotives:

Road No.	Cyln.	Type	Dvr. in.	Bldr.	Bldr. No.	Date	Weight	Effort	REmarks
1*	20x28	2-8-2	48	BLW	34563	4/10	171,700	32,800	new as M&M; to Newaukum Vy.
2*	15x16	3 truck	36	'	40664	9/13	150,000		one of BLW five "Shays"
17*	10x12	2T Shay	29½	Lima	1722	8/06	74,000	16,900	new as M&N; 1927 to dealer
20*	12x12	'	40	'	1829	5/07	110,000	21,575	new as M&N; 40" drivers?
242		'	28	'	242	6/89	56,000	13,180	to Campbell Bros. Lumber Co.
315*	10x11	'	29½	'	315	10/90		15,125	to Lincoln Creek Lumber Co.
659*?	10x12	'	'	'	659	6/01	64,000	11,250	to Regal Logging Co.
3?		3T Shay	36	'	2269	2/10	140,000	29,800	acq. 2d hand; to Brix Logging

Freight traffic: logging

Roster of 6/30/1910:
    (Marysville & Northern)
    3   geared engines
    8   flat cars
    130 logging trucks
    26½ miles of track

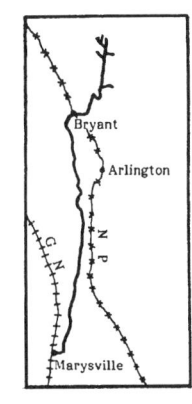

SULTAN RAILWAY & TIMBER COMPANY

					President
Incorp:	4/4/1903	**Operated:** 1903 to 1941		**HQ city:**	Sultan

Disposition: abandoned - corporation dissolved January 14, 1942

Purchased: Standard Railway & Timber Company   HQ at Hazel, 12 miles track   from: 1906 to 1913

Miles track: 20   **Gauge:** 56½"

Main line: Oso into the forest and also from Sultan

Rail wt.: 56 lbs.   **Max. grade:**   **Const. began:** grading   1903

Locomotives:

Road No.	Cyln.	Type	Dvr. in.	Bldr.	Bldr. No.	Date	Weight	Effort	REmarks
1*	11x12	2T Shay	32	Lima	803	7/03	90,000	18,750	to Puget Sound Mills & Tbr.
3*	12x15	3T Shay	36	'	2653	7/13	140,000	30,350	to Monroe Logging Co.
3-2d*	12x12	2T Shay	32	'	2945	2/18	120,000	23,890	sold into British Columbia
4*	14¼x15	3T Shay	36	'	3038	10/19	180,000	40,400	5/1930 to Lyman Timber Co.
5*	13½x15	'	'	'	3074	5/20	160,000	35,100	2/1940 to Monroe Logging Co.
21*	12x15	'	'	'	1810	1/07	130,000	29,825	to Sauk River Lumber Co.
		2T Shay	29½	'	2278	2/10	84,000	16,900	5/1922 to Lake Riley Lumber
(Standard Railway & Timber Co.)									
1*	16¼x14	2 truck	40	Heisler	1090	3/06	104,000		
2*	15x12	'	33	'	1122	2/07	74,000		to Sultan Ry. & Tbr. #2

Freight traffic: logging

Roster of 6/30/1910:
    (Sultan Ry. & Tbr. Co.)
    1   geared engine
    12   miles track at Sultan

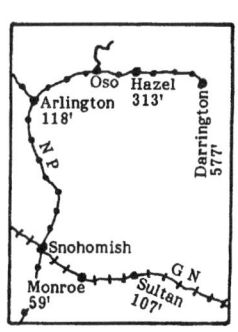

TACOMA & COLUMBIA RIVER RAILWAY COMPANY

						Wm. Bailey,	**President**
Incorp:	12/31/1895	Operated:	8/15/97	to	(1900)	**HQ city:**	Tacoma

Disposition: abandoned by June 30, 1901

Predecessor: Tacoma, Lake Park & Columbia River Railway Company   **Incorp.:** 4/4/1892 to 8/14/1897

Miles track: 18.50   **Gauge:** 56½"

Main line: Tacoma to Spanaway Park

Rail wt.: 56 lbs.   **Max. grade:**   **Const. began:** grading   1892

Locomotives:

Road
No.
1
2
3

Major business: common carrier, passengers

Roster of 4/1/1898:
- 3 locomotives
- 4 passenger cars
- 2 baggage cars

The predecessor company was first listed in ICC for 6/30/93 as an operating independent with 11 miles owned, not in use. It was placed in receivership on March 28, 1894, and was operating by 6/30/94. It continued to operate each year until reorganization in 1897.

First published timetable:
November, 1897
- 10:35 a.m. Tacoma
- 11:15 Lakeview 8.0
- 11:25 Parkland 11.0
- 11:35 Lake Park 13.4
- 11:40 terminus 15.5

The subject carrier was listed 6/30/98 with 10.4 miles owned and in use. It, too, was placed in recevership, April 4, 1899, but continued in business. By 6/30/00 it was operating eight miles, but was then abandoned.

Both corporations were dissolved August 23, 1909.

Construction notes from *Railroad Gazette:*
- April 15, 1892   Has purchased the ten-mile Tacoma and Lake Park line.
- March 3, 1893   To build from Center Street in Tacoma to Spanaway Lake.

And from *The Railway Age:*
- March 24, 1893   Twelve miles now in operation; to extend 140 miles more.

Bibliography: *Poor's 1895,* p. 302 and *1900,* p. 103

TACOMA & LAKE CITY RAILROAD & NAVIGATION COMPANY

						James D. Smith,	**President**
Incorp:	2/23/1889	Operated:	5/8/90	to	(1897)	**HQ city:**	Tacoma

Disposition: abandoned by June 30, 1897

Associate ? Portland & Puget Sound Railroad Company   **Incorp.:** 11/8/1889 to

Miles track: 11.10   **Gauge:** 42"

Main line: Tacoma (Union Avenue and 26th Street) to Lake City

Rail wt.:   **Max. grade:**   **Const. began:** grading (April 22, 1889)

                                                      laying rails   1890

Const. comp.: (June 30, 1890)   **First train operated:** May 8, 1890

Locomotive engine:

Road No.	Name	Type	Dvr. in.	Bldr.	Bldr. No.	Date	Weight	Effort	Remarks
1	Frank C. Ross	4-4-0	62	BLW	4927	1/80	58,300	10,900	ex Northern Pacific #316

Major business: common carrier, passengers

Roster of 6/30/1895:
- 1 locomotive
- 3 passenger cars
- 4 freight cars

First published timetable:
Tacoma Daily News
May 8, 1890
- 9:00 a.m. Tacoma
- Lake City 5:00 p.m.

fare: 30 cents each way.

It appears that Portland & Puget Sound Railroad Co. was an attempt by Union Pacific Railway Co. to develop real estate south of Tacoma without revealing the true buyer which would have advanced the asking prices for land.

Notes from *The Railway Age:*
    April 19, 1890   Now owns city tracks and a suburban line to American Lake.
    April 26, 1890   Expects to open on May first.

As the three passenger cars did not arrive until May 19, the May 8 "opening" must have been done with freight cars; with a 42-inch gauge, it could not borrow passenger cars from Northern Pacific.

The predecessor was first listed in ICC for 6/30/91 as an operating independent with 11 miles owned and in use. By 6/30/92 it was an operating subsidiary of Union Pacific Railway Co.; the same status in 1893 and 1894, except "not operating." The volume for 1895 changes the record - "No 11.1 miles road actually built; this track was really Tacoma & Lake City RR & N Co."

The subject carrier was listed 6/30/95 as an operating independent with 11 miles owned and in use; the same for 1896. The edition for 6/30/97 states "abandoned."

Bibliography: *Tacoma Daily News* - April 17, 1889 to March 20, 1890

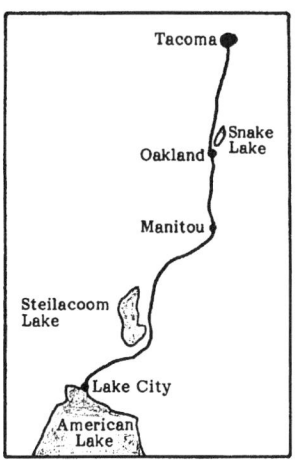

MORNING GLOBE, TACOMA, W. T., WEDNESDAY, MAY 1, 1889.

THE LAKE CITY LAND CO.

Will Offer for Sale on and after May 1, 1889, Lots in their Beautiful Surburban Townsite

LAKE CITY
—ON—
AMERICAN LAKE.

The Tacoma and Lake City Railroad and Navigation Company have placed on the Lake a

STEAMER AND FLEET OF ROW AND SAIL BOATS

And have Commenced Grading the Narrow Guage Railroad from Tacoma to the Lake.

It looks like there was more interest in real estate than railroading

TACOMA EASTERN RAILROAD COMPANY

Edward Cookingham, **President**

Incorp:	7/14/1890	**Operated:** 1/1/02 to 12/31/18	**HQ city:**	Tacoma
Disposition:	sold to Chicago, Milwaukee & St. Paul Railway Company on January 1, 1919			
Miles track:	96.621	**Gauge:** 56½"		
Main line:	Tacoma to Morton			
Rail wt.:	60/75 lb. steel	**Max. grade:**	**Const. began:** grading (October 6, 1890)	
			laying rails (April 6, 1891)	
Const. comp.:	(September 30, 1910)		**First train operated:** (April 11, 1891)	

Locomotives:

Road No.	Cyln.	Type	Dvr. in.	Bldr.	Bldr. No.	Date	Weight	Effort	Remarks
1		2-6-0	37	BLW	5034	3/80	48,000		acq. 3/1900 ex O.R.&N. #11
2		2-4-2T	44	'	9938	4/89			acq. (8/1900) ex Visalia & Tul.
3*	21x26	4-6-0	63	Cooke	2252	2/93	150,600	31,326	
4		4-4-0	62	BLW		/82	80,600		acq. 8/1901
5		2-8-0	50	Pitts.		/85	99,250		acq. 10/1901
6		'	'	Altoona		/80	97,700		acq. 5/1902 ex Pa. RR
7		4-6-0	'	'		/88	87,700		acq. 8/1902 ex Pa. RR
8		2-8-0	'	'		/80	97,700		acq. 1/1903 ex Pa. RR
9		'	'	'		'	'		acq. 8/1903 ex Pa. RR
10*	18x24	4-6-0	62	BLW	23682	2/04	150,500	29,467	to C.M.&St.P. #2334
11*		'	'	'	23673	'	119,500	20,980	to C.M.&St.P. #2007
12*	20x26	'	57	'	26638	10/05	150,500	29,467	to C.M.&St.P.
14*	22x28	2-8-0	50	'	29330	10/06	197,000	46,076	
15*	20x26	4-6-0	56	'	28486	6/06	150,500	31,017	to C.M.&St.P. #7565

Freight traffic: common carrier, logging and coal

Rosters of 6/30/1906 - 6/30/1911:

locomotives	10	12
passenger cars	8	7
freight cars	8	12
flat cars	265	616

First published "timetable:"
December, 1901
Tacoma
Kapowsin 23.0

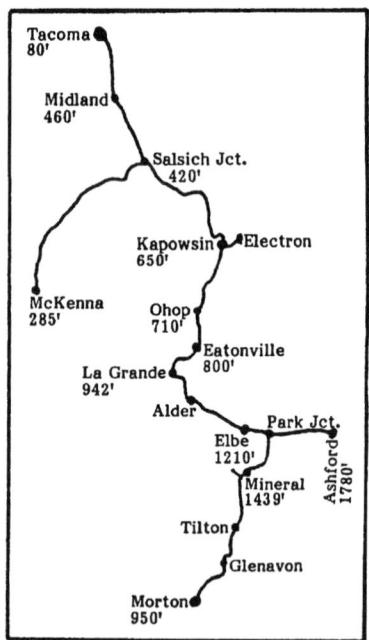

Published timetable dated:
May 7, 1916 - daily

8:50 a.m.	Tacoma	
9:20	Salich Jct.	11.0
9:52	Kapowsin	23.0
10:20	Eatonville	32.6
10:46	Alder	41.2
11:12	Park Jct.	49.6
11:27	Ashford	55.1
11:58	Mineral	53.7
12:50 p.m.	Morton	67.3

The road was opened on the dates shown from Tacoma to:

Kapowsin	23 miles	December, 1901
Eatonville	33	June 1, 1903
Elbe	47	June 1, 1904
Ashford	55	July, 1904
Mineral, Ladd	57	September 18, 1905
Tilton	60	September 9, 1906
Glenavon	63	June 23, 1907
McKenna	16	February 1, 1908
Morton	67	September 1, 1910

It appears that the carrier was first intended as a simple logging road when a locomotive engine was purchased in 1893 and a short section of track opened. It was reorganized February 17, 1903, and soon became a major secondary railroad.

The road cost $2,210,480 to build and $1,299,959 to equip.

First listed in ICC for 6/30/99 as an independent with six miles owned and operated. By 6/30/00 it was seven miles owned, not in use; by 6/30/01 it was 15 miles and still idle. By 6/30/02 it owned and operated 15 miles. It was extended to 41 miles by 6/30/03, to 62 miles the next year, 83 miles by 6/30/07 and 101 in 1908. By 6/30/09 it was an operating subsidiary of Chicago, Milwaukee & St. Paul Railway Co. with 103 miles; by 6/30/10 it had been reduced to 88 miles. By 6/30/11 this class II common carrier was 92 miles in length.

Bibliography: *Poor's 1010*, p. 756   *Valuation 44*, p. 810

WASHINGTON   291.

TACOMA, ORTING & SOUTHEASTERN RAILROAD COMPANY, THE   President

Incorp:	6/27/1888	**Operated:**	6/27/89 to 4/21/98	**HQ city:**	Orting

Disposition: sold to Northern Pacific Railway Company on April 21, 1898

Miles track: 10.92   **Gauge:** 56½"

Main line: Orting to Puyallup River

Rail wt.:   **Max. grade:**   **Const. began:** grading   September 25, 1888

                                                       laying rails   1889

Const. comp.: June 12, 1889   **First train operated:** June 24, 1889

Freight traffic: common carrier, lumber

Published timetable dated:
   January 1, 1893
      8:20 a.m.   Orting
                   Puyallup River   9:35 a.m.

The carrier was leased to Northern Pacific Railroad Company on June 24, 1889.

A note from *The Railway Age:*
   December 28, 1888   During the year 1888, eight miles of track was built.

First listed in ICC for 6/30/89 as a non-operating subsidiary of Northern Pacific Railroad Company with 7.6 miles owned. By 6/30/93 it was 10.61 miles and 11.04 by 6/30/95.

The *Valuation* series gives the final mileage as 7.64, similar to that found in ICC. *Poor's Manual* shows 10.92 miles, and ICC shows additional miles after 1889. It is possible that some sidings were added into the main line figures. Another factor would be whether the subject's track extended from Orting or from where it departed from the Northern Pacific main track.

Bibliography: *Poor's 1890*, p. 547   *Valuation 25*, p. 500

UNION LUMBER COMPANY   President

Incorp:	12/6/1902	**Operated:**	1902 to 1927	**HQ city:**	Tacoma

Disposition: abandoned

Miles track: 12   **Gauge:** 96" - pole road   **Date standardized:** by August, 1909

Main line: Long Lake and Union Mills into the forest

Rail wt.: 40 lbs.   **Max. grade:**   **Const. began:** grading   1902

Locomotives:

Road No.	Cyln.	Type	Dvr. in.	Bldr.	Bldr. No.	Date	Weight	Effort	Remarks
1*		2 truck	27	Climax	391	10/02	36,000	7,920	a pole road engine
3*	16x12	"	40	Heisler	1168	8/09	100,000		used at Union Mills
3-2d		2T Shay	28	Lima	646	4/01	56,000	11,125	used at Union Mills; scrapped 10/1929
4		3 truck	38	Heisler	1430	4/20	150,000		used at Union Mills; ex Wood/Iverson #5
5*	17x15	"	"	"	1444	9/20	"		used at Packwood; to Hedlund Lbr./Mfg.

Freight traffic: logging

Roster of 6/30/1910:
   2   geared engines
   1   rod engine
   20   flat cars

UNITED RAILROADS OF WASHINGTON, THE   President

Incorp:	8/2/1890	**Operated:**	2/13/92 to 4/20/98	**HQ city:**	Tacoma

Disposition: sold to Northern Pacific Railway Company on April 21, 1898

Predecessors: Tacoma, Olympia & Grays Harbor Railroad Company   **Incorp.:**   5/7/1890   to   2/13/1892

                    Yakima & Pacific Coast Railroad Company   5/1/1890   2/13/1892

Miles track: 182.45   **Gauge:** 56½"

Main line: Lakeview to Ocosta, Chehalis to South Bend and Centralia to Gate

Rail wt.:   **Max. grade:**   **Const. began:** grading   (May 12, 1890)

                                                       laying rails   (July 1, 1890)

Const. comp.: June 1, 1893 - main lines   **First train operated:** December 13, 1890

First published timetable:
```
July 27, 1893
   2:07 p.m.   Chehalis
               Frances     m.p. 35
               Menlo            46
   5:30        South Bend       57
```

First listed in ICC for 6/30/91 as a non-operating subsidiary of Northern Pacific Railroad Co. with 76 miles owned. It was increased to 120 miles by 6/30/92 and to 181 by 6/30/93 and then unchanged until its sale to Northern Pacific Railway Co. in 1898.

Official Guide, June, 1891, shows Tacoma, Olympia & Grays Harbor opening from Lakeview to Olympia and Centralia to Montesano. June, 1892, shows Montesano to South Aberdeen and November, 1892, to Ocosta.

Under title of Yakima & Pacific Coast, the May, 1893, *Guide* states "operated by the construction department."

The initial operation in 1890 was to three miles east of Centralia to the Florence Mine.

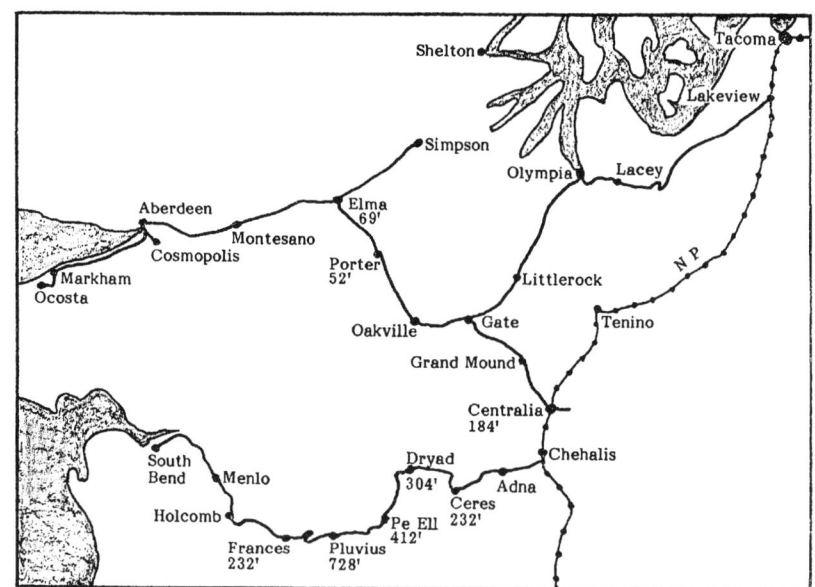

Constructed in part by Tacoma, Olympia & Chehalis Valley Railroad Co. and completed by Tacoma, Olympia & Grays Harbor Railroad Co. - Centralia to Elma - completed May 1, 1891.	32.57
Constructed by Tacoma, Olympia & Grays Harbor Railroad Co. - Lakeview to Lacey, 24.7 miles, completed May 1, 1891, and Lacey to Gate, finished August 10, 1891.	43.50
Also, as above, Junction to Cosmopolis, also completed in 1891.	1.60
Also, as above, Montesano to Ocosta, completed June 6, 1892.	24.70
Constructed in part by Yakima & Pacific Coast Railroad Co., 32.6 miles graded in 1890, rail laying about January 16, 1891, and completed by The United Railroads of Washington - Chehalis to South Bend, finished June 1, 1893.	56.68
Built by Puget Sound & Grays Harbor Railroad & Transportation Co. - Simpson to Montesano, opened January 15, 1891, and purchased by the carrier from the builder before October 31, 1892.	20.80
Constructed by The United Railroads of Washington - Junction to Aberdeen in 1895.	2.60

Notes from *Railroad Gazette:*

(Regarding Tacoma, Olympia & Grays Harbor Railroad Co.)

May 30, 1890	Contracts have been awarded for construction between Lakeview and Grays Harbor.
July 4, 1890	It is reported that about 1,100 men are working along the line at various points between Centralia and Grays Harbor. Several car loads of rails have arrived at Centralia and track laying is now in progress; it is expected to have 20 miles of track completed by July 10.
November 14, 1890	Ten miles of track has been laid from Lakeview toward the west.
December 19, 1890	The grading is now about completed over the entire line from Centralia to Ocosta and about 65 miles of track has been laid.

(Regarding Tacoma, Olympia & Chehalis Valley Railroad Co.)

June 27, 1890	Twelve miles have been built from Chehalis to the west; also, 3.5 miles east of Chehalis to reach the coal mines.

(Regarding Yakima & Pacific Coast Railroad Co.)

December 9, 1890	Track is now being laid at Chehalis.

Bibliography: *Poor's 1896*, p. 689 Spokane - *Spokesman-Review* - December 14, 1890 *Valuation 25*, p. 500
Tacoma - *Morning Globe* - November 27, 1890 to August 31, 1891

WALLA WALLA & COLUMBIA RIVER RAILROAD COMPANY

Dr. D. S. Baker, **Owner**

Incorp:	12/28/1868	**Operated:**	3/25/74 to 9/6/10		**HQ city:**	Walla Walla
Disposition:	sold to The Oregon Railroad & Navigation Company on September 6, 1910					
Miles track:	46.00	**Gauge:**	36"	**Date standardized:**		(May 25, 1881)
Main line:	Wallula to Walla Walla					

WASHINGTON   293.

Rail wt.:   25 lbs.   **Max. grade:**   **Const. began:**   grading   (January 16, 1872)

                                                                                                             laying rails   (July 23, 1873)

Const. comp.: October 23, 1875 - main line   **First train operated:**   (October 17, 1873)

Locomotive engines:

Road No.	Name	Type	Dvr. in.	Bldr.	Bldr. No.	Date	Weight	Effort	Remarks
1*	Walla Walla	0-4-0T		Porter	114	3/72	15,000		7/1881 to Columbia & Puget S. #7
2*	Wallula	'		'	124	8/72	'		12/1881 to Olympia & Chehalis Vy.
3*	Columbia	2-4-0		'	246	7/76	20,000		1881 to Cascades Railroad Co. #1
4*	Blue Mtn.	0-6-0		'	283	1/78	28,000		1896 to Cascades Railroad Co. #2
5*	Mtn. Queen	2-4-0	42	'	289	2/78	20,000	5,600	1881 to Mill Creek Flume & Mfg.
6*	J. W. Ladd	2-6-0	36	'	292	'	41,000		6/1881 to Mill Creek Flume & Mfg.

Freight traffic: common carrier, wheat and lumber

Rosters of   12/31/1876 - 12/31/1878:
    locomotive engines   3   3
    passenger cars   1   2
    freight cars   23   46

First published "timetable":
    March, 1877
    Walla Walla
    Whitman   5
    Touchet   15
    Wallula   32
    "Running time each way three hours."

The official construction record from Wallula to:
Touchet	16.00	March 25, 1874
Frenchtown	8.00	June 12, 1875
Whitman	3.00	September 10, 1875
Walla Walla	5.00	October 30, 1875
State line	3.00	September 15, 1879
Barrett	4.20	September 15, 1879
Blue Mtn.	6.80	September 15, 1879

Original construction was 6 x 6 timbers with 1/2 x 2 inch strap iron for the first 20 miles. In September, 1875, this was removed and replaced with light iron rails.

Construction of the branch into Oregon was begun in May of 1879. When completed, there were 35.00 miles in Washington Territory and 11.00 in Oregon. The 7.20 miles from Whitman to Barrett was dismantled in March, 1883, and the Barrett to Blue Mountain portion was made standard gauge about March 8, 1883.

Milton appears to be the new name for Barrett. A note in *Railroad Gazette*, December 22, 1882, regarding Oregon Railway & Navigation Co. states "Grading from Walla Walla to Milton, 13 miles, is completed and track laying has been begun. From Milton, a 3d rail will be laid on the narrow gauge branch to Blue Mountain, seven miles further. This branch will be extended next year to Weston, Centerville, Wild Horse Creek and Pendleton."

On December 31, 1876, the cost of building and equipment was placed at $323,269; by June 30, 1887, it had risen to $580,560.

The property was operated by its own organization from March 25, 1874, until December 31, 1881, and then under lease by Oregon Railway & Navigation Co. from January 1, 1882, until June 30, 1887. From that date until October 12, 1893, it was leased to Oregon Short Line & Utah Northern Railway Co. and finally, by Union Pacific Railway Co. receivers until August 17, 1896. Control passed to The Oregon Railroad & Navigation Co. on August 18, 1896.

The carrier was listed in first ICC (6/30/88) as a non-operating subsidiary of Oregon Railway & Navigation Co. with 36 miles owned.

Notes from *Railroad Gazette*:
April 23, 1873	Work has been resumed. Iron and two locomotives are at Wallula.
August 23, 1873	Bridges are being put up and tracklaying is actually begun.
October 11, 1873	Track has now been laid for 5¼ miles.
November 29, 1873	Ten miles are completed and regular trains are running.

Bibliography: *Poor's 1879*, p. 954   Oregon PUC report 1890, p. 208   *Valuation 44*, p. 271
                Walla Walla Statesman - October 18, 1873 and March 10, 1883   *Walla Walla Union* - July 26 to October 25, 1873
                             Union Pacific Railroad Company archives, p. 83 and 84

WALLA WALLA VALLEY RAILWAY COMPANY   Guy W. Talbot, **President**

Incorp: 4/30/1910   **Operated:**   5/1/10   to   5/26/85   **HQ city:**   Portland
Disposition: abandoned May 26, 1985
Predecessor: Walla Walla Valley Traction Company   **Incorp.:**   5/17/1905   to   4/30/1910
Miles track: 14.78   **Gauge:**   56½"
Main line: Walla Walla to Milton

Rail wt.:	60 lbs.	Max. grade:		Const. began:	grading	March 20, 1906
					laying rails	(Sept. 6, 1906)
Const. comp.:	July 1, 1907			First train operated:		September 11, 1906

Motive power:

Road No.	Type	Bldr.	Bldr. No.	Date	Weight	Effort	Remarks
500	0-4-4-0E	BLW	27927	4/06	90,000	360 h.p.	acquired in 1940; scrapped 1950
104	B-B			/39	202,064	24,000	ex Fort Worth & Denver City diesel

Major business: common carrier, passengers and agriculture

Roster of 6/30/1908:
- 8 passenger motors
- 1 freight motor
- 2 passenger cars
- 6 freight cars

Published timetable dated:
June, 1916

7:05 a.m.	Walla Walla	
7:19	Maple Street	4
7:49	Freewater	13
7:55	Milton	14

The property cost $492,887 to construct and equip.

Of the total trackage, 5.51 miles were in Oregon and 18.64 in Washington.

On January 1, 1950, its classification was changed from electric railway to a class II line-haul railroad. First listed in ICC for 12/31/50 as an operating subsidiary of Northern Pacific Railway Co. with 18 miles owned and 19 miles operated.

Electric lines were not included in ICC, hence the late inclusion. By 1952 the line was 19 miles owned and operated. Its status was then unchanged until 1970 when it was merged into Burlington Northern Railroad Co. as an operating subsidiary.

It was then abandoned as shown previously.

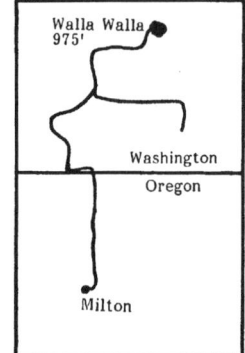

Bibliography: *Poor's 1909*, p. 1695

Walla Walla - *The Evening Statesman* - February 13 to September 11, 1906

Tacoma Public Library *Photo by Chapin Bowen*

Tacoma Railway & Power Co. cable winding machinery at 13th and A Streets on February 20, 1928. The cars were pulled up the 11th Street hill, out K Street and returned down 13th Street and to the power plant on A. The company was incorporated in February of 1899. By 1938, the gasoline driven bus was powerful enough for the hills and the electric cable system was retired.

WASHINGTON & COLUMBIA RIVER RAILWAY COMPANY, THE

W. D. Tyler, President

Incorp: 8/4/1892 **Operated:** 7/30/92 to 6/30/07 **HQ city:** Walla Walla

Disposition: sold to Northern Pacific Railway Company on June 18 to be effective July 1, 1907

Predecessors: Oregon & Washington Territory Railroad Company Renamed: 5/26/1887 to 10/5/1892
Oregon & Washington Territory Railroad Company, The Incorp.: 3/4/1886 5/25/1887

Purchased: Mill Creek Railroad Company 10/19/1903 9/8/1905

Miles track: 168.75 **Gauge:** 56½"

Main line: Pendleton to Dayton

Locomotives:

Road No.	Type	Dvr. in.	Bldr.	Bldr. No.	Date	Weight	Effort	Remarks
1	4-6-0	64	Grant	1766	3/88	110,300	18,700	to Northern Pacific #150
2	'	'	'	1767	'	'	'	to Northern Pacific #151
3	'	'	'	1768	'	'	'	to Northern Pacific #152
4	4-4-0	63	'	1783	12/88	94,400		to Northern Pacific #693
5	'	'	'	1780	4/88	'		to Northern Pacific #692
6	2-8-0	50	BLW	11914	5/91	160,000	33,800	ex Northern Pacific #66
7	'	'	'	11920	'	'	'	ex Northern Pacific #68

Freight traffic: common carrier, agriculture

Rosters of 6/30/1896 - 6/30/1906:
- locomotives 7 7
- passenger cars 3 5
- box cars 14 39
- flat cars 40 29

First published timetable:
November 4, 1892
- 7:00 a.m. Pendleton
- 10:15 Hunt's Jct. m.p. 40
- 1:33 p.m. Eureka Jct. 62
- 2:50 Walla Walla 93
- 3:26 Dixie 104
- 4:08 Waitsburg 117
- 4:30 Dayton 127

also the branches:
- Pleasant View 20
- Athena 14

Operations for year ending June 30, 1906:
- passenger income $64,160
- freight revenue 355,817
- other 13,394
- expenses 206,948
- net 226,423
- passenger miles 2,717,839
- freight ton miles 12,183,651
- cost of road $7,845,239

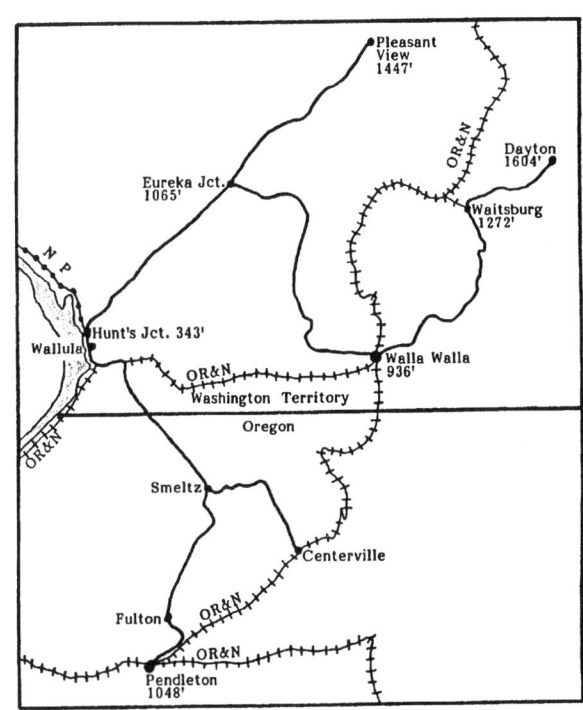

The Mill Creek Railroad Co. contributed 5.43 miles east from Walla Walla to Tracy which had been constructed as a narrow gauge by Mill Creek Flume & Mfg. Co. in 1880-1882. It was made standard gauge in 1905.

First listed in ICC for 6/30/93 as an operating independent with 162 miles owned and in use. By 6/30/97 it was an operating subsidiary of Northern Pacific Railway Co. with 163 miles each. It was increased to 169 miles each by 6/30/06 and then unchanged until it was sold in 1907.

Bibliography: *Poor's 1894*, p. 273 and *1907*, p. 802 *Valuation 25*, p. 503

WASHINGTON & GREAT NORTHERN RAILWAY COMPANY

Louis W. Hill, President

Incorp: 6/21/1901 **Operated:** 8/17/02 to 6/30/07 **HQ city:** Spokane

Disposition: sold to Great Northern Railway Company on July 1, 1907

Miles track: 83.68 **Gauge:** 56½"

Main line: Marcus Jct. to Republic

| Rail wt.: | 60/68 lbs. | Max. grade: | 3.50% | Const. began: | grading | (July 17, 1901) |
| | | | | | laying rails | (Nov. 4, 1901) |

Const. comp.: (December 31, 1905) **First train operated:** August 17, 1902

Freight traffic: common carrier, lumber

First published timetable:
    November 22, 1902
    2:05 p.m.   Marcus
    3:50   Grand Forks   42.0
    4:37   Curlew   52.0
    5:30   Republic   73.4

The date August 17, 1902, above refers to opening to Republic; there was doubtless an excursion before then.

The line was constructed in these sections:
    Marcus to Laurier   1901 - 1902   27.66 miles
    Danville to Eureka Gulch   1901 - August, 1902   41.50
    Curlew to Midway   1904 - December, 1905 14.52

It appears that construction of the portion in Canada was done in the name of Great Northern Railway Co.

As the track was operated as a part of Spokane Falls & Northern Railway Co. it is likely that SF&N rolling stock, rather than Great Northern, would have been found on this line.

Construction notes from *The Railway Age*:

    July 26, 1901   Construction contracts have been let.
    January 3, 1902   Tracklaying has just been commenced.
    March 7, 1902   Grading is completed from Marcus to Laurier and is being graded from there to Republic.
    June 2, 1902   The track has been laid to Curlew and expected to be at Republic by June 15, 1902.

And from *Railroad Gazette*:

    June 13, 1902   The Canadian section was completed on May 20, 1902.

First listed in ICC for 6/30/02 as an operating independent with 58 miles owned, not in use. By 6/30/03 it was 67 miles owned and in operation; the same in 1904. By 6/30/05 it was an operating subsidiary of Great Northern Railway Co. with 69 miles each. By 6/30/06 it was 84 miles each and 112 by 6/30/07.

The extra 28 miles referred to above must have been from the Canadian line above Molson to Oroville; a timetable dated June 9, 1907, shows this operation.

The carrier cost $4,555,392 to build and equip.

Bibliography: *Poor's 1903*, p. 580   *Valuation 133*, p. 191
                Spokane - *Twice-A-Week Spokesman=Review* - September 16, 1901 to July 3, 1902
                The Spokesman=Review - July 16 to November 5, 1901

WASHINGTON CENTRAL RAILROAD COMPANY, INC.   Nicholas B. Temple, President

| **Incorp:** | 7/28/1986 | **Operated:** | 10/13/86 to | **HQ city:** | Yakima |

Disposition: in operation 1993

Miles track: 292.00   **Gauge:** 56½"

Main line: Pasco to Cle Elum

Rail wt.: 66/132 lbs.   **Max. grade:** 1.00%

Locomotives:

Road No.	Type	Bldr.	Bldr. No.	Date	Weight	Effort	Remarks
201	B-B	EMD	31230	/66	249,700	1,200 h.p.	ex Mo. Pac. #1257
202	'	'	29801	/65	'	'	ex Mo. Pac. #1163
203	'	'	31222	/66	'	'	ex Mo. Pac. #1148
211	'	'	29784	/65	'	'	ex Mo. Pac. #1269
212	'	'	29788	'	'	'	ex Mo. Pac. #1273
301	'	'	22737	/57	255,400	1,750 h.p.	ex Burl. Northern #1919
302	'	'	22719	'	'	'	ex Burl. Northern #1754
401	'	AT&SFe		/73	249,600	1,500 h.p.	acq. 11/1987 ex AT&SFe #2578
402	'	'		/71	'	'	acq. 11/1987 ex AT&SFe #2636
2087	'	EMD		/67	266,500	2,000 h.p.	acq. 5/1992 ex CSX #2087
2184	'	'		'	'	'	acq. 3/1993 ex CSX #2184
4491	'	'		/52	230,600	1,500 h.p.	acq. 6/1991 ex C&NW #4491
4492	'	'		'	'	'	acq. 6/1991 ex C&NW #4492

Freight traffic: common carrier, agriculture

Roster of 12/31/1990:
    9   locomotives
  1,765 freight cars (leased)

Connection is also made at Kennewick with Union Pacific Railroad Co.

In 1993 it acquired two 1,500-h.p. EMDs for use at Renton in tourist service. Serial numbers are 16595 and 16596, both built in June, 1952, and ex B&LE.

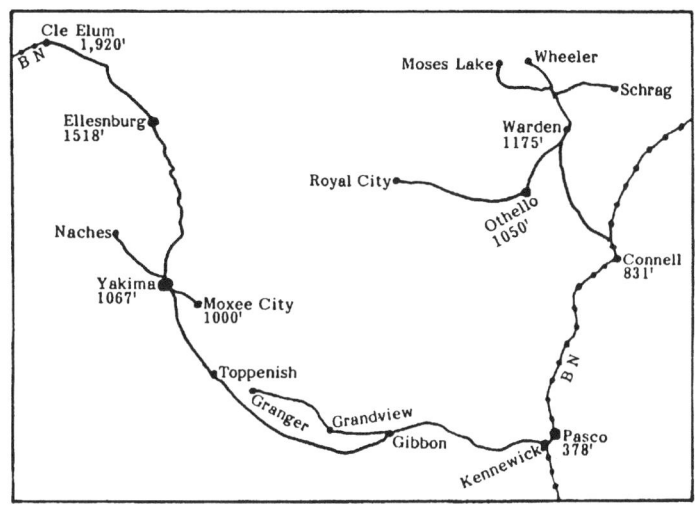

Bibliography: Direct communication

Official Open and Prepay Station List

WASHINGTON CENTRAL RAILWAY COMPANY, THE
    Howard Elliott, **President**

Incorp:	5/31/1898	**Operated:** 6/1/98 to 6/29/14		**HQ city:** Spokane
Disposition:	sold to Northern Pacific Railway Company on June 29, 1914			
Predecessor:	Central Washington Railroad Company, The		**Incorp.:**	3/2/1888 to 5/31/1898
Miles track:	129.76	**Gauge:** 56½"		
Main line:	Cheney to Adrian			
Rail wt.:	56 lbs.	**Max. grade:**	**Const. began:** grading	August 27, 1888
			laying rails	(October 8, 1888)
Const. comp.:	December 1, 1903		**First train operated:**	November 1, 1888

Locomotives:

Road No.	Cyln.	Type	Dvr. in.	Bldr.	Bldr. No.	Date	Weight	Effort	Remarks
5*	18x24	4-4-0	62	BLW	10247	9/89			to Northern Pacific #672
6*	'	'	'	'	10252	'			to Northern Pacific #673

Freight traffic: common carrier, agriculture

First published timetable:
  February 1, 1889
    12:00 m. Cheney
    3:00 p.m. Davenport 41
  November 24, 1889
    Cheney
    Adrian 87
  December 7, 1890
    Cheney
    Coulee City 108
  December, 1903
    Cheney
    Adrian 130

The construction record:

Cheney to Davenport	1888 to	7/1/1889	41.40
Davenport to Almira	1889 to	6/14/1890	46.10
Almira to Coulee City	1889 to	11/1/1890	21.16
Coulee Jct. to Adrian	1902 to	9/20/1903	21.10

Construction notes from *Railroad Gazette*:
  August 24, 1888 To begin construction at once.
  October 12, 1888 It is now being constructed.
  December 28, 1888 Nearly completed; to open on January 1, 1889.

And from *The Railway Age*:
  December 28, 1888 During the year 1888, 41.0 miles of track was laid.

The predecessor was first listed in ICC for 6/30/89 as a non-operating subsidiary of Northern Pacific Railroad Co. with 42 miles owned. It had been placed in operation November 1, 1888, by Northern Pacific and leased to it July 1, 1889. Mileage was increased to 87 by 6/30/90 and to 109 by 6/30/91. By 6/30/95 it was a 109-mile independent; it had been placed in receivership on October 6, 1893. By 6/30/96 it owned 109 miles and operated 126 (from Spokane). It was sold at foreclosure January 18, 1898, to Charles T. Barney, et al, who, by deed dated June 1, 1898, conveyed the property to The Washington Central Railway Co.

The subject was first included in ICC for 6/30/99 as a non-operating subsidiary of Northern Pacific Railway Co. with 109 miles owned; it had been leased to N.P. on June 1, 1898. The mileage was extended to 131 by 6/30/04 and then remained unchanged until it was sold in 1914.

Coulee Junction to Adrian was placed in commercial operation on December 8, 1903; it carried nine cars of wheat.

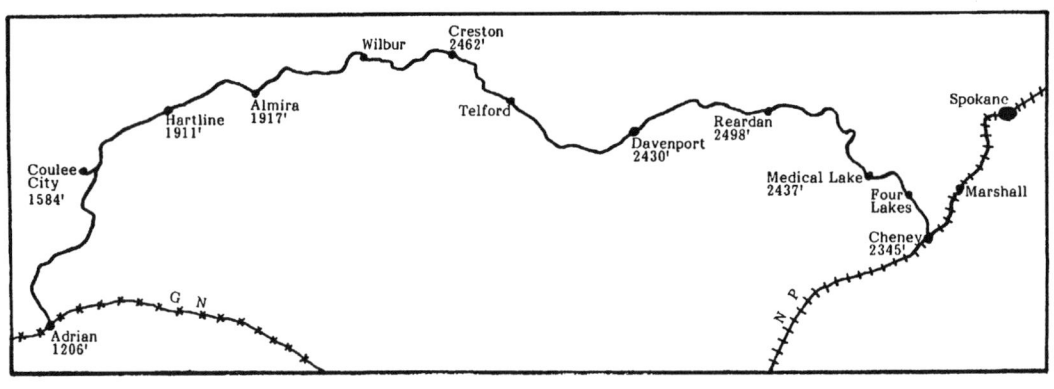

Bibliography: *Poor's 1890*, p. 545   Colfax - *Commoner* - April 6 to November 30, 1888   *Valuation 25*, p. 493
                                                Spokane - *Spokesman-Review* - November 10, 1903

WASHINGTON RAILWAY & NAVIGATION COMPANY   President
Incorp: 7/13/1903   **Operated:**   7/14/03   to   10/19/03   **HQ city:**   Yacolt
Disposition: sold to Northern Pacific Railway Company on October 19, 1903
Predecessors: Washington & Oregon Railway Company   **Incorp.:** 12/3/1900   to   7/13/1903
                    Portland, Vancouver & Yakima Railway Company   11/30/1897   7/13/1903
                    Vancouver, Klickitat & Yakima Railroad Company   1/29/1887   11/30/1897
Miles track: 59.02   **Gauge:** 56½"
Main line: Vancouver to Yacolt and Kalama to Vancouver
Rail wt.:   56 lbs.   **Max. grade:**   **Const. began:**   grading   February 1, 1888
                                                                                               laying rails (May 7, 1888)
Const. comp.:   (February 28, 1903)   **First train operated:**   December 19, 1888

Locomotives:

Road No.	Ctln.	Type	Dvr. in.	Bldr.	Bldr. No.	Date	Weight	Effort	Remarks
100*	11x12	2T Shay	32	Lima	783	10/03	90,000	18,750	to Northern Pac. #1098
101*	14x14	3T Shay	36	'	801	'	150,000	30,550	to Northern Pac. #1099
102*	11x12	2T Shay	32	'	848	2/04	90,000	18,750	to Northern Pac. #1097

Freight traffic: common carrier, lumber

First published "timetable":
    November, 1899
    Vancouver
    Barberton
    Thornton's
    Brush Prairie
    Salmon Creek   17 miles

The construction record:
    Vancouver, Klickitat & Yakima Railroad Co.
        Vancouver to Brush Prairie   1888 to 1889   12.10
        Brush Prairie to Salmon Creek   1895   1.40
    Portland, Vancouver & Yakima Railway Co.
        Brush Prairie to Salmon Creek   1899   2.50
        Salmon Creek to Daly's Road   1900   .30
        Daly's Road to Yacolt   1901 to 1902   14.10
        Connection at Vancouver   1903   .40
        Vancouver Jct. to Station 247   1903   2.60
    Washington & Oregon Railway Co.
        Commenced by Portland & Puget Sound Railroad
        and completed by Washington & Oregon Ry.
        Kalama to Vancouver   1901 to 3/1/1903   28.90

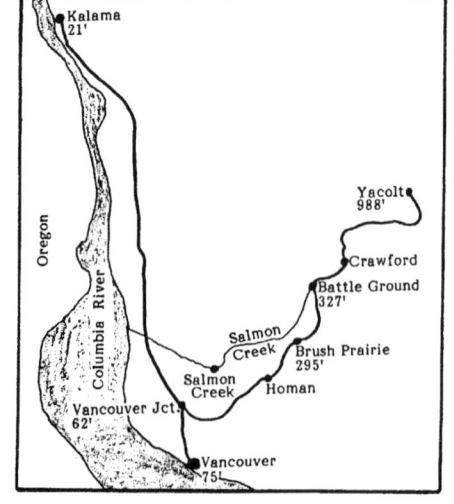

It should be noted that there was a town of "Salmon Creek" as well as a stream of the same name.

WASHINGTON

Construction notes from *The Railway Age:*
- March 22, 1888   A contract has been let for the first five miles and work is under way.
- May 4, 1888   Five miles are graded, ready for iron.
- September 7, 1888   Six miles are now ready for rails.

And from *Railroad Gazette:*
- March 16, 1888   Grading is under way.
- June 1, 1888   Five miles of track have been laid.
- March 29, 1889   Over five miles are in operation with ten miles graded; more track to be laid soon.

Vancouver, Klickitat & Yakima Railroad Co. was first listed in ICC for 6/30/90 as an operating independent with ten miles owned and in use. It was extended to 12 miles by 6/30/91 and to 15 by 6/30/96.

The carrier named above was succeeded by Portland, Vancouver & Yakima Railway Co. which was shown 6/30/98 with 16 miles owned and in use. A small increase was added to 17 miles by 6/30/99 and to 18 by 6/30/01. By 6/30/03 it was a 27-mile non-operating subsidiary of Northern Pacific Railway Co.

Washington & Oregon Railway Co. was listed 6/30/02 as an independent with 29 miles owned and in use. By 6/30/03 it too was a non-operating subsidiary of Northern Pacific Railway Co.

Northern Pacific extended the range of motive power beyond the Shays with engines number 4, 5, 6 and 771.

Bibliography: *Poor's 1900,* p. 103 and *1904,* p. 582   *Valuation 25,* p. 493
    Colfax - *Commoner* - December 28, 1888   *The Vancouver Independent* - February 1, 1888

WASHINGTON WESTERN RAILWAY COMPANY

B. W. Maguire, President

Incorp:	5/7/1912	**Operated:**	1912 to 1929		**HQ city:**	Three Lakes
Disposition:	abandoned November 15, 1929					
Purchased:	Panther Lake Lumber Company		12 miles in 1925	from:	1/1/1923 to	1929
Predecessors:	Three Lakes Lumber Company		16 miles in 1918		1904	12/31/1922
	Sterling Lumber Company				1902	1904

Miles track: 12.203   **Gauge:** 56½"

Main line: Machias to Woodruff

Rail wt.: 35/56 lbs.   **Max. grade:** 6.0%   **Const. began:** grading   1902

Const. comp.: August 9, 1912   **First train operated:** 1902

Locomotives:

Road No.	Cyln.	Type	Dvr. in.	Bldr.	Bldr. No.	Date	Weight	Effort	Remarks
1*	2	truck	33	Climax	351	/02	90,000	19,800	new as Sterling Mill Co. #1
2*	'	'	'	'	530	10/04	100,000	22,000	new as Three Lakes Lbr. #2
3*	'	'	35	'		5/09			new as Three Lakes Lbr. #3
4*	3	truck	'	'	1409	/16	140,000	30,800	new as Three Lakes #2-2d; P #4
5 ?	3T	Shay	36	Lima	716	7/02	130,000	20,475	2d hand to Panther Lake Lbr.
6	3	truck	'	Climax	1027	/10	160,000	35,200	3d hand to Panther Lake Lbr.
7 ?	2	truck	30	'	636	2/06	56,000		4th hand to Panther Lake Lbr.

Freight traffic: logging

Roster of 6/30/1910:
- 2   geared engines
- 70   logging trucks
- 9   miles track at Three Lakes

Published timetable dated:
February 15, 1916

10:45 a.m.	Machias	
10:55	Sinnetts	0.3
11:25	Three Lakes	4.0
1:15 p.m.	Three Lakes	
1:40	Williams	6.4
2:00	Roosevelt	9.3
2:10	Woodruff	10.7

Upon organization, the subject carrier purchased from Three Lakes Lumber Co. its logging railroad comprised of two disconnected sections - Machias to Three Lakes and from Three Lakes Jct. to Woodruff, a total of about ten miles. About one half mile was built in 1912 to join the two sections.

Washington Western Railway Co. was first listed in ICC for 6/30/14 as an operating independent with 11 miles owned and in use; a class II common carrier.

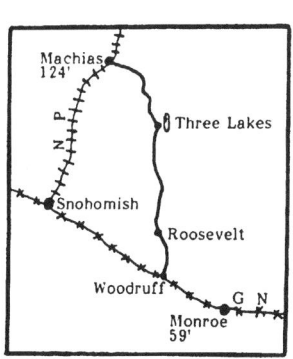

Bibliography: *Poor's 1915,* p. 532   *Valuation 116,* p. 492

WATERVILLE RAILWAY COMPANY

J. M. Fuel, **President**

Incorp:	8/30/1909	**Operated:**	8/19/10 to (6/11/48)	**HQ city:** Waterville
Disposition:	abandoned August 15, 1954			
Miles track:	5.092	**Gauge:**	56½"	
Main line:	Waterville to Douglas			
Rail wt.:	53 lbs.	**Max. grade:**	**Const. began:** grading October 14, 1909	
			laying rails (July 25, 1910)	
Const. comp.:	August 18, 1910		**First train operated:** August 19, 1910	

Locomotives:

Road No.	Type	Dvr. in.	Bldr.	Bldr. No.	Date	Weight	Effort	Remarks
299	4-6-0	56	Schen.	2861	5/89	77,000	16,820	acq. 2/1911 ex G.N. #299; SCR 1/1935
949	'	55	BLW	15059	9/96	85,000	20,090	acq. 5/1934 ex G.N. #949; SCR 5/1947

Freight traffic: common carrier, agriculture

Roster of 12/31/1923:
    1   locomotive
    2   passenger cars

Published timetable dated:
March, 1929
  9:45 a.m.   Waterville   11:30
  10:15   Douglas   11:00 a.m.
Operating two round trips on M-W-F

September, 1949 - "freight only"
March, 1950   "truck service only"
February, 1954   "wheat service only"
It was the final listing in *Official Guide*.

Rails, ties, etc. were loaned by Great Northern Railway Co. under agreement entered into November 22, 1909; no rental fee was charged. The material was valued at $48,577.

From 1910 through 1927 it had operating revenues of $219,403 and expenses of $225,675.

First listed in ICC for 6/30/15 as an operating independent with five miles owned and in use.

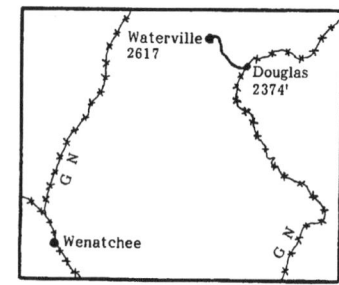

Bibliography: *Poor's 1924*, p. 2096

Waterville - *Big Bend Empire* - September 16, 1909 to August 18, 1910

WEYERHAEUSER COMPANY

Frederick Weyerhaeuser, **President**

Incorp:	1/28/1900	**Operated:**	1927 to	**HQ city:** Longview
Disposition:	in operation 1985			
Miles track:	125 at Vail and 195 from Ostrander Jct.	**Gauge:**	56½"	
Main line:	woods lines from Ostrander Jct. and Vail to Tidewater			
Rail wt.:		**Max. grade:**	**Const. began:** grading (May 1, 1923)	

Locomotives:

Road No.	Cyln.	Type	Dvr. in.	Bldr.	Bldr. No.	Date	Weight	Effort	Remarks
1		2T Shay	32	Lima	2030	11/07	100,000	22,600	used at Camp McDonald
2		3T Shay	36	'	3090	8/20	189,000	35,100	used at Vail; SCR 11/1943
3		2T Shay	'	'	2671	5/13	120,000	23,900	ex Cherry Vy. #3; used at Vail
4*	18¼x16	3 truck	40	Heisler	1573	4/29	180,000	38,480	at Vail; to Mud Bay Logging Co.
4		3T Shay	36	Lima	3317	2/28	184,800	38,200	at Headquarters Camp; sold 1947
5*	13x15	'	'	'	3316	'	'	'	at Vail; 1/1947 to British Col.
5		2T Shay	29½	'	486	2/95	64,000	14,075	ex Cherry Vy. #5; at Ostrander
6 ?		3T Shay	36	'	3253	3/24	172,400	30,350	3/1937 to N. Bend Tbr. Co. #6
7 ?		3 truck	'	Climax	1589	11/21	160,000	35,200	used at Vail
9*		2-6-6-2T	44	BLW	62068	/36	247,000	42,500	last new steam purchased
100		2-6-2	50	Cooke	62965	3/21	127,500	24,800	
101		2-8-2	48	BLW	37539	2/12	172,000	35,700	
101*	18¼x16	3 truck	40	Heisler	1562	6/28	180,000	38,480	at Ostrander; to Kosmos Tbr. #8
105*	23/35x28	2-6-6-2T	51	BLW	60784	4/29	245,800	44,800	
106*	'	'	'	'	60785	'	'	'	
107*		2-4-4-2	44	'	61355	5/30			
109		2-8-2	'	'	41710	9/14	135,000	27,100	ex Columbia & Nehalem #117
110*		2-6-6-2T	'	'	60561	9/28	222,000	37,500	
110*		'	'	'	62064	/36	247,000	42,500	
111*	23/35x28	'	51	'	60811	5/29	263,250	46,900	
112*	18/28x24	'	44	'	62065	/36	247,000	42,500	
120*		'	51	'	61904	'	293,000	59,600	
200*	23/35x28	2-8-8-2	51	'	60837	5/29	352,000	75,000	built to pull 100 loads up 3.7% grade - and they did
201*	'	'	'	'	61753	/33	'	'	

101-102*		BLW	74814-15	7/50	diesels
103*		'	75254	5/51	diesel
105*		'	75255	'	diesel
302-303-304	B-B				used at Ostrander in 1985

Freight traffic: logging

It should be noted that all of the locomotives on these pages probably do not belong on these pages. In addition to operations in Oregon, the company used numerous trade-styles in Washington.

These included Clark Timber Co., Twin Falls Logging Co., Columbia & Cowlitz Railway Co., Chehalis Western Railroad Co., Cherry Valley Logging Co., Snoqualmie Falls Lumber Co., Sound Timber Co., Washington Veneer Co. and Willapa Harbor Lumber Mills.

And builder records for rod engines do not show camp sites or movements amongst them.

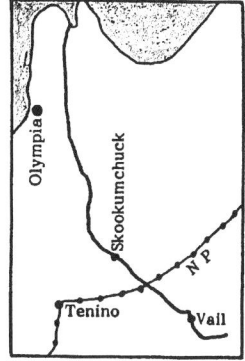
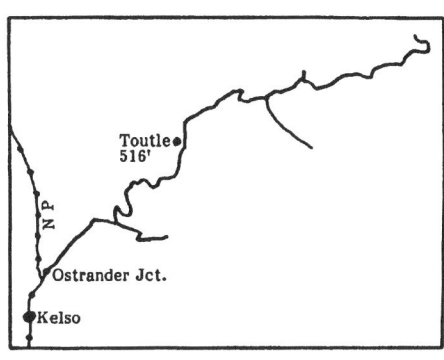

WHITE RIVER LUMBER COMPANY

Incorp:	1/13/1897	**Operated:**	1902 to 1949	**HQ city:**		Enumclaw
Disposition:	abandoned				**President**	
Miles track:	100	**Gauge:**	56½"			
Main line:	Enumclaw into the forest					
Rail wt.:	30/45/60 lbs.	**Max. grade:**	12.0%	**Const. began:**	grading	

Locomotives:

Road No.	Cyln.	Type	Dvr. in.	Bldr.	Bldr. No.	Date	Weight	Effort	Remarks
1*		2 truck		Climax		1/02	50,000		
1-2d*	12x15	3T Shay	36	Lima	2225	9/09	140,000	29,800	scrapped
2*		2 truck	35	Climax	417	/03	100,000	22,000	to Crown Willamette Paper Co.
2-2d*		3 truck	36	Willam.	12	12/23	140,000		
3*	18¼x16	'	40	Heisler	1569	9/28	180,000	43,600	wrecked in about 1948
4		3T Shay	36	Lima	3331	3/29	163,100	38,200	acq. 1/1936 2d hand; scrapped
5		2-8-2	48	BLW	45753	6/17			ex Silver Falls Timber Co. #102
6		3T Shay	36	Lima	3260	4/24	160,000	35,100	acq. 2/1941 3d hand
7		2-6-6-2T	44	BLW	58272	3/25			ex Saginaw Timber Co. #4
8 ?		3T Shay	36	Lima	3090	8/20	160,000	35,100	ex Cherry Vy. #2; SCR 11/1943
9		2T Shay	32	'	2547	5/12	100,000	22,575	acq. 3d hand; SCR 5/1941

Freight traffic: logging

Roster of 6/30/1910:
- 2 geared engines
- 1 rod engine
- 12 flat cars
- 7 miles of track

In January of 1903, it had two miles of track with a 12% maximum grade and 53° curve. By 1919 it had been extended to 30 miles. By 1926 the grade had been reduced to 7% and 12° curves.

It is interesting to note that an engine was purchased new from each of the geared-engine manufacturers.

Enumclaw was 20 miles east by South of Tacoma on the Northern Pacific Railway Co. main line.

WILLAPA LOGGING RAILROAD COMPANY

						Weyerhaeuser Co.,	**Owner**
Incorp:	3/21/1931	**Operated:**	1931 to 1944	**HQ city:**			Raymond
Disposition:	abandoned - corporation dissolved August 8, 1944						
Predecessors:	Willapa Harbor Lumber Mills	HQ: Raymond - 66 miles track			from: 1931	to 1942	
	Lewis Mills & Timber Co.	HQ: South Bend - 5 miles in 1926, 7% grade			1920	1931	
	Sunset Timber Company	HQ: Raymond - 21 miles, 56 lb. rail			1915	1931	
	South Bend Mills & Timber Company	HQ: South Bend - 6 miles track			1909	1921	

302.   ENCYCLOPEDIA OF WESTERN RAILROAD HISTORY

Miles track:		56			**Gauge:**	56½"			
Main line:		South Bend and Raymond into the forest							
Rail wt.:		56 lbs.			**Max. grade:**		**Const. began:**	grading	1909

Locomotives:

Road No.	Cyln.	Type	Dvr. in.	Bldr.	Bldr. No.	Date	Weight	Effort	Remarks
		Willapa Harbor Lumber Mills							
1		3T Shay	36	Lima	3010	10/18	146,000	30,350	acq. 1/1939; SCR 1943
2		2T Shay	32	'	2566	11/12	100,000	22,575	acq. 1931; sold 12/1938
2-2d		3T Shay	36	'	3019	4/19	146,000	30,350	ex Sunset Timber Co. #2
7 ?		3 truck	38	Heisler	1491	12/23	160,000		ex Greenwood Logging Co. #7
10 ?		3T Shay	40	Lima	3130	10/20	158,200	32,480	acq. 6/1933 ex Raymond Lbr. #10
12		'	36	'	2200	8/09	140,000	29,800	acq. 4th hand
103 ?		2 truck	40	Heisler	1342	7/16	130,000		ex Sunset Timber Co.
905		3 truck	38	'	1480	5/23	160,000		to Potlatch Forests #83
		Lewis Mills & Timber Co.							
1		2T Shay	26½	Lima	2173	2/10	72,000	14,800	acq. 11/1920 ex S. Bend Mills/T
2		'	32	'	2566	11/12	100,000	22,575	acq. 11/1920 ex S. Bend Mills/T
		Sunset Timber Co.							
1		3 truck	40	Heisler	1272	2/13	170,000		ex Dempsey Lumber Co. #1
2*	12x15	3T Shay	36	Lima	3019	4/19	146,000	30,350	6/1933 to Willapa Harbor Lbr. M.
101 ?		2 truck	'	Heisler	1172	11/09	84,000		ex Lebam Mill & Timber #101
103 ?		'	40	'	1342	7/16	130,000		ex Pacific & Eastern Ry. #103
		South Bend Mill & Timber Co.							
1 ?		2T Shay	26½	Lima	2173	2/10	72,000	14,800	ex M. D. Wright #1; sold 11/1920
2		'	32	'	2566	11/12	100,000	22,575	ex Silver Falls Timber Co. #1

Freight traffic: logging

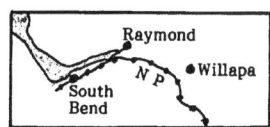

WINLOCK-TOLEDO LUMBER COMPANY

Incorp:	3/15/1926	**Operated:** 1929 to 1932	**HQ city:**	Winlock	**President**
Disposition:	abandoned - corporation dissolved July 1, 1937				
Predecessors:	Winlock & Toledo Logging & Railroad Company	25 miles track	**Incorp.:**	2/23/1924 to 1929	
	Winlock Lumber Company	8 miles track	**from:**	1916 1923	
	M. T. O'Connell Lumber Company	16 miles - dual gauge		1906 1916	
Miles track:	20	**Gauge:** 56½"			
Main line:	Winlock into the forest				
Rail wt.:		**Max. grade:** 6.0%	**Const. began:** grading	1906	

Locomotives:

Road No.	Cyln.	Type	Dvr. in.	Bldr.	Bldr. No.	Date	Weight	Effort	Remarks
		Winlock & Toledo Logging & Railway Co.							
3		2T Shay	29½	Lima	2770	6/15	84,000	16,900	sold to Portland dealer
4		'	32	'	3135	11/20	137,000	25,830	sold to dealer for scrap
7		2 truck	36	Heisler	1380	9/18	80,000		ex Washington Fir Timber Co.
		Winlock Lumber Co.							
1*	10x10	2T Shay	29½	Lima	2975	4/18	84,000	16,900	to Oregon-Kalama Lumber Co. #1
4 ?		'	32	'	3135	11/20	137,000	25,830	to Oregon-Kalama Lumber Co.
7 ?		2 truck	36	Heisler	1380	9/18	80,000		to Washington Fir Timber Co.
		M. T. O'Connell Lumber Co.							
2 ?		2T Shay	28	Lima	489	5/95	72,000	13,180	ex Salt Lake & Mercur #2
3*	8x10	'	26½	'	2137	1/09	56,000	13,300	42-inch gauge?
4*	10x12	'	29½	'	2651	5/13	84,000	16,900	sold to Seattle dealer
6*	'	'	'	'	2967	3/18	120,000	23,890	to California Barrell Co. #6
7*	'	'	'	'	2973	4/18	84,000	20,835	4/1923 to Bovill, Idaho
7-2d*	14x12	2 truck	36	Heisler	1380	9/18	80,000		to Winlock Lumber Co.

Freight traffic: logging

WASHINGTON

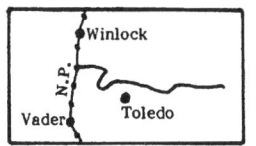

Roster of 6/30/1910:
1	geared engine	1	geared engine
1	rod engine	10	logging trucks
17	logging trucks	6	miles 56½" track
7	miles n.g. (42" ?) track		

WISCONSIN LOGGING & TIMBER COMPANY   President

Incorp:	4/14/1906	**Operated:**	(6/18/06) to 1923	**HQ city:**	Portland
Disposition:	abandoned - corporation dissolved July 1, 1926				
Predecessor:	Benson Logging & Lumbering Company	HQ at Stella - 20 miles track		from: 1891 to (6/1906)	
Miles track:	18	**Gauge:**	56½"		
Main line:	Oak Point into the forest				
Rail wt.:	45/60 lbs.	**Max. grade:** 6.0%	**Const. began:** grading		1891

Locomotives:

Road No.	Cyln.	Type	Dvr. in.	Bldr.	Bldr. No.	Date	Weight	Effort	Remarks
		Wisconsin Logging & Timber Co.							
1*	10x12	2T Shay	29½	Lima	1775	10/10	74,000	16,900	used at Oak Point
1*	17x14	2 truck	40	Heisler	1187	1/10	120,000		used at Stella; to Midway Logging
3		2T Shay	29½	Lima	884	5/04	74,000	15,625	Bessie; used at Midway
7		2-6-2	44	BLW	27379	1/06			ex Benson Logging #7
7-2d*		2-8-2		'	53251	5/20			
426 ?		2T Shay	29½	Lima	3005	4/19	85,000	16,900	ex Siems Carey #426; to Midway
		Benson Logging & Lumbering Co.							
5*	9x8	2T Shay	26	Lima	606	4/00	40,000	11,625	to Hammond Lumber Co.
5-2d	'	'	28	'	653	7/01	56,000	10,950	used at Midway; to Midway Logging
7*	16x24	2-6-2	44	BLW	27379	1/06			
8*	'	'	'	'	29822	12/06	108,000		to Benson @ Clatskanie, Oregon
528*	8x12	2T Shay	26½	Lima	528	3/97	34,000	9,350	used at Oak Point; sold 3/31/1904
554*	9x8	'	26	'	554	3/98	40,000	12,475	at Oak Point; 1903 to Coast Range
559*	'	'	'	'	559	7/98	'	11,625	at Oak Point; to L. B. Menefee
669*	10x10	'	28	'	669	10/01	56,000	9,875	at Oak Point; to Penn Lbr. Co.
671*	'	'	'	'	671	'	'	'	1908 to Bradley Logging Co.
884*	10x12	'	29½	'	884	5/04	74,000	15,625	used at Oak Point; to Wisc. #3

Freight traffic: logging

Roster of 6/30/1910:
- 4 geared engines
- 1 rod engine
- 40 sets logging trucks
- 2 flat cars
- 14 miles track at Oak Point

As the Benson company logged in Oregon (just across the Columbia River from Oak Point) between 1903 and 1936, some of these locomotives may not have been used in Washington.

A note in the February, 1907, *Western Lumberman* states that the new company is reducing the 6% grade to 1.5%.

YAKIMA VALLEY TRANSPORTATION COMPANY   H. B. Scudder, President

Incorp:	6/15/1906	**Operated:**	12/26/07 to 7/11/85	**HQ city:**	North Yakima
Disposition:	donated by Union Pacific Railroad Company to the City of Yakima on July 11, 1985				
Miles track:	34.0	**Gauge:**	56½"		
Main line:	North Yakima to Taylor, Henryboro and Wiley				
Rail wt.:		**Max. grade:** (2.0%)	**Const. began:** grading	(November 4, 1907)	
				laying rails	(Dec. 9, 1907)
Const. comp.:			**First train operated:**	December 25, 1907	

Electric motors:

297	0-4-4-0E	BLW	56937	8/23	500 h.p.	acq. 3/1942; 1/19/1986 to Orange Empire Museum	
298							
299	0-4-4-0E	BLW	32061	10/07	400 h.p.	ex United Railways (Oregon)	

Major business: common carrier, passengers and agriculture

Roster of 6/30/1914:
- 31 motors
- 13 passenger cars
- 1 express car
- 17 freight cars

The company franchise was granted October 1, 1906. Surveying of the route began on January 3, 1907. The first shipment of ties arrived - from Napavine - on May 16. The first rails were unloaded August 22 and power pole setting began October 26. All of this before grading began. A new Westinghouse generator arrived November 11 and operations began six weeks later.

The track to Wide Hollow, three miles, was completed December 16, 1907, and operations began a few days later as noted above.

The major lines were from North Yakima to
- Wiley   9.1 miles
- Taylor   7.1
- Harwood   7.3
- Orchard   4.6
- Fruitvale 3.1

Interurban service continued until May 15, 1935. From that date on, it was freight only, though it did continue to offer city street railway passenger service until February 1, 1947, when all passenger service was terminated.

In 1917, 2,048,117 passenger tickets were sold; in 1920 the population was 18,539. Passenger (tourist) service was resumed on November 12, 1974.

The Interstate Commerce Commission authorized the abandonment of 4.200 miles in 1943 and 1.850 miles in 1949.

The carrier ceased being an electrically operated freight carrier on May 16, 1983.

As previously noted, the property was donated to Yakima in 1985. It was made up of the following sections:
- Wide Hollow to Wiley   4.72 miles
- Eastman to Orchard   1.04
- Yakima to Selah   4.46
- Yakima to Henryboro   9.70
- total   19.92

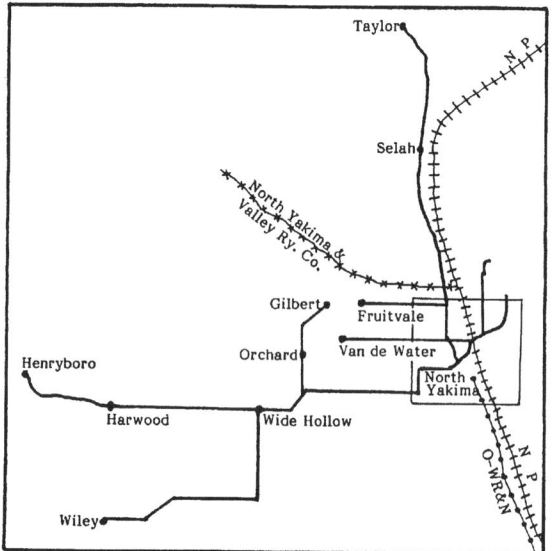

Bibliography: *Yakima Daily Herald* - July 31 to December 25, 1907

California State Railroad Museum Library *Gerald M. Best Collection*
Yakima Valley Transportation Co. service car <u>loaded</u> with gear in September, 1969

WASHINGTON

Extensions of old, opening of new roads, changes in name of roads, stations, @c. from *Official Guide*.

February, 1873
    Northern Pacific — Opened from Kalama to Tenino, 66 miles.

February, 1874
    Northern Pacific -- Opened Tenino to New Tacoma, 39 miles.

August, 1874
    Northern Pacific — Grand Prairie is now Winlock; Steilacoom is now Lake View.

October, 1878
    Northern Pacific — New Tacoma is now Tacoma.

July, 1880
    Walla Walla & Columbia River — Extended from Walla Walla south to Blue Mountain, 19 miles.

May, 1881
    Northern Pacific -- Wilkeson to Carbonado, 3 miles.

September, 1881
    Oregon Ry. & Navig. — Walla Walla northeast to Dayton, 39 miles.

January, 1882
    Oregon Ry. & Navig. -- Bolles Jct. northeast to Grange City and South Texas, 31 miles.

April, 1882
    Northern Pacific — Opened Ainsworth (on OR&N) to Lake Pend Oreille, Idaho Territory, 216 miles and 354 miles from The Dalles.

June, 1882
    Oregon Ry. & Navig. -- South Texas is now Riparia.

February, 1884
    Oregon Ry. & Navig. -- The Columbia & Palouse branch has been opened for business from Palouse Jct. eastward to Colfax, W. T., 88.8 miles.

February, 1885
    Columbia & Puget Sound — Renton southeast to Franklin, 20 miles.

December, 1886
    Oregon Ry. & Navig. -- Columbia & Palouse Farmington Branch has been opened for business from Colfax northeastward to Farmington, 27 miles.

March, 1887
    Puget Sound Shore — This division of Columbia & Puget Sound Shore has opened Stuck Jct. north to Seattle, 24 miles.

April, 1887
    Northern Pacific — Ellensburg to Roslyn, 28 miles.

May, 1888
    Seattle, Lake Shore & Eastern — Seattle northeast to Gilman, 42 miles.

July, 1888
    Northern Pacific -- Spokane & Palouse divn. opened Belmont to Genesee, Idaho Territory, 61 miles.

December, 1888
    Northern Pacific -- Palouse Jct. is now Connell.

January, 1889
    Oregon & Washington Territory -- Hunt's Jct. to Walla Walla, 53 miles; Eureka Jct. to Pleasant View, 20 miles and Hunt's Jct. (W. T.) to Fulton and Centerville, Oregon, 34 miles.
    Oregon Ry. & Navig. — Farmington north to Rockford, 34 miles.
    Seattle, Lake Shore & Eastern — Gilman to Raging River, 9.5 miles.

October, 1889
    Oregon Ry. & Navig. — (Oregon Railway Extensions Co., actually) Winona Jct. eastward to Seltice, 48 miles.

November, 1889
    Oregon Ry. & Navig. — (Washington & Idaho Railroad) Palouse Divn. extended Rockford to Spokane Falls, 27 miles.

February, 1890
    Spokane Falls & Northern — Opened Spokane Falls to Colville, 88 miles.

March, 1890
    Seattle, Lake Shore & Eastern — Snohomish north to Blackmans, 6 miles.

June, 1890
    Seattle, Lake Shore & Eastern — South Bend to Sallal Prairie, 3.2 miles.

July, 1890
    Spokane Falls & Northern — Colville northwest to Marcus, 14 miles.

August, 1890
    Seattle, Lake Shore & Eastern — Spokane Falls west to Davenport, 50 miles, and Blackmans to Arlington, 16 miles.
September, 1890
    Spokane Falls & Northern — Marcus north to Little Dalles, 25 miles.
December, 1890
    Seattle, Lake Shore & Eastern — Arlington north to Sedro Jct., 26 miles.
January, 1891
    Central Washington — Almira west to Coulee City, 21 miles.
February, 1891
    Tacoma, Orting & Southeastern — Orting to Puyallup River, 7 miles.
June, 1891
    Northern Pacific — Lakeview west to Olympia, 25 miles, and Centralia west to Montesano Wharf, 43 miles.
    Seattle, Lake Shore & Eastern — Sedro north to Sumas, 40 miles.
September, 1891
    Port Townsend Southern — Hooker's Lake south to Quilcene, 8 miles.
October, 1891
    Seattle, Lake Shore & Eastern — Sedro Jct. is now Woolley.
December, 1891
    Olympia & Chehalis Valley — It is now operated as Olympia Div. of Port Townsend Southern.
April, 1892
    Washington Southern — Shelton west to Satsop, 30 miles.
May, 1892
    Seattle, Lake Shore & Eastern — It is now operated as a portion of Northern Pacific Railroad Co.
June, 1892
    United Railroads of Washington — Montesano west to South Aberdeen, 14.2 miles.
November, 1892
    United Railroads of Washington — South Aberdeen to Ocosta, 13.1 miles.
December, 1892
    Great Northern — Spokane west to Wenatchee, 174 miles.
    Oregon & Washington Territory — The name has been changed to Washington & Columbia River Railway Co.
    Spokane Falls & Northern — Little Dalles north to Northport, 4 miles.
July, 1893
    Columbia & Puget Sound — Maple Valley east to Taylor, 10 miles.
    Great Northern — Spokane west to Seattle, 357.2 miles.
December, 1893
    Everett & Monte Cristo — Everett Jct. east to Monte Cristo, 72 miles.
March, 1894
    Spokane Falls & Northern — Northport northwest to Kootenay, B. C., 67.1 miles.
July, 1895
    Washington Southern — It has been reorganized as Peninsular Railroad company.
August, 1896
    Seattle, Lake Shore & Eastern — The name has been changed to Seattle & International Railway Co.
September, 1896
    Northern Pacific Railroad Co. — It is now Northern Pacific Railway Co.
February, 1897
    Columbia & Red Mountain — Opened from Northport to Rossland, B. C., 17 miles.
May, 1897
    Columbia & Puget Sound — Denny, three miles west of Black Diamond, is now Bruce.
January, 1898
    Pacific Coast Co. has assumed operation (from Oregon Improvement Co.) of Pacific Coast Railway Co., Columbia
        & Puget Sound Railroad Co., Seattle & Northern Railway Co. and Port Townsend Southern Railroad Co.
March, 1898
    Seattle & International — Deming (15 miles south of Sumas) is now Eureka.
April, 1898
    Northern Pacific — Pasco Jct. to Wallula is now a part of Washington & Columbia River Railway Co.
April, 1899
    Everett & Monte Cristo — Everett east to Canyon Head, 29 miles.
November, 1900
    Everett & Monte Cristo has been renamed Monte Cristo Railway Co., 61.7 miles.

WASHINGTON

April, 1901
    Seattle & International — Separate management terminated April 1, 1901, when that line became a part of Northern Pacific Railway Co.

July, 1901
    Northern Pacific — Opened for business from Arlington to Darrington, 28 miles.

September, 1901
    Northern Pacific — Wilkeson branch extended from Carbonado eastward to Fairfax, 7 miles.

November, 1901
    Bellingham Bay & British Columbia — The name of the northern terminal of this road, Hardan, is now Maple Falls.

December, 1901
    Great Northern — New Whatcom, 98 miles north of Seattle, is now Whatcom.

March, 1902
    Seattle & Northern — Extended from Hamilton to Rockport, 20 miles.

September, 1902
    Washington & Great Northern has opened for business from Marcus (on Spokane Falls & N.) north to Republic, 73 miles.

November, 1902
    Bellingham Bay & Eastern and Monte Cristo Railway are now a part of Northern Pacific Railway Co.

June, 1903
    Northern Pacific — Opened from Kalama to Vancouver, 28.5 miles.

July, 1903
    Bellingham Bay & British Columbia — Maple Falls east to Warnick, 5 miles.
    Tacoma Eastern — Holz east to Eatonville, 6 miles.

September, 1903
    Columbia River & Northern — Opened from Lyle to Goldendale, 42 miles.

February, 1904
    Bellingham Bay & British Columbia — Hampton to Lynden, 5 miles, and Warnick to Cornell, 3 miles.
    Great Northern — Whatcom is now Bellingham.

March, 1904
    Tacoma Eastern — Eatonville southward toward Alder, 9 miles.

April, 1904
    Columbia & Puget Sound — Extended from Newcastle to Coal Creek, 2 miles.
    Great Northern — Whatcom is now Bellingham.
    Northern Pacific — Yacolt branch is now open from Vancouver Jct. northward to Yacolt, 27 miles.

July, 1904
    Bellingham Bay & British Columbia — Cornell has been changed to Glacier.

August, 1904
    Tacoma Eastern — Elbe southeast to Ashford, 8 miles.

March, 1905
    Columbia & Puget Sound — Eddyville, 27 miles south of Seattle, is now Danville Jct.

December, 1905
    Northern Pacific — Lake Washington belt line branch of the Seattle Division extending from Woodinville to Black River, 24 miles, has been opened for business.

January, 1906
    Spokane Falls & Northern — Curlew, Wash., to Midway, Br. Col., 14.61 miles.

May, 1906
    Northern Pacific — Sunnyside branch extending from main line, 3.38 miles east of Toppenish, to Sunnyside, 11.98 miles, opened April 21, 1906.

July, 1906
    Northern Pacific — Grays Harbor branch extended from Hoquiam westward to Moclips, 28 miles.

December, 1906
    Spokane & Inland Empire — This company operates the Coeur d'Alene & Spokane Railway Co. and the Spokane & Inland Railway Co.

March, 1907
    Spokane & Inland — Extended from Waverly south to Rosalia, 12.2 miles.

April, 1907
    Great Northern — Spokane & Northern has been extended from Molson northward to Oroville, 25.3 miles.

May, 1907
    Spokane & Inland — Spring Valley south to Oakesdale, 13 miles.

June, 1907
    Spokane International -- Passenger service opened Spokane northeast to Eastport, Idaho, 140.8 miles.

July, 1907
    Northern Pacific -- Washington & Columbia River Railway Co. is now a Northern Pacific branch only.
    North Yakima & Valley — Opened North Yakima west to Naches, 14 miles.
    Spokane & Inland -- Oakesdale south to Palouse, 22.7 miles.
    Tacoma Eastern -- Extended from Tilton to Glenavon, 3 miles.

September, 1907
    Spokane & Inland Empire — - This road has been opened from Rosalia south to Colfax, 30.9 miles.

November, 1907
    Great Northern -- (Spokane Falls & Northern) Oroville to Keremos, B. C., 38 miles, opened for freight.

February, 1908
    Portland & Seattle -- Pasco west to Cliffs, 111.8 miles, was opened December 15, 1907, and Cliffs west to Lyle, 33.6 miles, on January 15, 1908.

March, 1908
    Idaho & Washington Northern -- Trains are now operating from Grand Jct., Idaho, to Spokane.
    Tacoma Eastern -- A new line has been opened from Tacoma eastward to McKenna, 27 miles.

April, 1908
    Spokane, Portland & Seattle — Lyle westward to Vancouver, 75.5 miles.

August, 1908
    Ilwaco Railroad — Extended east to Megler, 14 miles; steamer connection to Astoria is now made at Megler.

October, 1908
    Spokane & Inland Empire — Extended from Palouse to Moscow, 14.5 miles.

December, 1908
    Spokane, Portland & Seattle — The extension from Vancouver to Portland, 9.8 miles, has been completed; opened from Pasco to Portland, 230.7 miles, on November 17, 1908.

April, 1909
    Great Northern — A line from Blaine to New Westminster, B. C., 22.8 miles was opened March 15th.

May, 1909
    Spokane, Portland & Seattle — On May 3, 1909, the extension from Pasco to Spokane was opened, 146.8 miles.

June, 1909
    Not found to be reported — - Chicago, Milwaukee & Puget Sound completed from Chicago to tidewater.

October, 1909
    Idaho & Washington Northern — Train service extended from Newport to Usk, 18 miles.

December, 1909
    Idaho & Washington Northern -- Extended from Usk to Ione, 34 miles.
    Oregon Railroad & Navig. -- Dayton to Turner, 11.6 miles. (It was built in 1903; this was a reconstruction?).

January, 1910
    Oregon & Washington — On January 1, 1910, began operating trains between Portland and Seattle (on leased track).

July, 1910
    Northern Pacific — Roslyn Branch of Seattle Divn. was extended from Roslyn to Buckman, 3 miles.

September, 1910
    Tacoma Eastern — Opened from Tacoma to Morton, 67.3 miles.

October, 1910
    Chicago, Milwaukee & Puget Sound — A new section opened from McKenna west to Portola, 32.8 miles. Service is offered over Tacoma Eastern to McKenna, then CM&PS to Portola and thence over O-WR&N to S. Aberdeen.
    Oregon-Washington RR & Navig. — A new branch from Centralia via Portola to South Aberdeen, 52.8 miles.

December, 1910
    Connell & Northern -- Opened from Connell westward to Adco, 60.8 miles.
    Idaho & Washington Northern -- Extended from Ione northward to Metaline Falls, 10 miles.

January, 1911
    Chicago, Milwaukee & Puget Sound — A new branch has been opened from Warden west to Marcellus, 47 miles.
    North Yakima & Valley — A new branch has been opened from North Yakima to Moxee City.

April, 1911
    Oregon-Washington RR & Navig. — Has opened from Attalia westward to North Yakima, 98 miles.
    Spokane, Portland & Seattle -- It has purchased Astoria & Columbia River and the latter ceased to be an operating company.

June, 1911
    Not found to be reported — Chicago, Milwaukee & Puget Sound opened through passenger service on May 28, 1911.
    Spokane International — Opened from Corbin Jct. to Bayview, Idaho, 12 miles, and from Coeur d'Alene Jct. to Coeur d'Alene, Idaho, 10 miles.

WASHINGTON

March, 1912
    Northern Pacific -- Opened from Elma to McCleary, a distance of 8 miles.

June, 1912
    Washington Western — Has been opened from Machias southward via Harnett to Woodruff, 12 miles, and from Harnett eastward to Williams mill.

October, 1912
    North Yakima & Valley — The Zillah Branch, extending from North Yakima, Wash., southeastward to Granger, Wash., a distance of 25.2 miles, is operated for passenger and freight business.

February, 1913
    Western Washington — Extended from Sinnett's to Machias. (The company name has been reversed.)

June, 1913
    Chicago, Milwaukee & St. Paul -- Moses Lake line extended from Tiflis west to Neppel, 15 miles. Effective May 13, 1913, the new Beverly-Hanford extension was opened. Effective May 26, 1913, the Montesano line was opened for freight from South Montesano to Montesano.

November, 1913
    Chicago, Milwaukee & St. Paul -- Extended and opened Plummer Jct., Idaho, to Spokane, 41 miles, on Sept. 28, 1913.

August, 1914
    Great Northern — Pateros eastward (actually south) to Wenatchee, 58.9 miles.

October, 1914
    Oregon-Washington RR & Navig. -- A new line has been opened for business from Ayer Jct. north to Spokane, 104 miles.

January, 1915
    Northern Pacific -- The line between Tacoma and Tenino, 44 miles, opened December 15, 1914; it is jointly used by Northern Pacific and Oregon-Washington RR & Navig. (The Point Defiance line).

May, 1915
    Northern Pacific — Mixed train service now in operation on the Zillah branch (Pasco divn.) between Granger and Parker, 18 miles.

July, 1917
    Bellingham & Northern — A new line was opened from Goshen east to Kulshan, 12 miles.

Tacoma Public Library *Boland Collection #2731*
A sere scene of Far West Lumber Company locomotives west of Tacoma in about 1907

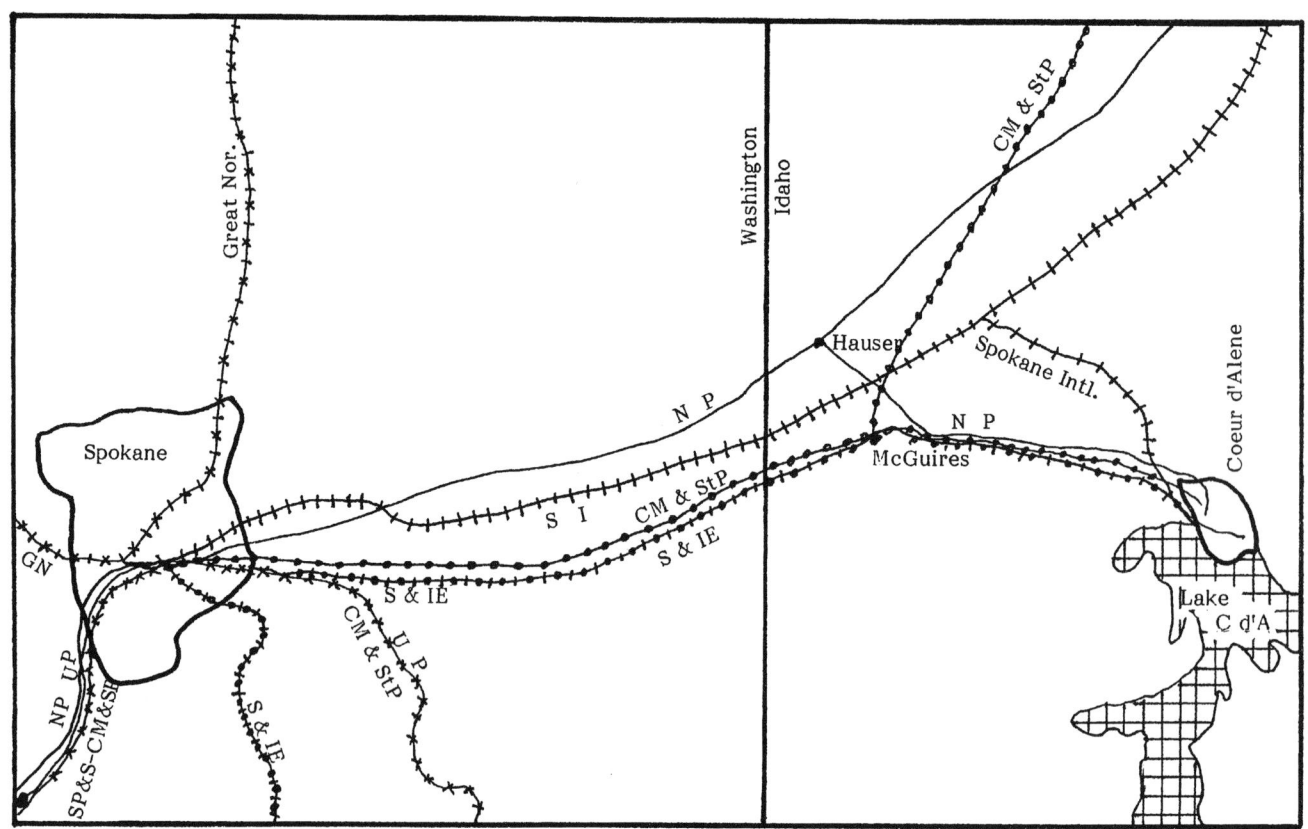

Detail maps of Spokane - Coeur d'Alene and Pasco areas.

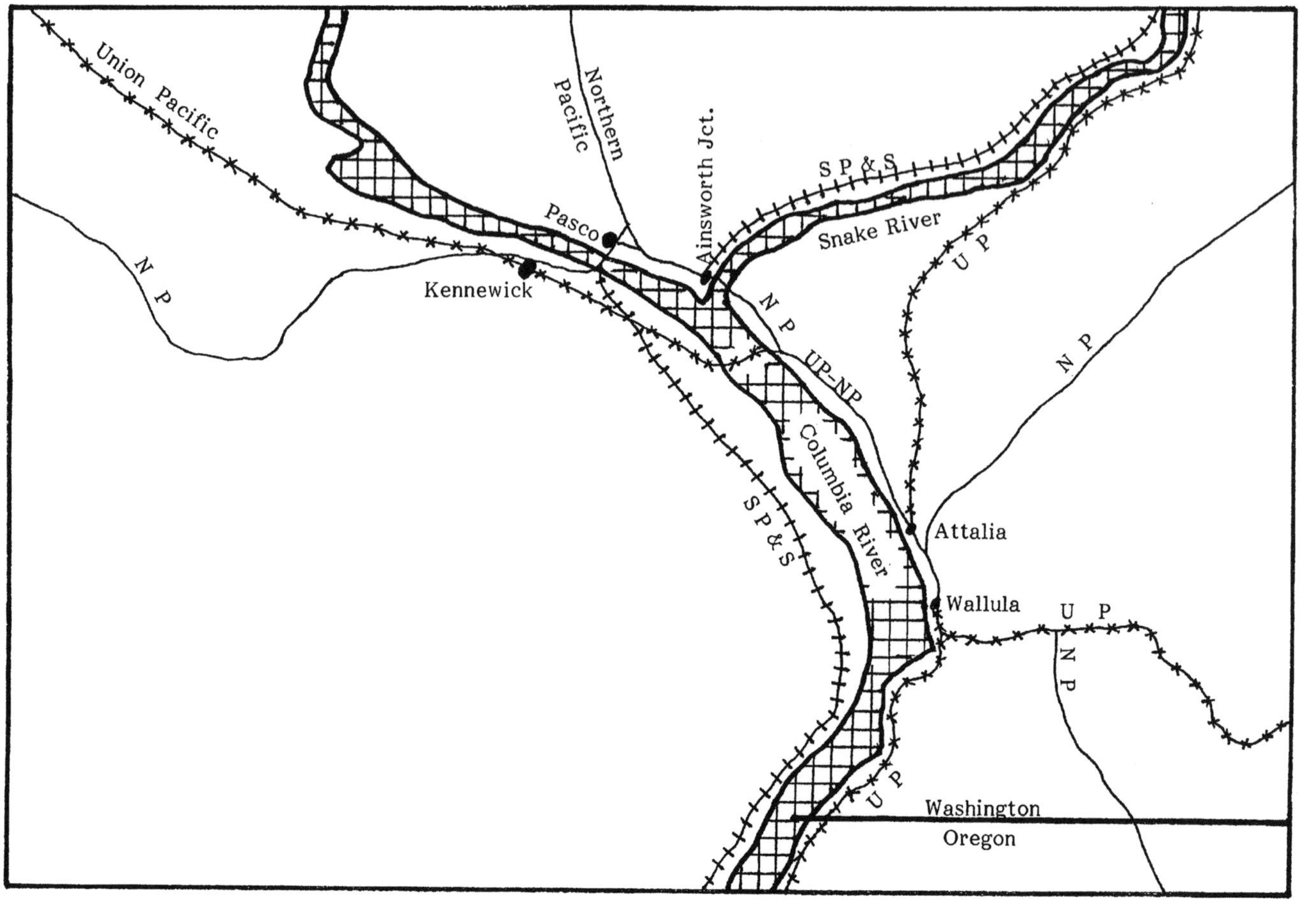

WASHINGTON 311.

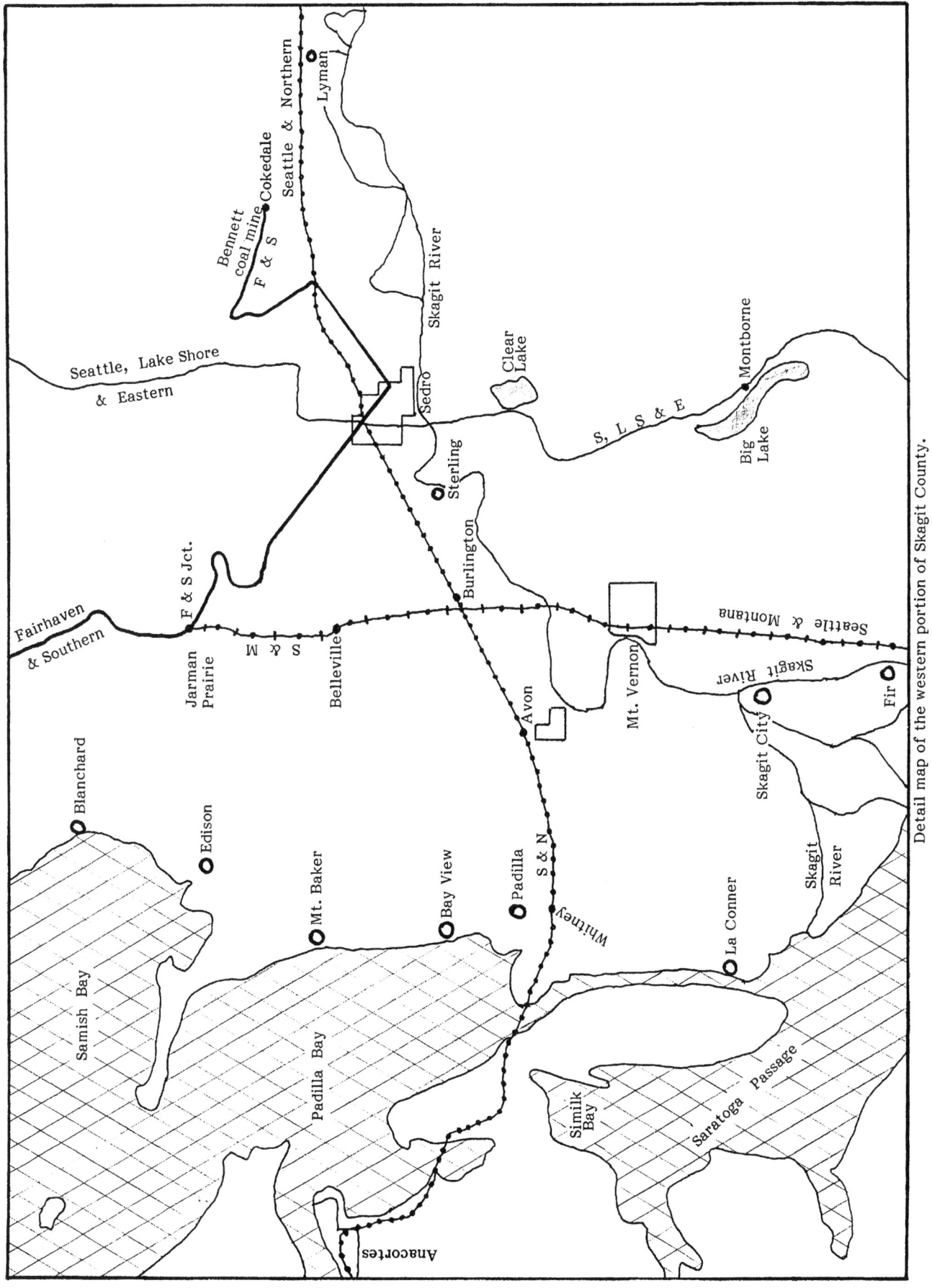

Detail map of the western portion of Skagit County.

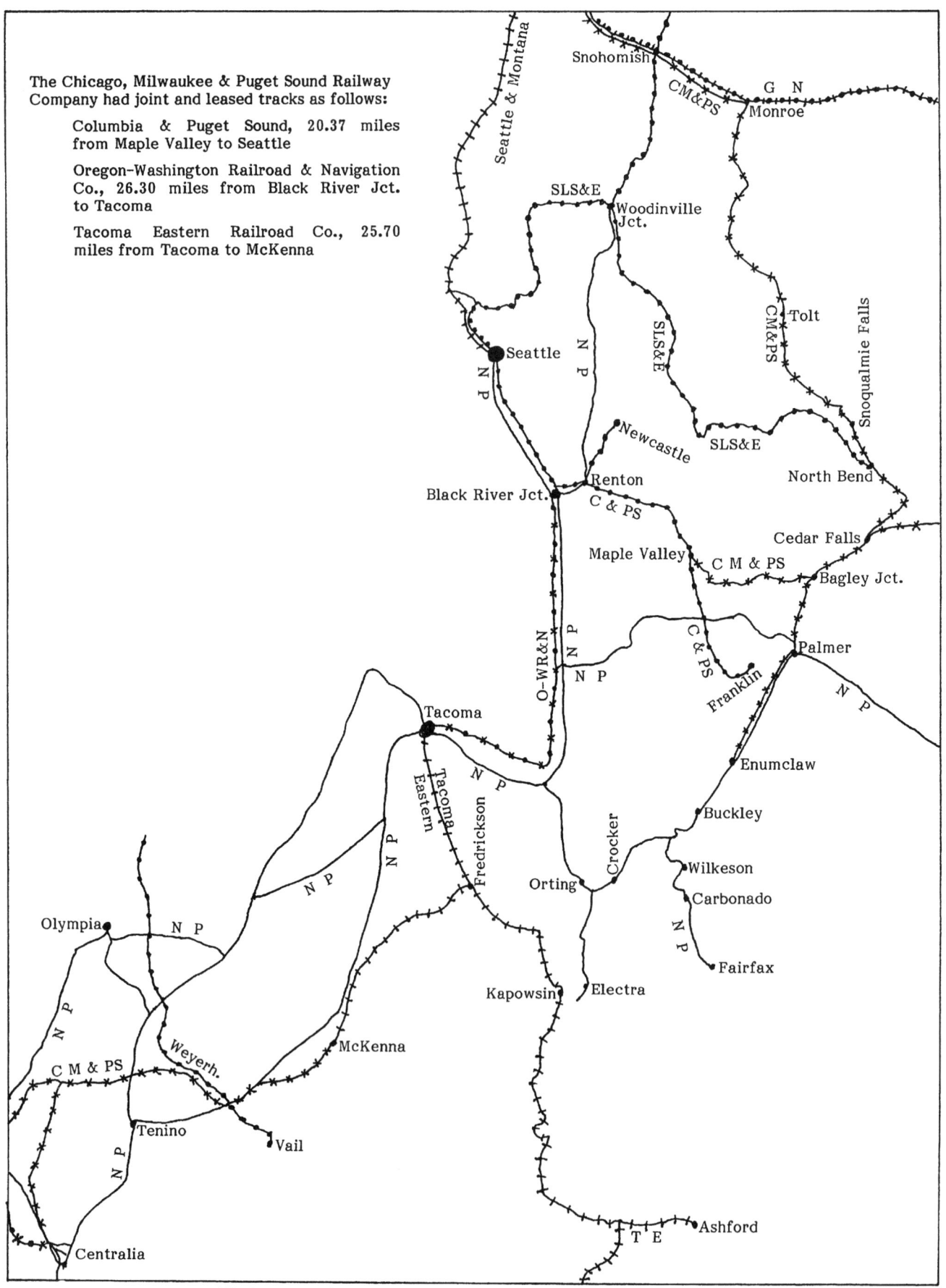

All-time map of west-central Washington showing major railroad lines.

CHRONOLOGY

Some of the major events in the development of the Territory/State of Washington.

1592	Juan de Fuca claimed the discovery of the strait that now bears his name.
1775	Bruno Heceta made the first recorded Europena landing on what is now the Washington coast.
1778	British captain James Cook (1728-1779) sighted and named Cape Flattery.
1788	Captain John Mears explored the Juan de Fuca Strait and named Mount Olympus and Cape Disappointment.
1790	Two Spanish navigators, Francisco Eliza and Manuel Quimper, explored to reinforce Spanish claims to the region.
1792	Captain George Vancouver explored present Puget Sound and took possession for King George III and named the land New Georgia.
1792	Captain Robert Gray discovered what became the Columbia River and Grays Harbor.
1804	Lewis and Clark expedition (1804-1806) from the Missouri River to the Pacific coast gave the nation claim to the Oregon country.
1810	Establishment of Spokane House by British North West Fur Co.; the first white settlement in eastern Washington.
1811	John J. Astor's Pacific Fur Co. founded Astoria and built Fort Okanogan in central part of the area.
1812	Fort Spokane established by Pacific Fur Co. near Spokane House.
1818	Fort Nez Perce was built by the Northwest Company near present day Walla Walla.
	British and United States governments agreed to joint occupancy of the Oregon country.
1825	Hudson's Bay Company established Fort Vancouver on the Columbia River.
1826	Hudson's Bay Company built Fort Colville and abandoned Spokane House.
1832	Captain Benjamin Bonneville, and later Nathaniel Wyeth, arrived at Fort Vancouver.
1833	Fort Nisqually built as the first trading post on Puget Sound.
1836	Waiilatpu Mission built by Marcus Whitman and associates.
1841	The Wilkes U.S. Exploring Expedition explored and mapped Puget Sound.
1843	Oregon provisional government established.
1844	Saint Ignatius Catholic mission was founded near present Spokane.
1845	First American settlement in Puget Sound region established at present Tumwater (Olympia).
1846	United States and Great Britain established boundary on the 49th parallel.
1848	Creation of Oregon Territory which included present day Washington.
1849	Fort Vancouver made U. S. Army headquarters in the Pacific northwest; Fort Steilacoom established.
1852	Monticello Convention requested that Congress create the Territory of Columbia.
1853	On March second, the Territory of Washington, population 3,965, was established.
	Isaac Stevens appointed Territorial Governor and Superintendent of Indian Affairs.
	First steam powered sawmill built on Puget Sound by Henry Yesler.
1854	Meeting of the first Territorial Legislature and first Federal Court in the territory.
1855	Indian wars break out; present eastern Washington closed to miners and settlers.
1856	Indians attack village of Seattle, but soon defeated at Connell's Prairie.
1857	Governor Stevens elected to Congress.
1859	Gold rush begins in eastern Washington Territory. With Oregon statehood, Territory reaches Rocky Mountains.
1860	United States completes acquisition of remaining Hudson's Bay Company properties.
1861	Territorial University opened at Seattle with Asa Mercer as the president and teacher.
1863	Territory of Idaho created and acquired eastern territory.
1867	Alaska purchased from Russia.
1870	Doctor Dorsey S. Baker established Territory's first bank at Walla Walla.
1871	First settlement at Spokane Falls.
1873	Northern Pacific Railroad reached New Tacoma from Kalama.
1885	The first paper mill in the northwest was opened at Camas.
1889	On November 11, the Territory of Washington became the 42nd state.
1891	U. S. Navy established the Puget Sound Navy Yard at Bremerton.
1892	Washington State College opened at Pullman.
1893	Great Northern Railway Co. completed route to Puget Sound.
1896	Trans-Pacific steamship service to Asia inaugurated.
1897	Klondike gold rush began with Seattle as the supply area.
1899	Mount Rainier National Park created.
1900	Frederick Weyerhaeuser purhcased timber land and started a lumbering empire.
1909	Alaska-Yukon-Pacific Esposition in Seattle.
1916	Boeing Company began the manufacture of airplanes in Seattle area.
1917	Fort Lewis established as a World War training center.
	Lake Washington ship canal opened.
1929	Great Northern Railway Co. Cascade tunnel completed.
1933	Works starts on Bonneville Dam and the Grand Coulee project was authorized.
1938	Boeing builds 74-passenger "Clipper" for Pan American Airways.
	Bonneville Dam completed.
1940	Aluminum plant established at Vancouver.
1941	Grand Coulee Dam completed.
1954	President Dwight D. Eisenhower dedicates McNary Dam.
1962	Seattle World's Fair "Century 21."
1974	Spokane World's Fair "Expo 74."

Source: *1986 Washington State Yearbook* from the Washington State Historical Society.

THE DAILY LEDGER, TACOMA, WASHINGTON, MONDAY, APRIL 4, 1892.

SHIPS NOW IN PUGET SOUND WATERS

Date of Arrival	Flag—Rig	NAME	Tons	MASTER	Loading Port	CARGO	DESTINAT'N
Dec.18,'91	Am bk	Shirley	997	Waldo	Tacoma		Waiting orders
Jan 15,'92	Br sp	Samaritan	1097	Dick	do		Disengaged
Feb 22	do sp	City of Benares	1674	Ingram	do	Lumber	Valparaiso
do 23	Swd sp	Hawksbury	1132	Nordfeldt	do	do	S. F.
March 26	Am sp	Alaska	1315	Worth	Seattle	Coal	do
do 26	Am bk	Germania	958	Lane	Whatcom	Lumber	do
do 26	Am bk	R. K. Ham	512	Gove	Blakeley	do	do
do 15	do sp	Eclipse	1535	Peterson	Tacoma	do	Guaymas
do 15	Br sp	Gen. Gordon	1615	Clayton	do	do	Port Pirie
Jan 14	do	Thomas Daua	1388	Meyers	do	do	Valparaiso
Feb 23	Br bk	Maude	1077	Evans	do	Lumber	Callao
Jan 30	Nor bk	Fristad	953	Fristad	Blakely		Repairing
Feb 23	Am sp	Daniel Barnes	1486	Stover	do	Spars	Philadelphia
do 29	Ger sp	Fanny	1800	Berholdt	do	do	Valparaiso
March 3	Nor bk	Hiawatha	1497	Jorgensen	do	do	Sydney
Feb 28	Am sp	Topgallant	1220	Jackson	do		Laid up
do 28	Swd bk	Belted Will	773	Hammergreen	do	Lumber	U. K.
March 13	Br bk	Archdale	1479	Rhode	do	do	Port Pirie
do 9	Nor bk	Orion	1235	Ulstup	Whatcom	do	Valparaiso
do 13	Am bk	Templar	910	Cardell	do		Laid up
do 11	do sp	Spartan	1376	Malgram	Pt Twnsd		Waiting orders
Jan 29	do sc	GovernorAmes	1090	Davis	Pt Town	Shpgcrw	Taku
March 10	do bk	Cowlitz	740	Miller	do	do	S. F.
Dec 2	do bk	Sagamore	1274	Moore	Ludlow		Laid up
Jan 4	do bk	James Cheston	948	Cushman	do	Lumber	Valparaiso
Feb 25	Br sp	Star of Austria	1633	Willis	do	do	Guaymas
do 26	Am bk	Harvester	1194	Beck	do	do	Australia
March 11	Swd bk	Albatros	957	Frockberg	do		Disengaged
Jan 1	Am bk	Nooantum	1110	McGuire	Madison		do
do 1	do bk	Tidal Wave	603	Wilson	do		do
do 5	do bk	Vidette	586	Pyle	do		do
do 10	do bk	Northwest	493	Swanton	do		do
do 12	do bk	Oakland	534	Welfaw	do		Dis'arging sugar
do 5	Br sp	Mount Carmel	1596	Livingston	Vancouver	Lumber	Valparaiso
Feb 29	do sp	British India	1199	Lines	do	do	Sydney
do 26	do bk	Mistletoe	821	Smith	do	do	Callao
Jan 21	do sp	Craigend	2218	Southwait	Hastings'ml	do	Valparaiso
do 15	do bk	Glenbervie	830	Gundualer	do	do	Sydney
Feb 29	do sp	Riversdale	1453	Farr	Esquimalt		Repairing
Jan 12	Nor bk	Dominion	1265		Chemainus		Laid up
Feb 23	do bk	Colorado	1036	Gibson	Nanaimo	Coal	San Pedro
do 25	Am sp	Kennebec	2025	Read	do	do	S F
March 13	do sp	Sea King	1436	Pierce	do	do	do
do 15	do sp	J. B. Brown	1473	Cameron	do	do	do
do 15	do sp	Commodore	1809	Davidson	do	do	S F
do	Am bt	Chenalis	656	Watts	Deep Bay	do	
do	Br bk	Argyleshire	1208	Stevens	Victoria	Disch'r'g	S F
Mch 19	Am bk	Sumatra	1015	Olsen	Tacoma	Lumber	S F
do	do	Mercury	1098	Killman	Blakely	do	S F
do	Am bk	Mary Glover	701	Seabury	Tacoma	Lumber	S F
do	Nor bk	Mynt	1257	Pederson	Blakely	do	Santos
do	Am sp	Highlander	1352	Edjett	Tacoma	do	Valparaiso
do	Am sc	Salvator	414	Petersen	Seattle		S F
do	Am bk	Carrolton	1390	Lewis	Nanaimo	Coal	S F
Mch 21	Br sp	Benares	1646	Mutch	Pt Townsnd	Lumber	Waiting orders
do	Am sc	Corona	375	McAllep	Seattle	do	S F
do	do sp	W F Babcock	2029	Graham	do	Coal	do
do	do sc	Martha W Tuft	165	Stockbye	do		
do	do	Excelsior	331	odeshom	Blakely	do	do
Mch 21	Am sp	Dshing Wave	1012	Moorhouse	Tacoma	Lumber	S. F.
do	Am bk	Bonanza	1293	Stetson	Gamble	do	do
do	Am bt	John Smith	565	Kustet	Ludlow	do	Launceston
do	Am bk	Louis Walsh	1197	Gammons	Nanaimo	Coal	S F
do	Br sp	Thermopylae	948	Wilson	Victoria		Discharging
do	Am bk	Canada	1149	Landcaster	Tacoma	Lumber	S F
Mch 25	Nor bk	Memento	650	Gunderson	Blakeley	do	Australia

As this century ends, railroads have major competition from millions of motor trucks operating on a right-of-way provided by taxpayers and government; a century-plus years ago it was thousands of small sailing vessels. In the data above it will be noted that Seattle was not the major site for their activity.

Denver Public Library - Western History Department #18141 *Photo by Otto C. Perry*
Union Pacific locomotive #2894, a 4-6-2, with a long train #12 at Spokane July 30, 1938

Denver Public Library - Western History Department #16929 *Photo by Otto C. Perry*
Union Pacific #3525, a 2-8-8-0, adds its mass to Wallowa's wood- and steel water tanks on July 29, 1938.

Tacoma Public Library
Anna Wright Seminary on Division Avenue in Tacoma, a private elite girls' school, circa 1885

Tacoma Public Library   *F. Jay Haynes Collection*
The Park Hotel, Centralia, in about 1890 bears a likeness to the Victorian shown above

Oregon State Library Collection - #757
Willamette steamer *Elk* was built at Canemah in October, 1857; it exploded at Davidson's Landing a few years later.

Tacoma Public Library
A Sunday outing at Frazer Hotel near South Tacoma Northern Pacific shops; railroaders boarded there when it opened in 1891

Tacoma Public Library   *Bolland Collection - B12953*
Puget Sound Electric Railway Co. depot at 702 A Street in Tacoma with its electric car, bus and taxies; the date was July 13, 1925.

Tacoma Public Library   *Boland Collection - B2240*
Western Washington motorized logging in about 1919; the truck was probably a Republic.

Photo by Ed Austin
A Union Pacific Railroad Company unit coal train westbound near Telocaset, Oregon, on August 25, 1992

Photo by Ed Austin
Amtrak southbound with a mixed consist of mismatched cars at Marion, Oregon, on March 7, 1993; awaiting the main line is a Southern Pacific Railroad Company freight train.

Special Collections Div. - Univ. of Washington Libraries
Clark Kinsey photo #1552
Independence Logging Co., headquartered in Aberdeen, trestles up to 112 feet tall and 1830 feet long

PHOTOGRAPH GALLERY

321.

Photo by *Ed Austin*
Union Pacific Railroad Co. eastbound freight on John Day bridge and dam of the same name in the background with five engines on their home rails and one carrying Frisco colors. The date was November 26, 1977.

Photo by Ed Austin
Southern Pacific eastbound wood products train on the Big Baldwin bridge of the Tillamook branch on July 11, 1976. There were four more SD-9s pushing on the rear.

GENERAL INDEX

Complete Index of Railroads Found in Volumes One, Two and Three

Admiralty Logging Company	P 189
Alamogordo & Sacramento Mountain Railway Company	D 187
Alamogordo Lumber Company	D 238
Albany & Lebanon Railroad Company	P 56
Albuquerque & Cerrillos Coal Company, Inc.	D 188
Albuquerque Eastern Railway Company, The	D 187
Alder Creek Railway Company	M 246
Algoma Lumber Company	P 56
American Fork Railroad Company	D 260
Anaconda Copper Mining Company	M 277
Anderson & Middleton Lumber Company of Oregon	P 56
Apache Lumber Company	D 106
Apache Railway Company, The	D 65
Arapahoe, Jefferson & South Park Railroad Company	M 64
Argentine & Grays Peak Railway Company	M 64
Argentine Central Railway Company	M 64
Arizona & California Railway Company	D 66
Arizona & Colorado Railroad Company	D 67
Arizona & Colorado Railroad of New Mexico, The	D 71
Arizona & New Mexico Railway Company	D 68
Arizona & South Eastern Rail Road Company, The	D 69
Arizona & Swansea Railroad Company	D 70
Arizona & Utah Railway Company, The	D 113
Arizona Central Railroad Company, The	D 91
Arizona Copper Company, Ltd.	D 68 and 80
Arizona Eastern Railroad Company	D 71
Arizona Eastern Railroad of New Mexico, The	D 71
Arizona Lumber & Timber Company	D 73
Arizona Mineral Belt Rail Road Company	D 73
Arizona Narrow-Gauge Railroad Company	D 109
Arizona Southern Railroad Company	D 74
Arkansas Valley Railroad Company, The	M 65
Arkansas Valley Railway Company	M 65
Armstrong, H. E.	P 208
Aspen & Western Railway Company, The	M 66
Astoria & Columbia River Railroad Company	P 57
Astoria & Portland Railway Company	P 134
Astoria & South Coast Railroad Company	P 134
Astoria Southern Railway Company	P 58
Atchison & Topeka Railroad Company	D 189
Atchison, Topeka & Santa Fe Rail Road Company, The	D 189
Atchison, Topeka & Santa Fe Railway Company, The	D 189
Atlantic & Pacific Railroad Company	D 75
Aurora Branch Railroad Company	M 384
Austin City Railway	D 132
Baird-Harper Lumber Company	M 347
Baker White Pine Lumber Company, The	P 145
Baldridge Logging Company	P 189
Ballard & Thompson Railroad Company	D 310
Bamberger Electric Railroad Company	D 261
Bamberger Railroad Company	D 261
Battle Mountain & Lewis Railway	D 133
Beaver, Penrose & Northern Railway Company, The	M 66
Beaverton & Willsburg Railroad Company	P 58
Big Blackfoot Milling Company	M 277
Big Blackfoot Railway Company	M 278
Big Horn Railroad Company	M 367
Big Horn Southern Railroad Company, The	M 367
Bellingham & Northern Railway Company	P 189
Bellingham Bay & British Columbia Rail Road Company	P 189
Bellingham Bay & Eastern Railroad Company	P 190
Bellingham Terminals & Railway Company	P 189
Benson Logging & Lumbering Company	P 59 and 303

Pages marked "D" will be found in volume one, The Desert States.
Pages marked "M" will be found in volume two, The Mountain States.
Pages marked "P" will be found in this volume, number three.

Big Blackfoot Milling Company	M 277
Big Blackfoot Railway Company	M 278
Big Creek Logging Company	P 60
Big Horn Railroad Company	M 367
Big Horn Southern Railroad Company, The	M 367
Billings & Central Montana Railway Company	M 278
Bingham & Garfield Railway Company	D 262
Bingham Canyon & Camp Floyd Rail Road Company	D 263
Black Hills & Northwestern Railway Company	P 228
Blackwell Lumber Company	M 246
Blakely Railroad Company	P 286
Bloedel-Donovan Lumber Mills	P 161
Blue Lake Logging Company	P 62
Blue Mountain Railroad, Inc.	P 192
Bluestone Mining & Smelting Company	D 133
Boise & Interurban Railway Company	M 202
Boise & Western Railroad Compnay	M 200
Boise City Railway & Terminal Company, The	M 200
Boise, Nampa & Owyhee Railway Company, Ltd.	M 201
Boise Payette Lumber Company	M 246
Boise Valley Railway Company	M 202
Boise Valley Traction Company	M 202
Bolcom-Riley Logging Company	P 193
Bolcom-Vanderhoof Logging Company	P 193
Bonners Ferry Lumber Company	M 246
Book Cliff Railroad Company	M 67
Booth-Kelly Lumber Company, The	P 60
Boston Consolidated Mining Company	D 263
Bowman-Hicks Lumber Company	P 61
Bozeman Street Railway Company	M 301
Bradley Logging Company	P 208
Bradshaw Mountain Railroad Company	D 77
Bratnober-Waite Lumber Company	P 200
Breece Lumber Company, Geo. E.	D 204
Bristol Silver Mines Company	D 133
Brix Logging Company	P 61
Brock Logging Company, B. F.	P 213
Brooks-Scanlon Lumber Company	M 347 and P 62
Brownlee-Olds Lumber Company	P 90
Brown's Bay Logging Company	P 189
Buckley Logging Company	P 212
Buffelen Lumber & Mfg. Company	P 193
Bullfrog Goldfield Railroad Company	D 134
Burlington & Colorado Railroad Company	M 68
Burlington & Missouri River Railroad Company (in Iowa)	M 384
Burlington & Missouri River Rail Road in Nebraska	M 69
Burlington Northern Railroad Company	M 279
Burro Mountain Railroad Company	D 205
Butte, Anaconda & Pacific Railway Company	M 282
Cadillac & Lake City Railway Company	M 71
Cady Lumber Corp.	D 106
Caliente & Pioche Railroad Company	D 135
California & Oregon Coast Railroad Company, The	P 62
California, Arizona & Santa Fe Railway Company, The	D 77
California Northeastern Railway Company	P 107
California Short Line Railway Company	D 286
Camas Prairie Railroad Company	M 203
Camp Creek Railway Company, The	M 283
Canon City & Cripple Creek Railroad Company, The	M 71
Canon City & San Juan Railway Company, The	M 153
Carbon County Railway Company	D 264
Carbon Cut-Off Railway Company, The	M 368
Carlisle Lumber Company	P 193
Carlisle-Pennell Lumber Company	P 193
Carlsborg Mill & Timber Company	P 216
Carlton & Coast Railroad Company	P 63
Carson & Colorado Railroad Company, The	D 136
Carson & Colorado Railway Company	D 136
Carson & Tahoe Railroad Company	D 142
Cascade Lumber Company	P 194
Cascade Timber Company	P 195
Cascades Railroad Company	P 195

Castle Valley Railroad Company	D 265
Castle Valley Railway Company	D 265
Cathlamet Timber Company	P 208
Central Arizona Railway Company	D 78
Central Idaho Railroad Company	M 204
Central Military Tract Railroad Company	M 384
Central Montana Rail, Inc.	M 283
Central Nevada Railroad Company	D 157
Central of Oregon Railway Company	P 121
Central Pacific Railway Company	see California
Central Railroad of Oregon	P 150
Central Railway Company of Oregon	P 150
Central Washington Railroad Company, The	P 297
Cerrillos Coal Railroad Company	D 188
Chambers Lumber Company, J. H.	P 56
Chehalis & Cowlitz Railway Company	P 208
Chehalis County Logging & Timber Company	P 260
Cherry Valley Logging Company	P 200
Cheyenne & Burlington Railroad Company	M 368
Cheyenne & Northern Railway Company	M 369
Chicago & Aurora Railroad Company	M 384
Chicago & North Western Railway Company	M 370
Chicago & Rock Island Rail Road Company	M 73
Chicago, Burlington & Quincy Railroad Company	M 384
Chicago, Kansas & Nebraska Railway Company, The	M 72
Chicago, Milwaukee & Puget Sound Railway Company	M 284
Chicago, Milwaukee & St. Paul Railway Company	M 284
Chicago, Milwaukee, St. Paul & Pacific Railroad Company	M 284
Chicago, Rock Island & El Paso Railway Company	D 205
Chicago, Rock Island & Pacific Railroad Company	M 73
Chicago, Rock Island & Pacific Railway Company	M 73
Chicago, St. Paul & Fond du Lac Rail Road Company	M 370
Cimarron & Northwestern Railway Company, The	D 206
City of Prineville Railway	P 64
Clallam County Railroad	P 250
Clark & Wilson Lumber Company	P 65
Clark County Timber Company	P 200
Clatsop Railroad Company	P 66
Clear Lake Lumber Company	P 200
Clearwater Short Line Railway Company	M 203
Clearwater Timber Company	M 229
Clemons Logging Company	P 201
Clifton & Lordsburg Railway Company	D 206
Clifton & Southern Pacific Railway Company	D 79
Cloudcroft Lumber & Land Company	D 204
Coalville & Echo Railway Company	D 288
Coats Logging Company, A. F.	P 211
Coats-Fordney Logging Company	P 211
Cobbs & Mitchell Lumber Company	P 66
Coeur d'Alene & Pend Oreille Railway Company	M 204
Coeur d'Alene & Spokane Railway Company, Ltd.	M 205
Coeur d'Alene Railway & Navigation Company	M 206
Coeur d'Alene Southern Railway Company	M 246
Colorado & Clear Creek Railroad Company	M 87
Colorado & New Mexico Railroad Company	M 153
Colorado & Northwestern Railroad Company	M 112
Colorado & North-Western Railway Company, The	M 112
Colorado & Southeastern Railroad Company, The	M 79
Colorado & Southeastern Railway Company, The	M 79
Colorado & Southern Railway Company, The	M 80
Colorado & Southwestern Railroad Company	M 152
Colorado & Wyoming Railroad Company, The	M 85
Colorado & Wyoming Railway Company, The	M 85
Colorado Central & Pacific Railroad Company	M 87
Colorado Central Rail Road Company	M 87
Colorado Central Railroad Company (Wyoming)	M 395
Colorado Eastern Railroad Company	M 89
Colorado Eastern Railway Company	M 89
Colorado-Kansas Railway Company, The	M 92
Colorado Midland Railroad Company, The	M 90
Colorado Midland Railway Company, The	M 90
Colorado Northern Railway Company, The	M 125

Colorado Railroad Company, The	M 91
Colorado Railroad, Inc.	M 92
Colorado Springs & Cripple Creek District Railway Co., The	M 93
Colorado, Wyoming & Eastern Railway Company, The	M 398
Colorado, Wyoming & Great Northern Railroad Company	M 67
Columbia & Cowlitz Railway Company	P 201
Columbia & Nehalem River Railroad Company	P 85
Columbia & Palouse Railroad Company, The	P 202
Columbia & Puget Sound Railroad Company	P 204
Columbia & Red Mountain Railway Company	P 205
Columbia Railway & Navigation Company, The	P 282
Columbia River & Northern Railway Company	P 206
Columbia River & Oregon Central Railroad Company	P 67
Columbia River Belt Line Railway	P 68
Columbia Southern Railway Company	P 69
Columbia Valley Railroad Company	P 222
Condon, Kinzua & Southern Railroad Company	P 69
Congress Gold Company	D 79
Connell Northern Railway Company	P 207
Consolidated Lumber Company	P 207
Coos Bay Lumber Company	P 82
Coos Bay, Roseburg & Eastern Railroad & Navigation Company, The	P 70
Copalis Lumber Company	P 193
Copper Belt Railroad Company	D 266
Coronado Railroad Company	D 80
Coronado Railway Company	D 80
Corvallis & Alsea River Railway Company	P 72
Corvallis & Eastern Railroad Company	P 72
Cowlitz, Chehalis & Cascade Railway Company	P 208
Craig Mountain Lumber Company	M 207
Craig Mountain Railway Company	M 207
Cripple Creek & Colorado Springs Railroad Company, The	M 94
Cripple Creek Central Railway Company, The	M 95
Cripple Creek District Railway	M 93
Crossett-Western Company	P 74
Crown Willamette Paper Company	P 74 and 208
Crown Zellerbach Corporation	P 74 and 208
Crystal Bay Railroad Company	D 137
Crystal River & San Juan Railroad Company, The	M 95
Crystal River Railroad Company	M 96
Crystal River Railway Company, The	M 96
Cuba Extension Railroad	D 232
Curtis Lumber Company	P 90
Curtis, Milburn & Eastern Railroad Company	P 209
Dawson Lumber Company	M 347
Dawson Railway Company	D 207
Dayton, Sheridan & Grande Ronde Railroad Company, The	P 158
Dayton, Sutro & Carson Valley Railroad	D 137
Deep Creek Railroad Company	D 266
Deep River Logging Company	P 210
Deer Park Central Railway Company	P 210
Deer Park Lumber Company	P 210
Deer Park Railway Company	P 210
Denver & Boulder Valley Railroad Company, The	M 97
Denver & Eastern Railway & Coal Company	M 89
Denver & Intermountain Railroad Company	M 98
Denver & Inter-mountain Railway Company	M 98
Denver & Middle Park Railroad Company, The	M 98
Denver & Montana Railroad Company, The	M 99
Denver & New Orleans Railroad Company, The	M 100
Denver & Rio Grande Railroad Company, The	M 101
Denver & Rio Grande Railway Company, The	M 101
Denver & Rio Grande Western Railroad Company, The	M 101
Denver & Rio Grande Western Railway Company, The	D 267
Denver & Salt Lake Railroad Company	M 110
Denver & Salt Lake Railway Company, The	M 101
Denver & Salt Lake Western Railroad Company, The	M 111
Denver & Santa Fe Railway Company, The	M 111
Denver & Scranton Railway Company	M 89
Denver & Southwestern Railway Company	M 95
Denver, Boulder & Western Railroad Company	M 112

Denver Circle Rail Road Company, The	M 113
Denver, Lakewood & Golden Railroad Company	M 113
Denver, Laramie & Northwestern Railroad Company	M 114
Denver, Laramie & Northwestern Railway Company	M 114
Denver, Leadville & Gunnison Railway Company, The	M 115
Denver, Longmont & Noland Stone & Railway Company	M 116
Denver, Longmont & Northwestern Railroad Company, The	M 125
Denver, Marshall & Boulder Railway Company, The	M 117
Denver, Northwestern & Pacific Railway Company	M 118
Denver Pacific Railway & Telegraph Company	M 119
Denver Railroad, Land & Coal Company	M 89
Denver Resort Railway & Telegraph Company	M 120
Denver, South Park & Hill Top Railway Company, The	M 120
Denver, South Park & Pacific Railroad Company	M 121
Denver, South Park & Pacific Railway Company	M 121
Denver, Texas & Fort Worth Railroad Company	M 123
Denver, Texas & Gulf Railroad Company	M 124
Denver, Utah & Pacific Railroad Company, The	M 125
Denver, Utah & Pacific Rail-road Company, The	M 125
Denver, Western & Pacific Railway Company, The	M 117
Des Chutes Railroad Company	P 76
Diamond Match Company	M 246
Dodge City & Cimarron Valley Railway Company	M 126
Dollar Company, Robert	P 76
Dolores, Paradox & Grand Junction Railroad Company	M 152
Donovan-Corkery Logging Company	P 211
Doty Lumber & Shingle Company	P 211
Doty Lumber Company	P 211
Drummond & Philipsburg Railroad Company, The	M 300
Durango & Silverton Narrow Gauge Railroad Company	M 101
Eagle Gorge Logging Company	P 212
Eagle Salt Works Railroad Company	D 138
Eastern & Western Lumber Company	P 77 and 213
Eastern Railway & Lumber Company	P 213
Eastern Railway Company of New Mexico, The	D 208
Eastern Washington Railway Company, The	P 276
East Portland Traction Company	P 78
East Side Logging Company	P 77
Eatonville Lumber Company	P 214
Eccles Lumber Company, W. H.	M 246
Echo & Park City Railway Company	D 268
Elk Creek & Grays Harbor Railway Company	P 211
El Paso & Northeastern Railway Company	D 210
El Paso & Rock Island Railway Company	D 211
El Paso & Southwestern Railroad Company	D 81
Emigration Canyon Railroad Company	D 268
Empire Copper Company	M 246
English Lumber Company	P 214
Eufaula Logging Company	P 213
Eugene & Eastern Railway Company	P 132
Eureka & Palisade Railroad Company	D 139
Eureka & Palisade Railway Company	D 139
Eureka & Ruby Hill Narrow Gauge Railroad	D 160
Eureka Hill Railroad Company	D 269
Eureka Lumber Company	M 347
Eureka-Nevada Railway Company	D 140
Everett & Monte Cristo Railway Company	P 231
Fairhaven & Southern Railroad Company	P 215
Farmers' Railway, Navigation & Steamboat Portage Company, The	P 282
Farmers' Transportation Company	P 282
Ferrocarril de Sonora	D 85
Fiberboard Products, Inc.	P 216
Flagstaff Lumber Mfg. Company	D 106
Flora Logging Company	P 79
Florence & Cripple Creek Railroad Company, The	M 127
Fort Collins Development Railway Company, The	M 128
Fremont, Elkhorn & Missouri Valley Rail Road Company	M 396
Fremont, Elkhorn & Missouri Valley Railroad Company	M 396

Galena & Chicago Union Rail Road Company	M 370
Gales Creek & Wilson River Railroad Company	P 79
Gallatin Light, Power & Railway Company	M 301
Gallatin Valley Electric Railway	M 301
Gallatin Valley Railway Company	M 301
Gaylord & Ruby Valley Railway Company	M 301
Georgetown & Grays Peak Railway Company, The	M 64
Georgetown, Breckenridge & Leadville Railway Company	M 128
Georgia-Pacific Corporation	P 82
Gila Valley, Globe & Northern Railway Company	D 87
Gilmore & Pittsburg Railroad Company, Ltd., The	M 208
Gilpin Railroad Company	M 129
Gilpin Tramway Company	M 129
Glendale Lumber Company	P 76
Goble, Nehalem & Pacific Railway Company	P 65
Golconda & Adelaide Railroad Company	D 141
Golden & South Platte Railroad Company	M 129
Golden, Boulder & Caribou Railway Company	M 130
Golden Circle Railroad Company, The	M 130
Golden City & South Platte Railway & Telegraph Company	M 131
Goldfield Consolidated Milling & Transportation Company	D 141
Goldfield Consolidated Mines Company	D 141
Goldfield Railroad Company	D 163
Goshen Valley Railroad Company	D 259
Grand Canyon Railway, The	D 88
Grande Ronde Lumber Company	P 145
Grand Island & Northern Wyoming Railroad Company, The	M 367
Great Falls & Canada Railway Company, The	M 302
Great Falls & Teton County Railway Company	M 302
Great Northern Lumber Company	P 217
Great Northern Railway Company	M 303
Great Salt Lake & Hot Springs Railway Company	D 270
Great Southern Railroad Company	P 148
Great Western Railway Company, The	M 132
Great Western Railway Company of Oregon, Inc.	P 83
Greeley, Salt Lake & Pacific Railway Company, The	M 133
Green River & Northern Railroad Company	P 217
Hamma Hamma Logging Company	P 220
Hallack & Howard Lumber Company	D 212 and M 246
Hammond Lumber Company	P 90
Hannibal & St. Joseph Railroad Company	M 384
Hanover Railroad Company	D 213
Hartford Eastern Railway Company	P 221
Helena & Jefferson County Railroad Company	M 315
Helena & Northern Railroad Company	M 317
Helena & Red Mountain Railroad Company, The	M 317
Helena, Boulder Valley & Butte Railroad Company	M 318
Heron Lumber Company	M 347
Hines Lumber Company, Edward	P 83
Holly & Swink Railway Company, The	M 133
Howe Lumber Mills, P. L.	M 347
Humbird Lumber Company	M 246
Idaho & Northwestern Railway Company	M 246
Idaho & Washington Northern Railroad	M 209
Idaho & Western Railway Company	M 210
Idaho Central Railway Company	M 210
Idaho Central Railway Company - 2d	P 278
Idaho Northern & Pacific Railroad Company	P 83
Idaho Northern Railroad Company	M 211
Idaho Northern Railway Company, Ltd., The	M 212
Idaho Railway, Light & Power Company	M 202
Idaho Southern Railroad Company	M 213
Illinois & Wisconsin Railroad Company	M 370
Ilwaco Railroad Company	P 222
Ilwaco Railway & Navigation Company, The	P 222
Ilwaco Steam Navigation Company, The	P 222
Ilwaco Wharf Company, The	P 222
Independence & Monmouth Railway Company, The	P 84
Independence Logging Company	P 260
Independent Coal & Coke Company	D 310

GENERAL INDEX

Ingham Lumber Company	P 76
Inland Empire Railroad Company	P 278
Inland Empire Railway Company	P 278
Inman-Poulsen Logging Company	P 222
Intermountain Railway Company	M 214
Intermountain Railway Company, The	M 98
Inter-Mountain Railroad Company	M 112
Intermountain Western Railroad	M 215
International Paper Company	P 85
Irving-Hartley Logging Company	P 216
Isthmus & Coquille Railroad Company	P 70
Izette Lumber Company	P 216
K-P Timber Company	P 85
Kansas & Colorado Railway Company	M 133
Kansas-Colorado Railroad Company	M 92
Kansas Pacific Railway Company	M 136
Kenilworth & Helper Railroad Company	D 270
Kennecott Copper Corp.	D 213
Kerry Timber Company	P 85
Kinzua Pine Mills Company	P 69
Klamath Falls Municipal Railway	P 104
Klamath Northern Railway Company	P 86
Klickitat Log & Lumber Company	P 223
Klickitat Northern Railroad Company	P 223
Kootenai Valley Railway Company	M 215
Kosmos Timber Company	P 223
Koster Products Company	P 86
La Dee Logging Company	P 86
Lake Creek & Coeur d'Alene Railroad Company	M 216
Lake Tahoe Narrow Gauge Railroad Company	D 142
Lake Whatcom Logging Company	P 189
Lamb-Davis Lumber Company	P 217
Lamm Lumber Company	P 87
Laramie, Hahns Peak & Pacific Railway Company	M 398
Laramie, North Park & Pacific Railroad & Telegraph Company, The	M 397
Laramie, North Park & Western Railroad Company	M 398
Laramie Valley Railway Company	M 399
Larimer & Routt County Railway Company, The	M 398
Larson Company	P 191
Las Vegas & Tonopah Railroad Company	D 143
Leavenworth, Pawnee & Western Railroad Company	M 136
Lewis & Clark Railroad Company	P 66
Lewis & Clark Railway Company	P 66
Lewis & Clark Railway Company - 2d	P 226
Lewis Lumber Company, B. R.	M 246
Lewis Mills & Timber Company	P 301
Lewiston, Nezperce & Eastern Railroad Company	M 218
Libby Lumber Company	M 347
Lincoln Logging & Lumber Company	M 347
Little Book Cliff Railway Company	M 67
Little Cottonwood Transportation Company	D 271
Little River Railway & Logging Company	P 232
Logan Rapid Transit Company	D 303
London, South Park & Leadville Railroad Company	M 138
Long-Bell Lumber Company	P 85 and 227
Longmont & Erie Railroad Company, The	M 125
Longview, Portland & Northern Railway Company	P 161 and 226
Lordsburg & Hachita Railroad Company	D 214
Los Angeles & Salt Lake Railroad Company	D 272
Lyman Timber Company	P 274
McCormick Lumber Company, Charles R.	P 250
McGaffey Company, The	D 214
McGoldrick Lumber Company	M 246
McKinley Land & Lumber Company	D 215
Magma Arizona Railroad Company	D 89
Malad Valley Railroad Company	M 216
Malheur Railroad Company	P 102
Malheur Valley Railway Company	P 87
Manitou & Pike's Peak Railway Company, The	M 139

329.

Manley-Moore Lumber Company	P 227
Mann Lumber Company	M 347
Maricopa & Phoenix & Salt River Valley Railroad Company, The	D 90
Maricopa & Phoenix Railroad Company, The	D 91
Marysville & Arlington Railway Company	P 228
Marysville & Northern Railway Company	P 286
Mascot & Western Railroad Company	D 92
Mason County Central Railroad Company	P 269
Mason County Logging Company	P 228
Mascot & Western Railroad Company	D 92
Masten Logging Company, C. C.	P 88
Medford & Crater Lake Railroad Company	P 127
Medford Coast Rail Road Company	P 88
Medford Corporation	P 90
Medford Logging Railroad Company	P 90
Melbourne & North River Railroad Company	P 201
Merrill & Ring Logging Company	P 229
Merrill & Ring Lumber Company	P 229
Mexico & Colorado Railroad Company	D 81
Midland Terminal Railway Company, The	M 140
Mill City Mfg. Company	P 90
Mill Creek Flume & Manufacturing Company	P 229
Mill Creek Railroad Company	P 229
Miller Logging Company	P 230
Milner & North Side Railroad Company	M 217
Milwaukee & Mississippi Rail Road Company	M 284
Milwaukee & Prairie du Chien Railway Company	M 284
Milwaukee & St. Paul Railway Company	M 284
Milwaukee & Waukesha Rail Road Company	M 284
Milwaukee Lumber Company	M 246
Minidoka & Southwestern Railroad Company	M 217
Minneapolis & Pacific Railway Company	M 319
Minneapolis & St. Cloud Railroad Company	M 303
Minneapolis, St. Paul & Sault Ste. Marie Railway Company	M 319
Minneapolis, Sault Ste. Marie & Atlantic Railway Company	M 319
Missoula & Bitter Root Valley Railroad Company, The	M 320
Missouri Pacific Railroad Company	M 141
Missouri Pacific Railway Company	M 141
Missouri River Railway Company	M 320
Mohave & Milltown Railway Company	D 92
Monroe Logging Company	P 230
Montana & Great Northern Railway Company	M 321
Montana Central Railway Company, The	M 322
Montana Eastern Railway Company	M 323
Montana Logging Company	M 347
Montana Rail Link, Inc.	M 324
Montana Railroad Company	M 325
Montana Railway Company	M 326
Montana Southern Railway Company	M 301
Montana Southern Railway Company - 2d	M 326
Montana Southwestern Railway Company	M 326
Montana Union Railway Company	M 327
Montana Western Railway Company, The	M 328
Montana, Wyoming & Southern Railroad Company	M 329
Monte Cristo Railway Company	P 231
Montezuma Lumber Company	M 152
Morenci Southern Railway Company	D 93
Mosquito & Coal Creek Railroad Company	P 213
Mount Emily Lumber Company	P 91
Mount Hood Railroad Company	P 92
Mount Hood Railway Company	P 92
Mount Hood Railway & Power Company	P 78
Mud Bay Logging Company	P 232
Mutual Lumber Company	P 232
Natches Pass Railroad Company	P 258
National Lumber & Mfg. Company	P 260
Neils Lumber Company, J.	M 347
Nelson Company, The, Charles	P 232
Nevada & California Railroad Company	D 145
Nevada & California Railway Company	D 146

Nevada & Oregon Railroad Company	D 147
Nevada & Oregon Railroad Company, The	D 147
Nevada-California-Oregon Railway	D 148
Nevada Central Railroad Company	D 157
Nevada Central Railroad Company - 2d	D 150
Nevada Central Railway Company	D 150
Nevada Copper Belt Railroad Company	D 151
Nevada Copper Belt Railway Company	D 151
Nevada Northern Railway Company	D 153
Nevada Railroad Company, The	D 154
Nevada Railway	D 150
Nevada Short Line Railway Company	D 155
Newaukum Railroad Company	P 193
Newaukum Valley Railroad Company	P 193
New East Tintic Railway Company	D 273
Newhouse, Copper Gulch & Sevier Lake Railroad Company	D 273
New Mexican Railroad Company, The	D 215
New Mexico & Arizona Railroad Company	D 94
New Mexico & Southern Pacific Railroad Company, The	D 216
New Mexico Central Railroad Company	D 218
New Mexico Central Railway Company	D 218
New Mexico Lumber Company	M 152
New Mexico Midland Railway Company, The	D 219
Nezperce & Idaho Railroad Company	M 218
Nezperce Railroad Company	M 218
Nooksack Timber Company	P 258
North & South Railway Company, The	M 400
North Bend Mill & Lumber Company	P 92
North Coast Railroad Company, The	P 233
North Coast Railway	P 233
Northern Pacific & Cascade Railroad Company	P 233
Northern Pacific & Montana Railroad Company	M 330
Northern Pacific & Puget Sound Shore Railroad Company	P 235
Northern Pacific Railroad Company	M 331 and P 236
Northern Pacific Railway Company	M 331
Northwestern Railroad Company	P 93
North Yakima & Valley Railway Company	P 240
Noyes-Holland Logging Company	P 94
O'Connell Lumber Company, M. T.	P 302
Ogden & Hot Springs Railway Company	D 273
Ogden & Northwestern Railroad Company	D 273
Ogden & Syracuse Railway Company, The	D 274
Ogden & Utah Hot Springs Railway Company	D 273
Ogden, Logan & Idaho Railway Company	D 303
Ogden Rapid Transit Company	D 303
Ohio Match Company	M 247
Olympia & Chehalis Valley Railroad Company, The	P 240
Olympia & Tenino Railroad Company	P 240
Olympia Railroad Union	P 240
Olympia Terminal Railway Company	P 122
Onalaska Lumber Company	P 193
Oregon & California Rail Road Company	P 96
Oregon & Northwestern Railroad Company	P 102
Oregon & Southeastern Railroad Company	P 102
Oregon & Washington Railroad Company	P 241
Oregon & Washington Territory Railroad Company	P 242
Oregon-American Lumber Company	P 85
Oregon, California & Eastern Railway Company	P 104
Oregon Central & Eastern Railroad Company	P 104
Oregon Central Railroad Company	P 106
Oregon Central Rail Road Company	P 106
Oregon Coast Range Lumber Company	P 130
Oregon Eastern Railway Company	P 107
Oregon Electric Railway Company	P 108
Oregon Lumber Company	P 111
Oregon Pacific & Eastern Railway Company	P 114
Oregon Pacific Railroad Company	P 157
Oregon Portage Rail Road	P 112
Oregon Railroad & Navigation Company, The	P 114
Oregon Railway & Navigation Company	P 117
Oregon Railway Company, Ltd., The (Oregon)	P 126

GENERAL INDEX

Oregon Railway Extensions Company, The	P 243
Oregon Short Line Railroad Company	M 219
Oregon Short Line Railway Company	M 223
Oregon Short Line & Utah Northern Railway Company	D 274
Oregon State Portage Railroad	P 119
Oregon Steam Navigation Company	P 121
Oregon Trunk Line, Inc.	P 121
Oregon Trunk Railway	P 121
Oregon, Washington & Idaho Railroad Company	P 243
Oregon-Washington Railroad & Navigation Company	P 122
Oregon Water Power & Railway Company, The	P 78
Oregon Western Railroad Company	P 126
Oregonian Railroad Company	P 126
Oregonian Railway Company, Ltd. (Scotland)	P 126
Ostrander Railroad Company, The	P 244
Owen-Oregon Lumber Company	P 90
Ozette Timber Company	P 256
Pacific & Eastern Railway Company	P 217
Pacific & Eastern Railway Company	P 254
Pacific & Idaho Northern Railway Company	M 226
Pacific Coast Railroad Company	P 244
Pacific National Lumber Company	P 245
Pacific Portland Cement Company	D 156
Pacific Railroad	M 141
Pacific Railway & Navigation Company	P 129
Pacific States Lumber Company	P 246
Page Lumber Company	P 193
Pagosa Lumber Company, The	D 219
Palmer Lumber Company, The George	P 61
Palouse River Railroad Company	P 192
Panhandle Lumber Company	M 247
Panther Lake Lumber Company	P 299
Parker-Bell Lumber Company	P 214
Payette Valley Extension Railroad Company	M 228
Payette Valley Railroad Company	M 228
Pecos Northern Railroad Company, The	D 222
Pecos Valley & Northeastern Railway Company, The	D 220
Pecos Valley Railroad Company, The	D 222
Pecos Valley Railway Company, The	D 222
Pelican Bay Lumber Company	P 129
Pend Oreille Valley Railroad	P 247
Pend Oreille Valley Railroad, Inc.	P 247
Peninsular Railway Company	P 292
Peoria & Oquawka Railroad Company	M 384
Phelps Dodge Corp.	D 80
Phoenix & Eastern Railroad Company	D 95
Phoenix Logging Company	P 247
Phoenix, Tempe & Mesa Railway Company, The	D 90
Pioche & Bullionville Railroad Company	D 157
Pioche & Pacific Transportation Company	D 158
Pioche Pacific Railroad Company	D 158
Pioche Pacific Railway Company	D 158
Pioche Pacific Transportation Company	D 158
Polk Operating Company	P 130
Polson Brothers Logging Company	P 248
Polson Logging Company	P 248
Pope & Talbot Lumber Company	P 250
Port Angeles Western Railroad Company	P 250
Portland & Oregon City Railway Company	P 65
Portland & Puget Sound Railroad Company	P 288
Portland & Seattle Railway Company	P 282
Portland & Southwestern Railroad Company	P 130
Portland & Willamette Valley Railway Company	P 131
Portland & Yamhill Railroad Company	P 131
Portland, Astoria & Pacific Railroad Company	P 151
Portland City & Oregon Railway Company	P 78
Portland Electric Power Company	P 78
Portland, Eugene & Eastern Railway Company	P 132
Portland Lumber Company	P 94
Portland Railway, Light & Power Company	P 78
Portland Southern Railroad Company	P 65

GENERAL INDEX

Portland, Vancouver & Yakima Railway Company	P 298
Port of Tillamook Bay Railroad	P 133
Port Ludlow, Port Angeles & Lake Crescent Railway	P 267
Port Townsend & Puget Sound Railway Company	P 252
Port Townsend Railroad	P 252
Port Townsend Southern Railroad Company	P 252
Potlatch Forests, Inc.	M 229
Potlatch Lumber Company	M 229
Prescott & Arizona Central Railway Company, The	D 96
Prescott & Eastern Railroad Company	D 97
Prestridge & Seligman	D 222
Prince Consolidated Mining Company	D 159
Pueblo & Arkansas Valley Railroad Company, The	M 153
Pueblo & Salt Lake Railway Company	M 153
Pueblo & State Line Railroad Company	M 154
Puget Mill Company	P 250
Puget Sound & Baker River Railway Company	P 253
Puget Sound & Cascade Railway Company	P 254
Puget Sound & Grays Harbor Railroad Company	P 286
Puget Sound & Grays Harbor Railroad & Transportation Company	P 286
Puget Sound & Willapa Harbor Railway Company	P 254
Puget Sound Mills & Timber Company	P 232
Puget Sound Pulp & Timber Company	P 255
Puget Sound Shore Railroad Company, The	P 255
Quarette Mining Company	D 159
Quincy & Chicago Railroad Company	M 384
Rarus Railway Company	M 343
Ray & Gila Valley Railroad Company	D 98
Rayonier Corporation	P 256
Republic & Kettle River Railway Company	P 275
Rio Grande & Pagosa Springs Railroad Company	M 155
Rio Grande & Santa Fe Railroad Company, The	D 223
Rio Grande & Southwestern Railroad Company	D 224
Rio Grande Eastern Railway Corp., The	D 224
Rio Grande Gunnison Railway Company	M 155
Rio Grande Junction Railway Company, The	M 156
Rio Grande, Mexico & Pacific Railroad Company	D 225
Rio Grande, Mexico & Pacific Railroad Company, The	D 225
Rio Grande, Pagosa & Northern Railroad Company, The	M 157
Rio Grande Railroad Company, The	M 158
Rio Grande Sangre de Cristo Railroad Company, The	M 158
Rio Grande Southern Railroad Company, The	M 159
Rio Grande Western Railway Company, The	D 276
Rock Island & La Salle Rail Road Company	M 73
Rock River Valley Union Railroad Company	M 370
Rocky Fork & Cooke City Railway Company	M 344
Rocky Mountain & Santa Fe Railway	D 227
Rocky Mountain Railroad Company of Montana	M 344
Rocky Mountain Railway Company	M 161
Rogue River Valley Railroad Company	P 88
Rogue River Valley Railway Company	P 88
Ruby Hill Railroad Company	D 160
Rucker Brothers Company	P 255
Rutledge Timber Company, Edward	M 247
St. Anthony Railroad Company	M 230
St. John & Ophir Railroad Company	D 310
St. Louis, Rocky Mountain & Pacific Railway Company	D 227
St. Maries Lumber Company	M 246
St. Maries River Railroad Company	M 230
St. Paul & Pacific Railroad Company, The	M 303
St. Paul & Tacoma Lumber Company	P 258
St. Paul, Minneapolis & Manitoba Railway Company, The	M 303
St. Regis Pulp & Paper Company	P 258
Sacramento Mountain Lumber Company	D 238
Saginaw & Manistee Lumber Company	D 99
Saginaw Southern Railroad Company	D 99
Saginaw Timber Company	P 258
Salem, Falls City & Western Railway Company	P 133
Salmon River Railroad Company	M 231

Saltair Railway Company, The	D 280
Salt Lake & Alta Railroad Company	D 279
Salt Lake & Eastern Railway Company	D 279
Salt Lake & Fort Douglas Railway Company	D 280
Salt Lake & Idaho Railroad Company	D 231
Salt Lake & Los Angeles Railway Company	D 280
Salt Lake & Mercur Railroad Company	D 281
Salt Lake & Ogden Railway Company	D 282
Salt Lake & Utah Railroad Corp., The	D 283
Salt Lake & Western Railway Company (of Utah)	D 284
Salt Lake, Garfield & Western Railway Company	D 285
Salt Lake, Sevier Valley & Pioche Railroad Company	D 285
San Luis Central Railroad Company, The	M 161
San Luis Southern Railway Company, The	M 165
San Luis Valley Southern Railway Company, The	M 165
San Manuel Arizona Railroad Company	D 100
San Pedro, Los Angeles & Salt Lake Railroad Company	see California
San Pete Valley Railway Company	D 286
Santa Barbara Tie & Pole Company	D 228
Santa Fe & Grand Canyon Railroad Company, The	D 88
Santa Fe, Albuquerque & Pacific Railroad Company	D 228
Santa Fe Central Railway Company	D 228
Santa Fe Northern Railroad	D 232
Santa Fe Northwestern Ry. Company	D 230
Santa Fe Pacific Railroad Company	D 101
Santa Fe, Prescott & Phoenix Railway Company, The	D 102
Santa Fe, Raton & Des Moines Railroad Company, The	D 231
Santa Fe, Raton & Eastern Railroad Company	D 231
Santa Fe, San Juan & Northern Railroad	D 232
Santa Fe Southern Railway Company, The	D 233
Santa Rita Mining Company	D 213
Santa Rita Railroad Company, The	D 233
Saratoga & Encampment Railroad Company	M 401
Saratoga & Encampment Railway Company	M 401
Saratoga & Encampment Valley Railroad Company	M 401
Sauk River Lumber Company	P 258
Satsop Rail Road Company	P 268
Schafer Brothers Logging Company	P 260
Seashore Railroad Company	P 134
Seattle & International Railway Company	P 261
Seattle & Montana Railroad Company	P 261
Seattle & Montana Railway Company	P 261
Seattle & North Coast Railroad Company	P 262
Seattle & Northern Railway Company	P 263
Seattle & Walla Walla Railroad & Transportation Company	P 265
Seattle & West Coast Railway Company	P 265
Seattle Coal & Transportation Company, The	P 265
Seattle, Lake Shore & Eastern Railway Company	P 265
Seattle Lumber Company	P 268
Seattle, Port Angeles & Lake Crescent Railway	P 267
Seattle, Port Angeles & Western Railway Company	P 267
Seattle Southeastern Railway Company	P 246
Sevier Railway Company	D 287
Shannon-Arizona Railway Company	D 103
Shaw-Bertram Lumber Company	P 135
Shelton Southwestern Railroad Company	P 268
Shelton Southwestern Railway Company, The	P 268
Sheridan & Willamina Railroad Company	P 135
Shevlin-Hixon Lumber Company	P 136
Shields River Valley Railway Company, The	M 345
Silver City & Northern Rail Road Company	D 234
Silver City, Deming & Pacific Railroad Company	D 235
Silver City, Pinos Altos & Mogollon Railroad Company	D 235
Silver Falls Timber Company	P 136
Silver Peak Railroad Company	D 160
Silverton, Gladstone & Northerly Railroad Company, The	M 162
Silverton Lumber Company	P 136
Silverton Northern Railroad Company, The	M 163
Silverton Railroad Company, The	M 164
Silverton Railway Company	M 164
Simpson Logging Company	P 268
Simpson Lumber Company	P 145

GENERAL INDEX

Simpson Timber Company	P 268
Six Companies, Inc.	D 161
Smith Lumber & Mfg. Company, C. A.	P 82
Smith-Powers Logging Company	P 82
Smith River & Northern Railway Company	P 137
Snake River Valley Railroad Company, The	P 273
Snohomish Logging Company	P 274
Snohomish, Skykomish & Spokane Railway & Transportation Company, The	P 231
Snoqualmie Falls Lumber Company	P 274
Somers Lumber Company	M 347
Soo Line Railroad Company	M 319
Soundview Pulp Company	P 274
South Bend Mills & Timber Company	P 301
Southern Oregon Traction Company	P 88
Southern Pacific Railroad Company (of Arizona), The	D 104
Southern Pacific Railroad Company of New Mexico	D 236
Southern Pacific Transportation Company	P 138
Southern San Luis Valley Railroad Company	M 165
Southern Utah Railroad Company	D 287
South Park & Leadville Short Line Railroad Company	M 138
Southwestern Railroad of Arizona	D 81
Southwestern Railroad of New Mexico	D 81
Southwest Forest Industries, Inc.	D 106
Southwest Lumber Company	D 238
Southwest Lumber Mills	D 106
Spaulding Logging Company, Chas. K.	P 144
Spaulding-Miami Lumber Company	P 144
Spokane & British Columbia Railway Company	P 275
Spokane & Eastern Railway & Power Company	P 278
Spokane & Inland Empire Railroad Company	P 278
Spokane & Inland Railway Company	P 278
Spokane & Palouse Railway Company	P 276
Spokane & Seattle Railway Company	P 277
Spokane, Coeur d'Alene & Palouse Railway Company	P 278
Spokane Falls & Idaho Railroad Company	M 223
Spokane Falls & Northern Railway Company, The	P 279
Spokane International Railroad Company	P 281
Spokane International Railway Company	P 281
Spokane Interurban System	P 278
Springdale & Long Lake Railway Company	P 210
Standard Logging Company	P 144
Standard Lumber Company	P 210
Standard Railway & Timber Company	P 287
State Line & Denver Railway Company, The	D 276
State Lumber Company	M 347
Sterling Mill Company	P 299
Stimson Mill Company	P 286
Stoddard Bros. Lumber Company	P 145
Stoddard Lumber Company	P 145
Stolz Land & Lumber Company, F. H.	M 347
Stout Lumber Company	P 145
Sultan Railway & Timber Company	P 287
Summit County Railroad Company, The	D 288
Sumpter Valley Railway Company	P 146
Sunset Logging Company	P 148
Sunset Timber Company	P 301
Sutro Tunnel Railroad	D 161
Tacoma & Columbia River Railway Company	P 288
Tacoma & Lake City Railroad & Navigation Company	P 288
Tacoma Eastern Railroad Company	P 290
Tacoma, Lake City & Columbia River Railway Company	P 288
Tacoma, Olympia & Chehalis Valley Railroad Company	P 213
Tacoma, Olympia & Grays Harbor Railroad Company	P 291
Tacoma, Orting & Southeastern Railroad Company, The	P 291
Texas-New Mexico Railway Company	D 238
Texas, Santa Fe & Northern Railroad Company	D 239
The Dalles & Southern Railroad Company	P 148
Three Lakes Lumber Company	P 299
Thurston County Railroad Construction Company	P 240
Thurston County Railway Company	P 232
Tierra Amarilla & Southern Ry.	D 239

Tintic Range Railway Company	D 289
Tintic Standard Mining Company	D 310
Tonopah & Goldfield Railroad Company	D 163
Tonopah & Tidewater Railroad Company	see California
Tonopah Railroad Company	D 163
Tooele Valley Railway Company	D 290
Toppenish, Simcoe & Western Railway Company	P 240
Tucson & Nogales Railroad Company	D 107
Tucson, Cornelia & Gila Bend Railroad Company	D 108
Tucson, Globe & Northern Railroad Company	D 109
Tucumcari & Memphis Railway Company	D 205
Twin Buttes Railroad Company, The	D 109
Twin Falls Logging Company	P 200
Uintah Railway Company, The	M 166
Umatilla Central Railroad Company	P 149
Union Lumber Company	P 291
Union Pacific, Denver & Gulf Railway Company	M 167
Union Pacific Railroad Company	M 233
Union Pacific Railroad Company, The	M 233
Union Pacific Railway Company, The	M 233
Union Pacific Railway Company - Eastern Division	M 136
Union Railroad of Oregon	P 150
Union Railway Company, The	P 150
Union River Logging Railroad Company	P 250
United Railroads of Washington, The	P 291
United Railways Company (Oregon)	P 151
United States Potash Company	D 240
United Verdi & Pacific Railway Company	D 110
Utah & Nevada Railway Company, The	D 291
Utah & Northern Railway Company	D 292
Utah & Pacific Railroad Company	D 295
Utah & Pleasant Valley Railway Company	D 296
Utah Central Rail Road Company, The	D 297
Utah Central Railroad Company	D 298
Utah Central Railway Company	D 299
Utah Central Railway Company - 2d	D 300
Utah Coal Railway Company	D 305
Utah Copper Company	D 310
Utah Eastern Rail Road Company	D 301
Utah Eastern Railway Company	D 302
Utah Idaho Central Railroad Company	D 303
Utah Idaho Central Railroad Corporation, The	D 303
Utah Idaho Central Railway	D 303
Utah Iron Ore Corp.	D 310
Utah, Nevada & California Railroad Company (of Nevada)	D 164
Utah Northern Railroad Company, The	D 304
Utah Railway Company	D 305
Utah Southern Railroad Company	D 306
Utah Southern Railroad Extension	D 307
Utah Western Railway Company	D 300
Utah Western Railway Company, The	D 308
Vale & Malheur Valley Railway Company	P 87
Valley & Siletz Railroad Company	P 159
Vance Lumber Company	P 228
Vancouver, Klickitat & Yakima Railroad Company	P 298
Verde Tunnel & Smelter Railroad Company	D 111
Verde Valley Railway Company	D 112
Verdi Lumber Company	D 165
Virginia & Truckee Rail Road Company	D 166
Virginia & Truckee Railroad Company	D 166
Virginia & Truckee Railway	D 166
WCTU Railway Company	P 153
Walla Walla & Columbia River Railroad Company	P 292
Walla Walla Valley Railway Company	P 293
Walla Walla Valley Traction Company	P 293
Walsenburg & Western Railway Company, The	M 91
Warland Lumber Company	M 347
Warren Spruce Company	P 152
Wasatch & Jordan Valley Railroad Company	D 309

Washington & Columbia River Railway Company, The	P 295
Washington & Great Northern Railway Company	P 295
Washington & Idaho Railroad Company	M 242
Washington & Oregon Railway Company	P 298
Washington Central Railroad Company, Inc.	P 296
Washington Central Railway Company, The	P 297
Washington Electric Railway Company	P 208
Washington, Idaho & Montana Railway Company	M 243
Washington Pulp & Paper Company	P 216
Washington Railway & Navigation Company	P 298
Washington Southern Railway Company	P 269
Washington Western Railway Company	P 299
Waterville Railway Company	P 300
Weed Lumber Company	P 107
Wenatchee Valley & Northern Railway Company	P 217
Western Arizona Railway Company	D 113
Western Lumber Company	M 277
Western Lumber Company	P 83
Western Lumber Company	P 213
Western Oregon Railroad Company	P 153
Western Pacific Railroad Company	see California
Western Pacific Railway Company	see California
Western Pine Lumber Company	P 223
Westfir Lumber Company	P 83
West Fork Logging Company	P 258
Weyerhaeuser Company	P 153 and 300
Wheeler, C. H.	P 154
White River Lumber Company	P 301
White Sulphur Springs & Yellowstone Park Railway Company	M 346
Willamette & Pacific Railroad Company	P 154
Willamette Pacific Railroad Company	P 155
Willamette Valley & Coast Rail Road Company	P 156
Willamette Valley Railroad Company	P 158
Willamette Valley Railroad Company - 2d	P 159
Willamette Valley Railway Company	P 160
Willamette Valley Railway Company - 2d	P 161
Willamette Valley Southern Railway Company	P 160
Willamina & Grande Ronde Railway Company	P 162
Willapa Harbor Lumber Mills	P 301
Willapa Logging Railroad Company	P 301
Wilson Bros. Company	P 260
Winlock & Toledo Logging & Railroad Company	P 302
Winlock Lumber Company	P 302
Winlock-Toledo Lumber Company	P 302
Winton Lumber Company	M 247
Winton-Rosenberry Lumber Company	M 247
Wisconsin Logging & Timber Company	P 302
Wood & Iverson	P 189
Wright Logging Company, Stacey E.	P 255
Wynoochee Timber Company	P 260
Wyoming & Colorado Railroad Company	P 163
Wyoming & Colorado Railroad, Inc.	M 403
Wyoming & Missouri River Railroad Company	M 404
Wyoming & Missouri River Railway Company	M 404
Wyoming & Northwestern Railway Company	M 405
Wyoming Central Railway Company	M 406
Wyoming North & South Railroad Company	M 400
Wyoming Railway Company	M 407
Wyoming Western Railroad Company	M 408
Yakima & Pacific Coast Railroad Company	P 291
Yakima Valley Transportation Company	P 303
Yellow Pine Mining Company	D 168
Yellowstone Park Railroad Company	M 244
Yellowstone Park Railroad Company	M 329
Yellowstone Park Railway Company	M 346
Yeon & Pelton Company	P 94
Yuma Valley Railroad	D 114
Zuni Mountain Railroad Company	D 240
Zuni Mountain Railway Company	D 240

INDEX-to-the-INDEX

The previous pages list 1,047 names; included here are the majors and some of the old and the famous.

Alamogordo & Sacramento Mountain Railway Company	D 187
Apache Railway Company, The	D 65
Arizona Eastern Railroad Company	D 71
Astoria & Columbia River Railroad Company	P 57
Atchison, Topeka & Santa Fe Railway Company, The	D 189
Atlantic & Pacific Railroad Company	D 75
Bullfrog Goldfield Railroad Company	D 134
Burlington & Missouri River Rail Road in Nebraska	M 69
Burlington Northern Railroad Company	M 279
Camas Prairie Railroad Company	M 203
Carson & Colorado Railway Company	D 136
Cheyenne & Northern Railway Company	M 369
Chicago & North Western Railway Company	M 370
Chicago, Burlington & Quincy Railroad Company	M 384
Chicago, Kansas & Nebraska Railway Company, The	M 72
Chicago, Milwaukee, St. Paul & Pacific Railroad Company	M 284
Chicago, Rock Island & Pacific Railroad Company	M 73
Colorado & Southern Railway Company, The	M 80
Colorado Central Rail Road Company	M 87
Denver & Boulder Valley Railroad Company, The	M 97
Denver & Rio Grande Western Railroad Company, The	M 101
Denver & Rio Grande Western Railway Company, The	D 267
Denver & Salt Lake Railway Company, The	M 101
Denver, Leadville & Gunnison Railway Company, The	M 115
Denver, Northwestern & Pacific Railway Company	M 118
Denver, South Park & Pacific Railroad Company	M 121
Denver, Texas & Fort Worth Railroad Company	M 123
Eastern Railway Company of New Mexico, The	D 208
El Paso & Southwestern Railroad Company	D 81
Fremont, Elkhorn & Missouri Valley Railroad Company	M 396
Gilmore & Pittsburg Railroad Company, Ltd., The	M 208
Great Northern Railway Company	M 303
Kansas Pacific Railway Company	M 136
Las Vegas & Tonopah Railroad Company	D 143
Los Angeles & Salt Lake Railroad Company	D 272
Missouri Pacific Railroad Company	M 141
Montana Central Railway Company, The	M 322
Montana Rail Link, Inc.	M 324
Nevada & California Railway Company	D 146
Nevada-California-Oregon Railway	D 148
New Mexico & Southern Pacific Railroad Company, The	D 216
Northern Pacific & Montana Railroad Company	M 330
Northern Pacific Railway Company	M 331
Oregon & California Rail Road Company	P 96
Oregon Electric Railway Company	P 108
Oregon Short Line Railroad Company	M 219
Oregon Steam Navigation Company	P 121
Oregon-Washington Railroad & Navigation Company	P 122
Oregonian Railroad Company	P 126
Pecos Northern Railroad Company, The	D 222
Pueblo & Arkansas Valley Railroad Company, The	M 153
Rio Grande, Mexico & Pacific Railroad Company, The	D 225
Rio Grande Southern Railroad Company, The	M 159
Rio Grande Western Railway Company, The	D 276
Santa Fe Pacific Railroad Company	D 101
Santa Fe, Prescott & Phoenix Railway Company, The	D 102
Seattle, Lake Shore & Eastern Railway Company	P 265
Soo Line Railroad Company	M 319
Southern Pacific Railroad Company (of Arizona), The	D 104
Southern Pacific Transportation Company	P 138
Spokane International Railroad Company	P 281
Sumpter Valley Railway Company	P 146
Uintah Railway Company, The	M 166
Union Pacific, Denver & Gulf Railway Company	M 167
Union Pacific Railroad Company	M 233
United Railroads of Washington, The	P 291
Utah & Northern Railway Company	D 292
Utah Central Railway Company	D 299
Virginia & Truckee Railway	D 166
Willamette Valley & Coast Rail Road Company	P 156

o 0000 o